S0-BMT-689

Introduction to Information Systems

Introduction to Information Systems

Eighth Edition

James A. O'Brien
College of Business Administration
Northern Arizona University

IRWIN

Chicago • Bogotá • Boston • Buenos Aires • Caracas
London • Madrid • Mexico City • Sydney • Toronto

© The McGraw-Hill Companies, Inc., 1975, 1978, 1982, 1985, 1988, 1991, 1994 and 1997
1982, 1985, 1988, 1991, 1994 and 1997

All rights reserved. No part of this publication may be
reproduced, stored in a retrieval system, or transmitted,
in any form or by any means, electronic, mechanical,
photocopying, recording, or otherwise, without the prior
written permission of the publisher.

Irwin Book Team
Publisher: *Tom Casson*
Senior sponsoring editor: *Rick Williamson*
Developmental editor: *Christine Wright*
Associate marketing manager: *Michelle Hudson*
Project supervisor: *Jean Lou Hess*
Production supervisor: *Dina L. Genovese*
Designer: *Matthew Baldwin*
Cover image by: *Boris Lyubner*
Photo research coordinator: *Keri Johnson*
Prepress buyer: *Charlene R. Perez*
Compositor: *PC&F, Inc.*
Typeface: *10/12 Berkeley Old Style*
Printer: *Von Hoffmann Press, Inc.*

Library of Congress Cataloging-in-Publication Data

O'Brien, James A.
   Introduction to information systems / James A. O'Brien.—8th ed.
     p. cm.
   ISBN 0-256-20937-5
   Includes index.
    1. Business—Data processing. 2. Management—Data processing. I.
Title
HF5548.2.O23   1997
658.4'038—dc20   96-34669

Printed in the United States of America
  2 3 4 5 6 7 8 9 0 VH 3 2 1 0 9 8 7

To all who read these words
May you love the Light within you
And in everyone you meet
And everything you experience

About the Author

James A. O'Brien is a professor of Computer Information Systems in the College of Business Administration at Northern Arizona University. He completed his undergraduate studies at the University of Hawaii and Gonzaga University and earned an M.S. and Ph.D. in Business Administration from the University of Oregon. He has been coordinator of the CIS area at Northern Arizona University, professor of Finance and Management Information Systems and chairman of the Department of Management at Eastern Washington University, and a visiting professor at the University of Alberta, the University of Hawaii, and Central Washington University.

Dr. O'Brien's business experience includes working in the Marketing Management Program of the IBM Corporation, as well as serving as a financial analyst for the General Electric Company. He is a graduate of General Electric's Financial Management Program. He has also served as an information systems consultant to several banks and computer services firms.

Jim's research interests lie in developing and testing basic conceptual frameworks used in information systems development and management. He has written eight books, including several that have been published in multiple editions, as well as in Dutch, French, or Japanese translations. He has also contributed to the field of information systems through the publication of many articles in business and academic journals, as well as through his participation in academic and industry associations in the field of information systems.

Preface

This text is written as an introduction to information systems for business students. As tomorrow's managers, entrepreneurs, or business specialists, business students need to know how to use and manage information technology in today's networked enterprises and global markets. In this dynamic environment, they will rely on interconnected networks of information systems for end user collaboration, including communications and computing among end user work groups and teams, and enterprisewide computing, including communications and information processing for business operations, managerial decision making, and strategic advantage.

Introducing Information Systems to Business Students

This is the business end user and networked enterprise perspective that the eighth edition brings to the study of information systems. Of course, as in the seventh edition, this edition:

- Loads the text with real world cases and problems about real people and companies in the business world.
- Organizes the text around a simple five level framework that emphasizes the IS knowledge a managerial end user needs to know.
- Distributes and integrates IS foundation theory throughout the text instead of concentrating it in several early chapters.
- Places a major emphasis on the strategic role of information systems in providing competitive advantage, as well as on the operational and decision support roles of information technology.

About the Text

This new eighth edition is a major revision that retains these important features, while significantly updating coverage of IS technology and its business and managerial applications. In addition, this edition includes a new chapter on the strategic use of IT for competitive advantage. Major revisions have been made to the organization of topics in many chapters, and new hands-on application exercises have been added to end-of-chapter materials. Finally, the eighth edition provides all new Real World Cases and Problems in every chapter.

This text is designed for use in undergraduate courses in Management Information Systems, which are required in many Business Administration or Management programs as part of the *common body of knowledge* required of all business majors. Thus, this text treats the subject area known as Information Systems (IS), Management Information Systems (MIS), or Computer Information Systems (CIS) as a major functional area of business that is as important to management education as are the areas of accounting, finance, operations management, marketing, and human resource management.

Like my other MIS texts, this text is designed to support the attainment of **information systems literacy** by students. That is, its objective is to build a basic understanding of the value and uses of information technology in information systems for business operations, managerial decision making, and strategic advantage. Although this text is not designed for courses in *computer literacy,* the four chapters of its *technology* module contain overviews of computer hardware, software, telecommunications, and database management that can be used as a refresher on such topics or to help remedy deficiencies in student computer literacy.

An Information Systems Framework

This text provides a teaching-learning resource that reduces the complexity of an introductory course in information systems by using a conceptual framework that organizes the knowledge needed by business students into five major areas:

- **Foundation Concepts.** Basic information systems concepts about the components and the operations, managerial, and strategic roles of information systems (Chapter 1). Other behavioral, managerial, and technical concepts are presented where appropriate in other chapters.
- **Technology.** Major concepts, developments, and managerial implications involved in computer hardware, software, database management, and telecommunications technologies (Chapters 2, 3, 4, and 5). Other technologies used in computer-based information systems are discussed where appropriate in selected chapters.
- **Applications.** How information technology is used in modern information systems to support end user collaboration, enterprise operations, managerial decision making, and strategic advantage (Chapters 6, 7, 8, and 9).
- **Development.** Developing information system solutions to business problems using a variety of approaches to application development and implementing change with IT (Chapter 10).
- **Management.** The challenges and methods of managing information systems technologies, activities, and resources, including information resource management, global IT management, and security and ethical challenges (discussed in many chapters, but emphasized in Chapters 11 and 12).

Real World Cases, Problems, and Exercises

This text makes extensive use of up-to-date "real world" case studies and problems. These are not fictional stories, but actual situations faced by business firms and other organizations as reported in current business and IS periodicals. This includes two real world case studies in each chapter that apply specifically to that chapter's contents, four real world problems provided at the end of every chapter, and a continuing case at the end of each module. In addition, each chapter contains several Application Exercises, including two hands-on spreadsheet or database software assignments in Chapters 2 through 11, and several Internet assignments in Chapter 4. The purpose of this variety of assignment options is to give instructors and students many opportunities to apply each chapter's material to real world situations, using managerial problem solving or end user development approaches.

Strategic, International, and Ethical Dimensions

This text contains substantial text material and cases reflecting the strategic, international, and ethical dimensions of information systems. This can be found not only in Chapter 9: *Information Systems for Strategic Advantage,* Chapter 11: *Enterprise and Global Management of Information Technology,* and Chapter 12: *Security and Ethical Challenges of Information Technology,* but in all other chapters of the text. This is especially evident in many real world cases and problems, such as Southwest Airlines, Satyam Computer Services, Catepillar, Inc., UPS, Federal Express, London Life, USAA Life, Bank of Montreal, Royal Bank of Canada, Columbia Sportswear, Dealer Net, Alaska Airlines, Eastman Kodak, Nestlé, Inc., Cisco Systems, Pacific Northwest National Laboratories, Database America, Yahoo Inc., and many, many others. These examples repeatedly demonstrate the strategic and ethical challenges of managing information technology for competitive advantage in global business markets and in the global information society in which we all live and work.

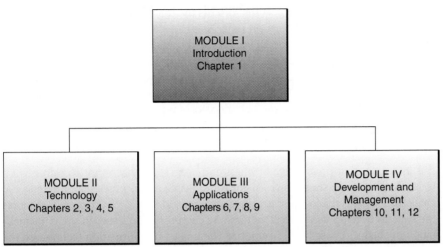

FIGURE 1

The modular organization of the text.

Modular Structure of the Text

The text is organized according to the five major areas of the framework for information systems knowledge mentioned earlier. Figure 1 illustrates how the text is organized into four modules. Also, each chapter is organized into two distinct sections. This is done to avoid proliferation of chapters, as well as to provide better conceptual organization of the text and each chapter. This organization increases instructor flexibility in assigning course material since it structures the text into modular levels (i.e., modules, chapters, and sections) while reducing the number of chapters that need to be covered.

Each chapter starts with a Chapter Outline and Learning Objectives and ends with a Summary, Key Terms and Concepts, a Review Quiz tied directly to the Key Terms and Concepts, Discussion Questions, Real World Problems, Application Exercises, Review Quiz Answers, and Selected References. Real World Cases are also provided at the end of each section and module of the book.

Module I: Introduction

The first chapter of this text is designed as an introductory core module of foundation concepts. Once instructors have covered Chapter 1, they can assign any other module depending on their pedagogical preferences. Chapter 1 introduces important topics and roles of information technology in business, a framework of information systems knowledge needed by business end users, the generic components and properties of information systems, and the major types of information systems.

Module II: Technology

Module II contains chapters on computer hardware (Chapter 2), software (Chapter 3), telecommunications (Chapter 4), and database management (Chapter 5). Its purpose is to give students an introduction to the technology used in modern computer-based information systems and its implications for end user management. This material is consolidated in an independent module since students may have already covered some of these topics in an earlier course. Thus, instructors can selectively use the chapters and sections of this module, depending on the preparation of their students. This is especially useful in the case of the important topics of business telecommunications and database management, to which many students have typically had only a brief exposure.

Module III: Applications

Module III contains four chapters that discuss the basic concepts and major applications of computer-based information systems. It emphasizes how information systems support end user productivity and the operations, managerial decision making, and competitive advantage of business firms and other organizations. Thus it includes coverage of concepts and applications in end user computing and collaboration and office automation (Chapter 6), business information systems and transaction processing (Chapter 7), management information, decision support, and executive information systems, and artificial intelligence and expert systems (Chapter 8), and information systems for strategic advantage (Chapter 9).

Module IV: Development and Management

It is important that prospective business end users learn that although information technology can help them solve business problems, it also poses major managerial challenges. That is the focus of the three chapters of Module IV. Chapter 10 explores the systems development process for and by end users, and issues in the implementation of changes caused by IT projects. The impact of information technology, the importance of information resource management, and the managerial implications of the global use of information technology are covered in Chapter 11. Chapter 12 explores the controls and safeguards needed to improve information system performance and security, as well as the ethical challenges posed by computer crime and other societal impacts of information technology.

Summary of Changes

Besides providing all new Real World Cases and Problems and Application Exercises, the eighth edition represents a major revision of chapter contents. Highlights of the changes made in the seventh edition material are found in the following eighth edition chapters:

Chapter 1:   *Introduction to Information Systems in Business.*
Section I of this chapter is a major revision that emphasizes the importance of IT in business with an overview of the impact of IT on business developments such as globalization, reengineering, and competitive advantage. The model of IS components in Section II has been revised to stress the role of network resources, and the overview of the types and roles of information systems has been expanded.

Chapter 2:   *Introduction to Computer Hardware.*
Updated and reorganized coverage of computer hardware, including moving more technical material to a *Technical Note* in Section I, and the elimination of Section III on the technical details of instruction execution and data representation.

Chapter 3:   *Introduction to Computer Software.*
Updated and reorganized coverage of computer software, with application software moved to Section I, and system software moved to Section II.

Chapter 4:   *Introduction to Business Telecommunications.*
A major revision and new topics such as open systems, client/server, the information superhighway, and business use of the Internet.

Chapter 5:   *Introduction to Database Management.*
Updated and reorganized coverage of the role of database management in managing organizational and end user data resources in Section I, and technical topics in database management in Section II.

Chapter 6:   *Information Systems for End User Computing and Collaboration.*
This revised chapter emphasizes the importance of end user computing and office automation applications, including new material on end user collaboration, work group computing, and hypertext and multimedia applications.

Chapter 7:   *Information Systems for Business Operations.*
Section I is a revision of material on IS support of the functional areas of business. Section II contains revised material on EDI, EFT, and transaction processing systems.

Chapter 8:   *Information Systems for Managerial Decision Support.*
Substantial new material has been added to Section I on online analytical processing (OLAP) and decision support and executive information systems. Section II features revised coverage of artificial intelligence and expert systems, and new material on case-based reasoning, neural networks, fuzzy logic, virtual reality, and intelligent agents.

Chapter 9:   *Information Systems for Strategic Advantage.*
Section I of this new chapter contains new and revised coverage of competitive strategy concepts formerly in Chapter 6. Section II contains much new material on the strategic use of IT for business process reengineering, total quality management, agile competition, virtual corporations, and strategic use of the Internet.

Chapter 10:   *Developing Business Solutions with Information Technology.*
Section I contains expanded coverage of end user development, and includes material on CASE formerly in Section III, which has been dropped. Section II contains new material on managing change caused by implementing new information technologies in an organization.

Chapter 11:   *Enterprise and Global Management of Information Technology.*
Section I is a revision of managerial issues in IT including management involvement in IS governance, trends in IS organization, and the managerial and organizational impact of IT. Section II contains much new and revised material on global IT management, including cultural challenges, global company requirements, and global business/IT strategies.

Chapter 12:   *Security and Ethical Challenges of Information Technology.*
Section I of this chapter contains new material on IS security and controls. Section II contains new material on computer crime and ethical controversies on the Internet, as well as revised coverage of ethical and societal IT issues.

Support Materials

The IRWIN Advantage and Effective Series are a collection of laboratory tutorials for the most popular microcomputer software packages available. There are numerous lab manuals available, so you can choose any combination to accommodate your individual class needs.

A revised **software casebook,** *Application Cases in MIS: Using Spreadsheet and Database Software,* second edition, by James N. Morgan of Northern Arizona University, is available to supplement the hands-on exercises in this edition. This optional casebook contains an extensive number of hands-on cases, many of which include a suggested approach for solving each case with spreadsheet or database management software packages to develop solutions for realistic business problems.

An **Instructor's Resource Manual,** revised by Margaret Edmunds of Mount Allison University, is available to instructors upon adoption of the text. It contains instructional aids and suggestions, detailed annotated chapter outlines with instructional suggestions for use in lectures, answers to chapter questions, and problems and case study questions. A data/solutions disk is included for use with the spreadsheet and database exercises in the text as well as the IRM on disk.

There is a **presentation graphics disk** in PowerPoint that supplies color slide shows for each chapter to support classroom discussion.

A **Test Bank,** which contains over 3,000 true-false, multiple choice, and fill-in-the-blank questions, has been prepared by Margaret Edmunds of Mount Allison University. It is available as a separate test manual and in computerized form on floppy disk for use with the Irwin Test Generator Program.

The *Irwin IS Video Library* contains 12 videos, approximately 10–12 minutes long, on various IS concepts like multimedia, business process reengineering, and client/server computing. These videos, along with two new 1997 updates, are available to adopters of the text.

Acknowledgments

The author wishes to acknowledge the assistance of the following reviewers whose constructive criticism and suggestions helped invaluably in shaping the form and content of this text:

Raymond D. Frost, Central Connecticut State University
Diane Graf, Waubonsee Community College
Mark Gruskin, University of Michigan-Dearborn
David W. Letcher, Trenton State College
Douglas Lund, University of Minnesota
Gail L. Rein, SUNY-Buffalo
Albert H. Segars, Boston College
Blair Smith, University of Phoenix
B. S. Vijayaraman, University of Akron
Richard Ye, CSU-Northridge

My thanks also go to James N. Morgan of Northern Arizona University, who authored the software casebook that can be used with this text and developed most of the hands-on Application Exercises in the text, as well as the Data/Solutions disk in the Instructor's Resource Manual. Additional acknowledgments are owed to Margaret Edmunds of Mount Allison University, who revised the Instructor's Resource Manual and prepared the Test Bank.

Much credit should go to several individuals who played significant roles in this project. Thus, my thanks go to the editorial and production team at Irwin, especially Rick Williamson, senior sponsoring editor, Christine Wright, developmental editor; Jean Lou Hess, project supervisor; and Matthew Baldwin, designer. Their ideas and hard work were invaluable contributions to the successful completion of the project. Thanks also to Michele Allen, whose word processing skills helped me meet many manuscript deadlines. The contributions of many authors, publishers, and firms in the computer industry who contributed case material, ideas, illustrations, and photographs used in this text are also thankfully acknowledged.

The unique contribution of over 100 business firms and other computer-using organizations that are the subject of the real world cases, problems, exercises, and case studies in each chapter is also gratefully acknowledged. The real-life situations faced by these firms and organizations provide the readers of this text with a valuable demonstration of the benefits and limitations of using information technology to support business operations, managerial decision making, and strategic advantage.

James A. O'Brien

Acknowledging the Real World of Business

Brief Contents

Contents

Introduction

Why study information systems? Why do businesses need information technology? What do you need to know about the use and management of information technology? The introductory chapter in Module I is designed to answer these fundamental questions.

Chapter 1, "Introduction to Information Systems in Business," introduces you to some key issues in the business use of information technology, the importance of information systems knowledge for business end users, careers in the information systems field, and the conceptual system components and basic types of information systems.

Introduction to Information Systems in Business

CHAPTER OUTLINE

LEARNING OBJECTIVES

After reading and studying this chapter, you should be able to:

1. Explain why knowledge of information systems is important for business end users and identify five areas of information systems knowledge they need.

2. Identify several types of jobs available in the information systems field.

3. Give examples to illustrate how information systems can help support a firm's business operations, managerial decision making, and strategic advantage.

4. Identify how businesses can use IT for strategic competitive advantage through programs of globalization and business process reengineering.

5. Identify and give examples of the components and functions of the generic concept of a system introduced in this chapter.

6. Provide examples of the components of real world information systems. Emphasize the concept that an information system uses people, hardware, software, data, and networks as resources to perform input, processing, output, storage, and control activities that transform data resources into information products.

7. Provide examples of several major types of information systems from your experiences with business organizations in the real world.

Section I

Why Businesses Need Information Technology

Why Information Systems Are Important

Why study **information systems?** That's the same as asking why anyone should study accounting, finance, operations management, marketing, human resource management, or any other major business function. Information systems have become a vital component of successful business firms and other organizations. They thus constitute an essential field of study in business administration and management. That's why most business majors must take a course in information systems. Since you probably intend to be a manager, entrepreneur, or business professional, it is just as important to have a basic understanding of information systems as it is to understand any other functional area in business.

Information System Resources and Technologies

An **information system** is an organized combination of people, hardware, software, communications networks, and data resources that collects, transforms, and disseminates information in an organization. See Figure 1.1. People have relied on information systems to communicate with each other using a variety of physical devices (hardware), information processing instructions (software), communications channels (networks), and stored data (data resources) since the dawn of civilization.

Today's end users rely on many types of information systems (IS). They might include *simple* manual (paper-and-pencil) hardware devices and *informal* (word-of-mouth) communications channels. However, in this text, we will concentrate on *computer-based information systems* that use computer hardware and software, telecommunications networks, computer-based data management techniques, and other forms of **information technology** (IT) to transform data resources into a variety of information products. We will discuss this concept further in the next section and in the chapters of Module II on Information Technology.

An End User Perspective

Anyone who uses an information system or the information it produces is an **end user.** This usually applies to most people in an organization, as distinguished from the smaller number of people who are *information system specialists*, such as systems analysts or professional computer programmers. A *managerial end user* is a manager, entrepreneur, or managerial-level professional who personally uses

FIGURE 1.1

Information systems use people, data, hardware, software, and communications network resources and technologies to collect, transform, and disseminate information in an organization.

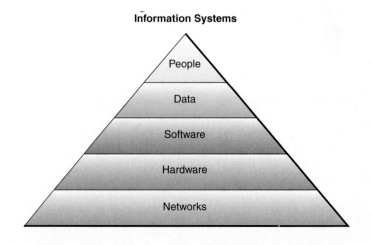

Information Systems

- People
- Data
- Software
- Hardware
- Networks

information systems. So most managers are managerial end users. This book is written for potential managerial end users like you and other students of business administration and management.

Whatever your career will be, you can increase your opportunities for success by becoming a knowledgeable end user of information technology. Businesses and other organizations need people who can use networked computer workstations to enhance their own personal productivity and the productivity of their work groups, departments, and organizations. For example, you should be able to use word processing and electronic mail to communicate more effectively, spreadsheet packages to more effectively analyze decision situations, database management packages to provide better reports on organizational performance, and specialized business software to support your specific work activities. You should also be aware of the management problems and opportunities presented by the use of information technology, and how you can effectively confront such challenges. Then you can play a major role in seeing that information system resources are used efficiently and effectively to benefit your career goals and the goals of the business firms or other organizations you may work for in the future.

An Enterprise Perspective

Information systems play a vital role in the business success of an enterprise. Information technology can provide the information a business needs for efficient operations, effective management, and competitive advantage. However, if information systems do not properly support the strategic objectives, business operations, or management needs of an enterprise, they can seriously damage its prospects for survival and success. So, the proper management of information systems is a major challenge for managers. Thus, the information systems function represents:

- A major functional area of business that is as important to business success as the functions of accounting, finance, operations management, marketing, and human resource management.
- A major part of the resources of an enterprise and its cost of doing business, thus posing a major resource management challenge.
- An important factor affecting operational efficiency, employee productivity and morale, and customer service and satisfaction.
- A major source of information and support needed to promote effective decision making by managers.
- An important ingredient in developing competitive products and services that give an organization a strategic advantage in the global marketplace.
- A vital, dynamic, and challenging career opportunity for millions of men and women.

A Global Society Perspective

We are living in a **global information society**, with a global economy that is increasingly dependent on the creation, management, and distribution of information resources. So information is a basic resource in today's society. People in many nations no longer live in agricultural societies, composed primarily of farmers, or even industrial societies, where a majority of the workforce consists of factory workers. Instead, the workforce in many nations consists primarily of workers in service occupations or **knowledge workers**, that is, people who spend most of their workday creating, using, and distributing information. See Figure 1.2.

Knowledge workers include executives, managers, and supervisors; professionals such as accountants, engineers, scientists, stockbrokers, and teachers; and staff personnel such as secretaries and clerical office personnel. Most of them are end users

FIGURE 1.2

Business end users are knowledge workers who are part of a global information society.

Charles Thatcher/Tony Stone Images.

who make their livings using information systems to create, distribute, manage, and use information resources. Thus, information systems help them manage the human, financial, material, energy, and other resources involved in their work responsibilities.

This brings up the question of what your responsibilities are in the ethical use of information technology. As a prospective managerial end user and knowledge worker, you should begin to think about what **ethical responsibilities** are generated by the use of information systems. For example, what uses of information technology might be considered improper or irresponsible to other individuals or to society? What is the proper use of an organization's information resources? What does it take to be a *responsible end user* of information technology and protect yourself from computer crime? These are some of the questions that outline the ethical dimensions of information systems that we will discuss in this text.

Information and information systems, then, are valuable resources for knowledge workers, their organizations, and society. A major challenge for our global information society is to manage its information resources to benefit all members of society while meeting the strategic goals of organizations and nations. This means, for example, using information systems to find more efficient, profitable, and socially responsible ways of using the world's limited supplies of material, energy, and other resources. Since the information systems of so many organizations are interconnected by local, regional, and global telecommunications networks, knowledge workers can now access and distribute information and manage resources all over the world. For these reasons, information systems play an increasingly vital role in our global economy, as many real world cases and problems in the text will demonstrate.

The Real World of Information Systems

Let's take a moment to bring the real world into our discussion of the importance of information systems. Read the Real World Case of California Pizza Kitchen on page 7. Then let's analyze it together.

CALIFORNIA PIZZA KITCHEN: IMPROVING EFFICIENCY AND PROFITS WITH IS

California Pizza Kitchen is relying on more than just new toppings and secret recipes to improve its profit margins.

A new computer network has improved the restaurant chain's profit margins by as much as 5 percent in some stores and has allowed California Pizza Kitchen to slice its costs, said Rick Smith, director of MIS at the company.

The setup also has allowed the company to automate and speed up the time it takes to perform routing tasks such as adding up the day's sales receipts. The biweekly payroll data, which used to take at least a day to tabulate, takes only eight minutes to transmit from 77 restaurants nationwide. The result: Store managers spend an "average of 15 percent more time in the restaurant assisting customers," Smith said.

To accomplish all this, California Pizza Kitchen recently installed a PC-based computer network using the Microsoft Windows NT network operating system and RemoteWare, a software telecommunications package from XcelleNet, Inc. This setup has been installed at corporate headquarters in Los Angeles and at restaurants nationwide. The company wanted a network environment that would let it use one network operating system for point-of-sale functions—including placing orders and paying the check—and back-office tasks such as tracking food costs and inventory.

RemoteWare lets the company's managers and district managers, who often travel among three or four restaurants a day, access the food cost system from the road. This lets them keep current with inventory levels, recipes, sales, and personnel schedules. RemoteWare's communications automation facility also ensures that the desktop environment is in sync for end users in corporate offices, the restaurants, and remote and mobile users' laptops.

This system has made operations more efficient at the restaurant chain. With the new network and remote computing package, California Pizza Kitchen managers can easily track and monitor every aspect of the operation. That includes making informed decisions about how much labor each restaurant requires, when to make all entrees and side dishes, and how much staff is needed.

Smith says the new setup has allowed the firm "to trim the fat from the organization and given us better control of the bottom line." And Smith has the stats to back him up:

- Store managers spend 15 percent more time with customers and less time performing administrative tasks.
- Labor scheduling and labor management tasks are automated.
- Information on itemized food spending is received quickly.
- Recipe development is faster.
- Daily sales receipts are processed quicker.
- Payroll data is collected from 77 stores in eight minutes.
- Profit margins have risen 5 percent.

CASE STUDY QUESTIONS

1. How important are computer-based information systems to the success of California Pizza Kitchen?

2. What business operations have been improved? What business benefits have resulted?

3. Could other types of businesses benefit by using a similar network? Give several examples.

Source: Adapted from Laura DiDio, "Pizzeria Eats Up Client/Server Pie," *Computerworld*, March 4, 1996, pp. 69–70.

We can learn a lot about the importance of computers and information systems from the Real World Case of California Pizza Kitchen.

This company's use of information technology has significantly improved their business efficiency and profitability. California Pizza Kitchen replaced their old computer system with a new computer network that gives their managers a faster, more powerful and versatile tool to control their business operations. The speed and efficiency of performing routine tasks such as adding up daily sales receipts, tabulating employee payroll, placing orders and paying suppliers, and tracking food costs and

Analyzing California Pizza Kitchen

inventory have all been dramatically improved with the new system. Just as importantly, managers can access their nationwide network from any store, or anywhere on the road to keep track of sales, inventory levels, and other key business results.

The new network has not only greatly improved the efficiency of California Pizza Kitchen's business operations, but has significantly improved the company's profitability. Store managers now have more time to spend assisting customers in their restaurants. The company's managers also have more time and the information resources they need to improve their decision making concerning key managerial and strategic issues that face any fast growing, successful company. So California Pizza Kitchen is just one more good example of the key role information technology plays in helping all kinds of businesses succeed in today's dynamic business environment.

Careers in Information Systems

Computers and their use in information systems have created interesting, highly paid, and challenging career opportunities for millions of men and women. Employment opportunities in the field of computers and information systems are excellent, as organizations continue to expand their use of computers. National employment surveys continually forecast shortages of qualified information systems personnel in many job categories. For these reasons, learning more about computers may help you decide if you want to pursue a computer-related career. Job opportunities in computers and information systems are continually changing due to dynamic developments in information technology, including computer hardware, software, telecommunications, and other technologies. One major source of jobs is the computer industry itself. Thousands of companies develop, manufacture, market, and service computer hardware and software, or provide related services such as computer training, telecommunications network services, or end user consulting. See Figure 1.3.

Academic Programs in IS

Graduates of computer science programs hold many of the more technical jobs in the computer industry. Their education helps prepare them for careers in the research and development of computer hardware, systems software, and application software packages. Graduates of college and university programs in information systems

FIGURE 1.3

Providing end user consulting services is a major career opportunity in information systems.

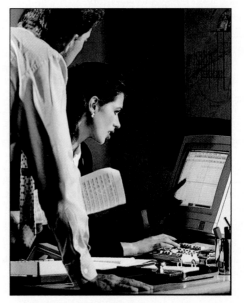

Frank Herholdt/Tony Stone Images.

(IS), management information systems (MIS), or computer information systems (CIS) hold millions of other computer-related jobs. The focus of these programs is training students to be information systems specialists. That's because the biggest source of jobs is the hundreds of thousands of businesses, government agencies, and other organizations that use computers. They need many types of IS managers and specialists to help them support the work activities and supply the information needs of their end users.

Information systems specialists are IS professionals who develop, implement, and operate computer-based information systems. Typical examples include systems analysts, programmers, and computer operators. Basically, systems analysts design information systems based on the information requirements of end users, programmers prepare computer programs based on the specifications of systems analysts, and computer operators operate large computer systems.

IS Specialists

Organizations also need many other managerial, technical, and clerical IS personnel. For example, the top IS management job in many organizations belongs to the *chief information officer* (CIO). This executive oversees the use of information technology throughout an organization, concentrating especially on IS planning and strategy. Examples of more technical job categories include database analysts and administrators who help develop and oversee the use of the common databases of an organization, telecommunications analysts and network managers who develop and supervise the use of the telecommunications network resources, and EDP (electronic data processing) auditors who audit the security and performance of computer-based systems. Examples of jobs in end user services include positions as user consultants, user trainers, and user liaisons. These IS specialists support efforts by employees to use computers to accomplish their work activities more easily and productively.

Figures 1.4 and 1.5 give valuable insight into the variety of job types and salaries commanded by many IS managers and specialists. Actual salaries range higher and lower than the average shown, depending on such factors as the size and geographic location of an organization. Note also that the career paths for IS professionals show how they can move upward into management or specialist positions.

FIGURE 1.4

Examples of important job categories and annual salaries in information services.

Top IS Management			
CIO/VP IS/ MIS/DP: $131,600	Director, systems development: $93,500	Director, networks: $90,700	Director, IS operations: $84,700
Networks			
Telecommunications manager: $69,700	Telecommunications specialist: $51,600	Network administrator: $47,400	LAN manager: $50,700
Systems Development			
Project manager, systems and programming: $62,900	Senior systems analyst: $56,800	Database manager: $61,100	Database analyst: $50,500
PC End User Support			
Microcomputer manager/End user computing manager: $59,300	Technical support manager/Help desk manager: $49,900	Business services analyst: $39,500	PC technical support specialist: $36,500

Source: Adapted from "Computerworld's Ninth Annual Salary Survey" by Alan Earls, *Computerworld*, Sept. 4, 1995, pp. 70–74. Copyright 1995 by Computerworld, Inc., Framingham, MA 01701—Reprinted from *Computerworld*.

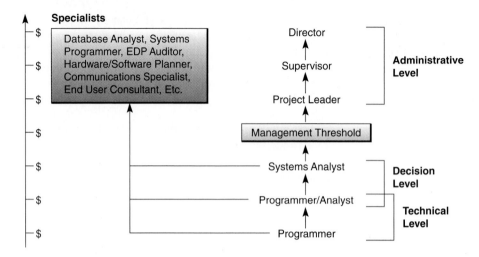

FIGURE 1.5

Career paths for systems development personnel can lead into management or branch into a variety of specialist positions.

The Fundamental Roles of Information Systems

Information technology is reshaping the basics of business. Customer service, operations, product and marketing strategies, and distribution are heavily, or sometimes even entirely, dependent on IT. The computers that support these functions can be found on the desk, on the shop floor, in the store, even in briefcases. Information technology, and its expense, have become an everyday part of business life [8].

Figure 1.6 illustrates the fundamental reasons for the use of information technology in business. Information systems perform three vital roles in any type of organization:

- Support of business operations.
- Support of managerial decision making.
- Support of strategic competitive advantage.

Let's take a retail store as an example to illustrate this important point. As a consumer, you have to deal regularly with the information systems that support business operations at the many retail stores where you shop. For example, most retail stores now use computer-based information systems to help them record customer purchases, keep track of inventory, pay employees, buy new merchandise, and evaluate sales trends. Store operations would grind to a halt without the support of such information systems. See Figures 1.7 and 1.8.

Information systems also help store managers make better decisions and attempt to gain a strategic competitive advantage. For example, decisions on what lines of merchandise need to be added or discontinued, or on what kind of investment they require, are typically made after an analysis provided by computer-based information systems. This not only supports the decision making of store managers but also helps them look for ways to gain an advantage over other retailers in the competition for customers.

For example, store managers might make a decision to install computerized touch-screen catalog ordering systems in all of their stores, tied in with computer-based telephone ordering systems and a home computer shopping network. This might lure customers away from other stores, based on the ease of ordering merchandise provided by such computer-based information systems. Thus, strategic information systems can help provide strategic products and services that give a business organization a comparative advantage over its competitors.

Information Systems

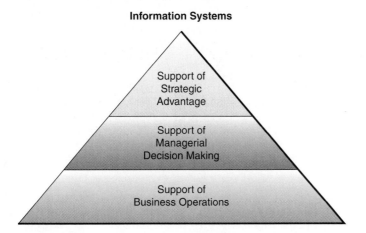

FIGURE 1.6

The three major roles of information systems. Information systems provide an organization with support for business operations, managerial decision making, and strategic advantage.

Today's managers need all the help they can get. Their firms are being buffeted on all sides by strong, frequently shifting winds of change. Organizations' strategic objectives (chosen markets, product strategy, expected outcomes) and their business processes (such as research and development, production, cash-flow management, and order fulfillment) are undergoing significant and volatile changes, placing great pressure on firms and their managers [2].

The shifting winds of change in today's business environment have made information systems and information technology vital components that help keep an enterprise on target to meet its business goals. Information technology has become an indispensable ingredient in several strategic thrusts that businesses have initiated to meet the challenge of change. These include globalization, business process reengineering, agile competition, and using information technology for competitive advantage. They are a major reason why today's businesses need information technology. We will introduce these topics here and cover them in greater detail in later chapters.

As we mentioned earlier, many companies are in the process of globalization; that is, becoming global enterprises. For example, businesses are expanding into global markets for their products and services, using global production facilities to manufacture or assemble products, raising money in global capital markets, forming alliances

The Winds of Change

Globalization

Robert Brenner/PhotoEdit.

FIGURE 1.7

Waldenbooks bookstores depend on computer-based information systems to support their business operations, managerial decision making, and competitive advantage.

FIGURE 1.8

Managers and employees at Waldenbooks bookstores depend on the hardware, software, telecommunications network, and database resources of their computer-based information systems.

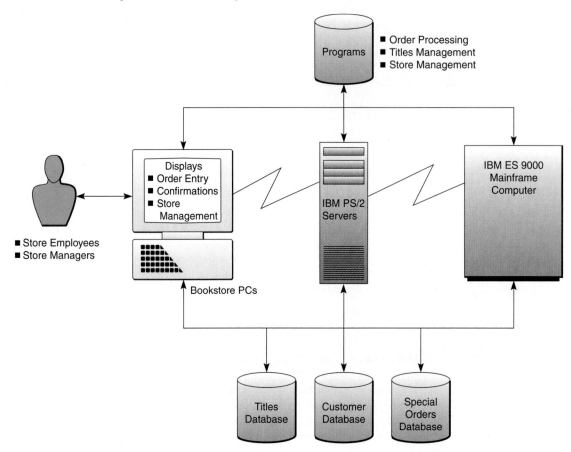

with global partners, and battling with global competitors for customers from all over the globe. Managing and accomplishing these strategic changes would be impossible without the global computing and telecommunications networks that are the central nervous system of today's global companies.

Figure 1.9 illustrates how information technology supports globalization. For example, global companies operate in a competitive environment in which networked computer systems make possible global markets that can instantly and cheaply process business transactions. So companies can now operate globally, sometimes by forming global business alliances with other organizations, including customers, suppliers, former competitors, consultants, and government agencies. Today's networked global corporation can collectively exploit many national market niches that would be too small for any one national company to service. They can also pool skills from many countries to work on projects that need workers with a variety of skills that cannot be found in any one country [1]. We will discuss managing global IT and its impact on global business operations further in Chapter 11.

Business Process Reengineering

When IT *substitutes* for human effort, it *automates* a task or process.
When IT *augments* human effort, it *informates* a task or process.
When IT *restructures*, it *transforms* a set of tasks or processes [2].

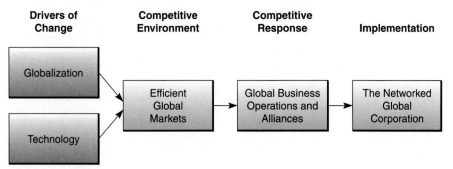

Source: Adapted and reprinted by permission of Harvard Business School Press from *Globalization, Technology, and Competition: The Fusion of Computers and Telecommunications in the 1990s* by Stephen P. Bradley, Jerry A. Hausman, and Richard L. Nolan. Boston: 1993, p. 4. Copyright © 1993 by the President and Fellows of Harvard College.

FIGURE 1.9

How information technology can support the globalization of business.

Businesses have used information technology for many years to automate tasks—from automated bookkeeping to automated manufacturing. More recently, businesses have used computer-based information systems to support the analysis, interpretation, and presentation of data in business decision making. Using a spreadsheet package to analyze business alternatives is a common example of *informating* a business task.

However, **business process reengineering** (BPR) is an example of how information technology is being used to restructure work by transforming business processes. A business process is any set of activities designed to produce a specified output for a customer or market. New product development or the purchase of inventory are typical examples. Reengineering guru Michael Hammer defines reengineering as "the fundamental rethinking and radical redesign of business processes to achieve dramatic improvements, such as cost, quality, service, and speed" [6]. Thus, reengineering questions all assumptions about "the way we do business." It focuses on the *how* and *why* of a business process so major changes can be made in how work is accomplished. BPR thus moves far beyond mere cost cutting or automating a process to make marginal improvements [2]. See Figure 1.10.

- *Old rule:* Managers make all decisions.

  Information technology: Decision support tools (database access, modeling software).

  New rule: Decision making is part of everyone's job.

- *Old rule:* Only experts can perform complex work.

  Information technology: Expert systems.

  New rule: A generalist can do the work of an expert.

- *Old rule:* Information can appear in only one place at one time.

  Information technology: Shared databases.

  New rule: Information can appear simultaneously in as many places as it is needed.

- *Old rule:* Field personnel need offices where they can receive, store, retrieve, and transmit information.

  Information technology: Wireless data communication and portable computers.

  New rule: Field personnel can send and receive information wherever they are.

FIGURE 1.10

How information technology can help reengineer business processes.

Source: Adapted from Michael Hammer and James Champy. *Reengineering the Corporation: A Manifesto for Business Revolution* (New York: HarperCollins, 1993), pp. 92–96. Copyright © 1993 by Michael Hammer and James Champy. Reprinted by permission of HarperCollins Publishers, Inc.

FIGURE 1.11

How information technology reengineered business processes at several levels of a business.

	IT Initiative	Process Changed	Business Benefit
Individual	Laptop System	Sales Call	Increased Sales
Work Group	Product Database	Product Distribution	Greater Customer Satisfaction
Business Unit	Product Management System	Marketing Channel Communications	Improved Competitive Position

Source: Adapted and reprinted by permission of Harvard Business School Press from *Process Innovation: Reengineering Work through Information Technology* by Thomas H. Davenport. Boston: 1993, p. 47. Copyright © 1993 by Ernst & Young.

Figure 1.11 illustrates how information technology was used to help reengineer several business processes at an agricultural chemical company. Notice that business processes at the individual, work group, and business unit levels can be changed by using information technologies to provide economic benefits. For example, the use of laptops for sales calls supported greater interaction between the individual salespeople and customers of an agricultural chemicals company and resulted in significantly greater sales [3].

Competitive Advantage

Using information technology for globalization and business process reengineering frequently results in the development of information systems that help give a company a **competitive advantage** in the marketplace. These *strategic information systems* use information technology to develop products, services, processes, and capabilities that give a business a strategic advantage over the competitive forces it faces in its industry. These forces include not only a firm's competitors but also its customers and suppliers, potential new entrants into its industry, and companies offering substitutes for its products and services. Information technology can be used to implement a variety of competitive strategies to confront these competitive forces [2, 8]. These include:

- **Cost strategies:** Becoming a low-cost producer, lowering your customers' or suppliers' costs, or increasing the costs your competitors must pay to remain in the industry.
- **Differentiation strategies:** Developing ways to differentiate your company's products or services from your competitors' so your customers perceive your products or services as having unique features or benefits.
- **Innovation strategies:** Introducing unique products or services, or making radical changes in your business processes that cause fundamental changes in the way business is conducted in your industry.

Figure 1.12 provides a variety of examples of how information technology has helped businesses gain competitive advantages using such strategies [9]. In Chapter 9, we will discuss in greater detail how businesses are using information technology to gain strategic competitive advantages.

What You Need to Know

The real world example of California Pizza Kitchen should help convince you that business end users need to know how information systems can be employed successfully in a global business environment. That's why this text contains more than 70 Real World Cases and Problems describing actual situations (not fictional stories)

FIGURE 1.12

Examples of the use of information technology to implement strategies for competitive advantage.

Strategy	Company	Strategic Information System	Business Benefit
Cost Leadership	Levitz Furniture	Centralized Buying	Cut Purchasing Costs
	Metropolitan Life	Medical Care Monitoring	Cut Medical Costs
	Deere & Company	Machine Tool Control	Cut Manufacturing Costs
Differentiation	Navistar	Portable Computer-Based Customer Needs Analysis	Increase in Market Share
	Setco Industries	Computer-Aided Job Estimation	Increase in Market Share
	Consolidated Freightways	Customer Online Shipment Tracking	Increase in Market Share
Innovation	Merrill Lynch	Customer Cash Management Accounts	Market Leadership
	Federal Express	Online Package Tracking and Flight Management	Market Leadership
	McKesson Corp.	Customer Order Entry and Merchandising	Market Leadership

occurring in real companies and organizations throughout the world. Business firms and other organizations need people who can help them manage their information resources. Knowledgeable managerial end users can play a major role in *information resource management* (IRM). That is, they can learn to manage information system hardware, software, data, and information resources so they are used for the efficient operation, effective management, and strategic success of their organizations.

However, what exactly does a business end user need to know about information systems? The answers are as diverse and dynamic as the area itself. As we have just mentioned, the field of information systems, like other areas in management and business administration, is based on a variety of academic disciplines and encompasses a great amount of technological and behavioral knowledge. The IS field is constantly changing and expanding as dramatic technological developments and behavioral research findings push back the frontiers of this dynamic discipline.

> Because many chief executive officers, if not most, are resigned to techno-illiteracy, they depend on resident technologists—usually at the chief information officer level—for critical decisions that may make or break the company. Unfortunately, as much as CEOs are unfamiliar with information technology, the CIOs are unfamiliar with the core businesses that technology is intended to support [10].

A Framework for Business End Users

That's the conclusion of Charles Wang, the chairman and CEO of Computer Associates International, a multibillion-dollar software company, after meeting with hundreds of CEOs throughout the world. So even top executives can feel overwhelmed by the complex technologies, abstract behavioral concepts, and specialized applications involved in the field of information systems. However, most managers and other end users do not have to absorb all of this knowledge. Figure 1.13 illustrates a useful conceptual framework that organizes the knowledge in this text and outlines what end users need to know about information systems. It emphasizes that you should concentrate your efforts in five areas of knowledge:

FIGURE 1.13
This framework outlines the major areas of information systems knowledge needed by business end users.

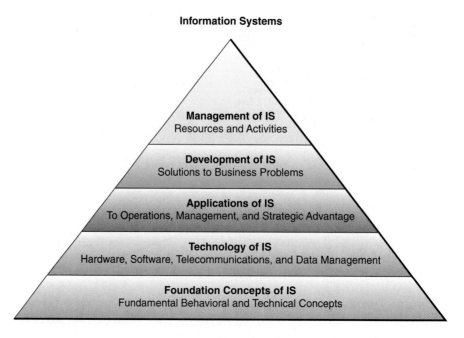

Information Systems

Management of IS
Resources and Activities

Development of IS
Solutions to Business Problems

Applications of IS
To Operations, Management, and Strategic Advantage

Technology of IS
Hardware, Software, Telecommunications, and Data Management

Foundation Concepts of IS
Fundamental Behavioral and Technical Concepts

- **Foundation Concepts.** Fundamental behavioral and technical concepts that will help you understand how information systems can support the business operations, managerial decision making, and strategic advantage of business firms and other organizations. Chapter 1 and other chapters of the text support this area of knowledge.

- **Technology.** Major concepts, developments, and management issues in **information technology**—that is, hardware, software, telecommunications, database management, and other information processing technologies. Chapters 2 through 5 of Module II along with other chapters of the text support this area of information systems knowledge.

- **Applications.** The major uses of information systems for end user computing and the operations, management, and competitive advantage of business firms and other organizations are covered in Chapters 6 to 9 of Module III.

- **Development.** How end users or information specialists develop information systems solutions to business problems using fundamental problem-solving and developmental methodologies. Chapter 10 of Module IV helps you gain such knowledge and begin applying it to simple business problems.

- **Management.** The challenges involved in managing the resources and technologies of information systems at the end user, enterprise, and global levels of a business. Chapters 11 and 12 of Module IV specifically cover these topics, but all of the chapters in the text emphasize the managerial challenges of information technology.

REAL WORLD CASE

AUTO-BY-TEL AND OTHERS: BUYING A CAR ON THE INTERNET

If buying a new car gives you about as much pleasure as scheduling a root canal, take heart. Computer technology, modern merchandising, and old-fashioned entrepreneurial spirit are about to put traditional car dealers on the endangered species list.

Let's say you're thinking of buying a car. You can visit a half-dozen dealers, kick tires, and dicker with the salespeople. Or you can dial up the World Wide Web and make your purchase in peace. Say you want a Ford Explorer, the third most popular vehicle in the United States. You need to make three online connections, all free.

Start by calling DealerNet (http://www.dealernet.com/), created by Reynolds & Reynolds, which provides computer services to dealers. You can see a picture of the Explorer and find out how it compares with competitors like the Jeep Grand Cherokee in such key areas as trunk space, fuel economy, and price.

Suppose you settle on a four-door, four-wheel-drive XLT model. Key over to the prices posted by Edmund Publications (http://www.news.com/magazines/edmunds), a longtime compiler of such information. There you discover that while the base XLT has a sticker price of $25,710, the dealer pays only $23,225. You also learn a little-known fact: The XLT carries a 3 percent holdback—essentially a rebate for each Explorer that Ford pays to the dealer at the end of the year. This may help you in evaluating the price your dealer quotes.

When you're ready to order, type in http://www.auto-bytel.com/. There are several buying services on the Web, but Auto-By-Tel is free. A few days after you've placed your order, you'll get a call from a nearby dealer. He will charge you a fixed amount over the invoice and deliver the car. Now, wasn't that easy!

The experience of George Chin, 43, a technical services manager in upstate New York, is typical. Using the Internet, he compared the specifications of various models and learned their retail and wholesale prices. Then he placed an electronic order for a Ford Explorer XLT with Auto-By-Tel, a computerized broker service. A few days later, he got a call from a nearby dealer, Bill Colb Ford,

who filled the order for a fixed amount over the wholesale price and delivered the vehicle. Says Chin: "The whole experience was painless. There was no price haggling. No psychological pressure. No surprises."

Auto-By-Tel is the creation of former California Ford and Chrysler dealer Peter Ellis. When his idea for selling cars on QVC television didn't work out two years ago, he decided to retail them in cyberspace. Ellis took sites on established online services like CompuServe, as well as on the World Wide Web, to solicit orders from customers. He relays an order to one of 1,200 dealers, each of which pays Ellis between $200 and $1,500 a month for referrals. The margins on each sale are low (about $600), but so are the costs. By snagging their customer electronically, the dealers can cut their marketing expense from $400 a car to $30. In one month, over 12,000 potential car buyers logged on to Auto-By-Tel.

Electronic shopping has the potential to add enormous value to the buying process and reduce costs to a minimum. Manufacturers should be able to get accurate and timely data about consumer preferences that will enable them to schedule parts deliveries and production runs more sensibly. Even better, cars can be sold without building showrooms.

Eventually a customer may be able to conduct an electronic auction, asking, say, all the Ford dealers in the Northeast to give him the price and availability of a particular Explorer—delivered to his driveway, of course—and seeing how much they will pay for his trade-in. Then he could dial up the factory where his car will be built, schedule it for the production queue, and get a date for its delivery.

Dealers won't become extinct, of course. But for a change, neither they nor the manufacturer will be in control of selling a car. With all these new ways to buy, it will be the customer, finally, who's in the driver's seat.

CASE STUDY QUESTIONS

1. How important are information technology and computer-based information systems for doing business on the Internet? Explain.

2. What are the benefits of electronic shopping to consumers and businesses?

3. Would you like to buy a car on the Internet? Why or why not?

Source: Adapted from Alex Taylor III, "How to Buy a Car on the Internet . . . and Other New Ways to Make the Second Biggest Purchase of a Lifetime," *Fortune*, March 4, 1996, pp. 164–68.

Section II   *Fundamentals of Information Systems*

System concepts underlie the field of information systems. That's why this section shows you how generic system concepts apply to business firms and the components and activities of information systems. Understanding system concepts will help you understand many other concepts in the technology, applications, development, and management of information systems that we will cover in this text. For example, system concepts help you understand:

- That computers are systems of information processing components.
- That business uses of computers are really interconnected business information systems.
- That developing ways to use computers in business includes designing the basic components of information systems.
- That managing information technology emphasizes the quality, business value, and security of an organization's information systems.

System Concepts

What is a system? A system can be simply defined as *a group of interrelated or interacting elements forming a unified whole.* Many examples of systems can be found in the physical and biological sciences, in modern technology, and in human society. Thus, we can talk of the physical system of the sun and its planets, the biological system of the human body, the technological system of an oil refinery, and the socioeconomic system of a business organization. However, the following generic system concept provides a more appropriate framework for describing information systems:

A **system** is a group of interrelated components working together toward a common goal by accepting inputs and producing outputs in an organized transformation process. Such a system (sometimes called a *dynamic system*) has three basic interacting components or functions:

- **Input** involves capturing and assembling elements that enter the system to be processed. For example, raw materials, energy, data, and human effort must be secured and organized for processing.
- **Processing** involves transformation processes that convert input into output. Examples are a manufacturing process, the human breathing process, or mathematical calculations.
- **Output** involves transferring elements that have been produced by a transformation process to their ultimate destination. For example, finished products, human services, and management information must be transmitted to their human users.

EXAMPLE   A manufacturing system accepts raw materials as input and produces finished goods as output. An information system also is a system that accepts resources (data) as input and processes them into products (information) as output. See Figure 1.14.

The system concept becomes even more useful by including two additional components: feedback and control. A system with feedback and control components is sometimes called a *cybernetic* system, that is, a self-monitoring, self-regulating system.

Feedback and Control

- **Feedback** is data about the performance of a system. For example, data about sales performance is feedback to a sales manager.
- **Control** involves monitoring and evaluating feedback to determine whether a system is moving toward the achievement of its goal. The control function then makes necessary adjustments to a system's input and processing components to ensure that it produces proper output. For example, a sales manager exercises control when he or she reassigns salespersons to new sales territories after evaluating feedback about their sales performance.

Feedback is frequently included as part of the concept of the control function because it is such a necessary part of its operation. Figure 1.14 shows the relationship of feedback and control to the other components of a system. Note the dashed arrows indicating the flow of feedback data to the managerial control component and the resulting control signals to the other components. This emphasizes that the role of feedback and control is to ensure that other system components properly transform inputs into outputs so a system can achieve its goal.

FIGURE 1.14

This manufacturing system illustrates the generic components of many types of systems.

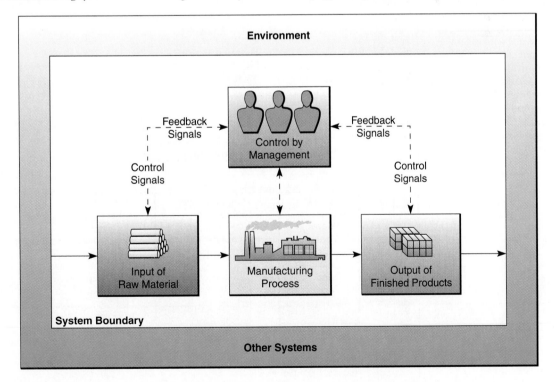

EXAMPLE   A familiar example of a self-monitoring, self-regulating system is the thermostat-controlled heating system found in many homes; it automatically monitors and regulates itself to maintain a desired temperature. Another example is the human body that can be regarded as a cybernetic system that automatically monitors and adjusts many of its functions, such as temperature, heartbeat, and breathing. A business also has many control activities. For example, computers may monitor and control manufacturing processes, accounting procedures help control financial systems, data entry displays provide control of data entry activities, and sales quotas and sales bonuses attempt to control sales performance.

Other System Characteristics

Figure 1.14 points out several other system characteristics that are important to a proper understanding of information systems. Note that a system does not exist in a vacuum; rather, it exists and functions in an *environment* containing other systems. If a system is one of the components of a larger system, it is a **subsystem**, and the larger system is its environment. Also, its system *boundary* separates a system from its environment and other systems.

Several systems may share the same environment. Some of these systems may be connected to one another by means of a shared boundary, or *interface*. Figure 1.14 also illustrates the concept of an *open system;* that is, a system that interacts with other systems in its environment. In this diagram, the system exchanges inputs and outputs with its environment. Thus we could say that it is connected to its environment by

FIGURE 1.15

A business is an organizational system where *economic resources* (input) are transformed by various *organizational processes* (processing) into *goods and services* (output). *Information systems* provide information (feedback) on the operations of the system to *management* for the direction and maintenance of the system (control), as it exchanges inputs and outputs with its environment.

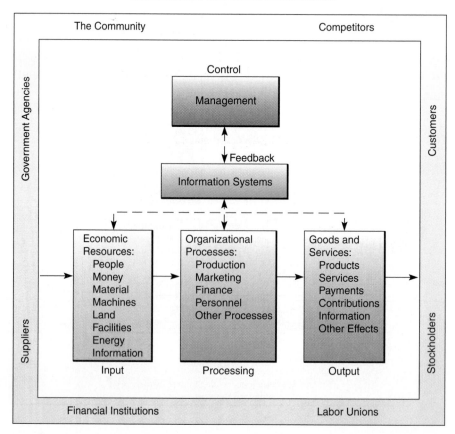

Stakeholders in the Business Environment

input and output interfaces. Finally, a system that has the ability to change itself or its environment in order to survive is an *adaptive system*. Now let's look at the example suggested by Figure 1.15.

EXAMPLE   Organizations such as businesses and government agencies are good examples of the systems in society, which is their environment. Society contains a multitude of such systems, including individuals and their social, political, and economic institutions. Organizations themselves consist of many subsystems, such as departments, divisions, and other work groups. Organizations are examples of open systems because they interface and interact with other systems in their environment. Finally, organizations are examples of adaptive systems, since they can modify themselves to meet the demands of a changing environment.

We are now ready to apply the system concepts we have learned to help us better understand how an information system works. For example, we have said that an information system is a system that accepts data resources as input and processes them into information products as output. How does an information system accomplish this? What system components and activities are involved?

Figure 1.16 illustrates an **information system model** that expresses a fundamental conceptual framework for the major components and activities of information systems.

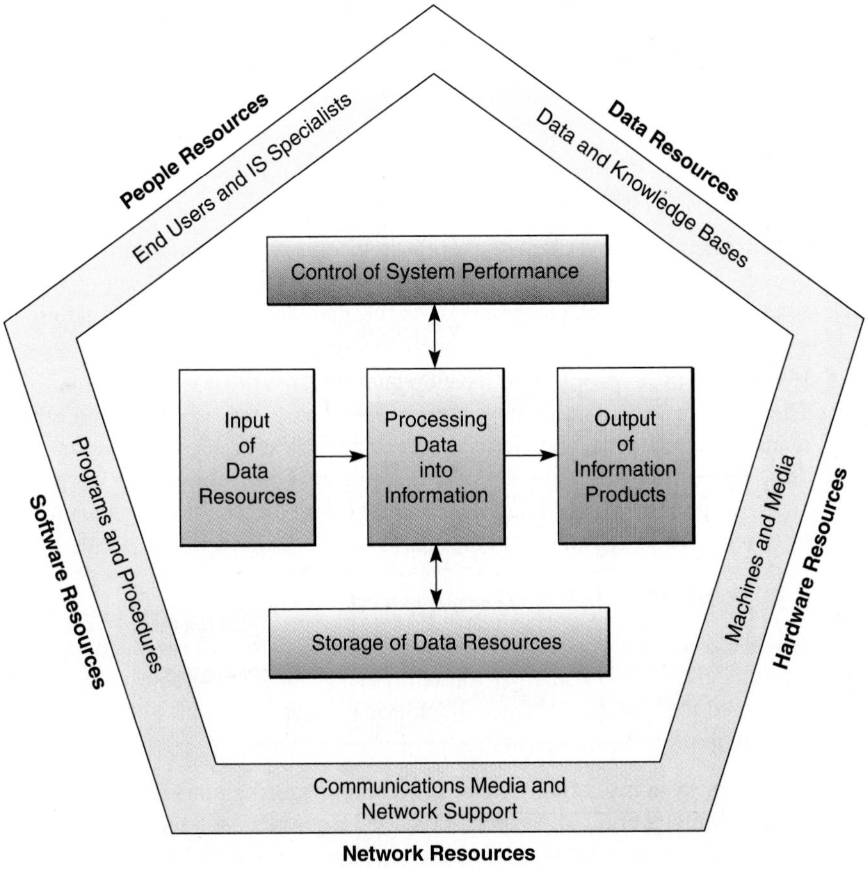

Components of an Information System

FIGURE 1.16

The components of an information system. All information systems use people, hardware, software, data, and network resources to perform input, processing, output, storage, and control activities that transform data resources into information products.

An information system uses the resources of people (end users and IS specialists), hardware (machines and media), software (programs and procedures), data (data and knowledge bases), and networks (communications media and network support) to perform input, processing, output, storage, and control activities that convert data resources into information products.

This information system model highlights the relationships among the components and activities of information systems. It provides a framework that emphasizes four major concepts that can be applied to all types of information systems:

- People, hardware, software, data, and networks are the five basic resources of information systems.
- People resources include end users and IS specialists, hardware resources consist of machines and media, software resources include both programs and procedures, data resources can include data and knowledge bases, and network resources can include communications media and network support.
- Data resources are transformed by information processing activities into a variety of information products for end users.
- Information processing consists of input, processing, output, storage, and control activities.

Information System Resources

Our basic IS model shows that an information system consists of five major resources: people, hardware, software, data, and networks. Let's briefly discuss several basic concepts and examples of the roles these resources play as the fundamental components of information systems. You should be able to recognize these five components at work in any type of information system you encounter in the real world. Figure 1.17 outlines several examples of typical information system resources and products.

People Resources

People are required for the operation of all information systems. These **people resources** include *end users* and *IS specialists*.

- **End users** (also called users or clients) are people who use an information system or the information it produces. They can be accountants, salespersons, engineers, clerks, customers, or managers. Most of us are information system end users.
- **IS specialists** are people who develop and operate information systems. They include systems analysts, programmers, computer operators, and other managerial, technical, and clerical IS personnel. Briefly, systems analysts design information systems based on the information requirements of end users; programmers prepare computer programs based on the specifications of systems analysts; and computer operators operate computer systems.

Hardware Resources

The concept of **hardware resources** includes all physical devices and materials used in information processing. Specifically, it includes not only **machines,** such as computers and calculators, but also all data **media,** that is, all tangible objects on which data is recorded from sheets of paper to magnetic disks. Examples of hardware in computer-based information systems are:

- **Computer systems,** which consist of central processing units (CPUs) and a variety of interconnected peripheral devices. Examples are large mainframe computer systems, midrange computer systems, and microcomputer systems.

- **Computer peripherals,** which are devices such as a keyboard or electronic mouse for input of data and commands, a video screen or printer for output of information, and magnetic or optical disks for storage of data resources.

The concept of **software resources** includes all sets of information processing instructions. This generic concept of software includes not only the sets of operating instructions called **programs,** which direct and control computer hardware, but also the sets of information processing instructions needed by people, called **procedures.** So even information systems that don't use computers have a software resource component. The following are examples of software resources:

Software Resources

- **System software,** such as an *operating system* program, which controls and supports the operations of a computer system.
- **Application software,** which are programs that direct processing for a particular use of computers by end users. Examples are a sales analysis program, a payroll program, and a word processing program.
- **Procedures,** which are operating instructions for the people who will use an information system. Examples are instructions for filling out a paper form or using a software package.

Data is more than the raw material of information systems. The concept of data resources has been broadened by managers and information systems professionals. They realize that data constitutes a valuable organizational resource. Thus, you should view data as **data resources** that must be managed effectively to benefit all end users in an organization.

Data Resources

People Resources

Specialists—systems analysts, programmers, computer operators.
End Users—anyone else who uses information systems.

Hardware Resources

Machines—computers, video monitors, magnetic disk drives, printers, optical scanners.
Media—floppy disks, magnetic tape, optical disks, plastic cards, paper forms.

Software Resources

Programs—operating system programs, spreadsheet programs, word processing programs, payroll programs.
Procedures—data entry procedures, error correction procedures, paycheck distribution procedures.

Data Resources

Product descriptions, customer records, employee files, inventory databases.

Network Resources

Communications media, communications processors, network access and control software.

Information Products

Management reports and business documents using text and graphics displays, audio responses, and paper forms.

FIGURE 1.17

Examples of information system resources and products.

Data can take many forms, including traditional *alphanumeric data*, composed of numbers and alphabetical and other characters that describe business transactions and other events and entities. *Text data*, consisting of sentences and paragraphs used in written communications; *image data*, such as graphic shapes and figures; and *audio data*, the human voice and other sounds, are also important forms of data.

The data resources of information systems are typically organized into:

- **Databases** that hold processed and organized data.
- **Knowledge bases** that hold knowledge in a variety of forms such as facts and rules of inference about various subjects.

For example, data about sales transactions may be accumulated and stored in a sales database for subsequent processing that yields daily, weekly, and monthly sales analysis reports for management. Knowledge bases are used by information systems called expert systems to give end users expert advice on specific subjects. We will explore these concepts further in later chapters.

Data versus Information

The word **data** is the plural of *datum*, though data commonly represents both singular and plural forms. Data are raw facts or observations, typically about physical phenomena or business transactions. For example, a spacecraft launch or the sale of an automobile would generate a lot of data describing those events. More specifically, data are objective measurements of the *attributes* (the characteristics) of *entities* (such as people, places, things, and events).

EXAMPLE   A spacecraft launch generates vast amounts of data. Electronic transmissions of data (*telemetry*) from thousands of sensors are converted to numeric and text data by computers. Voice and image data are also captured through video and radio monitoring of the launch by mission controllers. Of course, buying a car or an airline ticket also produces a lot of data. Just think of the hundreds of facts needed to describe the characteristics of the car you want and its financing, or the details for even the simplest airline reservation.

People often use the terms *data* and *information* interchangeably. However, it is better to view data as raw material *resources* that are processed into finished information *products*. Then we can define **information** as data that have been converted into a meaningful and useful context for specific end users. Thus, data are usually subjected to a value-added process (we call *data processing* or *information processing*) where (1) its form is aggregated, manipulated, and organized; (2) its content is analyzed and evaluated; and (3) it is placed in a proper context for a human user. So, you should view information as *processed data* placed in a context that gives it value for specific end users. See Figure 1.18.

FIGURE 1.18

Data versus information. Note that information is processed data placed in its proper context to give it value for specific end users.

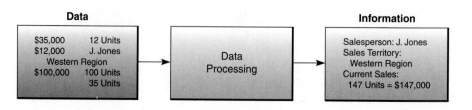

EXAMPLE Names, quantities, and dollar amounts recorded on sales forms represent data about sales transactions. However, a sales manager may not regard these as information. Only after such facts are properly organized and manipulated can meaningful sales information be furnished, specifying, for example, the amount of sales by product type, sales territory, or salesperson.

Network Resources

Telecommunications networks have become essential to the successful operations of modern organizations and their computer-based information systems. *Telecommunications networks* consist of computers, end user terminals, communications processors, and other devices interconnected by communications media and controlled by communications software. The concept of **network resources** emphasizes that communications networks are a fundamental resource component of all information systems. Network resources include:

- **Communications media.** Examples include twisted-pair wire, coaxial cable, fiber-optic cable, microwave systems, and communications satellite systems.
- **Network support.** This generic category includes all of the people, hardware, software, and data resources that directly support the operation and use of a communications network. Examples include communications processors such as modems and internetwork processors, and communications control software such as network operating systems and Internet access packages.

Information System Activities

Let's take a closer look now at each of the basic **information processing** (or **data processing**) activities that occur in information systems. You should be able to recognize input, processing, output, storage, and control activities taking place in any information system you are studying. Figure 1.19 lists business examples that illustrate each of these information system activities.

Input of Data Resources

Data about business transactions and other events must be captured and prepared for processing by *data entry* activities such as recording and editing. End users typically *record* data about transactions on some type of physical medium such as a paper form, or enter it directly into a computer system. This usually includes a variety of *editing* activities to ensure that they have recorded data correctly. Once entered, data may be transferred onto a *machine-readable* medium such as magnetic disk or tape, until needed for processing.

For example, data about sales transactions can be recorded on *source documents* such as paper sales order forms. (A **source document** is the original formal record of a transaction.) Alternately, salespersons can capture sales data using computer keyboards or optical scanning devices; they are visually prompted to enter data correctly by video displays. This provides them with a more convenient and efficient **user interface**; that

- **Input.** Optical scanning of bar-coded tags on merchandise.
- **Processing.** Calculating employee pay, taxes, and other payroll deductions.
- **Output.** Producing reports and displays about sales performance.
- **Storage.** Maintaining records on customers, employees, and products.
- **Control.** Generating audible signals to indicate proper entry of sales data.

FIGURE 1.19

Business examples of the basic activities of information systems.

is, methods of end user input and output with a computer system. Methods such as optical scanning and displays of menus, prompts, and fill-in-the-blanks formats make it easier for end users to enter data correctly into an information system.

Processing of Data into Information

Data is typically manipulated by such activities as calculating, comparing, sorting, classifying, and summarizing. These activities organize, analyze, and manipulate data, thus converting them into information for end users. The quality of any data stored in an information system must also be *maintained* by a continual process of correcting and updating activities.

For example, data received about a purchase can be (1) *added* to a running total of sales results, (2) *compared* to a standard to determine eligibility for a sales discount, (3) *sorted* in numerical order based on product identification numbers, (4) *classified* into product categories (such as food and nonfood items), (5) *summarized* to provide a sales manager with information about various product categories, and, finally, (6) used to *update* sales records.

Output of Information Products

Information in various forms is transmitted to end users and made available to them in the output activity. The goal of information systems is the production of appropriate **information products** for end users. Common information products are *video displays, paper documents,* and *audio responses* that provide us with *messages, forms, reports, listings, graphics displays,* and so on. We routinely use the information provided by these products as we work in organizations and live in society. For example, a sales manager may view a video display to check on the performance of a salesperson, accept a computer-produced voice message by telephone, and receive a printout of monthly sales results.

Storage of Data Resources

Storage is a basic system component of information systems. Storage is the information system activity in which data and information are retained in an organized manner for later use. For example, just as written text material is organized into words, sentences, paragraphs, and documents, stored data is commonly organized into *fields, records, files,* and *databases.* This facilitates its later use in processing or its retrieval as output when needed by users of a system. These common *data elements* are shown in Figure 1.20.

FIGURE 1.20

Common data elements. This is a common method of organizing stored data in information systems.

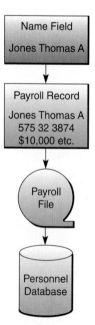

- A **field** is a grouping of characters that represent a characteristic of a person, place, thing, or event. For example, an employee's *name field.*

- A **record** is a collection of interrelated fields. For example, an employee's *payroll record* might consist of a name field, a social security number field, a department field, and a salary field.

- A **file** is a collection of interrelated records. For example, a *payroll file* might consist of the payroll *records* of all employees of a firm.

- A **database** is an integrated collection of interrelated records or files. For example, the *personnel database* of a business might contain payroll, personnel action, and employee skills files.

An information system should produce feedback about its input, processing, output, and storage activities. This feedback must be monitored and evaluated to determine if the system is meeting established performance standards. Then appropriate system activities must be adjusted so that proper information products are produced for end users. For example, a manager may discover that subtotals of sales amounts in a sales report do not add up to total sales. This might mean that data entry or processing procedures need to be corrected. Then changes would have to be made to ensure that all sales transactions would be properly captured and processed by a sales information system.

Control of System Performance

There are many kinds of information systems in the real world. All of them use hardware, software, network, and people resources to transform data resources into information products. Some are simple *manual* information systems, where people use simple tools such as pencils and paper, or even machines such as calculators and typewriters. Others are **computer-based information systems** that rely on a variety of computer systems to accomplish their information processing activities.

It is important not to confuse our discussion of *information systems* with the concept of *computer systems*. As we will see in Chapter 2, a computer system is a group of interconnected hardware components that may take the form of a *microcomputer,* or large *mainframe* computer system. However, whether it sits on a desk or is one of many computers in a telecommunications network, a computer system still represents only the *hardware resources* component of a computer-based information system. As we have just seen, an information system also consists of people, software, network, and data resources.

Overview of Information Systems

The roles given to the information systems function have expanded significantly over the years. Figure 1.21 summarizes these changes.

Until the 1960s, the role of information systems was simple: transaction processing, record-keeping, accounting, and other *electronic data processing* (EDP) applications. Then, another role was added, as the concept of *management information systems* (MIS) was conceived. This new role focused on providing managerial end users with predefined management reports that would give managers the information they needed for decision-making purposes.

By the 1970s, it was evident that the prespecified information products produced by such management information systems were not adequately meeting many of the decision-making needs of management. So the concept of *decision support systems* (DSS) was born. The new role for information systems was to provide managerial end users with ad hoc and interactive support of their decision-making processes. This support would be tailored to the unique decision-making styles of managers as they confronted specific types of problems in the real world.

In the 1980s, several new roles for information systems appeared. First, the rapid development of microcomputer processing power, application software packages, and telecommunications networks gave birth to the phenomenon of *end user computing*. Now, end users can use their own computing resources to support their job requirements instead of waiting for the indirect support of corporate information services departments.

Second, it became evident that most top corporate executives did not directly use either the reports of information reporting systems or the analytical modeling capabilities of decision support systems, so the concept of *executive information systems* (EIS) was developed. These information systems attempt to give top executives an easy way to get the critical information they want, when they want it, tailored to the formats they prefer.

Trends in Information Systems

Third, breakthroughs occurred in the development and application of artificial intelligence (AI) techniques to business information systems. *Expert systems* (ES) and other *knowledge-based systems* forged a new role for information systems. Today, expert systems can serve as consultants to users by providing expert advice in limited subject areas.

An important new role for information systems appeared in the 1980s and continues into the 1990s. This is the concept of a strategic role for information systems, sometimes called *strategic information systems* (SIS). In this concept, information technology becomes an integral component of business processes, products, and services that help a company gain a competitive advantage in the global marketplace.

FIGURE 1.21

Trends in information systems. Note how the roles of computer-based information systems have expanded over time. Also, note the impact of these changes on the end users and managers of an organization.

The Expanding Roles of IS in Business and Management

Data Processing: 1950s–1960s

Electronic data processing systems

  Transaction processing, record-keeping, and traditional accounting applications

Management Reporting: 1960s–1970s

Management information systems

  Management reports of prespecified information to support decision making

Decision Support: 1970s–1980s

Decision support systems

  Interactive ad hoc support of the managerial decision-making process

Strategic and End User Support: 1980s–1990s

End user computing systems

  Direct computing support for end user productivity and work group collaboration

Executive information systems

  Critical information for top management

Expert systems

  Knowledge-based expert advice for end users

Strategic information systems

  Strategic products and services for competitive advantage

Global Internetworking: 1990s–2000s

Internetworked information systems

  For end user, enterprise, and interorganizational computing, communications, and collaboration, including global operations and management on the Internet and other interconnected enterprise and global networks

The Expanding Participation of End Users and Managers in IS

Finally, the rapid growth of the Internet and other interconnected global networks in the 1990s is dramatically changing the capabilities of information systems in business as we move into the next century. Such **global internetworking** is revolutionizing end user, enterprise, and interorganizational computing, communications, and collaboration that supports the business operations and management of successful global enterprises.

Types of Information Systems

Conceptually, information systems in the real world can be classified several different ways. For example, several types of information systems can be classified conceptually as either *operations* or *management* information systems. Figure 1.22 illustrates this conceptual classification of information systems. Information systems are categorized this way to spotlight the major roles each plays in the operations and management of a business.

Figure 1.23 illustrates the relationship of *management support systems* and *operations support systems* to business operations and management. **Management support systems** support the decision-making needs of strategic (top) management, tactical (middle) management, and operating (supervisory)management. **Operations support systems** support the information processing requirements of the day-to-day operations of a business, as well as some lower-level operations management functions. Let's look briefly at some examples of how information systems exist in the business world.

Operations Support Systems

Information systems have always been needed to process data generated by and used in business operations. Such **operations support systems** produce a variety of information products for internal and external use. However, they do not emphasize producing the specific information products that can best be used by managers. Further processing by management information systems is usually required. The role

FIGURE 1.22

Operations and management classifications of information systems. Note how this conceptual overview emphasizes the main purpose of information systems that support business operations and managerial decision making.

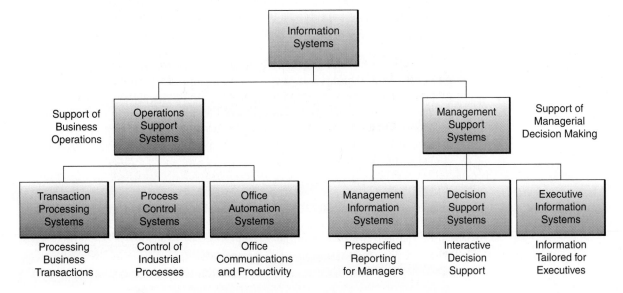

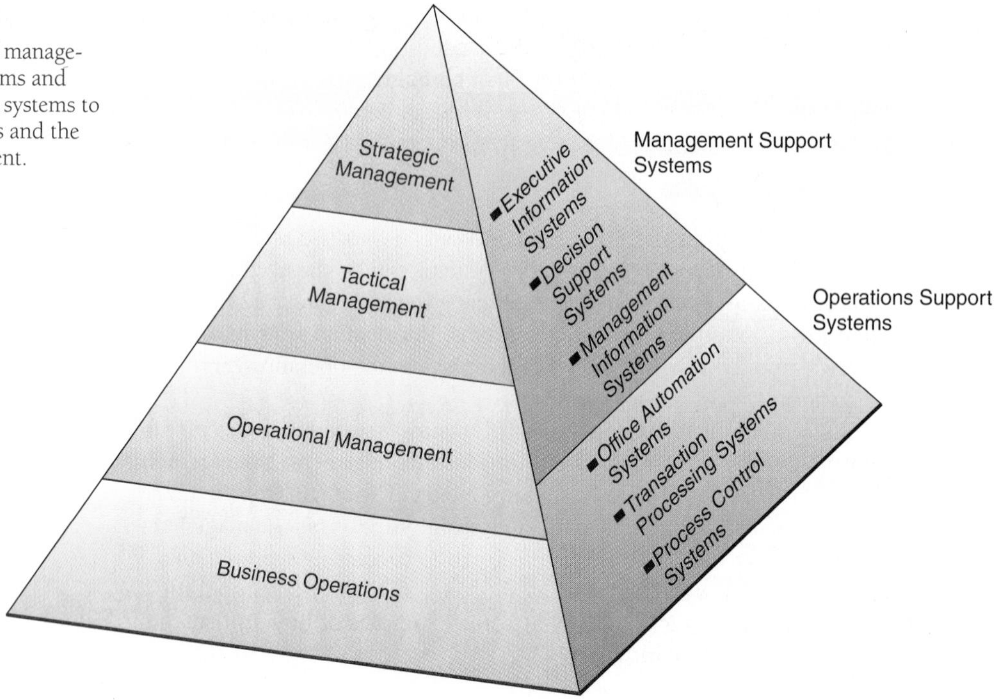

FIGURE 1.23

The relationship of management support systems and operations support systems to business operations and the levels of management.

of a business firm's operations support systems is to efficiently process business transactions, control industrial processes, support office communications and productivity, and update corporate databases.

Transaction processing systems are an important example of operations support systems that record and process data resulting from business transactions. They process transactions in two basic ways. In *batch processing,* transactions data is accumulated over a period of time and processed periodically. In *real-time* (or *online*) *processing,* data is processed immediately after a transaction occurs. For example, point-of-sale (POS) systems at many retail stores use electronic cash register terminals to electronically capture and transmit sales data over telecommunications links to regional computer centers for immediate (real-time) or nightly (batch) processing. See Figure 1.24.

Process control systems monitor and control physical processes. For example, a petroleum refinery uses electronic sensors linked to computers to continually monitor chemical processes and make instant (real-time) adjustments that control the refinery process. **Office automation systems** enhance office communications and productivity. For example, a corporation may use word processing for office correspondence, electronic mail to send and receive electronic messages, and teleconferencing to hold electronic meetings.

Management Support Systems

When information systems focus on providing information and support for effective decision making by managers, they are called **management support systems.** Providing information and support for decision making by all levels of management (from top executives to middle managers to supervisors) is a complex task. Conceptually, several major types of information systems support a variety of managerial end user responsibilities: (1) management information systems, (2) decision support systems, and (3) executive information systems. See Figure 1.25.

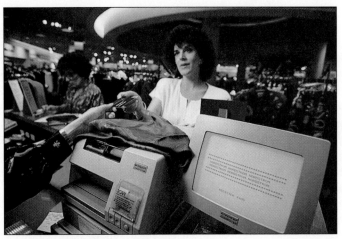

FIGURE 1.24
This sales transaction processing system captures sales transactions data, updates databases, and responds to end user inquiries.

Mark Richards/Photo Edit.

Management information systems provide information in the form of reports and displays to managers. For example, sales managers may use their computer workstations to get instantaneous displays about the sales results of their products and to access weekly sales analysis reports that evaluate sales made by each salesperson. **Decision support systems** give direct computer support to managers during the decision-making process. For example, advertising managers may use an electronic spreadsheet package to do what-if analysis as they test the impact of alternative advertising budgets on the forecasted sales of new products. **Executive information systems** provide critical information in easy-to-use displays to top and middle management. For example, top executives may use touchscreen terminals to instantly view text and graphics displays that highlight key areas of organizational and competitive performance.

FIGURE 1.25
Management support systems provide information and decision support to managers at all levels of an organization.

Jon Riley/Tony Stone Images.

Other Classifications of Information Systems

Several other categories of information systems provide more unique or broad classifications than those we have just mentioned. That's because these information systems can support either operations or management applications. For example, **expert systems** can provide expert advice for operational chores like equipment diagnostics, or managerial decisions such as loan portfolio management. Another example is **end user computing systems** that provide hardware, software, data, and network resources for direct hands-on computing by end users for either operational or managerial applications. Information systems that focus on operational and managerial applications in support of basic business functions such as accounting or marketing are known as **business information systems.** Finally, **strategic information systems** apply information technology to a firm's products, services, or business processes to help it gain a strategic advantage over its competitors.

It is also important to realize that information systems in the real world are typically integrated combinations of several types of information systems we have just mentioned. That's because conceptual classifications of information systems are designed to emphasize the many different roles of information systems. In practice, these roles are integrated into *composite* or **cross-functional information systems** that provide a variety of functions. Thus, most information systems are designed to produce information and support decision making for various levels of management and business functions, as well as do record-keeping and transaction processing chores. So whenever you analyze a business information system, you will probably see that it provides information for a variety of managerial levels and business functions.

Figure 1.26 summarizes the major categories of information systems we have introduced in this section. We will explore many examples of the use of such systems in the four chapters of Module III.

FIGURE 1.26

A summary of the major categories of information systems.

Operations support systems process data generated by business operations. Major categories are:

- **Transaction processing systems** process data resulting from business transactions, update operational databases, and produce business documents.
- **Process control systems** monitor and control industrial processes.
- **Office automation systems** automate office procedures and enhance office communications and productivity.

Management support systems provide information and support needed for effective decision making by managers. Major categories are:

- **Management information systems** provide information in the form of prespecified reports and displays to managers.
- **Decision support systems** provide interactive ad hoc support for the decision-making process of managers.
- **Executive information systems** provide critical information tailored to the information needs of executives.

Other categories of information systems can support either operations, management, or strategic applications.

- **Expert systems** are knowledge-based systems that provide expert advice and act as expert consultants to users.
- **End user computing systems** support the direct, hands-on use of computers by end users for operational and managerial applications.
- **Business information systems** support the operational and managerial applications of the basic business functions of a firm.
- **Strategic information systems** provide a firm with strategic products, services, and capabilities for competitive advantage.

As a business end user, you should be able to recognize the fundamental components of information systems you encounter in the real world. This means that you should be able to identify:

- The people, hardware, software, data, and network resources they use.
- The types of information products they produce.
- The way they perform input, processing, output, storage, and control activities.
- How they support the business operations, managerial decision making, or competitive advantage of a business.

This kind of understanding will help you be a better user, developer, and manager of information systems. And that, as we have pointed out in this chapter, is important to your future success as a manager, entrepreneur, or professional in business.

Read the Real World Case on ShuttleExpress on page 35. Then let's analyze the resources used, activities performed, and information products produced by their information systems. See Figure 1.27.

Figure 1.27 illustrates some of the components you might see in the ShuttleExpress information system. People resources include reservation agents, dispatchers, drivers, and managers who use the system. Hardware resources include machines such as the reservation and dispatcher PCs, the Digital Alpha server, and

Recognizing Information Systems

Analyzing the ShuttleExpress Information System

FIGURE 1.27

Information system components in the ShuttleExpress computer-based information system.

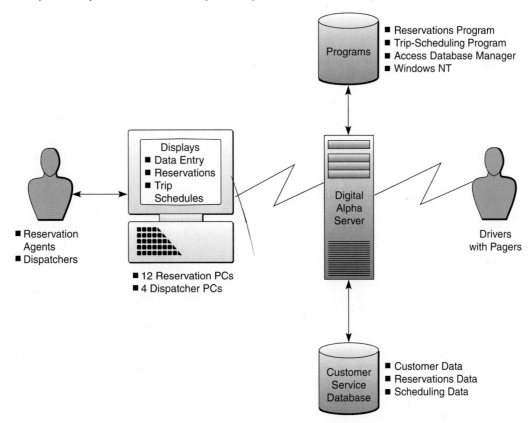

drivers' pagers as well as media such as magnetic disks. Software resources include reservations and trip-scheduling programs, the Access database management and Windows NT operating system programs, and the procedures followed by ShuttleExpress employees and managers. Data resources are contained in the customer, reservations, and scheduling data in the customer service database. Examples of network resources include the network management capabilities of Windows NT operating system, and the use of a mobile radio network for telecommunications with the drivers' pagers. Information products include video displays for data entry support, reservations information, and trip scheduling.

Customer reservations and dispatcher pickup data are entered into the system as input through the keyboards of the PCs. Processing is accomplished by PCs and the Digital Alpha server executing programs to accomplish reservation processing and trip scheduling. Output of information products produces video displays for data entry support, reservation information, and trip scheduling for dispatchers and drivers. Storage of data and software resources is provided by magnetic disk drives, which contain the customer service database, and reservations, trip-scheduling, database management, and operating system programs. Control is accomplished by ShuttleExpress's programs and procedures, which ensure quick and accurate customer service.

So you see, analyzing an information system to identify its basic components is not a difficult task. Just identify the resources that the information system uses, the information processing activities it performs, and the information products it produces. Then you will be better able to identify ways to improve these components, and thus the performance of the information system itself. That's a goal that every business end user should strive to attain.

SHUTTLEEXPRESS: FROM MANUAL TO COMPUTER-BASED IS

Your trip to Seattle is nearly over. You've concluded your business and had your last cup of espresso and checked out of the hotel. All that remains is to catch the shuttle van to the airport and fly home. In what is sometimes still called the Jet City, a van ride to the airport is just about the last thing you might expect to have a high-tech component.

Two years ago, you would have been correct but not today. Back then, the vans servicing customers of Seattle's ShuttleExpress were booked and dispatched using an entirely manual, paper-based system. Dispatchers tracked vans using a chalkboard and magnets to show each van's location on its routes.

"Sometimes the magnet designating a particular van got moved, and they missed the pickup so ShuttleExpress would have to call a cab at its own expense to take the customer to the airport," said Fred Taucher, chairman and chief executive officer of Corporate Computer, Inc.

The Seattle-based software development company replaced the chalkboard system with a computer-based system built on a network of PCs running the Microsoft Access database management package. The underlying network uses the Windows NT operating system.

The reservations system uses 12 NEC 486-based PCs networked to a Digital Equipment Alpha AXP server that has 128M-bytes of RAM and four 1.2G-byte hard disks. There are four more NEC 486 PCs for the dispatch systems that can also double as reservation systems when it gets exceptionally busy.

For ShuttleExpress, which was founded in 1987, computerizing its reservation and van dispatch system went extremely smoothly, according to company officials. Most of the system was finished in about six months, ShuttleExpress officials said.

One of the secrets to the system's successful development and deployment process was that ShuttleExpress involved people who would have to use the system, said John Bartanen, one of the company's dispatchers. "I find it easy to use, and we can carry at least twice as many people today as under the paper system," said Bartanen, who had no previous computer experience when the project started. "Everybody had an opportunity to get their input into it," said John Hagen, manager of ShuttleExpress's guest support center.

When the customer calls the reservations number, an agent enters all of the relevant information, including a customer's pickup location, destination, and any special instructions into the customer service database. The reservations portion of the program calculates fares based on location and generates a reservation confirmation number. Many common pickup points are preprogrammed, along with directions for drivers. The dispatchers then take the reservations data and assign them to a trip, which consists of a set of pickups for a particular van during a specific time period. Once trips are scheduled, they are dispatched to each van. The Access database program is set up to automatically dial out to drivers' alphanumeric pagers and give them all of the particulars for each customer on the trip.

Since the system became operational, the company has handled more than 695,000 reservations. On average, about 1,500 passengers travel to and from the airport daily in ShuttleExpress vans, which number approximately 75.

"Routing the vans used to take eight hours, but now it's down to three hours, and where it used to take three dispatchers each shift, now it's down to two in the morning and one in the afternoon," Hagen said.

CASE STUDY QUESTIONS

1. What people, hardware, software, data and network resources, and information products do you recognize at ShuttleExpress?

2. What IS input, processing, output, storage, and control activities do you recognize in ShuttleExpress's systems?

3. Does the use of information technology benefit the business operations, managerial decision making, or competitive advantage of ShuttleExpress? Explain.

Source: Adapted from Stuart Johnston, "Van Service Books Client/Server," *Computerworld*, April 17, 1995, p. 44. Copyright 1995 by Computerworld, Inc., Framingham, MA 01701—Reprinted from *Computerworld*.

Summary

- **Why Information Systems Are Important.** An understanding of the effective and responsible use and management of information systems is important for managers and other business knowledge workers in today's global information society. Information systems play a vital role in the efficient operations, effective management, and strategic success of businesses and other organizations that must operate in a global business environment. Thus, the field of information systems has become a major functional area of business administration.

- **Why Businesses Need Information Technology.** Information systems perform three vital roles in business firms. That is, they support an organization's business operations, managerial decision making, and strategic advantage. Information technology has also become an indispensable ingredient in several major strategies that businesses are implementing to meet the challenges of a rapidly changing business environment. These include globalization, business process reengineering, and using information technology for strategic competitive advantage.

- **System Concepts.** A system is a group of interrelated components working toward the attainment of a common goal by accepting inputs and producing outputs in an organized transformation process. Feedback is data about the performance of a system. Control is the component that monitors and evaluates feedback and makes any necessary adjustments to the input and processing components to ensure that proper output is produced.

- **Information System Concepts.** An information system uses the resources of people, hardware, software, data, and networks to perform input, processing, output, storage, and control activities that convert data resources into information products. Data is first collected and converted to a form that is suitable for processing (input). Then the data is manipulated and converted into information (processing), stored for future use (storage), or communicated to its ultimate user (output) according to correct processing procedures (control).

- **IS Resources and Products.** Hardware resources include machines and media used in information processing. Software resources include computerized instructions (programs) and instructions for people (procedures). People resources include information systems specialists and users. Data resources include alphanumeric, text, image, video, audio, tactile, and sensor data. Network resources include communications media and network support. Information products produced by an information system can take a variety of forms, including paper reports, visual displays, documents, messages, graphics, and audio responses.

- **Categories of Information Systems.** Major conceptual categories of information systems include operations support systems, such as transaction processing systems, process control systems, and automated office systems, and management support systems, such as management information systems, decision support systems, and executive information systems. Other major categories are end user computing systems, expert systems, strategic information systems, and business function information systems. However, in the real world, these conceptual classifications are typically combined into cross-functional information systems that provide information and decision support for managers and also perform operational information processing activities. Refer to Figure 1.26 for a summary of the major categories of information systems.

Key Terms and Concepts

These are the key terms and concepts of this chapter. The page number of their first explanation is in parentheses.

1. Business process reengineering (13)
2. Careers in information systems (8)
3. Competitive advantage (14)
4. Computer-based information system (27)
5. Control (19)
6. Data (24)
7. Data or information processing (24)
8. Data resources (23)
9. End user (4)
10. Environment (20)
11. Feedback (19)
12. Global information society (5)
13. Globalization (12)
14. Hardware resources (22)
    a. Machines
    b. Media
15. Information (24)
16. Information system (4)
17. Information system activities (25)
    a. Input
    b. Processing
    c. Output
    d. Storage
    e. Control
18. Information technology (4)
19. Interface (20)
20. Knowledge needed about information systems (15)
21. Knowledge workers (5)

22. Network resources (25)
23. People resources (22)
    a. IS specialists
    b. End users
24. Roles of information systems (10)

25. Software resources (23)
    a. Programs
    b. Procedures
26. Subsystem (20)
27. System (18)

28. Trends in information systems (27)
29. Types of information systems (29)
    a. Cross-functional systems (32)
    b. Management support systems (30)
    c. Operations support systems (29)

Review Quiz

Match one of the key terms and concepts listed above with one of the brief examples or definitions listed below. Look for the best fit for answers that seem to fit more than one key term or concept. Defend your choices.

_____ 1. You should know some fundamental concepts about information systems and their technology, development, applications, and management.

_____ 2. People who spend most of their workday creating, using, and distributing information.

_____ 3. We are living in a global economy that is dependent on information.

_____ 4. Computer hardware and software, telecommunications, data management, and other technologies.

_____ 5. Information systems support an organization's business operations, managerial decision making, and strategic competitive advantage.

_____ 6. Businesses are expanding into global markets and forming alliances with global partners.

_____ 7. The fundamental rethinking and redesign of business operations.

_____ 8. Using information technology to gain a strategic advantage over competitors.

_____ 9. A system that uses hardware, software, and people resources to perform information processing activities that transform data resources into information products for end users.

_____ 10. An information system that uses computers and their hardware and software.

_____ 11. Anyone who uses an information system or the information it produces.

_____ 12. Information systems professionals may help develop and operate information systems.

_____ 13. Examples include jobs such as computer programmers, systems analysts, network administrators, and end user consultants.

_____ 14. A group of interrelated components working together toward the attainment of a common goal.

_____ 15. Data about a system's performance.

_____ 16. Making adjustments to a system's components so that it operates properly.

_____ 17. A shared boundary between systems.

_____ 18. Facts or observations.

_____ 19. Data that have been placed into a meaningful context for an end user.

_____ 20. The act of converting data into information.

_____ 21. Programs and procedures.

_____ 22. A set of instructions for a computer.

_____ 23. A set of instructions for people.

_____ 24. Machines and media.

_____ 25. Computers, disk drives, video monitors, and printers are examples.

_____ 26. Magnetic disks, optical disks, and paper forms are examples.

_____ 27. Communications media, communications processors, and network access software are examples.

_____ 28. Using the keyboard of a computer to enter data.

_____ 29. Computing loan payments.

_____ 30. Printing a letter you wrote using a computer.

_____ 31. Saving a copy of the letter on a magnetic disk.

_____ 32. Having a sales receipt as proof of a purchase.

_____ 33. Information systems have evolved from a data processing orientation to the support of decision making, end users, and strategic initiatives.

_____ 34. Information systems can be classified into operations, management, and other categories.

_____ 35. Include transaction processing, process control, and office automation subsystems.

_____ 36. Management information, decision support, and executive information systems are examples.

_____ 37. End user computing, expert systems, and strategic information systems are examples.

Discussion Questions

1. How can a manager demonstrate that he or she is a responsible end user of information systems? Give several examples.
2. How can information systems support a company's business operations, decision making by their managers, and give them a competitive advantage? Give examples to illustrate your answer.
3. Refer to the Real World Case on California Pizza Kitchen in the chapter. Are the business benefits listed typical of those that can be gained by computerizing a business? Explain.
4. How important is information technology to the globalization of a business? Use examples to illustrate your answer.
5. Refer to the Real World Case on ShuttleExpress in the chapter. Why did computerizing their reservation and scheduling operations go so smoothly? Is this typical? Explain.
6. Would you be interested in a career in the information systems field? Why or why not?
7. In what major ways have the roles of information systems in business expanded during the last 40 years?
8. Why are there so many conceptual classifications of information systems? Why are they typically integrated in the information systems found in the real world?
9. Refer to the Real World Case on Auto-By-Tel in the chapter. Will the Internet make car dealers extinct in the future? Why or why not?
10. Can using information technology for business process reengineering help a company gain a competitive advantage? Give an example to illustrate your answer.

Real World Problems

1. Southwest Airlines: Reengineering for Strategic Advantage

The best on-time performance. The fewest customer complaints. The lowest number of lost bags. Southwest Airlines Co. has snared the U.S. Department of Transportation's coveted Triple Crown of airline service awards for an unprecedented four consecutive years. To keep a firm grasp on its number one ranking, the Dallas-based airline recently automated a gaggle of flight scheduling processes under an information systems project expected to deliver up to 20-to-1 productivity gains. And in keeping with its discount image, Southwest has so far spent a mere $300,000 to develop its new systems. That's more than cost effective when compared with the $1.2 million in packaged software that vendors pitched to Southwest—proposals that didn't include system interfaces in the airline's reservations and maintenance systems.

Most airlines already use information technologies to optimize flight and crew schedules, "but there's a lot more that airlines can do with technology to reengineer these processes," said Mark Shields, a principal in the aviation practice at Mercer Management Consulting in Washington. Unlike competitors such as United Airlines, which manages multiple aircraft types across international regions, Southwest flew only Boeing 737s on domestic routes. As such, Southwest would likely gain more from automating its flight planning activities than most airlines "since it has a formula that plays on simplicity," Shields added.

The airline is hoping to do just that. Its project, called the Southwest Airlines Integrated Flight Tracking System (Swift), is a reengineered system that the airlines' 37 dispatchers and routers began using in the fall of 1995 to track 2,200 daily flights. Dispatchers at high-powered Silicon Graphics workstations are now able to click onto buttons to calculate how much fuel is needed for a flight or to route a plane around bad weather, according to Mark Mortland, the lead programmer on the Swift project. Prior to Swift, dispatchers and routers had used a 17-foot-long flow sheet that contained all of Southwest's daily flight information. Although they had become proficient at scanning the flow sheet, dispatchers and routers often took up to 15 minutes to check the airline's reservation system and passenger lists before coming up with a set of rerouting options.

"We were missing opportunities to protect the customer because there was so much data to look for" on the flow sheets, said Dave Jordan, director of flight dispatch at Southwest. But by using their workstations, staffers can now get that information in just 15 seconds by accessing a Sybase database management system through Hewlett-Packard servers. That speed is critical to Southwest, which added 300 daily flights after expanding its arsenal from 191 planes to 226 aircraft in 1995.

a. How did Southwest Airlines use information technology to reengineer their flight tracking system?

b. What are the business benefits of their new system?

Source: Adapted from Thomas Hoffman, "Airline Turbo Charges Schedule Efficiency," *Computerworld*, March 25, 1996, pp. 1, 134. Copyright © 1996 by Computerworld, Inc., Framingham, MA 01701—Reprinted from *Computerworld*.

2. Music Boulevard: A Business on the Internet

"I listen to a lot of music," says John Pagakis, a technical specialist at The Options Clearing Corporation. "I'm a former professional rock guitarist—but I don't have time to go to as many music stores as I'd like. I'm in front of my computer at home a lot more than I'm out in stores. Music Boulevard (http://www.musicblvd.com) lets me look for and buy things I want quickly—and perhaps a bit too painlessly. Once they have your credit-card number (you can phone it in if you don't want it going over the 'net), ordering is as easy as point and click. According to my Visa card, I make a purchase there about twice a month.

"This music store is impressive; I have found CDs in its searchable database of 145,000 titles that I have been trying to find for years and have seen nowhere else. It's a very slick-looking Web site, too. The search engine is very helpful and makes it easy to choose a genre or search the whole database. Its speed is impressive. Even when you are searching all music, response time is quick. Your search choices are impressive, too. Via check boxes you can search all music or limit the search to certain genres. Within that, you can enter other criteria such as artist, album name, song, or record label.

"Plus, their customer service support has been excellent. If a search comes up empty, the Web page lets me send an electronic-mail query to them. They typically get back within a day or so. They may report they don't have something, but it's always a knowledgeable reply. They may suggest, for instance, another album with most of the same tracks.

"Another thing this site does is make recommendations. When you get information on an album you like, very often at the bottom of the page they'll say, 'If you like this artist, you may like these, too,' followed by links to one or more artists. You don't get features like this out of a company whose only motivation is profit. Music Boulevard knows enough about what they sell to make these kinds of extrapolations. I expect to see more companies adding on-line access like this . . . it makes it so darn easy to buy things."

a. Why does John Pagakis like shopping for CDs on the Internet's Music Boulevard?

b. What other types of businesses would be successful on the Internet? Explain.

Source: Adapted from Daniel Dern, "Fave Web Sites," *Computerworld*, March 11, 1996, pp. 97–98. Copyright © 1996 by Computerworld, Inc., Framingham, MA 01701—Reprinted from *Computerworld*.

3. Satyam Computer Services and Caterpillar Inc.: Globalizing Help-Desk Services

Satyam Computer Services Ltd. is a software export house based in Secunderabad, India, about 700 kilometers from Bangalore. Every day between the hours of 4:30 PM and 7:30 AM CST, Satyam provides first-level maintenance and help-desk services for users at Caterpillar, Inc., in Peoria, Illinois, more than 7,000 miles and 10 time zones away. This global alliance works because of the 10½-hour time difference between India and the United States.

To get help, a Caterpillar end user dials an independent service provider in Vienna, Virginia, that routes the call via Satyam hot lines to Secunderabad. There, engineers dedicated to the Caterpillar project handle technical and business-related problems. Satyam has been constantly tweaking the process with the objective of keeping communication, language, and other issues transparent to the end user, according to Rusi Brij, vice president of international marketing at Satyam.

Elaborate backup measures ensure that calls go through quickly. If the hot lines between the United States and Satyam's Secunderabad offices are busy or down, the call is rerouted to reach the Indian site. Problems are resolved over the phone or by logging on to a user's computer from Secunderabad. Every keystroke in that faraway city screams through local area networks and several communications processors to a government-owned satellite earth station about six kilometers away. A communications satellite picks up the signal and beams it down to an earth station in Amsterdam. From there it is blasted along fiber-optic cables under the Atlantic Ocean to Satyam's office in Iselin, New Jersey. A local circuit carries it to Vienna and on to Caterpillar's facility.

a. How has using global computer services benefited Caterpillar?

b. What other types of companies could use similar arrangements?

Source: Adapted from Julkumar Vijayan, "Lookout, Here Comes India," *Computerworld*, February 26, 1996, p. 102. Copyright © 1996 by Computerworld, Inc., Framingham, MA 01701—Reprinted from *Computerworld*.

4. Yahoo! and Others: Careers in Web Surfing

There is at least one group of folks who have figured out a way to make money on the Internet: professional Websurfers, who log on all day, every day, looking for sites that are useful, interesting, and rad. There are just over a hundred such positions out there, at online services such as AOL and at outfits dedicated to indexing the Web, such as Yahoo! and the McKinley Group. But the ranks of pro surfers promise to grow. Says Andy Beers, news director of Microsoft Network's online news service, which has two full-time "webmeisters" on staff: "For more and more businesses, it's going to become important to have someone whose job it is to sort all this stuff out."

Pro surfing sounds like a Gen-X, cyberpunk dream job, and it is, though it also tends to draw a fair number of journalists and librarians. But surfing is such a new profession that nothing's set in stone. The 18-person surf team at Yahoo!, a Sunnyvale, California, venture, includes an architect, an ex-lifeguard, and a person who taught English in Ecuador. These Surfing Yahoos! are working to assemble a sort of Internet yellow pages, free to users and supported by ad revenues. They check out some 2,500 sites every day and organize them under various categories—arts, science, business, and economy. Says, Srinija Srinivasan, aka Ninja, who manages the team and holds the title Ontological Yahoo!: "Curiosity is the key. Surfers are called upon to delve into topics you could comfortably remain ignorant about for your whole life."

That's certainly been the experience of Dorian Patchin, who works for FreeLoader, a Washington, D.C., startup that's developing a service to allow people to automatically download their favorite Websites on a regular basis. The 31-year-old former Washington *Post* researcher makes $45,000 for a job that's sent him surfing at sites as varied as a virtual frog-dissection kit and a Spanish wine of the week.

Julian Stewart, 23, a Websurfer at Infoseek, a Santa Clara, California, Internet indexing firm, is a recent graduate of UC Santa Cruz with a degree in modern literature. He's paid $25,000 to keep Infoseek's Cool Sites listings cool. Says he: "I'll be sitting there, playing with a bunch of pages, and it will hit me: Wow! They're paying me to amuse myself."

If this appeals to you, you should get out more. Still interested? Don't turn to the help wanted page. The key is networking, as in get on the Net and surf for job postings.

a. Do you agree with Andy Beers of Microsoft that businesses will increasingly need the services of professional Websurfers? Explain.

b. Would you like to be a professional Websurfer for a business? Why or why not?

Source: Adapted from Justin Martin, "Endless Summer on the Web," *Fortune,* March 4, 1996, p. 38. © 1996 Time Inc. All rights reserved.

Application Exercises

1. Auto Shack Stores

The president of Auto Shack Stores asked the following questions at a recent meeting of store managers and the vice president of information systems. Match each question with one of the major areas of information systems knowledge illustrated in Figure 1.13. Explain your choices.

a. How can we use information systems to support sales floor operations, store manager decision making, and gain a competitive advantage?

b. How can we involve store managers in developing such applications?

c. How can we use the latest developments in information technology to reach our customers, and build a "high-tech, high-touch" organization?

d. What hardware, software, telecommunications, and database management resources do we need to support our goals?

e. How are we going to manage the hardware, software, people, and data resources of our information systems at the store and corporate level?

2. Jefferson State University

Students in the College of Business Administration of Jefferson State University use its microcomputer lab for a variety of assignments. For example, a student may load a word processing program from a microcomputer's hard disk drive into main memory and then proceed to type a case study analysis. When the analysis is typed, edited, and properly formatted to an instructor's specifications, the student will save it on a floppy disk and print a copy on the microcomputer's printer. If the student tries to save the case study analysis using a file name he or she has already used for saving another document, the program will display a warning message and wait until it receives an additional command.

Make an outline to identify the information system components in the preceding example.

a. Identify the people, hardware, software, and data resources and the information products of this information system.

b. Identify the input, processing, output, storage, and control activities that occurred.

3. Office Products Corporation

Office Products Corporation has an IBM AS/400 computer that runs almost around the clock. More than 10,000 customer orders a month flow through the system, drawing on a combined inventory of over 1,000 office products stocked at the company's warehouse. More than 60 personal computer workstations, many with printers, are installed at Office Products headquarters, and many of its dealers are connected by telecommunications links to the AS/400. Orders are received by phone or mail and entered into the system by order entry personnel at video display terminals, or they are entered directly by dealers who have installed terminals to Office Products. Entry of orders is assisted by formatted screens that help operators follow data entry procedures to enter required information into the system, where it is stored on the magnetic disks of the AS/400.

As the order is entered, the AS/400 checks the availability of the parts, allocates the stock, and updates customer and part databases stored on the computer's magnetic disks. It then sends the order pick list to the warehouse printer, where it is used by warehouse personnel to fill the order. The company president has a PC workstation in her office, as do the controller, sales manager, inventory manager, and other executives. They use simple database management inquiry commands to get responses and reports concerning sales orders, customers, and inventory, and to review product demand and service trends.

Make an outline that identifies the information system components in Office Products' order processing system.

a. Identify the people, hardware, software, data, and network resources and the information products of this information system.

b. Identify the input, processing, output, storage, and control activities that occurred.

4. Western Chemical Corporation

Western Chemical uses telecommunications systems that connect its computers to those of its customers and suppliers to capture data about sales orders and purchases. Such data are processed immediately, and inventory and other databases are updated. Word processing and electronic mail services are also provided. Data generated by a chemical refinery process are captured by sensors and processed by a computer that also suggests answers to a complex refinery problem posed by an engineer. Managerial end users receive reports on a periodic, exception, and demand basis, and use computers to interactively assess the possible results of alternative decisions. Finally, top management can access text summaries and graphics displays that identify key elements of organizational performance and compare them to industry and competitor performance.

Western Chemical Corporation has started forming business alliances and building a global telecommunications network with other chemical companies throughout the world to offer their customers worldwide products and services.

Western Chemical is in the midst of making fundamental changes to their computer-based systems to increase the efficiency of their business operations and their managers' ability to react quickly to changing business conditions. Make an outline that identifies:

a. How information systems support (1) business operations, (2) management decision making, (3) strategic advantage, (4) globalization, and (5) business process reengineering at Western Chemical.

b. There are many different types of information systems at Western Chemical. Identify as many as you can in the preceding scenario. Refer to Figure 1.26 to help you. Explain the reasons for your choices.

Review Quiz Answers

1. *20*	11. *9*	21. *25*	31. *17d*
2. *21*	12. *23a*	22. *25a*	32. *17e*
3. *12*	13. *2*	23. *25b*	33. *24*
4. *18*	14. *29*	24. *14*	34. *29*
5. *26*	15. *11*	25. *14a*	35. *29c*
6. *13*	16. *5*	26. *14b*	36. *29b*
7. *1*	17. *19*	27. *22*	37. *29a*
8. *3*	18. *6*	28. *17a*	
9. *16*	19. *15*	29. *17b*	
10. *4*	20. *7*	30. *17c*	

Selected References

1. Bradley, Stephen P.; Jerry A. Hausman; and Richard L. Nolan, eds. *Globalization, Technology, and Competition: The Fusion of Computers and Telecommunications in the 1990s.* Boston: Harvard Business School Press, 1993.

2. Cash, James I., Jr.; Robert G. Eccles; Nitin Nohria; and Richard L. Nolan. *Building the Information-Age Organization: Structure, Control, and Information Technologies.* Burr Ridge, IL: Richard D. Irwin, 1994.

3. Davenport, Thomas H. *Process Innovation: Reengineering Work through Information Technology.* Boston: Harvard Business School Press, 1993.

4. Fried, Louis. "Information Security and Technology: Potential Threats and Solutions." *Information Systems Management,* Summer 1994.

5. Hammer, Michael, and James Champy. *Reengineering the Corporation: A Manifesto for Business Revolution.* New York: HarperCollins, 1993.

6. Jacobson, Ivar; Maria Ericsson; and Agneta Jacobson. *The Object Advantage: Business Process Reengineering with Object Technology.* New York: The ACM Press, 1995.

7. Keen, Peter G. W. *Shaping the Future: Business Design through Information Technology.* Cambridge: Harvard Business School Press, 1991.

8. Neumann, Seev. *Strategic Information Systems: Competition through Information Technologies.* New York: Macmillan College Publishing Co., 1994.

9. Tan, Djoen. "IT Management Plateaus: An Organizational Architecture for IS." *Information Systems Management,* Winter 1995.

10. Wang, Charles. "Technology Disconnect—Real World Danger." *Computerworld,* September 19, 1994.

Continuing Real World Case

Fast Freight, Inc.: Networking the Enterprise — Part I: The Importance of Information Systems

Introduction

Jim Kellogg, Fast Freight's senior systems engineer, glowed like a proud papa as he showed his visitors around the busy offices at the company headquarters in Wenatchee, Washington. Wenatchee proclaims itself to be the Apple Capital of the United States, but Jim was more interested in bragging about how much Fast Freight's newly installed computer network had improved its business operations.

"Everything we did was a slow and cumbersome process until the computer network came on line," he said. "Everything was keyed into our computers by hand from data on paper documents which we received by snail mail from customers or shippers. After processing, we would have to express mail reports to other company locations so they could get already outdated information faster," Jim said with a smile. "We had dissatisfied customers, dissatisfied shippers, dissatisfied employees, and dissatisfied management, especially since costs were too high and company profits too low. Things were a mess," he said. "Now that all our locations are interconnected in a nationwide computer network, our business operations are fast and efficient. Our costs are down, and sales and profits are up. We still have some problems, and a lot of ideas to make us even more efficient and competitive, but everyone is a lot happier now," said the still grinning systems engineer.

Company Background

Fast Freight, Inc., headquartered in Wenatchee, Washington, is a successful midsize corporation providing services primarily to the transportation industry. Fast Freight, Inc., serves as the parent company to seven subsidiary organizations. Although the Fast Freight divisions target various aspects of the transportation industry, their main business focus is intermodal trucking service. That is, they provide trucking services for transfer of shipments from railway railroad cars and cargo ships to their ultimate destinations. Fast Freight's subsidiaries include:

- **Fast Freight Company.** Provider of intermodal trucking service to the railroad industry across the United States, primarily through a master contract with Burlington Northern Railway and its affiliated companies.

Source: This case was developed by Charles N. Krasowski of Central Washington University and the author. It is based on real-life events and people in an actual freight company headquartered in Wenatchee, Washington.

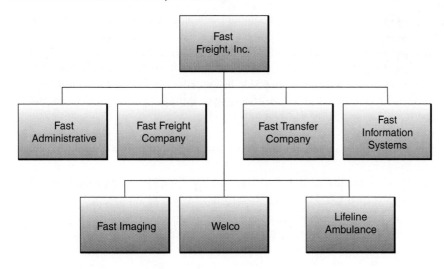

FIGURE 1

The subsidiaries of Fast Freight, Inc.

- **Fast Transfer Company.** A local franchise of United Van Lines providing moving and storage services to North Central Washington.
- **Welco.** An equipment leasing company serving the railroad industry and its affiliates.
- **Lifeline Ambulance.** Provider of emergency health care and transportation with four locations in North Central Washington.
- **Fast Administrative.** Provider of administrative services including accounting for all subsidiaries.
- **Fast Imaging.** Provider of electronic document imaging, storage, and retrieval services to business customers.
- **Fast Information Systems.** An authorized IBM general remarketer providing information system consultation, sales, installation, and service to business customers.

Fast Freight Company's mission is to provide efficient, on-time delivery of freight with proper documentation to and from railway depots across America, primarily through its master contract with Burlington Northern Railway and its affiliates. Fast Freight operates six depots in the Pacific Northwest: Seattle Harbor, South Seattle, Tukwilia, Spokane, and Wenatchee, Washington; and Portland, Oregon. Six other depots are in Billings, Montana; San Bernardino, California; Kansas City, Missouri; Omaha, Nebraska; Birmingham, Alabama; and Atlanta, Georgia. Fast Freight also operates four repair and maintenance facilities near several depots. Through this network, Fast Freight coordinates all the activities to assure that the freight of a Burlington Northern customer reaches its final destination on time and in good condition.

The success of Fast Freight's service depends on timing. Incoming orders received by mail or fax from Burlington Northern are processed by dispatch personnel at the closest Fast Freight depot. A dispatcher assigns either a company-owned or independent truck and driver to pick up and transport freight to the shipping railhead, or from the receiving railhead to the destination customer.

Business Requirements

Scheduling between Fast Freight and the railhead is critical because the operations of many business customers depend on just-in-time inventory systems. So Fast Freight's contracts provide for significant financial penalties for every five-minute delay in rail departure. After final delivery, all documentation (bills of lading, shipping manifests, etc.) are faxed or expressed to headquarters in Wenatchee for final processing, distribution, and storage, so that proper billing by Fast Freight's accounting department can be mailed to customers.

Case Study Questions

1. What business problems and opportunities do you recognize at Fast Freight, Inc.?
2. How has the use of information technology in the form of a computer network helped Fast Freight?
3. How might the use of other types of computer-based information systems benefit Fast Freight? Give several specific examples.

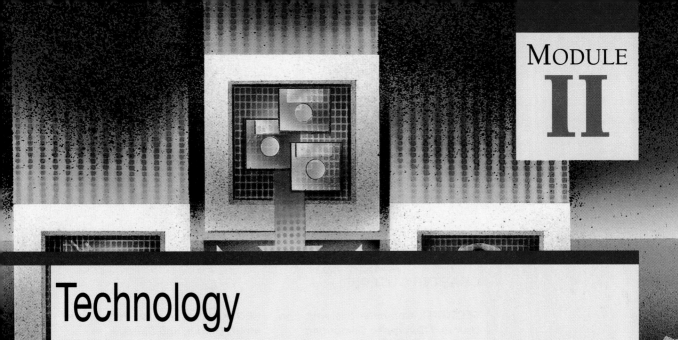

Technology

What challenges do information system technologies pose for business end users? What basic knowledge should you possess about information technology? The four chapters of this module give you an overview of the major technologies used in modern computer-based information systems and their implications for end users and managers.

Chapter 2, "Introduction to Computer Hardware," reviews microcomputers, midrange, mainframe, and networked computer systems, and the major types of peripheral devices used for computer input, output, and storage by end users.

Chapter 3, "Introduction to Computer Software," reviews the basic features and

functions of major types of system and application software packages used to support traditional and end user computing.

Chapter 4, "Introduction to Business Telecommunications," presents you with an overview of major trends, concepts, applications, and technical alternatives in telecommunications. It emphasizes the implications of telecommunications for managerial end users and the strategic success of organizations.

Chapter 5, "Introduction to Database Management," emphasizes management of the data resources of computer-using organizations. It outlines the managerial implications of basic concepts and applications of database management in organizational information systems.

Introduction to Computer Hardware

CHAPTER OUTLINE

LEARNING OBJECTIVES

After reading and studying this chapter, you should be able to:

1. Outline the major differences and uses of microcomputers, midrange, mainframe, and networked computers.

2. Identify the major types and uses of computer peripherals for input, output, and storage.

3. Explain the benefits, limitations, and trends in major types of computer systems and peripheral devices.

4. Identify the components and functions of a computer system.

Section I

Computer Systems: End User and Enterprise Computing

Computer Categories

Today's computer systems display striking differences as well as basic similarities. Differing end user needs and technological discoveries have resulted in the development of several major categories of computer systems with a variety of characteristics and capabilities. Thus, computer systems are typically classified as *microcomputers, midrange computers,* and *mainframe computers.* However, as Figure 2.1 illustrates, these are not precise classifications. For example, variations of these categories include *minicomputers, superminicomputers,* and *supercomputers.* Also, a variety of application categories, which describe major uses for various types of computers, are common. Examples are host computers, network servers, and technical workstations.

Such categories are attempts to describe the relative computing power provided by different *computing platforms,* or types of computers. Computers may differ in their processing speed and memory capacity, as well as in the number and capabilities of peripheral devices for input, output, and secondary storage they can support. However, you will find microcomputers that are more powerful than some midrange computers and midrange computers that are more powerful than some mainframe computers. So these computer classifications do overlap each other, as Figure 2.1 illustrates. In addition, experts continue to predict the merging or disappearance of several computer categories. For example, they argue that minicomputers and many mainframe computers are being made obsolete by the power and versatility of networks of microcomputer systems.

Computer manufacturers typically produce *families,* or product lines, of computers. So computer systems can have a variety of models with different processing speeds, memory capacities, and other capabilities. This allows manufacturers to provide a range of choices to customers, depending on their information processing needs. Most models in a family are compatible; that is, programs written for one model can usually be run on other models of the same family with little or no change. This allows customers to move up (*migrate*) to larger models of the same computer product line as their needs grow.

FIGURE 2.1

Computer system classifications. Note the overlap among the traditional and application categories of the three major classifications of computers.

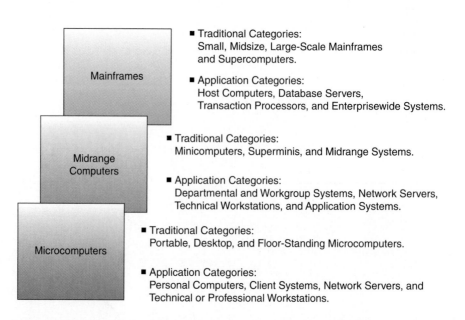

Mainframes

- Traditional Categories:
  Small, Midsize, Large-Scale Mainframes and Supercomputers.

- Application Categories:
  Host Computers, Database Servers, Transaction Processors, and Enterprisewide Systems.

Midrange Computers

- Traditional Categories:
  Minicomputers, Superminis, and Midrange Systems.

- Application Categories:
  Departmental and Workgroup Systems, Network Servers, Technical Workstations, and Application Systems.

Microcomputers

- Traditional Categories:
  Portable, Desktop, and Floor-Standing Microcomputers.

- Application Categories:
  Personal Computers, Client Systems, Network Servers, and Technical or Professional Workstations.

As an informed business end user, it is important that you recognize several major trends in computer systems. These trends have developed in the past during each major stage—or **generation**—of computers, and they are expected to continue into the future. The first generation of computers began in the early 1950s; the second generation in the late 1950s; the third generation in the mid-1960s; and the fourth generation began in the 1970s and continues to the present. A fifth generation of computers is expected to evolve by the end of the century. Figure 2.2 highlights trends in the characteristics and capabilities of computers. Notice that computers continue to become smaller, faster, more reliable, and less costly to purchase and maintain.

First-generation computers (1951–1958) used hundreds or thousands of **vacuum tubes** for their processing and memory circuitry. These computers were quite large and generated enormous amounts of heat; their vacuum tubes had to be replaced frequently. Thus, they had large electrical power, air conditioning, and maintenance requirements. First-generation computers had main memories of only a few thousand characters and millisecond processing speeds. They used magnetic drums or tape for secondary storage and punched cards or paper tape as input and output media.

Second-generation computers (1959–1963) used **transistors** and other *solid-state, semiconductor* devices that were wired to circuit boards. Transistorized circuits were much smaller and much more reliable, generated little heat, were less expensive,

Computer Generations

FIGURE 2.2

Major trends in computer characteristics and capabilities.

	First Generation	Second Generation	Third Generation	Fourth Generation	Fifth Generation
SIZE (Typical computers)	Room Size Mainframe	Closet Size Mainframe	Desk-Size Minicomputer	Desktop and Laptop Microcomputers	Credit Card-Size Micro?
CIRCUITRY	Vacuum tubes	Transistors	Integrated Semi-conductor Circuits	Large-Scale Integrated (LSI) Semi-Conductor Circuits	Very-Large-Scale Integrated (VLSI) Superconductor Circuits?
DENSITY (Circuits per component)	One	Hundreds	Thousands	Hundreds of Thousands	Millions?
SPEED (Instructions/second)	Hundreds	Thousands	Millions	Tens of Millions	Billions?
RELIABILITY (Failure of circuits)	Hours	Days	Weeks	Months	Years?
MEMORY (Capacity in characters)	Thousands	Tens of Thousands	Hundreds of Thousands	Millions	Billions?
COST (Per million instructions)	$10	$1.00	$.10	$.001	$.0001?

and required less power than vacuum tubes. Tiny *magnetic cores* were used for the computer's memory, or internal storage. Many second-generation computers had main memory capacities of less than 100 kilobytes and microsecond processing speeds. Removable *magnetic disk packs* were introduced, and magnetic tape emerged as the major input, output, and secondary storage medium for large computer installations.

Third-generation computers (1964–1979) began using **integrated circuits**, in which thousands of transistors and other circuit elements are etched on tiny chips of silicon. Main memory capacities increased to several megabytes and processing speeds jumped to millions of instructions per second (MIPS) as telecommunications capabilities became common. This made it possible for *operating system* programs to come into widespread use that automated and supervised the activities of many types of peripheral devices and processing of several programs at the same time, sometimes from networks of users at remote terminals. Integrated circuit technology also made possible the development and widespread use of small computers called **minicomputers** in the third computer generation.

Fourth-generation computers (1979 to the present) use LSI (large-scale integration) and VLSI (very-large-scale integration) technologies that cram hundreds of thousands or millions of transistors and other circuit elements on each chip. Main memory capacities ranging from a few megabytes to several gigabytes can be achieved by the memory chips that replaced magnetic core memories. LSI and VLSI technologies also allowed the development of **microprocessors**, in which all of the circuits of a CPU are contained on a single chip with processing speeds of millions of instructions per second. **Microcomputers,** which use microprocessor CPUs and a variety of peripheral devices and easy-to-use software packages to form small personal computer systems (PCs) or networks of linked PCs, are a hallmark of the fourth generation of computing.

Microcomputer Systems

Microcomputers are the smallest but most important category of computer systems for end users. Typically, we refer to a microcomputer as a *personal computer,* or PC. However, microcomputers have become much more than small computers used by individual persons. Their computing power now exceeds that of the mainframes of previous computer generations at a fraction of their cost. For this reason, they have become powerful *professional workstations* for use by end users in businesses and other organizations.

Microcomputers come in a variety of sizes and shapes for a variety of purposes, as Figure 2.3 illustrates. Microcomputers categorized by size include *handheld, notebook, laptop, portable, desktop,* and *floor-standing* microcomputers. Or, based on their use, they include *home, personal, professional, workstation,* and *multiuser* computers. Examples of special-purpose application categories include handheld microcomputer devices known as **personal digital assistants** (PDAs), designed for convenient mobile communications and computing, and **network computers** (NCs) that are designed primarily for "surfing" the Internet. However, the classifications of *desktop* versus *portable* are the most widely used distinctions. That is because most microcomputers are designed either to fit on top of an office desk, transforming it into an end user workstation, or to be conveniently carried by end users, such as by salespersons or consultants who do a lot of traveling.

Most microcomputers are single-user computers designed to support the work activities of a variety of end users. However, powerful **workstation computers** (*technical workstations*) are available that support applications with heavy mathematical computing and graphics display demands such as computer-aided design (CAD) in engineering, or investment and portfolio analysis in the securities industry. One of

FIGURE 2.3

Examples of microcomputer systems.

Courtesy of Compaq Computer Corporation.

a. A local area network of microcomputer systems.

Courtesy of Hewlett-Packard Company.

c. The microcomputer as a professional workstation.

Tom Tracy/The Stock Market.

b. The microcomputer as a technical workstation.

the fastest growing microcomputer application categories is **network servers.** They are usually more powerful microcomputers that coordinate telecommunications and resource sharing in local area networks (LANs) of interconnected microcomputers and other computer system devices.

Midrange computers, also called **minicomputers,** are larger and more powerful than most microcomputers but are smaller and less powerful than most large mainframe computer systems. However, this is not a precise distinction. High-end models of microcomputer systems (*supermicros*) are more powerful than some midrange computers, while high-end models of midrange systems (superminis) are more powerful than some smaller models of mainframe computers. In addition, midrange systems cost less to buy and maintain than mainframe computers. They can function in ordinary operating environments, and do not need special air conditioning or electrical wiring. See Figure 2.4.

Midrange Computer Systems

FIGURE 2.4

A midrange computer system, the HP 9000.

Courtesy of Hewlett-Packard Company.

Midrange computers are being used for many business and scientific applications. They first became popular as *minicomputers* for scientific research, instrumentation systems, engineering analysis, and industrial process monitoring and control. Minicomputers could easily handle such uses because these applications are narrow in scope and do not demand the processing versatility of mainframe systems. Thus, midrange computers serve as industrial process-control and manufacturing plant computers, and they play a major role in computer-aided manufacturing (CAM). They can also take the form of powerful *technical workstations* for computer-aided design (CAD) applications. Midrange computers are often used as *front-end* computers to help mainframe computers control data communications networks with large numbers of data entry terminals.

Midrange computers have also become popular as powerful *network servers* to help manage large interconnected local area networks that tie together many end user microcomputer workstations, and other computer devices in departments, offices, and other work sites. In addition, some midrange systems are used as departmental or office computers because they can provide large departments or offices more processing power and support more users at the same time than networked microcomputers.

Mainframe Computer Systems

Mainframe computers are large, powerful computers that are physically larger than micros and minis and usually have one or more central processors with faster instruction processing speeds. For example, they typically process hundreds of million instructions per second (MIPS). Mainframes have large primary storage capacities. For example, their main memory capacity can range from about 64 megabytes to several gigabytes of storage. Many mainframe models have the ability to service hundreds of users at once. For example, a single large mainframe can process hundreds of different programs and handle hundreds of different peripheral devices (terminals, disk and tape drives, printers, etc.) for hundreds of different users at the same time. See Figure 2.5.

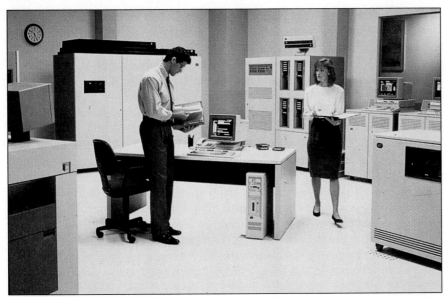

FIGURE 2.5

A large mainframe computer system, the IBM ES/9000.

Courtesy of International Business Machines Corporation.

Mainframe computers are designed to handle the information processing needs of major corporations and government agencies with many employees and customers or with complex computational problems. For example, large computers are necessary for organizations processing millions of transactions each day, such as major international banks, airlines, oil companies, and the national stock exchanges. They can also handle the processing of thousands of customer inquiries, employee paychecks, student registrations, sales transactions, and inventory changes, to give a few examples. Large mainframes can handle the great volume of complex calculations involved in scientific and engineering analyses and simulations of complex design projects, such as analyzing seismic data from oil field exploration, or designing aircraft. Mainframes are also becoming popular as superservers and corporate *database servers* for the large interconnected telecommunications networks of major corporations.

The term **supercomputer** describes a category of extremely powerful mainframe computer systems specifically designed for high-speed numeric computation. A small number of large supercomputers are built each year for government research agencies, military defense systems, national weather forecasting agencies, large time-sharing networks, and major corporations.

Supercomputer Systems

The leading maker of supercomputers is Cray Research, along with NEC, Fugitsu, and a few others. These models can process hundreds of millions of instructions per second (MIPS). Expressed another way, they can perform arithmetic calculations at a speed of billions of floating-point operations per second (gigaflops). *Teraflop* (1 trillion floating-point operations per second) supercomputers, which use advanced *massively parallel* designs, are becoming available.

Purchase prices for large supercomputers are in the $5 million to $50 million range. However, the use of *massively parallel processing* (MPP) designs of thousands of interconnected microprocessors has spawned a breed of *minisupercomputers* with prices less than $1 million. Thus, supercomputers continue to advance the state of the art for the entire computer industry.

Networked Computer Systems

Solitary computer systems are becoming a rarity in corporate computing. From the smallest microcomputer to the largest mainframe, computers are being *networked,* or interconnected by telecommunications links with other computer systems. This networked distribution of computer power throughout an organization is called **distributed processing.** It frequently takes the form of a **client/server** approach, with networks of end user microcomputers (*clients*) and network servers tied together, sometimes with midrange computers or mainframes acting as *superservers.* Networked computer systems allow end users and work groups to communicate electronically, and share the use of hardware, software, and data resources. For example, end users in an office **local area network** (LAN) of microcomputers can communicate with each other using electronic mail, work together on group projects, and share the use of software packages, laser printers, and work group databases. See Figure 2.6.

So, many computer systems consist of peripheral devices interconnected by communications links to one or more central processing units. Thus, networked computing depends on telecommunications. **Telecommunications,** or, more narrowly, *data communications,* is the use of networks of interconnected computers and peripheral devices to process and exchange data and information. Telecommunications networks use a variety of telecommunications media, hardware, and software to accomplish and control communications among computers and peripheral devices. For example, microcomputers rely on *modems* to convert data from digital to analog form and back, while *network operating system* programs control resource sharing and communications flow among computers and peripherals in a local area network. We will discuss telecommunications further in Chapter 4.

Networks of small computers have become a major alternative to the use of larger computer systems, as many organizations are **downsizing** their computing platforms. For example, a network of several midrange computers and many microcomputer workstations may replace a large mainframe computer system with many end user terminals. Alternately, networks of microcomputers can replace both minicomputers and mainframes in many organizations. Networked microcomputers have proven to be easier to install, use, and maintain; they provide a more efficient, flexible, lower-cost alternative to larger computer systems for many applications. See Figure 2.7.

FIGURE 2.6

The computer systems in client/server computing.

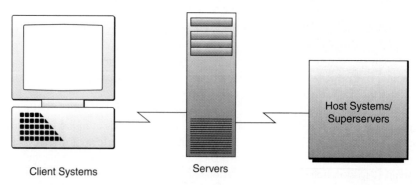

Client Systems

- Types: PCs, Workstations, Macintoshes.
- Functions: Provide user interface, perform some/most processing on an application.

Servers

- Types: Supermicros, Workstations, or Midrange Systems.
- Functions: Shared computation, application control, distributed databases.

Host Systems/Superservers

- Types: Mainframes and Midrange Systems.
- Functions: Central database control, security, directory management, heavy-duty processing.

Networked microcomputer systems are being used for jobs formerly given to large midrange or mainframe systems. Many LANs can easily handle the sharing of computing power, software, and databases that is required in time-sharing and resource-sharing applications. Networked computers also support *work group computing.* For example, end users in a work group can use their networked computers to communicate electronically and share data as they work together on joint projects. Finally, networked microcomputers are even being used for *transaction processing* applications. For example, some organizations are using networks of microcomputers to process thousands of daily credit card purchases, money transfers, credit checks, customer account inquiries, and other business transactions.

As a business end user, you do not need a detailed technical knowledge of computers. However, you do need to understand some basic facts and concepts about computer systems. This should help you be an informed and productive user of computer system resources. Therefore, this section presents basic concepts about the components and functions of a computer system. Other topics include the central processing unit, microprocessors, and computer memory concepts.

A computer is more than a high-powered collection of electronic devices performing a variety of information processing chores. A computer is a **system,** an interrelated combination of components that performs the basic system functions of *input, processing, output, storage,* and *control,* thus providing end users with a powerful information processing tool. Understanding the computer as a **computer system** is vital to the effective use and management of computers. You should be able to visualize any computer this way, from a microcomputer like that shown in Figure 2.8 to a large computer system whose components are interconnected by a telecommunications network and spread throughout a building or geographic area.

Technical Note: Computer System Concepts and Components

The Computer System Concept

Courtesy of Compaq Computer Corporation.

FIGURE 2.7

Networked microcomputers are replacing midrange computers and mainframes in many organizations.

FIGURE 2.8

A microcomputer is a system of computing components. This microcomputer system includes (1) a keyboard and mouse for input, (2) microprocessors and other circuitry in its main system unit for processing and control, (3) a video monitor and printer for output, and (4) memory chips and a built-in floppy disk drive and hard disk unit for storage.

John Curtis.

Figure 2.9 illustrates that a computer is a system of hardware devices organized according to the following system functions:

- **Input.** The input devices of a computer system include keyboards, touch screens, pens, electronic mice, optical scanners, and so on. They convert data into electronic *machine-readable* form for direct entry or through telecommunications links into a computer system.

- **Processing.** The *central processing unit* (CPU) is the main processing component of a computer system. (In microcomputers, it is the *main microprocessor.*) In particular, the electronic circuits of the *arithmetic-logic unit,* one of the CPU's major components, perform the arithmetic and logic functions required in computer processing.

- **Output.** The output devices of a computer system include video display units, printers, audio response units, and so on. They convert electronic information produced by the computer system into *human-intelligible* form for presentation to end users.

- **Storage.** The storage function of a computer system takes place in the storage circuits of the computer's *primary storage unit,* or *memory,* and in *secondary storage* devices such as magnetic disk and tape units. These devices store data and program instructions needed for processing.

- **Control.** The *control unit* of the CPU is the control component of a computer system. Its circuits interpret computer program instructions and transmit directions to the other components of the computer system.

The Central Processing Unit

The **central processing unit** is the most important hardware component of a computer system. It is also known as the CPU, the *central processor* or *instruction processor,* and the **main microprocessor** in a microcomputer. Conceptually, the CPU can be subdivided into two major subunits: the arithmetic-logic unit and the control unit. The CPU also includes specialized circuitry and devices such as *registers* for

FIGURE 2.9

The computer system concept. A computer is a system of hardware components and functions.

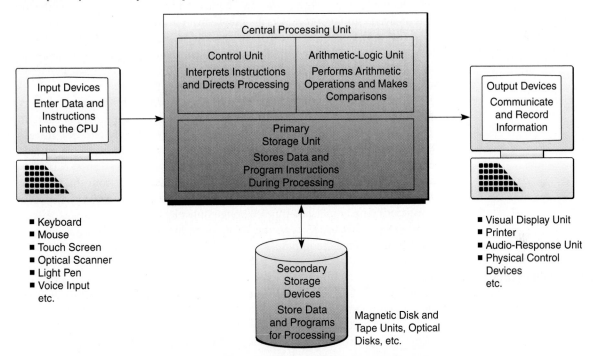

high-speed, temporary storage of instruction and data elements, and various sub-sidiary processors such as those for arithmetic operations, input/output, and telecommunications support. (Sometimes a computer's primary storage unit or memory is shown as part of a CPU.)

The **control unit** obtains instructions from those stored in the primary storage unit and interprets them. Then it transmits directions to the other components of the computer system, ordering them to perform required operations. The **arithmetic-logic unit** performs required arithmetic and comparison operations. A computer can make *logical* changes from one set of program instructions to another (e.g., overtime pay ver-sus regular pay calculations) based on the results of comparisons made in the ALU during processing.

Multiple Processors

Many current computers, from microcomputers to large mainframes, use **multiple processors** for their processing functions. Instead of having one CPU with a single control unit and arithmetic-logic unit, the CPUs of these computers contain several types of processing units. Let's briefly look at the major types of such **multiprocessor** designs.

A **support processor** design relies on specialized microprocessors to help the main CPU perform a variety of functions. These microprocessors may be used for input/output, memory management, arithmetic computations, and telecommunica-tions, thus freeing the main processor to do the primary job of executing program instructions. For example, many microcomputers rely on support microprocessors such as arithmetic co-processors, video display controllers, and magnetic disk controllers to reduce the processing load on their main microprocessors. A large computer may use support microprocessors called *channels* to control the movement of data between the CPU and input/output devices. Advanced microprocessor designs integrate the functions of several support processors on a single main microprocessor. See Figure 2.10.

A **coupled processor** design uses multiple CPUs or main microprocessors to do *multiprocessing,* that is, executing more than one instruction at the same time. Some configurations provide a *fault-tolerant* capability in which multiple CPUs provide a built-in backup to each other should one of them fail.

A **parallel processor** design uses a group of instruction processors to execute several program instructions at the same time. Sometimes, hundreds or thousands of processors are organized in clusters or networks in **massively parallel processor** (MPP) computers. Other parallel processor designs are based on simple models of the human brain called *neural networks.* All of these systems can execute many instructions at a time in *parallel.* This is a major departure from the traditional design of current computers, called the *Von Neumann design,* which executes instructions *serially* (one at a time). Though difficult to program, many experts consider parallel processor systems the key to providing artificial intelligence capabilities to fifth-generation computers.

RISC Processors

Many advanced technical workstations and other computers rely on a processor design called RISC (reduced instruction set computer). This contrasts with most current computers that use CISC (complex instruction set computer) processors. RISC processor designs optimize a CPU's processing speed by using a smaller *instruction set.* That is, they use a smaller number of the *basic machine instructions* that a processor is capable of executing. By keeping the instruction set simpler than CISC processors and using more complex software, a RISC processor can reduce the time needed to execute program instructions. Thus, RISC processors like Digital Equipment's Alpha chip have become popular for computers such as network

FIGURE 2.10

The Intel PentiumPro microprocessor contains more than 5 million transistors and features four execution units and high-speed memory caches that give it a top processing speed of over 200 million instructions per second.

Courtesy of Bonnie Kamin.

servers and technical workstations. Also, a new generation of powerful microcomputers is emerging that uses RISC microprocessors like the Power PC, codeveloped by Motorola, Apple, and IBM. See Figure 2.11.

How fast are computer systems? Computer operating speeds that were formerly measured in **milliseconds** (thousandths of a second) are now in the **microsecond** (millionth of a second) and **nanosecond** (billionth of a second) range, with **picosecond** (trillionth of a second) speed being attained by some computers. Such speeds seem almost incomprehensible. For example, an average person taking one step each nanosecond would circle the earth about 20 times in one second!

Computer Processing Speeds

Many microcomputers and midrange computers, and most mainframe computers, operate at nanosecond speeds and can thus process several *million instructions per second* (MIPS). Another measure of processing speed is megahertz (MHz), or millions of cycles per second. It is commonly called the *clock speed* of a microprocessor, since it is used to rate microprocessors by the speed of their timing circuits or internal clock. However, megahertz ratings can be misleading indicators of the effective processing speed of microprocessors as measured in MIPS and other measures. That's because processing speed depends on a variety of factors besides a microprocessor's clock speed. Important examples include the size of circuitry paths, or *busses,* that interconnect microprocessor components, the capacity of instruction processing *registers,* the use of high-speed *memory caches,* and the use of specialized microprocessors such as a *math co-processor* to do arithmetic calculations faster.

Note: Registers are small high-speed storage circuitry elements in a CPU used to temporarily store parts of an instruction or data element during the execution of an instruction. *Cache memory* is a high-speed temporary storage area in a CPU for storing parts of a program or data during computer processing.

For example, Intel's 80486 microprocessor, which has a cache memory and math co-processor built into the chip, is rated at 20 to 40 MIPS. This is about twice the processing speed of the Intel 80386 microprocessor, even when both chips run at the same megahertz speeds. Just for comparison, Intel's Pentium microprocessor runs at 66 to 133 MHz and is rated at over 100 MIPS. Supercomputers have been clocked at more than 1,000 MIPS and perform arithmetic computations in billions of floating-point operations per second, or *gigaflops.* See Figure 2.12.

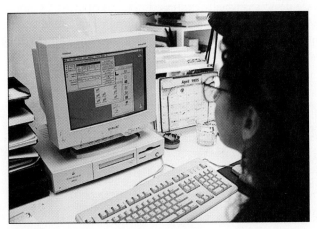

Ed Kashi.

FIGURE 2.11

This Apple Power Macintosh relies on a Power PC microprocessor as its central processing unit.

Primary and Secondary Storage

The **primary storage unit** (also called *main memory*) holds data and instructions between processing steps and supplies them to the control unit and arithmetic-logic unit during processing. All data and programs must be placed in memory before they can be used in processing. In modern computers, the primary storage unit consists of micro-electronic *semiconductor memory chips*. Most of memory is known as **RAM** (random access memory). The contents of these memory chips can be instantly changed to store new data. Other, more permanent memory chips are called **ROM** (read only memory).

Secondary storage devices like magnetic and optical disks, also store data and programs, and thus greatly enlarge the storage capacities of computer systems. Also, since memory circuits typically lose their contents when electric power is turned off, most secondary storage media provide a more permanent type of storage. However, the contents of secondary storage devices cannot be processed without first being brought into the primary storage unit. Thus, external secondary storage devices play a supporting role to the primary storage unit of a computer system. For example, programs and files are typically stored until needed on magnetic floppy disks and hard disks on microcomputer systems, and on large magnetic tape disk and tape units on larger computer systems.

Computer Storage Capacities

Data are processed and stored in a computer system through the presence or absence of electronic or magnetic signals in the computer's circuitry or in the media it uses. This is called a "two-state" or **binary representation** of data, since the computer and the media can exhibit only two possible states or conditions. For example, transistors and other semiconductor circuits are either in a conducting or nonconducting state. Media such as magnetic disks and tapes indicate these two states by having magnetized spots whose magnetic fields have one of two different directions, or polarities. This binary character-istic of computer circuitry and media is what makes the *binary number system* the basis for representing data in computers. Thus, for electronic circuits, the conducting (ON) state represents the number one, while the nonconducting (OFF) state represents the number zero. For magnetic media, the magnetic field of a magnetized spot in one direc-tion represents a one, while magnetism in the other direction represents a zero.

The smallest element of data is called a **bit,** or binary digit, which can have a value of either zero or one. The capacity of memory chips is usually expressed in terms of bits. A **byte** is a basic grouping of bits that the computer operates as a sin-gle unit. Typically, it consists of eight bits and represents one character of data in most computer coding schemes. Thus, the capacity of a computer's memory and sec-ondary storage devices is usually expressed in terms of bytes. Computer codes such as ASCII (American Standard Code for Information Interchange) use various arrangements of bits to form bytes that represent the numbers zero through nine, the letters of the alphabet, and many other characters. See Figure 2.13.

FIGURE 2.12

A comparison of five genera-tions of Intel microprocessors.

Intel Microprocessor	Bus Width (bits)	Register Size (bits)	Clock Speed (MHz)	MIPs
8088	8	8	5–8	0.33
80286	16	16	8–12	1.2
80386	32	32	16–33	2.5–6
80486	32	32	25–66	15–40
Pentium	64	64	66–200	112+
PentiumPro	64	64	133–200+	200+

Character	ASCII Code	Character	ASCII Code
0	00110000	I	01001001
1	00110001	J	01001010
2	00110010	K	01001011
3	00110011	L	01001100
4	00110100	M	01001101
5	00110101	N	01001110
6	00110110	O	01001111
7	00110111	P	01010000
8	00111000	Q	01010001
9	00111001	R	01010010
A	01000001	S	01010011
B	01000010	T	01010100
C	01000011	U	01010101
D	01000100	V	01010110
E	01000101	W	01010111
F	01000110	X	01011000
G	01000111	Y	01011001
H	01001000	Z	01011010

FIGURE 2.13
Examples of the ASCII computer code.

Storage capacities are frequently measured in **kilobytes** (abbreviated as KB or K) or **megabytes** (abbreviated as MB or M). Although *kilo* means 1,000 in the metric system, the computer industry uses K to represent 1,024 (or 2^{10}) storage positions. Therefore, a memory size of 640K, for example, is really 655,360 storage positions, rather than 640,000 positions. However, such differences are frequently disregarded in order to simplify descriptions of storage capacity. Thus, a megabyte is roughly 1 million bytes of storage, while a **gigabyte** is roughly 1 billion bytes and a **terabyte** represents about 1 trillion bytes. Typically, computer primary storage capacities now range from 4 to 64 megabytes for microcomputer memories to several gigabytes of memory for large mainframe computer systems. Magnetic disk capacities generally range from one to several megabytes for floppy disks, from more than 200 megabytes to several gigabytes for hard disk drives, and over 500 megabytes for an optical disk. Mainframe magnetic disk units supply many gigabytes of online storage. Figure 2.14 summarizes these important **storage capacity elements.**

Computer Time Elements	Storage Elements (approximate capacities)
Millisecond = One thousandth of a second	Kilobyte = One thousand bytes
Microsecond = One millionth of a second	Megabyte = One million bytes
Nanosecond = One billionth of a second	Gigabyte = One billion bytes
Picosecond = One trillionth of a second	Terabyte = One trillion bytes

FIGURE 2.14
Computer storage capacity and speed elements.

CENTEX GROUP AND CRSS CONSTRUCTORS: FROM DESKTOP TO LAPTOP PCs

The dominance of desktop PCs in corporate settings is on the wane. And portables will rise to take their place for mid- to upper-level users by the end of the century, industry observers say.

"Laptops are changing the scope of computing and the way we work today," explained Stephen Wittner, network manager at Centex Group, Inc., in Dallas. "To stay competitive, you have to stay as mobile as possible." Furthermore, users say that while notebooks can improve productivity, that benefit is difficult to quantify. "Notebooks still cost more, but the productivity gains are there," Wittner said. "Being able to take your work with you—and not need a bulky briefcase—makes a big difference."

The number of workers using portables will expand from about one in five today to one in three by the year 2000, predicted William Ablondi, an analyst at Giga Information Group. And of those portable users, Giga predicts, 80 percent will use notebooks as their primary PC, up from the current 30 percent.

Driving the switch to portables as primary computing devices is the migration to the virtual office concept of work, according to analysts. That's when users can compute from just about anywhere with access to corporate databases and networks. Information systems managers eventually will start to choose between notebooks and desktops, rather than providing both—and notebooks will win, according to industry analysts.

Users say this is already starting to happen. Support and administrative staff will always need desktops, they note, but among corporate professionals, the scale is beginning to tip toward notebooks.

"Eighty percent of my purchases in the past year have been notebooks," said Doug Moran, an IS manager at CRSS Constructors, Inc., in Denver. "I see the mix between desktop and portable users becoming more like 60–40, in favor of notebooks, in the next couple of years. And that is probably quite conservative."

Users say this trend is becoming easier to swallow financially because the price gap between desktops and notebooks—traditionally notebooks have cost almost double what a standard PC costs—is narrowing. Also aiding notebooks is the fact that notebooks have kept up with desktop microprocessor power trends, even as prices are declining.

There are less obvious financial gains. "If laptop users work an extra two to three hours a week, you are definitely getting your money's worth," Ablondi said. "They are more productive and less stressed out if they can pick up their computer and run and work when they can."

CASE STUDY QUESTIONS

1. Why are laptops overtaking desktop PCs in corporate business?

2. What are the advantages and limitations of laptop computers versus desktop PCs?

3. Would you prefer to have a laptop or a desktop PC for your future career in business? Explain.

Source: Adapted from Mindy Blodget, "Laptops Pushing PCs Off Corporate Desktop," *Computerworld,* April 8, 1996, pp. 1, 12. Copyright © 1996 by Computerworld, Inc., Framingham, MA 01701—Reprinted from *Computerworld.*

Computer Peripherals: Input, Output, and Storage Technologies

Section II

A computer is just a high-powered "processing box" without *peripherals*. **Peripherals** is the generic name given to all input, output, and secondary storage devices that are part of a computer system. Peripherals depend on direct connections or telecommunications links to the central processing unit of a computer system. Thus, all peripherals are **online** devices; that is, they are separate from, but can be electronically connected to and controlled by, a CPU. (This is the opposite of **offline** devices that are separate from and not under the control of the CPU.) The major types of peripherals and media that can be part of a computer system are discussed in this section.

Input/Output Hardware Trends

There are many technologies for input and output at the *user interface* between computer systems and end users. Figure 2.15 shows you the major trends in input/output media and methods that have developed over four generations of computers and are expected to continue into a future fifth generation.

Figure 2.15 emphasizes that there is a major trend toward the increased use of a variety of **direct input/output devices** to provide a more natural user interface. More and more, data and instructions are entered into a computer system directly, through input devices such as keyboards, electronic mice, pens, touch screens, and optical scanning wands. These direct input/output devices drastically reduce the need for paper source documents and their conversion to machine-readable media. Direct output of information through video displays of text and graphics and voice response devices is increasingly becoming the dominant form of output for end users.

Computer Terminal Trends

The most common user interface method still involves a keyboard for entry of data and a video display screen for output to users. **Computer terminals** of various types are widely used for such input and output. Technically, any input/output device connected by telecommunications links to a computer is called a terminal. However, most terminals use a keyboard for input and a TV-like screen for visual output, and

---

FIGURE 2.15

Input/output hardware trends. Note the trend toward direct input and output media and methods to provide a more natural user interface.

	First Generation	Second Generation	Third Generation	Fourth Generation	Fifth Generation?
INPUT MEDIA/ METHOD	Punched Cards Paper Tape	Punched Cards	Key to Tape/Disk	Keyboard Data Entry Direct Input Devices Optical Scanning	Speech Input Tactile Input
TREND: Towards Direct Input Devices that Are Easy to Use.					
OUTPUT MEDIA/ METHOD	Punched Cards Printed Reports	Punched Cards Printed Reports	Printed Reports Video Displays	Video Displays Audio Responses Printed Reports	Graphics Displays Voice Responses
TREND: Towards Direct Output Devices that Communicate Quickly and Clearly.					

are called **visual** (or video) **display terminals** (VDTs) or CRT (cathode ray tube) terminals. They allow keyed-in data to be displayed and edited before entry into a computer system.

There is a trend away from *dumb terminals,* which have no processing capabilities themselves, toward **intelligent terminals,** which have their own microprocessors and memory circuits. Many intelligent terminals are really desktop or portable microcomputers used as telecommunications terminals to larger computers. Therefore, they can perform data entry and other information processing tasks independently. Another trend is the widespread use of **transaction terminals** in banks, retail stores, factories, and other work sites. Examples are automated teller machines (ATMs), factory production recorders, and retail point-of-sale (POS) terminals. These terminals use a variety of input/output methods to capture data from end users during a transaction and transmit it over telecommunications networks to a computer system for processing.

Pointing Devices

Keyboards are the most widely used devices for entering data and text into computer systems. However, **pointing devices** are a better alternative for issuing commands, making choices, and responding to prompts displayed on your video screen. For example, pointing devices such as electronic mice and trackballs allow you to easily choose from menu selections and icon displays using *point-and-click* or *point-and-drag* methods. **Icons** are small figures that look like familiar devices, such as a file folder (for accessing a file), a wastebasket (for deleting a file), or scissors (for cut and paste operations), and so on. Using icons helps simplify computer use since they are easier to use with pointing devices than menus and other text-based displays. See Figure 2.16.

The **electronic mouse** is a pointing device used to move the cursor on the screen, as well as to issue commands and make icon and menu selections. Some mice contain a roller ball that moves the cursor in the direction the ball is rolled. Others use an optical sensing technology that recognizes points on a special pad. By moving the mouse on a desktop or pad, you can move the cursor onto an icon displayed on the screen. Pressing a button on the mouse begins the activity represented by the icon selected.

FIGURE 2.16

The keyboard and the mouse are the most widely used computer input devices.

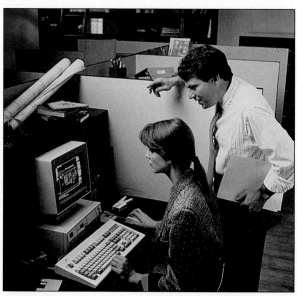

Sygma Photo News.

The trackball, pointing stick, and touch pad are other pointing devices most often used in place of the mouse. A **trackball** is a stationary device related to the mouse. You turn a roller ball with only its top exposed outside its case to move the cursor on the screen. A **pointing stick** (also called a *trackpoint*) is a small buttonlike device, sometimes likened to the eraserhead of a pencil. It is usually centered one row above the space bar of a keyboard. The cursor moves in the direction of the pressure you place on the trackpoint. The **touchpad** is a small rectangular touch-sensitive surface usually placed below the keyboard. The cursor moves in the direction your finger moves on the pad. Trackballs, pointing sticks, and touch pads are easier to use than a mouse for portable computer users and are thus built into many laptop computer keyboards. See Figure 2.17.

Touch-sensitive screens are devices that allow you to use a computer by touching the surface of its video display screen. Such screens emit a grid of infrared beams, sound waves, or a slight electric current that is broken when the screen is touched. The computer senses the point in the grid where the break occurs and responds with an appropriate action. For example, you could indicate your selection on a menu display by just touching the screen next to that menu item.

Pen-Based Computing

End users can write or draw directly on a video screen or on other surfaces using a variety of penlike devices. One example is the **light pen.** This pen-shaped device uses photoelectric circuitry to enter data into the computer through a video screen. A user can write on the video display because the light-sensitive pen enables the computer to calculate the coordinates of the points on the screen touched by the light pen. A **graphics tablet** is a form of *digitizer* that allows you to draw or write on its pressure-sensitive surface with a pen-shaped stylus. Your handwriting or drawing is digitized by the computer, accepted as input, and displayed on its video screen.

Light pen and graphics pad technologies are being used in a new generation of **pen-based** personal computers and personal digital assistants (PDAs) that recognize handwriting. These notebook PCs and PDAs are portable, tablet-style microcomputers that contain software that recognizes and digitizes handwriting, handprinting, and hand drawing. They have a pressure-sensitive layer like a graphics pad under their slatelike liquid crystal display (LCD) screen. So instead of writing on a paper form fastened to a clipboard, inspectors, field engineers, and other mobile workers can use a pen to enter handwritten data directly into a computer. See Figure 2.18.

Courtesy of International Business Machines Corporation.

FIGURE 2.17
The pointing stick is a popular pointing device for portable computers. Note that this multimedia laptop PC also includes a CD–ROM drive.

FIGURE 2.18
This pen-based notebook computer recognizes hand-writing on its display screen.

Courtesy of Compaq Computer Corporation.

Video Input/Output

Video and Multimedia Input

Video images can serve as input as well as output. For example, input from a TV receiver, camcorder, or VCR can be digitized and compressed for storage on magnetic or optical disks. Digitizing *snapshot* images can be done with an optical scanner. Digitizing *full motion* video images from camcorders and VCRs requires PCs that use technologies like *digital video interactive* (DVI). Equipping your PC with a DVI capability requires additional software, circuit boards, memory, and magnetic or optical disk capacity. This would give you a *multimedia development* capability. Then you could merge text, graphics, sound, and TV images to produce computer-generated video presentations. We will discuss multimedia technologies and applications further in Chapter 6. See Figure 2.19.

Video Output

Video displays are the most common type of computer output. Most video displays use a **cathode ray tube** (CRT) technology similar to the picture tubes used in home TV sets. Usually, the clarity of the display and the support of monochrome or color displays depend on the type of video monitor used and the graphics circuit board, or *video adapter,* installed in the microcomputer. These can provide a variety of graphics

FIGURE 2.19
This multimedia PC can help you develop multimedia video presentations.

Courtesy of International Business Machines Corporation.

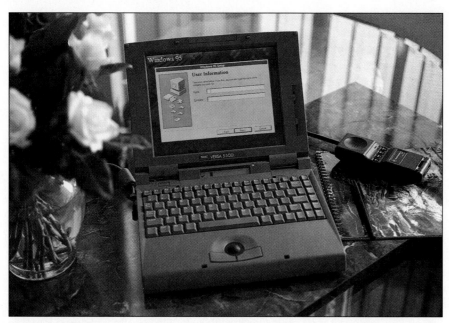

Bonnie Kamin/Offshoot.

FIGURE 2.20

This laptop microcomputer features an LCD display and built-in trackball.

modes of increasing capability. A high level of clarity is especially important to support the more complex graphical displays of many current software packages. These packages provide a *graphical user interface* (GUI), which uses icons and a variety of screen images and typically splits the screen into multiple *window* displays.

Liquid crystal displays (LCDs), such as those used in electronic calculators and watches, are also being used to display computer output. Their biggest use is to provide a visual display capability for portable microcomputers and terminals. Advances in technology have improved the clarity of such displays that were formerly hard to see in bright sunlight and artificial light. LCD displays need significantly less electric current and provide a thin, flat display. Full-color LCD displays are now available. See Figure 2.20.

Plasma display devices have replaced CRT devices in a limited number of applications where a flat display is needed. Plasma displays are generated by electrically charged particles of gas (plasma) trapped between glass plates. Plasma display units are significantly more expensive than CRT and LCD units. However, they use less power, provide faster display speeds, and produce clearer displays that are easier to see from any angle and in any lighting conditions.

Printed Output

After video displays, printed output is the most common form of visual output for the user interface. Most computer systems use **printers** to produce permanent (hard copy) output in human-readable form. End users need printed output if they want to take copies of output away from the computer to share with others. Hard copy output is also frequently needed for legal documentation. Thus, computers can usually produce printed reports and documents, such as sales invoices, payroll checks, and bank statements, as well as hard copy of graphics displays. **Plotters,** which draw graphics displays on paper, also produce printed paper output.

Many printers are **impact printers.** They form characters and other images on paper through the impact of a printing mechanism that presses a printing element (such as a print wheel or cylinder) and an inked ribbon or roller against the face of a sheet of paper. Multiple copies can be produced because the impact of the printing mechanism can transmit an image onto several layers of multiple copy forms. Popular impact printers for microcomputer systems use a **dot matrix** printing element that consists of short print wires that form a character as a grouping or matrix of dots. Speeds of several hundred characters per second are attainable. Mainframe computer systems typically use high-speed line printers that can print up to several thousand lines per minute. The printing element they use may be a moving metal chain or cylinder of characters.

Nonimpact printers are quieter than impact printers, since the sound of a printing element striking paper is eliminated. However, they do not produce multiple copies like impact printers. **Laser printers** and **ink jet printers** are examples of popular nonimpact printing methods for producing high-quality printed output. Laser printers allow companies to produce their own business forms, as well as formal reports and manuals. Such *desktop publishing* applications are discussed in Chapter 6. Laser printers for microcomputer systems have speeds from less than 5 to more than 200 pages per minute. See Figure 2.21.

Voice Recognition and Response

Voice recognition and *voice response* promise to be the easiest method of providing a user interface for data entry and conversational computing, since speech is the easiest, most natural means of human communication. Voice input and output of data have now become technologically and economically feasible for a variety of applications. A voice recognition capability can be added to a microcomputer by acquiring a voice recognition circuit board and software for less than $1,000. The circuit board contains a digital signal processor (DSP) microprocessor and other circuitry for voice recognition processing, and a vocabulary in ROM ranging from several hundred to more than 30,000 words. For example, personal dictation systems for word processing (including a circuit board and software) are now available for under $1,000 for a 34,000 word vocabulary system. See Figure 2.22.

Voice recognition systems analyze and classify speech or vocal tract patterns and convert them into digital codes for entry into a computer system. Most voice recognition systems require training the computer to recognize a limited vocabulary of standard words for each user. Operators train the system to recognize their voices by repeating each word in the vocabulary about 10 times. Trained systems regularly

FIGURE 2.21

A laser printer produces high-quality printed output.

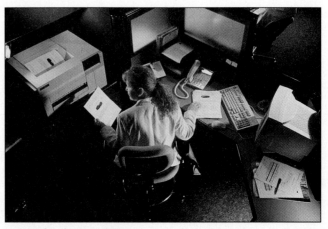

Courtesy of Hewlett-Packard Company.

achieve a 99 percent plus word recognition rate. Speaker-independent voice recognition systems, which allow a computer to understand a voice it has never heard before, are used in a limited number of applications.

Voice recognition devices in work situations allow operators to perform data entry without using their hands to key in data or instructions and to provide faster and more accurate input. For example, manufacturers use voice recognition systems for the inspection, inventory, and quality control of a variety of products; and airlines and parcel delivery companies use them for voice-directed sorting of baggage and parcels. Voice recognition is also available for software packages like spreadsheets and database managers for voice input of data and commands. In addition, voice input for word processing is becoming a popular application of voice recognition technology.

Voice response devices range from mainframe *audio-response* units to voice-messaging minicomputers to *speech synthesizer* microprocessors. Speech microprocessors can be found in toys, calculators, appliances, automobiles, and a variety of other consumer, commercial, and industrial products.

Voice-messaging minicomputer and mainframe audio-response units use voice-response software to verbally guide an operator through the steps of a task in many kinds of activities. They may also allow computers to respond to verbal and Touch-Tone input over the telephone. Examples of applications include computerized telephone call switching, telemarketing surveys, bank pay-by-phone bill-paying services, stock quotations services, university registration systems, and customer credit and account balance inquiries.

Optical and Magnetic Recognition

Optical Scanning

Optical scanning devices read text or graphics and convert them into digital input for a computer. They include **optical character recognition** (OCR) equipment that can read special-purpose characters and codes. Optical scanning of pages of text and graphics is especially popular in desktop publishing applications. Thus, optical scanning provides a method of direct input of data from source documents into a computer system.

There are many types of optical readers, but they all employ photoelectric devices to scan the characters being read. Reflected light patterns of the data are converted into electronic impulses that are then accepted as input into the computer

Martin Schneider and Associates.

FIGURE 2.22

Using voice recognition for word processing in a hospital patient care system.

system. Devices can currently read many types of printing and graphics. Progress is continually being made in improving the reading ability of scanning equipment. See Figure 2.23.

The credit card billing operations of credit card companies, banks, and oil companies use OCR-based optical scanning systems extensively. They also process utility bills, insurance premiums, airline tickets, and cash register machine tapes. OCR scanners can automatically sort mail, score tests, and process a wide variety of forms in business and government.

Optical scanning devices such as handheld **wands** read data on merchandise tags and other media. This frequently involves reading *bar coding,* a code that utilizes bars to represent characters. Thus, Universal Product Code (UPC) bar coding on packages of food items and other products has become commonplace. For example, the automated checkout scanners found in many supermarkets read UPC bar coding. Supermarket scanners emit laser beams that are reflected off a UPC bar code. The reflected image is converted to electronic impulses that are sent to the in-store minicomputer, where they are matched with pricing information. Pricing information is returned to the terminal, visually displayed, and printed on a receipt.

Magnetic Data Entry

The computer systems of the banking industry can magnetically read checks and deposit slips using **magnetic ink character recognition** (MICR) technology. Computers can thus sort, tabulate, and post checks to the proper checking accounts. Such processing is possible because the identification numbers of the bank and the customer's account are preprinted on the bottom of the checks with an iron oxide–based ink. The first bank receiving a check after it has been written must

FIGURE 2.23

Using an optical scanning wand to read bar coding of product data in a warehouse shipping and receiving system.

Jeff Zaruba/The Stock Market.

encode the amount of the check in magnetic ink on the check's lower right-hand corner. The MICR system uses 14 characters (the 10 decimal digits and 4 special symbols) of a standardized design.

MICR characters can be either preprinted on documents or encoded on documents using a keyboard-operated machine called a *proof-inscriber*. Equipment known as MICR *reader-sorters* read a check by first magnetizing the magnetic ink characters and then sensing the signal induced by each character as it passes a reading head. In this way, data are electronically captured by the computer system. The check is then sorted by directing it into one of the pockets of the reader-sorter. Reader-sorters can read more than 2,400 checks per minute, with a data transfer rate of over 3,000 characters per second. However, several large banks have begun replacing MICR technology with optical scanning systems.

Another familiar form of magnetic data entry is the **magnetic stripe** technology that helps computers read credit cards. The dark magnetic stripe on the back of credit and debit cards is the same iron oxide coating as on magnetic tape. Customer account numbers can be recorded on the stripe so it can be read by bank ATMs, credit card authorization terminals, and other *magnetic stripe readers*.

Storage Trends and Trade-Offs

Data and information need to be stored after input, during processing, and before output. Even today, many organizations still rely on paper documents stored in filing cabinets as a major form of storage media. However, computer-based information systems rely primarily on the memory circuits and secondary storage devices of computer systems to accomplish the storage function. Figure 2.24 illustrates major trends in primary and secondary storage methods. Continued developments in very-large-scale integration (VLSI), which packs millions of electronic circuit elements on tiny semiconductor memory chips, are responsible for a significant increase in the main memory capacity of computers. Secondary storage capacities are also expected to escalate into the billions and trillions of characters, due primarily to use of optical media.

There are many types of storage media and devices. Figure 2.25 illustrates the speed, capacity, and cost relationships of several alternative primary and secondary storage media. Note the cost/speed/capacity trade-offs as one moves from semiconductor memories to magnetic media, such as magnetic disks and tapes, to optical

FIGURE 2.24

Major trends in primary and secondary storage methods.

	First Generation	Second Generation	Third Generation	Fourth Generation	Fifth Generation?
PRIMARY STORAGE	Magnetic Drum	Magnetic Core	Magnetic Core	LSI Semiconductor Memory	VLSI Semiconductor Memory
TREND: Towards Large Capacities Using Smaller Microelectronic Circuits.					
SECONDARY STORAGE	Magnetic Tape Magnetic Drum	Magnetic Tape Magnetic Disk	Magnetic Disk Magnetic Tape	Magnetic Disk Optical Disk	Optical Disk Magnetic Disk
TREND: Towards Massive Capacities Using Magnetic and Optical Media.					

FIGURE 2.25

Storage media cost, speed, and capacity trade-offs. Note how cost increases with faster access speeds but decreases with increased capacity.

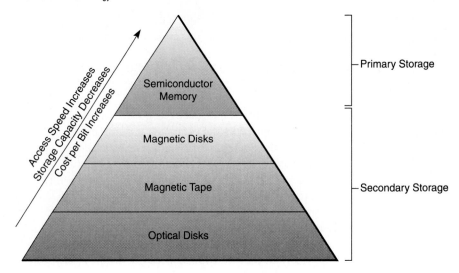

disks. High-speed storage media cost more per byte and provide lower capacities. Large-capacity storage media cost less per byte but are slower. This is why we have different kinds of storage media.

Note in Figure 2.25 that semiconductor memories are used mainly for primary storage, though they are finding increasing use as high-speed secondary storage devices. Magnetic disk and tape and optical disk devices, on the other hand, are used as secondary storage devices to greatly enlarge the storage capacity of computer systems. Also, since most primary storage circuits use RAM (random access memory) chips, which lose their contents when electrical power is interrupted, secondary storage devices provide a more permanent type of storage media for storage of data and programs.

Direct and Sequential Access

Primary storage media such as semiconductor memory chips are called **direct access** or *random access memories* (RAM). Magnetic disk devices are frequently called direct access storage devices (DASDs). On the other hand, media such as magnetic tapes are known as **sequential access** devices.

The terms *direct access* and *random access* describe the same concept. They mean that an element of data or instructions (such as a byte or word) can be directly stored and retrieved by selecting and using any of the locations on the storage media. They also mean that each storage position (1) has a unique address and (2) can be individually accessed in approximately the same length of time without having to search through other storage positions. For example, each memory cell on a microelectronic semiconductor RAM chip can be individually sensed or changed in the same length of time. Also any data record stored on a magnetic or optical disk can be accessed directly in approximately the same time period. See Figure 2.26.

Sequential access storage media such as magnetic tape do not have unique storage addresses that can be directly addressed. Instead, data must be stored and retrieved using a sequential or serial process. Data are recorded one after another in a predetermined sequence (such as in numeric order) on a storage medium. Locating an individual item of data requires searching much of the recorded data on the tape until the desired item is located.

FIGURE 2.26

Sequential versus direct access storage. Magnetic tape is a typical sequential access medium. Magnetic disks are typical direct access storage devices.

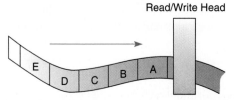

Sequential Access Storage Device

Read/Write Head

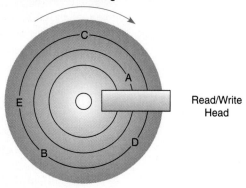

Direct Access Storage Device

Read/Write Head

The primary storage (main memory) of most modern computers consists of microelectronic **semiconductor memory** circuits. Millions of storage circuits can be etched on large-scale integrated (LSI) silicon chips. *Memory chips* with capacities of 256K bits, 1 million bits (1 megabit), 4 megabits, and 16 megabits are now used in many computers.

Some of the major attractions of semiconductor memory are small size, great speed, shock and temperature resistance, and low cost due to mass production capabilities. One major disadvantage of most semiconductor memory is its **volatility**. Uninterrupted electric power must be supplied or the contents of memory will be lost. Therefore, emergency transfer to other devices or standby electrical power (through battery packs or emergency generators) is required if data are to be saved. Another alternative is to permanently "burn in" the contents of semiconductor devices so that they cannot be erased by a loss of power.

Thus, there are two basic types of semiconductor memory: **random access memory** (RAM) and **read only memory** (ROM).

- **RAM: random access memory.** These memory chips are the most widely used primary storage medium. Each memory position can be both sensed (read) and changed (written), so it is also called read/write memory. This is a volatile memory.

- **ROM: read only memory.** Nonvolatile random access memory chips are used for permanent storage. ROM can be read but not erased or overwritten. Frequently used control instructions in the control unit and programs in primary storage (such as parts of the operating system) can be permanently burned in to the storage cells during manufacture. This is sometimes called firmware. Variations include PROM (programmable read only memory) and EPROM (erasable programmable read only memory) that can be permanently or temporarily programmed after manufacture.

Semiconductor Memory

Semiconductor Secondary Storage

Semiconductor memory chips serve as direct access primary and secondary storage media for both large and small computers. Plug-in memory circuit boards containing up to several megabytes of semiconductor memory chips (RAM cards) can be added to a microcomputer to increase its memory capacity. These provide additional primary storage, but they can also be used for secondary storage. A computer's operating system program can be instructed to treat part of RAM as if another disk drive has been added to the system. This provides a very-high-speed semiconductor secondary-storage capability, sometimes called a RAM *disk*. Semiconductor secondary storage devices also include removable credit-card-size "flash memory" RAM *cards*. They provide up to 40 megabytes of erasable direct access storage for some notebook or handheld PCs. Peripheral devices consisting of semiconductor memory chips are also marketed as high-speed alternatives to magnetic disk units for mainframe computers.

Magnetic Disk Storage

Magnetic disks are the most common form of secondary storage for modern computer systems. They provide fast access and high storage capacities at a reasonable cost. The two basic types of magnetic disk media are conventional (hard) metal disks and flexible (floppy) diskettes. Several types of magnetic disk peripherals are used as DASDs in both small and large computer systems. See Figure 2.27.

Magnetic disks are thin metal or plastic disks that are coated on both sides with an iron oxide recording material. Several disks may be mounted together in a vertical cylinder on a vertical shaft, which typically rotates the disks at speeds of 2,400 to 3,600 revolutions per minute (rpm). Electromagnetic read/write heads are positioned by access arms between the slightly separated disks to read and write data on concentric, circular **tracks.** Data are recorded on tracks in the form of tiny magnetized spots to form binary digits arranged in serial order in common computer codes. Thousands of bytes can be recorded on each track, and there are several hundred data tracks on each disk surface, each of which is subdivided into a number of **sectors.** See Figure 2.28.

Types of Magnetic Disks

There are several types of magnetic disk arrangements, including removable disk packs and cartridges as well as fixed disk units. The removable disk devices are popular because they can be used interchangeably in magnetic disk units and stored offline for convenience and security when not in use.

FIGURE 2.27

Magnetic disk media: A 3½-inch floppy disk and a hard magnetic disk drive.

Walter Bibikow/The Image Bank.   Courtesy of Quantum Corporation.

- **Floppy disks,** or *magnetic diskettes,* are disks that consist of polyester film covered with an iron oxide compound. A single disk is mounted and rotates freely inside a protective flexible or hard plastic jacket, which has access openings to accommodate the read/write head of a disk drive unit. The 3½-inch floppy disk, with capacities of 720 kilobytes and 1.44 or 2.8 megabytes, has rapidly replaced most of the older 5¼-inch size.

- **Hard disk drives** combine magnetic disks, access arms, and read/write heads into a sealed module. This allows higher speeds, greater data-recording densities, and closer tolerances within a sealed, more stable environment. Fixed or removable disk cartridge versions are also available. Capacities of hard drives typically range from 120 megabytes to several gigabytes of storage.

- **RAID.** Disk arrays of interconnected microcomputer hard disk drives are challenging large-capacity mainframe disk drives to provide many gigabytes of online storage. Known as **RAID** (redundant arrays of independent disks), they combine from 6 to more than 100 small hard disk drives and their control microprocessors into a single unit. RAID units provide large capacities with high access speeds since data are accessed in parallel over multiple paths from many disks. RAID units also provide a *fault tolerant* capability, since their redundant design offers multiple copies of data on several disks. If one disk fails, data can be recovered from backup copies automatically stored on other disks.

Magnetic tape is another widely used secondary storage medium. The read/write heads of magnetic tape drives record data in the form of magnetized spots on the iron oxide coating of the plastic tape. Magnetic tape usually has horizontal tracks to accommodate recording bits into common computer codes. Blank spaces, known as gaps, separate individual data records and blocks of grouped records. These gaps allow for such mechanical operations as the start/stop time of a magnetic tape unit. Most devices group records into blocks to conserve storage space instead of leaving gaps between each record.

Magnetic Tape Storage

FIGURE 2.28

Characteristics of magnetic disks. Note especially the concepts of cylinders, tracks, and sectors.

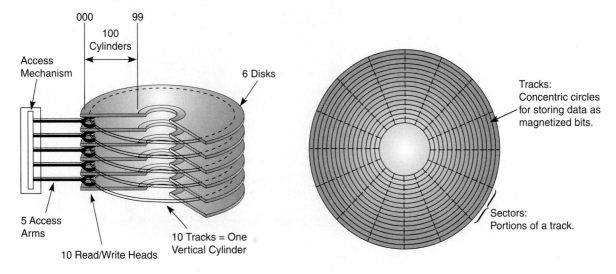

Magnetic tape comes in the form of tape reels and cartridges for mainframes and minicomputers, and small cassettes or cartridges for microcomputers. Mainframe magnetic cartridges are replacing tape reels and can hold over 200 megabytes. Small cartridges can store more than 100 megabytes and are a popular means of providing backup capabilities for microcomputer hard disk drives.

Optical Disk Storage

Optical disks are a fast-growing storage medium. Mainframe and midsize computer versions use 12-inch plastic disks with capacities of several gigabytes, with up to 20 disks held in "jukebox" drive units. The version for use with microcomputers is called **CD–ROM** (compact disk–read only memory). CD–ROM technology uses 12-centimeter (4.7-inch) compact disks (CDs) similar to those used in stereo music systems, and *CD–ROM drives* for microcomputer systems. Each disk can store more than 600 megabytes. That's the equivalent of over 400 1.44 megabyte floppy disks or more than 300,000 double-spaced pages of text. A laser records data by burning permanent microscopic pits in a spiral track on a master disk from which compact disks can be mass produced. Then CD–ROM disk drives use a laser device to read the binary codes formed by those pits. See Figure 2.29.

Other optical disk technologies produce **WORM** (write once, read many) and **CD–R** (compact disk–recordable) disks. This allows computers with the proper optical disk drive units to record their own data once on an optical disk, then be able to read it indefinitely. The major limitation of CD–ROM, CD–R, and WORM disks is that recorded data cannot be erased. However, **erasable optical disk** systems have now become available. This technology records and erases data by using a laser to heat a microscopic point of the disk's surface. In some versions, a magnetic coil

FIGURE 2.29

CD–ROM disks can hold more than 600 million characters of information.

David Pollack/The Stock Market.

changes the spot's reflective properties from one direction to another, thus recording a binary one or zero. A laser device can then read the binary codes on the disk by sensing the direction of reflected light.

One of the major uses of optical disks in mainframe and midrange systems is in *image processing,* where long-term *archival storage* of historical files of document images must be maintained. Financial institutions, among others, are using optical scanners to capture digitized document images and store them on WORM optical disks as an alternative to microfilm media. One of the major uses of CD–ROM disks is to provide companies with fast access to reference materials in a convenient, compact form. This includes catalogs, directories, manuals, periodical abstracts, part listings, and statistical databases of business and economic activity.

Interactive **multimedia applications** in business, education, and entertainment are another major use of CD–ROM disks. *Multimedia* is the use of a variety of media, including text and graphics displays, voice, music, and other audio, photographs, animation, and video segments. Multimedia has large storage requirements. For example, it takes one megabyte for a color picture, 2.4 megabytes for a four-minute song, and over 1 gigabyte for a minute of full motion video, though this can be reduced by video compression technologies. Thus, the large storage capacities of CD–ROM are a natural choice for computer video games, educational videos, multimedia encyclopedias, and advertising presentations. See Figure 2.30.

Optical disks have emerged as a popular storage medium for image processing and multimedia applications, and they appear to be a promising alternative to magnetic disks and tape for very large (mass) storage capabilities for enterprise and end user computing systems. However, erasable optical technologies are still being perfected. Also, optical disk devices are significantly slower and more expensive (per byte of storage) than magnetic disk devices. So optical disk systems are not expected to displace magnetic disk technology in the near future.

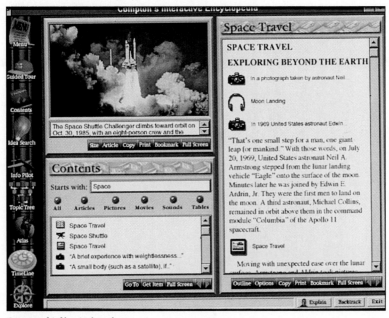

Courtesy of Softkey Multimedia, Inc.

FIGURE 2.30

A display screen from Compton's Multimedia Encyclopedia that is stored on a CD–ROM.

CHRYSLER CORPORATION: MULTIMEDIA TOUCH SCREEN PC KIOSKS

"May I help you?" These may be the four most dreaded words spoken in a new-car showroom. That's why Chrysler's Modus system lets customers steer themselves through the buying process. Under siege from on-line car brokers, warehouse clubs, and giant auto malls, Chrysler is banishing high-pressure salespeople and nitty-gritty haggling over prices.

The carmaker's bid for survival is its new system, called Modus, that provides car shoppers with touch screen kiosks to help them find information about new cars and the fixed price tags they carry. Consumers who want to comparison shop can tap into automotive sites on the World Wide Web from Modus kiosks that are equipped with a browser.

To get started, shoppers use touch screens at kiosks—which are actually Intel-based PCs that run Windows 95—to indicate the features they want, view video clips of different models, scan available inventory, look up fixed prices, and calculate finance options.

Behind the scenes, inventory, pricing, and manufacturer's information is stored on a Microsoft SQL Server database that runs on a Windows NT server. A separate network server handles communications and houses software that continually monitors the kinds of information customers request at the kiosks.

Once a buyer selects a car, financing can be secured on-line in less than five minutes from Chrysler Finance Corporation and NationsBank. Both are linked into Modus at the MidPark Jeep-Eagle dealership in Dallas, one of several pilot test sites in the United States. Other banks will join them, tying into the system via the Modus system's network.

After buying, customers are issued smart cards similar to automated teller machine banking cards. These will provide 24-hour access to MidPark's service center, where customers can view on-line the services available and charges. There is even cappuccino and popcorn for the thirsty and hungry, telephones and modem ports for mobile workers' laptop PCs, and a play area for the children.

CASE STUDY QUESTIONS

1. Why is Chrysler installing multimedia touch screen kiosks in their dealers' showrooms?

2. What computer systems and input/output technologies are involved in the Modus system? What are their benefits and limitations?

3. Would you like to buy a car using the Modus kiosk system? Why or why not?

Source: Adapted from Julia King, "High Tech Drives Automaker's Pitch," *Computerworld,* February 19, 1996, pp. 1, 105. Copyright © 1996 by Computerworld, Inc., Framingham, MA 01701—Reprinted from *Computerworld.*

Summary

- **Computer Systems.** A computer is a system of information processing components that perform input, processing, output, storage, and control functions. Its hardware components include input and output devices, a central processing unit (CPU), and primary and secondary storage devices. The major functions and hardware in a computer system are summarized in Figure 2.9. Major types and trends in computer systems are summarized in Figures 2.1 and 2.2.

- **Microcomputer Systems.** Microcomputers are used as personal computers, professional workstations, technical workstations, and network servers. Microcomputers typically use a keyboard for input, a system unit containing the main microprocessor for processing and control, semiconductor RAM and ROM circuits for primary storage, floppy disk and hard disk drives for secondary storage, and a video display monitor and printer for output. A wide variety of other hardware devices are available, as are thousands of application software packages.

- **Other Computer Systems.** Midrange computers are general-purpose computers that are larger and more powerful than most microcomputers. They are used as powerful network servers and for many business data processing and scientific applications. Mainframe computers are larger and more powerful than most minicomputers. They are usually faster, have more memory capacity, and can support more input/output and secondary storage devices. They are designed to handle the information processing needs of large organizations with many customers and employees, or with complex computational problems. Supercomputers are a special category of extremely powerful mainframe computer systems designed for massive computational assignments.

- **Peripheral Devices.** Refer to Figures 2.31 and 2.32 for summaries of the functions, characteristics, advantages, and disadvantages of peripheral devices for input, output, and storage discussed in this chapter.

Peripheral Equipment	Media	Primary Functions	Major Advantages and/or Disadvantages
Video display terminals	None	Keyboard input and video output	Conventional and inexpensive, but limited display capacity and no hard copy
Printers	Paper	Printed output of paper reports and documents	Hard copy, but inconvenient and bulky; many printers are relatively slow
Pointing devices	None	Input by mouse, trackball, pointing stick, pen, touch screen, and graphics pad. Video output.	Input devices are easy to use and inexpensive, but may have limited applications and software support
Voice input/ output devices	None	Voice input and output	Easiest I/O but is slow, has limited vocabulary, and has accuracy problems
Optical scanners	Paper documents	Direct input from written or printed documents	Direct input from paper documents, but some limitations on input format
Magnetic ink character recognition (MICR) readers	MICR paper documents	Direct input of MICR documents	Fast, high-reliability reading, but documents must be preprinted and the character set is limited

FIGURE 2.31

A summary of important input/output methods. Note especially the advantages and disadvantages of each method in providing hardware support of the user interface.

FIGURE 2.32

A summary of important computer storage methods. Note the advantages and disadvantages of each method.

Peripheral Equipment	Media	Primary Functions	Major Advantages and/or Disadvantages
Magnetic disk drive	Hard disk, Disk pack, Disk cartridge	Secondary storage (direct access) and input/output	Large capacity, fast, direct access storage device (DASD), but relatively expensive
Floppy disk drive	Magnetic diskette: 3½- and 5¼-inch diameters	Secondary storage (direct access) and input/output	Small, inexpensive, and convenient, but slower and smaller capacity than other DASDs
Magnetic tape drive	Magnetic tape reel and cartridge	Secondary storage (sequential access), input/output, and disk backup	Inexpensive, with a fast transfer rate, but only sequential access
Optical disk drive	Optical disk: CD–ROM, WORM, CD–R, and erasable	Secondary storage (direct access) and archival storage	Large capacity, high-quality storage of data, text, and images. Primarily a read-only medium

Key Terms and Concepts

These are the key terms and concepts of this chapter. The page number of their first explanation is given in parentheses.

1. Arithmetic-logic unit (57)
2. Binary representation (60)
3. Cathode ray tube (66)
4. Central processing unit (56)
5. Client/server (54)
6. Computer system (55)
7. Computer terminals (63)
8. Control unit (57)
9. Direct access (72)
10. Direct input/output devices (63)
11. Distributed processing (54)
12. Downsizing (54)
13. Generations of computing (49)
14. Graphics tablet (65)
15. Icon (64)
16. Light pen (65)
17. Liquid crystal displays (67)
18. Local area network (54)
19. Magnetic disk storage (74)
    a. Floppy disk
    b. Hard disk
20. Magnetic ink character recognition (70)
21. Magnetic tape (75)
22. Mainframe computer (52)
23. Microcomputer (50)
24. Microprocessor (50)
25. Midrange computer (51)
26. Minicomputer (51)
27. Multimedia (77)
28. Multiple processors (57)
29. Network server (51)
30. Networked computer systems (50)
31. Offline (63)
32. Online (63)
33. Optical character recognition (69)
34. Optical disk storage (76)
    a. CD–ROM
    b. Erasable disks
    c. WORM disks
35. Optical scanning (69)
36. Pen-based computing (65)
37. Peripheral devices (63)
38. Plasma displays (67)
39. Plotters (67)
40. Pointing devices (64)
    a. Electronic mouse
    b. Pointing stick
    c. Touchpad
    d. Trackball
41. Primary storage unit (60)
42. Printers (67)
43. Processing speeds (59)
44. Secondary storage device (60)
45. Semiconductor memory (73)
    a. RAM
    b. ROM
46. Sequential access (72)
47. Storage capacity elements (60)
    a. Bit
    b. Byte
    c. Kilobyte
    d. Megabyte
    e. Gigabyte
    f. Terabyte

48. Storage media trade-offs (71)
49. Supercomputer (53)
50. Time elements (59)
    a. Millisecond
    b. Microsecond

    c. Nanosecond
    d. Picosecond
51. Touch-sensitive screen (65)
52. Trends in computers (49)
53. Video input/output (66)

54. Voice recognition (68)
55. Voice response (69)
56. Volatility (73)
57. Wand (70)
58. Workstation (50)

Review Quiz

Match one of the key terms and concepts listed above with one of the brief examples or definitions listed below. Try to find the best fit for answers that seem to fit more than one term or concept. Defend your choices.

_____ 1. Computers will become smaller, faster, more reliable, easier to use, and less costly.

_____ 2. Major stages in the development of computers.

_____ 3. A computer is a combination of components that perform input, processing, output, storage, and control functions.

_____ 4. Contains the arithmetic-logic unit and control unit.

_____ 5. Performs computations and comparisons.

_____ 6. Interprets instructions and directs processing.

_____ 7. The memory of a computer.

_____ 8. Magnetic disks and tape and optical disks perform this function.

_____ 9. Capture data or communicate information without media.

_____ 10. Input/output and secondary storage devices for a computer system.

_____ 11. Connected to and controlled by a CPU.

_____ 12. Separate from and not controlled by a CPU.

_____ 13. Results from the presence or absence or change in direction of electric current, magnetic fields, or light rays in computer circuits and media.

_____ 14. The central processing unit of a microcomputer.

_____ 15. Can be a desktop or portable computer and a single- or multiuser unit.

_____ 16. A computer category between microcomputers and mainframes.

_____ 17. A computer that can handle the information processing needs of large organizations.

_____ 18. Dispersing networked computer power throughout an organization.

_____ 19. Many computer systems are now interconnected by telecommunications networks.

_____ 20. End user workstations are networked to server computers.

_____ 21. A computer with several CPUs is an example.

_____ 22. A computer that manages network communications and resources.

_____ 23. The most powerful type of computer.

_____ 24. A telecommunications network in an office or other worksite.

_____ 25. One billionth of a second.

_____ 26. Roughly one billion characters of storage.

_____ 27. Includes electronic mice, trackballs, and pointing sticks.

_____ 28. You can write on the pressure-sensitive LCD screen of notebook-size microcomputers with a pen.

_____ 29. Helps you write on a video screen with a light-sensitive pen.

_____ 30. Moving this along your desktop moves the cursor on the screen.

_____ 31. You can communicate with a computer by touching its display.

_____ 32. A peripheral device that digitizes data drawn on its pressure-sensitive surface.

_____ 33. Produces hard copy output such as paper documents and reports.

_____ 34. May use a mechanical arm with several pens to draw hard copy graphics output.

_____ 35. Promises to be the easiest, most natural way to communicate with computers.

_____ 36. Capturing data by processing light reflected from images.

_____ 37. Optical scanning of bar codes and other characters.

_____ 38. Bank check processing uses this technology.

_____ 39. Small figures are displayed to help you indicate activities to be performed.

_____ 40. A device with a keyboard and a video display connected to a computer is a typical example.

_____ 41. The most common video display technology.

_____ 42. Computer voice output.

_____ 43. Combining text, graphics, voice, and video in computer input and output.

_____ 44. A handheld device that reads bar coding.

_____ 45. Storage media cost, speed, and capacity differences.

_____ 46. You cannot erase the contents of these storage circuits.

_____ 47. The memory of most computers consists of these storage circuits.

_____ 48. The property that determines whether data are lost or retained when power fails.

_____ 49. Each position of storage can be accessed in approximately the same time.

_____ 50. Each position of storage can be accessed according to a predetermined order.

_____ 51. Microelectronic storage circuits on silicon chips.

_____ 52. Uses magnetic spots on metal or plastic disks.

_____ 53. Uses magnetic spots on plastic tape.

_____ 54. Uses a laser to read microscopic points on plastic disks.

Discussion Questions

1. Why is it important to think of a computer as a system instead of an information processing box?

2. What trends are occurring in the development and use of the major types of computer systems?

3. What is the difference between microcomputers used as professional or end user workstations and those used as workstation computers or technical workstations?

4. Refer to the Real World Case on Centex Group and CRSS Constructors in the chapter. Do you agree that "Laptops are changing the scope of computing and the way we work today"? Why or why not?

5. Are networked computers making minicomputers and mainframe computers obsolete? Explain.

6. What are the benefits and limitations of parallel processors? RISC processors?

7. Refer to the Real World Case on Chrysler Corporation in the chapter. What alternative input/output technologies would you suggest that Chrysler use to improve the business performance of their Modus kiosks?

8. Why are there so many types of peripheral devices for input and output? For secondary storage?

9. Refer to Real World Problem #1 on Oracle Corporation in the chapter. Do you think network computers will be a commercial success? Why or why not?

10. What trends are occurring in the development and use of peripheral devices? Why are these trends occurring?

Real World Problems

1. **Oracle Corporation: Network Computers and Network-Centric Computing**

Before a standing-room-only crowd of developers, Oracle Corporation CEO Larry Ellison held aloft the future of computing. Or so he hoped. Ellison displayed prototypes of the Network Computer (NC), a family of inexpensive, monitorless, and diskless Internet-access microcomputers that he proclaimed will outnumber PCs by the year 2000. In theory, information systems departments could deploy the computing appliances as on-line banking devices, retail kiosks, or low-cost terminals for thousands of employees. One prototype, a palmtop-size unit that cost $295 to build, was connected to a standard color television; it easily accessed the Internet and played audio and video samples in real time.

Sun Microsystems, whose slogan is "the network is the computer," and IBM have embraced this vision of network computers and "network-centric" computing, and are working on similar products. Microsoft and Intel call the idea misguided, and are promoting the Simply Interactive PC, a multimedia PC that is more powerful and simpler to operate, but more expensive than today's PCs. Revealing new details of Oracle's plan, Ellison said NC users will get word processing, spreadsheet, presentation, and data-access applications as well as scheduling and voice-mail capabilities, all provided by Internet or internal corporate servers. Thus, all NCs will depend on the Internet or internal company network servers for software and data storage and management to support their computing and communications activities.

a. What are the benefits and limitations of network computers compared to today's PCs? Compared to the Simply Interactive PC?

b. What are the advantages and disadvantages of network-centric computing compared to mainframe and client/server computing?

Source: Adapted from Dan Richman, "Oracle Bets on 'Net Appliances," *Computerworld*, March 4, 1996, p. 15. Copyright © 1996 by Computerworld, Inc., Framingham, MA 01701—Reprinted from *Computerworld*.

2. Bell Atlantic: Installing Intranet Web Servers

World Wide Web servers aren't just for the Internet any-more. Hooked by the lure of a new corporate market, Sun Microsystems and Silicon Graphics, Inc. (SGI), have loaded their powerful Web servers with bigger bundles of preinstalled software. The beefier servers are meant for customers who run applications on intranets. Intranets—internal corporate networks that make use of computing and communications capabilities and data resources simi-lar to those on the public Internet—are expected to grow much faster than Internet and other external Web-based applications.

Web servers with preinstalled software can ease installa-tion and configuration burdens on customers. For exam-ple, Sun officials vow that the company's powerful Netra servers can be up and running in less than 45 minutes. Several users who were drawn by the convenience factor said the increase in preinstalled software that Sun and SGI are offering should further automate the installation process. "I don't want to have to pay people to do that stuff," said Chris Keenan, director at Bell Atlantic Corp.'s southern regional operations center for data network ser-vices in Silver Spring, Maryland. Keenan recently bought one of SGI's WebForce servers for use in an intranet that Bell Atlantic is building to serve corporate users of their interconnected client/server networks.

a. What are intranets? What is the role of World Wide Web servers in corporate intranets?

b. Why do you think Sun and SGI are competing for the intranet server market?

Source: Adapted from Craig Steadman, "Serving Intranets," *Computerworld,* April 8, 1996, p. 45. Copyright © 1996 by Computerworld, Inc., Framingham, MA 01701—Reprinted from *Computerworld.*

3. GTE and Marist College: Mainframes versus Client/Server

Who needs client/server anyway? Not GTE Corp.'s tele-phone operation; it just junked a planned Unix-based cus-tomer service system and instead will put a friendlier user interface on an existing mainframe application. "Our strate-gy was 100 percent client/server," said Arnie Lumbers, man-ager of information technology asset management at GTE's systems unit in Tampa, Florida. "In fact, we were going to start pulling things off the mainframe. But it turns out that some of those mainframe applications weren't that bad."

Like many before it, GTE also ran into development delays and higher-than-expected costs on the client/server project, which was built around Hewlett-Packard PCs and servers. The company expects to finish overhauling its mainframe-based customer service application in a few months, Lumbers said.

Marist College also found nonmainframe platforms wanting for a digital library application that went into lim-ited use this academic year. "Some of the early tests were on smaller client/server systems, and they didn't fit the bill," said Harry Williams, manager of programming at the school. Marist instead returned to its mainframe and is "looking at scaling up to mainframes as a lot easier than we could have done otherwise," he said.

a. Why are GTE and Marist College deciding to use main-frames instead of client/server systems?

b. What are the advantages and limitations of client/server systems compared to mainframe systems?

Source: Adapted from Craig Steadman, "Big Iron Seeks Alternative Fuels to Sustain Revival," *Computerworld,* January 15, 1996, pp. 1, 28. Copyright © 1996 by Computerworld, Inc., Framingham, MA 01701—Reprinted from *Computerworld.*

4. Apria Healthcare Group: Moving To Midrange Computers

Take your AS/400 midrange medicine today, and tomorrow you'll get a client/server treat. That's the prescription Apria Healthcare Group, Inc.'s information systems department has written for its users. The $1.1 billion home health care company in Costa Mesa, California, is doing away with a mishmash of old and new systems and standardizing on IBM's AS/400, the best-selling midrange computers for business applications.

Apria, which was formed last June by the merger of two rivals, is expanding a network of low-end AS/400s that run homegrown, terminal-based applications to cover its 350 branch offices.

The move to midrange computers, due to be completed in a few months, will include the purchase of 150 new or upgraded AS/400s. This will push Apria's installed base to more than 200 AS/400s. Multiple offices in some areas will share one AS/400. In the near future, Apria wants to shift most processing to PCs and recast its AS/400s as database and network servers in interconnected client/server networks. Thus, running in parallel is a project to develop new client/server AS/400 application software for all business applications at Apria. Client/server versions of two corporate applications went into use in January, and end users at branch offices will see programs with graphical user interfaces (GUI) on their PCs and client-level processing soon, said John Farmer, vice president of information services at Apria.

a. Why do you think that Apria is standardizing on AS/400 midrange computers?

b. Why do you think Apria is converting their AS/400 ter-minal-based systems to client/server computing?

Source: Adapted from Craig Steadman, "Midrange Moxie," *Computerworld,* April 1, 1996, pp. 75, 77. Copyright © 1996 by Computerworld, Inc., Framingham, MA 01701—Reprinted from *Computerworld.*

Application Exercises

1. Input Alternatives

Which method of input would you recommend for the following activities? Explain your choices. Refer to Figure 2.31 to help you.

a. Entering data from printed questionnaires.
b. Entering data from telephone surveys.
c. Entering data from bank checks.
d. Entering data from merchandise tags.
e. Entering data from engineering drawings.

2. Output Alternatives

Which method of output would you recommend for the following information products? Explain your choices. Refer to Figure 2.31 to help you.

a. Visual displays for portable microcomputers.
b. Legal documents.
c. Engineering drawings.
d. Financial results for top executives.
e. Responses for telephone transactions.

3. Storage Alternatives

Indicate which secondary storage medium you would use for each of the following storage tasks. Select from the choices on the right, using Figure 2.32 to help you.

a. Primary storage	1. Magnetic hard disk
b. Large capacity, permanent storage	2. Floppy disk
c. Large capacity, fast direct access	3. Magnetic tape
d. Large files for occasional processing	4. Semiconductor memory
e. Inexpensive, portable direct access	5. Optical disk

4. Computer Hardware Prices

The following table shows some price and capacity figures for four important components of a computer system: the microprocessor, primary memory (RAM), secondary hard disk storage, and modems. These figures were gathered from old copies of PC magazines and are typical of the configurations and prices available in the years indicated. Although there have been improvements in these components that are not reflected in basic measures of their speed or capacity, it is interesting to examine trends in these measurable characteristics.

	1989	1991	1993	1995
Microprocessor				
Speed (Megahertz)	10	25	33	100
Cost	$245	$180	$125	$275
Random Access Memory				
Megabytes	1	1	4	4
Cost	$640	$55	$140	$140
Hard Disk Storage				
Megabytes	40	105	250	540
Cost	$435	$480	$375	$220
Modem				
Bits per second	2,400	9,600	14,400	28,800
Cost	$240	$400	$185	$160

Note: If you are not experienced in the use of spreadsheets and want some information on how to design and develop spreadsheet applications, see Application Exercise in Chapter 10.

a. Investigate current configurations and prices for these PC components.
b. Create a spreadsheet including the preceding figures and the current figures you got. In your spreadsheet, calculate a cost per unit of capacity (cost per megahertz of speed for microprocessor units, cost per megabyte for RAM and hard disk storage, and cost per BPS for modems).
c. Create a graph highlighting your results. What has been the trend in the prices of these components? Do you expect the trends you found to continue? Why or why not?

5. Computer Systems at ABC Company

You have been asked to assemble cost estimates for upgrades to your department's personal computer network. This upgrade involves purchasing 12 microcomputers for use as workstations, three laser printers, and a high-end workstation for use as a database server. The per-unit pricing offered by a local supplier is as follows:

Base workstation unit (Equipped with 16 megabytes RAM, 1 gigabyte hard drive, monitor separate)	$2,000
Options:	
RAM Upgrade (16 megabytes)	$ 425
Hard drive upgrade (to 2 gigabytes)	100
Monitor (15-inch)	275
Monitor (17-inch)	360
Laser printer (8 pages per minute, 600 dots per inch)	$ 625
Database server (fully equipped)	$7,200

After checking the needs of various users, you determine that five of the workstations will need to be upgraded to two gigabyte hard drives. Seven of the workstations will require 17-inch monitors, while five can be configured with 15-inch monitors.

a. Create a spreadsheet to analyze the cost of the needed equipment.

b. Suppose that the vendor offered to give either a 15 percent discount on the database server or a 50 percent discount on the printers. Modify your spreadsheet to show the effects of each discount.

c. Write a memorandum summarizing your results and including your recommendations for this purchase. Include copies of your spreadsheet analysis.

Review Quiz Answers

1. 52	15. 23	29. 16	43. 7
2. 13	16. 25	30. 40a	44. 57
3. 6	17. 22	31. 51	45. 48
4. 4	18. 11	32. 14	46. 45b
5. 1	19. 30	33. 42	47. 45a
6. 8	20. 5	34. 39	48. 56
7. 41	21. 28	35. 54	49. 9
8. 44	22. 29	36. 35	50. 46
9. 10	23. 49	37. 33	51. 45
10. 37	24. 18	38. 20	52. 19
11. 32	25. 50c	39. 15	53. 21
12. 31	26. 47e	40. 7	54. 34
13. 2	27. 40	41. 3	
14. 24	28. 36	42. 55	

Selected References

1. *Computerworld, Datamation, PC Week, PC Magazine,* and *PC World.* (Examples of good sources for current information on computer systems hardware and other developments in information systems technology.)

2. Datapro Corporation. *Datapro Reports.* (Series of regular, detailed reports on selected computer systems hardware.)

Introduction to Computer Software

CHAPTER OUTLINE

Chapter

3

LEARNING OBJECTIVES

After reading and studying this chapter, you should be able to:

1. Describe two major trends occurring in computer software.
2. Identify several major types of system and application software.
3. Explain the purpose of several popular microcomputer software packages for end user computing.
4. Outline the functions of operating systems and operating environments.
5. Describe the major differences between machine, assembler, high-level, fourth-generation, and object-oriented languages.
6. Explain the functions of programming language translators and programming tools.

Section I

Application Software: End User Applications

Introduction to Software

This chapter presents an overview of the major types of software you will depend on as you work with computers. It discusses their characteristics and purposes and gives examples of their uses. Information systems depend on software resources to help end users use computer hardware to transform data resources into a variety of information products. Software is needed to accomplish the input, processing, output, storage, and control activities of information systems. As we said in Chapter 1, computer software is typically classified into two major types of programs:

- **Application software.** Programs that direct the performance of a particular use, or *application,* of computers to meet the information processing needs of end users.
- **System software.** Programs that manage and support the resources and operations of a computer system as it performs various information processing tasks.

Let's begin our analysis of software by looking at an overview of the major types and functions of software available to computer users, shown in Figure 3.1. This figure summarizes the major categories of system and application software we will discuss in this chapter. Of course, this is a conceptual illustration. The types of software you will

FIGURE 3.1

An overview of computer software. Note the major types and examples of system and application software.

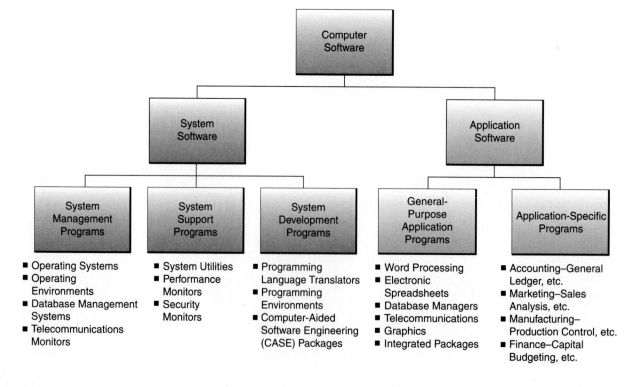

encounter depend primarily on the manufacturer and the model of the computer you use and then on what additional software is acquired to increase your computer's performance or to accomplish specific tasks for you and other end users.

Figure 3.2 emphasizes two major **software trends** important to managerial end users. First, there is a trend away from custom-designed one-of-a-kind programs developed by the professional programmers or end users of an organization. Instead, the trend is toward the use of off-the-shelf software packages acquired by end users from software vendors. This trend accelerated with the development of relatively inexpensive and easy-to-use productivity software packages for microcomputers, and it continues to grow, even for minicomputer and mainframe users.

Software Trends

    Second, there is a major trend away from (1) technical, machine-specific programming languages using binary-based or symbolic codes, and (2) *procedural languages,* which use brief statements and mathematical expressions to specify the sequence of instructions a computer must perform. Instead, the trend is toward *nonprocedural, natural languages* that are closer to human conversation. This trend has accelerated with the creation of easy-to-use, nonprocedural *fourth-generation languages* (4GLs). It continues to grow as developments in graphics and artificial intelligence produce natural language and *graphical user interfaces* that make software packages easier to use.

    In addition, expert system modules and other artificial intelligence features are built into a new generation of **expert-assisted software** packages. For example, many spreadsheet, database management, and graphics packages now provide *intelligent help* features. Sometimes called *wizards,* they help you perform common software functions like graphing parts of a spreadsheet or generating reports from a database. Other software packages use capabilities called *intelligent agents* to perform activities based on instructions from a user. For example, an electronic mail package could use an intelligent agent capability to organize, send, and screen E-mail messages for you. See Figure 3.3.

    These major trends seem to be converging to produce a fifth generation of powerful, multipurpose, expert-assisted software packages with natural language and graphical interfaces for end users.

FIGURE 3.2

Trends in computer software. The trend in software is toward multipurpose, expert-assisted packages with natural language and graphical user interfaces.

	FIRST GENERATION	SECOND GENERATION	THIRD GENERATION	FOURTH GENERATION	FIFTH GENERATION?
Trend: Toward Conversational Natural Programming Languages.					
Software Trends	User-Written Programs Machine Languages	Packaged Programs Symbolic Languages	Operating Systems High-Level Languages	Database Management Systems Fourth-Generation Languages Microcomputer Packages	Natural Languages Multipurpose Graphic-Interface Expert-Assisted Packages
Trend: Toward Easy-to-Use Multipurpose Application Packages.					

FIGURE 3.3

This software package provides intelligent help features
called wizards.

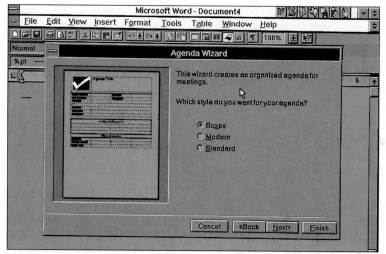

Sarah Evertson/Courtesy of Microsoft Corporation.

Application Software for End Users

Application software consists of programs that direct computers to perform specific information processing activities for end users. These programs are called
application packages because they direct the processing required for a particular
use, or *application,* that end users want accomplished. Thousands of application
packages are available because there are thousands of different jobs end users
want computers to do. The use of personal computers has multiplied the growth
of such programs.

General-Purpose Programs

Figure 3.1 showed that application software includes a variety of programs that can
be subdivided into *general-purpose* and *application-specific* categories. **General-purpose application programs** are programs that perform common information processing jobs for end users. For example, word processing programs, spreadsheet
programs, database management programs, integrated packages, and graphics programs are popular with microcomputer users for home, education, business, scientific, and many other purposes. Because they significantly increase the productivity
of end users, they are also known as *productivity packages.* We will briefly explain
some of the most popular types of such packages in this section.

Application-Specific Programs

Thousands of application software packages are available to support specific applications of end users. Major categories of such **application-specific programs** are:

- **Business Application Programs.** Programs that accomplish the information
  processing tasks of important business functions or industry requirements.
  Examples of such business functions and their corresponding applications are
  accounting (general ledger), marketing (sales analysis), finance (capital budgeting), manufacturing (material requirements planning), operations management (inventory control), and human resource management (employee
  benefits analysis).

- **Scientific Application Programs.** Programs that perform information processing tasks for the natural, physical, social, and behavioral sciences; and for
  mathematics, engineering, and all other areas involved in scientific research,
  experimentation, and development. Some broad application categories include
  scientific analysis, engineering design, and monitoring of experiments.

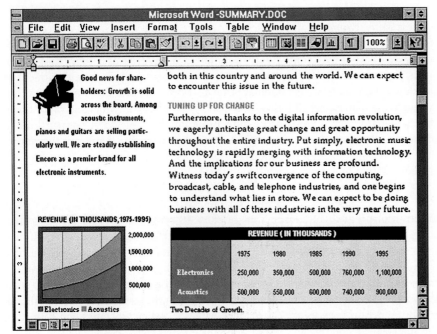

Courtesy of Microsoft Corporation.

FIGURE 3.4

Using the Microsoft Word for Windows word processing package.

- **Other Application Programs.** There are so many other application areas of computers that we lump them all into this category. Thus, we can talk of computer applications in education, entertainment, music, art, law enforcement, medicine, and so on. Some specific examples are computer-assisted instruction programs in education, video game programs in entertainment, and computer-generated music and art programs.

Word Processing Packages

Word processing packages are programs that computerize the creation, editing, and printing of *documents* (such as letters, memos, and reports) by electronically processing *text data* (words, phrases, sentences, and paragraphs). Thus, word processing is an important application of *office automation,* which we will discuss in Chapter 6. Figure 3.4 illustrates the use of a popular word processing package. With word processing packages such as WordPerfect and Microsoft Word, end users can:

- Use a computer to create and edit a document and have each line of text automatically adjusted to fit prespecified margins.
- Move to any point in a document and add, delete, or change words, sentences, or paragraphs.
- Move a block of text from one part of a document to another and insert standard text from another document file.
- Check a document for spelling or grammatical errors and selectively change all occurrences of a particular word or phrase.
- Store a document as a document file on a magnetic disk, retrieve it any time, and print it according to a variety of predesigned formats.

Many word processing packages provide advanced features or can be upgraded with supplementary packages. One example is a *spelling checker* program that uses built-in dictionaries to identify and correct spelling errors in a document.

Another is a *thesaurus program* that helps you find a better choice of words to express ideas. *Grammar* and *style checker* programs can identify and correct grammar and punctuation errors, as well as suggest possible improvements in your writing style. Another text productivity tool is an *idea processor* or *outliner* program. It helps you organize and outline your thoughts before you prepare a document or develop a presentation. Also popular is a *mail-merge* program that can automatically merge the names and addresses in a mailing list file with letters and other documents. Finally, many word processing programs are able to support a limited amount of *desktop publishing* activity. As we will discuss in Chapter 6, this allows end users to merge text, graphics, and other illustrations on each page to produce documents that look professionally published.

Electronic Spreadsheet Packages

Electronic spreadsheet packages are application programs used for analysis, planning, and modeling. They provide an electronic replacement for more traditional tools such as paper worksheets, pencils, and calculators. They generate an electronic spreadsheet, which is a worksheet of rows and columns stored in the computer's memory and displayed on its video screen. You use the computer's keyboard to enter data and relationships (formulas) into the worksheet. In response to your input, the computer performs necessary calculations based on the relationships you defined in the spreadsheet, and displays results immediately. See Figure 3.5.

An electronic spreadsheet package creates a *spreadsheet model* of the mathematical and other relationships within a particular business activity. It can thus record and analyze past and present activity. It can also act as a decision support tool to help you answer *what-if questions* you may have. For example, "**What** would happen to net profit **if** advertising expense increased by 10 percent?" To answer this question, you would simply change the advertising expense formula on an income statement worksheet. The computer recalculates the affected figures, producing a

FIGURE 3.5

Using an electronic spreadsheet. The Lotus 1–2–3 for Windows spreadsheet allows you to work with multiple related spreadsheets and graphics.

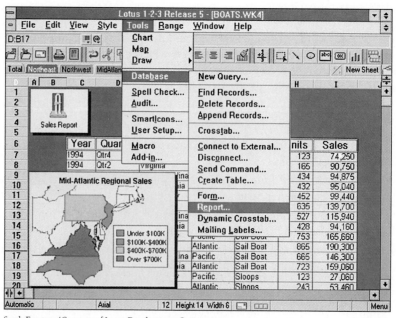

Sarah Evertson/Courtesy of Lotus Development Corporation.

new net profit figure. You would then have a better insight into whether advertising expense should be increased. The use of electronic spreadsheets for such decision support will be discussed further in Chapter 8.

Once an electronic spreadsheet has been developed, you can store it for later use or print it out as a report. Popular electronic spreadsheet packages for microcomputers include Lotus 1–2–3, Excel, and Quattro Pro. Mainframe and minicomputer users can also use the electronic spreadsheet modules of products such as Lotus 1–2–3M and Focus. Special-purpose spreadsheet models called *templates* are available for most spreadsheet packages. These worksheets are developed for many applications, such as tax accounting or real estate investment.

Database Management Packages

Microcomputer versions of database management programs have become so popular that they are now viewed as general-purpose *application software* packages like word processing and spreadsheet packages. **Database management packages** such as Access by Microsoft or Approach by Lotus Development allow end users to set up databases of files and records on their personal computer systems and quickly store data and retrieve information. As Figure 3.6 illustrates, most DBMS packages can perform four primary tasks, which we will discuss further in Chapter 5.

- **Database development.** Define and organize the content, relationships, and structure of the data needed to build a database.
- **Database interrogation.** Access the data in a database for information retrieval and report generation. End users can selectively retrieve and display information and produce printed reports and documents.
- **Database maintenance.** Add, delete, update, correct, and protect the data in a database.
- **Application development.** Develop prototypes of data entry screens, queries, forms, reports, and labels for a proposed application. Or use a 4GL or application generator to develop program codes.

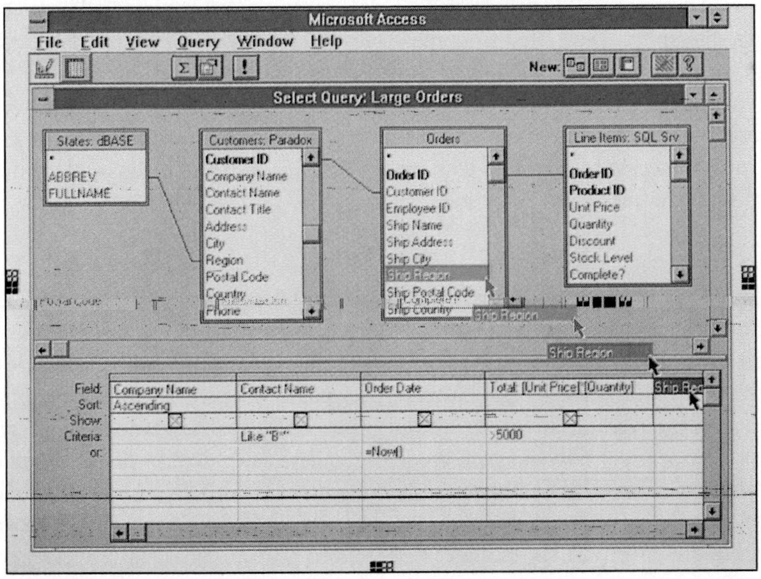

Courtesy of Microsoft Corporation.

FIGURE 3.6

Using a DBMS package. Note how the Microsoft Access database management package lets you easily obtain information from a customer order database.

FIGURE 3.7

Using the Crosstalk telecommunications package to transfer files on the Internet.

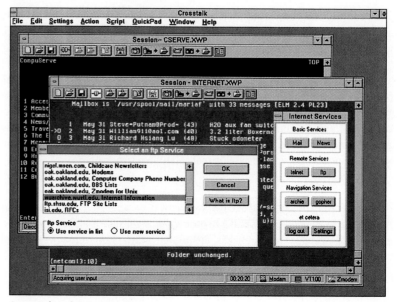

Courtesy of Attachmate Corporation.

Telecommunications Packages

Telecommunications packages for microcomputers have become general-purpose application packages for end users. These packages can connect a microcomputer equipped with a modem to the Internet or other public or private networks. However, communications control packages such as Procomm Plus and Crosstalk are being challenged by the networking capabilities of operating systems such as Windows 95 and OS/2 Warp. Other telecommunications software is provided by public information services like Prodigy, CompuServe, and America Online, or marketed for surfing the Internet's World Wide Web by companies such as Netscape Communications. See Figure 3.7.

Telecommunications software is also available from many other sources, including Internet local access providers, electronic mail software vendors, and fax/modem suppliers. All of these packages help your microcomputer act as an *intelligent terminal* so it can transmit, receive, and store messages, information, and files of data and programs. For example, files of data and programs can be downloaded from a host computer to a microcomputer and stored on a disk. Or files can be uploaded from the microcomputer to a host computer. Some programs even allow files to be transferred automatically between unattended computer systems. We will discuss telecommunications software further in Chapter 4.

Graphics Packages

Graphics packages convert numeric data into graphics displays such as line charts, bar graphs, and pie charts. Many other types of presentation graphics displays are possible. *Draw* and *paint* graphics packages support freehand drawing, while desktop publishing programs provide predrawn *clip art* graphics for insertion into documents. Images are displayed on your video monitor or copies can be made on your system printer or plotter. Not only are such graphics displays easier to comprehend and communicate than numeric data but multiple-color displays also can more easily emphasize strategic differences and trends in the data. Presentation graphics have proved to be much more effective than tabular presentations of numeric data for reporting and communicating in management reports or in presentations to groups of people.

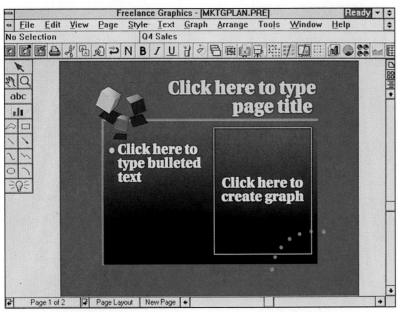

Courtesy of Lotus Development Corporation.

FIGURE 3.8

Using the Lotus Freelance graphics package.

Presentation graphics can be produced by graphics packages, such as Harvard Graphics and Lotus Freelance for microcomputers, and SAS Graph and Tell-A-Graph for minicomputers and mainframes, or by the graphics modules of electronic spreadsheets or integrated packages. To use such packages, typically you select the type of graph you want and enter the categories of data you want plotted. This is done in response to prompts displayed on your screen, or you can highlight the data you want graphed. The graphics program then analyzes the file of data you specify and generates the requested graphics. See Figure 3.8.

Integrated Packages and Software Suites

Integrated packages combine the abilities of several general-purpose applications in one program. Integrated packages were developed to solve the problems caused by the inability of individual programs to communicate and work together with common files of data. However, integrated packages typically reduce the functions they provide, and may compromise on the speed, power, and flexibility of some of their functions in order to achieve integration. Therefore, software vendors are now offering **software suites** that combine several individual packages that share a common graphical interface and are designed to easily transfer data between them.

Examples of popular integrated packages are Microsoft Works, Lotus Works, and IBM Works. Examples of popular software suites are Lotus Smart Suite, Microsoft Office, and Corel Office Professional. For example, the Microsoft Office suite consists of the Microsoft Word word processing package, Excel spreadsheet, Access database manager, and the Powerpoint graphics package. Such packages combine the functions of general-purpose application software such as electronic spreadsheets, word processing, graphics, database management, and data communications. Thus, you can process the same file of data with one package, moving from one function to the other by selecting a few icons on your video display. See Figure 3.9.

FIGURE 3.9

Using the Microsoft Works
integrated package. It provides word processing,
spreadsheet, file manage-
ment, telecommunications,
and graphics capabilities in
one package.

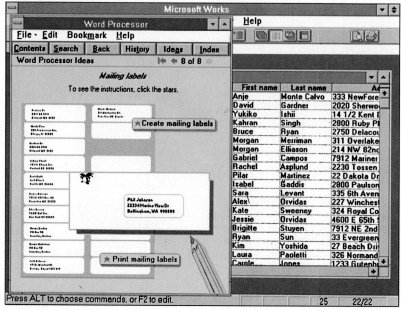

Courtesy of Microsoft Corporation.

Other End User Packages

We could spend a lot more time discussing the many application packages available to end users. Microcomputer application packages support managerial, professional, and business uses such as decision support, accounting, project management, investment analysis, and desktop publishing. Still other packages support end users by helping them organize random pieces of information and accomplish routine tasks (*personal information managers*). Other software packages help end users with personal finance, home management, entertainment, education, and using the Internet and other information services. These and other software packages are discussed in upcoming chapters on telecommunications, database management, end user computing, office automation, decision support, expert systems, and other information systems.

BARRIE CULVER AND NBC TV: SPREADSHEET STATS FOR THE SEATTLE SEAHAWKS

In the computer industry, where new products are continually introduced with great hype, it's easy to abandon well-used programs for the attractive newcomer in shrink wrap. But sometimes, it pays to look for new applications from the tools you already have. Often, the programs you have are every bit as powerful as that new entry packed with superfluous features. For example, take a look at what Barrie Culver does for the NBC TV network and the Seattle Seahawks NFL team using the Lotus 1–2–3 spreadsheet package.

Frequently during a sporting event, displays of statistics magically appear on your television screen, accompanying the broadcaster's commentary. Culver is one of the people who makes that possible. A stockbroker by profession, he has been tracking Seahawks game statistics for NBC since the team's entry into the NFL in 1976.

Many TV networks still track stats by hand—a tedious method with obvious limitations. Culver, however, developed an automated system with Lotus 1–2–3. He'd already used the flagship spreadsheet package in his brokering. With the advent of faster, more powerful PCs, Culver recognized the program's potential to help him provide NBC broadcast crews with a wider, more complete, and constantly updated array of statistics—and all within the five-second window between plays.

"I was trying to devise a better way of orchestrating the whole thing," Culver says. "I wanted a good way to keep things in sync between me, and the official yardage, and the sportscasters."

Culver customized the flexible Lotus 1–2–3 for the task. He designed a multipage spreadsheet containing more than 1,000 formulas, some macro buttons (to quickly record and retrieve the broadest or most specific of statistics), and custom icons. Not only do the icons make navigation easy, some represent events, such as a touchdown or punt, that activate "possession" strings. If the input is correct, the spreadsheet always knows which team has the ball.

"Basically, you formulate your own dialog boxes for exactly what you need," says Culver. "Then, between macros and icons I developed for myself, I manage a database within the spreadsheet. Say it's a pass completion. I click on the completion icon, and it takes me to that team's passing page, where I have team statistics. I can page down again to the quarterback's personal statistics, then I can page down again to the running database that keeps track of what he does on each drive. If I'm behind the official spot by a yard, I click the Plus-1 icon. It takes two seconds to update everything."

Culver says that with his customized Lotus system he produces from 200 percent to 500 percent more information in the five-second window between plays than he could tracking stats manually.

Not only can Culver continue expanding his capabilities with each new idea, building the spreadsheet himself ensures streamlined efficiency. Using the Lotus 1–2–3 program he already owns, Culver is creating a tool-in-progress based on exactly what he needs.

Culver has copyrighted his program under the name Stat US Pro. He's also pitching the package to other major networks for use in their television coverage of NFL games.

CASE STUDY QUESTIONS

1. Why do you think Barrie Culver chose a spreadsheet program to compute game statistics?

2. What spreadsheet features has Culver developed that you might use in your own spreadsheet applications?

3. How might Culver's spreadsheet system be used in other business situations?

Source: Adapted from Sean Doolittle, "Old Apps, New Tricks," *PC Today,* March 1996, p. 112. *PC Today,* 125 W. Harvest Drive, Lincoln, NE 68501.

Section II

System Software: Computer System Management

System Software Overview

System software consists of programs that manage and support a computer system and its information processing activities. These programs serve as a vital *software interface* between computer system hardware and the application programs of end users. See Figure 3.10. Note that we can group such programs into three major functional categories:

- **System management programs.** Programs that manage the hardware, software, and data resources of the computer system during its execution of the various information processing jobs of users. The most important system management programs are operating systems and operating environments, followed by telecommunications monitors and database management systems.
- **System support programs.** Programs that support the operations and management of a computer system by providing a variety of support services. Major support programs are system utilities, performance monitors, and security monitors.
- **System development programs.** Programs that help users develop information system programs and procedures and prepare user programs for computer processing. Major development programs are language translators, programming tools, and CASE (computer-aided software engineering) packages.

Operating Systems

The most important system software package for any computer is its **operating system.** An operating system is an integrated system of programs that manages the operations of the CPU, controls the input/output and storage resources and activities of the computer system, and provides various support services as the computer executes the application programs of users.

FIGURE 3.10

The system and application software interface between end users and computer hardware.

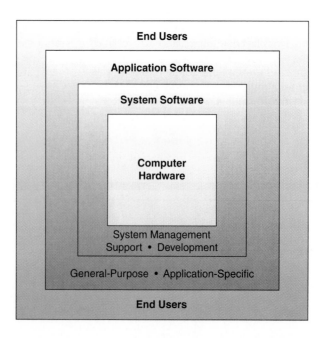

The primary purpose of an operating system is to maximize the productivity of a computer system by operating it in the most efficient manner. An operating system minimizes the amount of human intervention required during processing. It helps your application programs perform common operations such as entering data, saving and retrieving files, and printing or displaying output. If you have any hands-on experience on a computer, you know that the operating system must be loaded and activated before you can accomplish other tasks. This emphasizes the fact that operating systems are the most indispensable component of the software interface between users and the hardware of their computer systems.

An operating system performs five basic functions in the operation of a computer system: providing a user interface, resource management, task management, file management, and utilities and support services. See Figure 3.11.

Operating System Functions

The **user interface** is the part of the operating system that allows you to communicate with it so you can load programs, access files, and accomplish other tasks. Three main types of user interfaces are the *command-driven, menu-driven,* and *graphical user interfaces.* The trend in user interfaces for operating systems, operating environments, and other software is moving away from the entry of brief end user commands, or even the selection of choices from menus of options. Instead, the trend is toward an easy-to-use **graphical user interface** (GUI) that uses icons, bars, buttons, boxes, and other images. GUIs rely on pointing devices like the electronic mouse to make selections that help you get things done. See Figure 3.12.

The User Interface

The user interfaces of operating systems are typically enhanced by the use of **operating environments.** Examples include the graphical user interface of Microsoft Windows 95 and the Workplace Shell in IBM's OS/2 Warp, or add-on packages for Microsoft DOS such as Windows 3.1 and Desqview. Operating environments enhance the user interface by adding a graphical user interface between end users, the operating system, and their application programs. These packages serve as a shell to interconnect several separate application packages so that they can communicate and work together and share common data files. Operating environment packages provide icon displays and support the use of an electronic mouse or other pointing devices. They also allow the output of several programs to be displayed at the same time in multiple windows. Finally, several of these packages support some type of multitasking, where several programs or tasks can be processed at the same time.

Operating Environments

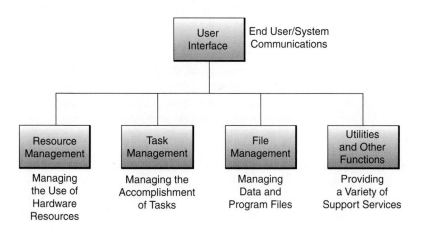

FIGURE 3.11

The basic functions of an operating system include a user interface, resource management, task management, file management, and utilities and other functions.

FIGURE 3.12

The graphical user interface of Microsoft's Windows 95 operating system.

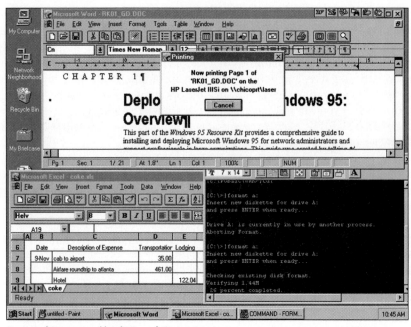

Courtesy of Computerworld and Microsoft Corporation.

Resource Management

An operating system uses a variety of **resource management** programs to manage the hardware resources of a computer system, including its CPU, memory, secondary storage devices, and input/output peripherals. For example, memory management programs keep track of where data and programs are stored. They may also subdivide memory into a number of sections and swap parts of programs and data between memory and magnetic disks or other secondary storage devices. This can provide a computer system with a **virtual memory** capability that is significantly larger than the real memory capacity of its primary storage unit. So, a computer with a virtual memory capability can process larger programs and greater amounts of data than the capacity of its memory circuits would normally allow.

File Management

An operating system contains **file management** programs that control the creation, deletion, and access of files of data and programs. File management also involves keeping track of the physical location of files on magnetic disks and other secondary storage devices. So operating systems maintain directories of information about the location and characteristics of files stored on a computer system's secondary storage devices.

Task Management

The **task management** programs of an operating system manage the accomplishment of the computing tasks of end users. They give each task a slice of a CPU's time and interrupt the CPU operations to substitute other tasks. Task management may involve a **multitasking** capability where several computing tasks can occur at the same time. Multitasking may take the form of *multiprogramming,* where the CPU can process the tasks of several programs at the same time, or *time-sharing,* where the computing tasks of several users can be processed at the same time. The efficiency of *multitasking* operations depends on the processing power of a CPU and the virtual memory and multitasking capabilities of the operating system it uses.

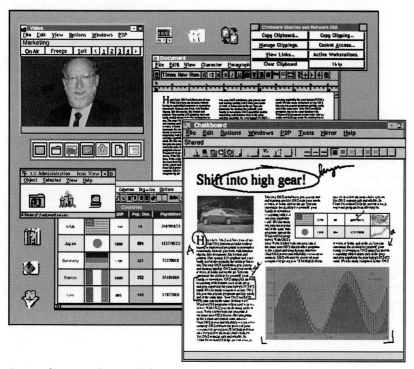

FIGURE 3.13

Multitasking with OS/2 Warp. Note how OS/2 Warp enables this end user to do word processing, page make-up, and video editing operations concurrently.

Courtesy of International Business Machines Corporation.

New microcomputer operating systems and most minicomputer and mainframe operating systems provide a multitasking capability. With multitasking, end users can do two or more operations (e.g., keyboarding and printing) or applications (e.g., word processing and financial analysis) *concurrently,* that is, at the same time. Multitasking on microcomputers has also been made possible by the development of more powerful microprocessors (like the Intel 80486) and their ability to directly address much larger memory capacities (up to 4 gigabytes). This allows an operating system to subdivide primary storage into several large partitions, each of which can be used by a different application program.

In effect, a single computer can act as if it were several computers, or *virtual machines,* since each application program is running independently at the same time. The number of programs that can be run concurrently depends on the amount of memory that is available and the amount of processing each job demands. That's because a microprocessor (or CPU) can become overloaded with too many jobs and provide unacceptably slow response times. However, if memory and processing capacities are adequate, multitasking allows end users to easily switch from one application to another, share data files among applications, and process some applications in a background mode. Typically, background tasks include large printing jobs, extensive mathematical computation, or unattended telecommunications sessions. See Figure 3.13.

MS–DOS (Microsoft Disk Operating System), along with the Windows operating environment, has been the most widely used microcomputer operating system. It is a single-user, single-tasking operating system, but was given a graphical user interface and limited multitasking capabilities by combining it with Microsoft Windows. Microsoft began replacing its DOS/Windows combination in 1995

Popular Operating Systems

with the **Windows 95** operating system. Windows 95 is an advanced operating system featuring a graphical user interface, true multitasking, networking, multimedia, and many other capabilities. Microsoft introduced another operating system, **Windows NT** (New Technology), in 1993. Windows NT is a powerful, multitasking, multiuser operating system that is being installed on network servers to manage local area networks and on powerful workstations with high-performance computing requirements.

OS/2 (Operating System/2) is a microcomputer operating system from IBM. Its latest version, **OS/2 Warp,** was introduced in 1994 and provides a graphical user interface, multitasking, virtual memory, telecommunications, and many other capabilities. Originally developed by AT&T, **UNIX** now is also offered by other vendors, including Solaris by Sun Microsystems, AIX by IBM, and Xenix by Microsoft. UNIX is a multitasking, multiuser, network-managing operating system whose *portability* allows it to run on mainframes, midrange computers, and microcomputers. UNIX is a popular choice for network servers in many client/server computing networks. **The Macintosh System** is an operating system from Apple for Macintosh microcomputers. Now in version 7.5, the system has a popular graphical user interface as well as multitasking and virtual memory capabilities. See Figure 3.14.

FIGURE 3.14

A comparison of popular operating systems.

Operating System	MS–DOS	OS/2 Warp	Windows 95	Macintosh System 7.5	Windows NT	UNIX
Developer	Microsoft	IBM	Microsoft	Apple	Microsoft	AT&T, Sun, IBM, etc.
Primary Market	PCs	PCs	PCs	Macintoshes	Servers	Workstations Servers Midrange Mainframes
Primary Micro-processors	Intel	Intel Power PC	Intel	Motorola Power PC	Intel Alpha	Many
GUI		X	X	X	X	X
Single User	X	X	X	X	X	
Multitasking		X	X	X	X	X
Virtual Memory		X	X	X	X	X
Networking		X	X	X	X	X
Multiuser					X	X
Network Management					X	X

In mainframe and midrange computer systems, a **database management system** (DBMS) is a system software package that controls the development, use, and maintenance of the databases of computer-using organizations. A DBMS program helps organizations use their integrated collections of data records and files known as databases. It allows different user application programs to easily access the same database. For example, a DBMS makes it easy for an employee database to be accessed by payroll, employee benefits, and other human resource programs. A DBMS also simplifies the process of retrieving information from databases in the form of displays and reports. Instead of having to write computer programs to extract information, end users can ask simple questions in a *query language*. Thus, many DBMS packages provide *fourth-generation languages* (4GLs) and other application development features. Examples of popular mainframe and midrange packages are DB2 by IBM and Oracle by Oracle Corporation. We will explore the use of database management packages in information systems in Chapter 5.

Database Management Systems

Modern information systems rely heavily on telecommunications networks to provide electronic communication links between end user workstations, other computer systems, and an organization's databases. This requires system software called **telecommunications monitors.** These programs are used by the main computer in a network (called the host), or in telecommunications control computers such as *front-end processors* and *network servers.* Telecommunications monitors and similar programs perform such functions as connecting or disconnecting communication links between computers and terminals, automatically checking terminals for input/output activity, assigning priorities to data communications requests from terminals, and detecting and correcting transmission errors. Thus, they control and support the data communications activities occurring in a telecommunications network. We will discuss communications software in more detail in Chapter 4.

Telecommunications Monitors

System support programs are a category of software that performs routine support functions for the users of a computer system. **Utility programs,** or *utilities,* are an important example. These programs perform miscellaneous housekeeping and file conversion functions. For example, *sort programs* are important utility programs that perform the sorting operations on data required in many information processing applications. Utility programs also clear primary storage, load programs, record the contents of primary storage, and convert files of data from one storage medium to another, such as from tape to disk. Many of the operating system commands used with microcomputers and other computer systems provide users with utility programs and routines for a variety of chores.

Other system support programs include performance monitors and security monitors. **Performance monitors** are programs that monitor the performance and usage of computer systems to help its efficient use. **Security monitors** are packages that monitor and control the use of computer systems and provide warning messages and record evidence of unauthorized use of computer resources. These packages will be discussed further in Chapters 11 and 12.

System Support Programs

Programming Languages

A proper understanding of computer software requires a basic knowledge of **programming languages.** A programming language allows a programmer or end user to develop the sets of instructions that constitute a computer program. To be a knowledgeable end user, you should know the basic categories of programming languages. Many different programming languages have been developed, each with its own unique vocabulary, grammar, and uses. Programming languages can be grouped into the five major categories shown in Figure 3.15.

Machine Languages

Machine languages (or *first-generation languages*) are the most basic level of programming languages. In the early stages of computer development, all program instructions had to be written using binary codes unique to each computer. This type of programming involves the difficult task of writing instructions in the form of strings of binary digits (ones and zeros) or other number systems. Programmers must have a detailed knowledge of the internal operations of the specific type of CPU they are using. They must write long series of detailed instructions to accomplish even simple processing tasks. Programming in machine language requires specifying the storage locations for every instruction and item of data used. Instructions must be included for every switch and indicator used by the program. These requirements make machine language programming a difficult and error-prone task. A machine language program to add two numbers together in the CPU of a specific computer and store the result might take the form shown in Figure 3.16.

Assembler Languages

Assembler languages (or *second-generation languages*) are the next level of programming languages. They were developed to reduce the difficulties in writing machine language programs. The use of assembler languages requires language translator programs called *assemblers* that allow a computer to convert the instructions of such languages into machine instructions. Assembler languages are frequently called *symbolic languages* because symbols are used to represent operation codes and storage locations. Convenient alphabetic abbreviations called mnemonics (memory aids) and other symbols represent operation codes, storage locations, and data elements. For example, the computation X = Y + Z in an assembler language might take the form shown in Figure 3.16.

Advantages and Disadvantages

An assembler language uses alphabetic abbreviations that are easier to remember in place of the actual numeric addresses of the data. This greatly simplifies programming, since the programmer does not need to know the exact storage locations of data and instructions. However, assembler language is still *machine oriented,* because assembler language instructions correspond closely to the machine language

---

FIGURE 3.15

Major categories of programming languages.

- **Object-Oriented Languages:** Use combinations of objects
- **Fourth-Generation Languages:** Use natural and nonprocedural statements
- **High-Level Languages:** Use brief statements or arithmetic notation
- **Assembler Languages:** Use symbolic coded instructions
- **Machine Languages:** Use binary coded instructions

instructions of the particular computer model being used. Also, note that each assembler instruction corresponds to a single machine instruction, and that the same number of instructions are required in both illustrations.

Assembler languages are still widely used as a method of programming a computer in a machine-oriented language. Most computer manufacturers provide an assembler language that reflects the unique machine language instruction set of a particular line of computers. This feature is particularly desirable to *system programmers,* who program system software (as opposed to *application programmers,* who program application software), since it provides them with greater control and flexibility in designing a program for a particular computer. They can then produce more *efficient* software; that is, programs that require a minimum of instructions, storage, and CPU time to perform a specific processing assignment.

High-Level Languages

High-level languages (or *third-generation languages*) use instructions, which are called statements, that closely resemble human language or the standard notation of mathematics. Individual high-level language statements are actually *macroinstructions;* that is, each individual statement generates several machine instructions when translated into machine language by high-level language translator programs called *compilers* or *interpreters.* The use of macroinstructions is also common in fourth-generation languages and software packages such as spreadsheet and database management programs. High-level language statements resemble the phrases or mathematical expressions required to express the problem or procedure being programmed. The *syntax* (vocabulary, punctuation, and grammatical rules) and the semantics (meanings) of such statements do not reflect the internal code of any particular computer. For example, the computation X = Y + Z would be programmed in the high-level languages of BASIC and COBOL as shown in Figure 3.16.

Advantages and Disadvantages

A high-level language is obviously easier to learn and understand than an assembler language. Also, high-level languages have less-rigid rules, forms, and syntaxes, so the potential for error is reduced. However, high-level language programs are usually less efficient than assembler language programs and require a greater amount of computer time for translation into machine instructions. Since most high-level languages are machine-independent, programs written in a high-level language do not have to be reprogrammed when a new computer is installed, and computer programmers do not have to learn a new language for each computer they program. Figure 3.17 highlights some of the major high-level languages in use today. Note that the most widely used languages include COBOL for business application programs, BASIC for microcomputer end users, and FORTRAN for scientific and engineering applications.

Machine Language 1010 11001 1011 11010 1100 11011	High-Level Languages BASIC: X = Y + Z COBOL: COMPUTE X = Y + Z
Assembler Language LOD Y ADD Z STR X	Fourth-Generation Language SUM THE FOLLOWING NUMBERS

FIGURE 3.16

Examples of four levels of programming languages. These programming language instructions might be used to compute the sum of two numbers as expressed by the formula X = Y + Z.

Fourth-Generation Languages

The term **fourth-generation language** describes a variety of programming languages that are more nonprocedural and conversational than prior languages. These languages are called fourth-generation languages (4GLs) to differentiate them from machine languages (first generation), assembler languages (second generation), and high-level languages (third generation). It should be noted that some industry observers have begun to use the term *fifth-generation language* to describe languages using artificial intelligence techniques to accomplish results for users.

Most fourth-generation languages are **nonprocedural languages** that encourage users and programmers to specify the results they want, while the computer determines the *sequence of instructions* that will accomplish those results. Users and programmers no longer have to spend a lot of time developing the sequence of instructions the computer must follow to achieve a result. Thus, fourth-generation languages have helped simplify the programming process. **Natural languages** are 4GLs that are very close to English or other human languages. Research and development activity in artificial intelligence (AI) is developing programming languages that are as easy to use as ordinary conversation in one's native tongue. For example, INTELLECT, a natural language 4GL, would use a statement like: "What are the average exam scores in MIS 200?" to program a simple average exam score task.

Advantages and Disadvantages

There are major differences in the ease of use and technical sophistication of 4GL products. For instance, INTELLECT and English Wizard are examples of natural query languages that impose no rigid grammatical rules, while SQL and FOCUS require concise structured statements. However, the ease of use of 4GLs is gained at the expense of some loss in flexibility. It is frequently difficult for an end user to override some of the prespecified formats or procedures of 4GLs. Also, the machine language code generated by a program developed by a 4GL is frequently much less efficient (in terms of processing speed and amount of storage capacity needed) than a program written in a language like COBOL. Major failures have occurred in some large transaction processing applications programmed in a 4GL. These applications were unable to provide reasonable response times when faced with a large amount of real-time transaction processing and end user inquiries. However, 4GLs have shown great success in end user and departmental applications that do not have a high volume of transaction processing.

FIGURE 3.17

Highlights of several important high-level languages. Note the differences in the characteristics and purposes of each language.

Ada: Named after Augusta Ada Bryon, considered the world's first computer programmer. Developed for the U.S. Department of Defense as a standard "high-order language" to replace COBOL and FORTRAN.

BASIC: (Beginner's All-Purpose Symbolic Instruction Code). A simple procedure-oriented language used for end user programming.

C: A mid-level structured language developed as part of the UNIX operating system. It resembles a machine-independent assembler language and is presently popular for system software programming and development of application software packages.

COBOL: (COmmon Business Oriented Language). Designed as an Englishlike language specifically for business data processing. It is the most widely used programming language for business applications.

FORTRAN: (FORmula TRANslation). The oldest of the popular high-level languages. It is still the most widely used programming language for scientific and engineering applications.

Pascal: Named after Blaise Pascal. Developed specifically to incorporate structured programming concepts.

Object-oriented programming (OOP) languages have been around since Xerox developed Smalltalk in the 1960s. However, object-oriented languages have become a major tool of software development. Briefly, while most other programming languages separate data elements from the procedures or actions that will be performed upon them, OOP languages tie them together into *objects*. Thus, an object consists of data and the actions that can be performed on the data. For example, an object could be a set of data about a bank customer's savings account, and the operations (such as interest calculations) that might be performed upon the data. Or an object could be data in graphic form such as a video display window, plus the display actions that might be used upon it. See Figure 3.18.

In procedural languages, a program consists of procedures to perform actions on each data element. However, in object-oriented systems, objects tell other objects to perform actions on themselves. For example, to open a window on a computer video display, a beginning menu object could send a window object a message to open and a window will appear on the screen. That's because the window object contains the program code for opening itself.

Object-oriented languages like Visual Basic and C++ are easier to use and more efficient for programming the graphics-oriented user interfaces required by many applications. Also, once objects are programmed, they are reusable. Therefore, reusability of objects is a major benefit of object-oriented programming. For example, programmers can construct a user interface for a new program by assembling standard objects such as windows, bars, boxes, buttons, and icons. Therefore, most object-oriented programming packages provide a GUI that supports a "point and click," "drag and drop" visual assembly of objects known as *visual programming*. Figure 3.19 shows a display of the Visual Basic object-oriented programming environment. Object-oriented technology is discussed further in the coverage of object-oriented databases in Chapter 5.

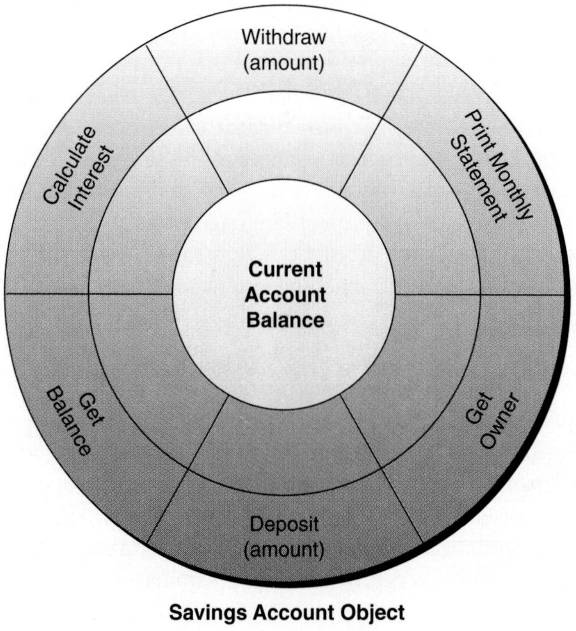

Object-Oriented Languages

Savings Account Object

FIGURE 3.18

An example of a bank savings account object. This object consists of data about a customer's account balance and the basic operations that can be performed on those data.

FIGURE 3.19

Using the Visual Basic
object-oriented program-
ming package.

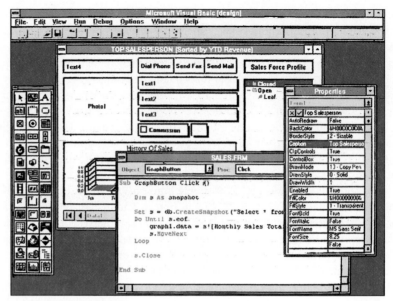

Courtesy of Microsoft Corporation.

Programming Packages

A variety of software packages are available to help programmers develop computer programs. For example, *programming language translators* are programs that translate other programs into machine language instruction codes that computers can execute. Other software packages called *programming tools* help programmers write programs by providing program creation and editing facilities.

Language Translator Programs

Computer programs consist of sets of instructions written in programming languages that must be translated by a **language translator** into the computer's own machine language before they can be processed, or *executed,* by the CPU. Programming language translator programs (or *language processors*) are known by a variety of names. An **assembler** translates the symbolic instruction codes of programs written in an assembler language into machine language instructions, while a **compiler** translates high-level language statements. An **interpreter** is a special type of compiler that translates and executes each program statement one at a time, instead of first producing a complete machine language program, like compilers and assemblers do.

Figure 3.20 illustrates the typical language translation process. A program written in a language such as BASIC or COBOL is called a *source program*. When the source program is translated into machine language, it is called the *object program,* which can then be executed by a computer.

Programming Tools

Many language translator programs are enhanced by a *graphical programming* interface and a variety of built-in capabilities or add-on packages. Language translators have always provided some editing and diagnostic capabilities to identify programming errors or bugs. However, many language translator programs now include powerful graphics-oriented *editors* and *debuggers*. These programs help programmers identify and avoid errors while they are programming. Such **programming tools** provide a computer-aided programming *environment* or *workbench*. Their goal

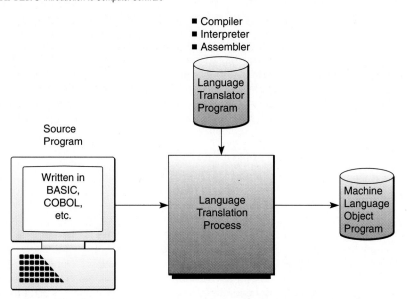

FIGURE 3.20

The language translation process. A program must be translated into machine language before it can be executed by a computer.

is to decrease the drudgery of programming while increasing the efficiency and productivity of programmers. Other programming tools include diagramming packages, code generators, libraries of reusable objects and program code, and prototyping tools. Many of these same tools are part of the toolkit provided by *computer-aided software engineering* (CASE) packages. See Figure 3.21.

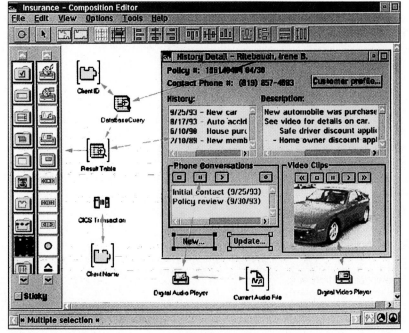

Courtesy of International Business Machines Corporation.

FIGURE 3.21

Using the graphical programming interface of Visual Age, IBM's object-oriented programming tool.

ARTHUR ANDERSEN AND OTHERS: WINDOWS 95 VERSUS WINDOWS NT

Arthur Andersen

The Andersen location in New York City runs Windows 95 in production mode on about 1,200 desktops and uses Microsoft's Office 95. The company expects to standardize on Windows 95 because it can run in 8 megabytes of memory on the company's 33-MHz Intel Corp. 486-based PCs. "If users go to all 32-bit applications, they will find Win 95 multitasks beautifully and works great," says systems analyst Lenworth D. Gordon. Andersen uses NT to support selected applications and also runs Microsoft SQL Server on three servers.

Christian Broadcast Network

Having recently moved off the mainframe, the network has 800 users supported by a mix of UNIX, Novell's NetWare, and Windows NT. The organization is moving to Microsoft SQL Server for its transaction processing but is debating whether to make NetWare or NT its core network operating system. Windows 95 is being used for selected applications. "Win 95 is ideal for our mobile users. It's easy to use and transport," says vice president of IS Paul Flanagan, citing Windows 95's power management and plug and play capabilities. However, he says he expects Christian Broadcast Network in Virginia Beach, Virginia, to be running NT Workstation on most desktops within two years.

Gould Evans Goodman Associates

About a quarter of the 120 users at this Kansas City, Missouri, architectural firm are running Windows 95 on new PCs. The 120-user network is built around servers based on Windows NT. "We get a lot of CAD work, and it is for that platform that we really want to go to NT over the long haul," says IS manager Rob White. "For the general user, such as our project managers, secretaries, and support staff, Windows 95 is adequate," he says.

Mobile Research and Development

This center in Paulsboro, New Jersey, has 600 workers who use PCs that primarily run Windows for Workgroups and about 50 Macintoshes. Microsoft's NT Server (for network servers) and NT Workstation (for PCs) support fewer than 25 percent of the users. A test of Windows 95 recently was abandoned because of difficulties running some of Microsoft's own software, including Access. As far as senior research engineer Allen Lovell is concerned, NT is almost identical to Windows, but users will experience far fewer problems.

Robbins Auto Parts

Windows NT seems to be the way to go for this company in Dover, New Hampshire The IS staff supports about 150 users; 80 percent of those users are connected through terminal servers on a statewide Novell LAN. One machine runs Windows NT Server. The company is testing Windows 95 and plans to expand its use of NT Server. However, it expects NT Workstation to be its primary desktop operating system in two years. "We will migrate for the security and stability of NT. I expect we will get everybody over to Win 95 in the next year," says Bill Pelletier, MIS manager at the firm. "Then, as soon as the Win 95 interface for Win NT is available, which will provide a nicer look and more functionality, we will move everybody over to NT," he says.

U.S. Department of Health and Human Services

The agency runs mission-critical applications on a mainframe and select UNIX systems, but it's testing Windows NT and Windows 95 on a few machines. Charles Hunter, director of IS, has major concerns about Windows 95 and NT. Those concerns include memory demands, software compatibility, scalability, and portability. "Overall, I still think OS/2 is a better choice for an operating system compared with Win 95," Hunter says. He cites OS/2's stability and his success with OS/2 as a database processor that runs browser software. However, Hunter anticipates that his site will primarily use UNIX and Windows NT two years from now.

CASE STUDY QUESTIONS

1. What are the benefits and limitations of Windows 95? Windows NT?

2. Which operating system seems to be preferred now and in the future by most of these organizations? Why?

3. Which operating system do you think businesses should install on their PCs? Why?

Source: Adapted from James Connolly. "Buyers' Guide: Win 95 and NT—Taking Root," *Computerworld*, March 11, 1996, pp. 87–92. Copyright © 1996 by Computerworld, Inc., Framingham, MA 01701—Reprinted from *Computerworld*.

Summary

- **Software.** Computer software consists of two major types of programs: (1) system software that controls and supports the operations of a computer system as it performs various information processing tasks, and (2) application software that directs the performance of a particular use, or application, of computers to meet the information processing needs of users. Refer to Figure 3.1 for an overview of the major types of software.

- **Application Software.** Application software includes a variety of programs that can be segregated into general-purpose, business, scientific, and other application-specific categories. General-purpose application programs perform common information processing jobs for end users. Examples are word processing, electronic spreadsheet, database management, telecommunications, and graphics programs. Business application programs accomplish information processing tasks that support specific business functions or industry requirements.

- **System Software.** System software can be subdivided into system management programs, system support programs, and system development programs. System management programs manage the hardware, software, and data resources of a computer system during its execution of information processing jobs. Major system management programs are operating systems, operating environments, database management systems, and communications monitors. System support programs support the operations, management, and users of computer systems by providing a variety of support services. Major support programs are system utilities, performance monitors, and security monitors. System development programs help users develop information processing programs and procedures and prepare user programs for computer processing. Major development programs are language translators, programming editors and other programming tools, code generators, and CASE tools.

- **Operating Systems.** An operating system is an integrated system of programs that supervises the operation of the CPU, controls the input/output storage functions of the computer system, and provides various support services. An operating system performs five basic functions: (1) a user interface for communication with users and operators, (2) resource management for managing the hardware resources of a computer system, (3) file management for managing files of data and programs, (4) task management for managing the tasks a computer must accomplish, and (5) utilities and other functions that provide miscellaneous support services.

- **Other System Software.** Operating environment programs add a graphical user interface to an operating system and may provide multitasking capabilities. Database management systems control the development, integration, and maintenance of databases. Telecommunications monitors control and support the telecommunications activities among the computers and terminals in a telecommunications network. Utilities are programs that perform routine computing functions, such as sorting data or copying files, as part of an operating system or as a separate package.

- **Programming Languages.** Programming languages are a major category of system software. They require the use of a variety of programming packages to help programmers develop computer programs, and language translator programs to convert programming language instructions into machine language instruction codes. The five major levels of programming languages are machine languages, assembler languages, high-level languages, fourth-generation languages, and object-oriented languages.

Key Terms and Concepts

These are the key terms and concepts of this chapter. The page number of their first explanation is given in parentheses.

1. Application software (88)
2. Application-specific programs (90)
3. Assembler language (104)
4. Database management package (93)
5. Electronic spreadsheet package (92)
6. File management (100)
7. Fourth-generation language (106)
8. General-purpose application programs (90)
9. Graphical user interface (99)
10. Graphics package (94)
11. High-level language (105)
12. Integrated package (95)
13. Language translator program (108)
14. Machine language (104)
15. Multitasking (100)
16. Natural language (106)
17. Nonprocedural language (106)
18. Object-oriented language (107)
19. Operating environment (99)
20. Operating system (98)
21. Programming tools (108)
22. Resource management (100)
23. Software suites (95)
24. System management programs (98)
25. System software (88)
26. System support programs (98)
27. Task management (100)
28. Telecommunications package (94)
29. Trends in software (89)
30. User interface (99)
31. Utility programs (103)
32. Virtual memory (100)
33. Word processing package (91)

Review Quiz

Match one of the key terms and concepts listed above with one of the brief examples or definitions listed below. Try to find the best fit for answers that seem to fit more than one term or concept. Defend your choices.

____ 1. Programs that manage and support the operations of computers.
____ 2. Programs that direct the performance of a specific use of computers.
____ 3. An integrated system of programs that manages the operations of a computer system.
____ 4. Managing the processing of tasks in a computer system.
____ 5. Managing the use of CPU time, primary and secondary storage, and input/output devices.
____ 6. Managing the input/output, storage, and retrieval of files.
____ 7. The function that provides a means of communication between end users and an operating system.
____ 8. The use of icons, bars, buttons, and other image displays to help you get things done.
____ 9. Provides a greater memory capability than a computer's actual memory capacity.
____ 10. Serves as an end user graphics-based interface that integrates the use of the operating system and application programs.
____ 11. Manages and supports the maintenance and retrieval of data stored in databases.
____ 12. Manages and supports telecommunications in a network.
____ 13. Translates high-level instructions into machine language instructions.
____ 14. Performs housekeeping chores for a computer system.
____ 15. A category of application software that performs common information processing tasks for end users.
____ 16. Allows you to create and edit documents.
____ 17. Software available for the specific applications of end users in business, science, and other fields.
____ 18. Creates and displays a worksheet for analysis.
____ 19. Produces line, bar, and pie charts and other displays.
____ 20. A program that performs several general-purpose applications in one package.
____ 21. A group of individual general-purpose application packages that work easily together.
____ 22. Uses instructions in the form of coded strings of ones and zeros.
____ 23. Uses instructions consisting of symbols representing operation codes and storage locations.
____ 24. Uses instructions called statements that resemble human language or the standard notation of mathematics.
____ 25. Might take the form of query languages and report generators.
____ 26. Languages that tie together data and the actions that will be performed upon the data.
____ 27. You don't have to tell the computer how to do something, just what result you want.
____ 28. As easy to use as one's native tongue.
____ 29. Performing two or more operations or applications at the same time.
____ 30. Includes programming editors, debuggers, code generators, and object libraries.
____ 31. Toward powerful, integrated, general-purpose, expert-assisted packages with easy-to-use graphic and natural language interfaces.

Discussion Questions

1. What major trends are occurring in software? What capabilities do you expect to see in future software packages?
2. How do the different roles of system software and application software affect you as an end user?
3. Refer to the Real World Case on Barrie Culver and NBC TV in the chapter. What pre-programmed business applications are available for the spreadsheet program you use? How effective are such spreadsheet templates?
4. Why is an operating system necessary? That is, why can't an end user just load an application program in a computer and start computing?
5. Which type of user interface do you prefer: command-driven, menu-driven, or graphical user interface? Explain why.
6. Refer to the Real World Case on Arthur Andersen and Others in the chapter. If you were Bill Gates of Microsoft, what would you do about the preference for Windows NT over Windows 95 by most companies in the case?
7. What capabilities does a multitasking virtual memory operating system give to a business end user?
8. Should a business end user know how to use a programming language to develop custom programs? Explain.

9. Refer to Real World Problem #1 on Dun & Bradstreet and Houghton Mifflin in the chapter. How do you think that applets on World Wide Web or intranet servers will affect the PC hardware and software needs of business end users?

10. Which application software packages are the most important for a business end user to know how to use? Explain the reasons for your choices.

Real World Problems

1. Dun & Bradstreet Software and Houghton Mifflin: Using Web Browser Applets

Dun & Bradstreet Software announced a series of small application software modules or "applets" designed for use over corporate intranets. One example is its requisitions applet, part of the SmartStream Web Series, a Web browser–based version of its popular SmartStream accounting and financial applications packages for client/server computing systems. The applet was developed with the Java programming language in conjunction with Sun Microsystems. It lets users execute a purchase request through a SmartStream system without having SmartStream software installed on their desktop PCs.

"It makes sense for managers to do their purchase requisitions electronically, but you wouldn't deploy client software to every manager just to do that," said Jeff Scherb, chief technology manager at D&B Software. "With a browser-based application, it's much easier and cheaper to extend access to casual users. You're not installing 50 or 100 megabytes of software code on every PC workstation," he explained. Instead, the D&B Software applet resides on a server and can be downloaded on an as-needed basis by browser software that is becoming ubiquitous at many large companies.

Houghton Mifflin Co., a $700 million publishing company and user of D&B Software's SmartStream, estimates it could save about $1,000 on each desktop PC that uses a browser instead of traditional SmartStream client software. "It would be a significant savings. With a browser, you also wouldn't need the disk space and RAM that the client software requires," said Daire Starr, a financial systems project manager at Houghton Mifflin in Boston. As a result, "we'd definitely like to use the new applet for casual users who do not need a complete SmartStream application on their PCs," Starr said.

a. What are applets? How are they related to Web browser software and application programs like SmartStream?

b. How would businesses like Houghton Mifflin benefit from using applets like D&B's requisition applet?

Source: Adapted from Julia King, "Intranet Applets," *Computerworld*, April 1, 1996, p. 45. Copyright © 1996 by Computerworld, Inc., Framingham, MA 01701—Reprinted from *Computerworld*.

2. Fireman's Fund and Sequus Pharmaceuticals: Sticking with OS/2 and UNIX

In the cacophony over Microsoft Windows 95 and Windows NT, it is easy to overlook other operating systems that are alive and well in corporate America. Among them are IBM's OS/2 and the various flavors of UNIX that continue to multiply.

Early on, OS/2 became known for robust and secure multitasking as well as some key applications such as Notes that were available only on that platform. This proved a boon for companies that decided to move to client/server technology before that trend caught on. For instance, Fireman's Fund Insurance Co. in Novato, California, committed to OS/2 more than six years ago. "In the late 1980s, OS/2 was the only operating system in town that could support our mission-critical needs on client PC workstations," said Robert O'Brien, systems adviser at Fireman's Fund. Fireman's Fund is happy with its OS/2 investment and will remain committed to the operating system for the foreseeable future, O'Brien said.

On the UNIX side, even some dyed-in-the-wool Windows shops still see the benefits of using UNIX in niche areas. For example, Menlo Park, California–based Sequus Pharmaceuticals, Inc., has chosen Windows 95 on the desktop and NT on servers. But the company also has a pair of Sun Microsystems servers that use Sun's Solaris version of UNIX. These servers run medical systems and laboratory analysis software packages that aren't available on NT, said Randy Dugger, director of IS.

a. Do you think Fireman's Fund should stick with OS/2? Explain.

b. Why is Sequus using UNIX? Is this an important reason for using an operating system? Explain.

Source: Adapted from Stuart Johnson. "UNIX, OS/2 Hold Their Ground Against NT," *Computerworld*, February 26, 1996, p. 54. Copyright © 1996 by Computerworld, Inc., Framingham, MA 01701—Reprinted from *Computerworld*.

3. London Life and USAA Life: Moving to Object-Oriented Applications

One of the insurance industry's early object technology pioneers, London Life Insurance Co. in London, Ontario, Canada, certainly has suffered its share of scrapes and bruises. In 1991, the company began using Trinzic Corp.'s KBMS software development tool to "objectize" its IBM mainframe, Digital Equipment midrange, and PC-based Windows applications. But after two years of development and nearly $500,000, KBMS turned out to be a bust. The development software was rigid, it chewed up too many PC resources, and the vendor didn't support it very well, said Sandro Palleschi, a senior consultant at London Life.

London Life has since shifted to Microsoft Visual Basic and Access object development kits to create business applications with GUIs and reusable objects for its three-tiered computer systems. The payoff has been impressive because of object technology's ability to reuse business methods and objects. For example, London Life was able to create objects for 35,000-plus business functions last year, some 13,000 more than it had anticipated.

In the United States, USAA Life Insurance Co. is implementing a set of 350 IBM DB2, object-oriented client/server–based health, annuities, and life (HAL) application systems. The HAL modules are expected to decrease systems training time for end users by 57 percent and improve the productivity of processing large transaction volumes by 50 percent. "This policy and administration system will allow us to build insurance products quickly," said Edwin L. Rosane, president and chief executive officer of the San Antonio–based firm.

a. Why was London Life's first experience with object-oriented software development a failure? What benefits finally resulted?

b. What are the benefits of object-oriented software for USAA Life?

Source: Adapted from Thomas Hoffman, "Agents of Change," *Computerworld*, March 18, 1996, p. 16. Copyright © 1996 by Computerworld, Inc., Framingham, MA 01701—Reprinted from *Computerworld*.

4. Information Presentation Technologies: Programming in Java

Think of it as "Visual Basic for Java." That's JFactory, a visual programming package for Java, Sun Microsystems' development language for the Internet's World Wide Web. And unlike most Java development systems, JFactory is much more than a gussied-up code editor.

"You can basically prototype your whole user interface, create menus, and hook up menus and buttons to dialogs and windows—without writing a single line of code," said user Mark Rhoads, vice president of software engineering at Information Presentation Technologies, Inc., in San Luis Obispo, California.

Java lets programmers create Internet applications that will run unchanged on Windows, UNIX, and other platforms. Developers can build small application programs or "applets" that can be downloaded and run as part of a World Wide Web page or as larger stand-alone applications.

Until now, developers have had to write virtually every line of Java code themselves. JFactory, developed by Rogue Wave Software, runs on Microsoft Windows 95, Windows NT, and Sun's Solaris. It lets developers use a mouse to drag and drop windows, menus, buttons, and other user interface elements. Common features of Java Web page applets, such as animations, also can be created without writing code. However, some application logic requires programmers to write Java code—for error handling and reading data from files, for example. Then JFactory, with a single mouse click, generates a working Java application program.

a. What are the benefits of JFactory as a Java software development tool?

b. What are the benefits of applets programmed in Java on the World Wide Web?

Source: Adapted from Frank Hayes, "Visual Tool Eases Java Development," *Computerworld*, February 26, 1996, pp. 1, 15. Copyright © 1996 by Computerworld, Inc., Framingham, MA 01701—Reprinted from *Computerworld*.

Application Exercises

1. ABC Department Stores

ABC Department Stores would like to acquire software to do the following tasks. Identify what software packages they need.

a. Support telecommunications among their end users.

b. Control access and use of the hardware, software, and data resources of the system.

c. Monitor and record how the system resources are being used.

d. Make it easier to update and integrate their databases.

e. Add a graphical user interface and multitasking capabilities to their microcomputer operating systems.

f. Type correspondence and reports.

g. Analyze rows and columns of figures.

h. Develop line, bar, and pie charts.

2. Evaluating Software Packages

Have you used one of the software packages mentioned in this chapter?

a. Briefly describe the advantages and disadvantages of one of the packages you have used so far.

b. How would such a package help you in a present or future job situation?

c. How would you improve the package you used?

3. Action Products Software Licensing Costs

Action Products Company wants to provide common application software packages for all its employees who need to use them. Sixty employees at Action Products have PCs on their desks. The plan is to provide E-mail software to each employee with a PC. In addition, 55 employees will need word processing software, 42 will need spreadsheet software, and 22 will need database software. The 22 users who need the database software will all be using the other three packages as well. Action Products has been offered the following pricing by a major application software supplier. The per-unit cost declines when the number of licenses reaches certain levels, and the supplier offers a bundled price for an applications suite including all four of the applications Action Products is considering.

Your task is to create a spreadsheet that will show the costs of acquiring the needed software licenses and allow management to assess all reasonable alternatives with respect to the licenses to be purchased. For instance, it may be cheaper to buy the suite package for everyone even though major parts of it will not be used by some workers, or it may pay to increase the order for certain packages to the next higher pricing threshold (e.g., 25 copies of the database software). Find the cheapest solution for Action Products. Make sure that your spreadsheet includes at least these three alternatives: (1) Buy just the number of units required of each package. (2) Buy a license to the suite package for everyone. (3) Buy 25 licenses for the suite package and buy just the number of additional licenses needed for the E-mail, word processing, and spreadsheet packages.

a. Get a printed listing of your spreadsheet showing the alternatives you examined and their costs.

b. Use a word processing package to write a brief memorandum describing your results and recommending the option you think should be chosen.

	Cost per License			
Application	1–9 Licenses	10–24 Licenses	25–49 Licenses	50 or More Licenses
E-mail	$ 45	$ 40	$ 37	$ 35
Word processing	75	65	60	55
Spreadsheet	95	85	77	72
Database	125	110	100	92
Integrated package	250	220	205	190

4. Employee Training at ABC's Marketing Department

You have been given the responsibility for planning and implementing a computer software training program for the marketing department at ABC Company. Training topics will include word processing, spreadsheet, database, and Internet use. Training will be provided by outside contractors. Eligibility for training will be based on the employee's job responsibilities and current knowledge level. Among those eligible, slots will be allocated based on seniority. You have surveyed each employee in your department about their level of knowledge for each type of software involved. A sample of relevant data for employees in your department follows.

a. Using a database software package, create an appropriate database table and enter the following sample data.

b. Use your database package's querying capabilities to generate a prioritized list of employees who will be offered slots for the following training sessions:

1. Introduction to Word Processing—Employees whose skill level is *none* or *low* and whose job type is not technical are eligible for this session.

2. Introduction to the Internet—All employees whose Internet use skill level is *none* are eligible.

3. Introduction to Database Systems—Employees whose database skill level is *low* or *none* and whose job type is managerial or technical are eligible.

			Self-Reported Skill Level			
Employee Name	Job Type	Hire Date	Word Processing	Spreadsheet	Database	Internet Use
S. Jones	Managerial	03-02-93	None	Low	None	Medium
L. Davis	Clerical	11-08-88	High	None	None	None
R. Smith	Clerical	12-02-92	Low	Low	None	None
M. Marx	Technical	04-06-91	Low	Medium	Low	Low
J. Lewis	Managerial	02-24-95	None	None	None	None
V. Adams	Clerical	04-21-86	High	Medium	None	Low
S. Vale	Technical	11-01-95	Medium	Medium	Medium	None
J. Cole	Clerical	08-22-87	Low	High	Medium	None
L. Evans	Clerical	11-03-94	None	None	None	None
T. Wall	Managerial	02-28-96	Medium	High	Low	Medium
J. Dorn	Technical	08-18-96	None	Medium	Medium	None

Note: If you are not familiar with the use of database software packages and would like additional information about how to design and implement a database application, see Application Exercise 3 in Chapter 10.

Review Quiz Answers

1. *25*	9. *32*	17. *2*	25. *7*
2. *1*	10. *19*	18. *5*	26. *18*
3. *20*	11. *4*	19. *10*	27. *17*
4. *26*	12. *28*	20. *12*	28. *16*
5. *22*	13. *13*	21. *23*	29. *15*
6. *6*	14. *31*	22. *14*	30. *21*
7. *30*	15. *8*	23. *3*	31. *29*
8. *9*	16. *33*	24. *11*	

Selected References

1. *Business Software Review, Computerworld, PC Magazine, PC Week,* and *Software Digest.* (Examples of good sources of current information on computer software packages.)

2. Datapro Corporation. *Datapro Reports.* (Series of regular detailed reports on selected software packages.)

3. Connolly, James. "Buyer's Guide: Win 95 and NT—Taking Root." *Computerworld,* March 11, 1996.

4. Jacobsen, Ivar; Maria Ericsson; and Ageneta Jacobsen. *The Object Advantage: Business Process Reengineering with Object Technology.* New York: ACM Press, 1995.

5. Simon, Barry. "Painless Programming." *Windows Sources,* June 1993.

6. Slitz, John. "Object Technology Profiles." Supplement to *Computerworld,* June 1994.

7. Special OS/2 Warp Edition, *Personal Systems,* January 1995.

8. "The CW Guide to Operating Systems." *Computerworld,* April 24, 1995.

Introduction to Business Telecommunications

CHAPTER OUTLINE

Chapter

4

LEARNING OBJECTIVES

After reading and studying this chapter, you should be able to:

1. Identify the basic components, functions, and types of telecommunications networks.

2. Identify several major developments and trends in the industries, technology, and applications of telecommunications.

3. Explain the functions of major types of telecommunications network hardware, software, and media.

Section I

A Manager's View of Telecommunications Networks

Why Telecommunications Is Important

Empower a business with a network that spans every location, and that organization can operate more efficiently and more creatively. By electronically linking workers, a network enables all employees to work together as efficiently as if they were in the same work group. A network allows people to make decisions based on the most current information; they don't have to rely on a report that was generated yesterday. This leads to better decisions and higher productivity. Propelled by the right corporate philosophy, an enterprisewide network can help even a monolithic corporation act like an agile start-up company [17].

End users need to communicate electronically to succeed in today's global information society. Managers, end users, and their organizations need to electronically exchange data and information with other end users, customers, suppliers, and other organizations. Only through the use of telecommunications can they perform their work activities, manage organizational resources, and compete successfully in today's fast-changing global economy. Thus, many organizations today could not survive without interconnected *networks* of computers to service the information processing and communications needs of their end users. As a managerial end user, you will thus be expected to make or participate in decisions regarding a great variety of telecommunications options. That's why you need to study the applications, technology, and managerial implications of telecommunications. See Figure 4.1.

Telecommunications is the sending of information in any form (e.g., voice, data, text, and images) from one place to another using electronic or light-emitting media. *Data communications* is a more specific term that describes the transmitting and receiving of data over communication links between one or more computer

FIGURE 4.1

Telecommunications networks are a vital part of today's businesses.

Seth Resnick.

systems and a variety of input/output terminals. The terms *teleprocessing, telematics,* and *telephony* may also be used since they reflect the integration of computer-based information processing with telecommunications and telephone technologies. However, all forms of telecommunications now rely heavily on computers and computerized devices. For this reason, the broader term *telecommunications* can be used as a synonym for data communications activities. Therefore, in this text, we will use these terms interchangeably.

Telecommunications networks provide invaluable capabilities to an organization and its end users. For example, some networks enable work groups to communicate electronically and share hardware, software, and data resources. Other networks let a company process sales transactions immediately from many remote locations, exchange business documents electronically with its customers and suppliers, or remotely monitor and control production processes. Telecommunications networks can also interconnect the computer systems of a business so their computing power can be shared by end users throughout an enterprise. And, of course, telecommunications networks enhance collaboration and communication among individuals both inside and outside an organization.

Figure 4.2 emphasizes the many possible applications of telecommunications. It groups a large number of telecommunications applications into the major categories of electronic communications systems, electronic meeting systems, and business process systems. Also note that these applications can be supported by several major types of telecommunications architectures. We will discuss these architectures in this chapter, and the end user and enterprise applications of telecommunications in Chapters 6 and 7.

Applications of Telecommunications

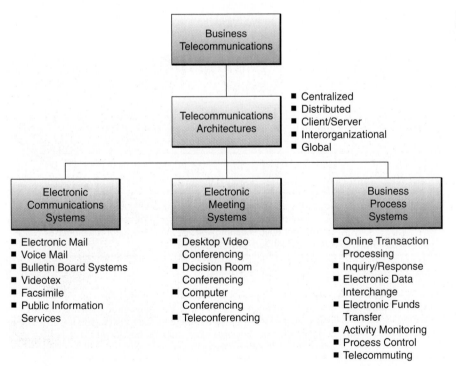

FIGURE 4.2

Applications of telecommunications. Note the major categories and types of applications supported by telecommunications networks.

Trends in Telecommunications

Major trends occurring in the field of telecommunications have a significant impact on management decisions in this area. Informed managerial end users should thus be aware of major trends in telecommunications industries, technologies, and applications that significantly increase the decision alternatives confronting their organizations. See Figure 4.3.

Industry Trends

The competitive arena for telecommunications service has changed dramatically in the United States, from a few government-regulated monopolies to many fiercely competitive suppliers of telecommunications services. With the breakup of AT&T and the Bell System in 1984, and the passage of the Telecommunications Act of 1996, local and global telecommunications networks and services are now available from a variety of large and small telecommunications companies. Hundreds of companies now offer businesses and consumers a choice of everything from long-distance telephone services and Internet access, to communications satellite channels, mobile radio, cable TV, and cellular phone services. The Internet and public information networks such as America Online, CompuServe, and Prodigy now offer electronic mail, bulletin board systems, multimedia marketing, electronic shopping, and many other services. Thus, the service and vendor options available to meet a company's telecommunications needs have increased significantly, as has a manager's decision-making alternatives.

The U.S. Telecommunications Deregulation and Reform Act of 1996 promises to accelerate the dynamic changes taking place in the telecommunications industry. With a few exceptions, the law overturns virtually all U.S. federal regulations that governed which companies could enter which communications businesses. This should result in the creation of even more telecommunications companies, telecommunications mergers and alliances, and telecommunications services [3, 26]. Key changes in the law include:

- Local telephone companies, including the regional Bell operating companies, can provide long distance telecommunications services.
- Long distance telephone companies can enter local telephone service markets.

FIGURE 4.3

Major trends in telecommunications.

Industry trends Toward a greater number of competitive vendors, carriers, alliances, and telecommunications network services.

Technology trends Toward open and interconnected local and global digital networks for voice, data, and video with heavy use of high-speed fiber optic lines and satellite channels to form a global information superhighway system.

Application trends Toward the pervasive use of the Internet and enterprise and interorganizational intranet networks to support collaborative computing, online business operations, and strategic advantage in local and global markets.

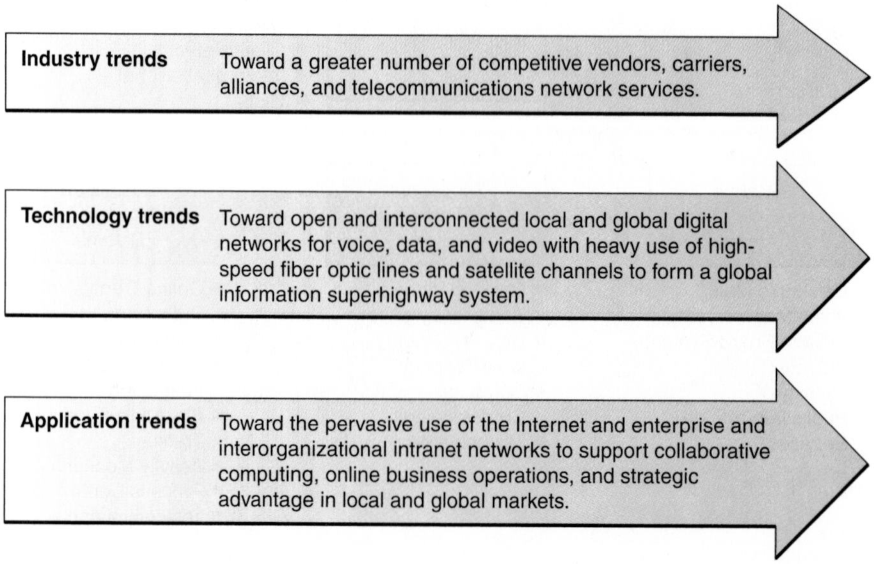

- Local and long distance telephone companies can expand into the cable TV business.
- Cable TV companies can provide local telephone services.
- Public utilities, such as electric, gas, and water companies, can offer a variety of telecommunications services.
- Telephone companies can offer television programming and other video communications services [3, 26].

Technology Trends

Digital technology will make the phones we use today seem like two cans joined by a string. Within perhaps four years, we will see cellular service that costs almost as little to use as the corner phone booth, handheld communicators that will let us scribble notes with an electronic stylus and zap them wirelessly anywhere on earth, and networks that will automatically deliver our calls to the people we want to reach, wherever they happen to be. Travelers will commune with the office network as fully and easily as if they were sitting at their desks; workers with computers will commingle video, voice, data, and images on a single line as they seamlessly collaborate with faraway colleagues [12].

Telecommunications is being revolutionized by a change from analog to digital network technologies. Telecommunications has always depended on voice-oriented analog transmission systems designed to transmit the variable electrical frequencies generated by the sound waves of the human voice. However, local and global telecommunications networks are rapidly converting to digital transmission technologies that transmit information in the form of discrete pulses, as computers do. This provides (1) significantly higher transmission speeds, (2) the movement of larger amounts of information, (3) greater economy, and (4) much lower error rates than analog systems. In addition, digital technologies, including ISDN (Integrated Services Digital Network), will allow telecommunications networks to carry multiple types of communications (data, voice, video) on the same circuits.

Another major trend in telecommunications technology is a change in communications media. Many telecommunications networks are switching from copper wire-based media (such as coaxial cable) and land-based microwave relay systems to fiber optic lines and communications satellite transmissions. Fiber optic transmission, which uses pulses of laser-generated light, offers significant advantages in terms of reduced size and installation effort, vastly greater communication capacity, much faster transmission speeds, and freedom from electrical interference. Satellite transmission offers significant advantages in speed and capacity for organizations that need to transmit massive quantities of data over global networks. These trends in technology give organizations more alternatives in overcoming the limitations of their present telecommunications systems.

Open Systems

Clearly, the direction of the computer field today is toward "increased connectivity"— where any computer in an organization, from mainframe to micro, can communicate with any other one. There are a lot of technical hurdles to overcome before reaching this goal. But there are also some key management decisions and policies that can help ease the task [16].

Another major telecommunications trend is toward easier access by end users to the computing resource of interconnected networks like the Internet, or Internet-like corporate *intranet* networks. This trend is based on both industry and technical moves toward building networks based on an open systems architecture. **Open systems** are information systems that use common standards for hardware, software, applications, and networking. Open systems create a computing environment that is open to easy access by end users and their networked computer systems. Open systems provide greater *connectivity,* that is, the ability of networked computers and other devices to easily access and communicate with each other and share information. An open systems architecture also provides a high degree of network *interoperability.* That is, open systems enable the many different applications of end users to be accomplished using the different varieties of computer systems, software packages, and databases provided by a variety of interconnected networks. Sometimes, software known as *middleware* may be used to help diverse systems work together. Networks like the Internet and network architectures like the Open Systems Interconnection (OSI) model of the International Standards Organization promote open, flexible, and efficient standards for the development of open telecommunications networks.

Application Trends

The changes in telecommunications industries and technologies just mentioned are causing a significant change in the business use of telecommunications. The trend toward more vendors, services, advanced technologies, and open systems, and the growth of the Internet and corporate intranets, dramatically increases the number of feasible applications. Thus, telecommunications is playing a more important role in support of the operations, management, and strategic objectives of both large and small companies. An organization's telecommunications function is no longer relegated to office telephone systems, long-distance calling arrangements, and a limited amount of data communications with corporate mainframes. Instead, it has become an integral part of local and global networks of computers that are used to cut costs, improve the collaboration of work groups, develop online operational processes, share resources, lock in customers and suppliers, and develop new products and services. This makes telecommunications a more complex and important decision area for businesses that must increasingly compete in both domestic and global markets.

The Information Superhighway

The trend toward open, high-speed, digital networks with fiber optic and satellite links has made the concept of an **information superhighway** technically possible and has captured the interest of both business and government. In this concept, local, regional, nationwide, and global networks will be integrated into a vast network of networks, with more advanced capabilities than the Internet. The information superhighway system would connect individuals, households, businesses, government agencies, libraries, universities, and all other institutions and would support interactive voice, data, video, and multimedia communications. See Figure 4.4.

Proponents of the information superhighway say it could provide a National Information Infrastructure (NII) and economic network with an economic impact equivalent to the transcontinental railway and interstate highway systems combined. Critics question whether the potential benefits of the superhighway would be worth its cost, especially given the rapid growth of the Internet [6]. The proposed national data highway system would be a massive undertaking, costing hundreds of billions of dollars and taking several decades to construct. For example, government estimates of the investment cost include investment by private industry of $2 trillion, with the government investing $200 billion over 10–50 years [5].

Why build such a superhighway network? Proponents argue that the information superhighway (or *infobahn*) would create a national information infrastructure that would dramatically increase business efficiency and competitiveness by improving economic communications, collaboration, and information gathering.

- **Names:** Information superhighway, national data highway, infobahn, national information infrastructure.
- **Purpose:** Create a national telecommunications infrastructure of interconnected local, regional, and global networks to support all economic, societal, and individual telecommunications.
- **Participants:** All individuals, households, businesses, government agencies, libraries, schools, universities, and other institutions.
- **Communications:** Interactive voice, video, data, and multimedia telecommunications.
- **Examples:** Universal electronic mail, videoconferencing, electronic data interchange, interactive home shopping, education, entertainment, and all forms of online, real-time computing.
- **Builders:** Private industry (telecommunications companies, entertainment companies, publishing companies, etc.) and the federal government.
- **Cost and time estimates:** From hundreds of billions to several trillions of dollars, over 10 to 50 years.

FIGURE 4.4

Overview of the information superhighway.

For example, the information superhighway could use electronic mail, videoconferencing, and electronic databank services to enable businesses throughout the country to build products faster through an electronic collaboration in the product design process. Or the highway could support an interactive video home shopping and entertainment system that could revolutionize the retailing and entertainment industries [5]. In any event, the information superhighway idea promises to be a catalyst for the development of the Internet and other changes in telecommunications services in the years to come.

Before we discuss the use and management of telecommunications, we should understand the basic components of a *telecommunications* network. Generally, a *communications network* is any arrangement where a *sender* transmits a *message* to a receiver over a *channel* consisting of some type of medium. Figure 4.5 illustrates a simple conceptual model of a **telecommunications network,** which shows that it consists of five basic categories of components:

A Telecommunications Network Model

- **Terminals,** such as networked microcomputer workstations or video terminals. Of course, any input/output device that uses telecommunications networks to transmit or receive data is a terminal, including telephones, office equipment, and the *transaction terminals* discussed in Chapter 2.
- **Telecommunications processors,** which support data transmission and reception between terminals and computers. These devices, such as modems and front-end processors, perform a variety of control and support functions in a telecommunications network. For example, they convert data from digital to analog and back, code and decode data, and control the accuracy and efficiency of the communications flow between computers and terminals in a telecommunications network.
- **Telecommunications channels and media** over which data are transmitted and received. Telecommunications channels use combinations of *media,* such as copper wires, coaxial cables, fiber optic cables, microwave systems, and communications satellites, to interconnect the other components of a telecommunications network.

FIGURE 4.5

The five basic components in a telecommunications network: (1) terminals, (2) telecommunications processors, (3) telecommunications channels and media, (4) computers, and (5) telecommunications software.

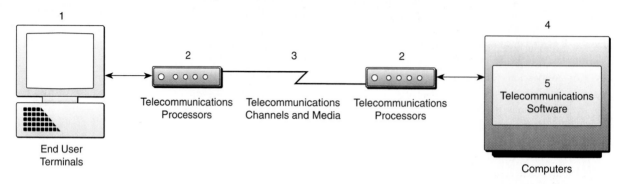

- **Computers** of all sizes and types are interconnected by telecommunications networks so that they can carry out their information processing assignments. For example, a mainframe computer may serve as a *host computer* for a large network, assisted by a midrange computer serving as a *front-end processor,* while a microcomputer may act as a *network server* for a small network of microcomputer workstations.
- **Telecommunications control software** consists of programs that control telecommunications activities and manage the functions of telecommunications networks. Examples include *telecommunications monitors* for mainframe host computers, *network operating systems* for microcomputer network servers, and *communications packages* for microcomputers.

No matter how large and complex real-world telecommunications networks may appear to be, these five basic categories of components must be at work to support an organization's telecommunications activities. Use this framework to help you understand the various types of telecommunications networks in use today.

Types of Telecommunications Networks

There are many different types of telecommunications networks. However, from an end user's point of view, there are two basic types: *wide area* and *local area* networks.

Wide Area Networks

Telecommunications networks covering a large geographic area are called *remote networks, long-distance networks,* or, more popularly, **wide area networks** (WANs). Networks that cover a large city or metropolitan area (*metropolitan area networks*) can also be included in this category. Such large networks have become a necessity for carrying out the day-to-day activities of many business and government organizations and their end users. Thus, WANs are used by manufacturing firms, banks, retailers, distributors, transportation companies, and government agencies to transmit and receive information among their employees, customers, suppliers, and other organizations across cities, regions, countries, or the world. Figure 4.6 illustrates an example of a global wide area network for a major multinational corporation.

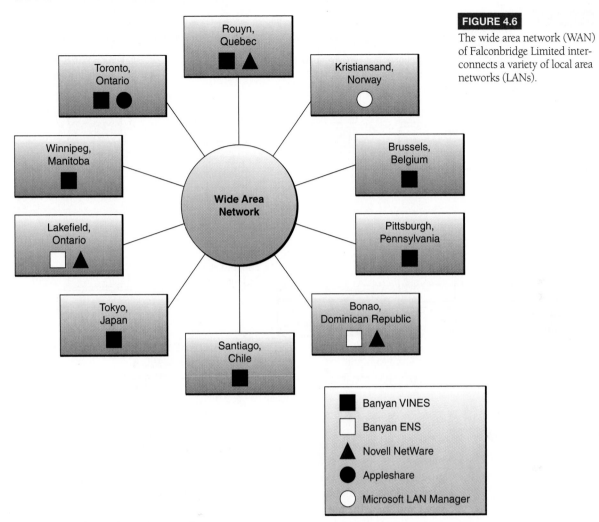

FIGURE 4.6

The wide area network (WAN) of Falconbridge Limited interconnects a variety of local area networks (LANs).

Source: Courtesy of Banyan Systems Incorporated.

Local Area Networks

Local area networks (LANs) connect computers and other information processing devices within a limited physical area, such as an office, a building, manufacturing plant, or other work site. LANs have become commonplace in many organizations for providing telecommunications network capabilities that link end users in offices, departments, and other work groups.

LANs use a variety of telecommunications media, such as ordinary telephone wiring, coaxial cable, or even wireless radio systems to interconnect microcomputer workstations and computer peripherals. To communicate over the network, each PC must have a circuit board called a *network interface card*. Most LANs use a powerful microcomputer having a large hard disk capacity, called a *file server* or **network server**, that contains a **network operating system** program that controls telecommunications and the use of network resources. For example, it distributes copies of common data files and software packages to the other microcomputers in the network and controls access to laser printers and other network peripherals. See Figure 4.7.

FIGURE 4.7

A local area network (LAN). Note how this LAN allows users to share hardware, software, and data resources.

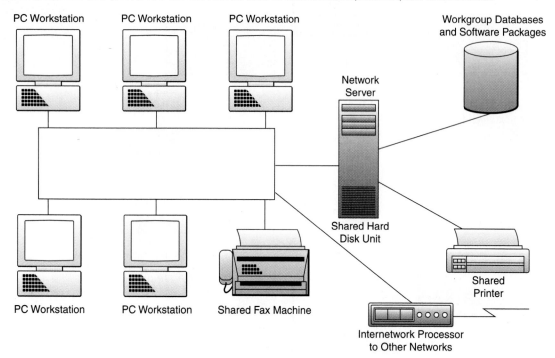

LANs allow end users in a work group to communicate electronically; share hardware, software, and data resources; and pool their efforts when working on group projects. For example, a project team of end users whose microcomputer workstations are interconnected by a LAN can send each other *electronic mail* messages and share the use of laser printers and hard magnetic disk units, copies of electronic spreadsheets or word processing documents, and project databases. LANs have thus become a more popular alternative for end user and work group computing than the use of terminals connected to larger computers.

Internetworks and Intranets

Most local area networks are eventually connected to other LANs or wide area networks to create **internetworks.** That's because end users need to communicate with the workstations of colleagues on other LANs, or to access the computing resources and databases at other company locations or at other organizations. Local area networks rely on **internetwork processors**, such as *bridges, routers, hubs,* or *gateways,* to make *internetworking* connections to other LANs and wide area networks.

The goal of many such internetwork architectures is to create a seamless network of networks or **intranet** within each organization that connects to the Internet and the networks of organizations that share business relationships. Intranets are designed to be secure Internet-like open systems, whose Weblike browsing software provides easy point-and-click access by end users to network resources. Intranets emphasize connectivity and interoperability among their interconnected workstations, servers, work group, business unit, and corporate

FIGURE 4.8

An example of the internetwork architecture of South Boston Savings Bank.

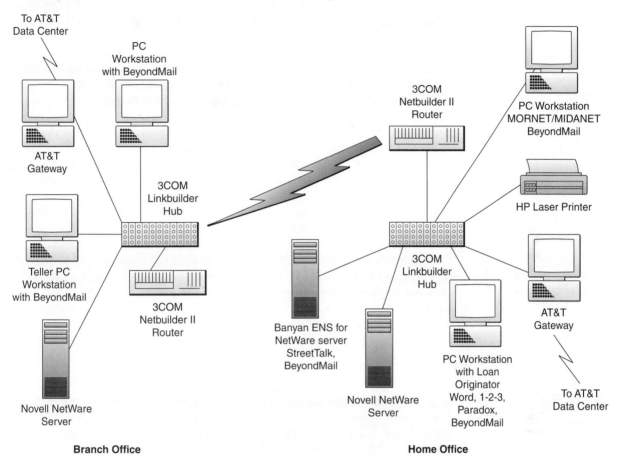

Source: Courtesy of Banyan Systems Incorporated.

databases, the Internet, and other networks. Many companies, universities, and other organizations are creating such intranet structures as their model for internetworking their diverse networks. Figure 4.8 is an example of an internetwork architecture for a savings bank.

> Client/server technology promises many things to many people: to end users, easier access to corporate and external data; to managers, dramatically lower costs for processing; to programmers, reduced maintenance; to corporate planners, an infrastructure that enables business processes to be reengineered for strategic benefits. Whether client/server lives up to these promises will depend in large part on how carefully it is planned for, and how intelligently policies are put forth to manage it [13].

Client/Server Computing

Client/server computing has become the model for a new *information architecture* that will take enterprisewide computing into the 21st century. We introduced client/server networks in Chapter 2, in our discussion of networked computer systems. Computing power has rapidly become distributed and interconnected throughout many organizations through networks of all types of computers. More and more, networked computer systems are taking the form of client/server networks. In a client/server network, end user microcomputer workstations are the **clients.** They are interconnected by local area networks and share application processing with LAN **servers,** which also manage the networks. These local area networks may also be interconnected to other LANs and wide area networks of client workstations and servers. See Figures 4.9 and 4.10.

With client/server computing, end users at client LAN workstations can handle a broad range of information processing tasks. They can thus perform some or most of the processing of their business applications. This includes data entry and other user interface activities, inquiry response, transaction processing, updating databases, generating reports, and providing decision support. LAN servers can share application processing, manage work group collaboration, and control common hardware, software, and databases. Thus, data can be completely processed locally, where most input and output (and errors and problems) must be handled anyway, while still providing access to the workstations and servers in other networks. This provides computer processing more tailored to the needs of end users and increases information processing efficiency and effectiveness as users become more responsible for their own application systems.

Client/server computing also lets large central-site computers handle those jobs they can do best, such as high-volume transaction processing, communications network security and control, and maintenance and control of large corporate databases. User clients at local sites can access these *superservers* to receive corporatewide management information or transmit summary transaction data reflecting local site activities.

FIGURE 4.9

Client/server networks enable cooperative processing among end user workstations and network servers.

Courtesy of Hewlett-Packard Company.

Client/server computing is the latest form of **distributed processing.** In *distributed processing,* information processing activities in an organization are accomplished by using a network of computers interconnected by telecommunications links instead of relying on one large *centralized* computer facility or on the *decentralized* operation of several independent computers. For example, a distributed processing network may consist of mainframes, minicomputers, and microcomputers,

Distributed Processing

FIGURE 4.10

A client/server model for distributed and cooperative processing. Note the functions performed by different types of computers acting as clients, servers, and superservers for the Westland Group, a Wisconsin banking and insurance company.

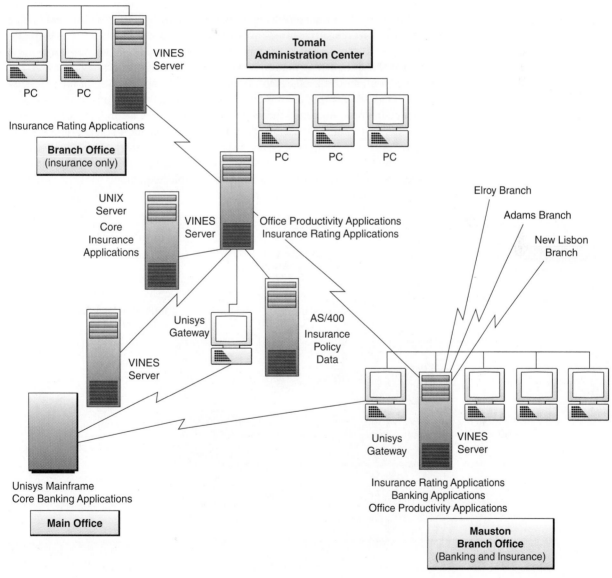

Source: Courtesy of Banyan Systems Incorporated.

dispersed over a wide geographic area and interconnected by wide area networks. Or it may take the form of a client/server network of end user workstations and network servers distributed within user departments in interconnected local area networks.

Cooperative Processing

Client/server computing may also involve **cooperative processing.** Cooperative processing allows the various types of computers in a distributed processing network to share the processing of parts of an end user's application. Application software packages are available that have common user interfaces and functions so they can operate consistently on networks of micro, mini, and mainframe computer systems. For example, end users could use a spreadsheet package provided to their microcomputer workstations by a local area network server to perform financial analysis on databases managed by a corporate mainframe.

Interorganizational Networks

Many of the applications of telecommunications we have just mentioned can be classified as **interorganizational networks.** As Figure 4.11 illustrates, such networks link a company's wide area and local area networks to the networks of its customers, suppliers, information service providers, and other organizations. For example, you can think of a computerized account inquiry system for access by customers as an example of an interorganizational network. So is the use of electronic document interchange that links the computers of a company with its suppliers and customers. Accessing information services such as Dow-Jones News Retrieval or the data banks of government agencies for information about market and economic conditions is another example. Electronic funds transfer applications also depend on interorganizational networks established among banks, businesses, employees, customers, and suppliers.

FIGURE 4.11

Interorganizational systems rely on network links between an organization and its customers, suppliers, and other organizations.

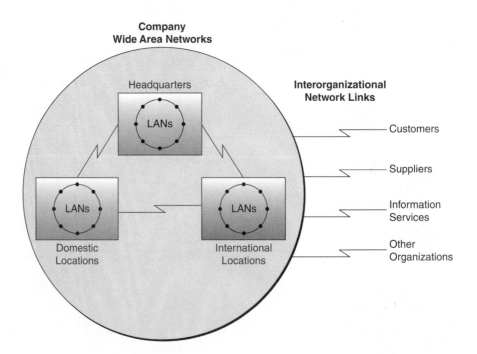

Thus, the business use of telecommunications has moved beyond the boundaries of work groups and the organization. Now many business firms have extended their telecommunications networks to their customers and suppliers, both domestically and internationally. As we will see in Chapter 9, such *inter-organizational systems* build new strategic business relationships and alliances with those *stakeholders* in an attempt to increase and lock in their business, while locking out competitors. Also, transaction processing costs are frequently reduced, and the quality of service increases. In addition, the availability of external information about industry, market, economic, and political developments provides better information for managerial decision making. Because of these benefits, the trend toward increased connectivity between the networks of an organization and its external stakeholders is expected to continue.

The Internet

The **Internet** is the largest network of networks today, and the closest model we have to the information superhighway of tomorrow. The Internet (the Net) is a rapidly growing global web of thousands of business, educational, and research networks connecting millions of computers and their users in more than 100 countries to each other. The Internet evolved from a research and development network (ARPANET) established in 1969 by the U.S. Defense Department to enable corporate, academic, and government researchers to communicate with E-mail and share data and computing resources. The Net doesn't have a central computer system or telecommunications center. Instead each message sent has an address code so any computer in the network can forward it to its destination [8, 9].

The Internet doesn't have a headquarters or governing body. The Internet society in Reston, Virginia, is a volunteer group of individual and corporate members who promote use of the Internet and the development of new communications standards or *protocols*. These common standards are the key to the free flow of messages among the widely different computers and networks in the system. The Internet is growing rapidly. For example, the Internet is more than doubling in size each year, growing to over 20 million host computer networks and more than 50 million users in early 1996. The monthly rate of growth of the Internet was estimated at between 7 to 10 percent. One of Internet's founders, Vinton Cerf, expects the Internet to eventually interconnect more than 1 billion networks [1, 2].

The most popular Internet applications are E-mail and browsing the sites on the World Wide Web. Internet E-mail is fast, faster than many public networks. Messages usually arrive in seconds or a few minutes, anywhere in the world. And Internet E-mail messages can take the form of data, text, fax, and video files. Graphical browser software like Netscape and Mosaic enable you to "surf" the World Wide Web by pointing and clicking your way to the information resources on the *home pages* of thousands of hyperlinked corporate, government, and other sites. Many Web sites provide multimedia displays of information to users.

The Internet also supports bulletin board systems formed by thousands of special interest groups. Anyone can post messages on thousands of topics for interested users to read. Other popular applications include accessing files and databases from libraries and thousands of organizations, logging on to other computers in the network, and holding real-time conversations with other Internet users. See Figure 4.12.

FIGURE 4.12
Important telecommunica-
tions services on the Internet.

- **E-mail:** Exchange electronic mail with millions of Internet users.
- **Usenet:** Post messages on bulletin board systems formed by thousands of special inter-est discussion groups.
- **Internet Relay Chat:** Hold real-time conversations with Internet users around the world on hundreds of discussion channels.
- **File Transfer Protocol (FTP):** Download data files, programs, reports, articles, maga-zines, books, pictures, sounds, and other types of files from thousands of sources to your computer system.
- **Telenet:** Log on to and use thousands of Internet computer systems around the world.
- **World Wide Web:** Point and click your way to thousands of hyperlinked Internet sites and resources using graphical browser software like Mosaic and Netscape.

Business on the Internet

No discussion of the business applications of telecommunications would be com-plete today without mention of the Internet. From small businesses to blue chip companies like General Electric, IBM, Merrill Lynch, Motorola, and Xerox, business use of the Internet has expanded rapidly. By 1995, over 1.5 million of the host net-works on the Internet belonged to businesses or their research labs [2, 16]. Businesses are connecting their networks to the Internet for several reasons. One is the ease of worldwide communications and collaboration through Internet's global E-mail and bulletin board systems. Another reason is the access to a vast range of information provided by the networks on the Internet.

Businesses are also connecting to the Internet because it represents the wave of the future in the competitive business use of telecommunications networks to access nation-al and global markets. Internet expert Mary Cronin, of Boston College, says that "the most compelling argument for connecting is that the Internet is the biggest and earliest manifestation of the way business is going to be conducted from now on. Networked information and communication are the standard for the future" [4]. For businesses, the information superhighway may be years away, but the Internet is available now.

Many businesses use the Internet primarily as a way to send E-mail messages to colleagues anywhere in the world. For example, IBM employees used the Internet to exchange 580,000 messages with outsiders in just one month [16]. Businesses also rely on the Internet to support worldwide collaboration among their employees and consultants, customers, and suppliers. They use the Internet to link their work-stations together to form *virtual work groups* to work on joint projects such as prod-uct development, marketing campaigns, and scientific research.

Another major business use of the Internet is gathering information. You can make online searches for information in a variety of ways, using World Wide Web browsing software like Netscape, or search engines such as Web Crawler and direc-tories like Yahoo. Hundreds of library catalogs from university libraries to the Library of Congress are available, as are electronic versions of numerous academic and industry publications. You can point and click your way to thousands of sites and their databases, downloading everything from the latest satellite weather photos from NASA to world almanac excerpts from the U.S. Central Intelligence Agency.

You can also gather information by sitting in electronically on thousands of com-puter conferences, work sessions, E-mail exchanges, and bulletin board postings run by the members of thousands of Internet special-interest groups. Or you could place your-self on the E-mail mailing list of any Internet special interest group, industry association, business, or government agency in which you have an interest. See Figure 4.13.

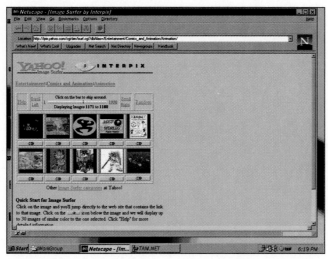

Courtesy of Yahoo.

Courtesy of Lycos.

FIGURE 4.13

You can access the resources of the Internet in a variety of ways, using directories like Yahoo or search engines like Lycos.

Other uses of the Internet are developing as more and more companies investigate its business potential. For example, many companies view the millions of members of the Internet as a vast market of potential customers. Thus, they have developed *home page* sites on the World Wide Web that provide multimedia versions of advertising, press releases, new product demonstrations, product catalogs, and shopping malls. However, since some early attempts by direct mail companies met with considerable resistance, and other businesses report little interest in their offerings, companies are now being more selective and creative in their approaches [15]. Still, the Internet is an electronic highway on which many companies are test driving their competitive business strategies to prepare for the information superhighway of the future. We will discuss such strategic business use of the Internet for competitive advantage in Chapter 9. See Figure 4.14.

FIGURE 4.14

Examples of corporate home
pages on the Internet's World
Wide Web. These are the
opening home pages of
Federal Express and UPS.

Courtesy of FedEx.

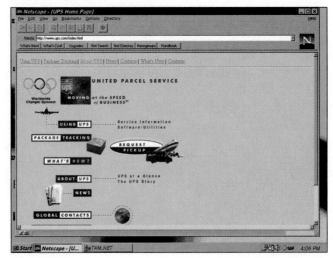

Courtesy of UPS.

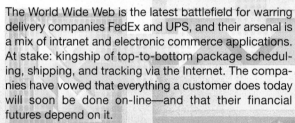

UPS VERSUS FEDEX: COMPETING ON THE WORLD WIDE WEB

The World Wide Web is the latest battlefield for warring delivery companies FedEx and UPS, and their arsenal is a mix of intranet and electronic commerce applications. At stake: kingship of top-to-bottom package scheduling, shipping, and tracking via the Internet. The companies have vowed that everything a customer does today will soon be done on-line—and that their financial futures depend on it.

"We're fanatics about the Web. It's hyperimportant to us," said Robert Hamilton, manager of electronic commerce marketing at FedEx Corp. in Memphis, Tennessee. The $9.4 billion company has a long-range goal of generating 100 percent of its business on-line.

No less adamant is United Parcel Service, Inc. "Our energy is the Internet. We know that's where we need to be," said Tom Hoffman, manager of public network access development in the customer automation group at UPS in Mahwah, New Jersey.

Many of the on-line applications that the firms have in the works aren't simple Web programs for interacting with customers. Nor are they strict, behind-the-firewall intranet applications. They are complicated hybrids—public Internet/intranet systems—that few users have tried. Let's look at some stats for both UPS and FedEx Systems:

UPS Internet Website
Web server software: Netscape Commerce Server
Hardware: Sun SPARCservers
Key services: Package tracking, rate calculations, transit maps
Traffic volume: 200,000 to 300,000 hits per week

UPS Intranet
Web browser: Netscape Navigator
Web server software: Netscape Communications Server
Hardware: Sun SPARCserver 1000s
Kinds of applications:
- Marketing and logistics groups analyze data collected from external Web site.
- Departmental newsgroups.
- Software distribution.

FedEx Internet Website
Web server software: Netscape Commerce Server
Hardware: Sun SPARC 1000s
Key services: Package tracking, delivery options, software downloads
Traffic volume: 280,000 to 420,000 hits per day

FedEx Intranet
Web browser: Netscape Navigator
Web server software: Netscape Communications Server
Hardware: Sun SPARCservers and HP 9000s
Kinds of applications:
- Mapping system to match customers with best or closest FedEx office.
- Imaging-based inventory system.
- Personnel manuals.

UPS beat FedEx to market with a Web site that can handle package scheduling and pickup from start to finish. That means anyone in a major metropolitan area who has a box to ship can surf to the UPS Web site, check delivery routes, calculate rates, and schedule a pickup. Payment is made off-line. Eventually, payment will be done on the Web by credit card or, for large, regular customers, via a tab tracked with on-line purchase orders.

Such a system requires data collected at the external Web site to be shunted in-house, melded with UPS's IBM mainframe and AS/400 scheduling system, and spit out in a Web-readable form for the waiting customer. UPS's information systems group has built connectors to translate Hypertext Markup Language and other Web languages to formats that are compatible with IBM databases. The tough part, Hoffman said, is designing a system that flows smoothly between the public Internet and the secured intranet realm.

Meanwhile, UPS and FedEx run neck-and-neck in Web-based package tracking functions that let users type in a package number and find out where it is. FedEx users track 13,000 packages daily that way. UPS customers track 10,000 packages per day.

CASE STUDY QUESTIONS

1. Why is the World Wide Web so important in the competition between UPS and FedEx?

2. How are the intranets of UPS and FedEx involved in their competition?

3. How might other kinds of businesses benefit from Internet/intranet systems like those of UPS and FedEx? Give several examples.

Source: Adapted from Kim Nash, "Overnight Services Duke It Out On-Line," *Computerworld,* April 22, 1996, pp. 1, 64. Copyright © 1996 by Computerworld Inc., Framingham, MA 01701—Reprinted from *Computerworld.*

Section II

Technical Telecommunications Alternatives

Telecommunications Alternatives

Telecommunications is a highly technical, rapidly changing field of information systems technology. Most end users do not need a detailed knowledge of its technical characteristics. However, it is necessary that you understand some of the important characteristics of the basic components of telecommunications networks. This understanding will help you participate effectively in decision making regarding telecommunications alternatives. Figure 4.15 outlines key telecommunications network components and alternatives. Remember, a basic understanding and appreciation, not a detailed knowledge, are sufficient for most business end users.

Telecommunications Media

Telecommunications channels (also called communications *lines* or *links*) are the means by which data and other forms of communications are transmitted between the sending and receiving devices in a telecommunications network. A telecommunications channel makes use of a variety of telecommunications media. These include twisted-pair wire, coaxial cables, and fiber optic cables, all of which physically link the devices in a network. Also included are terrestrial microwave, communications satellites, cellular and LAN radio, all of which use microwave and other radio waves, and infrared systems, which use infrared light to transmit and receive data. Figure 4.16 illustrates some of the major types of media used in modern telecommunications networks.

Twisted-Pair Wire

Ordinary telephone wire, consisting of copper wire twisted into pairs (*twisted-pair wire*) is the most widely used media for telecommunications. These lines are used in established communications networks throughout the world for both voice and data transmission. Thus, twisted-pair wiring is used extensively in home and office telephone systems and many local area networks and wide area networks. See Figure 4.17.

Coaxial Cable

Coaxial cable consists of a sturdy copper or aluminum wire wrapped with spacers to insulate and protect it. The cable's cover and insulation minimize interference and distortion of the signals the cable carries. Groups of coaxial cables may be bundled together in a big cable for ease of installation. These high-quality lines can be placed

---

FIGURE 4.15

Key telecommunications network components and alternatives.

Network Component	Examples of Alternatives
Media	Twisted-pair wire, coaxial cable, fiber optics, microwave radio, communications satellites, cellular and LAN radio, infrared
Processors	Modems, multiplexers, bridges, routers, hubs, gateways, front-end processors, private branch exchanges
Software	Telecommunications monitors, telecommunications access programs, network operating systems, end user communications packages
Channels	Analog/digital, switched/nonswitched, transmission speed, circuit/message/packet switching, simplex/duplex, asynchronous/synchronous
Topology/architecture	Point-to-point, multidrop, star/ring/bus, OSI, ISDN, TCP/IP

underground and laid on the floors of lakes and oceans. They allow high-speed data transmission and are used instead of twisted-pair wire lines in high-service metropolitan areas, for cable TV systems, and for short-distance connection of computers and peripheral devices. Coaxial cables are also used extensively in office buildings and other work sites for local area networks.

Fiber optics uses cables consisting of one or more hair-thin filaments of glass fiber wrapped in a protective jacket. They can conduct light pulses generated by lasers at transmission rates as high as 30 billion bits per second. This is about 60 times greater than coaxial cable and 3,000 times better than twisted-pair wire lines. Fiber optic cables provide substantial size and weight reductions as well as increased speed and greater carrying capacity. A half-inch-diameter fiber optic cable can carry up to 50,000 channels, compared to about 5,500 channels for a standard coaxial cable.

Fiber Optics

FIGURE 4.16

An example of the telecommunications media in a telecommunications channel. Note the use of a telecommunications satellite, earth stations with dish antennas, microwave links, fiber optic and coaxial cable, and a wireless LAN.

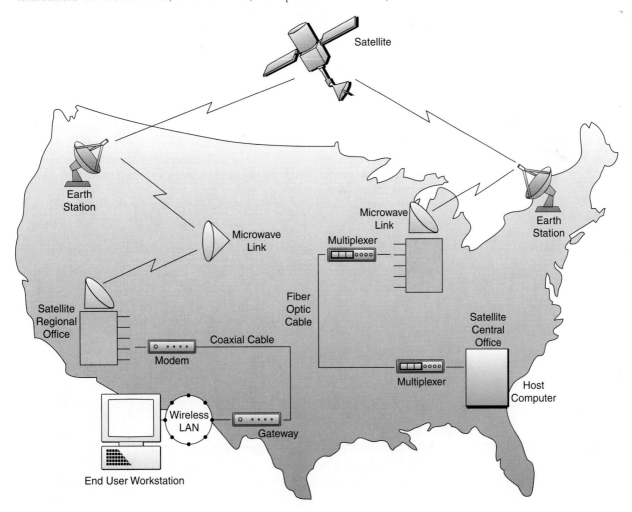

FIGURE 4.17

Telecommunications wire
and cable alternatives.

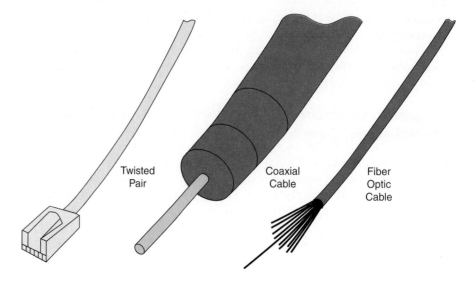

FIGURE 4.17

Telecommunications wire
and cable alternatives.

Fiber optic cables are not affected by and do not generate electromagnetic radiation; therefore, multiple fibers can be placed in the same cable. Fiber optic cables have a minimal need for repeaters for signal retransmissions, unlike electrical wire media. Fiber optics also has a much lower data error rate than other media and is harder to tap than electrical wire and cable. The biggest disadvantage of fiber optics has been the difficulty of splicing the cable to make connections, though this is also a security advantage that limits line tapping. However, new splicing techniques have made it easier to splice fiber cables. Fiber optic cables have already been installed in many parts of the United States, and they are expected to replace other communications media in many applications in the near future.

Terrestrial Microwave

Terrestrial microwave involves earthbound microwave systems that transmit high-speed radio signals in a line-of-sight path between relay stations spaced approximately 30 miles apart. Microwave antennas are usually placed on top of buildings, towers, hills, and mountain peaks, and they are a familiar sight in many sections of the country. They are still a popular medium for both long-distance and metropolitan area networks.

Communications Satellites

An important telecommunications medium is the use of **communications satellites** for microwave transmission. There are several dozen communications satellites from several nations placed into stationary *geosynchronous* orbits approximately 22,000 miles above the equator. Satellites are powered by solar panels and can transmit microwave signals at a rate of several hundred million bits per second. They serve as relay stations for communication signals transmitted from *earth* stations. Earth stations use *dish antennas* to beam microwave signals to the satellites that amplify and retransmit the signals to other earth stations thousands of miles away.

While communications satellites were used initially for voice and video transmission, they are now also used for high-speed transmission of large volumes of data. Because of time delays caused by the great distances involved, they are not suitable for interactive, real-time processing. Communications satellite systems are operated by several firms, including AT&T, Western Union, American Satellite Company, and Intellsat, an international consortium of more than 100 nations.

Many large corporations and other users have developed networks of small satellite dish antennas known as VSAT (very-small-aperture terminal) to connect their distant work areas. These satellite networks are also called *bypass networks* because firms are bypassing the regular communications networks provided by communications carriers.

Cellular radio is the radio communications technology that makes cellular phones possible. It divides a metropolitan area into a honeycomb of cells. This greatly increases the number of frequencies and users that can take advantage of mobile phone service. Each cell has its own low-power transmitter, rather than having one high-powered radio transmitter to serve an entire city. This significantly increases the number of radio frequencies available for mobile phone service. However, this technology requires a central computer and other communications equipment to coordinate and control the transmissions of thousands of mobile phone users as they drive from one cell to another.

Cellular Radio

Cellular radio has become an important communications medium for mobile voice and data communications. For example, Federal Express uses cellular radio for data communications with terminals in each of its thousands of delivery vans as part of its competitive edge. The integration of cellular and other mobile radio technologies is expected to accelerate in the next few years. This will provide a full range of mobile computing capabilities to laptop computer users [25].

Wiring an office or a building for a local area network is often a difficult and costly task. Older buildings frequently do not have conduits for coaxial cables or additional twisted-pair wire, and the conduits in newer buildings may not have enough room to pull additional wiring through. Repairing mistakes and damages to wiring is often difficult and costly, as are major relocations of LAN workstations and other components.

Wireless LANs

One increasingly popular solution to such problems is installing a wireless LAN, using one of several wireless technologies. One example is LAN radio that uses radio transmissions to interconnect LAN components. LAN radio may involve a high-frequency radio technology similar to cellular radio, or a low-frequency radio technology called *spread spectrum*. The other wireless LAN technology is called infrared because it uses beams of infrared light to establish network links between LAN components. See Figure 4.18.

Obviously, a wireless LAN eliminates or greatly reduces the need for wires and cables, thus making a LAN easier to set up, relocate, and maintain. However, current wireless technologies have higher initial costs and other limitations. For example, an infrared LAN transmits faster than radio LANs but is limited to line-of-sight arrangements to a maximum of about 80 feet between components. High-frequency radio LANs do not need line-of-sight links, but are limited to 40 to 70 feet between components in enclosed areas. Spread spectrum radio LANs can penetrate masonry walls and link components from 100 to 200 feet away in enclosed areas, but are more subject to receiving or generating radio interference. However, even with these limitations, the use of wireless LAN technologies is expected to increase significantly [3].

Telecommunications channels for wide area networks can be owned by an organization or provided by other companies. In the United States, several companies have traditionally used a variety of communications media to create networks that can provide a broad range of communications services.

Telecommunications Carriers

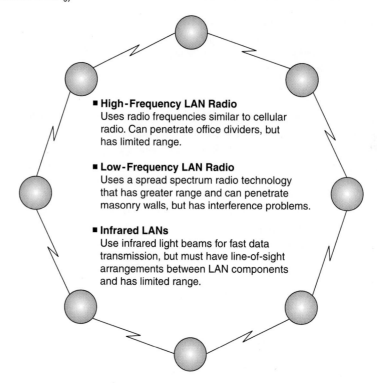

FIGURE 4.18

Three competing wireless LAN technologies. Note the benefits and limitations of each.

- **High-Frequency LAN Radio**
  Uses radio frequencies similar to cellular radio. Can penetrate office dividers, but has limited range.

- **Low-Frequency LAN Radio**
  Uses a spread spectrum radio technology that has greater range and can penetrate masonry walls, but has interference problems.

- **Infrared LANs**
  Use infrared light beams for fast data transmission, but must have line-of-sight arrangements between LAN components and has limited range.

Common Carriers

These **common carriers** provide the wide area communications networks used by most computer-using firms and individuals. They have traditionally been authorized by government agencies to provide a selected number of communication services to the public. Examples are the former Bell operating companies, General Telephone and Electronics, Western Union, and many independent telephone companies. Some common carriers specialize in selling long-distance voice and digital data communications services in high-density areas of the country and the world. Examples of such specialized carriers are AT&T Long Distance, ITT World Communications, Southern Pacific Communications, U.S. Sprint, and MCI Communications.

Common carriers can provide an organization needing the data communications capabilities of a wide area telecommunications network with several options. For example, an organization could use regular, voice-grade, direct-distance dialing (DDD) that is more expensive, slower, and less reliable than other options due to delays caused by excessive communications traffic and the noise of voice-switching circuits. Or it could sign up for a wide area telephone service (WATS) and pay a monthly fee and a per hour fee for use of a set amount of telephone line capacity. This would be cheaper for an organization with a lot of communications activity, but it would have the same reliability problem as DDD.

A company could lease its own communications lines (called *leased lines*) from telephone companies and be guaranteed exclusive use of a low-noise, fast communications channel. However, this is an expensive alternative that is economically feasible only for large corporations and government agencies with massive data communications needs. Another expensive option is the use of a company that provides communications satellite services. Or an organization could build a *bypass* system, in which it installs its own dish antennas and bypasses the common carrier networks and transmits directly to communications satellites. Once again, this is a more expensive alternative attractive only to organizations with a high volume of data communications.

Value-Added Carriers

Other major communications carriers are companies called value-added carriers. These are third-party vendors who lease communications lines from common carriers and offer communications services to customers. Typically, messages from customers are transmitted in groupings called packets, via *packet-switching* networks. However, the networks of such carriers are known as *value-added networks* (VANs), because they add value to their leased communications lines by using communications hardware and software and their expertise to provide not only packet switching but other data communications services. Value-added networks also take over the responsibility for the management of the network, thus relieving their customers of the technical problems inherent in long-distance communications.

Value-added carriers offer their customers, or *subscribers,* high-quality, relatively low-cost service in return for a membership fee and usage charges based on the amount of communications activity accomplished. By spreading the cost of leasing the lines among many subscribers and using the capacity of the lines intensively, they are able to sell their services at attractive prices and still make a profit. Examples of value-added companies are GTE Telenet, General Electric's Mark Net, and Compunet by CompuServe. These VANs have become so popular that common carriers such as the Bell operating companies, AT&T, MCI, and Western Union and large corporations such as IBM and RCA now offer VAN services.

Telecommunications Processors

Telecommunications processors such as modems, multiplexers, bridges, front-end processors, and other devices perform a variety of support functions between the terminals and computers in a telecommunications network. Let's take a look at some of these devices and their functions. See Figure 4.19.

Modems

Modems are the most common type of communications processor. They convert the digital signals from a computer or transmission terminal at one end of a communications link into analog frequencies that can be transmitted over ordinary telephone lines. A modem at the other end of the communications line converts the transmitted data back into digital form at a receiving terminal. This process is known as *modulation* and *demodulation,* and the word *modem* is a combined abbreviation of those two words. Modems come in several forms, including small stand-alone units, plug-in circuit boards, and microelectric modem chips. Many modems also support a variety of telecommunications interface functions, such as transmission error control, automatic dialing and answering, and a faxing capability.

Modems are used because ordinary telephone networks were primarily designed to handle continuous analog signals (electromagnetic frequencies), such as those generated by the human voice over the telephone. Since data from computers are in digital form (voltage pulses), devices are necessary to convert digital signals into appropriate analog transmission frequencies and vice versa. However, digital communications networks that transmit only digital signals and do not need analog/digital conversion are becoming commonplace. Since most modems also perform a variety of telecommunications support functions, modems may still be needed in digital networks. See Figure 4.20.

FIGURE 4.19

A summary of important communications processors.

- **Modem:** Serves as a telecommunications interface for personal computers and converts transmissions from digital to analog and back.
- **Multiplexer:** Allows a single communications channel to carry simultaneous data transmissions from many terminals.
- **Internetwork processor:** Includes bridges, routers, hubs, and gateways that interconnect a local area network with other local and wide area networks.
- **Private branch exchange:** Switches external and internal voice and data transmissions over telephone lines within an office or other work area.
- **Front-end processor:** Handles data communications control and network management functions for a larger computer.

Multiplexers

A **multiplexer** is a communications processor that allows a single communications channel to carry simultaneous data transmissions from many terminals. Thus, a single communications line can be shared by several terminals. Typically, a multiplexer merges the transmissions of several terminals at one end of a communications channel, while a similar unit separates the individual transmissions at the receiving end.

This is accomplished in two basic ways. In *frequency division multiplexing* (FDM), a multiplexer effectively divides a high-speed channel into multiple slow-speed channels. In *time division muliplexing* (TDM), the multiplexer divides the time each terminal can use the high-speed line into very short time slots, or time frames. The most advanced and popular type of multiplexer is the *statistical time division multiplexer,* most commonly referred to as a statistical multiplexer. Instead of giving all terminals equal time slots, it dynamically allocates time slots only to active terminals according to priorities assigned by a telecommunications manager.

Internetwork Processors

As we have previously mentioned, many local area networks are interconnected by **internetwork processors** such as *bridges, routers, hubs,* or *gateways* to other LANs or wide area networks. A *bridge* is a communications processor that connects two similar LANs, that is, LANs based on the same network standards or *protocols.* A *router* is a communications processor that connects LANs to networks based on different protocols. A *hub* is a port switching communications processor. Advanced versions of hubs provide automatic switching among connections called *ports* for shared access to a network's resources. LAN workstations, servers, printers, and other LAN resources are connected to ports, as are bridges and routers provided by the hub to other LANs and WANs. Networks that use different communications architectures are interconnected by using a communications processor called a *gateway.* All these

FIGURE 4.20

Modems perform a modulation-demodulation process that converts digital signals to analog and back.

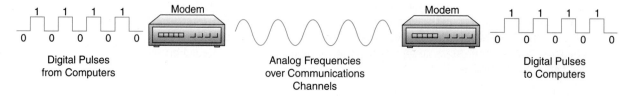

devices are essential to providing connectivity and easy access between the multiple LANs within an organization and the wide area networks connecting them to other company locations and organizations.

The **private branch exchange** (PBX) is a communications processor that serves as a switching device between the telephone lines within a work area and the local telephone company's main telephone lines, or *trunks*. PBXs can be as small as a telephone or as large as a minicomputer. They not only route telephone calls within an office but also provide other services, such as automatic forwarding of calls, conference calling, and least-cost routing of long-distance calls. Some PBX models can control communications among the terminals, computers, and other information processing devices in local area networks in offices and other work areas. Other PBXs can integrate the switching of voice, data, and images in *integrated services digital networks* (ISDN) that we will be discussing shortly.

A **front-end processor** is typically a minicomputer dedicated to handling the data communications control functions for large mainframe host computers. For example, a front-end processor uses telecommunications control programs to provide temporary buffer storage; data coding and decoding; error detection; recovery; and the recording, interpreting, and processing of control information (such as characters that indicate the beginning and end of a message). It can also poll remote terminals to determine if they have a message to send or if they are ready to receive a message.

A front-end processor also has other, more advanced responsibilities. It controls access to a network and allows only authorized users to use the system, assigns priorities to messages, logs all data communications activity, computes statistics on network activity, and routes and reroutes messages among alternative communication links. Thus, the front-end processor can relieve the host computer of its data communications control functions so it can concentrate on its other information processing chores.

Software is a vital component of all telecommunications networks. **Telecommunications control software** includes programs stored in the host computer as well as programs in front-end computers and other communications processors. Such software controls and supports the communications occurring in a telecommunications network. For example, telecommunications software packages for mainframe-based wide area networks are frequently called telecommunications monitors or *teleprocessing (TP) monitors*. CICS (Customer Identification Control System) for IBM mainframes is a typical example. Local area networks rely on software called **network operating systems,** such as Novell NetWare or Microsoft LAN Manager. Many times, telecommunications software known as *middleware* can help diverse systems communicate with each other. A variety of communications software packages are also available for microcomputers, including those for accessing the Internet, as we discussed earlier and in Chapter 3. See Figure 4.21.

Telecommunications software packages provide a variety of communications support services. The number and type of terminals, computers, communications processors, and communications activities involved determine the capabilities of the program required. However, several major functions are commonly provided by telecommunications packages.

Private Branch Exchange

Front-End Processors

Telecommunications Software

Common Software Functions

Access Control

This function establishes the connections between terminals and computers in a network. The software works with a communications processor (such as a modem) to connect and disconnect communications links and establish communications parameters such as transmission speed, mode, and direction. Access control may also involve automatic telephone dialing and redialing, logging on and off with appropriate account numbers and security codes, and automatic answering of telephone calls from another computer. Many communications packages include a *script language* that allows you to develop programs to customize access control, such as accessing other computers at night or while you are away.

Transmission Control

This function allows computers and terminals to send and receive commands, messages, data, and programs. Some error checking and correction of data transmissions may also be provided. Data and programs are usually transmitted in the form of files, so this activity is frequently called *file transfer*.

Network Management

This function manages communications in a telecommunications network. Software such as LAN network operating systems and WAN telecommunications monitors determines transmission priorities; routes (switches) messages, polls, and terminals in the network; and forms waiting lines (*queues*) of transmission requests. It also logs statistics of network activity and the use of network resources by end user workstations.

Error Control

This function involves detection and correction of transmission errors. Errors are usually caused by distortions in the communications channel, such as line noise and power surges. Communications software and processors control errors in transmission by several methods, including *parity checking*. Parity checking involves determining whether there is an odd or even number of *binary one digits* in a character being transmitted or received. Besides parity bits, additional *control codes* are usually added to the message

FIGURE 4.21

This display of a telecommunications monitor shows the status of local area and wide area networks.

Matthew Borkoski/Stock Boston.

itself. These specify such information as the destination of the data, their priority, and the beginning and end of the message, plus additional error detecting and correcting information. Most error correction methods involve retransmissions. A signal is sent back to the computer or terminal to retransmit the previous message.

This function protects a communications network from unauthorized access. Network operating systems or other security programs restrict access to data files and other computing resources in LANs and other types of networks. This restriction usually involves control procedures that limit access to all or parts of a network by various categories of users, as determined by the *network manager* or *administrator* of the network. Automatic disconnection and callback procedures may also be used. Data transmissions can also be protected by coding techniques called **encryption.** Data are scrambled into a coded form before transmission and decoded upon arrival.

Security Management

There are several basic types of network **topologies,** or structures, in telecommunications networks. The two simplest are *point-to-point* lines and *multidrop* lines. When point-to-point lines are used, each terminal is connected by its own line to a computer system. When multidrop lines are used, several terminals share each data communications line to a computer. Obviously point-to-point lines are more expensive than multidrop lines; all of the communications capacity and equipment of a communications line is being used by a single terminal. Therefore, point-to-point lines are used only if there will be continuous communications between a computer and a terminal or other computer system. A multidrop line decreases communications costs, because each line is shared by many terminals. Communications processors such as multiplexers and concentrators help many terminals share the same line. See Figure 4.22.

Telecommunications Network Topologies

Figure 4.23 illustrates three basic topologies used in wide area and local area telecommunications networks. A **star network** ties end user computers to a central computer. A **ring network** ties local computer processors together in a ring on a more equal basis. A **bus network** is a network in which local processors share the same bus, or communications channel. In many cases, star networks take the form of hierarchical networks. In hierarchical networks, a large headquarters computer at the top of the company's hierarchy is connected to medium-size computers at the divisional level that

Star, Ring, and Bus Networks

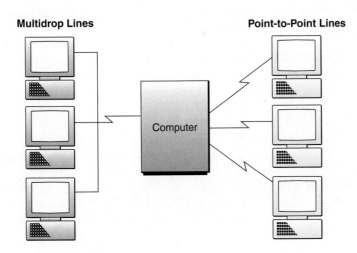

Multidrop Lines   **Point-to-Point Lines**

Computer

FIGURE 4.22

Multidrop lines allow terminals to share a communications line. Point-to-point lines provide a separate communications line for each terminal.

FIGURE 4.23

The star, ring, and bus network topologies.

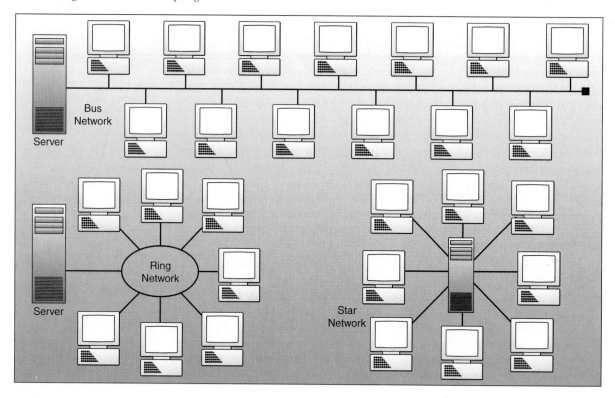

are connected to small computers at the departmental or work group level. A variation of the ring network is the *mesh* network. This uses direct communications lines to connect some or all of the computers in the ring to each other. Another variation is the tree network that joins several bus networks together.

In most cases, distributed processing systems use a combination of star, ring, and bus approaches. Obviously, the star network is more centralized, while ring and bus networks have a more decentralized approach. However, this is not always the case. For example, the central computer in a star configuration may be acting only as a **switch**, or message-switching computer, that handles the data communications between autonomous local computers.

Star, ring, and bus networks differ in their performances, reliabilities, and costs. A pure star network is considered less reliable than a ring network, since the other computers in the star are heavily dependent on the central host computer. If it fails, there is no backup processing and communications capability, and the local computers are cut off from the corporate headquarters and from each other. Therefore, it is essential that the host computer be highly reliable. Having some type of *multiprocessor architecture* to provide a *fault tolerant* capability is a common solution.

Star network variations are common because they can support the *chain-of-command* and hierarchical structures of most organizations. Ring and bus networks are most common in local area networks. Ring networks are considered more reliable and less costly for the type of communications in such networks. If one computer in the ring goes down, the other computers can continue to process their own work as well as to communicate with each other.

Until quite recently, there was a lack of sufficient standards for the interfaces between the hardware, software, and communications channels of data communication networks. For this reason, it is quite common to find a lack of compatibility between the data communications hardware and software of different manufacturers. This situation has hampered the use of data communications, increased its costs, and reduced its efficiency and effectiveness. In response, computer manufacturers and national and international organizations have developed standards called *protocols* and master plans called *network architectures* to support the development of advanced data communications networks.

A **protocol** is a standard set of rules and procedures for the control of communications in a network. However, these standards may be limited to just one manufacturer's equipment, or to just one type of data communications. Part of the goal of communications network architectures is to create more standardization and compatibility among communications protocols. One example of a protocol is a standard for the physical characteristics of the cables and connectors between terminals, computers, modems, and communications lines. Other examples are the protocols that establish the communications control information needed for *handshaking,* which is the process of exchanging predetermined signals and characters to establish a telecommunications session between terminals and computers. Other protocols deal with control of data transmission reception in a network, switching techniques, internetwork connections, and so on.

The goal of **network architectures** is to promote an open, simple, flexible, and efficient telecommunications environment. This is accomplished by the use of standard protocols, standard communications hardware and software interfaces, and the design of a standard multilevel interface between end users and computer systems.

The International Standards Organization (ISO) has developed a seven-layer Open Systems Interconnection (OSI) model to serve as a standard model for network architectures. By dividing data communications functions into seven distinct layers, the ISO hopes to promote the development of modular network architectures. This would assist the development, operation, and maintenance of large telecommunications networks. Figure 4.24 illustrates the functions of the seven levels of the OSI model architecture.

Examples of network architectures include IBM's System Network Architecture (SNA) and DECnet by the Digital Equipment Corporation. An important suite of protocols that has become so widely used that it is equivalent to a network architecture is the Internet's Transmission Control Protocol/Internet Protocol known as TCP/IP. Another example is the local area network architecture for automated factories sponsored by General Motors and other manufacturers called the Manufacturing Automation Protocol (MAP).

Related to the development of network architectures is the development of a set of standards for ISDN, the Integrated Services Digital Network. This is a set of international standards needed to establish public and private digital telecommunications networks capable of handling voice, data, image, and video communications throughout the world. Many communications carriers and corporations are developing, testing, and installing ISDN networks.

ISDN promises to revolutionize telecommunications and networking. If ISDN is fully implemented, voice, video, and data transmissions would be available through your telephone company and the normal twisted-pair telephone wiring of your office or

Network Architectures and Protocols

Protocols

Network Architectures

The OSI Model and Other Architectures

Integrated Services Digital Network

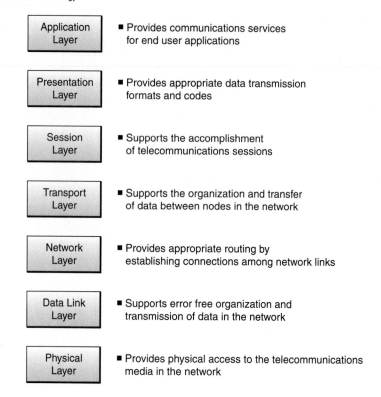

FIGURE 4.24
The seven layers of the OSI communications network architecture. The OSI model is recognized as an international standard for telecommunications networks.

home just by plugging your computer or *videophone* into a telephone wall socket. So ISDN will enable end users to enjoy multimedia computing and communications. However, much more development work remains to be done by communications carriers, computer manufacturers, and end user organizations. ISDN's technology must still be perfected, costs must become competitive, and organizations must learn how to use this new communications service. Only then will the promise of ISDN become a reality.

Communications Channel Characteristics

The communication capabilities of telecommunications channels can be classified by *bandwidth*. This is the frequency range of the channel; it determines the channel's maximum transmission rate. Data transmission rates are typically measured in bits per second (BPS). This is sometimes referred to as the *baud* rate, though baud is more correctly a measure of signal changes in a transmission line.

Transmission Speed

Voiceband, or low-speed analog, channels are typically used for transmission rates from 300 to 9,600 BPS, but can now handle up to 1 million BPS (MBPS). They are usually unshielded twisted-pair lines commonly used for voice communications, but are also used for data communications by microcomputers, video terminals, and fax machines. *Medium-band,* or medium-speed, channels use shielded twisted-pair lines for transmission speeds from 9,600 BPS up to 10 MBPS.

    Broadband, or high-speed digital, channels allow transmission rates at specific intervals from 256,000 BPS to several billion BPS. Typically, they use microwave, fiber optics, or satellite transmission. Examples are 1.54 million BPS for TI communications channels developed by AT&T and up to 100 MBPS for satellite channels used by many large private communications networks. See Figure 4.25.

Type of Media	Maximum Speeds
Twisted pair—unshielded	2 MBPS
Twisted pair—shielded	100 MBPS
Coaxial cable—baseband	264 MBPS
Coaxial cable—broadband	550 MBPS
Terrestrial microwave	100 MBPS
Satellite microwave	100 MBPS
LAN radio	3.3 MBPS
Infrared LAN	4 MBPS
Fiber optic cable	30 GBPS

FIGURE 4.25

Examples of telecommunications transmission speeds by type of media and type of network.

Type of Network	Typical Speeds
LAN (standard Ethernet or token ring)	10–16 MBPS
LAN (high-speed Ethernet)	100 MBPS
LAN (FDDI: fiber distributed data interface)	100 MBPS
WAN (DDN: digital data network)	2.4 KBPS–2 MBPS
WAN (PSN: packet switching network)	2.4 KBPS–64 KBPS
WAN (frame relay network)	9.6 KBPS–2 MBPS
WAN (ISDN: integrated services digital network)	64 KBPS–2MBPS
LAN and WAN (ATM: asynchronous transfer mode)	25–622 MBPS

KBPS = thousand BPS or kilobits per second.   GBPS = billion BPS or gigabits per second.
MBPS = million BPS or megabits per second.

Source: Adapted in part from John Vargo and Ray Hunt, *Telecommunications in Business: Strategy and Application* (Burr Ridge, IL: Richard D. Irwin, 1996), p. 173.

Transmission Mode

The two modes of transmitting data are called *asynchronous* and *synchronous* transmission. Asynchronous transmission transmits one character at a time, with each character preceded by a *start bit* and followed by a *stop bit*. Asynchronous transmission is normally used for low-speed transmission at rates less than 2,400 BPS. Synchronous transmission transmits groups of characters at a time, with the beginning and end of a character determined by the timing circuitry of a communications processor. Synchronous transmission is normally used for high-speed transmission exceeding 2,400 BPS.

Switching Alternatives

Regular telephone service relies on *circuit switching,* in which a circuit is opened to establish a link between a sender and receiver; it remains open until the communication session is completed. In *message switching,* a message is transmitted a block at a time from one switching device to another. This method is sometimes called store-and-forward transmission because messages may be temporarily stored by the switching device before being retransmitted.

Packet switching involves subdividing communications messages into groups called packets. For example, many packets are 128 characters long. The packet switching network is typically operated by a value-added carrier who uses computers and other communications processors to control the packet switching process and transmit the packets of various users over its leased lines.

Many packet switching networks are *X.25 networks.* The X.25 protocol is an international set of standards governing the operations of widely used, but relatively slow packet switching networks. *Frame relay* is another popular packet switching protocol. Frame relay is considerably faster than X.25, and is better able to handle the heavy telecommunications traffic of interconnected local area networks within a company's wide area network. ATM (*asynchronous transfer mode*) is an emerging high capacity packet switching technology based on the broadband ISDN (B-ISDN) international protocol. ATM networks are being developed by companies needing its fast, high-capacity multimedia capabilities for voice, video, and data communications among their internetworked end users.

Access Methods

How can terminals and other devices access and share a network to transmit and receive data? As Figure 4.26 indicates, a variety of *access methods* provide this capacity. In the *polling* approach, a host computer or communications processor polls (contacts) each terminal in sequence to determine which terminals have messages to send. The sequence in which the terminals are polled is based on the communications traffic expected from each terminal. Thus, the transmission of each terminal is based on a roll call of each terminal on the line. Polling can be an effective method because the speed of mainframe and communications processor computers allows them to poll and control transmissions by many terminals sharing the same line, especially if typical communications consist of brief messages and inquiries.

In the *contention approach,* line use is on a first-come, first-served basis, where a terminal can transmit data if the line is not in use but must wait if it is busy. One way to make contention work is a widely used method called *carrier-sense multiple access with collision detection* (CSMA/CD). This requires a terminal or other device to continually monitor the network and send a message only if it senses the network is not in use. If a collision is detected, the terminal must stop transmission, wait until the network is clear, and try again. This access method is used by the Ethernet standard for local area networks.

Another widely used method in local area networks is *token passing.* A token is a special signal code sent around the network. If a terminal or other device wants to transmit a message, it must wait for the token to come by, examine it to see if it is in use, and pass it on or use the token to help route its message to its destination on the network. After transmission is completed, the token is returned to the network by the receiving terminal if it is not needed. This access method is used in all *token ring* local area networks, the Datapoint and MAP *token bus* networks, and the high-speed fiber optic–based token ring LAN standard known as Fiber Distributed Data Interface or FDDI.

FIGURE 4.26

Common telecommunications access methods.

- **Polling.** A communications processor conducts a roll call of the terminals in a network to determine if they have messages to send.
- **Contention.** Terminals send messages on the network on a first-come, first-served basis.
- **Token passing.** Terminals use an electronic signal code, or *token,* to send messages that are passed on to the appropriate terminal in the network.

THE BOEING COMPANY: PIONEERING A CORPORATE INTRANET

In the fall of 1993, a handful of engineers, technologists, and researchers hovered over their PCs at the Seattle offices of the Boeing Co., trying to make sense of a graphical portal to the Internet known as Mosaic. The World Wide Web was in its infancy then, but the group, dubbed the Webmasters, looked into the future and saw the makings of an inexpensive network that would allow its employees to easily share information.

More than two years later, the Boeing Web has 300 servers and 20,000 users; by the end of the year, at least 80 percent of Boeing's 96,000 U.S. employees will have access to the corporate intranet, said Joe Meadows, one of the founders of the Boeing Web and product manager at Boeing's Information Support Services division in Seattle.

While the Webmasters could not quantify a return on investment for the intranet, they were able to sell Boeing's top management on the project's low cost and high flexibility. Freeware Web servers and browsers formed the software base, enabling any user on any platform to access and view documents, share information, and exchange E-mail.

"When we started this project, upper management wanted a business case made," said Meadows, "But the benefits of the Boeing Web are not easily found. How do you put a price on information? It's like trying to find a ROI for the telephone when it first appeared."

While Boeing's UNIX and mainframe LAN E-mail systems are still in place, the Boeing Web is poised to replace or consolidate UNIX and mainframe document management and communications platforms currently in use.

"The Boeing Web is used for just about everything today," said Meadows. "Web servers allow us to create a 'pull' information system, rather than pushing information out to employees, who could care less about certain items."

Access to the intranet is open to any employee, though one of the biggest challenges is to continue to enhance and preserve the security of the Boeing Web from outsiders, said Meadows. Currently, the Boeing Web is walled off from the rest of the Internet, with Boeing employees gaining access through two centrally managed servers.

Employees who log onto the Boeing Web are directed to a central directory server that highlights new or current Web sites. Boeing employees and business units, in fact, are encouraged to create Web sites of their own—using more freeware site-development tools—to keep the company informed of projects, meeting schedules, or other collaborations, said Meadows.

As the Internet matures, Boeing is looking to expand its use of Internet Web technologies both internally and externally. Over the next few months, it plans to convert to a commercial browser—it is evaluating Netscape Navigator, Microsoft Internet Explorer, and Spyglass Mosaic—to take advantage of encryption and authentication capabilities, said Ann Bassetti, Boeing's Web product manager. Boeing also is beginning to evaluate a Web server for Windows NT.

Another major project under way is the creation of a centralized authentication registry of users that will allow the company to post more sensitive documents on its Web servers, said Meadows.

Along the same lines, Boeing is looking to tie some of its 131 customers into its intranet to share maintenance information and manuals, which currently take up reams of paper. So the Boeing Web is expanding by interconnecting with the intranets of its airline and government customers.

CASE STUDY QUESTIONS

1. How important is the Boeing Web intranet to Boeing users and management?
2. Why is Boeing improving and expanding their intranet?
3. What are the uses and benefits of an intranet to a business?

Source: Adapted from Michael Moeller, "Boeing Network Takes Flight with Pioneering Intranet Project," *PC Week*, February 19, 1996, pp. 1, 105. Reprinted from *PC Week.* Copyright © 1996 Ziff-Davis Publishing Company, L.P.

Summary

- **Telecommunications Trends.** The information systems of many organizations depend on telecommunications networks to service the communications and information processing needs of their end users. Telecommunications has entered a competitive environment with many vendors, carriers, and services. Telecommunications technology is moving toward integrated digital networks for voice, data, and video, and the pervasive use of the technology to build interconnected global networks, like the Internet, that form information superhighways to support business operations, managerial decision making, and strategic advantage in a global economy.

- **Telecommunications Networks.** The major components of a telecommunications network are (1) terminals, (2) telecommunications processors, (3) communications channels and media, (4) computers, and (5) telecommunications control software. There are two basic types of telecommunications networks: wide area networks (WANs) and local area networks (LANs). WANs cover a wide geographic area, while LANs interconnect end user workstations and other devices at local work sites. Both types of networks are being interconnected to form internetworks such as the Internet, corporate intranets, and interorganizational networks.

- **Client/Server Computing.** Telecommunications networks are being used to support client/server computing as organizations move away from centralized mainframe-based networks. In client/server networks, end user microcomputer workstations (clients) are interconnected within a local area network whose hardware, software, and database resources are managed by a LAN server. Application processing may be shared among clients and servers within a LAN, or by interconnections with clients and servers in other LANs and wide area networks in a cooperative processing approach.

- **Network Alternatives.** Key telecommunications network alternatives and components are summarized in Figure 4.15 for telecommunications media, processors, software, channels, and network architectures. A basic understanding of these major alternatives will help managerial end users participate effectively in decisions involving telecommunications issues. Telecommunications processors include modems, multiplexers, and various devices to help enhance the capacity and efficiency of telecommunications channels. Telecommunications channels include such media as twisted-pair wire, coaxial cables, fiber optic cables, terrestrial microwave, communications satellites, cellular and LAN radio, and infrared systems. Use of public communications channels is provided by companies called common carriers and value-added carriers who offer a variety of telecommunications services. Telecommunications software consists of a variety of programs that control and support the communications occurring in a telecommunications network.

Key Terms and Concepts

These are the key terms and concepts of this chapter. The page number of their first explanation is in parentheses.

1. Applications of telecommunications (121)
2. Business use of the Internet (134)
3. Cellular radio (141)
4. Client/server computing (129)
5. Coaxial cable (138)
6. Common carriers (142)
7. Communications satellites (140)
8. Cooperative processing (132)
9. Distributed processing (131)
10. Fiber optic cables (140)
11. Front-end processors (145)
12. Host computer (126)
13. Information superhighway (124)
14. The Internet (133)
15. Internetwork processors (128)
16. Internetworks (128)
17. Interorganizational networks (132)
18. Intranets (128)
19. Local area network (127)
20. Modem (143)
21. Multiplexer (144)
22. Network operating system (127)
23. Network server (127)
24. Open systems (123)
25. Private branch exchange (145)
26. Protocol (149)
27. Telecommunications channels and media (125)
28. Telecommunications control software (126)
29. Telecommunications network (125)
    a. Architecture
    b. Components
    c. Topology
30. Telecommunications processors (125)
31. Trends in telecommunications (122)
32. Value-added carriers (143)
33. Wide area network (126)
34. Wireless LANs (141)

Review Quiz

Match one of the key terms and concepts listed above with one of the brief examples or definitions listed below. Try to find the best fit for answers that seem to fit more than one term or concept. Defend your choices.

_____ 1. Fundamental changes have occurred in the competitive environment, the technology, and the applications of telecommunications.

_____ 2. Includes terminals, telecommunications processors, channels and media, computers, and control software.

_____ 3. A communications network covering a large geographic area.

_____ 4. A communications network in an office, a building, or other work site.

_____ 5. Provide a variety of communications networks and services.

_____ 6. They lease lines from common carriers and offer telecommunications services.

_____ 7. Includes coaxial cable, microwave, fiber optics, and satellites.

_____ 8. A communications medium that uses pulses of laser light in glass fibers.

_____ 9. Supports mobile data communications in urban areas.

_____ 10. Includes modems, multiplexers, and front-end processors.

_____ 11. Includes programs for control of communications access, transmission, networks, errors, and security.

_____ 12. A common communications processor for microcomputers.

_____ 13. Helps a communications channel carry simultaneous data transmissions from many terminals.

_____ 14. The main computer in a data communications network.

_____ 15. A minicomputer dedicated to handling communications functions for a mainframe.

_____ 16. A computer that handles resource sharing and telecommunications in a local area network.

_____ 17. Handles the switching of both voice and data in an office.

_____ 18. The software that manages a local area network.

_____ 19. A standard, multilevel interface to promote compatibility among telecommunications networks.

_____ 20. A standard set of rules and procedures for control of communications in a network.

_____ 21. Information systems with common standards that provide easy access to end users and their networked computer systems.

_____ 22. Interconnected networks need communications processors such as bridges, routers, hubs, and gateways.

_____ 23. Most networks are connected to other local area or wide area networks.

_____ 24. A global network of millions of business, government, educational, and research networks, computer systems, and end users.

_____ 25. A proposed national network of interconnected local, regional, and global networks that would support interactive voice, data, video, and multimedia communications.

_____ 26. Telecommunications can support a wide range of business uses.

_____ 27. Using the Internet for corporate communications, information retrieval, collaborative computing, and marketing.

_____ 28. End user workstations are tied to LAN servers to share application processing.

_____ 29. Computers at central and local sites interconnected by a network.

_____ 30. Networked computers sharing the processing of parts of an end user's applications.

_____ 31. Telecommunications networks interconnect an organization with its customers and suppliers.

_____ 32. Internetlike organizational and interorganizational networks.

Discussion Questions

1. Some people argue that one can no longer separate telecommunications from computing in business. Do you agree or disagree? Why?

2. Why is there a trend toward open systems in computing and telecommunications?

3. In what way does the Internet and corporate intranets indicate a trend in the business use of telecommunications?

4. Refer to the Real World Case on UPS and FedEx in the chapter and the intranet applications for each company. What benefits do such applications provide by being available on an intranet to company employees?

5. Why have local area networks become so popular? What management problems are posed by the use of LANs?

6. What examples can you give that trends in telecommunications include: (*a*) more telecommunications providers, (*b*) a greater variety of telecommunications services, and (*c*) an increased use of telecommunications applications in business?

7. What telecommunications applications in business are most vital for business success? Defend your choices.

8. Refer to the Real World Case on the Boeing Company in the chapter. Should every business establish an intranet? Why or why not?

9. How realistic is the concept of a national information superhighway? How valuable would the superhighway be for consumers, business, and the nation's economy?

10. What is the Internet's business significance, compared to commercial networks such as America Online, CompuServe, and Prodigy?

Real World Problems

1. Tyson Foods: Creating an Intranet

The Internet is undeniably one of the hottest business tools around. Vendors use it to sell products. Companies use it to distribute information such as product specs and up-to-date price lists. Businesses use it to handle customer queries and complaints quickly and efficiently. But some businesses are using the concept of the Net for a lot more than simply servicing customers.

With more than 5,000 employees at 100 or so remote locations worldwide, Tyson Foods needed an easy way to keep its workers in touch with corporate headquarters. Early last year, it took advantage of Internet technology to create an internal corporate network known as an intranet. Intranets are becoming increasingly common as companies from AT&T to UPS are using an Internetlike network internally to distribute news, post notices, and connect remote employees cheaply and practically. Businesses can send text, graphics, and even video to thousands of employees with minimum cost, and they're doing so in increasingly large numbers.

Tyson Foods uses its internal network to distribute senior management reports, let buyers know the latest wholesale chicken prices, post MIS training schedules, and more. "We use it for several different things, and it can be accessed by any Web browser," says Jim Bennett, Tyson's PC LAN manager. "It's extremely valuable." Tyson Foods already had a corporate LAN in place that was running on a Windows NT server. The company bought a new Process Software server for $10,000, added Netscape Web browsers (at $36 a pop for each computer that uses one), and its intranet was born. "The advantage of our intranet is that it has a lower cost," Bennett says. And "being on an NT server we have it as secure as we want it."

a. What are the business benefits of Tyson's intranet?

b. How could other businesses benefit from an intranet like Tyson's?

Source: Adapted from Heidi Anderson, "Intranets Gain Popularity," *PC Today*, February 1996, p. 100. *PC Today*, 125 W. Harvest Drive, Lincoln, NE 68501.

2. Northeast Utilities: Moving into the Telecommunications Business

The signing of the Telecommunications Deregulation and Reform law, which opens up the industry to widespread competition, lit a lightbulb at Northeast Utilities. The Berlin, Connecticut, electric company quickly joined forces with Central Maine Power to bust bandwidth by building the New England Optical Network (NEON), a 410-mile fiber-optic network. Northeast Utilities can use NEON revenue to cut its bandwidth costs. And other users can cut their wide area network costs by buying NEON data services that are cheaper than those from established carriers.

Electric and gas utilities, railroads, and some other utility firms have so-called rights-of-way that let them lay fiber optic cable along their power lines, pipelines, and railroad tracks, and then become telecommunications carriers. "We think we have everything it takes to be successful in the venture, especially given our background in implementing advanced WAN technologies like frame relay and ATM," said John Boyd, chief networking technologist at Northeast Utilities. "There's serious money to be made in this business."

a. Why is Northeast Utilities moving into the telecommunications business?

b. What other telecommunications law changes might benefit business?

Source: Adapted from Bob Wallace, "Keeping the Bandwidth Beast in Check," *Computerworld*, April 1, 1996, p. 55. Copyright © 1996 by Computerworld, Inc., Framingham, MA 01701—Reprinted from *Computerworld*.

3. Best Western International: Installing a Global Network

In a $15 million systems modernization project, Best Western International is implementing a worldwide reservation system based on a client/server architecture. The move is expected to generate an estimated $44 million in incremental annual room revenue and reduced operating costs—such as training—for the group's member hotels worldwide.

Best Western, based in Phoenix, has more than 3,500 independently owned and operated member hotels in 62 countries. Under the two-phase project, Best Western has just deployed a communications network called Lynx at its central reservations offices in Wichita, Kansas; Phoenix, Arizona; Milan, Italy; and Dublin, Ireland. Best Western properties in North America are connected to the reservation offices via two-way satellite communications from Hughes Network Systems. Internationally, properties are connected via a combination of AT&T frame-relay and virtual private network services. New Windows 95 PCs are being deployed at each of the member hotels. They will tie into the central system in Phoenix; it is powered by two UNIX-based Digital Equipment AlphaServer 8400 enterprise servers using an Oracle7 database management system.

Baseline features of the new system include detailed guest histories, online packages, and group booking capabilities. Enhanced features include interactive maps to assist reservation agents in property location and selection. And to monitor employee productivity, the system features performance-tracking modules and revenue-management tools. The system also features a new graphical user interface.

Once the system goes fully on-line, reservation agents will be able to instantly give customers detailed descriptions, including pictures, pricing, and up-to-date availability, of Best Western properties anywhere in the world. Because of this improvement, the system will allow Best Western property owners to better manage their room inventory. Also, the availability of customer databases and on-line guest histories will allow individual hotels to apply frequent-guest discounts and track customer preferences worldwide. When fully implemented, the system will hold close to a terabyte of data, support 4 gigabytes of memory, and process 2.5 million "room-nights" and 15 million calls annually.

a. What telecommunications network components and functions (see Figure 4.5) can you identify in this case?
b. What are the business benefits of the Lynx network to Best Western?

Source: Adapted from Jaikumar Vijayan, "Best Western Checks in with Client/Server," *Computerworld*, May 6, 1996, pp. 85–86. Copyright © 1996 by Computerworld, Inc., Framingham, MA 01701—Reprinted from *Computerworld*.

4. Mary Ellen Bercik of Apple Computer: Using the Internet for Business Research

I am supervisor of Research Services at the corporate library at Apple Computer, Inc., headquarters. My work involves doing online research for Apple employees worldwide. I find information that my users need so they can create, market, and sell next-generation software and hardware. I also teach a class about navigating the Web.

Managers in most departments around Apple are mandating that employees learn the Internet. Marketing and product support groups have been told to get documents into Hypertext Markup Language (HTML) so they can be posted on Apple's Web server (http://www.apple.com/). Human resources has heard there are employment resources on the Net, but where? Benefits people need to get the employees handbook and thousands of other benefits-related documents into HTML in three weeks. Soon, Apple will be delivering its own corporate communications on a private intranet server that will be accessible only from within the company. Apple departments will publish internal documents from there.

Now let's look at a few examples of how I use the Internet for business research.

An employee from public relations is on the phone. Apple is issuing a release in New York related to our earnings—in an hour. She needs some background information: three competitors' financial results for this quarter. No problem. Used to be I would jump on Dow Jones or Dialog and check the business wire for this. That would cost anywhere from $10 to $35 per company, depending on the information needed. Now I just hop onto our competitors' corporate Web servers and look for press releases. Nine times out of 10, it's there, and I've just saved Apple upwards of $100 by using the Internet. Within 20 minutes, I've E-mailed the financial data to PR personnel, who use it to brief executives so they'll be prepared to answer questions at the press conference.

Howard, a hardware engineer who designs keyboards, comes in looking for the specifications of an ergonomic keyboard. He knows the manufacturer, so I jump on its Web site to look for technical documentation. Yup. It's there along with the specs: a three-page description of the design and a picture of the keyboard. Fifteen minutes after Howard arrives, he's trotting back to his office with the information I downloaded. He will compare the specs used against ones used by Apple on its keyboards. We used to pay good money (like thousands or tens of thousands of dollars) on an annual basis to get this kind of information from a market research firm. By using the Web, I just got this for nothing and retrieved it in a quarter of an hour. That's what you can do, too, on the Web.

a. How does Mary Ellen Bercik's research use of the Internet benefit Apple?
b. How could you benefit at school or at work by using the Internet for research? Give several examples.

Source: Adapted from Mary Ellen Bercik, "Cybrarian to the Rescue," *Computerworld*, March 18, 1996, pp. 84–86. Copyright © 1996 by Computerworld, Inc., Framingham, MA 01701—Reprinted from *Computerworld*.

Application Exercises

1. Hands-on Internet for Business Advantage

Learn to use the Internet to access online business information that can give you a competitive advantage. Each of the services listed below has a site or E-mail address that will take you there or help you get more information. Make sure you honor uppercase and lowercase letters when keying in these addresses—Internet addresses are case sensitive!

Internet Business Center

Visit this clearinghouse of current information on what companies are doing on the Internet and learn how you can conduct business on the 'net more effectively. Free.

Web: http://tig.com/IBC/idx.html

Best Markets Reports

Here you'll find information and analysis of markets, including apparel, auto parts and service equipment, software, electrical power systems, laboratory scientific equipment, telecommunications equipment, and so on. Free.

Web: http://Libfind.unl.edu:2020/alpha/Best_Market_Reports.html

Gopher: gopher://una.hh.Lib.umich.edu/11/ebb/bmr

Quotecom

The Quotecom server offers a wide variety of financial data. Offerings include free stock, commodity, and mutual fund quotes, Standard & Poor's Stock Guide, Hoover company profiles, European market data, BusinessWire news reports, and Freese-Notis weather reports. Some basic services are free, others require a subscription.

Web address: http://www.quote.com
E-mail address: info@quote.com

Infoseek

This makes searching the Internet fast, easy, and fun. You can access a large, up-to-date index of Web sites, Usenet news, computer periodicals, news wires, company profiles, and movie and book reviews. Enter a plain English query, and Infoseek will find the information for you in seconds. Free trial, subscription-based.

Web: http://www.infoseek.com/

City Net

This is a comprehensive international guide to communities around the world. City Net provides easy access to timely information on travel, entertainment, and local business, plus government and community services for all regions of the world. Free.

Web: http://www.city.net

Lycos, Webcrawler, and Yahoo

Check out these Web search engines and the Yahoo directory. They can help you find people, places, and things on the Web. By periodically traversing the Web, these services attempt to build comprehensive indices for the content of thousands of Internet sites. Each does a different type of indexing so try them all. Free.

Web: http://www.lycos.com/
Web: http://www.webcrawler.com/
Web: http://www.yahoo.com/

a. If the address for the service takes the form http://www.xxx.yyy, the site is a home page on the World Wide Web. Use a Web browser program such as Mosaic or Netscape to visit these sites.

b. If the address takes the form of gopher.xxx.yyy, use Xgopher, WinGopher, or other gopher software to access that site.

c. If you see an E-mail address such as info@xxx.com, simply send E-mail to the Internet address to get an automatic reply.

d. Send a short E-mail message to your instructor's Internet or other E-mail address summarizing something you learned when visiting one or more of the Internet sites in this exercise.

e. Prepare a one- or two-page summary of specific information gained from several of the above Internet sites that would help you start or expand a business, analyze an investment opportunity, or choose a business career.

Source: Adapted from Lori Dix, Kathie Gow, and Bob Rankin. "Cyberland: The Internet Game for Information and Business Professionals." *Computerworld,* April 17, 1995, pp 102–3. Copyright © 1995 by Computerworld, Inc., Framingham, MA 01701—Reprinted from *Computerworld.*

2. Visiting Corporate Internet Web Sites

Visit the Internet World Wide Web sites (home pages) of Fidelity Investments in Boston, Federal Express in Memphis, and Capital One in Richmond, Virginia.

a. Use the Fidelity Investment home page (http://www.fid-inv.com) to look up information on Fidelity and its mutual funds. Then fill out the worksheet form for calculating savings needed for a college fund, and print it out on your system printer.

b. Visit the FedEx home page (http://www.fedex.com) to review information on FedEx and its services. You would need a copy of their Powership package and a FedEx account number and package tracking number to check the status of a shipment. So just print out a screenful of information on FedEx services to document your visit.

c. Use Capital One's home page (http://www.capital1.com) to find out information about Capital One's banking and financial services. Then fill out and print out the application form for a Visa card offered by Capital One. Don't submit the application to Capital (you can cancel the session any time) unless you are really interested in applying for their Visa card!

159

3. Communications Costs at ABC Company

The ABC Company currently uses direct-distance dialing service for all of its long-distance voice and data communications. ABC has a central headquarters and assembly facility in Birmingham, Alabama, and assembly plants in Atlanta, Georgia, and Cincinnati, Ohio. There is substantial and growing volume of both voice and data communications among the three locations. Other outgoing communications consist of voice communications to a variety of vendors and customers throughout the country.

ABC also has communications expenses associated with incoming calls placed by members of ABC's sales force. Salespersons use telephone credit cards to call headquarters with orders and inquiries while they are in the field.

You have been asked to take a look at trends in ABC's long-distance communications expenses. You are to prepare materials for a presentation to upper management.

Your materials should highlight recent trends in ABC's long-distance communications services. You have been asked to also recommend changes in the way ABC purchases its long-distance communications services.

By examining billing records you have been able to obtain the following estimates. These figures describe long-distance communications expenses by category for the past four years.

a. Using spreadsheet software, create a spreadsheet application analyzing the following information, including appropriate reports and graphs to highlight trends in ABC's long-distance communications costs.
b. What changes in how they purchase long-distance communications services would you recommend that ABC consider?

	Year			
Type of call	1993	1994	1995	1996
Outgoing facility to facility				
Atlanta–Birmingham				
Voice	$ 8,307	$ 9,832	$11,083	$13,486
Data	5,252	7,893	9,672	12,679
Atlanta–Cincinnati				
Voice	1,307	1,608	1,964	2,102
Data	893	1,004	1,083	1,132
Cincinnati–Birmingham				
Voice	6,402	7,072	7,803	8,349
Data	4,682	6,192	7,093	9,737
Other outgoing calls	11,358	11,482	10,639	9,806
Incoming credit card calls	6,273	6,852	8,391	9,475

4. Action Products Data Communications

Action Products has a warehouse in Chicago and sales offices in Los Angeles and New York City. Order and invoicing information gathered on personal computers at the sales offices is transmitted to a minicomputer at the Chicago warehouse. On an average day, 20,000 invoices are sent by the Chicago office and 30,000 are sent by the New York City office.

Action Products can either lease telephone lines between its sales offices and the warehouse, or use standard dial-up phone services. If dial-up services are used, Action Products will batch its transactions at each sales office. That is, all of the transactions generated at each sales site will be stored all day on the PCs at the sales office and sent as a batch to the Chicago warehouse in a single phone call. Using this method, 100 transactions per minute can be sent. The cost of dial-up services is as follows:

	First Minute	Additional Minutes
Los Angeles to Chicago	$0.17	$0.13
New York City to Chicago	0.15	0.12

Leased phone lines normally have three components. Lines must be leased from the local phone company in each city to the nearest switching office (called a point-of-presence) of the long-distance phone company. Then a line must be leased from the long-distance company between that company's switching offices in the two cities. These are the circuit components and distances:

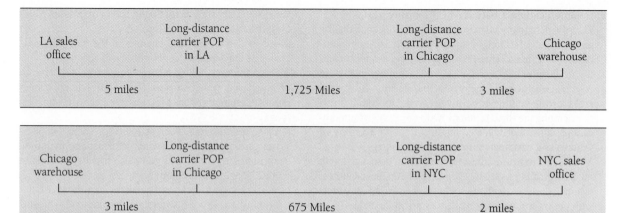

Leased line rates commonly have a fixed component and a per mile rate that declines as distance increases. If leased lines are used, invoices can be transmitted to the Chicago office immediately when the sale is made. Assume the following monthly rates apply for the phone companies that Action Products will be dealing with:

a. Based on the figures given, generate a spreadsheet to compute Action Product's monthly cost to transmit its invoices using dial-up lines and using leased lines.

b. Would you recommend that Action Products lease its lines or use dial-up services? What factors other than cost would influence your decision?

Local Phone Companies:			
	Los Angeles	**Chicago**	**New York City**
Fixed monthly charge	$40	$37	$42
Additional charge per mile	3.50	3.00	4.00
Long-Distance Carrier:			
Fixed monthly charge		$105	
Additional charge per mile			
1st 100 Miles		1.25	
101–1,000 Miles		0.72	
Over 1,000 Miles		0.44	

Review Quiz Answers

1. *31*	9. *3*	17. *25*	25. *13*
2. *29b*	10. *30*	18. *22*	26. *1*
3. *33*	11. *28*	19. *29a*	27. *2*
4. *19*	12. *20*	20. *26*	28. *4*
5. *6*	13. *21*	21. *24*	29. *9*
6. *32*	14. *12*	22. *15*	30. *8*
7. *27*	15. *11*	23. *16*	31. *17*
8. *10*	16. *23*	24. *14*	32. *18*

Selected References

1. Anthes, Gary. "In Depth: Interview with Vinton Cerf." *Computerworld,* February 7, 1994.

2. Booker, Ellis. "A Tangled Web." *Computerworld Client/Server Journal,* April 1995.

3. Carney, Dan. "Congress Fires First Shot in Information Revolution." *Congressional Quarterly Weekly,* February 3, 1996.

4. Cronin, Mary. *Doing More Business on the Internet.* New York: Van Nostrand Reinhold, 1995.

5. Eliot, Lance. "Data Highway Needs Fuzzy Look." *AI Expert,* January 1994.

6. Friend, David. "Client/Server versus Cooperative Processing: Two Downsizing Topologies Compared." *Information Systems Management,* Summer 1994.

7. Gilder, George. "Into the Telecosm." *Harvard Business Review,* March/April 1991.

8. Gleason, Tim. "The Information Hypeway." *Oregon Quarterly,* Spring 1994.

9. Green, James Harry. *The Irwin Handbook of Telecommunications.* 2nd ed. Burr Ridge, IL: Richard D. Irwin, 1992.

10. Keen, Peter G. W. *Shaping the Future: Business Design through Information Technology.* Boston: Harvard Business School Press, 1991.

11. Kehoe, Brandan. *Zen and the Art of the Internet: A Beginner's Guide.* 3rd ed. Englewood Cliffs, NJ: Prentice Hall, 1994.

12. Kupfer, Andrew. "The Future of the Phone Companies." *Fortune,* October 3, 1994.

13. Martin, E. Wainwright; Daniel DeHayes; Jeffrey Hoffer; and William Perkins. *Managing Information Technology: What Managers Need to Know.* 2nd ed. New York: Macmillan, 1994.

14. O'Mara, Brendan. "Information Superhighway." *Online Access,* Internet Special Issue, April 1994.

15. Roche, Edward M. *Telecommunications and Business Strategy.* Fort Worth, TX: Dryden Press, 1994.

16. Rochester, Jack, ed. "Plans and Policies for Client/Server Technology." *I/S Analyzer,* April 1992.

17. Schnaidt, Patricia. *Enterprise-wide Networking.* Carmel, IN: SAMS Publishing, 1992.

18. Sherman, Stratford. "Will the Information Highway Be the Death of Retailing?" *Fortune,* April 18, 1994.

19. Sprague, Ralph, Jr., and Barbara McNurlin. *Information Systems Management in Practice.* 3rd ed. Englewood Cliffs, NJ: Prentice Hall, 1993.

20. Stallings, William, and Richard Van Slyke. *Business Data Communications.* 2nd ed. New York: Macmillan, 1994.

21. Stamper, David. *Business Data Communications.* 3rd ed. Redwood City, CA: Benjamin Cummings Publishing Co., 1992.

22. Tetzelli, Rick. "The Internet and Your Business." *Fortune,* March 7, 1994.

23. Von Schilling, Peter, and John Levis. "Distributed Computing Environments: Process and Organization Issues." *Information Systems Management,* Spring 1995.

24. Wrobel, Leo. "Developing Information Highways." *Information Systems Management,* Spring 1995.

25. Yankee Group. "White Paper: Wireless Communications." *Computerworld,* November 14, 1994.

26. Zoglin, Richard. "We're All Connected." *Time,* February 12, 1996.

Introduction to Database Management

CHAPTER OUTLINE

LEARNING OBJECTIVES

After reading and studying this chapter, you should be able to:

1. Explain the importance of data resource management and how it is implemented by methods such as database administration, data administration, and data planning.

2. Outline the advantages of the database management approach.

3. Explain the functions of database management software in terms of end users and database management applications.

4. Provide examples to illustrate each of the following concepts:

   a. Logical data elements.

   b. Fundamental database structures.

   c. Major types of databases.

   d. Database development.

Section I

A Manager's View of Database Management

Data Resource Management

Data are a vital organizational resource that need to be managed like other important business assets. Most organizations could not survive or succeed without quality data about their internal operations and external environment.

> Organizations are under tremendous pressure to provide better quality decision-making information in forms easy to access and manipulate. Business users are reacting to their own mission-critical needs for better information due to rapidly changing, increasingly volatile and competitive markets, as well as ever-shortening product life cycles [13].

That's why organizations and their managers need to practice **data resource management**—a managerial activity that applies information systems technology and management tools to the task of managing an organization's data resources to meet the information needs of business users. This chapter will show you the managerial implications of using database management technologies and methods to manage an organization's data assets to meet the information requirements of a business. We will also introduce the concepts of database administration, data administration, and data planning, which are part of the data resource management function. See Figure 5.1.

Foundation Data Concepts

Before we go any further, let's review some fundamental concepts about how data are organized in information systems. As we first mentioned in Chapter 1, a hierarchy of several levels of data has been devised that differentiates between different groupings, or *elements,* of data. Thus, data may be logically organized into **characters, fields, records, files,** and **databases,** just as writing can be organized in letters, words, sentences, paragraphs, and documents. Examples of these **logical data elements** are shown in Figure 5.2.

FIGURE 5.1

Managing data as organizational assets is an important focus for today's managers.

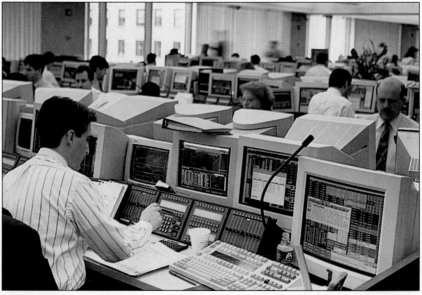

Reinhold Speigler.

The most basic logical data element is the **character,** which consists of a single alphabetic, numeric, or other symbol. One might argue that the *bit* or *byte* is a more elementary data element, but remember that those terms refer to the *physical* storage elements provided by the computer hardware, discussed in Chapter 2. From a user's point of view (that is, from a *logical* as opposed to a *physical* or *hardware* view of data), a character is the most basic element of data that can be observed and manipulated.

Character

The next higher level of data is the **field,** or *data item.* A field consists of a grouping of characters. For example, the grouping of alphabetic characters in a person's name forms a *name field,* and the grouping of numbers in a sales amount forms a sales *amount field.* Specifically, a data field represents an **attribute** (a characteristic or quality) of some **entity** (object, person, place, or event). For example, an employee's salary is an attribute that is a typical data field used to describe an entity who is an employee of a business.

Field

Related fields of data are grouped to form a **record.** Thus, a record represents a collection of attributes that describe an entity. An example is the payroll record for a person, which consists of data fields such as the person's name, Social Security number, and rate of pay. *Fixed-length records* contain a fixed number of fixed-length data fields. *Variable-length* records contain a variable number of fields and field lengths.

Record

A group of related records is a data **file,** or *table.* Thus, an *employee file* would contain the records of the employees of a firm. Files are frequently classified by the application for which they are primarily used, such as a *payroll file* or an *inventory file.* Files are also classified by their permanence, for example, a payroll *master file* versus a payroll weekly *transaction file.* A **transaction file,** therefore, would contain records of all transactions occurring during a period and would be used periodically to update the permanent records contained in a **master file.** A *history file* is an obsolete transaction or master file retained for backup purposes or for long-term historical storage called *archival storage.*

File

FIGURE 5.2

Examples of the logical data elements in information systems. Note especially the examples of how data fields, records, files, and databases are related.

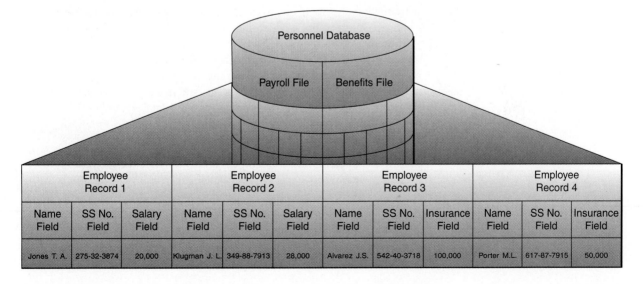

FIGURE 5.3

A personnel database consolidates data formerly kept in separate files.

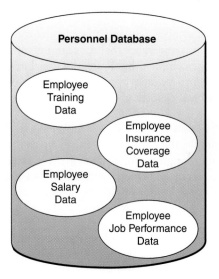

Database

A **database** is an integrated collection of logically related records or files. A database consolidates records previously stored in separate files into a common pool of data records that provides data for many applications. The data stored in a database are independent of the application programs using them and of the type of secondary storage devices on which they are stored. For example, a personnel database consolidates data formerly segregated in separate files such as payroll files, personnel action files, and employee skills files. See Figure 5.3.

The Database Management Approach

The development of *databases* and *database management software* is the foundation of modern methods of managing organizational data. The **database management approach** consolidates data records into databases that can be accessed by many different application programs. In addition, an important software package called a *database management system* (DBMS) serves as a software interface between users and databases. This helps users easily access the records in a database. Thus, database management involves the use of database management software to control how databases are created, interrogated, and maintained to provide information needed by end users and their organizations.

For example, customer records and other common types of data are needed for several different applications in banking, such as check processing, automated teller systems, bank credit cards, savings accounts, and installment loan accounting. These data can be consolidated into a common *customer database*, rather than being kept in separate files for each of those applications. See Figure 5.4.

Thus, the database management approach involves three basic activities:

- Updating and maintaining common databases to reflect new business transactions and other events requiring changes to an organization's records.

- Providing information needed for each end user's application by using application programs that share the data in common databases. This sharing of data is supported by the common software interface provided by a

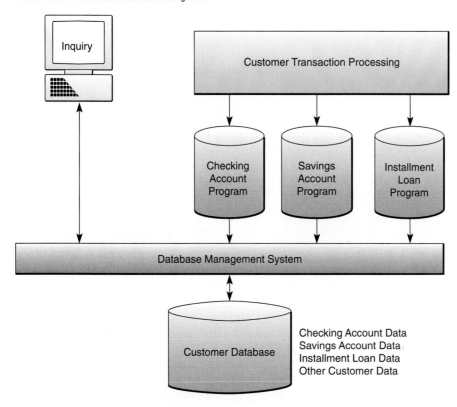

FIGURE 5.4

An example of a database management approach in a banking information system. Note how the savings, checking, and installment loan programs use a database management system to share a customer database. Note also that the DBMS allows a user to make a direct, ad hoc interrogation of the database without using application programs.

database management system package. Thus, end users and programmers do not have to know where or how data are physically stored.

- Providing an inquiry/response and reporting capability through a DBMS package so that end users can easily interrogate databases, generate reports, and receive quick responses to their ad hoc requests for information.

Using Database Management Software

Let's take a closer look at the capabilities provided by database management software. A **database management system** (DBMS) is a set of computer programs that controls the creation, maintenance, and use of the databases of an organization and its end users. As we said in Chapter 3, database management packages are available for micro, mini, and mainframe computer systems. The four major DBMS uses are illustrated in Figure 5.5. Let's take a look at each of them now.

Database Development

Database management packages allow end users to easily develop the databases they need. However, a DBMS allows organizations to place control of organizationwide database development in the hands of **database administrators** (DBAs) and other specialists. This improves the integrity and security of organizational databases. The database administrator uses a *data definition language* (DDL) to develop and specify the data contents, relationships, and structure of each database, and to modify these database specifications when necessary. Such information is cataloged and stored in a database of data definitions and specifications called a *data dictionary,* which is maintained by the DBA. We will discuss database development further in Section II of this chapter.

FIGURE 5.5

The four major uses of a DBMS package are database development, database interrogation, database maintenance, and application development.

- Database Development
- Database Interrogation
- Database Maintenance
- Application Development

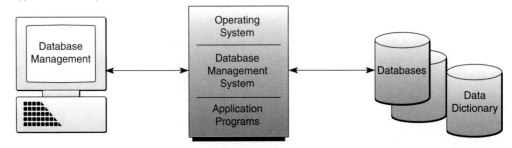

The Data Dictionary

Data dictionaries have become a major tool of database administration. A data dictionary is a computer-based catalog or directory containing *metadata;* that is, data about data. A data dictionary includes a software component to manage a database of *data definitions;* that is, metadata about the structure, data elements, and other characteristics of an organization's databases. For example, it contains the names and descriptions of all types of data records and their interrelationships, as well as information outlining requirements for end users' access, use of application programs, and database maintenance and security. See Figure 5.6.

Data dictionaries can be queried by the database administrator to report the status of any aspect of a firm's metadata. The administrator can then make changes to the definitions of selected data elements. Some *active* (versus *passive*) data dictionaries automatically enforce standard data element definitions whenever end users and application programs use a DBMS to access an organization's databases. For example, an active data dictionary would not allow a data entry program to use a nonstandard definition of a customer record, nor would it allow a data entry operator to enter a name of a customer that exceeded the defined size of that data element.

Database Interrogation

End users can use a DBMS by asking for information from a database using a *query language* or a *report generator.* They can receive an immediate response in the form of video displays or printed reports. No difficult programming is required. This **database interrogation** capability is a major benefit to ordinary end users. The **query language** feature lets you easily obtain immediate responses to ad hoc inquiries: you merely key in a few short inquiries. The **report generator** feature allows you to quickly specify a report format for information you want presented as a report. Figure 5.7 illustrates the use of a DBMS report generator.

SQL and QBE

SQL, or Structured Query Language, is a query language found in many database management packages. The basic form of an SQL query is:

SELECT . . . FROM . . . WHERE . . .

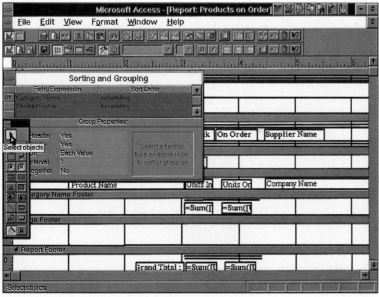

FIGURE 5.6

A display of part of the information in a data dictionary for a customer order number data element.

Courtesy Intersolv Inc.

After SELECT you list the data fields you want retrieved. After FROM you list the files or tables from which the data must be retrieved. After WHERE you specify conditions that limit the search to only those data records in which you are interested. For example, suppose a financial manager wanted to retrieve the names, Social Security numbers, departments, and salaries of all employees who are financial analysts from the employee and payroll files in the company's *human resources* database. Then she might use the SQL query shown in Figure 5.8 to display such information.

FIGURE 5.7

Using the report generator of Microsoft Access to produce an inventory report.

Sarah Evertson/Courtesy of Microsoft Corporation.

FIGURE 5.8

Using SQL (Structured Query Language) and QBE (query by example) to retrieve information about a company's financial analysts.

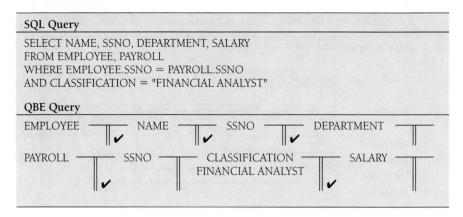

SQL Query

SELECT NAME, SSNO, DEPARTMENT, SALARY
FROM EMPLOYEE, PAYROLL
WHERE EMPLOYEE.SSNO = PAYROLL.SSNO
AND CLASSIFICATION = "FINANCIAL ANALYST"

QBE Query

EMPLOYEE — NAME — SSNO — DEPARTMENT
PAYROLL — SSNO — CLASSIFICATION FINANCIAL ANALYST — SALARY

Another query language in some database management packages is QBE, or *query by example*. QBE is a popular query language because its "point-and-click" capabilities make it easier for end users than SQL. This method displays boxes for each of the data fields in one or more files. You then use your keyboard or mouse to fill in, click on, query, or check boxes to indicate which information you want. For example, a QBE query that would retrieve information similar to the previous SQL query is shown in Figure 5.8.

Graphical and Natural Queries

Many end users (and IS professionals) have difficulty correctly phrasing SQL and other database language queries. So most end user database management packages offer GUI (graphical user interface) point-and-click methods, which are easier to use. See Figure 5.9. Other packages are available that use **natural language** query statements similar to conversational English (or other languages). See Figure 5.10.

FIGURE 5.9

Using the Query Wizard of the Microsoft Access database management package to develop a query using a graphical point-and-click process.

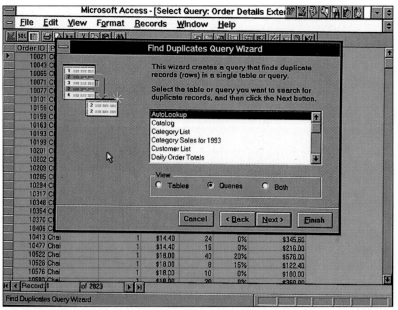

Sarah Evertson/Courtesy of Microsoft Corporation.

**A Sample English-to-SQL Translation for
Microsoft's Access Database Manager**

English Wizard

WHAT CUSTOMERS DIDN'T HAVE ANY ORDERS LAST MONTH?

SQL

SELECT [Customers].[Company Name],[Customers].[Contact Name]
FROM [Customers]
WHERE not Exists {SELECT [Ship Name] FROM [Orders]
    WHERE Month {[Order Date]}=1 and Year {[Order Date]}=1996 and
    [Customers].[Customer ID]=[Orders].[Customer ID]}

Source: Adapted from Kim Nash, "Wizard Turns English into Database Language," *Computerworld,* February 20, 1995,
p. 116. Copyright © 1995 by Computerworld, Inc., Framingham, MA 01701—Reprinted from *Computerworld.*

FIGURE 5.10

Comparing a natural language query with an SQL query.

Database Maintenance

The databases of an organization need to be updated continually to reflect new business transactions and other events. Other miscellaneous changes must also be made to ensure accuracy of the data in the databases. This **database maintenance** process is accomplished by transaction processing programs and other end user application packages, with the support of the DBMS. End users and information specialists can also employ various *utilities* provided by a DBMS for database maintenance.

Application Development

DBMS packages play a major role in **application development.** A DBMS makes the job of application programmers easier, since they do not have to develop detailed data-handling procedures using a conventional programming language (a host language, such as COBOL) every time they write a program. Instead, they can include in their application programs *data manipulation language* (DML) statements that let the DBMS perform necessary data-handling activities. Programmers can also use the internal programming language provided by many DBMS packages or a built-in application generator to develop complete application programs.

Types of Databases

The growth of distributed processing, end user computing, and decision support and executive information systems has caused the development of several major **types of databases.** Figure 5.11 illustrates six major types of databases that may be found in computer-using organizations.

- **Operational Databases.** These databases store detailed data needed to support the operations of the entire organization. They are also called *subject area databases* (SADB), *transaction databases,* and *production databases.* Examples are a customer database, personnel database, inventory database, and other databases containing data generated by business operations.

- **Analytical Databases.** These databases store data and information extracted from selected operational and external databases. They consist of summarized data and information most needed by an organization's managers and other end users. Analytical databases are also called *management databases* or *information databases.* They may also be called multidimensional databases, since they frequently use a multidimensional database structure to organize data. These are the databases accessed by the *online analytical processing* (OLAP) systems, decision support systems, and executive information systems we will discuss in Chapter 8 [2, 4].

FIGURE 5.11

Examples of the major types of databases used by organizations and end users.

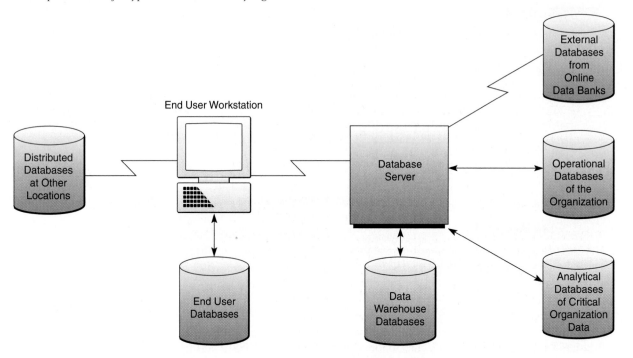

- **Data Warehouse Databases.** A *data warehouse* stores data from current and previous years that has been extracted from the various operational and management databases of an organization. It is a central source of data that has been standardized and integrated so it can be used by managers and other end user professionals throughout an organization. For example, a major use of data warehouse databases is *pattern processing,* where operational data are processed to identify key factors and trends in historical patterns of business activity [9, 13].
- **Distributed Databases.** These are databases of local work groups and departments at regional offices, branch offices, manufacturing plants, and other work sites. These databases can include segments of both common operational and common user databases, as well as data generated and used only at a user's own site. Ensuring that all of the data in an organization's distributed databases are consistently and concurrently updated is a major consideration of data resource management.
- **End User Databases.** These databases consist of a variety of data files developed by end users at their workstations. For example, users may have their own electronic copies of documents they generated with word processing packages or received by electronic mail. Or they may have their own data files generated from using spreadsheet and DBMS packages.
- **External Databases.** Access to external *online databases* or *data banks* is available for a fee from commercial information services, or without charge from many sources on the Internet. Data are available in the form of statistics

FIGURE 5.12

Examples of the information available in the online databases of commercial information services.

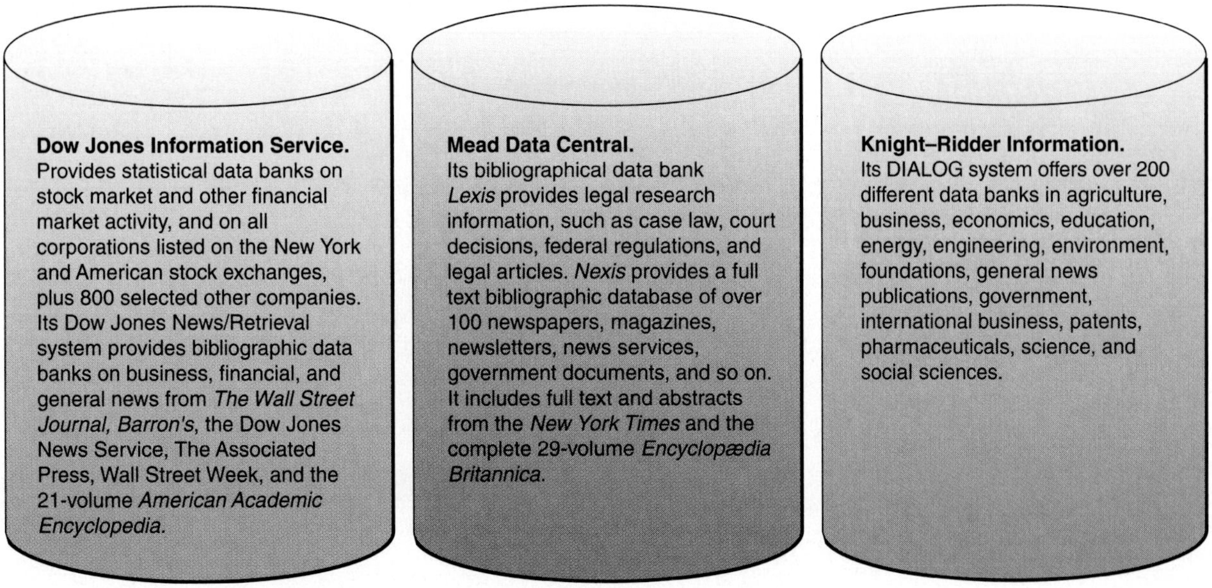

Dow Jones Information Service. Provides statistical data banks on stock market and other financial market activity, and on all corporations listed on the New York and American stock exchanges, plus 800 selected other companies. Its Dow Jones News/Retrieval system provides bibliographic data banks on business, financial, and general news from *The Wall Street Journal, Barron's*, the Dow Jones News Service, The Associated Press, Wall Street Week, and the 21-volume *American Academic Encyclopedia.*

Mead Data Central. Its bibliographical data bank *Lexis* provides legal research information, such as case law, court decisions, federal regulations, and legal articles. *Nexis* provides a full text bibliographic database of over 100 newspapers, magazines, newsletters, news services, government documents, and so on. It includes full text and abstracts from the *New York Times* and the complete 29-volume *Encyclopædia Britannica.*

Knight–Ridder Information. Its DIALOG system offers over 200 different data banks in agriculture, business, economics, education, energy, engineering, environment, foundations, general news publications, government, international business, patents, pharmaceuticals, science, and social sciences.

on economic and demographic activity from *statistical* data banks. Or you can receive abstracts from hundreds of newspapers, magazines, and other periodicals from *bibliographic* data banks. See Figure 5.12.

Text Databases

Text databases are a natural outgrowth of the use of computers to create and store documents electronically. Thus, online database services store bibliographic information such as publications in large text databases. Text databases are also available on CD–ROM optical disks for use with microcomputer systems. Major corporations and government agencies have developed large text databases containing documents of all kinds. They use *text database management systems* software to help create, store, search, retrieve, modify, and assemble documents and other information stored as text data in such databases. Microcomputer versions of this software help users manage their own text databases on CD–ROM disks.

Image and Multimedia Databases

Up to this point, we have discussed databases that hold data in traditional alphanumeric records and files or as documents in text databases. **Image databases** or **multimedia databases** can also store a wide variety of images electronically. For example, *electronic encyclopedias* on CD–ROM disks store thousands of photographs and many animated video sequences as digitized images, along with thousands of pages of text. The main appeal of image databases for business users is in *document image processing*. Thousands of pages of business documents, such as customer correspondence, purchase orders and invoices, as well as sales catalogs and service manuals, can be optically scanned and stored as document images on a single optical disk. Image database management software allows employees in many companies to quickly retrieve and display documents from image databases holding millions of pages of document images. Workers can view and modify documents at their workstations and electronically route them to the workstations of other end users in the organization. See Figure 5.13.

FIGURE 5.13

CD–ROM disks can hold image and multimedia databases.

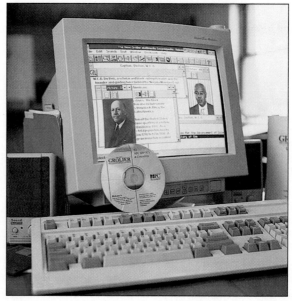

Scott Goodwin.

Managerial Considerations for Data Resource Management

Managerial end users should view data as an important resource that they must learn to manage properly to ensure the success and survival of their organizations. But this is easier said than done.

Database management is an important application of information systems technology to the management of a firm's data resources. However, other major data resource management efforts are needed in order to offset some of the problems that can result from the use of a database management approach. Those are (1) database administration, (2) data planning, and (3) data administration. See Figure 5.14.

Benefits and Limitations of Database Management

The database management approach provides managerial end users with several important benefits. Database management reduces the duplication of data and integrates data so that they can be accessed by multiple programs and users. Programs are not dependent on the format of the data and the type of secondary storage hardware being used. Users are provided with an inquiry/response and reporting capability that allows them to easily obtain information they need without having to write computer programs. Computer programming is simplified, because programs are not dependent on either the logical format of the data or their physical storage location. Finally, the integrity and security of the data stored in databases can be increased, since access to data and modification of the database are controlled by database management system software, a data dictionary, and a database administrator function.

The limitations of database management arise from its increased technological complexity. Thus, a database management approach can pose problems in data resource management. Developing a large database and installing a DBMS can be difficult and expensive. More hardware capability is required, since storage requirements for the organization's data, overhead control data, and the DBMS programs are greater. Longer processing times may result from high-volume transaction processing applications since an extra layer of software (the DBMS) exists between application

FIGURE 5.14

Data resource management includes database administration, data planning, and data administration activities.

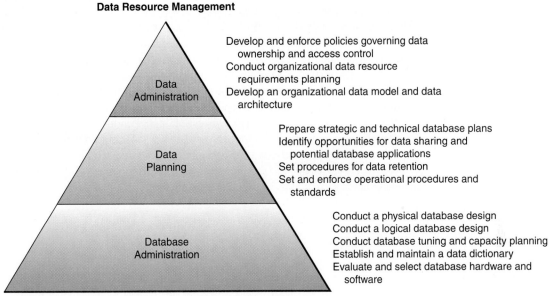

Data Resource Management

Data Administration
- Develop and enforce policies governing data ownership and access control
- Conduct organizational data resource requirements planning
- Develop an organizational data model and data architecture

Data Planning
- Prepare strategic and technical database plans
- Identify opportunities for data sharing and potential database applications
- Set procedures for data retention
- Set and enforce operational procedures and standards

Database Administration
- Conduct a physical database design
- Conduct a logical database design
- Conduct database tuning and capacity planning
- Establish and maintain a data dictionary
- Evaluate and select database hardware and software

Source: Adapted from Varun Grover, and James Teng, "How Effective Is Data Resource Management? Reassessing Strategic Objectives," *Journal of Information Systems Management* (New York: Auerbach Publications), Summer 1991, pp. 19–20. © 1991 Warren, Gorham & Lamont. Used with permission.

programs and the operating system. Finally, if an organization relies on centralized databases, its vulnerability to errors, fraud, and failures is increased. Yet problems of inconsistency of data can arise if a distributed database approach is used. Therefore, the security and integrity of an organization's databases are major concerns of an organization's data resource management effort.

Database Administration

Database administration is an important data resource management function responsible for the proper use of database management technology. Database administration has more operational and technical responsibilities than other data resource management functions. These include responsibilities for developing and maintaining the organization's data dictionary, designing and monitoring the performance of databases, and enforcing standards for database use and security. Database administrators work with systems analysts, programmers, and end users to provide their expertise to major systems development projects.

Data Planning

Data planning is a corporate planning and analysis function that focuses on data resource management. It includes the responsibility for developing an overall *data architecture* for the firm's data resources that ties in with the firm's strategic mission and plans, and the objectives and processes of its business units. Data planning is thus a major component of an organization's strategic planning process. It shows that an organization has made a formal commitment to long-range planning for the strategic use and management of its data resources. In the next section we will discuss how data planning is also an important first step in developing databases for an organization.

Data Administration

Data administration is another vital data resource management function. It involves the establishment and enforcement of policies and procedures for managing data as a strategic corporate resource. This means administering the collection, storage, and dissemination of all types of data in such a way that data become a standardized resource available to all end users in the organization. Thus, a data administrator must learn to work with the diverse business units and work groups in an organization, many of whom are uncomfortable with any attempt to dictate the use of "their data."

Data administration typically is an organizationwide managerial function without the operational and technical focus of database administration. Its focus is the planning and control of data in support of an organization's business functions and strategic business objectives. A major thrust of data administration, therefore, is the establishment of a data planning activity for the organization. Data administration may also include responsibility for developing policies and setting standards for corporate database design, processing, and security arrangements, and for selecting database management and data dictionary software.

VICTORIA'S SECRET: THE BUSINESS BENEFITS OF A DATA WAREHOUSE

In what observers said is a classic case of value gained by analyzing data in new ways, Victoria's Secret has embarked on a $5 million information technology project that its information systems and business managers say will benefit the bottom line. "We were spending way too much time trying to find information and not enough time analyzing it," said Rick Acari, vice president of IS at Victoria's Secret. So the lingerie chain started working with Tandem Computers to see if a data warehouse computer-based system could boost the $1.3 billion chain's fortunes.

Managers considered 25 items from the chain's 1,000-item inventory, Acari said. They learned that Victoria's Secret's system of allocating and pricing merchandise to its 678 shops, based on a mathematical store average, was wrong, he said. For example, although Victoria's Secret applied merchandise discounts across the board at its stores, geographic demand patterns showed that some outlets should be able to continue charging full price. Acari said a more precise application of discounts could boost sales by an estimated $3 million.

These revelations about sales and inventory yielded a new way of thinking at Victoria's Secret shops, Acari said. "Our processes and systems were built around an average-shop concept, when in reality, our chain has few average shops. We found we were missing opportunities. And from that, we recognized we needed deeper levels of information at a lower level of detail and with rapid access to it," he said.

Retail industry consultant Mohsen Moazami said the lingerie chain joins a growing army of merchants who are trying to understand their customers' behavior with precision. A data warehouse application is a competitive advantage now, but it may not be in a year, said Moazami, national director of the advanced technology group at Kurt Salmon Associates in Los Angeles. Food, clothing, and other retailers that fail to invest in such technology "are going to be out of the game," he said.

Sandy Taylor, an analyst at Standish Group International, said the experience of the Victoria's Secret chain highlights a common theme among companies that are having success with data warehouses.

"Data warehousing is one of the few technologies where you can get back some very visible payback," Taylor said. "We have seen situations where the company discovers an early trend in product inventory where they basically recoup the price of the system with just one decision."

The value of the information in its test last summer—along with technical support from Tandem—prompted Victoria's Secret to pick a 10-processor Himalaya server as the hardware platform for its data warehouse, Acari said. The $5 million project will be in full production in a few months, he said.

CASE STUDY QUESTIONS

1. How does a data warehouse differ from a typical business database?
2. How did Victoria's Secret benefit from using a data warehouse?
3. How can other types of businesses benefit from a data warehouse?

Source: Adapted from Michael Goldberg and Jaikumar Vijayan, "Data 'Wearhouse' Gains," *Computerworld,* April 8, 1996, pp. 6, 16. Copyright © 1996 by Computerworld, Inc., Framingham, MA 01701—Reprinted from *Computerworld.*

Section II

Technical Foundations of Database Management

Just imagine how difficult it would be to get any information from an information system if data were stored in an unorganized way, or if there was no systematic way to retrieve it. Therefore, in all information systems, data resources must be organized and structured in some logical manner so that they can be accessed easily, processed efficiently, retrieved quickly, and managed effectively. Thus, *data structures* and *access methods* ranging from simple to complex have been devised to efficiently organize and access data stored by information systems. In this section, we will explore these concepts, as well as more technical concepts of database management.

Database Structures

The relationships among the many individual records stored in databases are based on one of several logical *data structures* or *models*. Database management system packages are designed to use a specific data structure to provide end users with quick, easy access to information stored in databases. Five fundamental database structures are the *hierarchical, network, relational, object-oriented,* and *multidimensional models*. Simplified illustrations of the first three database structures are shown in Figure 5.15.

Hierarchical Structure

Early mainframe DBMS packages used the **hierarchical structure,** in which the relationships between records form a *hierarchy* or treelike structure. In the traditional hierarchical model, all records are dependent and arranged in multilevel structures, consisting of one *root* record and any number of *subordinate* levels. Thus, all of the relationships among records are *one-to-many,* since each data element is related to only one element above it. The data element or record at the highest level of the hierarchy (the department data element in this illustration) is called the *root* element. Any data element can be accessed by moving progressively downward from a root and along the *branches* of the tree until the desired record (for example, the employee data element) is located.

Network Structure

The **network structure** can represent more complex logical relationships, and is still used by some mainframe DBMS packages. It allows *many-to-many* relationships among records—that is, the network model can access a data element by following one of several paths, because any data element or record can be related to any number of other data elements. For example, in Figure 5.15, departmental records can be related to more than one employee record, and employee records can be related to more than one project record. Thus, one could locate all employee records for a particular department, or all project records related to a particular employee.

Relational Structure

The **relational model** has become the most popular of the three database structures. It is used by most microcomputer DBMS packages, as well as many minicomputer and mainframe systems. In the relational model, all data elements within the database are viewed as being stored in the form of simple **tables.** Figure 5.15 illustrates the relational database model with two tables representing some of the relationships among departmental and employee records. Other tables, or **relations,** for this organization's database might represent the data element relationships among projects,

HIERARCHICAL STRUCTURE

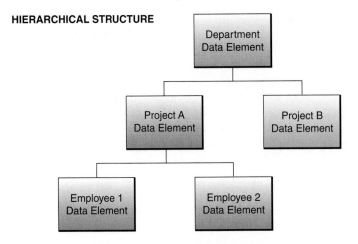

FIGURE 5.15

Examples of three fundamental database structures. They represent three basic ways to develop and express the relationships among the data elements in a database.

NETWORK STRUCTURE

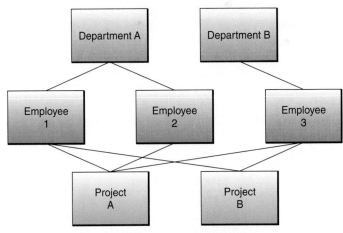

RELATIONAL STRUCTURE

Department Table

Deptno	Dname	Dloc	Dmgr
Dept A			
Dept B			
Dept C			

Employee Table

Empno	Ename	Etitle	Esalary	Deptno
Emp 1				Dept A
Emp 2				Dept A
Emp 3				Dept B
Emp 4				Dept B
Emp 5				Dept C
Emp 6				Dept B

divisions, product lines, and so on. Database management system packages based on the relational model can link data elements from various tables to provide information to users. For example, a DBMS package could retrieve and display an employee's name and salary from the employee table in Figure 5.15, and the name of his department from the department table, by using their common department number field (Deptno) to link or join the two tables.

Object-Oriented Structure

Other database models are being developed to provide capabilities missing from the hierarchical, network, and relational structures. One example is the **object-oriented** database model. We introduced the concept of objects when we discussed *object-oriented programming* in Chapter 3. As Figure 5.16 illustrates, an **object** consists of data values describing the attributes of an entity, plus the operations that can be performed upon the data. This *encapsulation* capability allows the object-oriented model to better handle more complex types of data (graphics, pictures, voice, text) than other database structures.

The object-oriented model also supports *inheritance;* that is, new objects can be automatically created by replicating some or all of the characteristics of one or more *parent objects*. Thus, in Figure 5.16, the checking and savings account objects can both inherit the common attributes and operations of the parent bank account object. Such capabilities have made object-oriented database management systems (OODBMS) popular in computer-aided design (CAD) and similar applications. For example, they allow designers to develop product designs, store them as objects in an object-oriented database, and replicate and modify them to create new product designs.

Multidimensional Structure

The **multidimensional** database model uses multidimensional structures to store data and relationships between data. You can visualize multidimensional structures as cubes of data—and cubes within cubes of data. Each side of the cube is considered a dimension of the data. Figure 5.17 is an example that shows that each dimension can represent a different category, such as product type, region, sales channel, and time.

Each cell within a multidimensional structure contains aggregated data related to elements along each of its dimensions. For example, a single cell may contain the total sales for a product in a region for a specific sales channel in a single month. A major benefit of multidimensional databases is that they are a compact and easy-to-understand

FIGURE 5.16

The checking and savings account objects can inherit common attributes and operations from the bank account object.

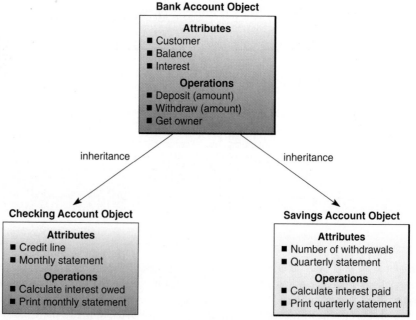

Source: Adapted from Ivar Jacobsen, Maria Ericsson, and Ageneta Jacobsen, *The Object Advantage: Business Process Reengineering with Object Technology* (New York: ACM Press, 1995), p. 65. Copyright © 1995, Association of Computing Machinery. By permission.

way to visualize and manipulate data elements that have many interrelationships. So multidimensional databases have become the most popular database structure for the *analytical databases* that support *online analytical processing* (OLAP) applications, in which fast answers to complex business queries are expected. We will discuss OLAP applications in Chapter 8.

The hierarchical data structure is a natural model for the databases used for many of the structured, routine types of transaction processing characteristic of many business operations. Data for many of these operations can easily be represented by groups of records in a hierarchical relationship. However, there are many cases where information is needed about records that do not have hierarchical relationships. For example, it is obvious that, in some organizations, employees from more than one department can work on more than one project (see Figure 5.15). A network data structure could easily handle this many-to-many relationship. It is thus

Evaluation of Database Structures

FIGURE 5.17

An example of the different dimensions of a multidimensional database.

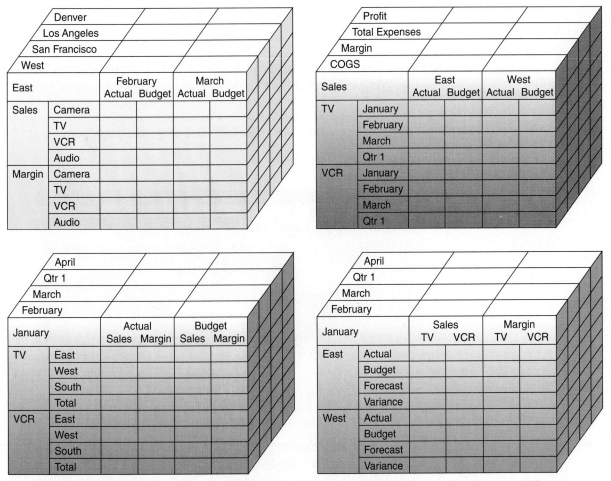

Source: Adapted from Richard Finkelstein, *Understanding the Need for On-Line Analytical Servers* (Ann Arbor, MI., *Arbor Software Corporation,* 1994), p. 9.

more flexible than the hierarchical structure in support of databases for many types of business operations. However, like the hierarchical structure, because its relationships must be specified in advance, the network model cannot easily handle ad hoc requests for information.

Relational databases, on the other hand, allow an end user to easily receive information in response to ad hoc requests. That's because not all of the relationships between the data elements in a relationally organized database need to be specified when the database is created. Database management software (such as Oracle, DB2, Access, and Approach) create new tables of data relationships using parts of the data from several tables. Thus, relational databases are easier for programmers to work with and easier to maintain than the hierarchical and network models.

The major limitation of the relational model is that database management systems based on it cannot process large amounts of business transactions as quickly and efficiently as those based on the hierarchical and network models, in which all data relationships are prespecified. However, this performance gap is narrowing with the development of advanced relational DBMS software. The use of database management software based on the object-oriented and multidimensional models is growing steadily, but these technologies are still not developed fully enough for widespread use in most business information systems.

Database Development

Developing small, personal databases is relatively easy using microcomputer database management packages. See Figure 5.18 and Figure 10.44 in Chapter 10. However, developing a large database can be a complex task. In many companies, developing and managing large corporate databases is the primary responsibility of the database administrator and database design analysts. They work with end users and systems analysts to determine (1) what data definitions should be included in the database and (2) what structure or relationships should exist among the data elements.

FIGURE 5.18

Creating a database with Microsoft Access. This display shows how a customer record is created and added to the Customers table that is part of a company database.

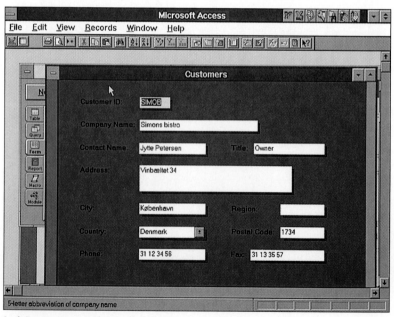

Sarah Evertson/Courtesy of Microsoft Corporation.

As Figure 5.19 illustrates, database development may start with a top-down **data planning** process. Database administrators and designers work with corporate and end user management to develop an *enterprise model* that defines the basic business processes of the enterprise. Then they define the information needs of end users in a business process, such as the purchasing/receiving process that all businesses have [17].

Next, end users must identify the key data elements that are needed to perform their specific business activities. This frequently involves developing *entity relationship diagrams* (ERDs) that model the relationships among the many entities involved in business processes. For example, Figure 5.20 illustrates some of the relationships in a purchasing/receiving system. End users and database designers could use ERD models to identify what supplier and product data are necessary in the purchasing/receiving process.

Such user views are a major part of a **data modeling** process where the relationships between data elements are identified. Each data model defines the logical relationships among the data elements needed to support a basic business process. For example, can a supplier provide more than one type of product to us? Can a customer have more than one type of account with us? Can an employee have several pay rates or be assigned to several project work groups? Answering such questions will identify data relationships that have to be represented in a data model that supports a business process.

Data Planning and Database Design

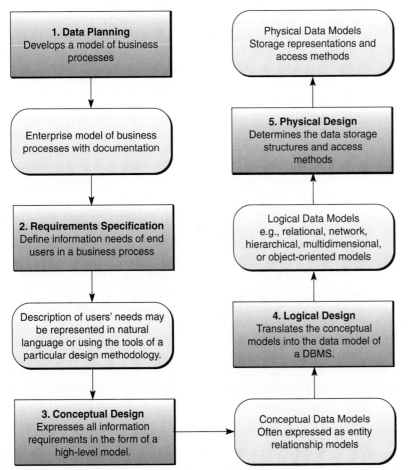

FIGURE 5.19

Database development involves data planning and database design activities. Data models that support business processes are used to develop databases that meet the information needs of users.

Source: Adapted from Veda Storey and Robert Goldstein, "Knowledge-Based Approaches to Database Design," *MIS Quarterly,* March 1993, p. 26. Reprinted with permission from the *MIS Quarterly.*

FIGURE 5.20

This entity relationship diagram illustrates some of the relationships among entities in a purchasing/receiving system.

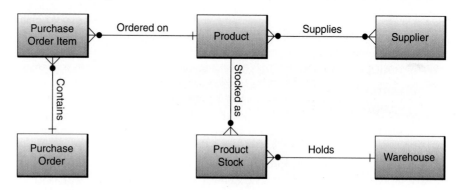

These data models then serve as logical frameworks (called *schemas* and *subschemas*) on which to base the *physical design* of databases and the development of application programs to support the business processes of the organization. A schema is an overall logical view of the relationships between data in a database, while the *subschema* is a logical view of the data relationships needed to support specific end user application programs that will access that database.

Remember that data models represent *logical views* of the data and relationships of the database. Physical database design takes a *physical view* of the data (also called the internal view) that describes how data are to be physically arranged, stored, and accessed on the magnetic disks and other secondary storage devices of a computer system. For example, Figure 5.21 shows these different database views and the software interface of a bank database processing system.

Accessing Files and Databases

Databases and files are stored on various types of storage media and are organized in a variety of ways to make it easier to access the data records they contain. In database and file maintenance, records have to be continually added, deleted, or updated to reflect business transactions. Data must also be accessed so information can be produced in response to end user requests. Thus, efficient access to data is important.

Key Fields

That's why all data records usually contain one or more identification fields, or keys, that identify the record so it can be located. For example, the Social Security number of a person is often used as a *primary* **key field** that uniquely identifies the data records of individuals in student, employee, and customer files and databases. Other methods also identify and link data records stored in several different database files. For example, hierarchical and network databases may use *pointer fields*. These are fields within a record that indicate (point to) the location of another record that is related to it in the same file, or in another file. Hierarchical and network database management systems use this method to link records so they can retrieve information from several different database files.

Relational database management packages use primary keys to link records. Each table (file) in a relational database must contain a primary key. This field (or fields) uniquely identifies each record in a file and must also be found in other related files. For example, in Figure 5.15, department number (Deptno) is the primary key in the Department table and is also a field in the Employee table. As we mentioned earlier, a relational database management package could easily provide you with information from both tables to join the tables and retrieve the information you want. See Figure 5.22.

FIGURE 5.21

Examples of the logical and physical database views and the software interface of a database processing system in banking.

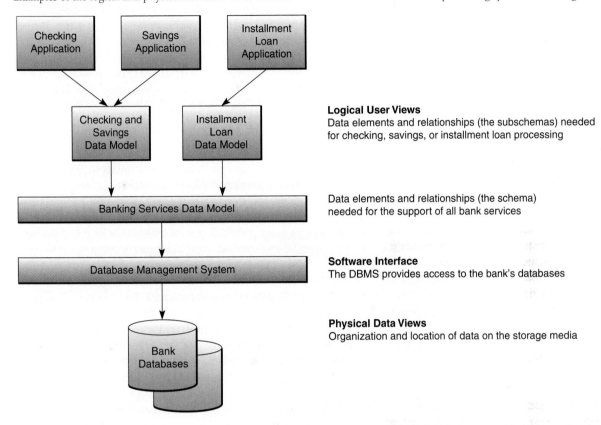

Logical User Views
Data elements and relationships (the subschemas) needed for checking, savings, or installment loan processing

Data elements and relationships (the schema) needed for the support of all bank services

Software Interface
The DBMS provides access to the bank's databases

Physical Data Views
Organization and location of data on the storage media

One of the basic ways to access data is to use a **sequential organization,** in which records are physically stored in a specified order according to a key field in each record. For example, payroll records could be placed in a payroll file in a numerical order based on employee Social Security numbers. **Sequential access** is fast and efficient when dealing with large volumes of data that need to be processed periodically. However, it requires that all new transactions be sorted into the proper sequence for

Sequential Organization and Access

FIGURE 5.22

Joining the Employee and Department tables in a relational database allows you to selectively access data in both tables at the same time.

Department Table

Deptno	Dname	Dloc	Dmgr
Dept A			
Dept B			
Dept C			

Employee Table

Empno	Ename	Etitle	Esalary	Deptno
Emp 1				Dept A
Emp 2				Dept A
Emp 3				Dept B
Emp 4				Dept B
Emp 5				Dept C
Emp 6				Dept B

sequential access processing. Also, most of the database or file may have to be searched to locate, store, or modify even a small number of data records. Thus, this method is too slow to handle applications requiring immediate updating or responses.

Direct Organization and Access

When using **direct access** methods, records do not have to be arranged in any particular sequence on storage media. However, the computer must keep track of the storage location of each record using a variety of **direct organization** methods so that data can be retrieved when needed. New transactions data do not have to be sorted, and processing that requires immediate responses or updating is easily handled. There are a number of ways to directly access records in the direct organization method. Let's take a look at three widely used methods to accomplish such *direct access processing.*

One common technique of direct access is **key transformation.** This method performs an arithmetic computation on a key field of record (such as a product number or Social Security number) and uses the number that results from that calculation as an address to store and access that record. Thus, the process is called *key transformation* because an arithmetic operation is applied to a key field to transform it into the storage location address of a record. Another direct access method used to store and locate records involves the use of an **index** of record keys and related storage addresses. A new data record is stored at the next available location, and its key and address are placed in an index. The computer uses this index whenever it must access a record.

In the **indexed sequential access method** (ISAM), records are physically stored in a sequential order on a magnetic disk or other direct access storage device based on the key field of each record. In addition, each file contains an index that references one or more key fields of each data record to its storage location address. Thus, an individual record can be directly located by using its key fields to search and locate its address in the file index, just as you can locate key topics in this book by looking them up in its index. As a result, if a few records must be processed quickly, the file index is used to directly access the record needed. However, when large numbers of records must be processed periodically, the sequential organization provided by this method is used. For example, processing the weekly payroll for employees or producing monthly statements for customers would be done using sequential access processing of the records in the file or database.

BOOZ ALLEN & HAMILTON AND VOICE I/S: DATABASES FOR MULTIPLE TYPES OF DATA

You won't be seeing voice and video or Internet transactions in your typical accounting database any time soon. But many information systems shops are laying the groundwork for a new generation of corporate databases that will manage a broad range of data types.

Object technology can stir up contentious technical debates: Are users better off with pure object databases or with hybrid systems that meld relational and object functions? According to industry consultants and IS managers, there is no clear right or wrong choice. Instead, companies need to make decisions based on their current database investments and predictions of how significant a role they expect objects to play.

For years, companies have worked with object technology and found ways to incorporate nonrelational data types into their IS operations with dedicated systems, such as imaging or text-retrieval systems. The difference today, according to many observers, is there are more substantial business reasons to integrate these functions directly into the corporate database environment. The most compelling business driver today is the Internet. Because so much of the information flying across the Internet is nonrelational, companies need databases that can store, retrieve, and manage other data types, particularly documents, video, and sound.

As a result, the big database software developers are shipping tools to "Internet-enable" their software. This—among other things—lets users from a remote World Wide Web browser directly access the database. With this capability, companies can move from static Internet activity—essentially publishing company information—to an interactive environment of electronic commerce.

"There has to be a business reason before these technologies become attractive," says Yogesh Gupta, a senior vice president of product strategy at Computer Associates, "For relational, it was ad hoc queries. People are now making audio, video, and graphics an integral part of their business. To do that, you need to have a database that supports these rich data types."

Booz Allen & Hamilton, Inc., a consulting firm in New York and an Oracle user, has been developing a worldwide knowledge database that its consultants can tap into and use on consulting assignments. Aron Dutta, a principal and member of the knowledge team developing this database, says, "we have to handle more than relational data" because data exists in so many different formats.

The company has used separate subsystems from several vendors to manage various data sources such as document images. But the firm wanted one integrated platform to manage all data types. It now uses the relational database and Web server components of Oracle's Universal Server. It will evaluate this platform for managing other data types as well, Dutta says.

Bryan Knox, president of Voice I/S, Inc., a customer-support software provider in Dallas, Texas, is testing object extensions for IBM's DB2 Relational DBMS so his company can integrate voice data into its DB2-based system.

"This swings the door wide open," Knox says. Voice I/S plans to sell new customer service software that can handle relational, image, and voice data. "Historically, voice-processing solutions didn't talk to relational databases," he says. His company had to link its DB2-based system to images stored in image databases. By using the DB2 object extenders, the company will be able to provide application software that uses one database for different data types.

As an example, the customer service application will not only store voice messages but also eventually store images of letters and documents such as contracts and related product information that are associated with customer accounts, Knox says.

CASE STUDY QUESTIONS

1. What is the impact of the Internet on databases that Booz Allen & Hamilton can use to store, retrieve, and manage multiple data types?

2. Why does Voice I/S have a business need for a hybrid relational/object database system?

3. How could a typical business use relational/object databases that hold multiple types of data? Give several examples.

Source: Adapted from Rosemary Cafassso, "Busting Loose," *Computerworld*, April 15, 1996, pp. 93, 96. Copyright © 1996 by Computerworld, Inc., Framingham, MA 01701—Reprinted from *Computerworld*.

Summary

- **Data Resource Management.** Data resource management is a managerial activity that applies information systems technology and management tools to the task of managing an organization's data resources. It includes the database administration function that focuses on developing and maintaining standards and controls for an organization's databases. Data administration, however, focuses on the planning and control of data to support business functions and strategic organizational objectives. This includes a data planning effort that focuses on developing an overall data architecture for a firm's data resources.

- **Database Management.** The database management approach affects the storage and processing of data. The data needed by different applications is consolidated and integrated into several common databases, instead of being stored in many independent data files. Also, the database management approach emphasizes updating and maintaining common databases, having users' application programs share the data in the database, and providing a reporting and an inquiry/response capability so end users can easily receive reports and quick responses to requests for information.

- **Database Software.** Database management systems are software packages that simplify the creation, use, and maintenance of databases. They provide software tools so end users, programmers, and database administrators can create and modify databases, interrogate a database, generate reports, do application development, and perform database maintenance.

- **Types of Databases.** Several types of databases are used by computer-using organizations, including central, distributed, end user, management, data warehouse, and online databases. Text databases consist of data in text form, while image databases contain digitized images of documents, photographs, and other visual media. Special database management software can catalog and index such databases for quick retrieval of text and images of documents or other forms of information.

- **Database Development.** The development of databases can be easily accomplished using microcomputer database management packages for small end user applications. However, the development of large corporate databases requires a top-down data planning effort. This may involve developing enterprise and entity relationship models, subject area databases, and data models that reflect the logical data elements and relationships needed to support the operation and management of the basic business processes of the organization.

- **Data Organization and Access.** Data must be organized in some logical manner on physical storage devices so that they can be efficiently processed. For this reason, data are commonly organized into logical data elements such as characters, fields, records, files, and databases. Database structures, such as the hierarchical, network, relational, and object-oriented models, are used to organize the relationships among the data records stored in databases. Databases and files can be organized in either a sequential or direct manner and can be accessed and maintained by either sequential access or direct access processing methods.

Key Terms and Concepts

These are the key terms and concepts of this chapter. The page number of their first explanation is in parentheses.

1. Data administration (176)
2. Data dictionary (168)
3. Data modeling (183)
4. Data planning (175)
5. Data resource management (164)
6. Database administration (175)
7. Database administrator (167)
8. Database management approach (166)
9. Database management system (167)
10. Database and file access (184)
    a. Direct (186)
    b. Sequential (185)
11. Database structures (178)
    a. Hierarchical (178)
    b. Network (178)

c. Multidimensional (180)
d. Object-oriented (180)
e. Relational (178)
12. DBMS uses (167)
    a. Application development (171)
    b. Database development (167)
    c. Database interrogation (168)
    d. Database maintenance (171)
13. Key field (184)
14. Logical data elements (164)
    a. Character (165)
    b. Field (165)
    c. Record (165)
    d. File (165)
    e. Database (166)

15. Query language (168)
16. Report generator (168)
17. Types of databases (171)
    a. Analytical (171)
    b. Data warehouse (172)
    c. Distributed (172)
    d. End user (172)
    e. External (172)
    f. Image (173)
    g. Multimedia (173)
    h. Operational (171)
    i. Text (173)

Review Quiz

Match one of the key terms and concepts listed above with one of the brief examples or definitions listed below. Try to find the best fit for answers that seem to fit more than one term or concept. Defend your choices.

_____ 1. The use of integrated collections of data records and files for data storage and processing.

_____ 2. A DBMS allows you to create, interrogate, and maintain a database, create reports, and develop application programs.

_____ 3. A specialist in charge of the databases of an organization.

_____ 4. This DBMS feature allows users to easily interrogate a database.

_____ 5. Defines and catalogs the data elements and data relationships in an organization's database.

_____ 6. Helps you specify and produce reports from a database.

_____ 7. The main software package that supports a database management approach.

_____ 8. Databases are dispersed throughout an organization.

_____ 9. Your own personal databases.

_____ 10. Databases of documents.

_____ 11. Applies information systems technology and management tools to the management of an organization's data resources.

_____ 12. Developing databases and maintaining standards and controls for an organization's databases.

_____ 13. The planning and control of data to support organizational objectives.

_____ 14. A top-down effort that ties database development to the support of basic business processes.

_____ 15. Developing conceptual views of the relationships among data in a database.

_____ 16. A customer's name.

_____ 17. A customer's name, address, and account balance.

_____ 18. The names, addresses, and account balances of all of your customers.

_____ 19. An integrated collection of all of the data about your customers.

_____ 20. An identification field in a record.

_____ 21. A treelike structure of records in a database.

_____ 22. A tabular structure of records in a database.

_____ 23. Records are stored as cubes within cubes in a database.

_____ 24. Transactions are sorted in ascending order by Social Security number before processing.

_____ 25. Unsorted transactions can be used to immediately update a database.

_____ 26. Databases that support the major business processes of an organization.

_____ 27. A centralized and integrated database of current and historical data about an organization.

_____ 28. Databases provided by online information services.

_____ 29. Databases that store data as text, images, sound, and video.

Discussion Questions

1. Organizations could not survive or succeed without quality data about their internal operations and external environment. Do you agree? What examples can you give to defend your position?

2. If data are an important resource and asset to a firm, they must be managed properly. What role does database management and data administration play in managing data?

3. What are the advantages of the database management approaches to managing an organization's data resources? Give examples to illustrate your answer.

4. Refer to the Real World Case on Victoria's Secret in the chapter. How could a company "recoup the price of a data warehouse system with just one decision"?

5. What is a database management system? What functions does it enable end users and IS professionals to accomplish?

6. Databases of information about a firm's internal operations were formerly the only databases that were considered to be important to a business. What other kinds of databases are there? What is their importance to end users and their organizations?

7. Refer to the Real World Case on Booz Allen & Hamilton and Voice I/S in the chapter. Do you agree that "people are now making audio, video, and graphics an integral part of their business"? Give several examples to back up your answer.

8. Why has the relational database model become more important than the hierarchical and network structures? Why do you think object-oriented database models are gaining in popularity?

9. Do you think that developing a company's databases might require a data planning effort that is part of that organization's strategic planning process? Explain.

10. How have the Internet and the World Wide Web affected end user access to external text, image, and multimedia databases?

Real World Problems

1. CVS/Pharmacies: Building a Data Warehouse

For the IS managers and business decisionmakers at CVS/Pharmacy, building a data warehouse was more than an attempt to gain a strategic advantage—it was a matter of survival. Before raising a data warehouse in 1993, CVS, a division of Melville Corp., was managing all the information from its chain of 1,400 pharmacies in the Northeast on an IBM mainframe using applications developed in the 1970s and early 1980s. Howard Edels, MIS senior vice president, said CVS had nowhere else to go: Changes in the health care system made information that could cut costs vital. "This project is critical to this company's future," he said.

After completing the first phase of its data warehouse, CVS is already reaping just that kind of data, according to Edels. For instance, CVS can now analyze when stores are busiest and which stores sell the most of what kinds of retail items and prescriptions, according to Shafi Shilad, MIS vice president for pharmacy systems. CVS can also verify HMO-based prescriptions online. Edels said CVS also envisions being able to market specials to individual consumers based on their buying patterns, make more use of less costly generic drugs, send customers reminders about taking medicine that could keep them out of the hospital, and even offer pharmacists' services for a fee.

Edels said the project has cost unspecified millions of dollars for equipment and consultants, required eight monthly meetings with management to detail the system's strategic importance and work challenges, and entailed hours of training for 100 IS staff and 35 end users. CVS uses an Oracle7 database management system on a 10-processor UNIX-based Nile server. It has two dual-processor Nile servers for online transaction processing of prescriptions.

a. Why did CVS/Pharmacies need a data warehouse?

b. What business benefits resulted from their data warehouse? Was it worth the cost? Explain.

Source: Adapted from Michael Goldberg, "Data Warehouse Fills CVS Prescription," *Computerworld*, April 1, 1996, p. 77. Copyright © 1996 by Computerworld, Inc., Framingham, MA 01701—Reprinted from *Computerworld*.

2. America Online: Linking Web Servers to Corporate Databases

Linking World Wide Web servers to corporate databases can be a royal pain, partly because there is no single way to do it. The high price of siting a database behind a Web application also has deterred some users. But making a Web/database connection is often necessary for many intranet systems, such as simple telephone directories or more complicated customer service applications. Some external Internet applications—order taking, package tracking—couldn't exist without Web/database links. Fortunately, some creative information systems groups have found ways around the high price and high tension.

For example, America Online's Netscape Web server can talk directly to an Illustra Information Technologies object database management system. Illustra programmers can embed SQL, the language understood by relational databases, in Hypertext Markup Language (HTML) documents stored in America Online's Web site object database. One scenario in which that would matter is online shopping. Orders placed by Internet users can quickly update a relational inventory. Although few Web servers can communicate directly with databases, more will have that capability soon, says Jean Anderson, an independent Web and database consultant in San Diego, California.

a. Why is there a business need to link Internet Web servers with corporate databases?

b. How does America Online link its Web sites to corporate databases?

Source: Adapted from Kim Nash, "Rethink Those Links," *Computerworld*, April 15, 1996, p. 75. Copyright © 1996 by Computerworld, Inc., Framingham, MA 01701—Reprinted from *Computerworld*.

3. DbIntellect and MCI: Fast Answers to Database Queries

It sounds too good to be true: Database management software that speeds most queries 10, 40, or even 500 times faster than conventional relational database management systems (RDBMS). But it seems true nonetheless. Sybase, Inc.'s IQ is turning out results that have impressed users and analysts.

IQ achieves its speed by storing data from a data warehouse in columns rather than tables. It uses an indexing technology called bit-mapping, where each data element is represented by a single digit rather than by a word or phrase. In addition to bit maps, IQ also uses special indexes that excel at finding specific records or ranges of records. The combination of indexes, plus an optimizer that picks the right scheme for the job, produces IQ's high performance.

"A very wide range of things that an RDBMS can do, IQ can do faster," said James McElhiney, a senior principal consultant at DbIntellect Technologies, a database application developer in Hull, Quebec. DbIntellect tested data similar to what its end users use and achieved speeds an average of 44 times faster. Nineteen queries ran 500 times faster. At worst some queries ran at half the speed they had.

Other users report similar experiences. "We had one complex decision-support query . . . that we called The Stinker," said a database specialist at a financial services company in Cincinnati, Ohio. "It took an hour to run on an RDBMS. With IQ, it took one minute. I don't see a reason why we shouldn't move our entire decision support database into IQ." Scott F. Barnes, a senior manager at MCI Telecommunications Corp. in Atlanta, Georgia, said IQ let MCI improve its telemarketing efforts by sifting through lists of prospective customers quickly. "It would have taken us three days to do what IQ does in five minutes, so we simply didn't bother," he said.

a. Why do you think IQ's database technology is faster than that used by relational database management systems?

b. Why is it important for MCI and other businesses to have fast answers to database queries?

Source: Adapted from Dan Richman, "Engine that Could," *Computerworld,* April 15, 1996, pp. 53, 56. Copyright © 1996 by Computerworld, Inc., Framingham, MA 01701—Reprinted from *Computerworld.*

4. Motorola, Inc.: Using a Distributed Data Warehouse

A division of Motorola, Inc., in Tempe, Arizona, has built a data warehouse that provides the benefits of both distributed data marts and a centralized data store. The warehouse, which contains product and financial information, lets about 400 users analyze the efficiency of several manufacturing facilities and better manage order fulfillment. The contents of the data warehouse are divided into nine data warehouse segments or "data marts" on Oracle database servers, with information most often accessed by end users kept on the servers closest to them.

Key to the warehouse is a centrally updated repository that contains information about what data exist and where they are housed. The metadata repository is accessible locally by any end user and can be used to locate and access information stored in the nine data marts.

These data warehouse segments, spread across the United States and Europe, and in Tokyo, Japan, are connected via a network of high-speed lines. Motorola loads about 2 gigabytes of data from mainframes and minicomputers into the warehouse each day. At the end of each month, about 20 gigabytes of additional data are loaded, then the distributed database servers are updated. The warehouse is based on a global database format that gives it a common look and feel. End users also have access to a library of queries and formatted reports.

"As a result of the warehouse, we are able to measure the performance of our manufacturing plants in a consistent way," said Barbara Martensen, vice president and director of information systems for the data warehouse sector at Motorola. "We're also using the warehouse to improve quality and deliver products in a more timely way."

a. How does Motorola use the concepts of a distributed data warehouse and data marts?

b. What are the business benefits of this approach?

Source: Adapted from Bard Cole, "Motorola Unit Builds Distributed Warehouse," *Network World,* April 1, 1996, p. 47. Copyright © 1996 by Network World, Inc., Framingham, MA 01701—Reprinted from *Network World.*

Application Exercises

1. An Employee Database Table

Action Products Company's sales department wants to establish a database to track key information about its salespersons. Salespersons are assigned to either industrial or commercial customers and to one of four sales regions (East, South, Midwest, and West). Action Products wishes to record the following information for each salesperson: Their name, the date they were hired, their sales commission rate, their sales region, and the category of customer served. The table below shows this information for Action's sales staff.

a. Using a database software package, create a table to store the preceding information and enter the sample data provided.

b. Generate database queries or reports to answer these questions and get a printed listing of your results.

1. Get a listing of the name, commission rate, and hire date of all salespersons who sell to commercial customers. Sort your listing in order from the first hired to the most recently hired salesperson.
2. Get a listing of the names and commission rates of all salespersons in the eastern region sorted from the lowest to the highest commission rate.
3. Get a listing showing the number of salespersons receiving each commission rate.

Note: If you are not familiar with the use of database software packages and would like additional information about how to design and implement a database application, see Application Exercise 3 in Chapter 10.

Salesperson Name	Hire Date	Commission Rate	Customer Type	Region
E. Lewis	01-18-92	1.50%	Industrial	West
B. Davis	07-03-89	1.75	Commercial	East
S. Arnold	08-22-94	1.25	Commercial	East
B. Smith	11-05-88	1.75	Industrial	Midwest
C. Travis	05-22-96	1.25	Industrial	South
L. Evers	12-09-86	1.75	Commercial	South
T. Turner	09-07-93	1.50	Industrial	East
J. Morris	09-18-87	1.75	Commercial	Midwest
L. Johnson	11-23-95	1.25	Commercial	West
D. Franks	02-11-93	1.50	Commercial	South
C. Norris	06-24-95	1.25	Commercial	Midwest

2. Sales and Commissions at Action Products

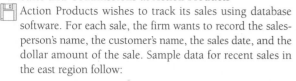

Action Products wishes to track its sales using database software. For each sale, the firm wants to record the sales-person's name, the customer's name, the sales date, and the dollar amount of the sale. Sample data for recent sales in the east region follow:

Salesperson Name	Customer Name	Sales Date*	Sales Dollar Amount
B. Davis	Pace Products	10-07-96	$ 3,540.00
T. Turner	Cyber Inc.	10-07-96	14,875.00
B. Davis	DEF Sales	10-07-96	2,270.00
S. Arnold	Landers'	10-08-96	4,255.00
T. Turner	DDC Inc.	10-08-96	5,240.00
B. Davis	Pace Products	10-09-96	1,692.50
S. Arnold	Tech21	10-09-96	10,247.00
T. Turner	DDC Inc.	10-09-96	8,712.50
B. Davis	DEF Sales	10-10-96	6,805.00
S. Arnold	Landers'	10-10-96	8,150.00
T. Turner	HyTech	10-10-96	3,845.00
B. Davis	Pace Products	10-10-96	12,705.00
T. Turner	Cyber Inc.	10-11-96	7,850.00
B. Davis	Lyons Ltd.	10-11-96	9,885.00

a. Using database software, create an appropriate table for these sales data. If you completed Application Exercise 5–1, add this new table to the database where you stored the employee table. Enter the sample sales data into your sales database table.

b. Using your table of sample data, prepare and get printed listings of the following:

1. A report of sales by the salesperson T. Turner showing detailed information (customer name, date, and amount) for each sale and showing the total dollar amount of sales.

2. A report grouped by customer name showing detailed information (date and amount) for each sale and showing total dollar amount of all sales to each customer.

3. (If you completed Application Exercise 5–1) Join the employee and sales tables appropriately to produce a table showing commissions earned. (The commission earned equals the commission rate from the employee table times the dollar amount from the sales table.) Your report should be grouped by salesperson and should show the customer name, date, sales dollar amount, and commission earned for each sale. It should also show totals for sales dollar amount and commission earned for each salesperson.

Review Quiz Answers

1. 8
2. 12
3. 7
4. 15
5. 2
6. 16
7. 9
8. 17c
9. 17d
10. 17i
11. 5
12. 6
13. 1
14. 4
15. 3
16. 14b
17. 14c
18. 14d
19. 14e
20. 13
21. 11a
22. 11e
23. 11c
24. 10b
25. 10a
26. 17h
27. 17b
28. 17e
29. 17g

Selected References

1. Ahrens, Judith, and Chetan Sankar. "Tailoring Database Training for End Users." *MIS Quarterly,* December 1993.

2. Babcock, Charles. "OLAP Leads Way to Post-Relational Era." *Computerworld,* November 21, 1994.

3. Bruegger, Dave, and Sooun Lee. "Distributed Database Systems: Accessing Data More Efficiently." *Information Systems Management,* Spring 1995.

4. Cafasso, Rosemary. "Multidimensional DB on Comeback Trail." *Computerworld,* October 24, 1994.

5. Chan, Hock Chuan; Kee Wei Kwock; and Keng Leng Siau. "User-Database Interface: The Effect of Abstraction Levels on Query Performance." *MIS Quarterly,* December 1993.

6. Courtney, James, and David Paradice. *Database Systems for Management.* 2nd ed. Burr Ridge, IL: Richard D. Irwin, 1992.

7. Grover, Varun, and James Teng. "How Effective Is Data Resource Management? Reassessing Strategic Objectives." *Journal of Information Systems Management,* Summer 1991.

8. Jacobsen, Ivar; Maria Ericsson; and Ageneta Jacobsen. *The Object Advantage: Business Process Reengineering with Object Technology.* New York: ACM Press. 1995.

9. Jenkings, Avery. "Warehouse Woes." In Depth. *Computerworld,* February 6, 1995.

10. Kroenke, David. *Database Processing: Fundamentals, Design, Implementation.* New York: Macmillan, 1992.

11. Nash, Kim. "Wizard Turns English into Database Language." *Computerworld,* February 20, 1995.

12. Pei, Daniel, and Carmine Cutone. "Object-Oriented Analysis and Design: Realism or Impressionism." *Information Systems Management,* Winter 1995.

13. "Shedding Light on Data Warehousing for More Informed Business Solutions." Special Advertising Supplement. *Computerworld,* February 13, 1995.

14. Slitz, John. "Object Technology Profiles." Special Advertising Supplement. *Computerworld,* June 13, 1994.

15. Smith, Lavica. "Developers Eye Object Databases." *PC Week,* February 15, 1993.

16. Spiegler, Israel. "Toward a Unified View of Data: Bridging Data Structure and Content." *Information Systems Management,* Spring 1995.

17. Storey, Veda, and Robert Goldstein. "Knowledge-Based Approaches to Database Design." *MIS Quarterly,* March 1993.

18. Tasker, Daniel. "Object Lesson." *Computerworld,* April 22, 1991.

19. Wylder, John. "The Network as the Enterprise Database." *Information Systems Management,* Spring 1995.

Continuing Real World Case

Fast Freight, Inc.: Networking the Enterprise—Part II: Hardware, Software, Data, and Network Resources

Fast Freight's Computer Network

Fast Information Systems has developed a computer network designed uniquely for Fast Freight's transportation services. See Figure 2. In-house developers, with assistance from IBM, developed what Jim Kellogg, Fast Freight's senior systems engineer, calls a "three-layer network" to link and assist all divisions of the company. But nowhere is the computer network more important than to the company's intermodal trucking service. Through the hardware configurations and the developed software, the overall system impacts the service in three areas: day-to-day dispatch operations, depot and home office administration, and record storage and retrieval. Fast Freight's triple layer system has been geared to support the heart of the business.

The first layer consists of a network of IBM AS/400 midrange computers installed at 11 rail depot offices and the headquarters in Wenatchee. As an example, the Wenatchee AS/400 has 82 megabytes of main RAM with a 98-gigabyte hard disk drive storage capacity along with a 5-gigabyte, 8mm magnetic tape backup system. Video terminals with keyboards and mouse devices handle input of data by office personnel, while output is displayed on 14-inch color monitors. Depending on the office, each unit connects to one or several laser printers and facsimile machines. A token ring network using the Novell NetWare network operating system, installed on a network server, connects all peripheral devices with the AS/400. Thus, all units in the field can connect with the home office computer via regular telecommunications lines.

At the terminals, dispatchers, operators, and managers process data by means of customized software packages, including Walldata and Rumba, through a Windows interface. This software helps employees to enter and process incoming orders, updates the company database, allows dispatchers to assign trucks and drivers, coordinates rail schedules, and records the freight to be handled. An information card is then printed and posted on a master schedule board for dispatchers to monitor. Once initial orders are processed, all documents are faxed to the home office in Wenatchee.

The second layer of Fast Freight's system enhances the administration of the company. Each depot manager and repair facility, as well as all key administration personnel, have an IBM 486 DX250 PC at their disposal. These units have 16

FIGURE 2

Fast Freight's computer network.

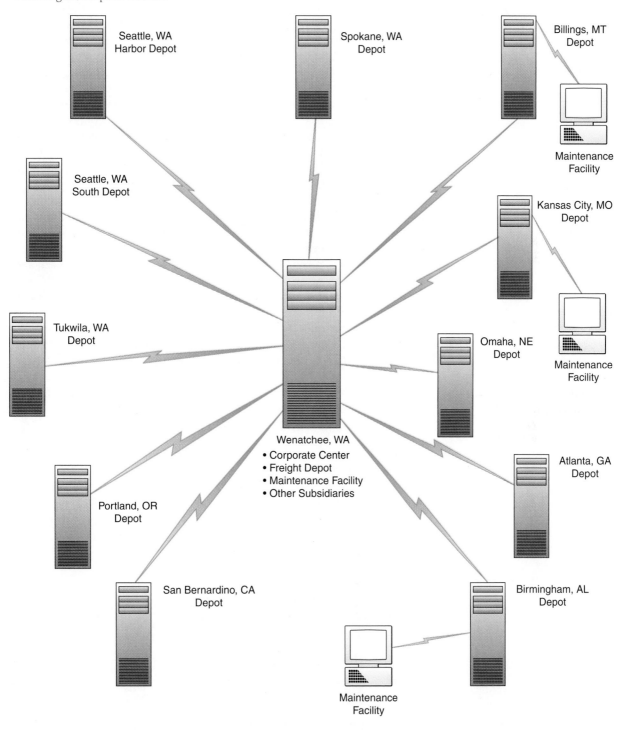

megabytes of RAM, a 250 megabyte hard disk along with keyboard, mouse, and 16-inch color monitor. A variety of business applications are accomplished through the Microsoft Office software suite using Windows for Work Groups as the operating system interface. Each PC is connected via the token ring network server to office peripherals and telecommunications lines for access and exchange of information with other depots and the home office.

Sometimes Fast Freight needs to quickly access and produce documents from past business transactions. That is accomplished through the third layer of Fast Freight's system. Fast Imaging Services was set up to provide electronic document management (EDM) services for the subsidiaries of Fast Freight and its customers. However, the bulk of the transaction document image processing comes from the company's intermodal trucking service.

The heart of the EDM system is a Novell server, a Pentium 66 computer with 72 megabytes of main RAM and 22 gigabytes of disk storage. Documents are captured by a Hewlett-Packard image scanner and displayed on 18-inch full document monitors. A DAT 42-gigabyte tape subsystem backs up data every noon of the workweek. The unit is connected via the token ring network to Fast Freight's other two systems and office peripheral devices.

All documents that come into the home office are captured, processed, and stored. Appropriate copies are mailed out to customers who do not use EDM, and then all documents are destroyed by shredding. Therefore, a corporate database of transaction documents is maintained for Fast Freight, Inc., as well as for its major customer, Burlington Northern. Having this EDM layer aligned with the other two gives Fast Freight an invaluable multilevel computer network that has improved the efficiency and effectiveness of Fast Freight's service to the transportation industry.

Case Study Questions

1. What are the following components of Fast Freight's computer network?
   a. Hardware resources.
   b. Software resources.
   c. Data resources.
   d. Network resources.
2. Why does Jim Kellogg call Fast Freight's computer network a three-layer network? Explain the business role of each layer.
3. Given current hardware and software developments in the business world, would you upgrade any of Fast Freight's hardware and software? Explain your suggestions with several examples.

III

Applications

How are information systems used to support end user computing, business operations, managerial decision making, and strategic advantage? The four chapters of this module show you how such applications are accomplished in modern organizations.

Chapter 6, "Information Systems for End User Computing and Collaboration," discusses the resource requirements and managerial challenges of end user and work group computing applications. It also discusses the benefits and limitations of major types of office automation information systems.

Chapter 7, "Information Systems for Business Operations," describes how information systems support the business functions of marketing, manufacturing, human resource management, accounting, and finance. It also

shows the various ways that information systems support the processing of transactions generated by business operations.

Chapter 8, "Information Systems for Managerial Decision Support," shows how management information systems, decision support systems, executive information systems, expert systems, and artificial intelligence technologies have been developed and applied to business operations and decision-making situations faced by managers.

Chapter 9, "Information Systems for Strategic Advantage," introduces fundamental concepts of strategic advantage through information technology, and illustrates strategic applications of information systems that can gain competitive advantages for an organization.

Information Systems for End User Computing and Collaboration

CHAPTER OUTLINE

LEARNING OBJECTIVES

After reading and studying this chapter, you should be able to:

1. Discuss the reasons for the growth of end user computing and collaboration.

2. Identify the major components and resources needed to support end user computing.

3. Identify and give examples for each of the major application categories of end user and work group computing.

4. Give examples of several risks in end user computing and possible managerial solutions to reduce such risks.

5. Discuss the purposes and activities of the major types of office automation systems.

6. Identify several types of electronic office communications and their benefits for end users.

7. Discuss the benefits and limitations of office automation systems.

Section I — *End User Computing and Collaboration*

End User Computing

The days of relying primarily on information systems professionals to meet our information processing needs are over. Most organizations can't keep up with the information demands of their end users. So today's knowledge workers use networked microcomputers as professional workstations to get the information they need to accomplish their jobs successfully. That's what **end user computing** is all about. It's the direct, hands-on use of computers by end users, instead of the indirect use provided by the hardware, software, and professional resources of an organization's information services department. This doesn't mean that end users don't rely on IS resources. However, in end user computing, an information services department plays only a supportive role to an end user's own computing resources and efforts.

Why has end user computing grown? Because information services departments have shown that they cannot keep up with the information demands of end users. Developing computer-based information system solutions for users by teams of systems analysts and programmers is costly and time-consuming. Thus, many organizations estimate they have a backlog of unfilled user requests for information systems development of two to five years. This backlog includes the development of new applications as well as the changes made to improve existing information systems in the systems maintenance activity. To make matters worse, the backlog discourages users from making additional requests for systems development. Experts estimate that this creates a *hidden backlog* of unsubmitted requests that is even greater than the apparent backlog of formal user requests.

Another major reason for the growth of end user computing lies in the dramatic improvements in the capabilities and availability of computer hardware, software, and networks. The development of networked microcomputers has brought computing power down to the departmental, work group, and individual levels. Also, software packages for end users for all types of applications have proliferated and improved in their power and ease of use. These improvements have made computer hardware, software, and networks affordable and attractive to many individuals and organizations. These developments are reinforced by the growing familiarity of many end users with computers, caused by their longtime and widespread use in schools, businesses, and other organizations. Thus, end users are able to turn to the direct use of information technology to solve their information processing problems.

End User Collaboration

The cooperation of individuals produces the finest end results, yet balancing cooperation and individualism is a never-ending challenge. The 1980s delivered a revolution in work and computing: The personal computer freed workers to compute independently. The information systems revolution of the 1990s is the local area network. Networks encourage people to work individually while fostering cooperation among them [15].

Most of us have to interact with others to get things done. And as you can see, information technology is changing the way we work. Telecommunications networks enable us to collaborate: To share resources, communicate ideas, and coordinate our

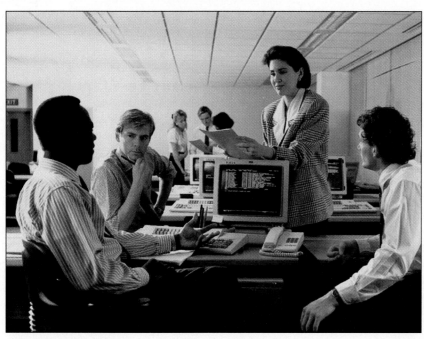

Tim Brown/Tony Stone Images.

FIGURE 6.1

Information technology
enhances end user
collaboration.

efforts as members of the many formal and informal *work groups* that make up
today's organizations. For example, the members of many office work groups depend
on local area networks to communicate with electronic mail and share hardware
devices, software packages, and work group databases. At large multinational corporations, work groups use global telecommunications networks to communicate with
and coordinate the activities of their counterparts at various overseas locations. Thus
in this chapter, we will explore the many types of applications that enhance the communications and coordination, and thus the collaboration of end user work groups
and their organizations. See Figure 6.1.

It is important to think of end user computing in an information system context.
Figure 6.2 shows the resource components and application outputs of an end user
computing system. It illustrates the major categories of end user computing applications, and the hardware, software, people, data, and network resources required.
As you can see, end user computing systems are microcomputer-based information
systems that directly support both the operational and managerial applications of
end users.

Figure 6.2 also shows that many end users do not rely solely on their own
microcomputer workstations, software packages, and databases. They can also rely
on the support of software packages, databases, and networked computer systems at
the work group, departmental, and corporate levels. In addition, many organizations
provide information centers as another source of support for end user computing.
Information center specialists serve as consultants to users who need assistance in
their computing efforts. In this way, organizations hope to improve the efficiency and
effectiveness of end user computing.

Components of an End User Computing System

Resources for End User Computing

Figure 6.2 emphasizes that hardware, software, people, data, and network resources are needed for end user computing. Let's briefly consider each of these resources.

Hardware Resources: End User Workstations

The hardware resources for end user computing consist primarily of microcomputer workstations. Microcomputer systems (including their peripheral devices) provide the information processing capabilities needed for most user applications. Though dumb terminals connected to minicomputers or mainframes are sometimes used, they have been largely replaced by networks of microcomputer workstations. Therefore, as Figure 6.2 shows, microcomputer workstations may be tied by telecommunications links to other workstations in a local area network, with a more powerful microcomputer operating as a network server. Or they may be connected to larger networks, using departmental minicomputers or corporate mainframes as hosts. Server computer systems (1) help control communications in the network including serving as gateways between networks, (2) oversee the sharing of software packages and databases among the workstations in the network, and (3) perform time-sharing processing services for jobs that are too big for the workstations to handle.

FIGURE 6.2

An end user computing system. Note the major categories of end user computing applications and the hardware, software, people, data, and network resources required.

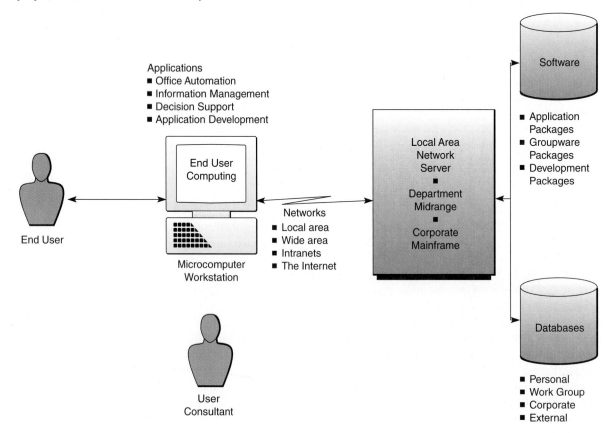

Application software packages for microcomputer systems are the primary software resources needed for end user computing. These include general-purpose *productivity packages* for word processing, electronic spreadsheets, database and information management, graphics, data communications, and integrated packages, as discussed in Chapter 3. Other software resources include packages for *office automation* applications such as desktop publishing, electronic mail, and office support services. We will discuss such packages in Section II of this chapter. Of course, many other types of application software can be used, depending on the business needs of end users.

Groupware is a fast-growing category of software for end user computing. Groupware is *collaboration software,* that is, software that helps work groups of end users work together to accomplish group assignments. As we will discuss in more detail shortly, this includes software for applications like electronic mail, joint word processing and spreadsheet analysis, file sharing, computer conferencing, scheduling meetings, project management, and so on. See Figure 6.3.

Application development packages are another major category of software resources shown in Figure 6.2. This includes fourth-generation languages and other application development packages. As discussed in Chapter 3, 4GL packages allow users to specify what information they want, rather than how the computer system should do it. Major categories of 4GLs include natural and structured query languages, such as Intellect and SQL, and the report generators found in many spreadsheet programs, integrated packages, database management systems, and decision support system packages. Such tools allow end users to make ad hoc inquiries and generate their own reports. The application generators found in database management and other application development packages are also included in this category. These packages provide *visual programming* tools that allow experienced end users to interactively develop their own application programs, instead of relying on professional systems analysts and programmers.

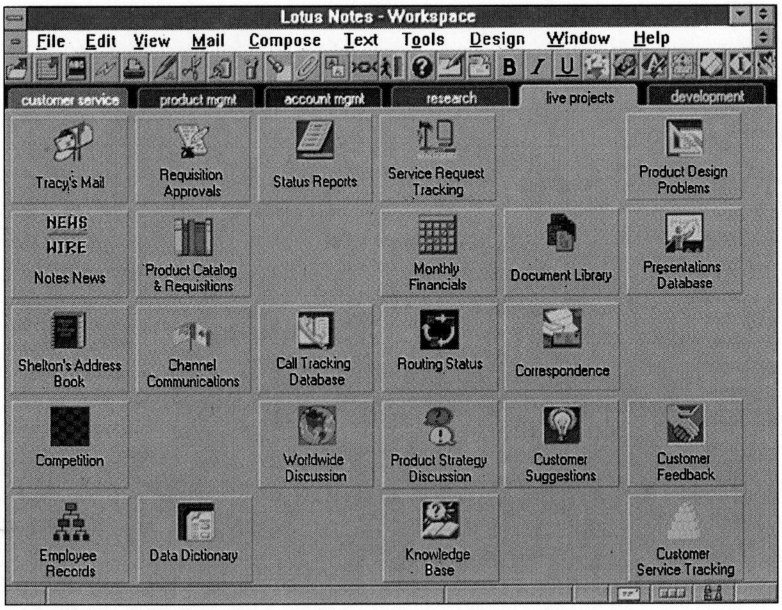

Software Resources: End User Packages

Courtesy of Lotus Development Corporation.

FIGURE 6.3

Lotus Notes is a popular groupware package. Notice how it organizes end user activities to support end user collaboration.

Data Resources: Multiple Databases

Figure 6.2 emphasizes that end user computing relies on several major types of databases introduced in Chapter 5. Personal databases are created and maintained by end users to support their individual professional activities. For example, personal databases may have files of correspondence created by word processing or spreadsheets created by electronic spreadsheet packages. End users may also have access to work group and corporate databases through telecommunications network links. This allows end users to transfer data files among themselves and work group and corporate offices. Finally, end users can use the telecommunications capabilities of their workstations to access external databases. This allows them to access a wealth of economic and other types of information from the data banks of commercial information services.

Network Resources: Networking End Users

Telecommunications networks have become a fundamental resource of end user computing. Just think of how common it is for end user computers to be networked together in local area networks, connected to wide area networks, and able to access corporate intranets and the Internet. Most of today's business end users work in networked work groups, departments, enterprises, and global markets. They rely on interconnected networks of information systems to share ideas, information, and computing resources. These networks support information technologies such as E-mail, file transfer, and video conferencing that enable fast communications and easy collaboration across the enterprise and among organizations. Thus, businesspeople can work together productively no matter where they are located. And that has become an essential ingredient for success in today's fast-changing global business environment.

People Resources: End User Support Groups

Figure 6.2 emphasizes that many organizations have made a major commitment of human resources to end user computing. This commitment may take the form of an **information center,** which is an organizational unit that supports the end users in an organization. In any case, an organization's biggest contribution to end user computing is a staff of **user consultants** consisting of systems analysts, programmers, and technicians. Their primary role is to educate and assist users in the effective use of microcomputer systems and their many software packages. They also work as consultants to end users to help them develop new applications using a variety of application development tools.

An information center is an organizational subunit that provides hardware, software, and people support to end users in an organization. Typically, it has been part of an organization's information services department, but it can also be found in individual end user departments. Figure 6.4 summarizes many of the services provided by information centers or other end user support groups. As you can see, most of the services can be categorized as dealing with end user education and training, assistance with applications development, hardware/software sharing and evaluation, or the development of administrative control methods for end user applications.

The concept of providing support facilities for end user computing has grown so popular that it has become a major factor in organizational computing. However, in recent years, many organizations have distributed responsibility for end user support to their business units and have abolished their centralized information centers. Instead, they have established user liaison or user consultant positions within each business unit to support end users' computing activities.

Basic Services	Enhanced Services
▪ Computer literacy education	▪ Development of telecommunications software
▪ Training on use of products	▪ Data administration
▪ Hardware/software sharing	▪ Installing and testing new software product releases
▪ Application consulting	
▪ Help center with hotline telephone service	▪ Maintenance of PC equipment
▪ Hardware/software evaluation	▪ Project management for user-development projects
▪ Hardware and software standards	▪ Quality assurance of user-written software
▪ Support for standard products	
▪ Security support	▪ Prototype development for end users

FIGURE 6.4

End user support services. Note the variety of services that may be provided by information centers or other end user support groups.

Source: Adapted and reprinted by permission, Barbara C. McNurlin and Ralph H. Sprague, Jr., *Information Systems Management in Practice,* 2nd ed. (Englewood Cliffs, NJ: Prentice Hall, 1989), pp. 328–29.

End User Computing Applications

Figure 6.2 listed four major categories of **end user computing applications:** (1) office automation, (2) information management, (3) decision support, and (4) application development. These categories define what end users do when they do their own computing. Let's take a brief look at what's involved in each of them.

Office Automation

Office automation (OA) applications are a major category of end user computing, since much end user and work group computing takes place in office settings. Office automation will be discussed in detail in Section II of this chapter. OA applications enhance end user productivity and communications within work groups and organizations, and with external contacts such as customers and suppliers. This, typically, involves applications such as word processing, electronic mail, desktop publishing, and presentation graphics. For example, you could compose a business letter using word processing, send electronic messages to colleagues using electronic mail, and prepare graphic displays for a formal presentation using the hardware and software capabilities of your microcomputer workstation.

Information Management Applications

End users are inundated with data and information that must be organized, stored, and retrieved. Thus, one major application of end user computing is the use of database management packages to manage the creation, access, and maintenance of databases and files. In Chapter 3, we discussed how DBMS packages help end users create data files and databases to store data and retrieve information. The query languages and report generators of such packages allow end users to retrieve information from personal, work group, corporate, and external databases. Query languages allow simple inquiries to be made quickly and easily by end users. Report generators help end users prepare reports that extract, manipulate, and display information in a variety of formats. In Chapter 5, we saw how end users can make inquiries using a query language like SQL or QBE and receive immediate displays of information.

Another software package used for information management and retrieval is the **personal information manager** (PIM). These packages help end users store, organize, and retrieve text and numerical data in the form of notes, lists, clippings, tables, memos, letters, reports, and so on. For example, information can be entered randomly about people, companies, deadlines, appointments, meetings, projects, and financial results. The PIM package will automatically organize such data with minimal instructions from the end user. Then portions of the stored information can be retrieved in any order, and in a variety of forms, depending on the relationships established among pieces of data by the software and the user. For example, information can be retrieved as a list of appointments, meetings, or other things to do; the timetable for a project; or a display of key facts and financial data about a competitor [18]. See Figure 6.5.

In Chapter 8, we will discuss how an executive information system (EIS) enables end users who are corporate executives to easily retrieve information tailored to their strategic information needs. So end user computing allows managerial end users at all levels to bypass the periodic reporting process of traditional information system applications. Instead, they can receive directly at their workstations much of the information they need.

Decision Support Applications

Software packages such as electronic spreadsheets, integrated packages, and other decision support system (DSS) software allow end users to build and manipulate analytical models of business activities. End users can thus create their own **decision support** systems with the use of such tools and the variety of databases previously mentioned. As we will discuss in Chapter 8, this allows end users to pose *what-if* questions by entering different alternatives into a spreadsheet or other model. They can then see the results displayed immediately on their workstation screens.

FIGURE 6.5

An example of a personal information manager (PIM). Notice some of the ways that information is recorded and presented by Lotus Organizer.

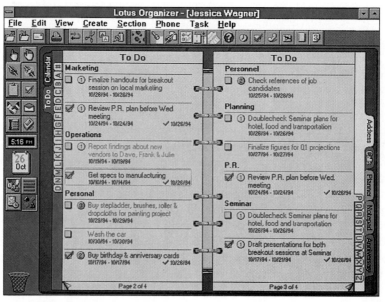

Courtesy of Lotus Development Corporation.

Thus, managerial end users can use an interactive modeling process to analyze alternatives and help them make or recommend decisions. Besides spreadsheet programs, a variety of 4GL products and financial, statistical, and mathematical analysis packages can be used by end users for decision support applications. This includes *group decision support system* (GDSS) software that enhances the joint decision making of work groups and other organizational units.

End User Application Development

Another major category of end user computing is the development of new or improved computer applications by users. That is, end users can develop new or improved ways to perform their jobs without the direct involvement of professional systems analysts. Users themselves can accomplish the steps of information systems development discussed in Chapter 10. The primary reasons for this phenomenon are the application development capabilities of electronic spreadsheet, database management, and other microcomputer software packages. These software resources make it easier for end users to develop their own computer-based information systems. See Figure 6.6. Figures 10.40 and 10.44 in the *Application Exercises* at the end of Chapter 10 outline the basic activities of the database and spreadsheet application development process for end users.

Work Group Computing

Work is fundamentally social. Most activity, and certainly its meaning, arises in a context of cooperation [12].

Much of end user computing is a group effort known as **work group computing.** More formal terms include *computer-supported collaboration* (CSC), *computer-based systems for collaborative work* (CSCW), and *collaborative work support systems* (CWSS). But no matter what you call it, the fact is that end users are now using

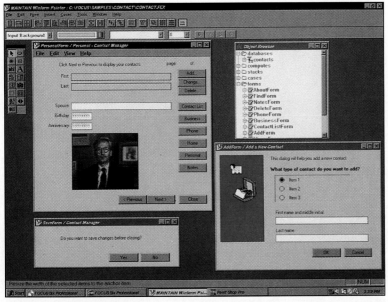

FIGURE 6.6

Using Focus Six Professional Developer's Kit for end user application development, such as developing this contact manager system.

Courtesy of Information Builders.

computers, software, and telecommunications networks to communicate and coordinate with each other about work assignments. For example, members of an office sales team may use interconnected local area networks and *groupware* software packages to communicate with electronic mail and jointly do the word processing, spreadsheet analysis, and report generation needed to accomplish a particular sales presentation assignment. Or they may use networked workstations in a *decision room* and *electronic meeting systems* (EMS) or *group decision support systems* (GDSS) software to help them make better group decisions at a project planning meeting. See Figure 6.7.

Electronic Work Groups

There are many types of work groups, each with its own work styles, agendas, and computing needs. A **work group** can be defined as two or more people working together on the same task or assignment. Thus, a work group can be as small as 2 persons or as large as 30 or more people. Work groups can be as formal and structured as a traditional office or department dedicated to one type of business activity—an *Accounts Payable Department,* for example. Or they can be as informal

FIGURE 6.7

Much of end user computing is a work group effort.

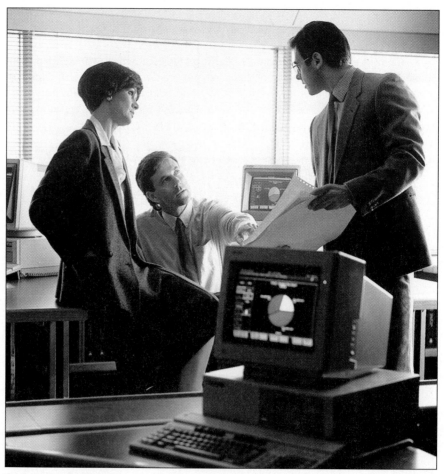

Tim Brown/Tony Stone Images.

and unstructured as an ad hoc task force whose members work for different organizations in different parts of the world—the planning committee for a major international conference, for example.

Therefore, the members of a work group don't have to work in the same physical location. They can be members of a *virtual work group;* that is, one whose members are united by the tasks on which they are collaborating, not by geography or membership in a larger organization. In sociology and cultural anthropology, these work groups are called *social fields*—semiautonomous and self-regulating associations of people with their own work agendas, rules, relationships, and norms of behavior. Work group computing makes *electronic social fields* possible. Computers, groupware, and telecommunications allow end users to work together without regard to time constraints, physical location, or organizational boundaries [14].

Figure 6.8 shows that **groupware** is designed to make communication and coordination of work group activities and cooperation among end users significantly easier, no matter where the members of the work group are located. So, though groupware packages provide a variety of software tools that can accomplish many important jobs, the work group cooperation and coordination they make possible is their key feature. That's why groupware is also known as *collaboration software.* It helps the members of a work group collaborate on group projects, at the same or different times and at the same or different places. So groupware provides some of the office automation, information management and retrieval, decision support, and application development tools work groups need to accomplish specific work assignments.

The Role of Groupware

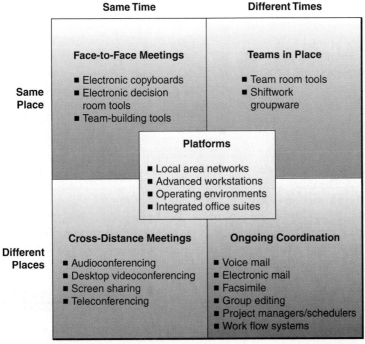

FIGURE 6.8

Groupware is collaboration software that uses a variety of software tools to support work activities and foster cooperation among work group members at the same or different times and places.

Source: Adapted by permission of Prentice Hall Inc., Upper Saddle River, NJ, from Sprague/McNurlin, *Information Systems Management in Practice,* 3rd ed. (© 1993), p. 416.

FIGURE 6.9

Applications of groupware for
work group computing.

- **Electronic Messaging.** Sending electronic messages to work group members using electronic mail, voice mail, bulletin board systems, facsimile, and desktop videoconferencing.
- **Electronic Meetings.** Holding electronic meetings of work groups using computer conferencing and teleconferencing, and group decision support systems.
- **Scheduling Management.** Scheduling work group appointments and meetings using electronic calendars and appointment books.
- **Task and Project Management.** Managing work group tasks and projects by project scheduling, resource allocation, tracking, reminding, and record-keeping.
- **Document Creating and Management.** Joint work group editing and annotation of documents. Electronic filing, retrieval, and routing of documents to work group members.
- **Data Management.** Managing the storage and retrieval of work group data files and databases.
- **Decision Support.** Joint work group spreadsheet development and analysis. Using other types of group decision software.

Figure 6.9 outlines the major types of work group computing applications that may be supported by groupware packages. Some groupware packages support only one of these application areas, while others attempt to integrate several applications in one groupware package. For example, some software packages may be used primarily for document retrieval, while Lotus Notes, a top-selling groupware package, supports E-mail, document management, computer conferencing, and many other functions.

Management Implications of End User Computing

Managers face significant challenges in managing end user computing in their organizations. Managing the hardware, software, people, data, and network resources of end user computing systems is a major challenge. Workstations, computers, telecommunications networks, and software packages must be evaluated, budgeted for, and acquired. End users must be properly trained and assisted. The integrity and security of the databases that are created and available to end users must be ensured. Finally, the applications end users develop and implement must be evaluated for their efficiency and effectiveness in meeting the objectives of the business. Figure 6.10 illustrates some of the managerial challenges of end user computing.

So managing end user computing is not an easy job. However, it is a responsibility shared by every managerial end user, as well as by the management of an organization's information systems function. Business firms, typically, make a variety of organizational, policy, and procedural arrangements to support and control end user computing. Previously mentioned was the creation of information centers with user consultants in the business units of a company. Organizations also develop formal and informal methods to deal with data resource management, application development, and acquisition of end user computing resources.

The creation and access of data resources by end users makes the integrity and security of end user and corporate databases a major concern of data resource management. For example, passwords and other safeguards for proper access to sensitive corporate data must be developed. Also, end user databases extracted from corporate

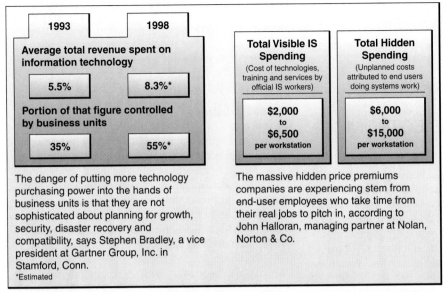

FIGURE 6.10

The costs and risks of end user computing are a major managerial challenge.

Source: Gartner Group, Inc., Stamford, CT (left chart); 1993 Survey of End User Computing, Nolan, Norton & Co. (right chart) adapted from Alice Laplante, "In Depth: End-User Invasion," *Computerworld*, July 18, 1994, p. 98. Copyright © 1994 by Computerworld, Inc., Framingham, MA 01701—Reprinted from *Computerworld*.

databases may become out-of-date or incorrect if they are not properly updated and maintained. So policies such as automatic monitoring and updating of workgroup databases may be implemented.

Application development guidelines for end user computing encourage end users to develop the information systems they need to do their jobs. However, end users may have to demonstrate that their system is well documented with built-in controls that make efficient use of computing resources and does not threaten the integrity of the company's databases. Information center consultants and employees with user liaison responsibilities in the business units are a common way that companies use to help end users develop applications that meet such standards.

Managing end user computing also requires the development of policies and procedures concerning hardware and software acquisition by end users. So corporate or business unit guidelines regulating the cost and types of hardware and software end users can purchase are common. What managers are trying to do is to control the costs of end user computing and avoid proliferation of hardware and software, while ensuring compatibility with the organization's computing and telecommunications networks.

REAL WORLD CASE

CUSHMAN & WAKEFIELD AND MARSHALL INDUSTRIES: GROUPWARE, CORPORATE INTRANETS, AND ELECTRONIC COMMERCE

Fans of Lotus Notes, the most widely used groupware in corporate America, say its security and replication features and ready development tools make Notes the best choice for populating the World Wide Web outside company walls and for supporting mission-critical applications underpinning electronic commerce. Intranet boosters argue that low cost and a standard Web platform make it a smarter bet.

Experienced hands say before choosing groupware or intranets—Web-based networks for internal use—it's wise to think about what kind of electronic commerce with your customers and suppliers your company plans to conduct on the Internet or other networks. Transaction processing? Information delivery? Data access? All three?

Most companies probably will end up using whatever works. Let's look at two examples.

Cushman & Wakefield

Notes groupware was not the answer for New York–based Cushman & Wakefield, Inc., a commercial real estate company. "You can do a lot of things with groupware like Notes if you're willing to sell your soul to it, but you don't do that lightly," says David Solomon, C&W's director of office technology. Besides lower per user cost, he says, the Web offers easier updating than Notes.

The company's intranet runs on Netscape Web browser software installed on a server that allows users access to human resources policies, a national employee directory, sales proposals, and cobroker listings. The IS department currently is mounting a proprietary database of property listings on the intranet for remote access by the firm's national sales force.

C&W plans to leverage intranet knowledge outside the firewall to benefit customers on the Internet. For example, Solomon says, the SiteSolutions property tracking database may be made available to corporate services clients after it's mounted on the company's intranet. The big advantage of having the database on the external Internet Web, Solomon says, is that it works with any customer's system. "We just say, 'get a browser' and give them the Web address and a password. C&W's Web address is (www.cushwake.com).

Marshall Industries

The real question, says Rob Rodin, CEO and president of Marshall Industries, Inc., isn't groupware versus the intranet. Rather, it's how best to meet idiosyncratic customer needs. For the El Monte, California, distributor of industrial electronics, the answer includes Notes, intranets, electronic data interchange (EDI), and any other technology that allows customers and suppliers to conduct electronic commerce around the clock.

Marshall Industries has avoided an either-or approach in giving customers and suppliers 24-hour access to its products and services. The $1.9 billion industrial electronics distributor has been taking customer orders via its Web site (www.marshall.com) since late 1994. And Lotus Notes also plays an important role.

Marshall probably will have 1,000 Lotus Notes clients (PC end users) and hundreds of intranet clients by the end of this quarter, Rodin says. Notes lets the company replicate from all its databases and provide the data to both internal and external Web users. Notes databases also store a wealth of marketing information, such as customer presentations and an opportunities database that captures customer feedback on products and services.

In addition, Notes allows management of the tools at the back end of the process, Rodin says—tools that let the company analyze customer needs and sales and delivery performance, for instance.

Michael Sullivan-Trainor, research director of electronic messaging and Internet commerce for International Data Corporation, agrees that using both groupware like Notes and intranets makes sense for many companies. "Ultimately, a mixed approach is best," he says.

CASE STUDY QUESTIONS

1. What are the advantages and limitations of using groupware like Lotus Notes for end-user collaboration and electronic commerce?

2. What are the benefits and limitations of using a corporate intranet instead?

3. What do you think a company should implement for such applications? Explain.

Source: Adapted from Kathleen Gow, "Intranet versus Notes," *Computerworld*, February 5, 1996, pp. 76–77. Copyright © 1996 by Computerworld, Inc., Framingham, MA 01701—Reprinted from *Computerworld*.

| Office Automation Systems | Section II |

Introduction

Office automation (OA) has changed the equipment and work habits of today's end users and work groups. Of course, none of us would like to work in an office where all information processing activities are done manually or mechanically. So the *mechanized office* has given way to the *automated office*. Investment in networks of computer-based workstations and other automated equipment is transforming traditional manual office methods and paper communications media. This transformation has resulted in the development of automated systems that rely on electronic collaboration and communication networks, text processing, image processing, and other information technologies.

Office automation systems are telecommunications-based information systems that collect, process, store, and distribute electronic messages, documents, and other forms of communications among individuals, work groups, and organizations. Such systems can improve the collaboration and productivity of end users and work groups by significantly reducing the time and effort needed to produce, distribute, and share business communications. Figure 6.11 outlines major office automation systems.

Electronic Communications Systems

One way people interact is by meeting together. Meetings can be supported by equipping conference rooms with computers and sophisticated software. Alternatively, videoconferencing and desktop conferencing enable people to meet without physically moving. Another way people interact is by speaking, which computers support with voice mail and voice annotation. People interact by writing, supported by collaborative writing tools and electronic mail applications. Electronic bulletin boards and newsgroups support broader communications [11].

Electronic communications systems are the central nervous systems of today's organizations. *Electronic mail, voice mail, bulletin board systems,* and *facsimile* allow organizations to send messages in text, video, or voice form or transmit copies

FIGURE 6.11

An overview of office automation systems.

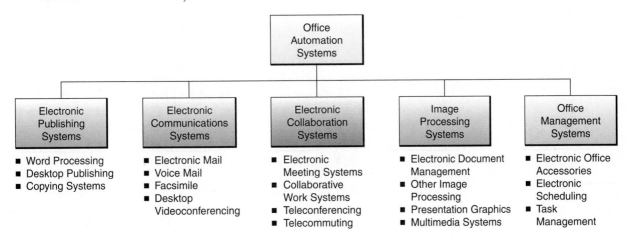

FIGURE 6.12

A summary of electronic
communications systems.

- **Electronic Mail.** Using telecommunications networks to transmit, store, and distribute electronic text messages among the computer workstations of end users. (May also include audio, video, and image media.)

- **Voice Mail.** Using the telephone system and a voice mail computer to transmit, store, and distribute digitized voice messages among end users.

- **Bulletin Board Systems.** A service offered by public information networks or the networks of businesses and other organizations in which electronic messages and data, programs, and other types of files can be stored by end users for other end users to read or copy.

- **Videotex.** An interactive video service provided by cable TV or telephone networks.

- **Facsimile.** Using the telephone system to transmit images of documents and reproduce them on paper at a receiving station.

of documents and do it in seconds, not hours or days. Such systems transmit and distribute text and images in electronic form over telecommunications networks. This enhances the communications and coordination among work groups and organizations. Electronic communications systems help reduce the flow of paper messages, letters, memos, documents, and reports that floods our present interoffice and postal systems. However, in many cases, this paper flood has become an electronic one. For example, some end users routinely send unsolicited copies of E-mail to many of their colleagues, instead of being more selective in their E-mail messaging. Figure 6.12 summarizes electronic communications systems.

Electronic Mail

Electronic mail has changed the way people work and communicate. Millions of end users now depend on electronic mail (E-mail) to send and receive electronic messages. You can send E-mail to anyone else on your network for storage in their *electronic mailboxes* on magnetic disk drives. Whenever they are ready, they can read their electronic mail by displaying it on the video screens at their workstations. So, with only a few minutes of effort (and a few microseconds of transmission), a message to one or many individuals can be composed, sent, and received.

Many organizations and work groups now depend on E-mail packages and their wide and local area networks for electronic mail. As we mentioned in Chapter 4, the Internet has become the E-mail network of choice for millions of networked end users. Communications companies such as GTE, TELENET, and MCI also offer such services, as do personal computer networks such as CompuServe, GEnie, and Prodigy, many of which provide access to the Internet for E-mail. Figure 6.13 shows a video display provided by an electronic mail package.

Many E-mail packages (such as CC:Mail by Lotus or Exchange by Microsoft) can route messages to multiple end users based on predefined mailing lists and provide password security, automatic message forwarding, and remote user access. They also may allow you to store messages in *folders* with provisions for adding attachments to message files. Other E-mail packages may allow you to edit and send graphics as well as text, and provide bulletin board and computer conferencing capabilities. Finally, some E-mail packages can automatically filter and sort incoming messages (even news items from online services such as Dow Jones News/Retrieval Service) and route them to appropriate user mailboxes and folders [6].

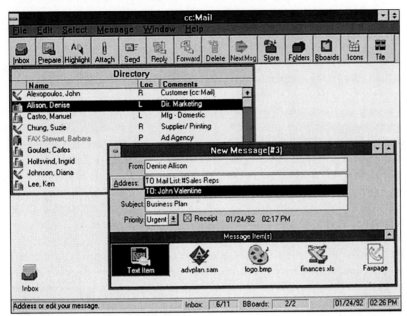

FIGURE 6.13

Using an electronic mail package.

Courtesy of Lotus Development Corporation.

Another variation of electronic mail is **voice mail** (also called *voice store-and-forward*) where digitized voice messages, rather than electronic text, are used. In this method, you first dial the number of the voice mail service. In some secure systems, you may be asked to enter an identification code. Once you are accepted, you dial the voice mail number of the person you wish to contact and speak your message. Your analog message is digitized and stored on the magnetic disk devices of the voice mail computer system. Whenever you want to hear your voice mail, you simply dial your mailbox and listen to the stored message that the computer converts back into analog voice form.

Voice Mail

Bulletin board systems (BBS) are a popular telecommunications service provided by the Internet, public information services, and thousands of business firms, organizations, and user groups. An electronic bulletin board system allows you to post public or private messages that other end users can read by accessing the BBS with their computers. Establishing a small BBS for a business is not that difficult. Minimum requirements are a microcomputer with a hard disk drive, custom or packaged BBS software, modem, and a telephone line.

Bulletin board systems serve as a central location to post and pick up messages or upload and download data files or programs 24 hours a day. A BBS helps end users ask questions, get advice, locate and share information, and get in touch with other end users. Thus, internal company bulletin board systems are being used by many business firms as a convenient, low-cost way to enhance the flow of information among their employees, while an external BBS helps them keep in touch with their customers and suppliers.

Bulletin Board Systems

Public information services are another major category of telecommunications applications. The Internet provides a wealth of information for free, while companies such as CompuServe, GEnie, and Prodigy offer a variety of information services for a fee to anyone. Gaining access to these services is easy if you have a personal computer

Public Information Services

equipped with a modem and a communications software package. They offer such services as electronic mail, bulletin board systems, financial market information, airline reservations, use of software packages for personal computing, electronic games, home banking and shopping, news/sports/weather information, and access to a variety of specialized data banks as discussed in Chapter 5. See Figures 6.14 and 6.15.

Videotex

Another way end users can get information using an information services network is **videotex.** Videotex is a computer-based interactive information service provided over phone lines or cable TV channels to access and selectively view text and graphics. End users can select specific video displays of data and information, such as electronic Yellow Pages and personal bank checking account registers. Thus, you can use a special terminal, intelligent TV set, or personal computer to do banking and shopping electronically. Videotex is widely used in France, where the Teletel system (popularly known as Minitel) has more than 6 million subscribers and 20,000 services, and handles over 2 billion calls a year [3]. Many companies tried pilot programs of videotex services in the 1980s, but most efforts failed to generate sufficient consumer interest. Videotex services are currently available from several sources, including personal computer networks such as Prodigy, and the CompuServe Bank-at-Home and Shop-at-Home services. Several large companies like Viacom and Time Warner have started major pilot programs for new interactive video services. These programs are spurred by the desire to capitalize on the business potential of the future information superhighway [14].

Facsimile

Facsimile (fax) is not a new office telecommunications service. However, advances in digital imaging technology and microelectronics have caused a sharp drop in prices and a significant increase in capabilities. As a consequence, sales of fax machines have skyrocketed in the last few years, and faxing has become a commonplace business term. Facsimile allows you to transmit images of important documents over telephone or other telecommunication links. Thus, "long-distance copying" might be an appropriate nickname for this telecommunications process.

FIGURE 6.14

A menu of Internet services provided by CompuServe.

Courtesy of CompuServe Corporation.

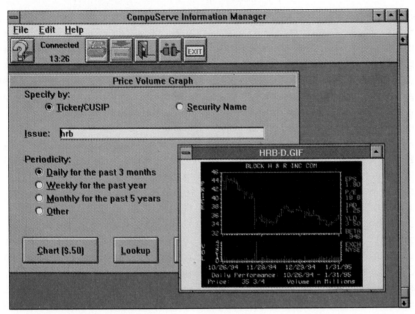

Courtesy of CompuServe Corporation.

FIGURE 6.15

Stock market information provided by CompuServe.

Usually, a fax machine at one office location transmits to a fax machine at another location, with both units connected to high-speed modems. Transmission speeds for digital office fax machines range from one to four pages per minute, with quality equivalent to an office copier. However, facsimile circuit boards and fax modems are also available for microcomputers. Installing a fax board or fax modem and using a fax software package allows a personal computer to transmit copies of word processing, spreadsheet, and other files to fax machines anywhere. Thus, fax machines can now become remote dial-up printers for microcomputer systems. See Figure 6.16.

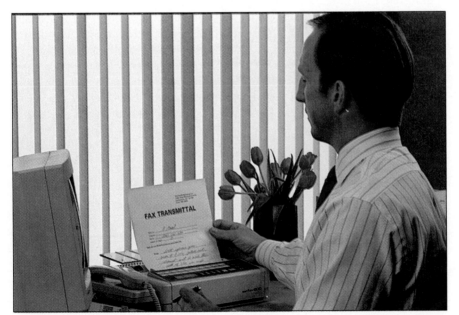

Jon Feingersh/The Stock Market.

FIGURE 6.16

Fax machines and PCs with fax modems have become a common and important component of telecommunications networks.

Electronic Meeting Systems

Why do people have to spend travel time and money to attend meetings away from their normal work locations? They don't have to if they use several types of **electronic meeting systems** (EMS), a growing method of electronic office telecommunications. Electronic meeting systems involve the use of video and audio communications to allow conferences and meetings to be held with participants who may be scattered across a room, a building, a country, or the globe. Reducing the need to travel to and from meetings should save employee time, increase productivity, and reduce travel expenses and energy consumption.

Electronic meeting systems are also being promoted as a form of *group decision support systems* (GDSS). Since EMS software can encourage, organize, and prioritize ideas from meeting participants, they promote more efficient and effective decision making by groups of people [10]. We will explore group decision support systems in Chapter 8.

There are several variations of electronic meeting systems, as summarized in Figure 6.17. In some versions, participants at remote sites key in their presentations and responses whenever convenient from their online terminals or workstations connected to a central conference computer. Since not all participants have to do this at the same time, this form of EMS is called *computer conferencing* and is like a form of interactive electronic mail. Group decision support systems for small groups may use a network of workstations and large-screen projection in a *decision room*. Both of these forms of electronic meeting systems provide computer and video facilities for their participants. Direct **desktop videoconferencing** between the workstations of end users is another promising development. The convenience of desktop videoconferencing promises to significantly enhance collaboration among the members of workgroups. See Figure 6.18.

Teleconferencing

Teleconferencing is an important form of EMS. Sessions are held in real time, with major participants being televised while participants at remote sites usually take part with voice input of questions and responses. See Figure 6.19. Teleconferencing can also consist of using closed-circuit television to reach multiple small groups, instead of using television broadcasting to reach large groups at multiple sites.

Several major communications carriers and hotel chains now offer teleconferencing services for such events as sales meetings, new product announcements, and employee education and training. However, organizations have found that teleconferencing and some forms of EMS are not as effective as face-to-face meetings, especially when important participants are not trained in how to communicate using these systems. Also, the cost of providing some electronic meeting services and facilities can be substantial and make EMS not as cost-effective as traditional meetings.

FIGURE 6.17

Major categories of electronic meeting systems.

- **Computer Conferencing.** Using online terminals and workstations to conduct conferences among participants at remote sites over a period of time, without the use of interactive video.
- **Desktop Videoconferencing.** Using appropriately equipped end user workstations to hold two-way interactive video conferences.
- **Decision Room Conferencing.** Using a meeting room with a network of workstations and large-screen video projection to hold meetings.
- **Teleconferencing.** Using interactive video telecommunications to hold conferences among many participants at remote sites.

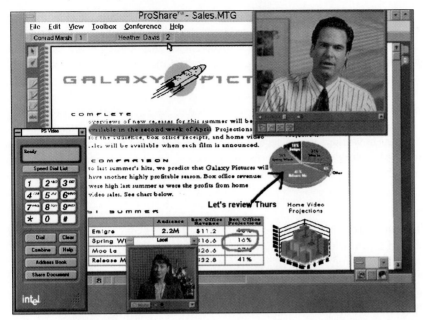

Courtesy of Intel Corporation.

FIGURE 6.18

Using desktop videoconferencing. This is an example of using Intel's ProShare system for two-way interactive videoconferencing.

Telecommuting

Telecommuting is the use of telecommunications by workers to replace commuting to work from their homes. Telecommuting also describes the use of telecommunications to carry on work activities from temporary locations other than offices and homes. Some people refer to telecommuting as the creation of virtual offices. Workers use a computer terminal or microcomputer with telecommunications capability to access their company's computer network and databases. Telecommuting workers and their colleagues also use electronic mail or voice mail to communicate with each other about job assignments.

Matthew Borkoski/Stock Boston.

FIGURE 6.19

Teleconferencing in action.

Telecommuting is becoming a significant work alternative at major corporations and a common approach for many independent professionals. It seems to be most attractive to people whose jobs involve a lot of individual work, such as programmers, systems analysts, writers, consultants, and so on. It is especially helpful for persons with disabilities and working parents of young children. Telecommuting is also being promoted as a way to conserve resources that would have been used by employees to commute to work. However, studies have shown that telecommuting is not appropriate for many jobs and people. Productivity and job satisfaction seem to suffer unless workers spend several days each week at the office or other work sites with their colleagues. So telecommuting is considered only a temporary or partial work alternative for many knowledge workers [9].

Electronic Publishing Systems

Electronic publishing systems have transformed today's office into an in-house publisher of business documents. *Word processing* and *desktop publishing* are the information technologies that give the modern workplace electronic publishing capabilities. **Word processing** was the first, and is still the most common, office automation application. Word processing is the use of computer systems to create, edit, revise, and print text material. As we mentioned in Chapter 3, word processing involves manipulating **text data** (characters, words, sentences, and paragraphs) to produce information products in the form of **documents** (letters, memos, forms, and reports).

Desktop Publishing

One of the major applications in office automation is **desktop publishing**. Organizations can use desktop publishing systems to produce their own printed materials. They can design and print their own newsletters, brochures, manuals, and books with several type styles, graphics, and colors on each page. What constitutes a desktop publishing system? Minimum hardware and software requirements include:

- A personal computer with a hard disk.
- A laser printer or other printer capable of high-quality graphics.
- Software that can do word processing, graphics, and page makeup.

Word processing packages and **page composition** packages are used typically to do word processing, graphics, and page makeup functions. For higher-quality printing, end users need to invest in a more powerful computer with advanced graphics capabilities, a more expensive graphics and page makeup package with more extensive features, and a laser or other printer with a greater variety of capabilities.

How does desktop publishing work? Here are the major steps in the process.

1. Prepare your text and illustrations with a word processing program and a graphics package. Use an optical scanner to input text and graphics from other sources. You can also use files of **clip art**, predrawn graphic illustrations provided by your software or available from other sources.

2. Use the page composition program to develop the format of each page. This is where desktop publishing departs from standard word processing and graphics. Your video screen becomes an *electronic pasteup board* with rulers, column guides, and other page design aids.

Richard Pasley.

FIGURE 6.20

Desktop publishing in action. The video display shows the use of page makeup software to produce a newsletter on a laser printer.

3. Now merge the text and illustrations into the page format you designed. The page composition software will automatically move excess text to another column or page and help size and place illustrations and headings. Most page composition packages provide WYSIWYG (What You See Is What You Get) displays so you can see what the finished document will actually look like.

4. When the pages on the screen look the way you want them, you can store them electronically on your hard disk, then print them on a laser printer or other printer to produce the finished printed material. See Figure 6.20.

Many word processing packages now provide limited desktop publishing features. However, the desktop publishing process is not as easy as it sounds for the casual end user. Projects involving complex layouts require experience, skill, and a knowledge of graphics design techniques. Advances in software have made the job easier in terms of ease of use and helping end users do a better job of graphics design. For example, many software packages frequently provide predesigned forms for various types of printed material (called *templates* or *style sheets*).

Image Processing

Image processing is another fast-growing area of office automation. It allows end users to electronically capture, store, process, and retrieve images of documents that may include numeric data, text, handwriting, graphics, and photographs. **Electronic document management** (EDM) is based on image processing technology. However, it views a document as "something that has been authored for human comprehension." Thus, an electronic document is not just an electronic image of traditional documents as described earlier. It may also take the form of a digitized "voice note" attached to an electronic mail message, or electronic images for a color graphics presentation [6, 21].

FIGURE 6.21

An image processing system.

Courtesy of International Business Machines Corporation.

Electronic document management may interface with other electronic document preparation systems such as word processing, desktop publishing, electronic mail, and voice mail. However, one of the fastest growing application areas is *transaction document image processing*. Documents such as customer correspondence, sales orders, invoices, application forms, and service requests are captured electronically and routed to end users throughout the organization for processing. For example, a customer application form for a bank loan can be captured by optical scanning, indexed by the image database management system, stored on optical disk drives, electronically routed to various end user workstations for editing and financial and credit analysis, and then rerouted to a loan officer's workstation where the loan application decision is made. Such image processing and document management systems have shown productivity improvements of 20 to 25 percent, as well as significant cost savings [2, 11]. See Figure 6.21.

Computer Graphics

Which type of output would you rather see: columns of numbers or a graphics display of the same information? Most people find it difficult to quickly and accurately comprehend numerical or statistical data that are presented in a purely numerical form (such as rows or columns of numbers). That is why typically presentation graphics methods, such as charts and graphs, are used in technical reports and business meetings. As we mentioned in Chapter 3, microcomputer and graphics software packages give end users a variety of computer graphics capabilities, ranging from computer-aided design to computer art to presentation graphics. Graphics can be presented as video displays, printed material, transparencies, and color slides. Computer-based presentations containing many different graphics display screens are common, and the use of multimedia presentations with sound, animation, and video clips is growing. See Figure 6.22.

Computer graphics have been used for many years in design applications called computer-aided design (CAD). Engineers use CAD to design complex mechanical and electronic products and physical structures. Architects use CAD to help them

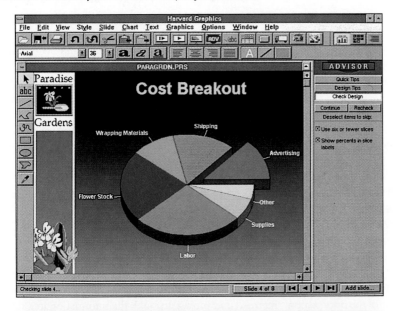

FIGURE 6.22

Presentation graphics displays. Note the use of color, line and bar graphs, three-dimensional graphics, and other graphics images.

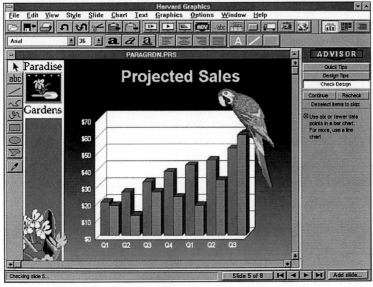

Courtesy of Software Publishing Corporation.

design buildings, work spaces, and other environments. Computer graphics also assist researchers in analyzing volumes of data and process control technicians in monitoring industrial processes.

The goal of **presentation graphics** is to provide information in a graphical form that helps end users and managers understand business proposals and performance and make better decisions about them. This includes the use of line and bar graphs, pie charts, and pictorial charts using a variety of symbols. So instead of being overwhelmed by large amounts of computer-produced data, graphics displays can assist managers in analyzing and interpreting information presented to them.

Presentation Graphics

Presentation graphics does not totally replace reports and displays of numbers and text material. Such methods are still needed to present the detailed information that many applications require. However, presentation graphics is becoming the usual method of presenting business information in reports, meetings, and other business presentations. That's because trends, problems, and opportunities hidden in data are easier to spot and communicate when using graphics displays. For example, presentation graphics makes it easier for a marketing manager to see complex market trends and communicate potential market problems and opportunities to the members of a sales team.

Multimedia Presentations

Information technology is enabling **multimedia presentations** for training employees, educating customers, making sales presentations, and adding impact to other business presentations. Business multimedia goes far beyond traditional forms of numeric, text, and graphics presentations. Multimedia methods of presentation give end users information in a variety of media, including text and graphics displays, voice and other digitized audio, photographs, and video clips. However, many multimedia systems go beyond one-way information presentations. They allow end users to select the form and content of the information presented and browse through the information in a random way, instead of being tied to the sequential access of information. Let's take a closer look now at the information technologies that make multimedia possible. See Figure 6.23.

Multimedia Hardware and Software

Figure 6.24 outlines the basic hardware and software requirements of a typical microcomputer system that enables you to create as well as enjoy multimedia presentations. Of course, owners of low cost *multimedia PCs* marketed for home use do not need *authoring software* or high-powered hardware capabilities in order to enjoy multimedia games and other entertainment and educational multimedia products.

FIGURE 6.23

An example of a multimedia business presentation.

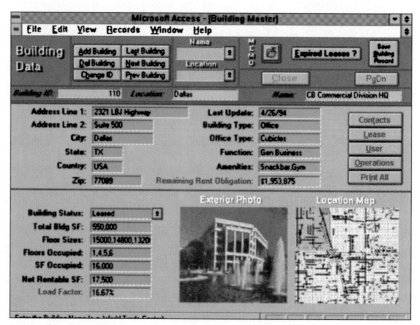

Courtesy of *Computerworld*.

But if you want to create your own multimedia productions, you will have to spend several thousand dollars to put together a high-performance multimedia system. As Figure 6.24 shows, this includes CD-ROM players, stereo speakers, high-resolution color graphics monitors, sound boards, video capture boards, a high-performance microprocessor, at least 16 megabytes of RAM, and over 300 megabytes of hard disk capacity. Software such as authoring tools and programs for image editing and graphics creation can add several thousand more dollars to the startup costs of your multimedia authoring system [19].

Hypertext and hypermedia are foundation technologies for multimedia presentations. **Hypertext** is a methodology for the construction and interactive use of text databases. By definition, hypertext contains only text and a limited amount of graphics. **Hypermedia** are electronic documents that contain multiple forms of media, including text, graphics, video, and so on. A hypertext or hypermedia document is a body of text of any size in electronic form that is indexed so that it can be quickly searched by the reader. For example, if you highlight a term on a hypermedia document displayed on your computer video screen and click your mouse button, the computer could instantly bring up a display of a passage of text and graphics related to that term. Once you finished viewing that pop-up display, you could return to what you were reading originally, or jump to another part of the document instantly.

Hypertext and Hypermedia

FIGURE 6.24

What you need to create multimedia productions.

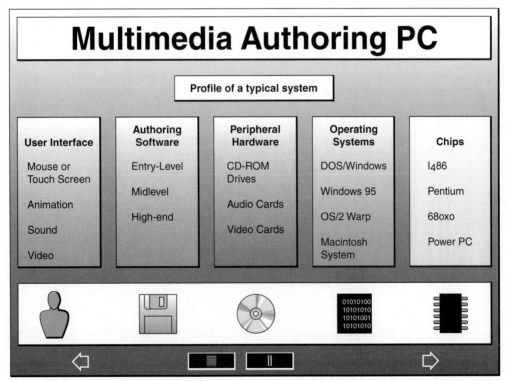

Source: Adapted from Elizabeth Wood, "Multimedia Comes Down to Earth," *Computerworld,* August 1, 1994, p. 71. Copyright © 1994 by Computerworld, Inc., Framingham, MA 01701—Reprinted from *Computerworld.*

FIGURE 6.25

A display of a popular hyper-
text/hypermedia development
package, which uses the
Hypertext Markup Language
(HTML) to develop hyper-
linked documents.

Courtesy of SoftQuad Inc.

Hypertext and hypermedia are developed using specialized programming languages like Java and the *Hypertext Markup Language* (HTML), which create *hyperlinks*
to other parts of the document, or to other documents and media. Hypertext and
hypermedia documents can thus be programmed to let a reader *navigate* through a
multimedia database by following a chain of hyperlinks through various documents.
The *home pages* on the World Wide Web of the Internet are a popular example of this
technology. Thus, the use of hypertext and hypermedia provides an environment for
online interactive presentations of multimedia. See Figure 6.25.

Interactive Video

Interactive video is another important multimedia technology that integrates
computer and video technologies. Using technologies like digital video interactive
(DVI) allows end users to digitally capture, edit, and combine video with text,
pictures, and sound into multimedia business and educational presentations. For
example, an interactive video session for training airline flight attendants can be
produced on CD-ROM disks. It can combine animated graphics displays of different airplane configurations, presentation graphics of airline statistics, lists of
major topics and facts, video clips of flight attendants working on various air-
planes, and various announcements and sounds helpful in managing emergen-
cies. Figure 6.26 summarizes many of the technologies that are used to create
multimedia presentations.

Office Management Systems

Office management systems are an important category of office automation systems. They include electronic calendars, tickler files, electronic mail directories,
schedulers, and task management systems. They provide computer-based support
services to managers and other office professionals to help them organize their work
activities. Office management software computerizes manual methods of planning

- **Authoring Language.** A high-level computer programming facility with English language commands specifically designed to implement multimedia applications.

- **Compact Disk Interactive.** A multimedia standard proposed by Philips Corp. A specification to read data from a CD containing audio, image, graphics, and computer data.

- **Compressed Audio.** A method of digitally encoding and decoding several seconds of voice-quality audio per single videodisc frame. This increases the storage capability to several hours of audio per videodisc.

- **Computer Edit System.** A video editing system controlled by a computer and interfaced to several playback and record machines. This type of system is capable of making precise frame-accurate edits.

- **Digital Audio.** A technique that stores audio as a series of numbers.

- **Digital Video Interactive.** This technology compresses video images and, in its latest version, can produce animated scenes at 30 frames per second. The current compression ratio is 160-to-1.

- **Interactive Video.** The convergence of video and computer technology. A user has control over a coordinated video program and computer program through the user's actions, choices, and decisions, which affect how the program unfolds.

- **Musical Instrument Digital Interface.** Serial data transmission protocol for transporting musical information between compatible electronic musical devices.

- **Sound Board.** An add-in card with software that captures and plays back sound or music.

- **Storyboard:**

  1. A visualization of the order of a piece, using representative frames from each shot or sequence to show a visual skeleton of the piece.

  2. Documentation for video production that contains the audio script and a complete description of the visual content often in the form of pictures or sketches.

- **Video Capture Card.** An add-in card that digitizes analog video from a VCR, video camera, or still-image camera. Video can be digitized as a single frame or multiple frames per second to produce full-motion video.

Source: Adapted from Elizabeth Wood, "Multimedia Comes Down to Earth," *Computerworld*, August 1, 1994, p. 70. Copyright © 1994 by Computerworld, Inc., Framingham, MA 01701—Reprinted from *Computerworld*.

FIGURE 6.26

Technologies for multimedia production and presentation.

such as paper calendars, appointment books, directories, file folders, memos, and notes. Microcomputer users can get some of the benefits of office management systems by using *desktop accessory* and *personal information manager* packages. **Groupware** packages also enable members of work groups on local area networks to share a variety of office management services and help end users and work groups organize routine office tasks.

For example, you could enter the date and time of a meeting into an electronic calendar. An electronic tickler file will automatically remind you of important events. Electronic schedulers use the electronic calendars of several people to help you schedule meetings and other activities with them. Desktop accessories provide features such as a calculator, notepad, alarm clock, phone directory, and appointment book that pop up in a window on the display screen of your workstation at the touch of a key. Electronic mail directories help you contact people easily. And electronic task management packages help you plan a series of related activities so that scheduled results are accomplished on time. Figure 6.27 shows the use of an office management system.

FIGURE 6.27

Using an office management
system for task management.

Courtesy of International Business Machines Corporation.

Management Implications of Office Automation

Office automation systems help end users achieve the benefits of (1) more cost-effective communications and (2) more *time-effective* communications than traditional written and telephone communications methods. For example, electronic mail and facsimile systems are designed to minimize *information float* and *telephone tag*. **Information float** is the time (at least several days) when a written letter or other document is in transit between the sender and receiver, and thus unavailable for any action or response. **Telephone tag** is the process of (1) repeatedly calling people, (2) finding them unavailable, (3) leaving messages, and (4) finding out later you were unavailable when they finally returned your calls.

Electronic mail, voice mail, and facsimile systems can also eliminate the effects of mail that is lost in transit or phone lines that are frequently busy. They reduce the costs of labor, materials, and postage for office communications (from more than $5 for a written message to less than 50 cents for an electronic message is one estimate). Also, the amount of time wasted in regular phone calls can be reduced (by one-third, according to another estimate) [2, 20].

Of course, these advantages are not acquired without some negative effects. First, the cost of automated office hardware is significantly higher than the equipment it replaces. Second, the ease of use and lack of security of many office automation systems have also caused problems. Inefficient and unauthorized use of electronic mail, voice mail, and facsimile services can significantly impair office productivity. One example is sending copies of electronic mail messages to people who do not need or want them. Another is "junk fax"—receiving unauthorized advertisements and unrequested documents that disrupt the normal use of office fax machines. Programs of employee education and policies that stress efficient use of OA services are a natural solution for such problems. Software that monitors and protects against improper use of OA systems is another controversial but fast-growing alternative.

REAL WORLD CASE

MCI COMMUNICATIONS: CREATING THE VIRTUAL OFFICE

Words such as *hearth* and *cafe* might bring to mind homey images of a country inn, but at the MCI Rally Center in Boston these are parts of a futuristic virtual office. The Boston Rally Center is the first of 200 such offices that MCI Communications Corp. plans to roll out in the next year or so. The rally center concept is the second phase of MCI's approximately $75 million investment in a mobile client/server project.

This is one of the largest sales force automation plans ever undertaken. Eventually, more than 5,600 field service representatives will work out of rally centers throughout the country. The Boston center is notable for its mobile workforce deployment, its state-of-the-art technology, and advanced office design.

Instead of having to report to an office and a designated cubicle every day, the center's approximately 120 sales representatives can work anywhere, anytime, by using loaded IBM 755CD ThinkPad laptops that connect via client/server software.

Sales representatives can share tips and retrieve data from resources that include a business library that lets users download pamphlets and product features.

The center of the office is the "hearth," a large, wide-open room with muted colors. Modular furniture—including small tables, comfortable chairs, and laptop stands—is scattered around and can be moved to suit an individual's needs. Plugs allow laptops to be connected via floors or walls. Large, rolling whiteboards are provided as planning tools or to close off areas during meetings.

In one corner of the room is the "cafe," a coffee bar with laptop connections where field representatives can meet to compare notes. A large video monitor is in another corner.

"Home base" is a locker area where sales representatives keep small rolling files. Before moving into the virtual office, representatives were required to throw out anything they don't really need and fit everything they consider essential into the folding storage bins.

Representatives can set up shop for the day in the "heads down" area that was devised for quiet work.

"The managers roam around too; we share three glassed-in offices among 18 managers," said Susan Beckmann, the branch director at the Boston Rally Center. "And we're out on the floor more often than not, not holed up in our offices."

"What MCI has done right is to treat this center concept as a technological development issue as much as a business development issue," said Gill Gordon, a telecommuting analyst at Gill Gordon Associates in Monmouth Junction, New Jersey. "And not so much for what this will do for space-saving costs, although that will happen, too.

"The other thing that will likely make this a successful rollout is that this is very aggressive. This isn't a pilot or a toe-in-the-water project; the Boston center is actually a prototype," Gordon said. "It's the first one out of the box."

Beckmann said MCI hopes the center will raise sales and revenue by as much as 30 percent in the first year of operation.

CASE STUDY QUESTIONS

1. Why is MCI implementing a nationwide system of rally centers for its field service reps?

2. Do you see any disadvantages in this concept? Explain.

3. Would you like to work in and out of a rally center like MCI's? Why or why not?

Source: Adapted from Mindy Blodgett, "Virtual Office Prototype Puts Field Service Reps to Work at 'Hearth' of MCI," *Computerworld*, February 26, 1996, pp. 73, 76. Copyright © 1996 by Computerworld, Inc., Framingham, MA 01701—Reprinted from *Computerworld*.

Summary

- **End User Computing.** End user computing is the direct, hands-on use of computers by end users to perform the information processing needed to accomplish their work activities. End user computing has grown dramatically because information services have been unable to keep up with the information processing requests of users. Also, improvements in microcomputer hardware, software, and networking capabilities have made end user computing attractive, affordable, and effective for today's organizations. Major application areas of end user computing include office automation, information management and retrieval, decision support, and application development.

- **End User Computing Systems.** End user computing should be viewed as systems of people, hardware, software, network, and data resources. Hardware resources include microcomputer workstations, local area network servers, departmental minicomputers, and corporate mainframes. Software resources consist of application packages, groupware packages, and application development packages. People resources include end users and information center and other user consultants. Data resources include personal, work group, corporate, and external databases.

- **Work Group Computing.** Much of end user computing is a collaborative effort known as work group computing. End users are using networked computers and groupware packages to collaborate on work assignments without regard to time constraints, physical location, or organizational boundaries. Groupware packages can accomplish many applications, as summarized in Figure 6.9. However, the key features of such collaboration software are the work group communications and coordination that it makes possible.

- **Office Automation.** Office automation systems include electronic communications and collaboration systems, text processing, image processing, and other information technologies to develop computer-based information systems that collect, store, and transmit electronic messages, documents, and other forms of communications. Office automation systems include work processing, desktop publishing, graphics and multimedia presentations, electronic mail, voice mail, facsimile, image processing, electronic meeting systems, and office management systems.

Key Terms and Concepts

These are the key terms and concepts of this chapter. The page number of their first explanation is in parentheses.

1. Bulletin board systems (215)
2. Computer graphics (222)
3. Desktop publishing (220)
4. Desktop videoconferencing (218)
5. Document (220)
6. Electronic document management (221)
7. Electronic mail (214)
8. Electronic meeting systems (218)
9. End user collaboration (200)
10. End user computing (200)
    a. Rationale (200)
    b. Management implications (210)
    c. Resources (202)
11. End user computing applications (205)
    a. Office automation (205)
    b. Information management (205)
    c. Decision support (206)
    d. Application development (207)
12. Facsimile (216)
13. Groupware (203)
14. Hypermedia (225)
15. Hypertext (225)
16. Image processing (221)
17. Information center (204)
18. Information float (228)
19. Interactive video (226)
20. Multimedia presentations (224)
21. Office automation (213)
    a. Management implications (228)
    b. Types of systems (213)
22. Office management systems (226)
23. Personal information manager (206)
24. Presentation graphics (223)
25. Public information services (215)
26. Telecommuting (219)
27. Teleconferencing (218)
28. Telephone tag (228)
29. Text data (220)
30. User consultant (204)
31. Videotex (216)
32. Voice mail (215)
33. Word processing (220)
34. Work group (208)
35. Work group computing (207)

Review Quiz

Match one of the key terms and concepts listed above with one of the brief examples or definitions listed below. Try to find the best fit for answers that seem to fit more than one term or concept. Defend your choices.

_____ 1. The direct, hands-on use of computers by users.

_____ 2. End user applications frequently lack adequate controls.

_____ 3. Examples are microcomputer workstations, application packages, information center consultants, and external databases.

_____ 4. Using your workstation to prepare documents and communicate with your colleagues.

_____ 5. Managing databases and generating reports.

_____ 6. Using an electronic spreadsheet for what-if analysis.

_____ 7. Developing new ways to use computers to perform jobs for you.

_____ 8. Software that helps people collaborate on group work assignments.

_____ 9. Members of an organization and its business partners communicate and coordinate on joint projects.

_____ 10. Members of a work group share computer resources to jointly accomplish work assignments.

_____ 11. Organizations have established these end user support groups.

_____ 12. Automates office work activities and communications, but may disrupt traditional work roles.

_____ 13. Includes word processing, desktop publishing, electronic mail, and teleconferencing.

_____ 14. Text data are manipulated and documents are produced.

_____ 15. Characters, words, sentences, and paragraphs.

_____ 16. Letters, memos, forms, and reports.

_____ 17. Users can produce their own brochures and manuals.

_____ 18. Includes computer-aided design, presentation graphics, and computer art.

_____ 19. Easier to understand than columns of numbers.

_____ 20. Presenting information in a variety of forms of media.

_____ 21. Helps you interactively browse through a text database.

_____ 22. A multimedia form of hypertext technology.

_____ 23. Allows end users to capture video and sound for computer-based presentations.

_____ 24. Use your workstation to send and receive messages.

_____ 25. Use your telephone as an electronic message terminal.

_____ 26. The time a document is in transit between sender and receiver.

_____ 27. You and the person you want to contact repeatedly miss each other's phone calls.

_____ 28. Transmitting images of documents electronically.

_____ 29. Saves travel time and money spent on meetings.

_____ 30. Realtime televised electronic meetings at remote sites.

_____ 31. Using telecommunications so you can work at home.

_____ 32. End users can electronically capture, store, process, and retrieve images.

_____ 33. Customer correspondence and sales orders can be optically captured and routed to end users for processing.

_____ 34. Helps end users store information in a variety of forms and retrieve it in many different ways.

_____ 35. Integrates calculator, calendar, address book, notepad, and other functions.

_____ 36. Provides a variety of office automation services such as electronic calendars and meeting scheduling.

_____ 37. End users can post public or private messages for other computer users.

_____ 38. They specialize in providing a range of computing and communications services to microcomputer users.

_____ 39. An interactive information service for home computers.

_____ 40. Interactive video communications between end user workstations.

Discussion Questions

1. What developments are responsible for the growth of end user computing? Do you expect this growth to continue? Explain.

2. What changes do you expect in the future in the types of hardware, software, people, network, and data resources typically used in end user computing systems? In the four major application areas of end user computing?

3. Refer to the Real World Case on Cushman & Wakefield and Marshall Industries in the chapter. How does an internal corporate intranet support an external application like electronic commerce?

4. Why is work group computing becoming an increasingly important form of end user computing? What is the role of groupware in supporting this trend?

5. Why do you think some organizations are closing their information centers and distributing end user support to departments and other business units?

6. Refer to the Real World Case on MCI Communications in the chapter. How do you think a company should provide office support to a mobile sales force? Defend your proposals.

7. If you were a manager, how would you manage some of the risks of end user computing?

8. What office automation developments are moving us toward a "virtual" office? What circumstances inhibit movement in that direction?

9. How will the growth of graphics and multimedia presentations affect the information presentation preferences of managers? Explain.

10. Would you like to take part in electronic meetings such as teleconferences? Would you like to telecommute to work? Why or why not?

Real World Problems

1. VeriFone, Inc.: Supporting Remote End Users

"You need to resist the temptation to have too many people involved" in supporting remote workers, says Kathy Cruz, chief information officer at VeriFone, Inc. The Redwood City, California, firm, which helps retailers and others automate sales transactions, comes as close as any to a virtual company. Many of its 2,800 workers in 38 countries work daily at a customer site, at home, or in a satellite office. "Everyone has connectivity, including voice mail, E-mail, and intranet access, from everywhere," Cruz says. A local call connects users worldwide to VeriFone's private leased-line network, intranets, VMS mail, and Novell LANs, she says.

All help calls from VeriFone employees are routed to an 800 number at a 24-hour, seven-day-a-week help desk staffed by IS user consultants in Honolulu, Hawaii. (A separate help desk handles customer calls.) The small percentage of problems that help desk workers can't handle are passed on to experts at the appropriate technical competency center. Cruz says having a central focal point builds confidence in IS support and reassures remote workers. "If I am an end user, I know I can call a single number," she says. "I don't need to worry if the help desk is open."

She says every company system, connection, and network is monitored constantly, so help desk staffers can usually tell callers how widespread the problem is. "If users call and say, 'The network is slow. What's going on?' the help desk can say, 'It's a lot bigger problem than you.'" Cruz says. Even language is standardized: English or Chinese.

a. Do you like how VeriFone provides end user support services? Why or why not?

b. Should other types of companies adopt similar help desk systems? Explain.

Source: Adapted from Joseph Maglitta, "Think Simple," *Computerworld*, May 13, 1996, pp. 77, 80. Copyright © 1996 by Computerworld, Inc., Framingham, MA 01701—Reprinted from *Computerworld.*

2. Sun Microsystems and Others: Telecommuting's Cost/Benefit

Your company has decided to support telecommuting. What will it cost? That depends on your approach. Some cases in point:

- When Sun Microsystems, Inc., created a telecommuting program for 700 of its San Francisco–area employees, it opted for high-end ISDN lines and Sun SPARC-stations that cost $5,000. Sun pays about $180 per worker per month for its ISDN connections, which includes usage charges and support from Pacific Bell.

- Aegon USA, Inc.'s Advanced Financial Services Division in Clearwater, Florida, is implementing telecommuting programs that will cost between $6,000 and $8,000 per worker and $300 in monthly communication and support expenses. The price includes extras, such as furniture for the insurer's home offices, and standard items including 486-based PCs and 28.8K bit/sec. dial-up access to the corporate LAN.

- Nynex Corp. employees in Boston are telecommuting on an ad hoc basis until a formal policy is unveiled later this year. Joan O'Brien, a staff manager, telecommutes two days a week and uses her own PC and printer. Aside from an extra phone line, Nynex bears none of the cost of O'Brien's telecommute.

So the tab for telecommuting can vary widely depending on the amount of information technology employed, and who picks up the tab. But let's take a look at some estimates.

The tab for telecommuting
Sample estimated costs for a home-based teleworker:
    Support: $500 one-time fee, $347 in annual costs.
    Network: $203 one-time fee, $1,282 in annual costs.
    Home equipment: $3,522 one-time fee, $494 in annual costs.
    Corporate setup: $237 one-time fee, $35 in annual costs.
    Total: $4,462 one-time fee, $2,158 in annual costs.

Source: Forrester Research, Inc.

The payback

Three areas where you could expect to recoup the cost of telecommuting

25–75 percent reduction in office space and associated costs.

10–50 percent increase in productivity.

20–40 percent reduction in recruitment and turnover costs.

Source: Telework Training International

a. How much should a business invest in information technology to support telecommuting by its employees? Explain.

b. Should most businesses implement telecommuting? Why or why not?

Source: Adapted from Suzanne Hildreth, "Trimming Telecommuting's Price Tag," *Computerworld*, April 8, 1996, p. 100. Copyright © 1996 by Computerworld, Inc., Framingham, MA 01701—Reprinted from *Computerworld*.

3. State Street Bank and Worcester Polytechnic: Using Desktop Videoconferencing

Until recently, desktop videoconferencing systems had a reputation for jerky, flickering pictures and poor reliability exacerbated by an absence of standards. Getting different brands of equipment to communicate was problematic at best. But the situation has changed almost overnight. Driven by increasing competition, the desktop video market is growing rapidly in both the number of users and the systems capabilities being offered to them. Because of the introduction of inexpensive, clonelike video cameras for use with PCs, hundreds of thousands of desktop video users are expected to become part of the videoconferencing universe this year.

James Miades, a communications specialist at Boston-based State Street Bank & Trust Co., uses a $2,000 PictureTel desktop system to connect with an elaborate room setup at the company's London office. With the PictureTel system, Miades can pan and zoom to focus on individuals in London. Images are sharp, which gives a you-are-there feel to the experience, he says. Miades says effective desktop videoconferencing could cut company travel costs dramatically. A trip to London, he notes, "could easily cost $5,000 compared to $295 per hour for videoconferencing time."

Desktop videoconferencing isn't used just to reduce expensive executive travel. Penny S. Turgeon, director of the Institutional Media Center at Worcester Polytechnic Institute, says desktop systems are used to provide "electronic office hours" for faculty working with distance learning programs. Employers also use the systems to interview graduating seniors. Turgeon says industry desktop videoconferencing standards have made incompatibility problems a nonissue.

a. What are the benefits of desktop videoconferencing for State Street Bank and Worcester Polytechnic?

b. What limitations do you see for this technology?

Source: Adapted from Alan Earls, "PCs Bring People Face to Face," *Computerworld*, April 29, 1996, p. 95. Copyright © 1996 by Computerworld, Inc., Framingham, MA 01701—Reprinted from *Computerworld*.

4. Federal Express: Training Employees with Interactive Multimedia

In the transportation business, time is of the essence. And no one knows that better than Federal Express (FedEx), the world's largest express transportation company with 1995 revenue of $9.4 billion. That's why when the Memphis, Tennessee–based employer of 119,000 workers in 210 countries decided on multimedia training—it's automatically a crucial application. FedEx recently deployed an interactive multimedia training system that will reach some 45,000 customer-contact employees, including couriers and service agents nationwide. Up to 3 percent of yearly revenue is devoted to training.

"Technology is one way we differentiate ourselves. Interactive multimedia, for us, is the best and most effective training approach out there," says Cynthia Hubard Spangler, vice president of corporate headquarters systems at FedEx. For almost a decade, FedEx used a laser disk–based training system. The technology, however, was beginning to age: The disks were wearing out, and replacement parts were difficult to obtain. "There was no question about it; we needed to upgrade our training system," she says.

Interactive multimedia was chosen for training because it satisfies corporate criteria for flexibility, retention, ease of use, user autonomy, and the ability to revise and update. Additionally, the interactive multimedia solution will allow FedEx to do more training without spending more. "It's a cost-effective way to reduce the number of classroom training sessions we hold," Spangler says. In fact, FedEx estimates it will be able to cut its classroom training in half when interactive multimedia training is fully implemented. The company spent several million dollars over three years on the multimedia training system.

Initial courseware focuses on new hires. The training—which FedEx field workers have dubbed "edutainment"—combines text, graphics, audio, animation, and video. The multimedia courseware will be distributed on CD–ROM and the material downloaded onto a workstation's hard drive. High-powered training workstations were purchased specifically from Silicon Graphics for the custom interactive multimedia training system and outfitted with 10-gigabyte hard drives. As revisions and updates are required, FedEx will distribute the new material electronically over its nationwide network.

a. What benefits does FedEx expect in their use of interactive multimedia for employee training?

b. Should other businesses, schools, and universities implement similar systems? Why or why not?

Source: Adapted from Lynn Haber, "Corporate Giants Test the Waters," *Communications Week*, March–April 1996, pp. S22–S23.

Application Exercises

1. End User Office Automation

Match one of the following office automation systems with the examples listed below:

a. Desktop publishing
b. Electronic mail
c. Office management systems
d. Teleconferencing
e. Voice mail
f. Word processing
g. Image processing
h. Facsimile
i. Electronic meetings
j. Desktop videoconferencing

_____ 1. Composing, editing, and printing a letter to a customer.

_____ 2. Producing a company newsletter with text and graphics.

_____ 3. Being prompted that you have scheduled a meeting.

_____ 4. Visually displaying messages that have been sent to you.

_____ 5. Listening to a computer-generated message from an associate.

_____ 6. Participating in a companywide TV workshop.

_____ 7. Conducting a meeting where all participants use computers.

_____ 8. Sending a copy of a letter electronically using the telephone system.

_____ 9. Optically capturing and using document images instead of paper documents.

_____ 10. Using video communications with colleagues at their workstations.

2. Tracking Training at ABC Company

As the manager of computer training for marketing department employees at ABC Company, you need to record summary information about training seminars attended by the employees. Information like the following sample is reported to you each time an employee completes a training session.

a. Using a database package, create an appropriate table and record the sample data shown. (If you have completed Application Exercise 3–4, add your new table to the database you created for that exercise.)

b. Using the table(s) you have created, produce the following:

1. A report on the introduction to word processing class listing the name of each employee attending that class and the number of hours attended. The report should also show the total of class hours attended by all marketing employees.

2. A report for each employee listing each class attended by the employee and indicating the number of hours attended. This report also should show the total hours of training (in all classes) attended by the employee.

3. A summary report showing the total hours of each type of training received by marketing department employees of ABC Company.

Employee Name	Class	Type of Training	Hours
S. Jones	Introduction to Spreadsheets	Spreadsheet	24
J. Lewis	Introduction to Word Processing	Word Processing	20
S. Jones	Intermediate Spreadsheets	Spreadsheet	16
J. Dorn	Intermediate Spreadsheets	Spreadsheet	16
J. Dorn	Introduction to the Internet	Internet	16
M. Marx	Introduction to the Internet	Internet	16
L. Evans	Introduction to Word Processing	Word Processing	20
M. Marx	Introduction to Word Processing	Word Processing	20
S. Vale	Introduction to the Internet	Internet	16
T. Wall	Intermediate Spreadsheets	Spreadsheet	16
M. Marx	Introduction to Databases	Database	24
S. Jones	Introduction to Databases	Database	24
V. Adams	Intermediate Word Processing	Word Processing	32
J. Lewis	Introduction to Spreadsheets	Spreadsheet	24
J. Dorn	Introduction to Spreadsheets	Spreadsheet	24
S. Jones	Introduction to Word Processing	Word Processing	20
T. Wall	Intermediate Word Processing	Word Processing	32
S. Vale	Intermediate Spreadsheets	Spreadsheet	16
T. Wall	Introduction to Databases	Database	24
J. Lewis	Introduction to Databases	Database	24
S. Jones	Intermediate Word Processing	Word Processing	32
L. Evans	Intermediate Word Processing	Word Processing	32
L. Davis	Introduction to the Internet	Internet	16
R. Smith	Introduction to the Internet	Internet	16
L. Evans	Introduction to the Internet	Internet	16
V. Adams	Introduction to the Internet	Internet	16

4. If you have completed Application Exercise 3–4, create a query appropriately linking the employee and training tables to produce the following report: A listing showing the total hours of word processing classes attended by each employee together with the person's initial word processing skill level. Group this report by the initial word processing skill level of the employee.

3. A Document Tracking System at Action Products

Action Products sells electronic equipment covered by a one-year warranty. At the end of the warranty period, customers can purchase an extended service contract (ESC). The ESC covers all repairs needed for an additional two years and includes a free on-site checkup and cleaning at the beginning of the service period. Customers wishing to purchase the ESC mail in request forms that are processed by the service department staff.

Each request is processed in four stages. First, there is the Prod_ID stage where the identity of the product to be covered is checked to ensure that it was purchased from Action Products and is eligible for the ESC coverage. Then, the Cust_Chk stage verifies the customer's method of payment and does any necessary credit checking. Next, the Serv_Sch stage schedules a time for the on-site checkup. Finally, in the Ctrct_Prep stage, the service contract, with all of the appropriate identifying information, is drawn up and mailed to the customer.

Each stage of the processing of these contracts is handled by a different staff member of Action Products. This promotes efficiency but sometimes makes it difficult to track the status of an individual contract request. Action Products has decided to create a tracking file, using a database software package, for its ESC requests. This file should allow Action Products to track the status of each contract request and to generate summary reports showing how long the firm takes to process a typical request. The tracking file contains the following information for each request: a request ID number, the customer's name, the product ID number, the current location of the request, and the number of days the request spent at each stage completed. A sample set of data follow.

a. Create an appropriate database table and add the set of sample data shown.

b. Create a query that will retrieve all available information for Request 1347.

c. Create a query that will list all requests whose Location is Serv_Sch.

d. Create a report showing the average number of days requests spend in each processing stage and a report showing the maximum number of days spent in each processing stage.

Request	Customer Name	Product ID	Current Location	Product Identification	Credit Checking	Service Scheduling	Contract Preparation
1276	Lewis, J.	28376	Completed	2	3	3	1
1288	Davis, R.	17382	Completed	3	1	4	3
1294	Jarvis, L.	57926	Completed	3	2	4	2
1297	Thomas, P.	31033	Completed	4	3	2	3
1304	Baker, B.	14082	Ctrct_Prep	5	4	5	
1314	Allen, S.	26308	Completed	2	2	4	2
1324	Mason, J.	48160	Completed	3	3	2	3
1341	Nance, R.	78917	Ctrct_Prep	4	3	4	
1347	Evers, M.	32018	Serv_Sch	4	5		
1364	Flowers, W.	52095	Ctrct_Prep	3	2	3	
1374	Vickers, D.	17830	Serv_Sch	4	3		
1386	Carney, L.	37954	Ctrct_Prep	2	1	3	
1392	Giles, N.	43084	Serv_Sch	3	3		
1405	Lamb, G.	26974	Cust_Chk	4			
1409	Morris, Z.	62037	Serv_Sch	2	3		
1422	Owens, V.	83910	Cust_Chk	3			
1428	Powers, P.	39046	Prod_ID				

Review Quiz Answers

1. *10*	11. *17*	21. *15*	31. *26*
2. *10b*	12. *21a*	22. *14*	32. *16*
3. *10c*	13. *21b*	23. *19*	33. *6*
4. *11a*	14. *33*	24. *7*	34. *23*
5. *11b*	15. *29*	25. *32*	35. *3*
6. *11c*	16. *5*	26. *18*	36. *22*
7. *11d*	17. *3*	27. *28*	37. *1*
8. *13*	18. *2*	28. *12*	38. *25*
9. *9*	19. *24*	29. *8*	39. *31*
10. *35*	20. *20*	30. *33*	40. *4*

Selected References

1. Amoroso, Donald, and Paul Cheney. "Testing a Causal Model of End User Application Effectiveness." *Journal of Management Information Systems,* Summer 1991.

2. Carlson, Patricia Ann, and Michael Slave. "Hypertext Tools for Knowledge Workers: The Next Frontier: Tools that Teach." *Information Systems Management,* Spring 1992.

3. Cats-Baril, William, and Tawfik Jelassi. "The French Videotex System Minitel: A Successful Implementation of a National Information Technology Infrastructure." *MIS Quarterly,* March 1994.

4. Chidambaram, Laku, and Beth Jones. "Impact on Communication Medium and Computer Support on Group Perceptions and Performance: A Comparison of Face-to-Face and Dispersed Meetings." *MIS Quarterly,* December 1993.

5. Doll, William, and Gholamreza Torkzadeh. "A Congruence Construct for User Involvement." *Decision Science Journal,* Spring 1991.

6. "Groupware: The Team Approach." Supplement to *PC Week,* October 14, 1991.

7. Hershey, Gerald, and Donna Kizzier. *Planning and Implementing End User Information Systems.* Cincinnati: SouthWestern, 1992.

8. Karten, Naomi. "Standards for User-Driven Applications Development." *Information Systems Management,* Summer 1991.

9. Kling, Rob. "Cooperation, Coordination and Control in Computer Supported Work." *Communications of the ACM,* December 1991.

10. Kyng, Morten. "Designing for Cooperation: Cooperating in Design." *Communications of the ACM,* December 1991.

11. Lasher, Donald; Blake Ives; and Sirkka Jarvenpaa. "USAA-IBM Partnership in Information Technology: Managing the Image Project." *MIS Quarterly,* December 1991.

12. Lee, Allen. "Electronic Mail as a Medium for Rich Communications: An Empirical Investigation Using Hermeneutic Interpretation." *MIS Quarterly,* June 1994.

13. Nunamaker, Jay; Alan Dennis; Joseph Valacich; Douglas Vogel; and Joey George. "Electronic Meeting Systems to Support Group Work." *Communications of the ACM,* July 1991.

14. Perin, Constance. "Electronic Social Fields in Bureaucracies." *Communications of the ACM,* December 1991.

15. Schnaidt, Patricia. *Enterprisewide Networking.* Carmel, IN: SAMS Publishing, 1992.

16. Sprague, Ralph, and Barbara McNurlin, eds. *Information Systems Management in Practice.* 3rd ed. Englewood Cliffs, NJ: Prentice Hall, 1993.

17. Tayntor, Christing. "New Challenges or the End of EUC?" *Information Systems Management,* Summer 1994.

18. Vessey, Iris, and Ajay Paul Sravanapudi. "CASE Tools as Collaborative Support Technologies." *Communications of the ACM,* January 1995.

19. Wood, Elizabeth. "Multimedia Comes Down to Earth," *Computerworld,* August 1, 1994.

20. Zigurs, Ilze, and Kenneth Kozar. "An Exploratory Study of Roles and Computer-Supported Groups." *MIS Quarterly,* September 1994.

Information Systems for Business Operations

CHAPTER OUTLINE

LEARNING OBJECTIVES

After reading and studying this chapter, you should be able to:

1. Give examples of how information systems support the business functions of accounting, finance, human resource management, marketing, and production and operations management.

2. Identify the major activities of transaction processing systems, and give examples of how they support the operations of a business.

3. Identify the advantages and disadvantages of traditional data entry versus source data automation, and batch processing versus realtime processing.

4. Provide business examples that demonstrate the benefits and limitations of electronic data interchange and online transaction processing systems.

Section I   *Business Information Systems*

IS in Business

Business managers are moving from a tradition where they could avoid, delegate, or ignore decisions about IT to one where they cannot create a marketing, product, international, organizational, or financial plan that does not involve such decisions [12].

There are as many ways to use information systems in business as there are business activities to be performed, business problems to be solved, and business opportunities to be pursued. As a prospective managerial end user, you should have a general understanding of the major ways information systems are used to support each of the **functions of business**. We will use the term **business information systems** to describe a variety of types of information systems (transaction processing, information reporting, decision support, etc.) that support a business function such as accounting, finance, marketing, or human resource management. Thus, applications of information systems in the functional areas of business are called *accounting information systems, marketing information systems, human resource information systems,* and so on. See Figure 7.1.

As a business end user, you should also have a *specific* understanding of how information systems affect a particular business function—marketing, for example—or a particular industry (e.g., banking) that is directly related to your career objectives. For example, someone whose career objective is a marketing position in banking should have a basic understanding of how information systems are used in banking and how they support the marketing activities of banks and other firms.

FIGURE 7.1

Examples of business information systems. Note how they support the major functional areas of business.

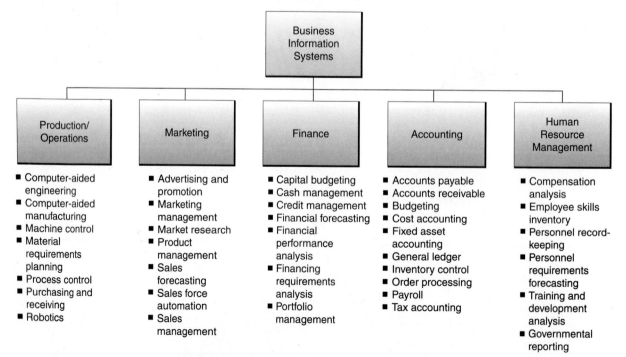

Figure 7.1 illustrates how information systems can be grouped into business function categories. Information systems in this section will be analyzed according to the business function they support to give you an appreciation of the variety of business information systems that both small and large business firms may use. However, as we emphasized in Chapter 1, information systems in the real world typically are integrated combinations of functional information systems. There is a strong emphasis in many organizations to develop such *composite* or **cross-functional information systems.** These organizations view cross-functional information systems as a strategic way to share information resources and improve the efficiency and effectiveness of a business, thus helping it attain its strategic objectives.

Cross-Functional Information Systems

The business function of **marketing** is concerned with the planning, promotion, and sale of existing products in existing markets, and the development of new products and new markets to better serve present and potential customers. Thus, marketing performs a vital function in the operation of a business enterprise. Business firms have increasingly turned to computers to help them perform vital marketing functions in the face of the rapid changes of today's environment. Computers have been a catalyst in the development of **marketing information systems** that integrate the information flows required by many marketing activities.

Figure 7.2 illustrates how marketing information systems provide information for planning, control, and transaction processing in the marketing function. Strategic, tactical, and operational information systems assist marketing managers in

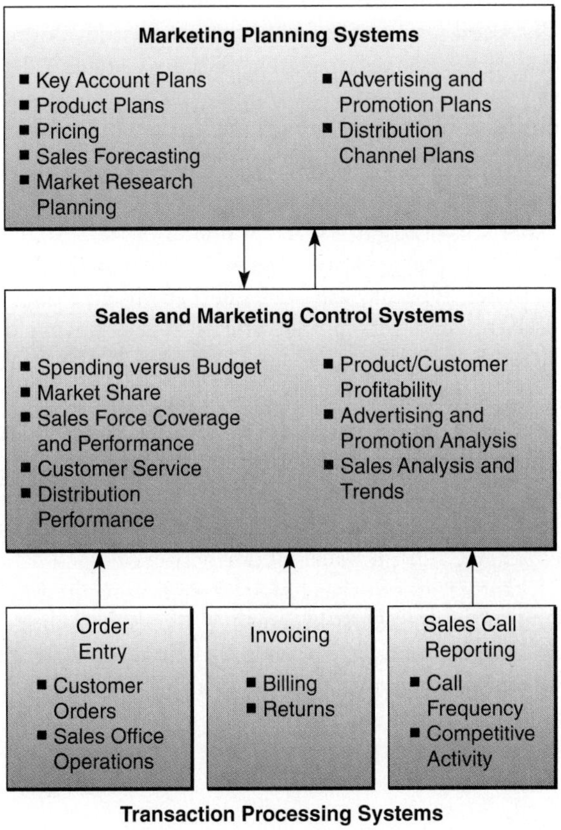

Marketing Information Systems

Marketing Planning Systems

- Key Account Plans
- Product Plans
- Pricing
- Sales Forecasting
- Market Research Planning
- Advertising and Promotion Plans
- Distribution Channel Plans

Sales and Marketing Control Systems

- Spending versus Budget
- Market Share
- Sales Force Coverage and Performance
- Customer Service
- Distribution Performance
- Product/Customer Profitability
- Advertising and Promotion Analysis
- Sales Analysis and Trends

Order Entry

- Customer Orders
- Sales Office Operations

Invoicing

- Billing
- Returns

Sales Call Reporting

- Call Frequency
- Competitive Activity

Transaction Processing Systems

FIGURE 7.2

Marketing information systems provide information for the planning and control of major components of the marketing function.

FIGURE 7.3

Examples of important
computer-based information
systems in marketing.

- **Sales Management**
  Plan, monitor, and support the performance of salespeople and sales of products and services.
- **Sales Force Automation**
  Automate the recording and reporting of sales activity by salespeople and the communications and sales support from sales management.
- **Product Management**
  Plan, monitor, and support the performance of products, product lines, and brands.
- **Advertising and Promotion**
  Help select media and promotional methods and control and evaluate advertising and promotion results.
- **Sales Forecasting**
  Produce short- and long-range sales forecasts.
- **Market Research**
  Collect and analyze internal and external data on market variables, developments, and trends.
- **Marketing Management**
  Develop marketing strategies and plans based on corporate goals and market research and sales activity data, and monitor and support marketing activities.

product planning, pricing decisions, advertising and sales promotion strategies and expenditures, forecasting market potential for new and present products, and determining channels of distribution. Control reporting systems support the efforts of marketing managers to control the efficiency and effectiveness of the selling and distribution of products and services. Analytical reports provide information on a firm's actual performance versus planned marketing objectives. Figure 7.3 summarizes several important ways that computer-based information systems could be used to support the marketing function.

Sales Management

Sales managers must plan, monitor, and support the performance of the salespeople in their organizations. So in most firms, computer-based systems produce sales analysis reports (such as that shown in Figure 7.4) that analyze sales by product, product line, customer, type of customer, salesperson, and sales territory. Such reports help marketing managers monitor the sales performance of products and salespeople and help them develop sales support programs to improve sales results.

Sales Force Automation

However, sales analysis is only one aspect of the use of computers for sales management and support. Increasingly, computer-based information systems are providing the basis for **sales force automation.** In many companies, the sales force is being outfitted with laptop computers, hand-held PCs, or even pen-based tablet computers. This not only increases the personal productivity of salespeople, but dramatically speeds up the capture and analysis of sales data from the field to marketing managers at company headquarters. In return, it allows marketing and sales management to improve the support they provide to their salespeople. Therefore, many companies are viewing sales force automation as a way to gain a strategic advantage in sales productivity and marketing responsiveness.

For example, salespeople use their PCs to record sales data as they make their calls on customers and prospects during the day. Then each night sales reps in the

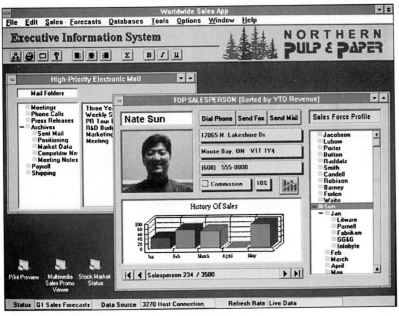

Courtesy of Comshare, Inc.

FIGURE 7.4

An example of a sales analysis display produced by an executive information system.

field can connect their computers by modem and telephone links to the mainframe computer at company headquarters and upload information on sales orders, sales calls, and other sales statistics, as well as send electronic mail messages and other queries. In return, the host computer may download product availability data, prospect lists of information on good sales prospects, E-mail messages, and other sales support information.

Advertising and Promotion

Marketing managers need information to help them achieve sales objectives at the lowest possible costs for advertising and promotion. Computers use market research information and promotion models to help (1) select media and promotional methods, (2) allocate financial resources, and (3) control and evaluate results of various advertising and promotion campaigns. For example, Figure 7.5 illustrates the INFOSCAN system of Information Resources Incorporated (IRI). It tracks the sales of over 800,000 products by their universal product code (UPC) to more than 70,000 U.S. households at over 2,400 retail stores. INFOSCAN measures the effect of promotional tactics such as price discounts, coupon offers, and point-of-purchase (POP) promotions. Then INFOSCAN's computer-based marketing models produce forecasts and other analyses of marketing strategy [11].

Product Management

Product managers need information to plan and control the performances of specific products, product lines, and brands. Computers can help provide price, revenue, cost, and growth information for existing products and new product development. Information and analysis for pricing decisions is a major function of this system. Information is also needed on the manufacturing and distribution resources proposed products will require. Computer-based models may be used to evaluate the performances of current products and the prospects for success of proposed products.

Sales Forecasting

The basic functions of sales forecasting can be grouped into the two categories of short-range forecasting and long-range forecasting. Short-range forecasting deals with forecasts of sales for periods up to one year, whereas long-range forecasting is concerned with sales forecasts for a year or more into the future. Marketing managers use systems like INFOSCAN (Figure 7.5) to capture market research data, historical sales data, and promotion plans, and to manipulate statistical forecasting models to generate short-range and long-range sales forecasts.

Market Research

The market research information system provides marketing intelligence to help managers make more effective marketing decisions. It also provides marketing managers with information to help them plan and control the market research projects of the firm. As the INFOSCAN system in Figure 7.5 illustrates, computers help the

FIGURE 7.5

INFOSCAN analyzes the effect of promotional devices on the sales of over 800,000 products.

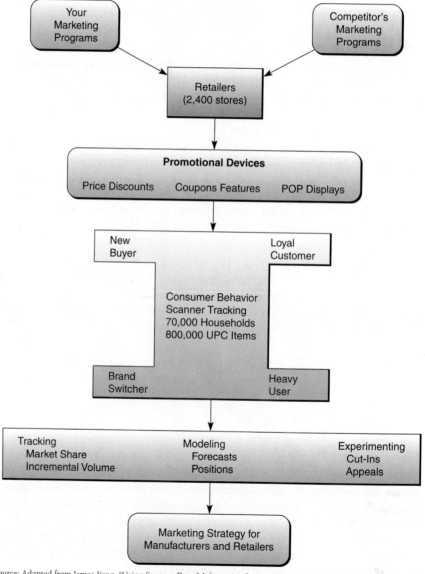

Source: Adapted from James Jiang, "Using Scanner Data," *Information Systems Management* (New York: Auerbach Publications), Winter 1995, p. 62. © 1995 Warren, Gorham & Lamont. Used with permission.

market research activity collect, analyze, and maintain an enormous amount of information on a wide variety of market variables that are subject to continual change. This includes information on customers, prospects, consumers, and competitors. Market, economic, and demographic trends are also analyzed. Data can be purchased in computer-readable form from external sources, or computers can help gather data through telemarketing and computer-aided telephone interviewing techniques. Finally, statistical analysis software packages help managers analyze market research data and spot important marketing trends.

Marketing managers use computer-based information systems to develop short- and long-range plans outlining product sales, profit, and growth objectives. They also provide feedback and analysis concerning performance-versus-plan for each area of marketing. Computer-based marketing models in decision support systems and expert systems are also being used to investigate the effects of alternative marketing plans. In addition, the fast capture of sales and marketing data by sales force automation systems helps marketing management respond faster to market shifts and sales performance trends and develop more timely marketing strategies.

Marketing Management

Manufacturing information systems support the **production/operations** function that includes all activities concerned with the planning and control of the processes producing goods or services. Thus, the production/operations function is concerned with the management of the *operational systems* of all business firms. The planning and control information systems used for operations management and transaction processing support *all* firms that must plan, monitor, and control inventories, purchases, and the flow of goods and services. Therefore, firms such as transportation companies, wholesalers, retailers, financial institutions, and service companies must use production/operations information systems to plan and control their operations. In this section, we will concentrate on computer-based manufacturing applications to illustrate information systems that support the production/operations function. See Figure 7.6.

Manufacturing Information Systems

Computer-based manufacturing information systems use several major techniques to support **computer-integrated manufacturing** (CIM). CIM is an overall concept that stresses that the goals of computer use in factory automation must be to:

Computer-Integrated Manufacturing

- **Simplify** (reengineer) production processes, product designs, and factory organization as a vital foundation to automation and integration.
- **Automate** production processes and the business functions that support them with computers and robots.
- **Integrate** all production and support processes using computers and telecommunications networks [2].

Thus, computers are simplifying, automating, and integrating many of the activities needed to produce products of all kinds. For example, computers are used to help engineers design better products using both *computer-aided engineering* (CAE) and *computer-aided design* (CAD), and better production processes with *computer-aiding process planning* (CAPP). They are also used to help plan the types of material needed in the production process, which is called **material requirements planning** (MRP), and to integrate MRP with production scheduling and shop floor control, which is known as *manufacturing resource planning* (MRPII). **Computer-aided**

FIGURE 7.6

Manufacturing information systems. Note the levels of planning, control, and transaction processing information systems.

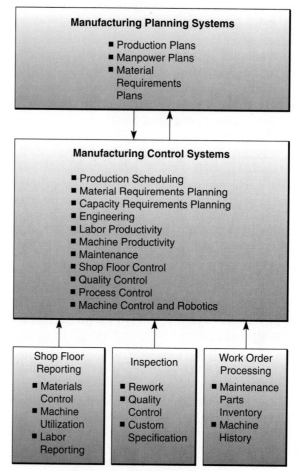

Manufacturing Planning Systems

- Production Plans
- Manpower Plans
- Material Requirements Plans

Manufacturing Control Systems

- Production Scheduling
- Material Requirements Planning
- Capacity Requirements Planning
- Engineering
- Labor Productivity
- Machine Productivity
- Maintenance
- Shop Floor Control
- Quality Control
- Process Control
- Machine Control and Robotics

Shop Floor Reporting
- Materials Control
- Machine Utilization
- Labor Reporting

Inspection
- Rework
- Quality Control
- Custom Specification

Work Order Processing
- Maintenance Parts Inventory
- Machine History

Transaction Processing Systems

manufacturing (CAM) may be used to help manufacture products. This could be accomplished by monitoring and controlling the production process in a factory (*shop floor control*) or by directly controlling a physical process (*process control*), a machine tool (*machine control*), or a machine with some humanlike capabilities (robots). See Figures 7.7 and 7.8.

Some of the benefits of computer integrated manufacturing systems are:

- Increased efficiency through work simplification and automation, better production schedule planning, and better balancing of production workload to production capacity.

- Improved utilization of production facilities, higher productivity, and better quality control resulting from continuous monitoring, feedback, and control of factory operations, equipment, and robots.

- Reduced investment in production inventories and facilities through work simplification, just-in-time inventory policies, and better planning and control of production and finished goods requirements.

- Improved customer service by drastically reducing out-of-stock situations and producing high-quality products that better meet customer requirements.

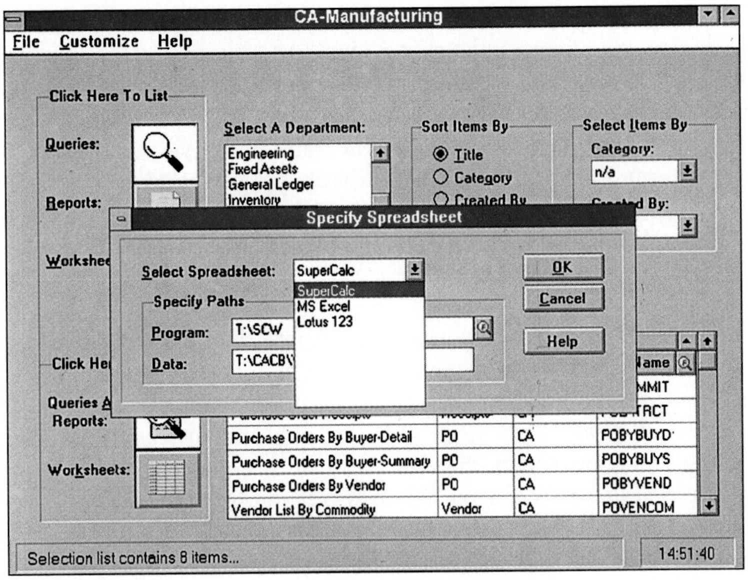

Courtesy of Computer Associates, Inc.

FIGURE 7.7

A display of a manufacturing resource planning package.

Process control is the use of computers to control an ongoing physical process. Process control computers control physical processes in petroleum refineries, cement plants, steel mills, chemical plants, food product manufacturing plants, pulp and paper mills, electric power plants, and so on. Many process control computers are special-purpose minicomputer systems. A process control computer system requires the use of special sensing devices that measure physical phenomena such as temperature or pressure changes. These continuous physical measurements are converted to digital form by analog-to-digital converters and relayed to computers for processing.

Process Control

- **Computer-Aided Design**
  Create, simulate, and evaluate models of products and manufacturing processes.

- **Computer-Aided Manufacturing**
  Use computers and robots to fabricate, assemble, and package products.

- **Factory Management**
  Plan and control production runs, coordinate incoming orders and raw material requests, and oversee cost and quality assurance programs.

- **Quality Management**
  Evaluate product and process specifications, test incoming materials and outgoing products, test production processes in progress, and design quality assurance programs.

- **Logistics**
  Purchase and receive materials, control and distribute materials, and control inventory and shipping of products.

- **Maintenance**
  Monitor and adjust machinery and processes, perform diagnostics, and do corrective and preventive maintenance.

FIGURE 7.8

Examples of computer-based systems in manufacturing.

Process control software uses mathematical models to analyze the data generated by the ongoing process and compare them to standards or forecasts of required results. Then the computer directs the control of the process by adjusting control devices such as thermostats, valves, switches, and so on. The process control system also provides messages and displays about the status of the process so a human operator can take appropriate measures to control the process. In addition, periodic and on-demand reports analyzing the performance of the production process can be produced. Personal computers have become a popular method of analyzing and reporting process control data. See Figure 7.9.

Machine Control

Machine control is the use of a computer to control the actions of a machine. This is also popularly called *numerical control*. The control of machine tools in factories is a typical numerical control application, though it also refers to the control of typesetting machines, weaving machines, and other industrial machinery.

Numerical control computer programs for machine tools convert geometric data from engineering drawings and machining instructions from process planning into a numerical code of commands that control the actions of a machine tool. Machine control may involve the use of special-purpose microcomputers called programmable logic controllers (PLCs). These devices operate one or more machines according to the directions of a numerical control program. Specially equipped personal computers that can withstand a factory environment are being used to develop and install numerical control programs in PLCs. They are also used to analyze production data furnished by the PLCs. This analysis helps engineers fine-tune machine tool performance.

Robotics

An important development in machine control and computer-aided manufacturing is the creation of smart machines and robots. These devices directly control their own activities with the aid of microcomputers. **Robotics** is the technology of building and using machines (robots) with computer intelligence and computer-controlled humanlike physical capabilities (dexterity, movement, vision, etc.). Robotics has also become a major thrust of research and development efforts in the field of artificial intelligence.

Robots are used as "steel-collar workers" to increase productivity and cut costs. For example, one robot regularly assembles compressor valves with 12 parts at the rate of 320 units per hour, which is 10 times the rate of human workers. Robots are also particularly valuable for hazardous areas or work activities. Robots follow programs loaded into separate or on-board special-purpose microcomputers. Input is

FIGURE 7.9

Process control computer systems control the galvanized steel process at this automated factory in Germany.

Michael Rosenfeld/Tony Stone Images.

received from visual and/or tactile sensors, processed by the microcomputer, and translated into movements of the robot. Typically, this involves moving its "arms" and "hands" to pick up and load items or perform some other work assignment such as painting, drilling, or welding. Robotics developments are expected to make robots more intelligent, flexible, and mobile by improving their computing, visual, tactile, and navigational capabilities [16]. See Figure 7.10.

Manufacturing engineers use **computer-aided engineering** to simulate, analyze, and evaluate the models of product designs they have developed using **computer-aided design** methods. Powerful *engineering workstations* with enhanced graphics and computational capabilities can analyze and design products and manufacturing facilities. They design products according to product specifications determined in cooperation with the product design efforts of marketing research and product development specialists. One of the final outputs of this design process is the bill of materials (specification of all required materials) used by the MRP application. The engineering subsystem is frequently responsible for determining standards for product quality (i.e., *quality assurance*). It also is responsible for the design of the production processes needed to manufacture the products it designs. This function depends heavily on the use of computers to perform the necessary analysis and design, and it is known as *computer-aided process planning*.

Computer-Aided Engineering

FIGURE 7.10

This robot consists of a computer-controlled robotic arm assembly that prints electronic circuits on computer circuit boards.

Tony Stone Images.

FIGURE 7.11

Computer-aided design is a vital component of computer-integrated manufacturing.

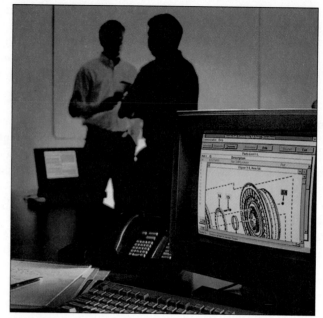

Matthew Borkoski/Folio.

Computer-aided design packages and engineering workstations are the software and hardware resources that make computer-aided engineering possible. Engineers use these high-powered computing and advanced graphics workstations for the design and testing of products, facilities, and processes. Input is by light pen, joystick, or keyboard, with the CAD package refining an engineer's initial drawings. Output is in two- or three-dimensional **computer graphics** that can be rotated to display all sides of the object being designed. The engineer can zoom in for close-up views of a specific part and even make parts of the product appear to move as they would in normal operation. The design can then be converted into a finished mathematical model of the product. This is used as the basis for production specifications and machine tool programs. See Figure 7.11.

Human Resource Information Systems

The **human resource management** (or personnel) function involves the recruitment, placement, evaluation, compensation, and development of the employees of an organization. Originally, businesses used computer-based information systems to (1) produce paychecks and payroll reports, (2) maintain personnel records, and (3) analyze the use of personnel in business operations. Many firms have gone beyond these traditional functions and have developed **human resource information systems** (HRIS) that also support (1) recruitment, selection, and hiring; (2) job placement; (3) performance appraisals; (4) employee benefits analysis; (5) training and development; and (6) health, safety, and security. See Figure 7.12.

Human resource information systems support the concept of *human resource management*. This business function emphasizes (1) *planning* to meet the personnel needs of the business, (2) *development* of employees to their full potential, and (3) *control* of all personnel policies and programs. The goal of human resource management is the effective and efficient use of the human resources of a company. The major applications and objectives of information systems in human resource management are summarized in Figure 7.13.

FIGURE 7.12

Human resource information systems support the strategic, tactical, and operational use of the human resources of an organization.

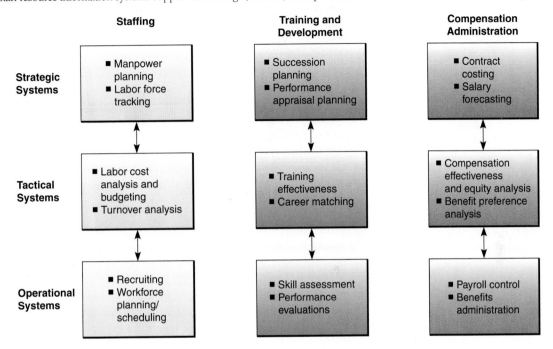

FIGURE 7.13

Examples of the objectives of human resource information systems.

- **Flexible Compensation Administration**
  Contain benefits costs, while offering benefits program choices
- **Benefits Administration**
  Cost-effective plan administration
- **Compensation Management**
  Salary planning and budget impact analysis
- **Payroll Administration**
  Accurate, timely payroll with controls
- **Personnel Management**
  Instant access to employee information
- **Defined Contributions**
  Provide pre-tax benefits to employees and employer
- **Position Control**
  Manage the mix of job positions in your organization
- **Historical Record-Keeping**
  Perform point-in-time and trend analysis to assist in legislative compliance and compensation planning
- **Recruiting and Applicant Tracking**
  Identify and attract qualified candidates
- **Career Development**
  Match employee skills to employer needs, to provide organizational flexibility
- **Pension Administration**
  Reduce administration costs for retirement planning

Staffing

These information systems record and track human resources within a company to maximize their use. For example, a *personnel record-keeping* system keeps track of additions, deletions, and other changes to the records in a personnel database. Changes in job assignments and compensation, or hirings and terminations, are examples of information that would be used to update the personnel database. Another example is an *employee skills inventory* system that uses the employee skills data from a personnel database to locate employees within a company who have the skills required for specific assignments and projects.

    A final example is doing *personnel requirements forecasting* to assure a business of an adequate supply of high-quality human resources. This application provides information required for forecasts of personnel requirements in each major employment category for various company departments or for new projects and other ventures being planned by management. Such long-range planning may use a computer-based simulation model to evaluate alternative plans for recruitment, reassignment, or retraining programs.

Training and Development

Information systems help human resource managers plan and monitor employee recruitment, training, and development programs by analyzing the success history of present programs. They also analyze the career development status of each employee to determine whether development methods such as training programs and periodic performance appraisals should be recommended. Computer-based training programs and appraisals of employee job performance are available to help support this area of human resource management. See Figure 7.14.

Compensation Analysis

Information systems can help analyze the range and distribution of employee compensation (wages, salaries, incentive payments, and fringe benefits) within a company and make comparisons with compensation paid by similar firms or with various economic indicators. This information is useful for planning changes in

---

FIGURE 7.14

An example of a performance evaluation display. Note how this employee's behavior on the job is being evaluated.

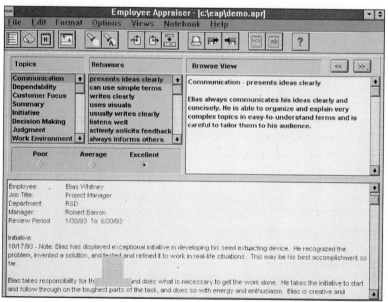

© Sarah Evertson.

compensation, especially if negotiations with labor unions are involved. It helps keep the compensation of a company competitive and equitable, while controlling compensation costs.

Nowadays, reporting to government agencies is a major responsibility of human resource management. So organizations use computer-based information systems to keep track of the statistics and produce reports required by a variety of government laws and regulations. For example, in the United States, statistics on employee recruitment and hiring must be collected for possible use in Equal Employment Opportunity Commission (EEOC) hearings; statistics for employee health, workplace hazards, accidents, and safety procedures must be reported to the Occupational Safety and Health Administration (OSHA); and statistics on the use of hazardous materials must be reported to the Environmental Protection Agency (EPA). Software packages to collect and report such statistics are available from a variety of software vendors.

Governmental Reporting

Accounting information systems are the oldest and most widely used information systems in business. They record and report business transactions and other economic events. Accounting information systems are based on the double-entry bookkeeping concept, which is hundreds of years old, and other, more recent accounting concepts such as responsibility accounting and profitability accounting. Computer-based accounting systems record and report the flow of funds through an organization on a historical basis and produce important financial statements such as balance sheets and income statements. Such systems also produce forecasts of future conditions such as projected financial statements and financial budgets. A firm's financial performance is measured against such forecasts by other analytical accounting reports.

Operational accounting systems emphasize legal and historical record-keeping and the production of accurate financial statements. Typically, these systems include transaction processing systems such as order processing, inventory control, accounts receivable, accounts payable, payroll, and general ledger systems. *Management accounting systems* focus on the planning and control of business operations. They emphasize cost accounting reports, the development of financial budgets and projected financial statements, and analytical reports comparing actual to forecasted performance.

Figure 7.15 illustrates the interrelationships of several important accounting information systems commonly computerized by both large and small businesses. Many accounting software packages are available for these applications. Let's briefly review how several of these systems support the operations and management of a business firm. Figure 7.16 summarizes the purpose of six common, but important, accounting information systems.

Accounting Information Systems

Order processing, or *sales order processing,* is an important transaction processing system that captures and processes customer orders and produces invoices for customers and data needed for sales analysis and inventory control. In many firms, it also keeps track of the status of customer orders until goods are delivered. Computer-based sales order processing systems provide a fast, accurate, and efficient method of recording and screening customer orders and sales transactions. They also provide inventory control systems with information on accepted orders so they can be filled as quickly as possible. Figure 7.17 is an example of an invoicing display of an integrated accounting package.

Order Processing

FIGURE 7.15

Important accounting information systems for transaction processing and financial reporting. Note how they are related to each other in terms of input and output flows.

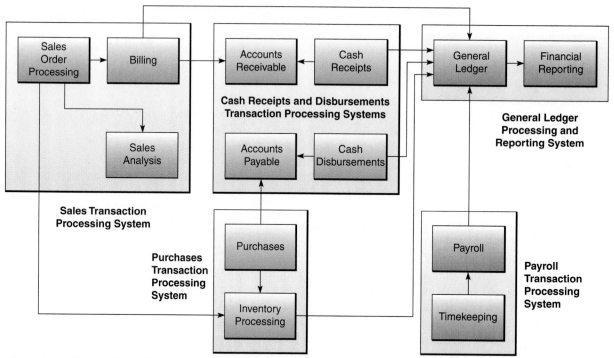

Source: Adapted from Joseph W. Wilkinson, *Accounting Information Systems: Essential Concepts and Applications.* Copyright © 1989 by John Wiley & Sons, Inc. Reprinted by permission of John Wiley & Sons, Inc.

Inventory Control

Inventory control systems process data reflecting changes to items in inventory. Once data about customer orders are received from an order processing system, a computer-based inventory control system records changes to inventory levels and prepares appropriate shipping documents. Then it may notify managers about items that need reordering and provide them with a variety of inventory status reports. Computer-based inventory control systems thus help a business provide high-quality service to customers while minimizing investment in inventory and inventory carrying costs.

Accounts Receivable

Accounts receivable systems keep records of amounts owed by customers from data generated by customer purchases and payments. They produce monthly customer statements and credit management reports, as illustrated in Figure 7.15. Computer-based accounts receivable systems stimulate prompt customer payments by preparing accurate and timely invoices and monthly statements to credit customers. They provide managers with reports to help them control the amount of credit extended and the collection of money owed. This activity helps to maximize profitable credit sales while minimizing losses from bad debts.

Accounts Payable

Accounts payable systems keep track of data concerning purchases from and payments to suppliers. They prepare checks in payment of outstanding invoices and produce cash management reports. Computer-based accounts payable systems help ensure prompt and accurate payment of suppliers to maintain good relationships,

- **Order Processing**
  Captures and processes customer orders and produces customer invoices.
- **Inventory Control**
  Processes data reflecting changes in inventory and provides shipping and reorder information.
- **Accounts Receivable**
  Records amounts owed by customers and produces monthly customer statements and credit management reports.
- **Accounts Payable**
  Records purchases from, amounts owed to, and payments to suppliers, and produces cash management reports.
- **Payroll**
  Records employee work and compensation data and produces paychecks and other payroll documents and reports.
- **General Ledger**
  Consolidates data from other accounting systems and produces the periodic financial statements and reports of the business.

FIGURE 7.16

A summary of six widely used accounting information systems.

ensure a good credit standing, and secure any discounts offered for prompt payment. They provide tight financial control over all cash disbursements of the business. They also provide management with information needed for the analysis of payments, expenses, purchases, employee expense accounts, and cash requirements.

Payroll systems receive and maintain data from employee time cards and other work records. They produce paychecks and other documents such as earning statements, payroll reports, and labor analysis reports. Other reports are also prepared for management and government agencies. Computer-based payroll systems help businesses make prompt and accurate payments to their employees, as well as reports to management, employees, and government agencies concerning earnings, taxes, and other deductions. They may also provide management with reports analyzing labor costs and productivity.

Payroll

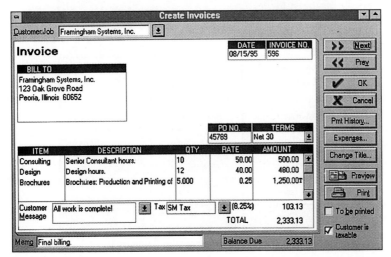

FIGURE 7.17

An example of an invoice display of a popular accounting software package, Quickbooks, by Intuit.

Courtesy of Intuit, Inc.

General Ledger

General ledger systems consolidate data received from accounts receivable, accounts payable, payroll, and other accounting information systems. At the end of each accounting period, they close the books of a business and produce the general ledger trial balance, the income statement and balance sheet of the firm, and various income and expense reports for management. Computer-based general ledger systems help businesses accomplish these accounting tasks in an accurate and timely manner. They typically provide better financial controls and management reports and involve fewer personnel and lower costs than manual accounting methods.

Financial Information Systems

Computer-based **financial information systems** support financial managers in decisions concerning (1) the financing of a business and (2) the allocation and control of financial resources within a business. Major financial information system categories include cash and securities management, capital budgeting, financial forecasting, and financial planning. Accounting information systems are frequently included as a vital category of financial information systems. Figure 7.18 illustrates

FIGURE 7.18

Financial planning, reporting, and transaction processing information systems support decisions concerning the financing and the allocation and control of funds within a business.

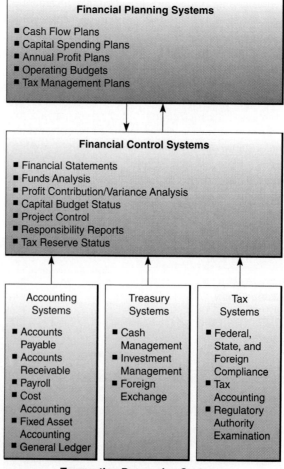

that the financial manager of a business may rely on a variety of financial planning, reporting, and transaction processing information systems to make financing, investment, and accounting decisions. Let's take a brief look at the functions of these computer-based financial systems. Figure 7.19 summarizes examples of important financial information systems.

Cash and Securities Management

Information systems collect information on all cash receipts and disbursements within a company on a realtime or periodic basis. Such information allows businesses to deposit or invest excess funds more quickly, and thus increase the income generated by deposited or invested funds. These systems also produce daily, weekly, or monthly forecasts of cash receipts or disbursements (cash flow forecasts) that are used to spot future cash deficits or surpluses. Mathematical models frequently can determine optimal cash collection programs and determine alternative financing or investment strategies for dealing with forecasted cash deficits or surpluses.

Many businesses invest their excess cash in short-term marketable securities (such as U.S. Treasury bills, commercial paper, or certificates of deposit) so that investment income may be earned until the funds are required. The portfolio of such securities can be managed by portfolio management software. It helps a financial manager make buying, selling, or holding decisions for each type of security so that the optimum mix of securities is developed that minimizes risk and maximizes investment income.

Capital Budgeting

The capital budgeting process involves evaluating the profitability and financial impact of proposed capital expenditures. Long-term expenditure proposals for plants and equipment can be analyzed using a variety of techniques incorporating present value analysis of expected cash flows and probability analysis of risk. This application makes heavy use of spreadsheet models that are designed for corporate financial planning.

Financial Forecasting

A business must make financial and other forecasts of economic trends. A variety of statistical forecasting packages provide analytical techniques that result in economic or financial forecasts of national and local economic conditions, wage levels, price levels, and interest rates. This forecasting may involve the use of data about the external business environment obtained from proprietary financial and demographic data banks provided by the information services described in Chapter 6.

- **Cash and Securities Management**
  Record data and produce forecasts of cash receipts and disbursements and manage investment in short-term securities.
- **Capital Budgeting**
  Evaluate the profitability and financial impact of proposed capital expenditures.
- **Financial Forecasting**
  Forecast business and economic trends and financial developments.
- **Financial Planning**
  Evaluate the present and projected financial performance and financing needs of the business.

FIGURE 7.19

Examples of important financial information systems.

Financial Planning

Financial planning systems use **financial planning models** to evaluate the present and projected financial performance of a business or of one of its divisions or subsidiaries. They also help determine the financing needs of a business and analyze alternative methods of financing the business. Financial analysts use information concerning the economic situation, business operations, types of financing available, interest rates, and stock and bond prices to develop an optimal financing plan for the business. Frequently they use electronic spreadsheet packages and DSS generators to build and manipulate these models. Answers to what-if and goal-seeking questions can be explored as financial analysts and managers evaluate their financing and investment alternatives. Figure 7.20 displays an example of projected operating data generated by an electronic spreadsheet as part of a financial planning process.

FIGURE 7.20

An example of projected operating data generated by a spreadsheet as part of a financial planning process.

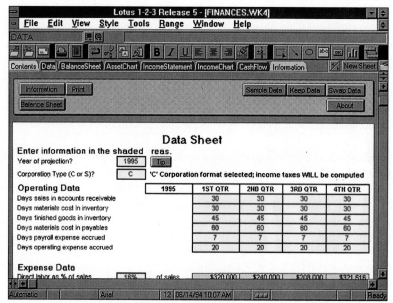

Courtesy of Lotus Development Corporation.

REAL WORLD CASE

GERLAND'S FOOD FAIR: COMPETING WITH A MARKETING DATABASE SYSTEM

What do you do if you're a small local chain and the big guys decide to move in on you? You fight back. And that's just what Gerland's Food Fair markets did when a nationally known chain set up shop in the Houston, Texas, area.

The first step was putting together a frequent shopper program to increase customer loyalty and give Gerland's 20 stores a personality distinct from its competitors. It helped—sales per customer are up over last year. But was there a way to take the program further? Kevin Doris, Gerland's chief operating officer, thought so.

The store receives a windfall of customer data every time a purchase is made because customers must hand the clerk a membership card with every purchase. So all the relevant data are recorded. Then the information is shipped to a centralized Compaq server, where Gerland's can slice it with a reporting application called the Marketing Database Application from S2 Systems Inc. of Dallas.

Now Gerland's can identify its most loyal customers. The S2 reports show how often customers come into the store and how they spend their money—all vital competitive information. "Thirty percent of the customers generate 80 percent of the business," Doris said. "Now that we know who the transactions are and know more about them, we'll be able to reward them better than before, and consequently they'll continue to shop with us over a longer period of time."

Before Gerland's set up its frequent-shopper program, the company used the Access reporting program and its cash register PC system to keep track of what items were purchased, the number of transactions per week, and the amount of each transaction, but the company was not able to tie a particular transaction to a particular customer, as it can now. For example, Gerland's has discovered that some of its customers shop the store three to four times a week, whereas another group comes in much less often.

Every week, Gerland's uses predefined reports from S2 to track how many club members came into the store that week, what portion of total sales they represent, and what the average shopper spends in one store versus another. One report compares previous and current shopping patterns to tell Gerland's if particular customers are defecting. Gerland's plans to use the information to send these customers special coupons and direct mailings in the hopes of winning them back, Doris said. A monthly report shows which stores and departments within stores are above or below the average in sales to club members.

Since Gerland's is a relatively small business with a small IT department, it chose to outsource its marketing system to another company that maintained the Compaq server and sent data to Gerland's in the form of weekly paper reports. Now the company has a dedicated line into Gerland's headquarters, so the five PCs there can access the marketing database program directly. The program runs on an Informix database management system and UnixWare, which Gerland's did not have the resources to support, Doris says.

Gerland's keep-it-simple approach made S2 a natural for the company, which liked the marketing database system's Windows-compatible format, easy-to-use GUI interface, and standard reports, Doris says.

At the end of the day, the system tells Gerland's what it needs to know. "It's our report card," Doris says.

CASE STUDY QUESTIONS

1. What marketing strategies do you recognize in Gerland's response to its new competition?

2. How does the marketing database system of Gerland's help the chain implement those strategies?

3. Could other types of businesses use a similar system? Give several examples.

Source: Adapted from Cate Corcoran, "In the Bag," *PC Week/Executive*, April 1, 1996, p. E5. Reprinted from *PC Week*. Copyright © 1996 Ziff-Davis Publishing Company.

Section II — *Transaction Processing Systems*

Transaction Processing

Transaction processing systems (TPS) are information systems that process data resulting from the occurrence of business transactions. Figure 7.21 illustrates this concept. **Transactions** are events that occur as part of doing business, such as sales, purchases, deposits, withdrawals, refunds, and payments. Think, for example, of the data generated whenever a business sells something to a customer on credit. Data about the customer, product, salesperson, store, and so on, must be captured and processed. This in turn causes additional transactions, such as credit checks, customer billing, inventory changes, and increases in accounts receivable balances that generate even more data. Thus, transaction processing activities are needed to capture and process such data, or the operations of a business would grind to a halt. Therefore, transaction processing systems play a vital role in supporting the operations of an organization.

Strategic TPS

Transaction processing systems can play strategic roles in gaining competitive advantages for a business. For example, many firms have developed *interorganizational* transaction processing systems that tie them electronically to their customers or suppliers with telecommunications network links. *Electronic data interchange* (EDI) systems (which exchange electronic copies of transaction documents) are an important example that we will discuss in this chapter. Many companies have also found that *realtime* or *online* transaction processing (OLTP) systems, which capture and process transactions immediately, can help them provide superior service to customers. This capability *adds value* to their products and services, and thus gives them an important way to differentiate themselves from their competitors [7, 9].

The Transaction Processing Cycle

Transaction processing systems capture and process data describing business transactions. Then they update organizational files and databases, and produce a variety of information products for internal and external use. You should think of these activities as a cycle of basic transaction processing activities. As Figure 7.22 illustrates, in the **transaction processing cycle,** systems go through a five-stage cycle of (1) data entry activities, (2) transaction processing activities, (3) file and database processing activities, (4) document and report generation, and (5) inquiry processing activities.

The Data Entry Process

The input activity in transaction processing systems involves a **data entry** process. In this process, data are captured or collected by recording, coding, and editing activities. Data may then be converted to a form that can be entered into a computer system. Data entry activities have always been a bottleneck in the use of computers for transaction processing. It has always been a problem getting data into computers accurately and quickly enough to match their awesome processing speeds. Thus, traditional *manual* methods of data entry that make heavy use of *data media* are being replaced by *direct automated* methods. These methods are more efficient and reliable and are known as *source data automation.* Let's take a look at both types of data entry. See Figure 7.23.

FIGURE 7.21

The role of transaction processing systems in a business. Note how business transactions such as sales to customers and purchases from suppliers are generated by the physical operations systems of this manufacturing firm. Documents describing such transactions are subsequently processed by the firm's transaction processing systems, resulting in updated databases and a variety of information products.

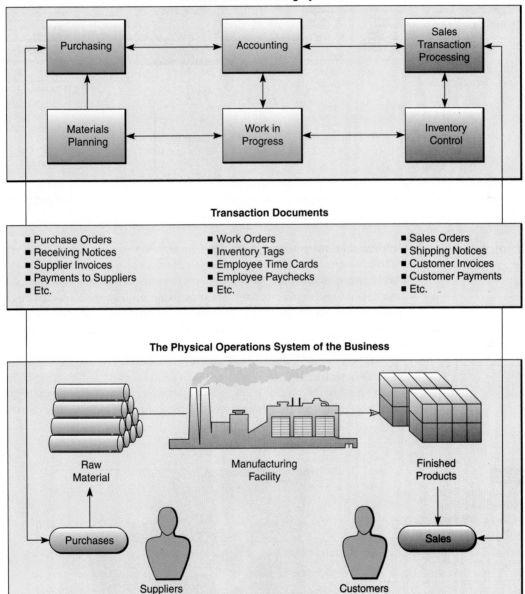

FIGURE 7.22

The transaction processing cycle. Note that transaction processing systems use a five-stage cycle of data entry, transaction processing, database maintenance, document and report generation, and inquiry processing activities.

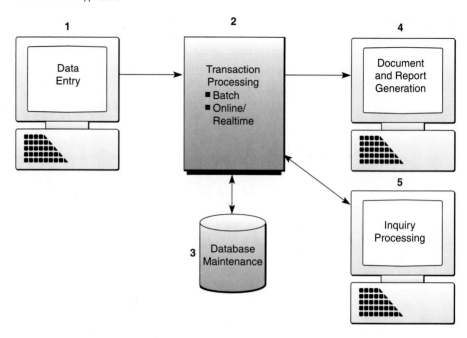

Traditional Data Entry

Traditional data entry methods typically rely on the end users of an information system to capture data on **source documents** such as purchase orders, payroll time sheets, and sales order forms. These source documents are then usually accumulated into batches and transferred to data processing professionals specializing in data entry. Periodically, the source documents are entered into a computer system. This is accomplished typically by employees or data entry specialists who must enter the data using the keyboards of data entry terminals or PCs.

It should not be surprising to discover that there has been a major shift away from traditional data entry. First, it requires too many activities, people, and data media. Second, it results in high costs and increases the potential for errors. Therefore, the response of both users and the computer industry has been to move toward *source data automation*.

FIGURE 7.23

Traditional computer-based data entry involves keying data from source documents into a computer system.

Richard Pasley.

The use of automated methods of data entry is known as **source data automation.** Several methods have been developed to accomplish this automation, though very few completely automate the data entry process. They are all based on trying to reduce or eliminate many of the activities, people, and data media required by traditional data entry methods. Figure 7.24 is an example of source data automation. Notice that this sales transaction processing system:

Source Data Automation

- Captures data *as early as possible* after a transaction or other event occurs by using POS terminals.
- Captures transaction data *as close as possible* to the source that generates the data. Salespersons at POS terminals capture and edit data right on the sales floor.
- Captures data by using *machine-readable media* initially (bar-coded tags and magnetic (mag) stripe credit cards), instead of preparing written source documents.
- Captures data that rarely changes by *prerecording* it on machine-readable media, or by storing it in the computer system.
- Captures data directly *without the use of data media* by optical scanning of bar code packaging.

The example in Figure 7.24 reveals some of the many types of devices used in source data automation. These include *transaction terminals,* such as POS terminals and automated teller machines (ATMs), and *optical character recognition* (OCR) devices, such as optical scanning wands and grocery checkout scanners. Many other input/output devices and telecommunications technologies discussed in Chapters 2 and 4 also play a role in source data automation. These include the use of PCs with cash drawers as intelligent POS terminals, portable digital radio terminals and pen-based tablet PCs for remote data entry, or touch screens and voice recognition systems for data entry. Organizations may also use local area networks of microcomputer workstations to accomplish data entry activities at regional centers, and then upload the data to corporate mainframes for further processing. Other organizations depend on LANs of networked PCs to accomplish their transaction processing activities [9].

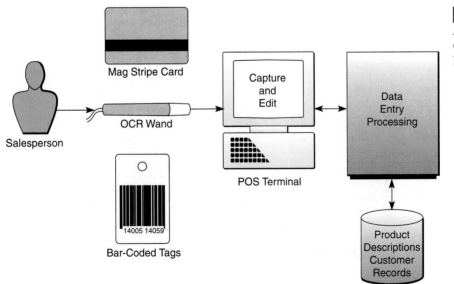

FIGURE 7.24

An automated data entry example: Sales transaction processing.

Mag Stripe Card

OCR Wand

Salesperson

Bar-Coded Tags

14005 14059

Capture and Edit

POS Terminal

Data Entry Processing

Product Descriptions Customer Records

Electronic Data Interchange

The ultimate in source data automation in many transaction processing systems is called **electronic data interchange**, or EDI. This involves the electronic transmission of business transaction data over telecommunications links between the computers of *trading partners* (organizations and their customers and suppliers). Data representing a variety of business *transaction documents* (such as purchase orders, invoices, requests for quotations, and shipping notices) are electronically transmitted using standard document message formats. Thus, EDI is an example of the almost complete automation of the data entry process.

Formatted transaction data are transmitted over telecommunications links directly between computers, without paper documents or human intervention. Besides direct network links between the computers of trading partners, third-party services are widely used. Value-added telecommunications carriers like GE Information Services, IBM, Control Data, and McDonnell Douglas offer EDI services, including an *electronic mailbox* for EDI documents [3, 16]. If necessary, EDI software is used to convert a company's own document formats into standardized EDI formats as specified by various industry and international protocols.

Figure 7.25 is an example of EDI in action. In this example, Motorola Codex has EDI links with its supplier, Texas Instruments, for the exchange of a variety of electronic transaction documents. In addition, it "closes the loop" by using *electronic funds transfer* (EFT) links to its banks so it can make electronic payments to its supplier [18].

FIGURE 7.25

An example of EDI. Motorola Codex uses EDI links to its supplier, Texas Instruments, for the exchange of business documents. Codex also makes electronic funds transfers to its banks to pay its suppliers.

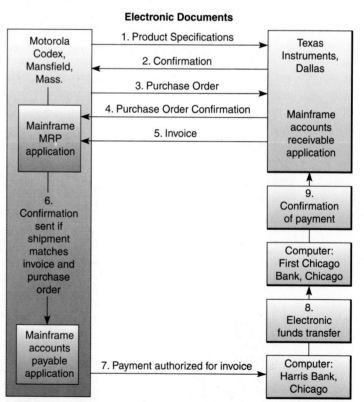

Electronic Documents

Source: Adapted from Clinton Wilder, "Codex Goes Paperless with EDI," *Computerworld,* January 13, 1992, p. 6. Copyright © 1992 by Computerworld, Inc., Framingham, MA 01701—Reprinted from *Computerworld.*

EDI eliminates the printing, mailing, checking, and handling by employees of numerous multiple-copy forms of business documents. Also, since standard document formats are used, the delays caused by mail or telephone communication between businesses to verify what a document means are drastically reduced. Some of the benefits of EDI that result are reductions in paper, postage, and labor costs; faster flow of transactions; reductions in errors; increases in productivity; support of just-in-time (JIT) inventory policies; reductions in inventory levels; and better customer service. For example, companies report decreases of 25 to 50 percent in the total time it takes to receive, process, package, and ship customer orders. Annual savings of $300 million in the grocery industry and $12 billion in the textile industry are expected. RCA expects the cost of processing a purchase order to drop from $50 to $4, and EDI is estimated to save $200 per automobile in the auto industry [16].

However, EDI is more than a way to increase efficiency, cut costs, and provide better service. In many industries, it has become an absolute business requirement. EDI is now a *strategic application* of information systems in many industries, where the message is "link up or lose out." Or, as Edward Lucente, IBM vice president, says: "Doing business without EDI will soon be like trying to do business without a telephone. No EDI, no business." General Motors proved that point when it made EDI a requirement for thousands of its suppliers, as did the U.S. Department of Defense. Experts predict that by the end of the decade over one-third of all business documents will involve EDI. Thus, EDI promises to revolutionize data entry in many transaction processing systems while promoting strategic relationships between industry trading partners [3, 16].

Electronic funds transfer (EFT) systems are a major form of transaction processing systems in banking and retailing industries. EFT systems use source data automation technologies to capture and process money and credit transfers between banks and businesses and their customers. For example, bank telecommunications networks support teller terminals at all branch offices and automated teller machines (ATMs) at locations throughout a city or region. Also supported are pay-by-phone services allowing bank customers to use their telephones as computer terminals to electronically pay bills. In addition, bankwide area networks may connect POS terminals in retail stores to bank EFT systems. This makes it possible for you to use a credit card or debit card to instantly pay for gas, groceries, or other purchases at participating retail outlets. See Figure 7.26.

Benefits of EDI

Electronic Funds Transfer

Courtesy of International Business Machines Corporation.

FIGURE 7.26

Banks use networks of ATM terminals to provide convenient electronic funds transfer services.

Batch Processing

Transaction processing systems process data in two basic ways: (1) **batch processing**, where transactions data are accumulated over a period of time and processed periodically, and (2) **realtime processing** (also called *online processing*), where data are processed immediately after a transaction occurs. Transaction processing systems still make heavy use of batch processing. However, the use of realtime processing is growing and expected to eventually become the primary form of transaction processing.

Batch Processing Activities

In **batch processing**, transactions data are accumulated over a period of time and processed periodically. Batch processing usually involves:

- Gathering *source documents* originated by business transactions, such as sales orders and invoices, into groups called batches.
- Recording transaction data on some type of input medium, such as magnetic disks or magnetic tape.
- Sorting the transactions in a *transaction file* in the same sequence as the records in a sequential *master file*.
- Processing transaction data and creating an updated master file and a variety of *documents* (such as customer invoices and paychecks) and reports.
- Capturing and storing batches of transaction data at remote sites, and then transmitting them periodically to a central computer for processing. This is known as *remote job entry,* or RJE.

Batch processing not only accumulates the transaction data for a particular application into batches but also runs (processes) a number of different transaction processing jobs periodically (daily, weekly, monthly). The rationale for batch processing is that the grouping of data and the periodic processing of jobs uses computer system resources more efficiently, compared to allowing data and jobs to be processed in an unorganized, random manner. Of course, this efficiency, economy, and control are accomplished by sacrificing the immediate processing of data for end users.

EXAMPLE In a typical example of batch processing, the banking industry usually accumulates all checks deposited during the day into batches for processing each evening. Thus, customer bank balances are updated on a daily basis and many management reports are produced daily. Figure 7.27 illustrates a batch processing system where transaction data in the form of batches of deposited checks are captured each day by MICR reader/sorters that read the data recorded in magnetic ink on the bottom of each check. Transaction data are then processed to update customer and other databases and produce a variety of customer documents and management reports.

Advantages and Disadvantages

Batch processing is an economical method when large volumes of transactions data must be processed. It is ideally suited for many applications where it is not necessary to update databases as transactions occur, and where documents and reports are required only at scheduled intervals. For example, customer statements may be prepared on a monthly basis, whereas payroll processing might be done on a weekly basis.

However, batch processing has some real disadvantages. Master files are frequently out-of-date between scheduled processing, as are the periodic scheduled reports that are produced. Also, immediate updated responses to inquiries cannot be made. For these reasons, more and more computer applications use realtime processing systems. However, batch processing systems are still widely used, and some of their disadvantages are overcome by using realtime processing for some transaction processing functions, such as data entry or inquiry processing.

FIGURE 7.27

A batch processing system example. Batches of deposited checks are accumulated and processed daily in the banking industry.

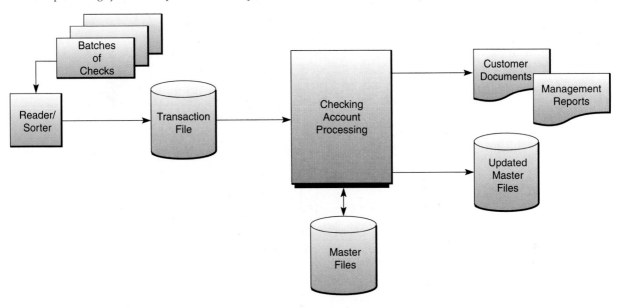

In transaction processing systems, a **realtime processing** capability allows transaction data to be processed immediately after they are generated and can provide immediate output to end users. Full-fledged realtime systems for transaction processing are popularly called **online transaction processing** (OLTP) systems. Transaction data are processed as soon as they are originated or recorded, without waiting to accumulate batches of data. Data are fed directly into the computer system from online terminals, without being sorted, and they are always stored online in direct access files. Files and databases are always up-to-date since they are updated whenever data are originated, regardless of their frequency. Responses to end users' inquiries are immediate, since information stored on direct access devices can be retrieved almost instantaneously. Realtime processing depends on wide area and local area networks to provide telecommunications links between transaction terminals, workstations, and other computers. A summary of the important capabilities differentiating batch processing and realtime processing is shown in Figure 7.28.

Realtime Processing

FIGURE 7.28

Batch versus realtime processing. Note the major differences.

Characteristic	Batch Processing	Realtime Processing
Processing of transactions	Transaction data are recorded, accumulated into batches, sorted, and processed periodically	Transaction data are processed as generated
File update	When batch is processed	When transaction is processed
Response time/turnaround time	Several hours or days after batches are submitted for processing	A few seconds after each transaction is captured

FIGURE 7.29

Example of a realtime sales processing system. Note that sales transaction processing, inquiries and responses, and database updates are accomplished immediately using online devices.

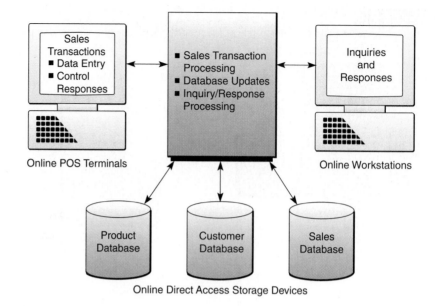

EXAMPLE   An example of a realtime sales transaction processing system is shown in Figure 7.29. Note how POS terminals are connected by telecommunications links to a computer for immediate entry of sales data and control responses (such as customer credit verification). The customer, product, and sales databases are stored on online direct access devices (typically, magnetic disk drives) and can be updated immediately to reflect sales transactions. Finally, an inquiry processing capability and telecommunication links to employee workstations allow them to make inquiries and display responses concerning customers, sales activity, inventory status, and so on.

Fault Tolerant Processing

Many airlines, banks, telephone companies, and other organizations depend on **fault tolerant systems** to protect themselves against failure of their strategic online transaction processing applications. For example, airline reservation systems and bank electronic funds transfer systems use fault tolerant computers that provide a nonstop realtime transaction processing capability that allows them to continue operating even if parts of the system fail. As we mentioned in Chapter 2, fault tolerant computers may use a multiprocessor design of several coupled CPUs or a parallel processor design of many networked microprocessors to provide a built-in backup capability in case one or more processors fail. In addition, fault tolerant computers have redundant memory units, disk drives, and other devices, as well as duplicate copies of software, including, in some cases, redundant operating systems [11]. See Figure 7.30.

Advantages and Disadvantages

Realtime processing provides immediate updating of files and immediate responses to user inquiries. Realtime processing is particularly important for applications where a high frequency of changes must be made to a file during a short time to keep it updated. Only the specific records affected by transactions or inquiries need to be processed, and several files can be processed or updated concurrently.

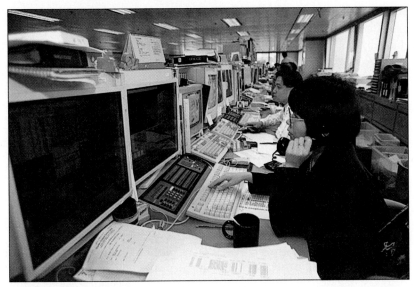

Greg Girard/Contact Press.

FIGURE 7.30

These securities traders in the Morgan Stanley trading room in Hong Kong depend on fault tolerant transaction processing systems.

Realtime processing has its disadvantages. Because of the online, direct-access nature of realtime processing, special precautions must be taken to protect the contents of databases. Thus, many realtime systems use magnetic tape files as *control logs* (to record all transactions made) or as *backup files* (by periodically making a magnetic tape copy of a file). Also, more controls have to be built into the software and processing procedures to protect against unauthorized access or the accidental destruction of data. In addition, organizations with critical OLTP applications have to pay a high cost premium for the security of fault tolerant computer systems. Thus, the many advantages of realtime processing must be balanced with the extra costs and security precautions that are necessary. However, many computer-using firms are willing to pay this price for the speed, efficiency, and superior service that realtime processing provides.

Database Maintenance

Database maintenance is a major activity of transaction processing systems. An organization's databases must be maintained by its transaction processing systems so that they are always correct and up-to-date. Therefore, transaction processing systems update the corporate databases of an organization to reflect changes resulting from day-to-day business transactions. For example, credit sales made to customers will cause customer account balances to be increased and the amount of inventory on hand to be decreased. Database maintenance ensures that these and other changes are reflected in the data records stored in the company's databases.

In addition, transaction processing systems process data resulting from miscellaneous adjustments to the records in a file or database. For example, name and address changes may have to be made to customer records, and tax withholding changes may have to be made to employee payroll records. Thus, one of the major functions of transaction processing systems is to update and make changes to an organization's corporate databases. These databases then provide the data resources that can be processed and used by information reporting systems, decision support systems, and executive information systems.

Document and Report Generation

The final stage in the transaction processing cycle is the generation of information products such as documents and reports. Figure 7.31 illustrates several examples. Documents produced by transaction processing systems are called **transaction documents.**

There are several major types of such documents:

- **Action Documents.** These are documents that initiate actions or transactions on the part of their recipient. For example, a purchase order authorizes a purchase from a supplier, and a paycheck authorizes a bank to pay an employee.

- **Information Documents.** These documents relate, confirm, or prove to their recipients that transactions have occurred. Examples are sales receipts, sales order confirmations, customer invoices and statements, and credit rejection notices. Information documents can be used as control documents, since they document the fact that a transaction has occurred.

- **Turnaround Documents.** Some types of transaction documents are designed to be read by magnetic or optical scanning equipment. Forms produced in this manner are known as turnaround documents because they are designed to be returned to the sender. For example, many computer-printed invoices consist of a turnaround portion that is returned by a customer along with his or her payment. The turnaround document can then be automatically processed by optical scanning devices. Thus, turnaround documents combine the functions of an action document (the turnaround portion) and an information document (the receipt portion).

Transaction processing systems also produce several types of reports and displays designed to document and monitor the results of business transactions occurring or processed during a specific time period. They are not specifically tailored for

FIGURE 7.31

Examples of information products produced by transaction processing systems. Transaction documents such as customer statements must be prepared and mailed to customers on a monthly basis. The cash requirements register is a control listing of the checks that must be prepared in payment of amounts owed to vendors.

management use, though they may be used by managers. Such reports can provide an audit trail for transaction control purposes. Examples are:

- **Control Listings.** These are detailed reports that describe each transaction occurring during a period. They are also called *transaction logs*. For example, a listing known as a payroll register lists every paycheck printed on a specified payday by a payroll system.
- **Edit Reports.** These are reports that describe errors detected during processing. For example, invalid account numbers, missing data, and incorrect control totals would be presented in edit reports.
- **Accounting Statements.** These are reports that legally document the financial performance or status of a business. Examples are general ledger summaries, statements of cash flow, balance sheets, and income statements.

Transaction processing and information reporting systems frequently support the realtime interrogation of online files and databases by end users. As we have previously mentioned, this **inquiry processing** capability can be provided by either batch or realtime processing. End users at workstations in wide area and local area networks can use database management query languages to make inquiries and receive responses concerning the results of transaction activity. Typically, responses are displayed in a variety of prespecified formats or *screens*. For example, employees can check on the status of a sales order, the balance in an account, or the amount of stock in inventory and receive immediate responses at their workstations. Or managers can receive responses and reports on demand concerning the performance of their employees, work groups, or departments. See Figure 7.32.

Inquiry Processing

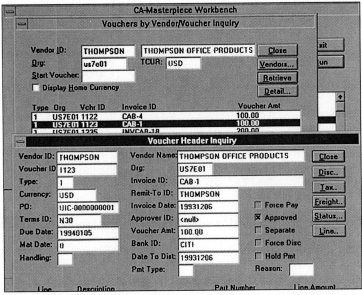

FIGURE 7.32

A vendor and voucher inquiry display provided by a transaction processing system.

Courtesy of Computer Associates, Inc.

REAL WORLD CASE

CAMPBELL SOUP CO.: TRACKING INVENTORY AND ELECTRONIC COMMERCE

When it comes to managing its finished goods inventory, Campbell Soup Co. has had a pretty good system going—if it needed to manage only 30 percent of its inventory. A 3090 mainframe receives daily updates from participating supermarkets, and when inventory dips, the system automatically replenishes their soup, salsa, or whatever other Campbell product is needed.

The problem, according to Ron Ferner, vice president of low-cost business systems at Camden, New Jersey–based Campbell, is the other 70 percent of inventory not managed on the system. Many of Campbell's customers are not comfortable handing over such purchasing decisions to Campbell.

So Campbell, which has been running the main-frame-based customer replenishment system for about four years, is trying to create a system that will cut inventory costs as dramatically as the mainframe system did. Not an easy task considering the mainframe system lopped $60 million off hundreds of millions of dollars of annual inventory costs.

However, Ferner is anxious to implement the new system since the balance of orders the mainframe replenishment systems don't process are paper-based and prone to ending up in the wrong Campbell plants and offices.

The new electronic commerce system, which Ferner is installing this year, will be based on an IBM RS/6000 parallel processor server running an Oracle database management system. It will house two components that take finished goods inventory information off an AS/400 midrange computer and whip it into electronic commerce action.

Campbell has hired IBM's Integrated Systems Solutions Corp. to deploy and maintain the system. One piece, an order processing application from Industri-Matematick,

Inc., in Sweden, will let Campbell centralize orders now scattered throughout 13 regional offices. A second piece, from Rockville, Maryland–based Manugistics, Inc., will facilitate sales order forecasting and assist Campbell's inventory planning.

Here's how the electronic commerce system works: Customers send an order to Campbell via MCI Mail. The Industri-Matematick system processes the order and feeds it to the Manugistics program. Manugistics compares the order against inventory and rolling sales information, which can help sales managers decide how much of which products to make and where.

The system also tracks inventory and can advise customers when to replenish. It then electronically tells customers which goods are on their way and when they'll arrive. "Today, they have to wait until the truck shows up to see if they got what they asked for," Ferner said.

He declined to say how much the two components cost but said they are part of a $26 million reengineering project that affects other aspects of the company as well. For instance, the Oracle database serving the inventory and product planning applications will anchor a central customer support and complaint center in Cherry Hill, New Jersey.

Ferner declined to elaborate on Campbell's predicted return on its investment except to say that given the economies of scale derived from leveraging the RS/6000 hardware and software investment across various operations, "we justified it easily."

CASE STUDY QUESTIONS

1. What steps of the transaction processing cycle (see Figure 7.22) do you recognize in Campbell's electronic commerce system? Explain.

2. Why can computerizing inventory like Campbell Soup did result in major cost savings to a business?

3. What benefits to Campbell and its customers do you see in their electronic commerce system?

Source: Adapted from Mark Halper, "Campbell Soups Up Inventory," in "Get Vertical," *Computerworld Electronic Commerce Journal*, April 29, 1996, pp. 11–12. Copyright © 1996 by Computerworld, Inc., Framingham, MA 01701—Reprinted from *Computerworld*.

Summary

- **IS in Business.** Business information systems support the functional areas of business (marketing, production/operations, accounting, finance, and human resource management) through a wide variety of computer-based operational and management information systems.

- **Marketing.** Marketing information systems provide information for the planning and control of the marketing function. Marketing planning information assists marketing managers in product planning, pricing decisions, planning advertising and sales promotion strategies and expenditures, forecasting the market potential for new and present products, and determining channels of distribution. Marketing control information supports the efforts of management to control the efficiency and effectiveness of the selling and distribution of products and services. The major types of marketing information systems are sales management, sales force automation, product management, advertising and promotion, sales forecasting, market research, and market management systems.

- **Manufacturing.** Computer-based manufacturing information systems use several major subsystems to achieve computer-aided manufacturing (CAM). Computers are automating many of the activities needed to produce products in manufacturing industries. For example, computer-aided design (CAD) systems help engineers design products. Then material requirements planning (MRP) systems help plan the types of material needed in the production process. Finally, computers may be used to manufacture products on the factory floor by directly controlling a physical process (process control), a machine tool (numerical control), or machines with some humanlike physical capabilities (robotics).

- **Human Resource Management.** Human resource information systems support human resource management in organizations. They include information systems for staffing, training and development, compensation administration, and performance appraisal.

- **Accounting and Finance.** Accounting information systems record and report business transactions and events for business firms and other organizations. Operational accounting systems emphasize legal and historical record-keeping and the production of accurate financial statements. Management accounting systems focus on the planning and control of business operations. Common operational accounting information systems include order processing, inventory control, accounts receivable, accounts payable, payroll, and general ledger systems. Information systems in finance support financial managers in decisions regarding the financing of a business and the allocation of financial resources within a business. Financial information systems include cash and securities management, capital budgeting, financial forecasting, and financial planning.

- **Transaction Processing.** Transaction processing systems play a vital role in processing data resulting from business transactions. They involve the basic activities of (1) data entry, (2) transaction processing, (3) database maintenance, (4) document and report generation, and (5) inquiry processing. However, transaction processing systems can also play a strategic role in gaining competitive advantages for a business.

- **Data Entry.** Traditional data entry methods in transaction processing systems requiring too many activities, people, and forms of data media are being replaced by more direct, automated methods known as source data automation. The high cost and potential for errors characteristic of traditional data entry methods can be minimized with source data automation that captures data as early and as close as possible to the source generating the data. Data are captured by using machine-readable media, prerecording data, or capturing data directly without the use of data media. Electronic data interchange methods allow the direct electronic transmission of source documents between companies.

- **Batch and Realtime Processing.** Two basic categories of transaction processing systems are batch processing, in which data are accumulated and processed periodically, and realtime (or online) processing, which processes data immediately. Realtime processing can be subdivided into several levels: inquiry, data entry, file processing, full capability, and process control.

Key Terms and Concepts

These are the key terms and concepts of this chapter. The page number of their first explanation is in parentheses.

1. Accounting information systems (253)
2. Accounts payable (254)
3. Accounts receivable (254)
4. Batch processing (266)
5. Business information systems (240)
6. Computer-aided design (249)
7. Computer-aided engineering (249)
8. Computer-aided manufacturing (245)
9. Computer graphics (250)
10. Computer-integrated manufacturing (245)
11. Control listing (271)

12. Cross-functional information systems (241)
13. Edit report (271)
14. Electronic data interchange (264)
15. Electronic funds transfer (265)
16. Fault tolerant system (268)
17. Financial information systems (256)
18. Financial planning models (258)
19. General ledger (256)
20. Human resource information systems (250)
21. Inquiry processing (271)

22. Inventory control (254)
23. Machine control (248)
24. Manufacturing information systems (245)
25. Marketing information systems (241)
26. Material requirements planning (245)
27. Online transaction processing (267)
28. Order processing (253)
29. Payroll (255)
30. Process control (247)
31. Realtime processing (266)

32. Robotics (248)
33. Sales force automation (242)
34. Source data automation (263)
35. Source document (262)
36. Strategic transaction processing systems (260)
37. Traditional data entry (262)
38. Transaction (260)
39. Transaction document (270)
40. Transaction processing cycle (260)
41. Transaction processing system (260)
42. Turnaround document (270)

Review Quiz

Match one of the key terms and concepts listed above with one of the brief examples or definitions listed below. Try to find the best fit for answers that seem to fit more than one term or concept. Defend your choices.

_____ 1. An example is making a sale or a payment.

_____ 2. Process data resulting from business transactions.

_____ 3. Data entry, transaction processing, database maintenance, document and report generation, and inquiry processing.

_____ 4. Has too many activities, people, media, costs, and errors.

_____ 5. The automatic capture of data at the time and place of transactions.

_____ 6. The electronic transmission of source documents between companies.

_____ 7. Collecting and periodically processing transaction data.

_____ 8. Processing transaction data immediately after they are captured.

_____ 9. A sales order form is an example.

_____ 10. Examples are paychecks, customer statements, and sales receipts.

_____ 11. Part of a customer's invoice is returned for automated data entry.

_____ 12. A payroll register is an example.

_____ 13. Reports that identify errors occurring during transaction processing.

_____ 14. Allows end users to check on the status of an order or the balance in an account and receive an immediate response.

_____ 15. A nonstop transaction processing capability.

_____ 16. A popular name for realtime transaction processing.

_____ 17. Transaction processing systems can build strong relationships with customers and suppliers.

_____ 18. Support marketing, production, accounting, finance, and human resource management with computer-based information systems.

_____ 19. Information systems must integrate the activities and resources of the functional areas of a business.

_____ 20. Information systems for sales management, product management, and promotion management.

_____ 21. Uses computers to automate sales recording and reporting by salespeople.

_____ 22. Information systems that support manufacturing operations and management.

_____ 23. Using computers in a variety of ways to help manufacture products.

_____ 24. Helps the design process using advanced graphics, workstations, and software.

_____ 25. Helps engineers evaluate products and processes.

_____ 26. A conceptual framework for all aspects of factory automation.

_____ 27. Using computers to operate a petroleum refinery.

_____ 28. Using computers to help operate machine tools.

_____ 29. Computerized devices can take over some production activities from human workers.

_____ 30. Translates the production schedule into a detailed plan for all materials required.

_____ 31. Information systems to support staffing, training and development, and compensation administration.

_____ 32. Accomplish legal and historical record-keeping and gather information for the planning and control of business operations.

_____ 33. Handles sales orders from customers.

____ 34. Keeps track of items in stock.

____ 35. Keeps track of amounts owed by customers.

____ 36. Keeps track of purchases from suppliers.

____ 37. Produces employee paychecks.

____ 38. Produces the financial statements of a firm.

____ 39. Information systems for cash and securities management, capital budgeting, and financial forecasting.

____ 40. Provides a DSS capability for financial planning.

____ 41. Systems for the capture and processing of money and credit transactions.

Discussion Questions

1. How can transaction processing systems play a strategic role in gaining competitive advantages for a business?

2. Why would electronic data interchange be "the ultimate in source data automation"?

3. Refer to the Real World Case on Gerland's Food Fair in the chapter. In what other ways could Gerland's use information technology to compete against a national chain of supermarkets? Give examples to illustrate your answer.

4. What are several reasons for the continued growth of online transaction processing? When would an OLTP system need a fault tolerant capability?

5. What is sales force automation? How does it affect salesperson productivity, marketing management, and competitive advantage?

6. Refer to the Real World Case on Campbell Soup Co. in this chapter. Why would Campbell use a database that serves order processing and inventory planning applications to "anchor a central customer support and complaint center?"

7. What is computer-integrated manufacturing? What is the role of computer-aided manufacturing, computer-aided engineering, and robotics in CIM?

8. How can computer-based information systems support human resource management in a business? Give a few examples.

9. What are the most common applications of computers in accounting? Why do most businesses computerize these accounting systems?

10. What are cross-functional information systems? Why is there a trend toward such systems?

Real World Problems

1. VIK Brothers Insurance Group:
Using IT for Sales Success

VIK Brothers Insurance Group deals in property and casualty insurance coverage for individuals and businesses. The national firm relies on a group of 30 salespeople to sell its policies through more than 3,000 independent agents. The primary tools of the trade for VIK's sales force used to be a briefcase and a pad of paper. "The basic problem was that we had our salespeople trying to sell insurance, but they didn't have the tools to do it," says Frank Neis, manager of sales at VIK's home office in Milwaukee. "We were only achieving a 20 percent success rate."

The solution was Saratoga Systems SPS, an opportunity management and sales information software system. SPS acts as a central database providing the sales rep easy access to multiwindow, multilevel customer profiles and sales-related information. SPS also functions as a distributed database, with end users uploading and downloading information from the central database through their PCs.

VIK does business in 39 states, but it doesn't have offices in all of those states. Although VIK doesn't have an agency in Montana, for example, the company has an agent who works using SPS. "He'll dial up the central database every night and upload what he has, and he gets what he needs

from us in exchange," Neis says. With SPS, management has more control of what its agents are sending. And the information they receive is much more current. VIK salespeople dial into servers at its four regional offices which, in turn, connect to the central server in Milwaukee every night. The regional offices hold only the information for that territory, so these servers can work much faster.

With SPS, VIK's sales success rates have increased to 35 percent. "We can't live without it," Neis says. "Our people are operating without paper now. It does call planning, takes the notes, and after the call they can post the call report." Neis says SPS has changed how its agents work. Now, they can give quotes on the spot. Agents make calls to fewer places now, too, concentrating more on high-impact locations, Neis says, and they get a lot more done. "Instead of a lot of 45-minute calls, they are spending a half a day at one call with greater results."

a. How do laptop PCs and software like SPS help the selling process? The sales management process?

b. What other types of products and sales situations could be helped by systems like SPS?

Source: Adapted from Richard Egan, "Software Boosts Sales Success," *PC Today*, June 1996, p. 110. *PC Today*, 125 W. Harvest Drive, Lincoln, NE 68501.

2. Marriott Castle Harbour Resort: Computerizing Human Resource Management

Even in Bermuda, life's no vacation when you're wading through piles of paperwork. Just ask Zehena Davis, human resources director for Marriott's Castle Harbour Resort in Tucker's Town, Bermuda. Davis uses *ICONtrol Human Resources*, a comprehensive management software package, to operate the resort's personnel office, where she's in charge of the 450 to 500 employees that service the hotel and resort.

"We saw that human resources needed to be more than just the old personnel, paper-pushing department," she says. Filing resumes, tracking salary histories and training, and keeping grievance and disciplinary records were sapping the human resources of Davis's department. There was little time to plan ahead, much less to document the recruiting, training, and hiring costs of the department. As a result, Davis says, suggestions from her department carried little weight with management since they couldn't be backed up with good, hard figures. "The paper was piling up," she says. "I figured there had to be a more efficient way."

Although manufactured in the United States, ICONtrol is flexible enough to handle Bermuda's laws. For instance, there is no Social Security system in the island country, but Bermuda does have social insurance. The Castle Harbour Marriott hires many nonresidents and several stay at company-owned housing, which requires extra tracking and deductions. The software was easily adapted to these circumstances, Davis says.

The HR office has increased its efficiency and has more time to manage workers. The click of an icon, Davis says, can produce a salary history that used to require wading through paper files. It's also a breeze to organize interviews. "We have a sizable number of people come through this office. If we have one job in the paper, we could have 20 to 30 people come in," she says. "We used to spend an hour and a half to get the applications together to give to management to screen. Now, we can do that in a few minutes."

a. How does the ICONtrol software help Castle Harbour's human resource management function?

b. How does an efficiently run HRM function (like Castle Harbour's is now) benefit a business?

Source: Adapted from Paul Hammel, "Paperless in Paradise," *PC Today*, March 1996, p. 115. *PC Today*, 125 W. Harvest Drive, Lincoln, NE 68501.

3. John Connolly of Sybase, Inc.: Browsing The Investors Edge

"The Investors Edge Web site is a great home page," says John Connolly, a senior analyst at Sybase, Inc. "Companies pay to have their investor relations materials made available on The Investors Edge (http://www.irnet.com). For users, it's a popular financial information source enhanced by stocks and mutual funds price data. I use it to track my stocks and the progress of the mutual funds in my 401(k) plan. The site also has a nice feature, its most active page, that shows the stock gainers and losers.

"The stock pages are nicely laid out for users—you can see the charts and addresses all in one place as opposed to seeing only a stock's symbol and price. It also has links so you can get telephone numbers and addresses quickly. Other excellent links include being able to get a stock quote and then go to links to other companies in that industry.

"For example, I can click on the auto industry from the General Motors stock page (http://server1.irnet.com/scripts/ethos.exe? www+p_IEStockInfo+'GM') and get a list of all the companies in the auto industry. I can also hot-link to GM's Web site from the stock page. It's also very easy to access; it doesn't require a login or authentication to get quotes. Because it doesn't use graphics extensively, as other financial sites do, each page doesn't take forever to download.

"I usually check the page about once a day, but if there's something I'm thinking of buying or selling, I can even leave the window running in the background on my screen. The information automatically refreshes at regular intervals, and it only takes me a few seconds during my work breaks to click it to the front and check.

"I also use the site to pull information about my stocks into Quicken (Intuit's personal finance management package). There's an option I can click on that generates a spreadsheet I can download as a file and then import into Quicken."

a. Why do you think John Connolly nominated The Investors Edge as one of the top business home pages on the World Wide Web?

b. Check out The Investors Edge on the Web. Do you agree with Connolly? Why or why not? Which business home page would you nominate as one of the best? Explain.

Source: Adapted from Daniel Dern, "Fave Web Sites," *Computerworld*, March 11, 1996, pp. 97–98. Copyright © 1996 by Computerworld, Inc., Framingham, MA 01701—Reprinted from *Computerworld*.

4. Motor and Equipment Manufacturers Association: Using Electronic Data Interchange

Once upon a time, six automotive parts manufacturers banded together to embark on what was then a radical concept: They created an industrywide electronic system for ordering parts, using electronic data interchange (EDI) technology. Twenty-two years later, the MISG/Transnet system is revving faster than ever. It established a record last year by processing 103 million lines of purchase orders for 230 manufacturers and 3,000 distributors in the $160 billion market for used car-replacement parts.

Transnet has helped industry participants dramatically slash their order-entry costs. For example, Gates Rubber Co. in Denver, Colorado, would have had to pay nine additional data-entry clerks at least $75,000 to type in the 6 million line items it sold through Transnet last year. So says Jim Bonham, electronic commerce manager at Gates, the world's largest maker of belts and hoses.

Management Information Systems Group, Inc. (MISG), in Research Triangle Park, North Carolina, is a division of the Motor and Equipment Manufacturers Association (MEMA).

It oversees Transnet's client and technical services. Transnet runs on the global access network of General Electric Co.'s General Electric Information Services (GEIS).

By using dial-up connections, distributors connect to the GEIS-based service and request parts from manufacturers. Manufacturers download the electronic requests, process the purchase orders, and send confirmations back to the distributors.

Transnet manufacturers pay about 4 to 5 cents for each line item that traverses the GEIS network, said Allan Evans,

director of marketing at MISG. Distributors don't pay for the Transnet service, which is funded by member manufacturers.

a. What steps of the transaction processing cycle (see Figure 7.22) do you recognize in the Transnet system? Explain.

b. What are the business benefits of EDI applications like the Transnet system?

Source: Adapted from Thomas Hoffman, "Net May Rev Up Auto Aftermarket," *Computerworld*, April 8, 1996, pp. 71–72. Copyright © 1996 by Computerworld, Inc., Framingham, MA 01701—Reprinted from *Computerworld*.

Application Exercises

1. ABC Department Stores

ABC Department Stores use POS terminals connected to a minicomputer in each store to capture sales data immediately and store them on a magnetic disk unit. Each night, the central computer in Phoenix polls each store's minicomputer to access and process the day's sales data, update the corporate database, and produce management reports. The next morning, managers use their terminals to interrogate the updated corporate databases.

Identify how each of the following types of computer processing is occurring in the example above:

a. Batch
b. Realtime
c. Online
d. Transaction
e. Data entry
f. Database maintenance
g. Inquiry processing

2. Business Information Systems

Which business information systems should be improved if the following complaints were brought to your attention? Identify the business function (accounting, finance, marketing, production/operations, or human resource management) and the specific information system in that functional area that is involved. (Refer to Figure 7.1.)

a. "Nobody is sure which of our sales reps is our top producer."
b. "Why was this part left out of the bill of materials?"
c. "I don't know why I didn't get a raise this year."
d. "Why were we overinvested in short-term securities?"
e. "Why are the balance sheet and income statement late this month?"
f. "Our sales reps are spending too much time on paperwork."
g. "The ROI and payback on this deal are all wrong."
h. "Which of our managers have overseas experience?"
i. "We need a workstation to design this product."
j. "Why are we being stuck with home office overhead expenses?"

3. Accounting Information Systems

Which common accounting information systems should be improved if the following complaints were brought to your attention? (Refer to Figure 7.16.)

a. "Month-end closings are always late."
b. "We are never sure how much of a certain product we have on the shelves."
c. "Many of us didn't get an earnings and deductions statement this week."
d. "We're tired of manually writing up a receipt every time a customer orders something."
e. "Our suppliers are complaining that they are not being paid on time."
f. "Our customers resent being sent notices demanding payment when they have already paid what they owe."

4. Strategic Sales Information at Action Products

All members of the Action Products sales force have portable computers to transmit orders and make inquiries while making sales calls on Action's customers. The marketing director believes that these portables could be put to strategic use if each salesperson could provide customers with information about recent trends in their sales of Action's products. This information could help make the case for additional counter space being allocated to Action Products. In addition, it would help customers make better stocking decisions and thus improve goodwill.

The information systems department could provide a set of information like the following sample for each customer that Action Products serves. You have been asked to take the sample data and develop a spreadsheet application that will produce reports and graphs highlighting the most important sales trends. The reports produced should show comparisons in percentage terms, where appropriate to highlight trends. When you have completed your work, information systems personnel will write a utility application using your spreadsheet as a template and allowing the set of data for any customer to be automatically loaded into it.

a. Based on the sample of data, create a spreadsheet application with appropriate reports and graphs to highlight the sales trends described.

	Two Years Ago		Prior Year		Current Year	
XYZ Company's Sales of Products Supplied by Action Products						
Product	**Current Quarter**	**Year to Date**	**Current Quarter**	**Year to Date**	**Current Quarter**	**Year to Date**
External Modem 14,400 BPS	325	718	340	785	310	675
Internal Modem 14,400 BPS	245	415	308	647	480	825
External Modem 28,800 BPS	503	1,154	515	1,148	532	1,195
Internal Modem 28,800 BPS	240	515	475	1,028	780	1,494

5. A Transactions File for Boat Rentals

Bayside Mart is a convenience store located on a lake in a resort area. Recently, the owner of Bayside Mart decided to add boat rentals to her products and services. The set of available boats includes a canoe, a kayak, and a rowboat. Bayside Mart has a PC and currently uses a popular accounting software package to handle basic transactions for the store. However, this accounting package does not track rental items.

When a boat is rented, the customer is required to either leave a credit card at the store or pay a cash deposit. Bayside's owner would like to have an application that would record for each rental the customer's name, the type of deposit, the type of boat rented, the date, the time the boat was taken, and the time it was returned. This information will be used to calculate how long a boat was rented so that customers are charged the correct amount. It will also track deposit infor-

mation. Finally, this information should allow summary reports about the usage of each type of boat to be produced.

You have been asked to create an appropriate database application to produce the information just described. A set of sample data from last week's rentals follows.

NOTE: The treatment of time mathematically varies substantially across different software products. The time-out and time-in values shown in the sample data are based on a 24-hour clock and can be stored as time variables or as integers. We are assuming that check-out and check-in times are always rounded off to the nearest hour. The number of hours a boat was rented is simply the time-in minus the time-out. If these variables are stored as integers, standard math is used. If you store them as times, you must use the time and data math functions of your database package to calculate how long the boat was used.

Customer's First Name	Last Name	Type of Deposit	Date	Boat Type	Time Out	Time In
Bayside Mart Sample Rental Data						
Susan	Jones	Cash	04/05/96	Canoe	10:00	13:00
Alan	Davis	Credit Card	04/05/96	Kayak	12:00	14:00
Louis	Cole	Cash	04/05/96	Rowboat	15:00	16:00
Louis	Cole	Cash	04/05/96	Canoe	15:00	16:00
Ed	Evans	Credit Card	04/06/96	Rowboat	9:00	14:00
Janet	Rand	Cash	04/06/96	Canoe	13:00	15:00
Sue	Thomas	Credit Card	04/07/96	Canoe	9:00	10:00
Joe	Smith	Cash	04/07/96	Rowboat	11:00	13:00
Lance	Edwards	Credit Card	04/07/96	Canoe	12:00	15:00
Ann	Gale	Credit Card	04/07/96	Rowboat	16:00	18:00
Joy	Miller	Cash	04/08/96	Canoe	11:00	16:00
Ed	Sampson	Cash	04/08/96	Kayak	15:00	17:00
Alice	Jackson	Cash	04/09/96	Rowboat	10:00	12:00
Alice	Jackson	Cash	04/09/96	Canoe	10:00	12:00
Mitch	Owens	Credit Card	04/09/96	Canoe	14:00	17:00
Al	Lawrence	Credit Card	04/11/96	Rowboat	9:00	11:00
Mac	Bush	Credit Card	04/11/96	Canoe	12:00	14:00
Len	Barnes	Cash	04/11/96	Kayak	16:00	17:00

a. Create a database table for this application and store the sample data shown.

b. Write a set of instructions for adding a new record to your database table when a boat is rented, for updating a record when a boat is returned, and for doing a query to show the data for boats that are currently rented (records with a checkout time but no return time).

c. Create a summary report that will list the number of rentals and the hours of rental time for each type of boat, based on the sample data.

Review Quiz Answers

1. 38	12. 11	23. 8	34. 22
2. 41	13. 13	24. 6	35. 3
3. 40	14. 21	25. 7	36. 2
4. 37	15. 16	26. 10	37. 29
5. 34	16. 27	27. 30	38. 19
6. 14	17. 36	28. 2	39. 17
7. 4	18. 5	29. 32	40. 18
8. 31	19. 12	30. 26	41. 15
9. 35	20. 25	31. 20	
10. 39	21. 33	32. 1	
11. 42	22. 24	33. 28	

Selected References

1. Andersen Consulting. *Foundations of Business Systems.* 2nd ed. Fort Worth, TX: Dryden Press, 1992.
2. Bakos, J. Yannis. "A Strategic Analysis of Electronic Marketplaces." *MIS Quarterly,* September 1991.
3. Blattberg, Robert C.; Rashi Glazer; and John D. C. Little, eds. *The Marketing Information Revolution.* Boston: The Harvard Business School Press, 1994.
4. Cushing, Barry, and Marshal Romney. *Accounting Information Systems.* 6th ed. Reading, MA: Addison-Wesley Publishing, 1994.
5. Dams, Leila. "On the Fast Track to HR Integration." *Datamation,* September 15, 1991.
6. Douglass, David. "Computer Integrated Manufacturing." *SIM Executive,* First Quarter 1991.
7. Eliason, Alan. *Online Business Computer Applications.* 3rd ed. New York: Macmillan, 1991.
8. Fitzgerald, Michael. "Users Trying Again with Sales Force Automation." *Computerworld,* November 28, 1994.
9. Hess, Christopher, and Chris Kemerer. "Computerized Loan Origination Systems: An Industry Case Study of the Electronic Markets Hypothesis." *MIS Quarterly,* September 1994.
10. "Integration Strategies: Manufacturing." *Computerworld,* October 28, 1991.
11. Jiang, James. "Using Scanner Data." *Information Systems Management,* Winter 1995.
12. Keen, Peter. *Shaping This Future: Business Design through Information Technology.* Cambridge: Harvard Business School Press, 1991.
13. McWilliams, Bryan. "Delighting the Marketer?" *Computerworld,* November 14, 1994.
14. Moad, Jeff. "Relational Takes on OLTP." *Datamation,* May 15, 1991.
15. Senn, James. "Electronic Data Interchange." *Information Systems Management,* Winter 1992.
16. Sloan, Robert, and Hal Green. "Manufacturing Decision Support Architecture: Achieving Effective Information Delivery." *Information Systems Management,* Winter 1995.
17. Snell, Ned. "Software to Tame the Sales Force." *Datamation,* June 1, 1991.
18. Trippi, Robert, and Efraim Turban. *Investment Management: Decision Support and Expert Systems.* Boston: boyd & fraser publishing co., 1990.
19. Wilder, Clinton. "Codex Goes Paperless with EDI." *Computerworld,* January 13, 1992.

Information Systems for Managerial Decision Support

CHAPTER OUTLINE

LEARNING OBJECTIVES

After reading and studying this chapter, you should be able to:

1. Identify the role and reporting alternatives of management information systems.

2. Describe how online analytical processing can meet key information needs of managers.

3. Explain the decision support system concept and how it differs from traditional information reporting systems.

4. Explain how executive information systems can support the information needs of top and middle managers.

5. Describe how group decision support systems can support group decision making.

6. Identify how neural networks, fuzzy logic, virtual reality, and intelligent agents can be used in business.

7. Give examples of several ways expert systems can be used in business decision-making situations.

Section I

Management Information and Decision Support Systems

Introduction

Previous chapters of this text have emphasized that information systems can support the diverse information and decision-making needs of managers. Figure 8.1 emphasizes the differing conceptual focuses of major types of information systems. In this section, we will explore in more detail how this is accomplished by management information, decision support, and executive information systems. We will concentrate our attention on how these information technologies have significantly strengthened the role information systems play in supporting the decision-making activities of managerial end users. See Figure 8.2.

Information, Decisions, and Management

Figure 8.3 emphasizes that the type of information required by managers is directly related to the level of management and the amount of structure in the decision situations they face. Decisions at the operational level tend to be more structured, those at the tactical level more semistructured, and those at the strategic level more unstructured. *Structured decisions* involve situations where the procedures to follow when a decision is needed can be specified in advance. The inventory reorder decisions faced by most businesses are a typical example.

Unstructured decisions involve decision situations where it is not possible to specify in advance most of the decision procedures to follow. At most, many decision situations are *semistructured*. That is, some decision procedures can be prespecified, but not enough to lead to a definite recommended decision. For example, decisions involved in starting a new line of products or making major changes to employee benefits would probably range from unstructured to semistructured. Figure 8.4 provides a variety of examples of business decisions by type of decision structure and level of management.

Therefore, information systems must be designed to produce a variety of information products to meet the changing decision needs of managers at different levels of an organization. For example, the strategic management level requires more summarized, ad hoc, unscheduled reports, forecasts, and external intelligence to support its more unstructured planning and policy-making responsibilities. The operational management level, on the other hand, may require more regular internal reports emphasizing detailed current and historical data comparisons that support its more structured control of day-to-day operations. Thus, we can generalize that higher levels of management require more ad hoc, unscheduled, infrequent summaries, with a wide, external, forward-looking scope. On the other hand, lower levels of management require more prespecified, frequently scheduled, and detailed information, with a more narrow, internal, and historical focus.

FIGURE 8.1

The differing focuses of major types of information systems.

Type of Information System	Focus
Expert systems	Knowledge—from experts
Decision support systems	Decisions—interactive support
Executive information systems	Information—for executives
Management information systems	Information—for managerial end users
Transaction processing systems	Data—from business operations

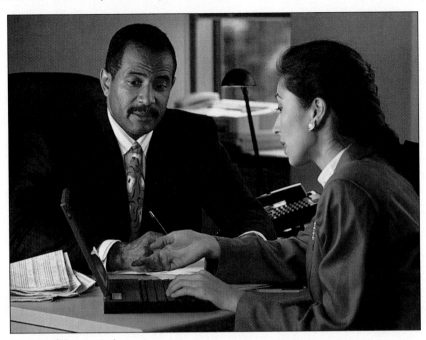

Steve Niedorf/The Image Bank.

FIGURE 8.2

Every manager relies on information systems for information and decision support.

FIGURE 8.3

Information requirements by management level. The type of information required by managers is directly related to their level of management and the structure of decision situations they face.

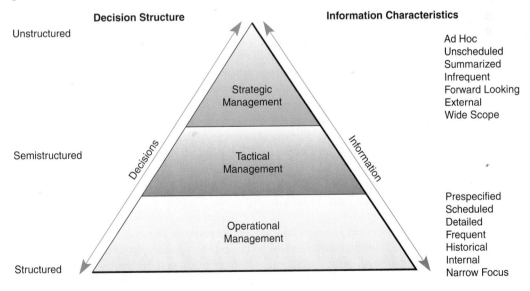

FIGURE 8.4

Examples of decisions by the type of decision structure and by level of management.

Decision Structure	Operational Management	Tactical Management	Strategic Management
Unstructured		Work group reorganization	New business planning
	Cash management	Work group performance analysis	Company reorganization
Semistructured	Credit management	Employee performance appraisal	Product planning
	Production scheduling	Capital budgeting	Mergers and acquisitions
	Daily work assignment	Program budgeting	Site location
Structured	Inventory control	Program control	

Information Quality

What characteristics make information meaningful and useful to managers? What qualities give it value for end users? One way to answer these important questions is to examine the characteristics or attributes of **information quality.** Information that is outdated, inaccurate, or hard to understand would not be very meaningful, useful, or valuable to managers. They want information of high quality, that is, information products whose characteristics, attributes, or qualities help make it valuable to them. It is useful to think of information as having the three dimensions of time, content, and form. Figure 8.5 summarizes the important attributes of information and groups them into these three dimensions.

Management Information Systems

Management information systems, also called *information reporting systems,* were the original type of management support systems, and are still a major category of information systems. MIS produce information products that support many of the day-to-day decision-making needs of management. Reports, displays, and responses produced by such systems provide information that managers have specified in advance as adequately meeting their information needs. Such predefined information products satisfy the information needs of managers at the operational and tactical levels of the organization who are faced with more structured types of decision situations. For example, sales managers rely heavily on sales analysis reports to evaluate differences in performance among salespeople who sell the same types of products to the same types of customers. They have a pretty good idea of the kinds of information about sales results they need to manage sales performance effectively.

Figure 8.6 illustrates the components of a management information system. Managers can receive information at their workstations that supports their decision-making activities. This information takes the form of periodic, exception, and demand reports and immediate responses to inquiries. Application programs and database management software provide access to information in the corporate databases of the organization. Remember, these databases are maintained by transaction processing systems. Data about the business environment are obtained from external databases when necessary.

Management Reporting Alternatives

Management information systems provide a variety of information products to managers. The three major reporting alternatives provided by such systems are summarized on page 285. See Figure 8.7.

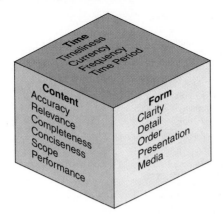

FIGURE 8.5

A summary of the attributes of information quality. This outlines the attributes that should be present in high-quality information products.

Time Dimension

Timeliness	Information should be provided when it is needed
Currency	Information should be up-to-date when it is provided
Frequency	Information should be provided as often as needed
Time Period	Information can be provided about past, present, and future time periods

Content Dimension

Accuracy	Information should be free from errors
Relevance	Information should be related to the information needs of a specific recipient for a specific situation
Completeness	All the information that is needed should be provided
Conciseness	Only the information that is needed should be provided
Scope	Information can have a broad or narrow scope, or an internal or external focus
Performance	Information can reveal performance by measuring activities accomplished, progress made, or resources accumulated

Form Dimension

Clarity	Information should be provided in a form that is easy to understand
Detail	Information can be provided in detail or summary form
Order	Information can be arranged in a predetermined sequence
Presentation	Information can be presented in narrative, numeric, graphic, or other forms
Media	Information can be provided in the form of printed paper documents, video displays, or other media

- **Periodic Scheduled Reports.** This traditional form of providing information to managers uses a prespecified format designed to provide managers with information on a regular basis. Typical examples of such periodic scheduled reports are weekly sales analysis reports and monthly financial statements.

- **Exception Reports.** In some cases, reports are produced only when exceptional conditions occur. In other cases, reports are produced periodically but contain information only about these exceptional conditions. For example, a credit manager can be provided with a report that contains only information on customers who exceed their credit limits. Such exception reporting promotes management *by exception,* instead of overwhelming management with periodic detailed reports of business activity.

- **Demand Reports and Responses.** Information is provided whenever a manager demands it. For example, DBMS query languages and report generators

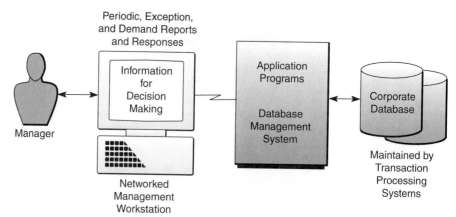

FIGURE 8.6

The management information system concept. Note especially that periodic, exception, and demand reports and responses are the information products produced for managers by this type of information system.

allow managers at online workstations to get immediate responses or reports as a result of their requests for information. Thus, managers do not have to wait for periodic reports to arrive as scheduled.

Online Analytical Processing

The competitive and dynamic nature of today's global business environment is driving demands by business managers and analysts for information systems that can provide fast answers to complex business queries. The IS industry has responded to these demands with developments like the analytical databases, data warehouses, and multidimensional database structures introduced in Chapter 5, and with specialized servers and software products that support **online analytical processing** (OLAP). Online analytical processing is a capability of management, decision support, and

FIGURE 8.7

An example of how the Selection function of the Express Analyzer package helps managers do exception analysis and reporting.

Select by Exception				
⦿ Select	○ Add	○ Keep	○ Remove	OK
		at level(s)		Cancel
⦿ Numeric	○ Measure	All		Preview...
		Global		
Geographical Areas where		Continents/Regions		Help
Sales		Countries/Areas		
		Cities		
is				
Greater than		for		
the value		Product:	Portable CD Player	
10,000		Distribution Channel:	Catalog	
		Time Period:	Quarter 2, 1995	
exclude				
☒ zeros				

Select Geographical Areas where Sales is greater than 10,000 at the Cities level in the Standard hierarchy for the Portable CD Player Product, Catalog Distribution Channel and Quarter 2, 1995 Time Period. Exclude zeros.

Courtesy of Oracle Corporation.

executive information systems that enables managers and analysts to interactively examine and manipulate large amounts of detailed and consolidated data from many perspectives. OLAP involves analyzing complex relationships among thousands or even millions of data items stored in multidimensional databases to discover patterns, trends, and exception conditions. An OLAP session takes place online in realtime, with rapid responses to a manager's or analyst's queries, so that their analytical or decision-making process is undisturbed [19]. See Figure 8.8.

Online analytical processing involves several basic analytical operations, including consolidation, "drill-down," and "slicing and dicing" [19]. See Figure 8.9.

- **Consolidation.** Consolidation involves the aggregation of data. This can involve simple roll-ups or complex groupings involving interrelated data. For example, sales offices can be rolled up to districts and districts rolled up to regions.

- **Drill-Down.** OLAP can go in the reverse direction and automatically display detail data that comprises consolidated data. This is called drill-down. For example, the sales by individual products or sales reps that make up a region's sales totals could be easily accessed.

- **Slicing and Dicing.** Slicing and dicing refers to the ability to look at the database from different viewpoints. One slice of the sales database might show all sales of product type within regions. Another slice might show all sales by sales channel within each product type. Slicing and dicing is often performed along a time axis in order to analyze trends and find patterns.

EXAMPLE   A marketing manager or analyst might use online analytical processing to access a multidimensional database consisting of sales data that has been aggregated by region, product type, and sales channel. In a typical OLAP query, a manager might access a multigigabyte/multiyear sales database in order to find all product sales in each region for each product type. After reviewing the results, the manager might refine his or her query to find the sales volume for each marketing channel within each sales region and product classification. Finally, the marketing manager might perform quarter-to-quarter or year-to-year comparisons for each marketing channel.

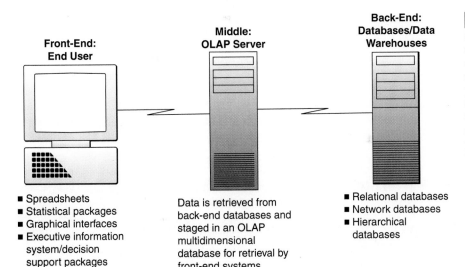

Front-End:
End User

Middle:
OLAP Server

Back-End:
Databases/Data
Warehouses

- Spreadsheets
- Statistical packages
- Graphical interfaces
- Executive information system/decision support packages

Data is retrieved from back-end databases and staged in an OLAP multidimensional database for retrieval by front-end systems

- Relational databases
- Network databases
- Hierarchical databases

FIGURE 8.8

Online analytical processing may involve the use of specialized servers and multidimensional databases. OLAP provides fast answers to complex queries posed by managers and analysts using management, decision support, and executive information systems.

FIGURE 8.9

An example of a display produced by an online analytical processing package.

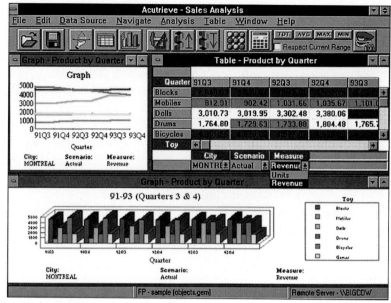

Courtesy of Kenan Systems, Inc.

In summary, online analytical processing can provide rapid responses to complex queries for managers and analysts using management, decision support, or executive information systems. OLAP applications:

- Access very large amounts of data—for example, several years of sales data in a data warehouse.

- Analyze the relationships between many types of business elements—such as sales, products, regions, and channels.

- Involve aggregated data—examples are sales volumes, budgeted dollars, and dollars spent in a region.

- Compare aggregated data over hierarchical time periods—monthly, quarterly, yearly, and the like.

- Present data in different perspectives—such as sales by region versus sales by channels and by product within each region.

- Involve complex calculations between data elements. For example, expected profits can be calculated as a function of sales revenue for each type of sales channel in a particular region.

- Are able to respond quickly to user requests so that managers or analysts can pursue an analytical or decision thought process without being hindered by the system [19].

Decision Support Systems

Decision support systems are a major category of management support systems. They are computer-based information systems that provide interactive information support to managers during the decision-making process. Decision support systems use (1) analytical models, (2) specialized databases, (3) a decision maker's own insights and judgments, and (4) an interactive, computer-based modeling process to support the making of semistructured and unstructured decisions by individual managers.

Therefore, they are designed to be ad hoc, quick-response systems that are initiated and controlled by managerial end users. Decision support systems are thus able to directly support the specific types of decisions and the personal decision-making styles and needs of individual managers.

Management Reporting versus Decision-Making Support

Management information systems focus on providing managers with prespecified information products that report on the performance of the organization. Decision support systems, however, focus on providing information interactively to support specific types of decisions by individual managers. Managers at the tactical and strategic levels of an organization need ad hoc types of information products to support their planning and control responsibilities. Decision support systems help such managers solve the typical semistructured and unstructured problems they face in the real world. In contrast, management information systems are designed to indirectly support the more structured types of decisions involved in operational and tactical planning and control.

Figure 8.10 summarizes and contrasts the differences between decision support and management information systems. Note that the objective of decision support systems is to provide information and decision support techniques needed to solve specific problems or pursue specific opportunities. In contrast, the objective of management information systems is to provide information about the performance of basic organizational functions and processes, such as marketing, manufacturing, and finance. Thus, decision support systems have a much more specific role in the decision-making process. Note also that a DSS is designed to support all four stages (intelligence, design, choice, and implementation) of decision making. Management information systems, on the other hand, are designed to provide information for the intelligence phase, which starts the decision-making process, and the implementation stage, which monitors its success.

EXAMPLE   An example might help at this point. Sales managers typically rely on management information systems to produce sales analysis reports. These reports contain sales performance figures by product line, salesperson, sales region, and so on. A decision support system, on the other hand, would also interactively show a sales manager the effects on sales performance of changes in a variety of factors (such as promotion expense and salesperson compensation). The DSS could then use several criteria (such as expected gross margin and market share) to evaluate and rank several alternative combinations of sales performance factors.

Examples of DSS Applications

Decision support systems are used for a variety of applications in both business and government. When a DSS is developed to solve large or complex problems that continually face an organization, it is called an *institutional* DSS. Decision support systems used for strategic corporate planning are an example of this type of DSS. Other DSS applications are developed quickly to solve smaller or less-complex problems that may be one-time situations facing a manager. These are called *ad hoc* DSS. Also, many decision support systems are developed to support the types of decisions faced by a specific industry (such as the airline, banking, or automotive industry) or by a specific functional area (such as marketing, finance, or manufacturing). Let's take a brief look at three examples to demonstrate the variety of DSS applications.

FIGURE 8.10
Comparing decision support systems and management information systems. Note the major differences in the information and decision support they provide.

	Management Information Systems	Decision Support Systems
Information Provided		
Information form and frequency	Periodic, exception, and demand reports and responses	Interactive inquiries and responses
Information format	Prespecified, fixed format	Ad hoc, flexible, and adaptable format
Information processing methodology	Information produced by extraction and manipulation of operational data	Information produced by analytical modeling of operational and external data
Decision Support Provided		
Type of support	Provide information about the performance of the organization	Provide information and decision support techniques to confront specific problems or opportunities
Stages of decision making supported	Support the intelligence and implementation stages of decision making	Support the intelligence, design, choice, and implementation stages of decision making
Types of decisions supported	Structured decisions for operational and tactical planning and control	Semistructured and unstructured decisions for tactical and strategic planning and control
Type of decision maker supported	Indirect support designed for many managers	Direct support tailored to the decision-making styles of individual managers.

Airline DSS

The American Analytical Information Management System (AAIMS) is a decision support system used in the airline industry. It was developed for American Airlines but is used by other airlines, aircraft manufacturers, airline financial analysts, consultants, and associations. AAIMS supports a variety of airline decisions by analyzing data collected on airline aircraft utilization, seating capacity and utilization, and traffic statistics. For example, it produces forecasts of airline market share, revenue, and profitability. Thus, AAIMS helps airline management make decisions on aircraft assignments, route requests, ticket classifications, pricing, and so on [39].

Another successful decision support system for American Airlines is its *yield management* system. This DSS helps managers and analysts decide how much to overbook and how to set prices for each seat so that a plane is filled up and profits are maximized. American's yield management system deals with more than 250 decision variables. The system generates an estimated 5 percent of American Airlines' revenue [5].

Real Estate DSS

RealPlan is a DSS used in the real estate industry to do complex analyses of investments in commercial real estate. For example, investing in commercial real estate properties typically involves highly detailed income, expense, and cash flow projections. RealPlan easily performs such analyses, even for properties with multiple units, lease terms, rents, and cost-of-living adjustments. Since RealPlan can also make forecasts of property values up to 40 years into the future, it helps decision makers not only with acquisition decisions but with real estate improvement and divestment decisions as well [39].

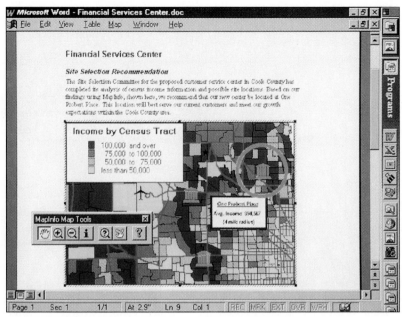

Courtesy of MapInfo, Inc.

FIGURE 8.11

Using a geographic information system package to support a site selection decision for a customer service center.

Geographic DSS

Geographic information systems (GIS) are a special category of DSS that integrate computer graphics and geographic databases with other DSS features. A geographic information system is a DSS that constructs and displays maps and other graphics displays that support decisions affecting the geographic distribution of people and other resources. Many companies are using GIS technology to choose new retail store locations, optimize distribution routes, or analyze the demographics of their target audiences. For example, companies like Levi Strauss, Arby's, Consolidated Rail, and Federal Express use GIS packages to integrate maps, graphics, and other geographic data with business data from spreadsheets and statistical packages. GIS software for microcomputers such as MapInfo and Atlas GIS are used for most business GIS applications. The use of the GIS for decision support should accelerate now that mapping capabilities have been integrated in the latest versions of spreadsheet packages such as Lotus 1-2-3 and Microsoft Excel [25]. See Figure 8.11.

Components of a Decision Support System

Figure 8.12 illustrates the **components of a DSS** present in any decision support system. Note the hardware, software, network, data, model, and people resources needed to provide interactive decision support for managers. Let's first outline the functions of these components and then discuss DSS model and software requirements in more detail.

- **Hardware and Network Resources.** Personal computer workstations provide the primary hardware resource for a DSS. They can be used on a stand-alone basis, but are typically connected by wide area or local area networks to servers and other computer systems for access to other DSS software, model, and data resources.
- **Software Resources.** DSS software packages (DSS generators) contain software modules to manage DSS databases, decision models, and end user/system dialogue.

FIGURE 8.12

The decision support system concept. Note that hardware, software, network, data, model, and people resources provide interactive decision support for managers.

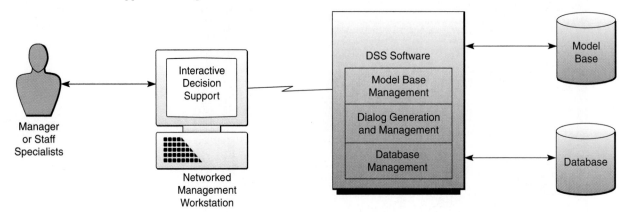

- **Data Resources.** A DSS database contains data and information extracted from the databases of the organization, external databases, and a manager's personal databases. It includes summarized data and information most needed by managers for specific types of decisions.
- **Model Resources.** The model *base* includes a library of mathematical models and analytical techniques stored as programs, subroutines, spreadsheets, and command files.
- **People Resources.** Managers or their staff specialists can use DSS to explore decision alternatives. Such end users can also develop their own simple decision support systems. However, they typically leave the development of large or complex decision support systems and DSS software packages to information systems specialists.

Models for Decision Support

Unlike management information systems, decision support systems rely on model bases as well as databases as vital system resources. A DSS **model base** is an organized collection of mathematical models. It includes models developed to support specific decisions as well as general-purpose models. The model base can include models representing simple computational and analytical routines, or models that mathematically express complex relationships among many variables.

For example, models might express simple accounting relationships among variables, such as Revenue − Expenses = Profit. Or the DSS model base could include models and analytical techniques used to express much more complex relationships among variables. For example, it might contain linear programming models, multiple regression forecasting models, and capital budgeting present value models. Such models may be stored in the form of spreadsheet models or templates, programs and program modules, and command files. Model base management software packages can combine models and model components to create integrated models that support specific types of decisions.

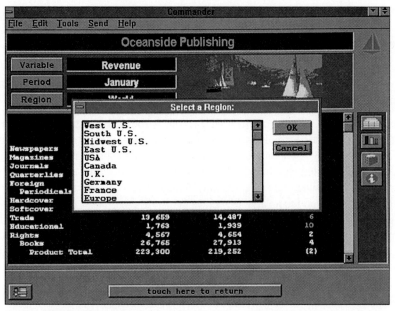

Courtesy of Comshare, Inc.

FIGURE 8.13
Using EXPRESS/EIS—a decision support/executive information system package. This analysis of revenue by product and region can help a marketing manager evaluate decision alternatives.

Software for Decision Support

The software resources needed by decision support systems must integrate the management and use of the model bases, databases, and dialogue generation capabilities of a decision support system. **DSS software** ranges from special-purpose and full-featured **DSS generators** to more modest electronic spreadsheet and integrated packages.

DSS software packages (such as IFPS/PLUS, ENCORE, STRATEGEM, and System W) or DSS/EIS packages (such as Express/EIS and Commander EIS) are available from independent consulting firms and computer manufacturers. Many are now available in microcomputer versions (e.g., PC/FOCUS, IFPS Personal, and ENCORE). In addition, electronic spreadsheet packages (such as Microsoft Excel and Lotus 1-2-3) are limited DSS generators. They provide some of the model building (spreadsheet models), analytical modeling (what-if and goal-seeking analysis), database management, and dialogue management (menus, icons, and prompts) offered by more powerful DSS generators. See Figure 8.13.

Using Decision Support Systems

Using a decision support system involves an interactive **analytical modeling** process. Typically, managers or staff specialists use DSS software packages at their workstations. This allows managers to make inquiries and responses and issue commands using a keyboard, an electronic mouse, a touch screen, or possibly voice input. Output is typically in the form of text and graphics visual displays, but printed reports may be produced.

For example, using a DSS software package for decision support may result in a series of displays in response to alternative what-if changes keyed in by a manager. This differs from the demand responses of information reporting systems, since managers are not demanding prespecified information. Rather, they are exploring possible alternatives. Thus, they do not have to specify their information needs in advance. Instead, the DSS interactively helps them find the information they need to make a decision. That is the essence of the decision support system concept.

Analytical Modeling Alternatives

Using a decision support system involves four basic types of analytical modeling activities: (1) what-if analysis, (2) sensitivity analysis, (3) goal-seeking analysis, and (4) optimization analysis. Let's briefly look at each type of analytical modeling that can be used for decision support. See Figure 8.14.

What-If Analysis

In **what-if analysis,** an end user makes changes to variables, or relationships among variables, and observes the resulting changes in the values of other variables. For example, if you were using a spreadsheet, you might change a revenue amount (a variable) or a tax rate formula (a relationship among variables) in a simple financial spreadsheet model. Then you could command the spreadsheet program to instantly recalculate all affected variables in the spreadsheet. A managerial user would be very interested in observing and evaluating any changes that occurred to the values in the spreadsheet, especially to a variable such as net profit after taxes. To many managers, net profit after taxes is an example of the bottom line, that is, a key factor in making many types of decisions. This type of analysis would be repeated until the manager was satisfied with what the results revealed about the effects of various possible decisions. Figure 8.15 is an example of what-if analysis.

Sensitivity Analysis

Sensitivity analysis is a special case of what-if analysis. Typically, the value of only one variable is changed repeatedly, and the resulting changes on other variables are observed. So sensitivity analysis is really a case of what-if analysis involving repeated changes to only one variable at a time. Some DSS packages automatically make repeated small changes to a variable when asked to perform sensitivity analysis. Typically, sensitivity analysis is used when decision makers are uncertain about the assumptions made in estimating the value of certain key variables. In our previous spreadsheet example, the value of revenue could be changed repeatedly in small increments, and the effects on other spreadsheet variables observed and evaluated. This would help a manager understand the impact of various revenue levels on other factors involved in decisions being considered.

FIGURE 8.14

Activities and examples of the major types of analytical modeling.

Type of Analytical Modeling	Activities and Examples
What-if analysis	Observing how changes to selected variables affect other variables. *Example:* What if we cut advertising by 10 percent? What would happen to sales?
Sensitivity analysis	Observing how repeated changes to a single variable affect other variables. *Example:* Let's cut advertising by $100 repeatedly so we can see its relationship to sales.
Goal-seeking analysis	Making repeated changes to selected variables until a chosen variable reaches a target value. *Example:* Let's try increases in advertising until sales reach $1 million.
Optimization analysis	Finding an optimum value for selected variables, given certain constraints. *Example:* What's the best amount of advertising to have, given our budget and choice of media?

Goal-seeking analysis reverses the direction of the analysis done in what-if and sensitivity analysis. Instead of observing how changes in a variable affect other variables, goal-seeking analysis (also called *how can* analysis) sets a target value (a goal) for a variable and then repeatedly changes other variables until the target value is achieved. For example, you could specify a target value (goal) of $2 million for net profit after taxes for a business venture. Then you could repeatedly change the value of revenue or expenses in a spreadsheet model until a result of $2 million is achieved. Thus you would discover what amount of revenue or level of expenses the business venture needs to achieve in order to reach the goal of $2 million in after-tax profits. Therefore, this form of analytical modeling would help answer the question, "How can we achieve $2 million in net profit after taxes?" instead of the question, "What happens if we change revenue or expenses?" Thus, goal-seeking analysis is another important method of decision support.

Goal-Seeking Analysis

Optimization analysis is a more complex extension of goal-seeking analysis. Instead of setting a specific target value for a variable, the goal is to find the optimum value for one or more target variables, given certain constraints. Then one or more other variables are changed repeatedly, subject to the specified constraints, until the best values for the target variables are discovered. For example, you could try to determine the highest possible level of profits that could be achieved by varying the values for selected revenue sources and expense categories. Changes to such variables could be subject to constraints such as the limited capacity of a production process or limits to available financing. Optimization, typically, is accomplished by special-purpose software packages for optimization techniques such as linear programming, or by advanced DSS generators. The RealPlan DSS, mentioned earlier, is an example of a DSS that uses optimization and sensitivity analysis to support commercial real estate investment decisions.

Optimization Analysis

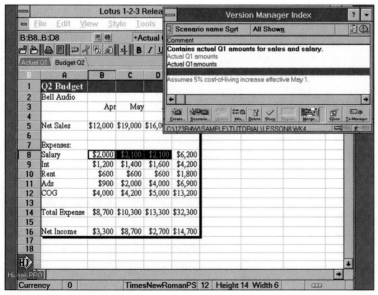

Courtesy of Lotus Development Corporation.

FIGURE 8.15

This example shows how what-if analysis involves the development of alternative scenarios based on changing assumptions.

Executive Information Systems

Executive information systems (EIS) are information systems that combine many of the features of management information systems and decision support systems. However, when they were first developed, their focus was on meeting the strategic information needs of top management. Thus, the first goal of executive information systems was to provide top executives with immediate and easy access to information about a firm's *critical success factors* (CSFs), that is, key factors that are critical to accomplishing an organization's strategic objectives. For example, the executives of a department store chain would probably consider factors such as its sales promotion efforts and its product line mix to be critical to its survival and success.

Rationale for EIS

Studies have shown that top executives get the information they need from many sources. These include letters, memos, periodicals, and reports produced manually or by computer systems. Other major sources of executive information are meetings, telephone calls, and social activities. Thus, much of a top executive's information comes from noncomputer sources. Computer-generated information has not played a major role in meeting many top executives' information needs [41].

Therefore, computer-based executive information systems were developed to meet the information needs of top management that were not being met by other forms of MIS. Executives and IS specialists have capitalized on advances in computer technology to develop attractive, easy-to-use ways to provide executives with the information they need. Software packages are now available that support EIS on mainframe, midsize, and networked microcomputer systems.

Executive information systems are still faced with resistance by some executives, are plagued by high costs, and have had many publicized failures. However, the use of executive information systems is growing rapidly. They have spread into the ranks of middle management as more executives come to recognize their feasibility and benefits, and as less-expensive microcomputer-based systems for client/server networks become available.

For example, according to one recent study, 25 percent of the world's corporate executives are likely to be using an EIS [20]. One popular EIS software package reports that only 3 percent of its users are top executives [20]. Another example is the EIS of Conoco, one of the world's largest oil companies. Conoco's EIS is used by most senior managers, and by over 4,000 employees located at corporate headquarters in Houston and throughout the world [4].

Thus, executive information systems are becoming so widely used by managers, analysts, and other knowledge workers that they are sometimes humorously called "everyone's information systems." More popular alternative names are **executive support systems** (ESS), *enterprise information systems* (EIS), and *management support systems* (MSS). These names also reflect the fact that more features, such as DSS and expert system capabilities, electronic mail, and personal productivity aids such as electronic calendars, are being added to many systems to make them more attractive to executives [41, 42]. See Figure 8.16.

Components of an EIS

As Figure 8.17 illustrates, executive workstations in an EIS are typically networked to mainframe or midsize systems or LAN servers for access to EIS software. The EIS package works with database management and telecommunications software to provide easy access to internal, external, and special management databases (such as multidimensional *analytical databases*) with almost instantaneous response times. Executive information systems provide information about the current status and projected trends in a company's critical success factors, as determined by its executive users. An analytical modeling capability to evaluate alternatives for decision support is also provided by newer EIS packages, as are some expert system features, such as an *explain* capability.

Executive Information Systems (EIS)

- Are tailored to individual executive users.
- Extract, filter, compress, and tract critical data.
- Provide online status access, trend analysis, exception reporting, and "drill-down" capabilities.
- Access and integrate a broad range of internal and external data.
- Are user-friendly and require minimal or no training to use.
- Are used directly by executives without intermediaries.
- Present graphical, tabular, and/or textual information.

Executive Support Systems (ESS)

- Are EIS with additional capabilities.
- Support electronic communications (e.g., E-mail, computer conferencing, and word processing).
- Provide data analysis capabilities (e.g., spreadsheets, query languages, and decision support systems).
- Include personal productivity tools (e.g., electronic calendars, Rolodex, and tickler files).

Source: Adapted from "Executive Information Systems: A Framework for Development and a Survey of Current Practices," by Hugh Watson, R. Kelly Ranier, and Chang Koh, *MIS Quarterly,* Volume 15, Number 1, March 1991. Reprinted with permission from the *MIS Quarterly.*

FIGURE 8.16
Capabilities of executive information and support systems.

Of course, in an EIS, information is presented in forms tailored to the preferences of the executives using the system. For example, most executive information systems stress the use of a graphical user interface and graphics displays that can be customized to the information preferences of executives using the EIS. Other information presentation methods used by an EIS include exception reporting and trend analysis. The ability to drill down, which allows executives to quickly retrieve displays of related information at lower levels of detail, is another important capability of an EIS [4, 41, 42].

FIGURE 8.17
The executive information system concept. Note the hardware, software, network, and data resources involved.

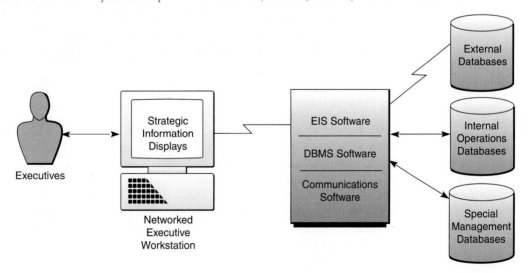

FIGURE 8.18

Displays provided by the
Commander executive information system. Note the simplicity and clarity in which
key information is provided,
and the ability to drill down
to lower levels of detail.

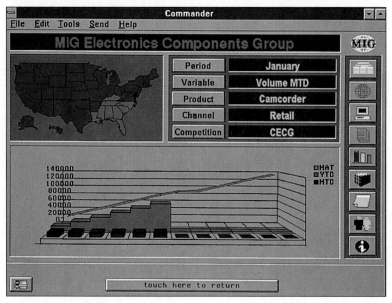

Courtesy of Comshare, Inc.

Examples of EIS

Figure 8.18 shows actual displays provided by the Commander executive information system. Notice how simple and brief these displays are. Also note how they provide executives with the ability to drill down quickly to lower levels of detail in areas
of particular interest to them. This drill-down capability is related to the hypertext
technology (discussed in Chapter 6), which allows end users to interactively retrieve
related pieces of information from text databases. That is why many EIS packages for
microcomputers rely heavily on hypertext technology. Besides the drill-down capability, the Commander also stresses trend analysis and exception reporting. Thus, an
executive can quickly discover the direction key factors are heading and the extent to
which critical factors are deviating from expected results [10, 41].

Top Management Involvement and Commitment
Identify a dedicated executive sponsor with a strategic vision for information systems and a commitment to the strategic use of information technology.

Understanding Data Sources
A successful EIS implementation depends on the availability of accurate and complete data. For many organizations, this could mean that a significant investment in existing business systems is needed prior to implementing EIS.

Focusing on What Is Important
Organization CSFs, exception reporting, accessing information with drill-down capability are a key to success of an EIS.

Response Time
A successful EIS will increase in use, functionality, and scope over time. Ongoing system performance monitoring is key.

Understanding of Computer Literacy Level of Executives
Dictates presentation format, degree of use of graphics, text, mouse, touch screen, etc. The EIS must be easy to use.

Learning Curve for Development Team
Tools to be used are key, especially if developing a system. Familiar tools are best. Vendor support for an EIS package is essential.

Flexibility
Executives' needs will continue to evolve and change with time. As much flexibility as possible should be included.

Ongoing Support
EIS cannot be implemented and forgotten. Continuing support is critical to satisfy changing needs.

FIGURE 8.19
Key factors needed for a successful EIS.

Source: Adapted from John Southcott and Bruce Hooey, "EIS Big League Decision Support," *Edge,* November/December 1989, p. 29, and Chris Gibbons, Corrine Chaves, Ronald Wilkes, and Mark Frolick, "Management Support System at Promus," *Information Systems Management* (New York: Auerbach Publications), Summer 1994, p. 55. © 1994 Warren, Gorham & Lamont. Used with permission.

As we mentioned earlier, Conoco, Inc., has a widely used EIS. Conoco's EIS is a large system with 75 different applications and hundreds of screen displays. Senior executives and over 4,000 managers and analysts worldwide use EIS applications ranging from analyzing internal operations and financial results to viewing external events that affect the petroleum industry. Conoco's EIS is popular with its users and has resulted in improved employee productivity and decision making, and significant cost savings compared to alternative methods of generating information for managers and analysts [4].

The Promus Companies developed another successful EIS [20]. Promus calls their EIS a *Management Support System* (MSS) since it combines office automation, decision support, and executive information services needed by managers in the hotel industry. Key factors recommended by Promus and others that should be considered in developing a successful EIS are shown in Figure 8.19.

Group Decision Support Systems

Decision making by groups of people is an important dimension of managerial decision making. In the real world, many decisions are not made by solitary decision makers. Instead, decisions are frequently made by groups of people coming to an agreement on a particular issue. Between these two extremes is a consultative type of decision making, combining both individual and group characteristics. For example, a manager may ask advice from other people individually before making a particular decision. Or the manager may bring a group of people together to discuss an issue but still make the final decision.

Group Decision Making

Thus, managers are frequently faced with decision-making situations that require interaction with groups of people. Figure 8.20 outlines some of the major factors that affect group decision making. The success of **group decision making** depends on such factors as (1) the characteristics of the group itself, (2) the characteristics of the task on which the group is working, (3) the organizational context in which the group decision-making process takes place, (4) the use of information technology such as electronic meeting systems and group decision support systems, and (5) the communication and decision-making processes the group utilizes [9, 31].

Information technology can provide a variety of computer-based tools to increase the effectiveness of group decision making. Known generically as *group support systems* (GSS), these technologies include **group decision support systems** (GDSS), electronic meeting systems (EMS), and *computer mediated communications systems* (CMCS) such as electronic media. We discussed these systems in Chapter 6 in the context of work group computing and office automation. Research studies indicate that group support systems produce several important benefits. For example, computer support makes group communications easier, protects the anonymity of participants, and provides a public recording of group communications (*group memory*). This significantly improves the efficiency, creativity, and quality of group decision making in business meetings [9, 23, 31].

GDSS Packages

The unique needs of decision making by groups of people have spawned a variety of software packages for group decision support systems. For example, extensive electronic meeting systems packages are available that support the group decision-making activities that may take place in a computer-based *decision room* setting. Other GDSS software may be designed to support a specific application or task, such as a package for labor/management negotiations or a package that merely supports anonymous voting by members of a group. Figure 8.21 illustrates the group decision-making activities supported by the software tools in the GroupSystems EMS software package developed at the University of Arizona [31]. Figure 8.22 shows a typical EMS/GDSS decision room in action.

Groupware that supports work group computing activities for members of a work group whose workstations are interconnected by local or wide area networks may also support group decision making. As we mentioned in Chapter 6, these packages are designed to support work group collaboration and communications by providing *computer-based systems for collaborative work* (CSCW) or *distributed group support systems* (DGSS). For example, they can support new product design and decision making, sales proposal preparation, financial planning, and other activities of work groups whose members may be located anywhere in the world [32, 40].

FIGURE 8.20

Important factors affecting success of group decision making.

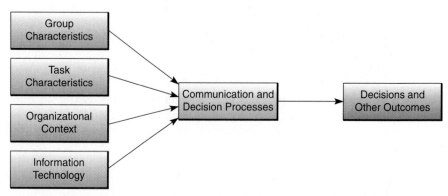

Source: Adapted from Jay Nunamaker et al., "Electronic Meetings to Support Group Work," *Communications of the ACM*, July 1991, p. 44. Copyright © 1991, Association for Computing Machinery, Inc. By permission.

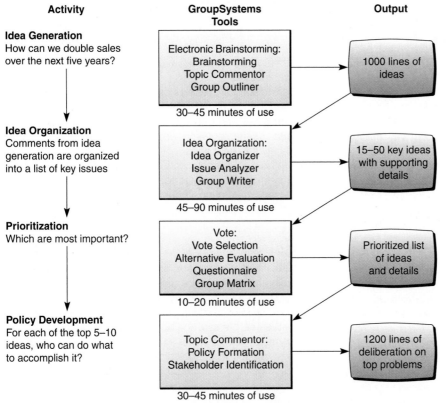

Activity	GroupSystems Tools	Output

Idea Generation
How can we double sales over the next five years?

Electronic Brainstorming:
Brainstorming
Topic Commentor
Group Outliner

30–45 minutes of use

1000 lines of ideas

Idea Organization
Comments from idea generation are organized into a list of key issues

Idea Organization:
Idea Organizer
Issue Analyzer
Group Writer

45–90 minutes of use

15–50 key ideas with supporting details

Prioritization
Which are most important?

Vote:
Vote Selection
Alternative Evaluation
Questionnaire
Group Matrix

10–20 minutes of use

Prioritized list of ideas and details

Policy Development
For each of the top 5–10 ideas, who can do what to accomplish it?

Topic Commentor:
Policy Formation
Stakeholder Identification

30–45 minutes of use

1200 lines of deliberation on top problems

Source: Adapted from Jay Nunamaker et al., "Electronic Meetings to Support Group Work," *Communications of the ACM,* July 1991, p. 44, and H. Chen, P. Hsu, R. Orwig, L. Hoopes, and J. F. Nunamaker, "Automatic Classification from Electronic Meetings," *Communications of the ACM,* October 1994, p. 57. Copyright © 1991 and 1994, Association for Computing Machinery, Inc. By permission.

FIGURE 8.21

An example of the use of the software tools in the GroupSystems software package for conducting electronic meetings. Note the various group activities supported by the modules of this GDSS package.

Courtesy of Ventana Corporation.

FIGURE 8.22

Using a group decision support system in a decision room setting.

REAL WORLD CASE

BANK OF MONTREAL: ONLINE DECISION SUPPORT IN BANKING

Imagine securing approval for a home mortgage loan in about the time it takes to get a pepperoni pizza. That's the goal of Lending On Pathway, an application that is part of a multimillion-dollar client/server initiative at the $41 billion (U.S.) Bank of Montreal. This object-oriented application is intended to compress the mortgage loan approval process from the current 24 hours to about 12 minutes.

It does this by automating many of the decisions now made by human underwriters. Where a person looks over a combination of paper-based applications and online credit bureau files to establish an applicant's creditworthiness, the system analyzes this information and weighs it against predefined lending criteria.

In a four-month pilot test, the average time it took the system to issue a decision—once all data were piped into the system—was 30 to 45 seconds. Said Jane Weatherbie, the bank's Toronto-based vice president of personal lending services, "The idea is for customers to call in, we'd take the application, and by the time the conversation was finished, they'd have an approval," Weatherbie explained.

During the pilot testing, more than 350 mortgages were processed—and the bank's booking ratio increased by 20 percent. Now the bank is deploying the application to its 1,200 branches.

At the heart of Bank of Montreal's application is an automated decision support engine that essentially acts as a computerized underwriter. Developed by American Management Systems, Inc., in Fairfax, Virginia, the engine is object-oriented software. It simultaneously analyzes the financial data from applicants, online information from credit bureaus, and customer data from a data warehouse.

The software resides on a Sybase relational database management system that runs on an IBM RS/6000 server. It lets loan officers perform what-if analyses, such as manipulating terms and loan amounts to determine what best suits a customer's needs.

When customers call in for the Bank of Montreal's streamlined home mortgage loans, bank staff at OS/2-based workstations input the applicant's detail in English on a series of graphically oriented screens. Unlike the previous and more rigid forms-based interface, the screens can be easily negotiated in any order. During the application interview, "We can jump between assets and liabilities for a husband and wife. The system is also so easy that you can be using it and still converse with a client," said Frances Ruibal, a project coordinator who used the system during the four-month pilot program.

Weatherbie said the bank intends to tap much of the same data warehouse and decision support technology that is used in the Lending On Pathway application to push other kinds of loans and services. "As we populate our credit warehouse, we'll be able to branch out and do much more sophisticated predictive modeling," she said. "We'll be able to look at customers' activities and what they tell us about their needs for banking services."

CASE STUDY QUESTIONS

1. What characteristics and capabilities make Lending On Pathway a decision support system?

2. Do you think Lending On Pathway could also be an expert system? Why or why not?

3. Could other industries benefit from similar technology? Explain.

Source: Adapted from Julia King, "Decision Support Software Cuts Loan Processing Time," *Computerworld*, February 19, 1996, pp. 63–64. Copyright © 1996 by Computerworld, Inc., Framingham, MA 01701—Reprinted from *Computerworld*.

Artificial Intelligence Technologies in Business

Section II

An Overview of Artificial Intelligence

Managerial decision making and business operations are being increasingly affected by developments in the field of artificial intelligence. Developments such as natural languages, industrial robots, expert systems, and "intelligent" software are some examples of this impact. As a potential business end user, you should be aware of the importance of such developments. Businesses and other organizations are significantly increasing their attempts to assist the human intelligence and productivity of their knowledge workers with artificial intelligence tools and techniques.

But what is artificial intelligence? **Artificial intelligence** (AI) is a science and technology based on disciplines such as computer science, biology, psychology, linguistics, mathematics, and engineering. The goal of AI is to develop computers that can think, as well as see, hear, walk, talk, and feel. A major thrust of artificial intelligence is the development of computer functions normally associated with human intelligence, such as reasoning, learning, and problem solving, as summarized in Figure 8.23. That's why the term *artificial intelligence* was coined by John McCarthy at MIT in 1956. Besides McCarthy, AI pioneers included Herbert Simon and Allen Newell at Carnegie-Mellon, Norbert Wiener and Marvin Minsky at MIT, Warren McCulloch and Walter Pitts at Illinois, Frank Rosenblatt at Cornell, Alan Turing at Manchester, Edward Feigenbaum at Stanford, Roger Shank at Yale, and many others [28].

Debate has raged around artificial intelligence since serious work in the field began in the 1950s. Not only technological, but moral and philosophical questions abound about the possibility of intelligent, "thinking" machines. For example, British AI pioneer Alan Turing in 1950 proposed a test for determining if machines could think. According to the Turing test, a computer could demonstrate intelligence if a human interviewer, conversing with an unseen human and an unseen computer, could not tell which was which [28].

Though much work has been done in many of the subgroups that fall under the AI umbrella, critics believe that no computer can truly pass the Turing test. They claim that developing intelligence to impart true humanlike capabilities to computers is simply not possible. But progress continues, and only time will tell if the ambitious goals of artificial intelligence will be achieved and equal the popular images found in science fiction.

- Think and reason.
- Use reason to solve problems.
- Learn or understand from experience.
- Acquire and apply knowledge.
- Exhibit creativity and imagination.
- Deal with complex or perplexing situations.
- Respond quickly and successfully to new situations.
- Recognize the relative importance of elements in a situation.
- Handle ambiguous, incomplete, or erroneous information.

FIGURE 8.23

Attributes of intelligent behavior. AI is attempting to duplicate these capabilities in computer-based systems.

The Domains of Artificial Intelligence

Figure 8.24 illustrates the major domains of AI research and development. Note that AI applications can be grouped under the four major areas of cognitive science, computer science, robotics, and natural interfaces, though these classifications do overlap each other, and other classifications can be used. Also note that expert systems are just one of many important AI applications. Let's briefly review each of these major areas of AI and some of their current applications.

Cognitive Science

This area of artificial intelligence is based on research in biology, neurology, psychology, mathematics, and many allied disciplines. It focuses on researching how the human brain works and how humans think and learn. The results of such research in *human information processing* are the basis for the development of a variety of computer-based applications in artificial intelligence.

Applications in the cognitive science area of AI include the development of expert systems and other *knowledge-based* systems that add a knowledge base and some reasoning capability to information systems. Also included are *adaptive learning* systems that can modify their behaviors based on information they acquire as they operate. Chess-playing systems are primitive examples of such applications, though many more applications are being implemented. *Fuzzy logic systems* can process data that are incomplete or ambiguous, that is, *fuzzy data*. Thus, they can solve unstructured problems with incomplete knowledge by developing approximate inferences and answers, as humans do.

Computer Science

This area of AI applications focuses on the computer hardware and system software needed to produce the powerful supercomputers required for many AI applications. At the forefront of this area are efforts to create a *fifth generation* of "intelligent" computers, which use the *parallel processing* architecture discussed in Chapter 2. Such computers will be designed for optimum *logical* inference processing that depends on symbolic processing instead of the numeric processing of traditional computing. Other attempts are being made to develop *neural networks,* including massively parallel, neurocomputer systems whose architecture is based on the human brain's

FIGURE 8.24

The major application areas of artificial intelligence. Note that the many applications of AI can be grouped into the four major areas of cognitive science, computer science, robotics, and natural interfaces.

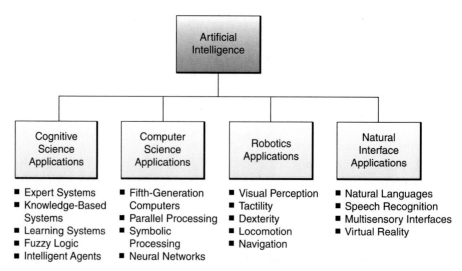

Artificial Intelligence

Cognitive Science Applications	Computer Science Applications	Robotics Applications	Natural Interface Applications
■ Expert Systems ■ Knowledge-Based Systems ■ Learning Systems ■ Fuzzy Logic ■ Intelligent Agents	■ Fifth-Generation Computers ■ Parallel Processing ■ Symbolic Processing ■ Neural Networks	■ Visual Perception ■ Tactility ■ Dexterity ■ Locomotion ■ Navigation	■ Natural Languages ■ Speech Recognition ■ Multisensory Interfaces ■ Virtual Reality

meshlike neuron structure. Neural network computers can process many different pieces of information simultaneously. Neural network software for traditional computers can learn by being shown sample problems and their solutions. As they start to recognize patterns, they can begin to program themselves to solve such problems on their own.

AI, engineering, and physiology are the basic disciplines of **robotics.** This technology produces robot machines with computer intelligence and computer-controlled, humanlike physical capabilities. This area thus includes applications designed to give robots the powers of sight or visual *perception,* touch or tactile capabilities, *dexterity* or skill in handling and manipulation, *locomotion* or the physical ability to move over any terrain, and *navigation* or the intelligence to properly find one's way to a destination [26]. The use of robotics in computer-aided manufacturing was discussed in Chapter 7.

Robotics

The development of natural *interfaces* is considered a major area of AI applications and is essential to the natural use of computers by humans. The development of natural languages is a major thrust of this area of AI. Being able to talk to computers and robots in conversational human languages and have them "understand" us as easily as we understand each other is the goal of many AI researchers. Thus, this application area involves research and development in linguistics, psychology, computer science, and other disciplines. Applications include human language understanding, speech recognition, and the development of multisensory devices that use a variety of body movements to operate computers. Thus, this area of AI drives developments in the voice recognition and response technology discussed in Chapter 2, and the natural programming languages discussed in Chapter 3. Finally, an emerging application area in AI is *virtual reality.* This field is developing multisensory human/computer interfaces that enable human users to experience computer-simulated objects, spaces, activities, and "worlds" as if they actually exist.

Natural Interfaces

Neural networks are computing systems modeled after the brain's meshlike network of interconnected processing elements, called *neurons.* Of course, neural networks are a lot simpler in architecture (the human brain is estimated to have over 100 billion neuron brain cells!). However, like the brain, the interconnected processors in a neural network operate in parallel and interact dynamically with each other. This enables the network to "learn" from data it processes. That is, it learns to recognize patterns and relationships in the data it processes. The more data examples it receives as input, the better it can learn to duplicate the results of the examples it processes. Thus, the neural network will change the strengths of the interconnections between the processing elements in response to changing patterns in the data it receives and the results that occur [37].

Neural Networks

Note in Figure 8.25 that before training, the neural net gave equal weight to all six neurons that represent possible criteria for credit risk determination and their "synapses," or connections, to the *profitable customer* and *default customer* neurons that are the next level of the net. Then the net was given several rounds of training that consists of processing data about actual credit applications and whether the resulting loans were paid back properly or not [37].

FIGURE 8.25

Training a neural network for a credit application evaluation system. Note how training has changed the strength of the connections between the credit criteria and customer neurons. The untrained neural net is on the left; the net after one round of training is on the right.

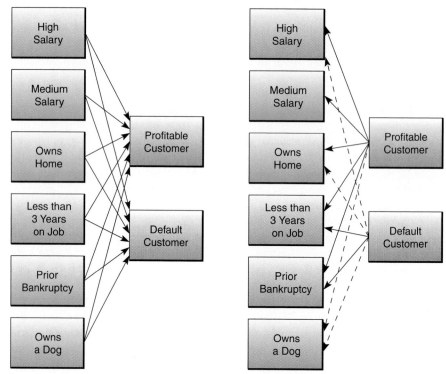

Source: Adapted by permission of Prentice Hall, Upper Saddle River, NJ, from Ralph Sprague and Barbara McNurlin, *Information Systems Management in Practice,* 3rd ed. (1993), p. 443.

After the first round of training, the neural net has kept its strong connections to the profitable customer neuron by sending "strengthen your signal" messages back to credit criteria like "high salary" and "own home." But it has weakened several connections to the default customer neuron by sending "send a weaker signal" messages back to some of the other criteria. It has also weakened the connection between the irrelevant "own a dog" criterion and the customer neurons.

Thus, the neural network begins to learn which credit characteristics result in good or bad loans. The developers of the neural network would provide it with many more examples of credit applications and loan results to process, and opportunities to adjust the signal strengths between its neurons. The neural network would continue to be trained until it demonstrated a high degree of accuracy in correctly duplicating the results of recent cases. At that point it would be trained enough to begin making credit evaluations on its own.

Neural networks can be implemented on microcomputers and other traditional computer systems by using software packages that simulate the activity of a neural network. Specialized neural network coprocessor circuit boards for PCs are also available that provide significantly greater processing power. In addition, special-purpose neural net microprocessor chips are being used in specific application areas such as military weapons systems, image processing, and voice recognition. However, most business applications depend primarily on neural net software packages to accomplish applications ranging from credit risk assessment to check

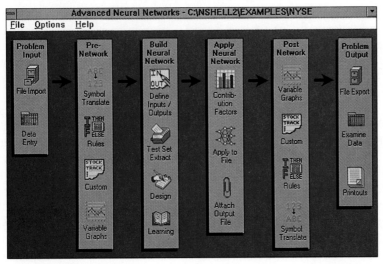

Courtesy of Ward Systems Group, Inc.

FIGURE 8.26

A display of a neural net software development package. Notice the variety of options for building and using the neural network.

signature verification, investment forecasting, and manufacturing quality control [26, 37]. See Figure 8.26. Let's take a closer look at a business example to get a better feel for a neural network application.

Consumer Lending

Security Pacific Bank of California has developed a neural net system for helping it make consumer lending decisions. Most banks rely on a *credit scoring* service provided by outside companies that collect and analyze statistics on the credit patterns of consumers that wish to qualify for a bank loan. Security Pacific replaced these "score card vendors" with a loan-underwriting neural net system it developed with the help of an AI consulting firm. They designed the net and then "trained" it by having it review 6,000 previous loan-underwriting cases in the bank's files.

The loan-underwriting system analyzes 27 credit factors about a potential borrower and makes one of two possible recommendations: (1) strongly applicable to an accept or (2) strongly indicative of a decline. If a decline recommendation is made by the system, the loan application is referred to a human loan officer for review. But all other loan requests are approved by the bank, which rates its neural net system as very successful [26].

Fuzzy Logic Systems

In spite of the funny name, **fuzzy logic** systems represent a small, but serious and growing, application of AI in business. Fuzzy logic is a method of reasoning that resembles human reasoning since it allows for approximate values and inferences (fuzzy logic) and incomplete or ambiguous data (fuzzy data) instead of relying only on *crisp data*, such as binary (yes/no) choices. For example, Figure 8.27 illustrates a partial set of rules (fuzzy rules) and a fuzzy SQL query for analyzing and extracting credit risk information on businesses that are being evaluated for selection as investments. Notice how fuzzy logic uses terminology that is deliberately imprecise, such as *very high, increasing, somewhat decreased, reasonable,* and *very low.* This enables fuzzy systems to process incomplete data and quickly provide approximate, but acceptable, solutions to problems that are difficult for other methods to solve [11, 13].

Fuzzy logic queries of a database, such as the SQL query shown in Figure 8.27, promise to improve the extraction of data from business databases. Queries can be stated more naturally in words that are closer to the way business specialists think about the topic for which they want information. Figure 8.28 illustrates the components of a fuzzy credit analysis, screening, and selection system that uses fuzzy SQL queries to interrogate company and external financial databases [12].

Examples of applications of fuzzy logic are numerous in Japan, but rare in the United States. The United States has tended to prefer using AI solutions like expert systems or neural networks. But Japan is a hotbed of fuzzy logic applications, especially the use of special-purpose fuzzy logic microprocessor chips, called *fuzzy process controllers*. Thus, the Japanese ride on subway trains, use elevators, and drive cars that are guided or supported by fuzzy process controllers made by Hitachi and Toshiba. They can even trade shares on the Tokyo Stock Exchange using a stock-trading program based on fuzzy logic rules. Many new models of Japanese-made products also feature fuzzy logic microprocessors. The list is growing, but includes auto-focus cameras, auto-stabilizing camcorders, energy-efficient air conditioners, self-adjusting washing machines, and automatic transmissions [30].

Virtual Reality

Virtual reality (VR) is computer-simulated reality. Virtual reality is a fast-growing area of artificial intelligence that had its origins in efforts to build more natural, realistic, multisensory human/computer interfaces. So virtual reality relies on multisensory input/output devices such as a headset with video goggles and stereo earphones or a *data glove* or jumpsuit with fiber-optic sensors that track your body movements. Then you can experience computer-simulated "virtual worlds" three-dimensionally through sight, sound, and touch. Thus, virtual reality is also called *telepresence*. For example, you can enter a computer-generated virtual world, look around and observe its contents, pick up and move objects, and move around in it at will. Thus virtual reality allows you to interact with computer-simulated objects, entities, and environments as if they actually exist [29, 33]. See Figure 8.29.

FIGURE 8.27

An example of fuzzy logic rules and a fuzzy logic SQL query in a credit risk analysis application.

Fuzzy Logic Rules

Risk should be acceptable
If debt-equity is very high
   then risk is positively increased
If income is increasing
   then risk is somewhat decreased
If cash reserves are low to very low
   then risk is very increased
If PE ratio is good
   then risk is generally decreased

Fuzzy Logic SQL Query

Select companies
   from financials
      where revenues are very large
      and pe_ratio is acceptable
      and profits are high to very high
      and (income/employee_tot) is reasonable

Source: Adapted from Earl Cox, "Solving Problems with Fuzzy Logic," *AI Expert,* March 1992, p. 30, and "Applications of Fuzzy System Models," *AI Expert,* October 1992, p. 37.

Current applications of virtual reality are wide ranging and include computer-aided design (CAD), medical diagnostics and treatment, scientific experimentation in many physical and biological sciences, flight simulation for training pilots and astronauts, and entertainment, especially 3-D video arcade games. CAD is the most widely used industrial VR application. It enables architects and other designers to design and test electronic 3-D models of products and structures by entering the models themselves and examining, touching, and manipulating sections and parts from all angles. This *scientific-visualization* capability is also used by pharmaceutical and biotechnology firms to develop and observe the behavior of computerized models of new drugs and materials, and by medical researchers to develop ways for physicians to enter and examine a virtual model of a patient's body.

VR designers are creating everything from virtual weather patterns and virtual wind tunnels to virtual cities and virtual securities markets. For example, by converting stock market and other financial data into three-dimensional graphic form, securities analysts can use VR systems to more rapidly observe and identify trends and exceptions in financial performance. Also promising are applications in information technology itself. This includes the development of 3-D models of telecommunications networks and databases. These virtual graphical representations of networks and databases make it easier for IS specialists to visualize the structure and relationships of an organization's telecommunications networks and corporate databases, thus improving their design and maintenance.

FIGURE 8.28

The components of a fuzzy logic credit analysis, screening, and selection system.

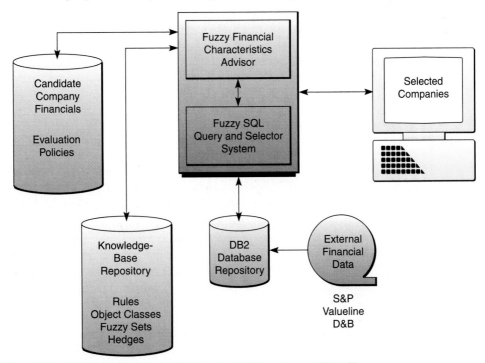

Source: Adapted from Earl Cox, "Relational Database Queries Using Fuzzy Logic," *AI Expert,* January 1995, p. 29.

FIGURE 8.29

Using virtual reality in product design. This Ford Motor Company engineer is using a virtual reality headset and data glove to help design improved car interiors at Ford's Advanced Engineering Center in Dearborn, Michigan.

Courtesy of Ford Motor Company.

VR becomes *telepresence* when users that can be anywhere in the world use VR systems to work alone or together at a remote site. Typically, this involves using a VR system to enhance the sight and touch of a human who is remotely manipulating equipment to accomplish a task. Examples range from *virtual surgery* where surgeon and patient may be on either side of the globe, to the remote use of equipment in hazardous environments such as chemical plants or nuclear reactors.

The use of virtual reality seems limited only by the newness and cost of its technology. For example, a VR system consisting of a headset with goggles and headphones, a fiber-optic data glove, a motion-sensing device, and a microcomputer workstation with 3-D modeling software may cost up to $50,000. If you want less-cumbersome devices, more realistic displays, and a more natural sense of motion in your VR world, costs can escalate into several hundred thousand dollars. Organizations such as NASA, the Department of Defense, IBM, Digital Equipment Corporation, Lockheed, Matsushita Electric, and several universities are investing millions of dollars in virtual reality R&D projects involving the use of supercomputers, complex modeling software, and custom-made sensing devices. However, the cost of highly realistic multisensory VR systems is expected to drop substantially in the future, making virtual reality available for a wide array of business and end user applications [2, 29, 33].

Expert Systems

One of the most practical and widely implemented applications of artificial intelligence in business is the development of *expert systems* and other *knowledge-based* information systems. A **knowledge-based information system** (KBIS) adds a knowledge base to the major components found in other types of computer-based information systems. An **expert system** (ES) is a knowledge-based information system that uses its knowledge about a specific, complex application area to act as an expert consultant to end users. As we said in Chapter 1, expert systems can be classified conceptually as either operations or management support systems, depending on whether they are giving expert advice to control operational processes or helping managers make decisions. See Figure 8.30.

Expert systems are related to knowledge-based decision support systems that add a knowledge base to the database and model base of traditional decision support systems. However, unlike decision support systems, expert systems provide answers

FIGURE 8.30

Large banks have been heavy users of expert systems and other AI technologies for applications such as screening loan applications and detecting credit card fraud.

Roger Tully/Tony Stone Images.

to questions in a very specific problem area by making humanlike inferences about knowledge contained in a specialized knowledge base. They must also be able to explain their reasoning process and conclusions to a user. So expert systems can provide decision support to managers in the form of advice from an expert consultant in a specific problem area [3, 38].

The **components** of an expert system include a knowledge base and software modules that perform inferences on the knowledge and communicate answers to a user's questions. Figure 8.31 illustrates the interrelated components of an expert system. Note the following components:

Components of an Expert System

- **Knowledge Base.** The knowledge base of an expert system contains (1) facts about a specific subject area (for example, *John is an analyst*) and (2) heuristics (rules of thumb) that express the reasoning procedures of an expert on the subject (for example: IF John is an analyst, THEN he needs a workstation). There are many ways that such knowledge is represented in expert systems. Examples are *rule-based, frame-based, object-based,* and *case-based* methods of knowledge representation. See Figure 8.32.

- **Software Resources.** An expert system software package contains an **inference engine** and other programs for refining knowledge and communicating with users. The inference engine program processes the knowledge (such as rules and facts) related to a specific problem. It then makes associations and inferences resulting in recommended courses of action for a user. User interface programs for communicating with end users are also needed, including an explanation program to explain the reasoning process to a user if requested.

  Knowledge acquisition programs are not part of an expert system but are software tools for knowledge base development. Other software packages, such as expert system shells, are important software resources for developing expert systems.

- ■ **Hardware and Network Resources.** These include stand-alone microcomputer systems, as well as microcomputer workstations and terminals connected to servers and midsize computers or mainframes in local and wide area telecommunications networks.
- ■ **People Resources.** An expert system provides expert advice to end users. This expertise is captured in a knowledge base by a knowledge engineer from facts and rules provided by one or more experts. Or experts and end users can be their own knowledge engineers and use expert system shells as development tools to build their own knowledge bases and expert systems.

Examples of Expert Systems

Using an expert system involves an interactive computer-based session, in which the solution to a problem is explored, with the expert system acting as a consultant to an end user. The expert system asks questions of the user, searches its knowledge base for facts and rules or other knowledge, explains its reasoning process when asked, and gives expert advice to the user in the subject area being explored. For example, Figure 8.33 illustrates one of the displays of an expert system.

FIGURE 8.31

Components of an expert system. The software modules perform inferences on a knowledge base built by an expert and/or knowledge engineer. This provides expert answers to an end user's questions in an interactive process.

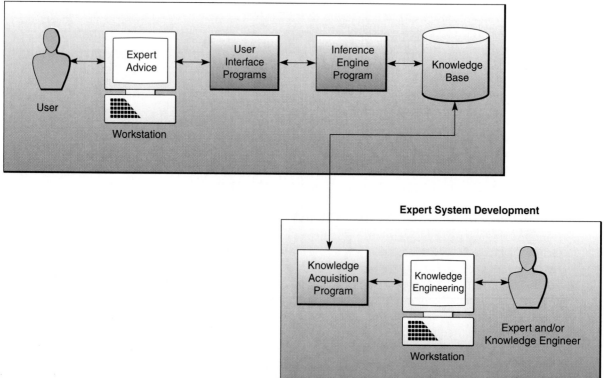

- **Case-Based Reasoning.** Representing knowledge in an expert system's knowledge base in the form of *cases,* that is, examples of past performance, occurrences, and experiences.
- **Frame-Based Knowledge.** Knowledge represented in the form of a hierarchy or network of *frames.* A frame is a collection of knowledge about an entity consisting of a complex package of data values describing its attributes.
- **Object-Based Knowledge.** Knowledge represented as a network of *objects.* An object is a data element that includes both data and the methods or processes that act on that data.
- **Rule-Based Knowledge.** Knowledge represented in the form of *rules* and statements of fact. Rules are statements that typically take the form of a premise and a conclusion such as: If (condition), Then (conclusion).

FIGURE 8.32

A summary of four ways that knowledge can be represented in an expert system's knowledge base.

Expert systems are being used for many different types of applications, and the variety of applications is expected to continue to increase. However, you should realize that expert systems typically accomplish one or more generic uses. Figure 8.34 outlines six generic categories of expert system activities, with specific examples of actual expert system applications. As you can see, expert systems are being used in many different fields, including medicine, engineering, the physical sciences, and business. Expert systems now help diagnose illnesses, search for minerals, analyze compounds, recommend repairs, and do financial planning. So from a strategic business standpoint, expert systems can and are being used to improve every step of the product cycle of a business, from finding customers to shipping products to them. Let's look at three actual examples more closely.

Expert System Applications

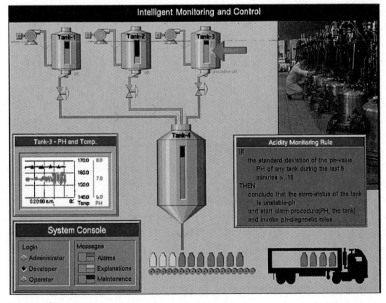

Courtesy of Gensym Corporation.

FIGURE 8.33

One of the displays of a chemical process monitoring expert system. Note one of the acidity monitoring rules in its knowledge base.

FIGURE 8.34

Major application categories and examples of typical expert systems. Note the variety of applications that can be supported by such systems.

Application Categories and Typical Uses

Decision management—Systems that appraise situations or consider alternatives and make recommendations based on criteria supplied during the discovery process:
- Loan portfolio analysis
- Employee performance evaluation
- Insurance underwriting
- Demographic forecasts

Diagnostic/troubleshooting—Systems that infer underlying causes from reported symptoms and history:
- Equipment calibration
- Help desk operations
- Software debugging
- Medical diagnosis

Maintenance/scheduling—Systems that prioritize and schedule limited or time-critical resources:
- Maintenance scheduling
- Production scheduling
- Education scheduling
- Project management

Design/configuration—Systems that help configure equipment components, given existing constraints:
- Computer option installation
- Manufacturability studies
- Communications networks
- Optimum assembly plan

Selection/classification—Systems that help users choose products or processes, often from among large or complex sets of alternatives:
- Material selection
- Delinquent account identification
- Information classification
- Suspect identification

Process monitoring/control—Systems that monitor and control procedures or processes:
- Machine control (including robotics)
- Inventory control
- Production monitoring
- Chemical testing

Advertising Strategy

ADCAD (ADvertising Communications Approach Designer) is an expert system that assists advertising agencies in setting marketing and communications objectives, selecting creative strategies, and identifying effective communications approaches. In particular, it is designed to help advertisers of consumer products with the development of advertising objectives and ad copy strategy, and the selection of communications techniques. Figure 8.35 illustrates the stages in the advertising design process and some of the factors affecting advertising design decisions on which ADCAD is based. ADCAD's knowledge base consists of rules derived from various sources, including consultations with the creative staff of the Young & Rubicam advertising agency. For example, here are two of the hundreds of rules in ADCAD's knowledge base:

- **IF** ad objective = convey brand image or reinforce brand image
  AND brand purchase motivation = sensory stimulation,
  AND message processing motivation = high
  THEN emotional tone = elation.

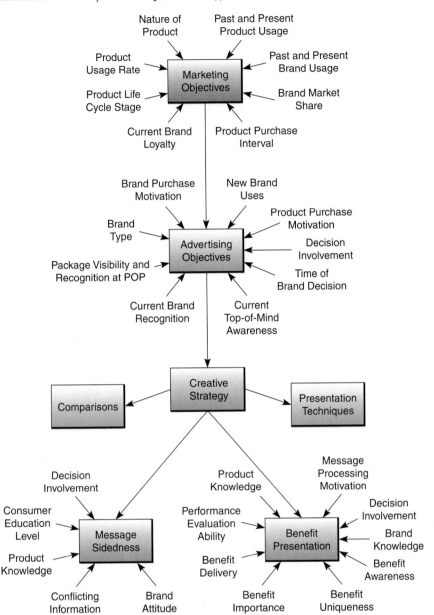

FIGURE 8.35

Some of the stages and factors in the advertising design process on which the ADCAD expert system is based.

Source: Adapted and reprinted by permission of Harvard Business School Press from Robert C. Blattberg, Rashi Glazer, and John D. C. Little, *The Marketing Information Revolution*, Boston: 1994, p. 213. Copyright © 1994 by The President and Fellows of Harvard College.

- **IF** ad objective = change brand beliefs
  AND message processing motivation = low,
  AND purchase anxiety = low,
  AND brand use avoids fearful consequences = yes
  THEN emotional tone = high fear.

ADCAD uses a question and answer format, asking the user a series of questions about the advertising problem. It then searches through its knowledge base, matching user answers against its rules to draw inferences. Then ADCAD presents its recommendations, along with a rationale for each recommendation if asked. For example, here's how ADCAD responded when asked to explain its recommendation to use a celebrity to present an ad on television for a shampoo product:

- Just a moment please . . .
  The advertising objective is to communicate or reinforce your brand's image, mood, or an associated lifestyle to consumers who are not highly motivated to process your ad message. A celebrity presenter can attract the consumer's attention, enhance your brand's image, and become a memorable cue for brand evaluation.

ADCAD has been popular with advertising and brand managers since it provides them with a rationale for their current advertising, as well as ideas for new communications approaches. Another benefit of ADCAD is its support of what-if analysis of advertising options. ADCAD allows users to easily change their responses to questions and investigate the impact of alternative product or market assumptions. This feature has also made ADCAD a valuable training tool for students and novice advertising managers [6].

Insurance Evaluation

The Kaiser Foundation Health Plan uses an expert system known as SIMR (System for Individual Marketing and Review) to evaluate applications for health insurance coverage. SIMR helps evaluate applicants to determine whether they medically qualify for membership with Kaiser. Processing such applications used to take four to six weeks since every application had to be reviewed by doctors or other medical staffers. Kaiser used the Aion DS expert system development tool to develop a knowledge base of rules extracted from the rules that medical staffers use when they review applications.

The SIMR expert system now automatically handles 40 percent of all insurance applications without requiring a review by medical personnel. For example, SIMR has been recommending 28 percent immediate acceptances and 12 percent immediate rejections of applications it reviews. SIMR also has cut in half the time a doctor or other medical staffer needs to review the remaining applications. By simplifying and automating what was formerly a manual process, SIMR has significantly improved some of Kaiser's business processes, cut operating expenses, and provided better service to customers [3].

Bank Auditing

Banks have been at the forefront of using expert systems, neural nets, and other AI technologies to audit key financial operations [38]. For example, Royal Bank of Canada has implemented an expert system for credit card fraud detection that has cut millions of dollars of losses each year, while reducing the operating costs of their fraud analysis operations by $200,000 a year. Royal Bank's system helps their fraud analysts quickly identify and analyze suspected fraudulent activity, so that they can shut down bad accounts within hours of the first transactions.

Banque Populaire De Lorraine, of France, has developed an expert system for the analysis and control of customer loans and other liabilities. Called SESAME, this expert system reviews the status of over 25,000 large and complex business customer accounts each month. It analyzes a client's business activity, identifies any irregularities, and makes recommendations on actions to be taken.

Chemical Bank of New York uses an expert system, called Inspector, and a communications network spanning 23 countries to review over a billion dollars in worldwide foreign exchange transactions each day. Because of the large dollar amounts involved in such transactions, Inspector paid for itself many times over, the first time it identified a fraudulent trade.

As the previous examples show, many organizations are developing expert system solutions to business problems. However, before developing an expert system, the following questions need to be answered:

- What applications are suitable for expert systems?
- What benefits and limitations of expert systems should be considered?
- Should the expert system be (1) purchased as a completely developed system, (2) developed with an expert system shell, or (3) developed from scratch as a custom system?

Developing Expert Systems

Obviously, expert systems are not the answer to every problem facing an organization. People using other types of information systems do quite well in many problem situations. So what types of problems are most suitable to expert system solutions? One way to answer this is to look at examples of the applications of current expert systems, including the generic tasks being accomplished, as were summarized in Figure 8.34. Another way is to identify criteria that make a problem situation suitable for an expert system. Figure 8.36 outlines some important criteria.

Figure 8.36 should emphasize that many real-world situations do not fit the suitability criteria for expert system solutions. Therefore, expert systems should be developed cautiously, especially if sensitive or strategic applications are involved. Hundreds of rules may be required to capture the assumptions, facts, and reasoning that are involved in even simple problem situations. For example, a task that might take an expert a few minutes to accomplish might require an expert system with hundreds of rules and take several months to develop. A task that may take a human expert several hours to do may require an expert system with thousands of rules and take several years to build [8, 28].

Expert System Suitability

Once the suitability and feasibility of a proposed expert system application have been evaluated, it's time to confront the make-or-buy decision. As you saw in a previous example, complete expert system packages like the ADCAD can be purchased by advertising companies and other businesses. Many other packages are available in a variety of application areas, and the number is increasing each year.

Expert Systems: Make or Buy?

Suitability Criteria

Domain: The domain, or subject area, of the problem is relatively small and limited to a well-defined problem area.

Expertise: Solutions to the problem require the efforts of an expert. That is, a body of knowledge, techniques, and intuition is needed that only a few people possess.

Complexity: Solution of the problem is a complex task that requires logical inference processing, which would not be handled as well by conventional information processing.

Structure: The solution process must be able to cope with ill-structured, uncertain, missing, and conflicting data, and a problem situation that changes with the passage of time.

Availability: An expert exists who is articulate and cooperative, and who has the support of the management and end users involved in the development of the proposed system.

FIGURE 8.36

Criteria for applications that are suitable for expert systems development.

As in other make-or-buy decisions, the suitability of the expert system package for an end user's needs must be balanced against the cost in time and money of developing a custom system.

Expert System Shells

The easiest way to develop your own expert system is to use an **expert system shell** as a developmental tool. An expert system shell is a software package consisting of an expert system without its kernel, that is, its knowledge base of facts and rules. This leaves a *shell* of software (the inference engine and user interface programs) with generic inferencing and user interface capabilities. Other development tools (such as rule editors and user interface generators) are added in making the shell a powerful expert system development tool.

Expert system shells are now available as relatively low cost software packages that help users develop their own expert systems on microcomputers. They allow trained users to develop the knowledge base for a specific expert system application. For example, one shell uses a spreadsheet format to help end users develop IF-THEN rules, automatically generating rules based on examples furnished by a user. Once a knowledge base is constructed, it is used with the shell's inference engine and user interface modules as a complete expert system on a specific subject area. Expert system shells have accelerated the widespread development and use of expert systems. See Figure 8.37.

Custom Expert System Development

Instead of using an expert system shell, an expert system can be developed from scratch. This requires using one or more programming languages to develop the inference engine and user interface programs and to build a knowledge base. For example, two programming languages, LISP and PROLOG, have long been used for expert systems development. LISP is a procedural, list processing language specifically designed to handle many types of logical text processing (symbolic processing). PROLOG is a nonprocedural language that uses statements defining values and relationships between objects to produce logical inferences. It thus is more efficient than LISP in constructing rule-based knowledge bases. Obviously, this is a much more difficult, time-consuming, and costly undertaking. However, early expert systems were developed this way, as are many large expert system

FIGURE 8.37

Using the Exsys Professional expert system shell to develop an expert system for a chemical refining process.

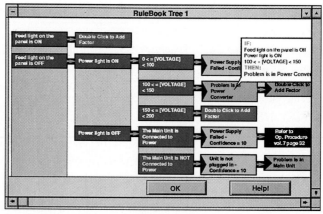

Courtesy of Exsys Expert Systems.

projects. Their developers want the design flexibility that is not supported by the generic nature and basic capabilities of many shells. Thus, they prefer to develop an expert system that is more tailored to their specific needs.

Knowledge Engineering

Expert systems are developed using a prototyping process, as explained in Chapter 10. However, developing expert systems is different because it results in the development of a knowledge base, and it frequently requires the services of a knowledge engineer.

A **knowledge engineer** is a professional who works with experts to capture the knowledge (facts and rules of thumb) they possess. The knowledge engineer then builds the knowledge base (and the rest of the expert system if necessary), using an iterative, prototyping process until the expert system is acceptable. Thus, knowledge engineers perform a role similar to that of systems analysts in conventional information systems development. Obviously, knowledge engineers must be able to understand and work with experts in many subject areas. Therefore, this new information systems specialty requires good people skills, as well as a background in artificial intelligence and information systems.

Once the decision is made to develop an expert system, a team of one or more domain experts and a knowledge engineer may be formed. Or experts skilled in the use of expert system shells could develop their own expert systems. If a shell is used, facts and rules of thumb about a specific domain can be defined and entered into a knowledge base with the help of a rule editor or other knowledge acquisition tool. A limited working prototype of the knowledge base is then constructed, tested, and evaluated using the inference engine and user interface programs of the shell. The knowledge engineer and domain experts can modify the knowledge base, then retest the system and evaluate the results. This process is repeated until the knowledge base and the shell result in an acceptable expert system.

The Value of Expert Systems

Benefits of Expert Systems

Before deciding to acquire or develop an expert system, it is important that managerial end users evaluate its **benefits and limitations.** In particular, they must decide whether the benefits of a proposed expert system will exceed its costs.

An expert system captures the expertise of an expert or group of experts in a computer-based information system. Thus, it can outperform a single human expert in many problem situations. That's because an expert system is faster and more consistent, can have the knowledge of several experts, and does not get tired or distracted by overwork or stress.

Expert systems also help preserve and reproduce the knowledge of experts. They allow a company to preserve the expertise of an expert before she leaves the organization. This expertise can then be shared by reproducing the software and knowledge base of the expert system. This allows novices to be trained and supported by copies of an expert system distributed throughout an organization. Finally, expert systems can have the same competitive advantages as other types of information technology. That is, the effective use of expert systems can allow a firm to (1) improve the efficiency of its operations, (2) produce new products and services, (3) lock in customers and suppliers with new business relationships, and (4) build knowledge-based strategic information resources.

Limitations of Expert Systems

The major limitations of expert systems arise from their limited focus, inability to learn, maintenance problems, and developmental cost. Expert systems excel only in solving specific types of problems in a limited domain of knowledge. They fail miserably in solving problems requiring a broad knowledge base and subjective problem solving. They do well with specific types of operational or analytical tasks, but falter at subjective managerial decision making. For example, an expert system might help a financial consultant develop alternative investment recommendations for a client. But it could not adequately evaluate the nuances or current political, economic, and societal developments, or the personal dynamics of a session with a client. These important factors would still have to be handled by the human consultant before a final investment decision could be reached.

Expert systems may also be difficult and costly to develop and maintain properly. The costs of knowledge engineers, lost expert time, and hardware and software resources may be too high to offset the benefits expected from some applications. Also, expert systems can't maintain themselves. That is, they can't learn from experience but must be taught new knowledge and modified as new expertise is needed to match developments in their subject areas. However, some of these limitations can be overcome by the use of expert system shells and other developmental tools that make the job of development and maintenance easier.

Intelligent Agents

In the case of the intelligent agent, we are seeing such AI-ish routines embedded in our latest spreadsheet and word processing packages and made available for use on networks such as the Internet. Indeed, almost any software package in the late 1990s will have to have an intelligent agent capability if it hopes to compete in the competitive software marketplace [16].

Intelligent agents are growing in popularity as a way to use artificial intelligence routines in software to help users accomplish many kinds of tasks. An intelligent agent is a *software surrogate* for an end user or a process that fulfills a stated need or activity. An intelligent agent uses its built-in and learned knowledge base about a person or process to make decisions and accomplish tasks in a way that fulfills the intentions of a user. Many times, an intelligent agent is given a graphic representation or persona, such as Einstein for a science advisor, Sherlock Holmes for an information search agent, and so on. Thus, intelligent agents (also called intelligent assistants and *Wizards*) are special-purpose knowledge-based information systems that accomplish specific tasks for users. Figure 8.38 illustrates the components of an intelligent agent for commodity buying [27, 32].

As we mentioned in Chapter 3, intelligent agents are evidence of a trend toward *expert-assisted* software packages. One of the most well-known uses of intelligent agents are the *Wizards* found in Microsoft Word, Excel, Access, and PowerPoint. These Wizards are built-in capabilities that can analyze how an end user is using a software package and offer suggestions on how to complete various tasks. Thus, Wizards might help you change document margins, format spreadsheet cells, query a database, or construct a graph. Wizards and other software agents are also designed to adjust to your way of using a software package so that they can anticipate when you will need their assistance. See Figure 8.39.

The use of intelligent agents is expected to grow rapidly as a way to simplify software use, access to network resources, and information screening and retrieval for users. Intelligent agents are becoming necessary as software packages become more

FIGURE 8.38

Components of an intelligent agent for commodity buying.

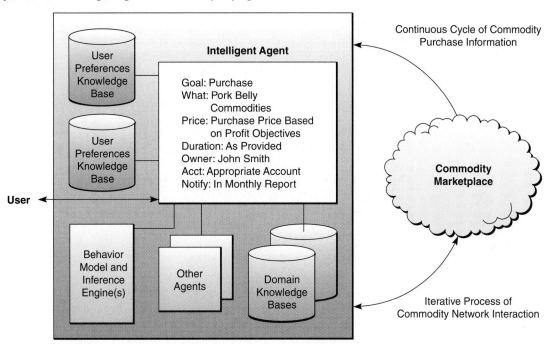

Source: Adapted from James King, "Intelligent Agents: Bringing Good Things to Life," *AI Expert*, February 1995, p. 18.

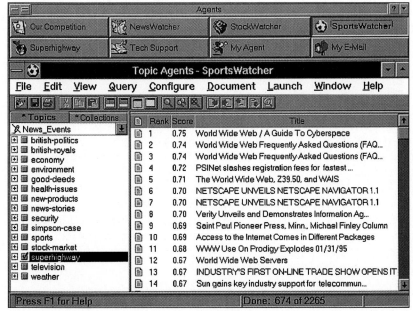

Courtesy of Verity, Inc.

FIGURE 8.39

Intelligent agents like those in Verity's Topic Information Server help you find information in a variety of categories from many online sources.

FIGURE 8.40

Examples of intelligent agents.

User Interface Agents

- **Interface Tutors.** Observe user computer operations, correct user mistakes, and provide hints and advice on efficient software use.

- **Presentation Agents.** Showing information in a variety of reporting and presentation forms and media based on user preferences.

- **Network Navigation Agents.** Discover paths to information and provide ways to view information that are preferred by a user.

- **Role-Playing Agents.** Play what-if games and other roles to help users understand information and make better decisions.

Information Management Agents

- **Search Agents.** Help users find files and databases, search for desired information, and suggest and find new types of information products, media, and resources.

- **Information Brokers.** Provide commercial services to discover and develop information resources that fit the business or personal needs of a user.

- **Information Filters.** Receive, find, filter, discard, save, forward, and notify users about products received or desired, including E-mail, voice mail, and all other information media.

sophisticated and powerful, as networks like the Internet became more vast and complex, and as information sources and media proliferate exponentially. In fact, some commentators forecast that much of the future of computing will consist of intelligent agents performing their work for users. So instead of using agents to help us accomplish computing tasks, we will be managing the performance of intelligent agents as they perform computing tasks for us. Figure 8.40 summarizes a few of the many types of intelligent agents that are in use or currently being developed [27].

REAL WORLD CASE

BUCKMAN LABORATORIES, HUGHES, AND CIGNA: CREATING KNOWLEDGE MANAGEMENT

Building systems to manage organizational know-how—until recently just another nice idea—has become real work for real information systems people at Monsanto Co.; Bechtel, Inc.; Cigna Corp.; and dozens of others. Although approaches vary, **knowledge management** in general tries to organize and make available important know-how, wherever and whenever it's needed. This includes processes, procedures, patents, reference works, formulas, "best practices," forecasts, and fixes. Technologically, intranets, groupware, data warehouses, networks, bulletin boards, and videoconferencing are key tools for storing and distributing this intelligence. Let's look at several examples.

Buckman Laboratories

"If you can bring shared company experience and knowledge to solve a customer problem, why reinvent the wheel?" asks Victor Baillargeon, vice president of knowledge transfer at Buckman Laboratories International, Inc. The Memphis-based maker of specialty chemicals credits much of a 250 percent growth in sales in the past decade to its brainpower-sharing via online forums. Buckman Labs' 1,200 employees in 80 countries have round-the-clock access to K'Netix—a rich global web of electronic forums, bulletin boards, virtual conference rooms, online libraries, knowledge bases, and electronic mail accessed via IBM PC ThinkPad 755 laptops.

As it celebrates its 50th anniversary, the company is adding Lotus Notes groupware and Internet support. It also has overhauled its worldwide network and is pulling data from Oracle databases onto internal Web servers, says Baillargeon, a Ph.D. chemist who oversees IS, telecommunications, and research and development. "We can save a lot of money doing work internally on our intranet," he explains.

Hughes Space & Communications

"There are no cookie-cutter solutions," says Arian Ward, leader of learning and change for Hughes Space & Communications Co. The El Segundo, California, aerospace giant decided the best approach was to create "The Hughes Knowledge Highway."

Described by Ward, a former IS consultant, as "a human network that uses technology," the highway employs videoconferencing, Lotus Notes, employee home pages, and other technologies. Among other things, the highway is used to spread new management practices, track patents and licenses, and gather competitive intelligence.

CIGNA Property & Casualty

CIGNA's Property and Casualty division, a $4 billion specialty insurer, set out to create a new desktop knowledge system for underwriters. So far, some 300 customized IBM PS/2 Model 70 client/server systems have been installed in 30 branch offices. With a few mouse clicks, underwriters can invoke worksheets, forms, motor vehicle and financial reports, and lists of company experts.

CIGNA uses knowledge management to discover and maintain profitable niches. The skills and experience of its people in underwriting and claims are being used to determine which niches to enter and to what extent. "Knowledge held by the individual worker is one of the most critical components to CIGNA's new strategy," says Tom Valerio, senior vice president, transformation.

Of course, getting people to share information willingly is one of the most difficult aspects of knowledge management. "You have to create an upward spiral for know-how to be shared," says Valerio. In an upward spiral, knowledge and information contributed by employees is processed by "knowledge editors"—such as experienced underwriters and other senior officials. They process information submitted by sales agents, claims agents, and others in the organization and then distribute it via the client/server network throughout the company, thus creating a learning loop. "If you can create a learning loop, where you're constantly creating and accessing individual knowledge, and if you have the right infrastructure, you're creating organizational know-how," Valerio says.

CASE STUDY QUESTIONS

1. What is knowledge management? Is it an application of artificial intelligence or human intelligence? Explain.

2. What information technologies and organizational practices can be used to implement knowledge management in a business?

3. What are the business benefits of knowledge management? Use Buckman, Hughes, and CIGNA as examples.

Source: Adapted from Joseph Maglitta, "Know-How, Inc.," *Computerworld,* January 15, 1996, pp. 73–75, and Harry Lasker and David Norton, "The New CIO/CEO Partnership," *Computerworld Leadership Series,* January 22, 1996, pp. 6–7. Copyright © 1996 by Computerworld, Inc., Framingham, MA 01701—Reprinted from *Computerworld.*

Summary

- **Information, Decisions, and Management.** Information systems can support a variety of management levels and decisions. These include the three levels of management activity (strategic, tactical, and operational planning and control), and three types of decision structures (structured, semistructured, and unstructured). Information systems provide a wide range of information products to support these types of decisions at all levels of management.

- **Information Quality.** Managers have to be provided with information products that possess many attributes of information quality in each of the three dimensions of time (timeliness, currency, frequency, and time period), content (accuracy, relevance, completeness, conciseness, scope, and performance), and form (clarity, detail, order, presentation, and media).

- **Online Analytical Processing.** Management, decision support, and executive information systems can be enhanced with an online analytical processing capability. OLAP typically relies on specialized servers and software to interactively analyze complex relationships among large amounts of data stored in multidimensional databases. Managers and analysts can then discover patterns, trends, and exception conditions in an online, realtime process that supports their business analysis and decision making.

- **Decision Support Systems.** Decision support systems are interactive, computer-based information systems that use a model base and a database to provide information tailored to support semistructured and unstructured decisions faced by individual managers. They are designed to use a decision maker's own insights and judgments in an ad hoc, interactive, analytical modeling process leading to a specific decision.

- **Analytical Modeling.** Using a decision support system is an interactive, analytical modeling process, consisting of what-if analysis, sensitivity analysis, goal-seeking analysis, and optimization analysis activities. Decision support system applications may be institutional or ad hoc but are typically developed to support the types of decisions faced by specific industries, functional areas, and decision makers.

- **Executive Information Systems.** Executive information systems are management information systems designed to support the strategic information needs of top management. However, their use is spreading to lower levels of management. EIS are easy to use and enable executives to retrieve information tailored to their needs and preferences. Thus, EIS can provide information about a company's critical success factors to executives to support their planning and control responsibilities.

- **Group Decision Support.** Managers are frequently faced with decision-making situations that require interactions with groups of people. Also, many decisions are made by groups of people coming to an agreement on a particular issue. The success of group decision making depends on many factors that can be enhanced by group decision-making

methodologies and facilitated by using the computer-based facilities and software tools of electronic meeting systems and group decision support systems.

- **Artificial Intelligence.** The major application domains of artificial intelligence (AI) include a variety of applications in cognitive science, computer science, robotics, and natural interfaces. The goal of AI is the development of computer functions normally associated with human physical and mental capabilities, such as robots that see, hear, talk, feel, and move, and software capable of reasoning, learning, and problem solving. Thus AI is being applied to many applications in business operations and managerial decision making, as well as in many other fields.

- **Expert Systems.** Expert systems are knowledge-based information systems that use a knowledge base about a specific, complex application area and an inference engine program to act as an expert consultant to users. An expert system consists of hardware, software, network, knowledge, and people resources. Hardware and network resources include workstations and other computers in local and wide area telecommunications networks. Software includes an inference engine program that makes inferences based on the facts and rules stored in a knowledge base. Other software includes user interface programs and expert system shells for expert system development. A knowledge base consists of facts about a specific subject area and heuristics (rules of thumb) that express the reasoning procedures of an expert. Users, domain experts, and knowledge engineers are the people resources of an expert system.

- **Expert System Development.** Expert systems can be purchased or developed if a problem situation exists that is suitable for solution by expert systems rather than by conventional experts and information processing. The benefits of expert systems (such as preservation and replication of expertise) must be balanced with their limited applicability in many problem situations. If the decision is made to develop an expert system, the use of an expert system shell may allow end users to develop their own expert systems in an interactive prototyping process.

- **Other AI Technologies.** The many application areas of AI are summarized in Figure 8.24, including neural networks, fuzzy logic, virtual reality, and intelligent agents. Neural nets are hardware or software systems based on simple models of the brain's neuron structure that can learn to recognize patterns in data. Fuzzy logic systems use rules of approximate reasoning to solve problems where data are incomplete or ambiguous. Virtual reality systems are multisensory systems that enable human users to experience computer-simulated environments as if they actually existed. Intelligent agents are knowledge-based software surrogates for a user or process in the accomplishment of selected tasks.

Key Terms and Concepts

These are the key terms and concepts of this chapter. The page number of their first explanation is in parentheses.

1. Analytical modeling (293)
   a. Goal-seeking analysis (295)
   b. Optimization analysis (295)
   c. Sensitivity analysis (294)
   d. What-if analysis (294)
2. Artificial intelligence (303)
   a. Application areas (304)
   b. Objectives (303)
3. Components of a DSS (291)
4. Decision structure and management level (282)
5. Decision support versus management reporting (289)
6. Decision support system (288)
7. DSS model base (292)
8. DSS software (293)
9. Executive information system (296)
10. Executive support system (296)
11. Expert system (310)
    a. Benefits and limitations (319)
    b. Components (311)
    c. Generic applications (313)
    d. Suitable applications (317)
12. Expert system development (317)
13. Expert system shell (318)
14. Fuzzy logic (307)
15. Group decision making (300)
16. Group decision support system (300)
17. Inference engine (311)
18. Information quality (284)
19. Intelligent agent (320)
20. Knowledge base (311)
21. Knowledge-based systems (310)
22. Knowledge engineer (319)
23. Management information system (284)
24. Neural network (305)
25. Online analytical processing (286)
26. Reporting alternatives (286)
27. Robotics (305)
28. Virtual reality (308)

Review Quiz

Match one of the key terms and concepts listed above with one of the brief examples or definitions listed below. Try to find the best fit for answers that seem to fit more than one term or concept. Defend your choices.

_____ 1. Provide an interactive modeling capability tailored to the specific information needs of managers.

_____ 2. Interactive responses to ad hoc inquiries versus prespecified information.

_____ 3. A management workstation, DSS software, database, model base, and manager or staff specialist.

_____ 4. A collection of mathematical models and analytical techniques.

_____ 5. Produce predefined reports for management.

_____ 6. Managers can receive reports periodically, on an exception basis, or on demand.

_____ 7. Analyzing the effect of changing variables and relationships and manipulating a mathematical model.

_____ 8. Changing revenues and tax rates to see the effect on net profit after taxes.

_____ 9. Changing revenues in many small increments to see revenue's effect on net profit after taxes.

_____ 10. Changing revenues and expenses to find how best to achieve a specified amount of net profit after taxes.

_____ 11. Changing revenues and expenses subject to certain constraints in order to achieve the highest net profit after taxes.

_____ 12. People coming to an agreement on an issue.

_____ 13. Computer-based tools can enhance the effectiveness of group decision making.

_____ 14. Information systems for the strategic information needs of top and middle managers.

_____ 15. Executive information systems that may have DSS, expert system, and office automation features.

_____ 16. Whether information is valuable and useful to you.

_____ 17. Information should be provided whenever it is needed and should be up-to-date.

_____ 18. Information should be accurate, relevant, complete, and concise.

_____ 19. Information should be presented clearly and attractively.

_____ 20. Realtime analysis of complex business data.

_____ 21. Information technology that focuses on the development of computer functions normally associated with human physical and mental capabilities.

_____ 22. Applications in cognitive science, computer science, robotics, and natural interfaces.

_____ 23. Development of computer-based machines that possess capabilities such as sight, hearing, dexterity, and movement.

_____ 24. Computers can provide you with computer-simulated experiences.

_____ 25. An information system that has a knowledge base as a major system component.

_____ 26. A knowledge-based information system that acts as an expert consultant to users in a specific application area.

_____ 27. A workstation, user interface programs, inference engine, knowledge base, and an end user.

_____ 28. Applications such as diagnosis, design, prediction, interpretation, and repair.

_____ 29. Small, well-defined problem areas that require experts and logical inference processing for solutions.

_____ 30. They can preserve and reproduce the knowledge of experts but have a limited application focus.

_____ 31. A collection of facts and reasoning procedures in a specific subject area.

_____ 32. A software package that manipulates a knowledge base and makes associations and inferences leading to a recommended course of action.

_____ 33. A software package consisting of an inference engine and user interface programs used as an expert system development tool.

_____ 34. One can either buy a completely developed expert system package, develop one with an expert system shell, or develop one from scratch by custom programming.

_____ 35. An analyst who interviews experts to develop a knowledge base about a specific application area.

_____ 36. Knowledge-based software surrogates who do things for you.

_____ 37. AI systems that use neuron structures to recognize patterns in data.

_____ 38. AI systems that use approximate reasoning to process ambiguous data.

Discussion Questions

1. What is the difference between the ability of a manager to retrieve information instantly on demand using a networked workstation, and the capabilities provided by a DSS?

2. Refer to the Real World Case on Bank of Montreal in the chapter. How could a mortgage approval decision support/expert system be used "to push other kinds of loans and services?"

3. In what ways does using an electronic spreadsheet package provide you with the components and capabilities of a decision support system?

4. How do electronic meeting systems support group decision making? What benefits and limitations do you see to using an EMS for group decision support?

5. Why is the use of executive information systems expanding into the ranks of middle management?

6. Refer to the Real World Case on Buckman Laboratories, Hughes, and CIGNA in the chapter. Compare a knowledge management system and the knowledge base of an expert system. Which supports business operations and management better? Explain your answer.

7. Can computers think? Will they ever be able to? Explain why or why not.

8. What are some of the most important applications of AI in business? Defend your choices.

9. What are several good applications of expert systems in business? Defend your choices based on the content of Figures 8.34 and 8.36.

10. What are some of the limitations or dangers you see in the use of AI technologies such as expert systems, virtual reality, and intelligent agents? What could be done to minimize such effects?

Real World Problems

1. **PepsiCo Restaurants International:**
   Doing Online Analytical Processing
   Those who analyze data to plot the future of PepsiCo Restaurants International have a lot on their plate. But at least the data are more accessible these days. A reorganization last year brought fast-food restaurants Pizza Hut, Kentucky Fried Chicken, and Taco Bell together in a single division and swelled the amount of financial data to be handled. The company has more than 3,000 stores in 29 countries from Hawaii to Morocco and handles 20 currencies.

   "Suddenly, we came to an issue of how to handle a huge database which was not consistent in different markets and not consistent between Kentucky Fried Chicken and Pizza Hut," said Ernest Luk, Asia region planning manager for PepsiCo Restaurants. And so the company began evaluating two online analytical processing (OLAP) tools—Sinper Corp.'s TM/1 and Hyperion Software's Hyperion.

   "What we need is a central data warehouse to put together all the information that we gather from the different markets," Luk said. Specifically, PepsiCo planners wanted to be able to drill down into financial data, consolidate different divisions' results, compare actual results to the forecasts, and translate foreign currencies to U.S. dollars.

Although PepsiCo Restaurants' U.S. headquarters uses the Hyperion OLAP tool, the Asian headquarters decided to go with TM/1. Besides meeting business requirements, Luk said, TM/1 was selected because it was easier to get it up and running than Hyperion. And Luk, as a finance professional and a self-proclaimed "noncomputer guy," is pleased with TM/1's ease of use. "You use a Lotus 1–2–3 spreadsheet as the user interface and just drill into the database and look at the numbers and try to make sense of it," he said.

a. Why did PepsiCo need to buy software for online analytical processing?

b. Why did they choose the TM/1 package? What business benefits can they derive from using this OLAP tool?

Source: Adapted from Jacqueline Mailloux, "New Menu at PepsiCo," *Computerworld*, May 6, 1996, p. 86. Copyright © by Computerworld, Inc., Framingham, MA 01701—Reprinted from *Computerworld*.

2. SystemSoft Corporation: Using an Expert System for PC Maintenance

SystemSoft Corp., a Natick, Massachusetts–based vendor of system-level software, has developed a Windows 95 and Windows NT–based package that can automatically identify, diagnose, and resolve common PC hardware, software, and system configuration problems. The software was developed with funding from Digital Equipment Corporation and Intel. Users of PCs equipped with the software will be able to automatically solve problems, such as a sound card configuration issue or a general protection fault, without help from technical support staff.

Call Avoidance is an integrated package that contains a wide knowledge base of general and system-specific hardware problems—and resolutions to those problems—culled from Digital's multivendor customer support group. Built into the package is an artificial intelligence engine that determines the cause of a specific problem and resolves it. The software takes advantage of system data available through Windows 95 or NT registries, the Plug and Play BIOS, and other system data files to help diagnose and resolve problems. Here's an example of how Call Avoidance software works:

The Problem

You've just installed a popular DOS game on your new PC. The background music works fine when playing the game, but other sounds don't seem to work.

The Fix

- Call Avoidance automatically examines the system and determines there is a conflict with the port that the sound card needs to use.
- The software reassigns the card to an open port and reloads the game.
- Total time for the fix is under 2 minutes, according to SystemSoft.

a. What expert system components and capabilities do you recognize in the Call Avoidance package?

b. Do you think this is a good application of expert system technology? Explain.

Source: Adapted from Jalkumar Vijayan, "Help Desk in a Box for Win95, NT," *Computerworld*, February 26, 1996, p. 44. Copyright © by Computerworld, Inc., Framingham, MA 01701—Reprinted from *Computerworld*.

3. Sedgwick James, Inc., and PepsiCo: Using a DSS/EIS for Risk Management

"We wanted to take the risk out of risk management," says Alan R. Josefsek, managing director, Information Systems Division, Sedgwick James, Inc. The world's second largest insurance broker, Sedgwick was hired by PepsiCo, Inc., to develop a new risk management information system.

PepsiCo, Inc.'s losses from accident, theft, and seasonal risks come right off the bottom line. And that means PepsiCo subsidiaries and divisions like the Pepsi-Cola Company, Frito-Lay, Taco Bell, KFC, and Pizza Hut had to get a handle on these risks to be able to create profitable real-world business plans. So Sedgwick developed a new risk management system called INFORM for PepsiCo.

Every week, Sedgwick loads the latest casualty claims data from the nation's leading insurance carriers into a FOCUS database resident on IBM RS/6000 servers in a distributed network. The database is then accessed via the PepsiCo wide area network by managers and analysts using more than 50 desktop PCs and remote laptops equipped with the INFORM risk management system. Both the RS/6000 servers and local PCs use Information Builders' EDA/SQL middleware to provide PepsiCo managers and business analysts with transparent data access from a variety of hardware/software configurations.

The INFORM risk management system combines the number-crunching power of FOCUS decision support modeling with the graphical analysis capabilities of FOCUS/EIS for Windows. As a result, PepsiCo managers at all levels can pinpoint critical trends, drill down for detailed back-up information, identify potential problems, and plan intelligently to minimize risks and maximize profits.

a. Is INFORM an example of an MIS, DSS, or EIS? Explain.

b. How is PepsiCo benefiting from the use of INFORM?

Source: Adapted from Jacqueline Mailloux, "New Menu at PepsiCo," *Computerworld*, May 6, 1996, p. 86. Copyright © by Computerworld, Inc., Framingham, MA 01701—Reprinted from *Computerworld*.

4. A.B. Data and Morgan Stanley: Neural Nets and Virtual Reality

A.B. Data

A.B. Data in Milwaukee is a direct marketer that specializes in fund-raising. For a telemarketing campaign, it developed a neural network application that increased profit per donor from $1.22 to $1.62 in eight months. Research director Gary Plouff says the system predicts which donors are "highly likely to be very profitable" in the next year. That lets fund-raisers focus on them, a switch from targeting Daddy Warbucks donors who may require extensive coaxing.

Plouff built the system, which contains 12 individual neural network models that analyze past data on donors in a donor database, using neural network software on a 486-based PC. The neural net software is from Advanced Software Applications in Pittsburgh. A.B. Data received an Information Technology and Analysis Award from the Database Marketing Association for this application.

Morgan Stanley

Morgan Stanley & Co. is experimenting with VRML (virtual reality modeling language) as a way to display the results of risk analyses in three dimensions on PCs in a corporate intranet. (VRML allows developers to create hyperlinks between 3-D objects in files and databases on the World Wide Web and corporate intranets.) Morgan's Market Risks Department uses Discovery software by Visible Decisions, Inc., to model risks of financial investments in varying market conditions. Discovery displays three-dimensional results using a powerful Silicon Graphics workstation. But Harry Mendell, a department vice president, is experimenting with displaying the results on ordinary PCs in a virtual reality experience over an intranet connection to a Sun Microsystems SPARCstation server running a Sun VRML browser.

By seeing data in three dimensions and experiencing relationships among data in a virtual reality process, it is easier for analysts to make intuitive connections than with a 2-D chart or table of numbers. "It allows side-by-side comparison with lots of data," Mendell said. "We've been looking at this data for over a year now, and when we got this running, I saw things I've never seen before."

a. Do you agree with the Database Marketing Association that A.B. Data's neural net application is a good application of neural network technology? Why or why not?

b. Why do you think that virtual reality 3-D modeling is helpful in analyzing the risks of financial investments?

Source: Adapted from Allan Alter, "FYI: Database Dynamos," *Computerworld*, March 25, 1996, p. 84, and Mitch Wagner, "Reality Check," *Computerworld*, February 26, 1996, p. 65. Copyright © 1996 by Computerworld, Inc., Framingham, MA 01701—Reprinted from *Computerworld*.

Application Exercises

1. The ADCAD System

Evaluate the ADCAD expert system on page 314 in the chapter. Write up your evaluation based on the following points.

a. The components of an expert system that you recognize. (See Figure 8.31.)

b. How well it fits the suitability criteria and application categories for expert systems. (See Figures 8.34 and 8.36.)

c. The benefits and limitations of this expert system.

2. The Kaiser Foundation

Evaluate the SIMR expert system of the Kaiser Foundation on page 316 in the chapter. Write up your evaluation based on the following points:

a. The components of an expert system that you recognize. (See Figure 8.31.)

b. How well it fits the suitability criteria and application categories for expert systems. (See Figures 8.34 and 8.36.)

c. The benefits and limitations of this expert system.

3. Computer Systems at Action Products

Your department is planning to purchase new personal computers for as many staff members as possible, up to 20. All PCs purchased are to be identically configured. From discussions with employees, you have determined a set of minimum requirements and a set of desired features for the PCs. You have gotten a price quote from a local vendor for these units. The quote received was in the form of a base price per unit for the minimum configuration, plus an indication of the added cost for upgrading to each of the desired features. The price quoted is valid for purchases of 15 or more units. The information on the price quote is as follows:

Action Products PC Purchase Quote (All prices are per unit based on purchase of at least 15 units.)	
Base price	$1,899
Upgrades	
To 16 megabytes RAM	325
To 17-inch monitor	129
To 2.5 gigabyte hard drive	159
To 8X CD–ROM drive	89

Assume that the upgrade items are listed in order from highest to lowest priority and that there is a fixed budget of $45,000 for the purchase of these PCs.

a. Create a spreadsheet that will allow you to analyze the possible configuration alternatives and their impact on costs. Modify your spreadsheet to analyze the three alternatives and any additional ones you would recommend. Attach a printed listing of each alternative to a memo summarizing your results.

1. Purchase 20 units and get as many upgrades as possible in priority order as previously described. Your spreadsheet should show the total cost and how many upgrade features could be purchased.

2. Purchase units with all of the upgrades listed and buy as many units as you can under the $45,000 budget.

3. Purchase 20 units and get as many upgrades as possible except for the RAM upgrades. This upgrade might be shifted to the lowest priority, because it would be easier to add RAM at a later time than to add any of the other upgrades.

4. Jackson City School District

The Jackson City School District has five high schools. The following table lists current enrollment and the number of teachers currently assigned to each high school. The district has established a goal of ensuring that there is at least one teacher for every 25 students in each high school. (You can divide the number of students by the number of teachers to determine this ratio for each school.) Is it possible to achieve this goal without increasing the number of teachers in the district?

School	Students	Teachers
Lincoln High	1,587	67
Kennedy High	1,704	65
Canaveral High	1,438	59
Washington High	1,699	63
Granite High	1,505	66

a. One suggested method for achieving this goal is to pay transportation expenses for students who are willing to transfer from overcrowded schools to less crowded schools. Use the goal-seeking analysis capabilities of your spreadsheet software to determine the number of students who would have to transfer to get all of the schools below the 1 to 25 ratio.

b. A second alternative is to transfer teachers from less crowded schools to schools that are overcrowded. Use goal-seeking analysis to determine the number of teachers who would have to transfer to each overcrowded school to get all schools below the 1 to 25 ratio.

Review Quiz Answers

1. *6*	11. *1b*	21. *2*	31. *20*
2. *5*	12. *15*	22. *2a*	32. *17*
3. *3*	13. *16*	23. *27*	33. *13*
4. *7*	14. *9*	24. *28*	34. *12*
5. *23*	15. *10*	25. *21*	35. *22*
6. *26*	16. *16*	26. *11*	36. *19*
7. *1*	17. *16c*	27. *11b*	37. *24*
8. *1d*	18. *16a*	28. *11c*	38. *14*
9. *1c*	19. *16b*	29. *11d*	
10. *1a*	20. *25*	30. *11a*	

Selected References

1. Allen, Bradley. "Case-Based Reasoning: Business Applications." *Communications of the ACM,* March 1994.

2. Ashline, Peter, and Vincent Lai. "Virtual Reality: An Emerging User-Interface Technology." *Information Systems Management,* Winter 1995.

3. Ballou, Melinda-Carrol. "Expert System Modernizes Kaiser." *Computerworld,* November 14, 1994.

4. Belcher, Lloyd, and Hugh Watson. "Assessing the Value of Conoco's EIS." *MIS Quarterly,* September 1993.

5. Betts, Mitch. "Efficiency Einsteins." *Computerworld,* March 22, 1993.

6. Blattberg, Robert; Rashi Glazer; and John Little. *The Marketing Information Revolution.* Boston: The Harvard Business School Press, 1994.

7. Burden, Kevin. "The CW Guide to Business Intelligence Software." *Computerworld,* December 19, 1994.

8. Buta, Paul. "Mining for Financial Knowledge with CBR." *AI Expert,* February 1994.

9. Chen, H.; P. Hsu; R. Orwig; L. Hoopes; and J. F. Nunamaker. "Automatic Concept Classification of Text from Electronic Meetings." *Communications of the ACM,* October 1994.

10. *Commander EIS: Delivering the Complete EIS Solution.* Ann Arbor, MI: Comshare, 1993.

11. Cox, Earl. "Application of Fuzzy System Models." *AI Expert,* October 1992.

12. Cox, Earl. "Relational Database Queries Using Fuzzy Logic." *AI Expert,* January 1995.

13. Cox, Earl. "Solving Problems with Fuzzy Logic." *AI Expert,* March 1992.

14. Dibbell, Julian. "The Race to Build Intelligent Machines." *Time,* March 25, 1996.

15. Dickson, Gary; Joo-Eng Lee Partridge; and Lora Robinson. "Exploring Modes of Facilitative Support for GDSS Technology." *MIS Quarterly,* June 1993.

16. Eliot, Lance. "Intelligent Agents Are Watching You." *AI Expert,* August 1994.

17. Enrado, Patty. "Giving Credit Where It Is Due." *AI Expert,* September 1991.

18. Finkelstein, Richard. *Understanding the Need for Online Analytical Servers.* Ann Arbor, MI: Comshare, 1994.

19. Finkelstein, Richard. "When OLAP Does Not Relate." *Computerworld,* December 12, 1994.

20. Gibbons, Chris; Corrine Chaves; Ronald Wilkes; and Mark Frolick. "Management Support System at Promus." *Information Systems Management,* Summer 1994.

21. Gorry, G. Anthony, and Michael Scott Manon. "A Framework for Management Information Systems." *Sloan Management Review,* Fall 1971; republished Spring 1989.

22. Jablonowski, Mark. "Fuzzy Risk Analysis: Using AI Systems." *AI Expert,* December 1994.

23. Jessup, Leonard, and David Tansuk. "Decision Making in an Automated Environment: The Effects on Anonymity and Proximity with a Group Decision Support System." *Decision Sciences Journal,* Spring 1991.

24. Jiang, James. "Using Scanner Data." *Information Systems Management,* Winter 1995.

25. Johnson, Mary Fran. "GIS Popularity Growing." *Computerworld,* March 22, 1993.

26. Keyes, Jessica. "Getting Caught in a Neural Network." *AI Expert,* July 1991.

27. King, James. "Intelligent Agents: Bringing Good Things to Life." *AI Expert,* February 1995.

28. Kurszweil, Raymond. *The Age of Intelligent Machines.* Cambridge, MA: The MIT Press, 1992.

29. Larijani, L. Casey. *The Virtual Reality Primer.* New York: McGraw-Hill, 1994.

30. McNeill, F. Martin, and Ellen Thro. *Fuzzy Logic: A Practical Approach.* Boston: AP Professional, 1994.

31. Nunamaker, Jay; Alan Dennis; Joseph Valacich; Douglas Vogel; and Joey F. George. "Electronic Meetings to Support Group Work." *Communications of the ACM,* July 1991.

32. *On the Cutting Edge of Technology.* Carmel, IN: SAMS Publishing, 1993.

33. Pimentel, Ken, and Kevin Teixeira. *Virtual Reality: Through the New Looking Glass.* 2nd ed. New York: Intel/McGraw-Hill, 1995.

34. Radding, Alan. "Is OLAP the Answer?" *Computerworld,* December 19, 1994.

35. Rhingoid, Howard. "How Real Is Virtual Reality?" *Beyond Computing,* March–April 1992.

36. Sengupta, Kishore, and Dov Te'eni. "Cognitive Feedback in GDSS: Improving Control and Convergence." *MIS Quarterly,* March 1993.

37. Sprague, Ralph, and Barbara McNurlin. *Information Systems Management in Practice.* 3rd ed. New York: Prentice Hall, 1993.

38. Trinzic Corporation. *An Introduction to Business Process Automation.* Palo Alto, CA: 1993.

39. Turban, Efraim. *Decision Support and Expert Systems: Management Support Systems.* 2nd ed. New York: Macmillan, 1990.

40. Turoff, Murray; Starr Roxanne Hiltz; Ahmed Bahgat; and Ajaz Rava. "Distributed Group Support Systems." *MIS Quarterly,* December 1993.

41. Watson, Hugh, and Mark Frolick. "Determining Information Requirements for an EIS." *MIS Quarterly,* September 1993.

42. Watson, Hugh, and John Satzinger. "Guidelines for Designing EIS Interfaces." *Information Systems Management,* Fall 1994.

43. Wright, Robert. "Can Machines Think?" *Time,* March 25, 1996.

Information Systems for Strategic Advantage

CHAPTER OUTLINE

LEARNING OBJECTIVES

After reading and studying this chapter, you should be able to:

1. Identify several basic competitive strategies and explain how they can be used to confront the competitive forces faced by a business.

2. Identify several strategic roles of information systems and give examples of how information technology can implement these roles and give competitive advantages to a business.

3. Give examples of how information technology can break time, geographic, cost, and structural barriers in business.

4. Give examples of how business process reengineering involves the strategic use of information technology.

5. Identify how total quality management differs from business process reengineering in its use of information technology.

6. Identify how information technology can be used strategically to help a company be an agile competitor.

7. Explain how information technology can be used to form a virtual company to meet strategic business opportunities.

8. Identify several strategic business uses of the Internet and give examples of each.

Section I

Fundamentals of Strategic Advantage

Introduction

What are the new skills demanded of effective managers in the 1990s? Competence and comfort in handling information technology (IT) will be high on the list. IT—computers plus telecommunications plus workstations plus information stores—is one of the major forces reshaping competition [20].

As a prospective manager, it is important that you view information systems as more than a set of technologies that support end user computing and collaboration, efficient business operations, or effective managerial decision making. Information systems can change the way businesses compete. So you should also view information systems strategically, that is, as competitive networks, as a means of organizational renewal, and as a vital investment in technologies that help an enterprise achieve its strategic objectives. See Figure 9.1.

Thus, the strategic role of information systems involves using information technology to develop products, services, and capabilities that give a company strategic advantages over the competitive forces it faces in the global marketplace. This creates **strategic information systems,** information systems that support or shape the competitive position and strategies of an enterprise. So a strategic information system can be any kind of information system (TPS, MIS, DSS, etc.) that helps an organization gain a competitive advantage, reduce a competitive disadvantage, or meet other strategic enterprise objectives [26]. Let's look at several basic concepts that define the role of such strategic information systems.

Competitive Strategy Concepts

How should a managerial end user think about competitive strategies? How can competitive strategies be applied to the use of information systems by an organization? Several important conceptual frameworks for understanding and applying competitive strategies (which we briefly introduced in Chapter 1), have been developed by Michael Porter [28, 29], Charles Wiseman [35], and others. Figure 9.2 illustrates several important concepts. A firm can survive and succeed in the long run if it successfully develops strategies to confront five **competitive forces** that shape the structure of competition in its industry. These are: (1) rivalry of competitors within its industry, (2) threat of new entrants, (3) threat of substitutes, (4) the bargaining power of customers, and (5) the bargaining power of suppliers.

A variety of **competitive strategies** can be developed to help a firm confront these competitive forces. For example, businesses may try to counter the bargaining power of their customers and suppliers by developing unique business relationships with them. This effectively locks in customers or suppliers by creating "switching costs" that make it expensive or inconvenient for them to switch to another firm. Thus, competitors are also locked out by such strategies. Companies may use other strategies to protect themselves from the threat of new businesses entering their industry, or the development of substitutes for their products or services. For example, businesses may try to develop legal, financial, or technological requirements that create barriers to entry to discourage firms from entering an industry, or make substitution unattractive or uneconomical.

Another way that businesses can counter the threats of competitive forces that confront them is to implement five basic competitive strategies [27, 34]. As Figure 9.3 illustrates, they include the following:

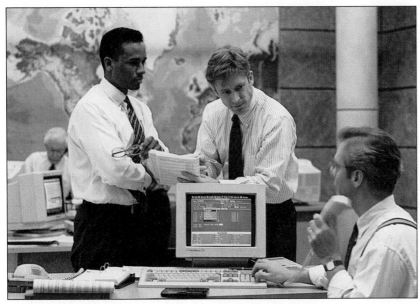

Jon Feingersch/The Stock Market.

FIGURE 9.1

Information systems can involve the strategic use of information technology to gain competitive advantages.

- **Cost Leadership Strategy.** Becoming a low-cost producer of products and services in the industry. Also, a firm can find ways to help its suppliers or customers reduce their costs or to increase the costs of their competitors.
- **Differentiation Strategy.** Developing ways to differentiate a firm's products and services from its competitors' or reduce the differentiation advantages of competitors. This may allow a firm to focus its products or services to give it an advantage in particular segments or niches of a market.
- **Innovation Strategy.** Finding new ways of doing business. This may involve the development of unique products and services, or entry into unique markets or market niches. It may also involve making radical changes to the business processes for producing or distributing products and services that are so different from the way business has been conducted that they alter the fundamental structure of an industry.

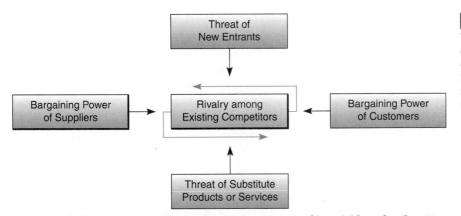

FIGURE 9.2

The competitive environment of an industry. Note the five competitive forces that determine the profitability and survival of the firms within an industry.

Source: Adapted and reprinted with the permission of The Free Press, an imprint of Simon & Schuster from *Competitive Advantage: Creating and Sustaining Superior Performance,* by Michael E. Porter. Copyright © 1985 by Michael E. Porter.

FIGURE 9.3

Businesses can develop competitive strategies to counter the actions of the competitive forces they confront in the marketplace.

Competitive Forces

Competitive Strategies	Supplier	Customer	Competitor	New Entrant	Substitute
Differentiation					
Cost					
Innovation					
Growth					
Alliance					
Other Strategies					

- **Growth Strategies.** Significantly expanding a company's capacity to produce goods and services, expanding into global markets, diversifying into new products and services, or integrating into related products and services.
- **Alliance Strategies.** Establishing new business linkages and alliances with customers, suppliers, competitors, consultants, and other companies. These linkages may include mergers, acquisitions, joint ventures, forming of "virtual companies," or other marketing, manufacturing, or distribution agreements.

Strategic Roles for Information Systems

How can the preceding competitive strategy concepts be applied to the **strategic role of information systems** in an organization? Put another way, how can managers use investments in information technology to directly support a firm's competitive strategies? These questions can be answered in terms of the key strategic roles that information systems can perform in a firm. Figure 9.4 summarizes how information technology can be used to implement a variety of competitive strategies. These include not only the five basic competitive strategies, but also other ways that companies can use information systems strategically to gain a competitive edge. Figure 9.5 on page 338 provides examples of how many corporations have used strategic information systems to implement each of the five basic strategies for competitive advantage [21, 22, 26, 35]. In the rest of this chapter, we will discuss and provide other examples of such strategic uses of information technology.

Improving Business Operations

Using information technology to improve a company's operations can have many strategic effects. Investments in information technology can help make a firm's operations substantially more efficient. Improvements to its business processes could enable a company to cut costs dramatically and improve the quality and

Lower Costs
- Use IT to substantially reduce the cost of business processes.
- Use IT to lower the costs of customers or suppliers.

Differentiate
- Develop new IT features to differentiate products and services.
- Use IT features to reduce the differentiation advantages of competitors.
- Use IT features to focus products and services at selected market niches.

Innovate
- Create new products and services that include IT components.
- Make radical changes to business processes with IT.
- Develop unique new markets or market niches with the help of IT.

Promote Growth
- Use IT to manage regional and global business expansion.
- Use IT to diversify and integrate into other products and services.

Develop Alliances
- Use IT to create virtual organizations of business partners.
- Develop interorganizational information systems that create strategic business relationships with customers, suppliers, subcontractors, and others.

Improve Quality and Efficiency
- Use IT to dramatically improve the quality of products and services.
- Use IT to make continuous improvements to the efficiency of business processes.
- Use IT to substantially shorten the time needed to develop, produce, and deliver products and services.

Build an IT Platform
- Leverage investment in IS people, hardware, software, and networks from operational uses into strategic applications.
- Build a strategic information base of internal and external data collected and analyzed by IT.

Other Strategies
- Use interorganizational information systems to create switching costs that lock in customers and suppliers.
- Use investment in IT to build barriers to entry against industry outsiders.
- Use IT components to make substitution of competing products unattractive.

FIGURE 9.4

A summary of how information technology can be used to implement competitive strategies.

delivery of its products and services. For example, manufacturing operations for everything from automobiles to watches have been automated and significantly improved by computer-aided manufacturing (CAM) technologies. In the automobile industry, the distribution of cars and parts and the exchange of vital business data have been substantially improved by telecommunications networks that electronically connect an automobile manufacturer's distribution facilities with car dealers. In the next section, we will discuss some of the major ways that using information technology for *business process reengineering* can improve the operational efficiency of business processes.

Operational efficiency may allow a firm to adopt a low-cost leadership strategy. However, a firm could decide instead to use its operational efficiency to increase quality and service by choosing a product differentiation strategy. This strategy would stress the unique quality of a firm's products and services. In either case, a firm would be better able to deter competitive threats. Its industry rivals and firms seeking to enter the industry using similar or substitute products would have a harder time beating an efficient competitor.

FIGURE 9.5

Examples of how companies used information technology to implement five competitive strategies for strategic advantage.

Strategy	Company	Strategic Information System	Business Benefit
Cost leadership	Levitz Furniture	Centralized buying	Cut purchasing costs
	Metropolitan Life	Medical care monitoring	Cut medical costs
	Deere & Company	Machine tool control	Cut manufacturing costs
Differentiation	Navistar	Portable computer-based customer needs analysis	Increase in market share
	Setco Industries	Computer-aided job estimation	Increase in market share
	Consolidated Freightways	Customer online shipment tracking	Increase in market share
Innovation	Merrill Lynch	Customer cash management accounts	Market leadership
	Federal Express	Online package tracking and flight management	Market leadership
	McKesson Corp.	Customer order entry and merchandising	Market leadership
Growth	Citicorp	Global telecommunications network	Increase in global market
	Wal-Mart	Merchandise ordering by satellite network	Market leadership
	Toys 'Я' Us Inc.	POS inventory tracking	Market leadership
Alliance	Wal-Mart/Procter & Gamble	Automatic inventory replenishment by supplier	Reduced inventory costs/increased sales
	Levi Strauss/Designs Inc.	Electronic data interchange	Just-in-time merchandise replenishment
	Airborne Express/Rentrak Corp.	Online inventory management/shipment tracking	Increase in market share

Promoting Business Innovation

Investments in information systems technology can result in the development of unique products and services or processes. This can create new business opportunities, and enable a firm to expand into new markets or into new segments of existing markets. The use of automated teller machines (ATMs) in banking is a classic example of an innovative investment in information systems technology.

By employing ATMs, Citibank and several other large banks were able to gain a strategic advantage over their competitors that lasted for several years [20, 21]. ATMs lured customers away from other financial institutions by cutting the cost of delivering bank services and increasing the convenience of such services. The more costly and less convenient alternative would have been to establish new bank branch offices. ATMs are also an example of product differentiation, since bank services are now provided in a new way. ATMs raised the cost of competition, which forced some smaller banks that could not afford the investment in new technology to merge with larger banks. ATMs represented an attractive and convenient new banking service produced and distributed to customers by making innovative changes in the delivery of bank services. Thus, information systems technology was used to develop a strategic new distribution process for bank services.

Locking in Customers and Suppliers

Investments in information technology can also allow a business to **lock in customers and suppliers** (and lock out competitors) by building valuable new relationships with them. This can deter both customers and suppliers from abandoning a firm for its competitors or intimidating a firm into accepting less profitable relationships. Early attempts to use information systems technology in these relationships focused on significantly improving the quality of service to customers and suppliers in a firm's distribution, marketing, sales, and service activities. Then businesses moved to more innovative uses of information technology.

For example, many telecommunications networks were designed to provide salespeople and customer service staffs with up-to-date sales, shipping, inventory, and account status information for relay to their customers. Firms began to use the operational efficiency of such information systems to offer better-quality service and thereby differentiate themselves from their competitors. Some firms then began to extend these networks to their customers and suppliers in order to build innovative relationships that would lock in their business. This creates **interorganizational information systems** in which telecommunications networks electronically link the terminals and computers of businesses with their customers and suppliers, resulting in new business alliances and partnerships. Electronic data interchange (EDI) links between a business and its suppliers such as those between Motorola Codex and Texas Instruments are one example. (See Figure 7.25 in Chapter 7.) An even stronger link is the automatic inventory replenishment system that Procter & Gamble has with Wal-Mart [8, 20].

Creating Switching Costs

A major emphasis in strategic information systems is to build **switching costs** into the relationships between a firm and its customers or suppliers. That is, investments in information systems technology can make customers or suppliers dependent on the continued use of innovative, mutually beneficial interorganizational information systems. Then, they become reluctant to pay the costs in time, money, effort, and inconvenience that it would take to change to a company's competitors.

A classic example is the computerized airline reservation systems used by most travel agents such as the SABRE system of AMR Corporation (American Airlines) and the APOLLO system of COVIA (United Airlines). Once a travel agency has invested a substantial sum in installing such an interorganizational system, and travel agents have been trained in its use, the agency is reluctant to switch to another reservation system. Thus, what seemed to be just a more convenient and efficient way of processing airline reservations has become a strategic weapon that gives these providers a major competitive advantage. Not only does an airline reservation system raise competitive barriers and increase switching costs, it also gives their providers an advantage in gaining reservations for themselves and provides them with a major new line of information products. Thus, computer-based reservation services are a major source of revenue for their providers, which charge a variety of fees to travel agencies and airlines who use their systems.

Raising Barriers to Entry

By making investments in information technology to improve its operations or promote innovation, a firm could also erect **barriers to entry** that would discourage or delay other companies from entering a market. Typically, this happens by increasing the amount of investment or the complexity of the technology required to compete in an industry or a market segment. Such actions would tend to discourage firms already in the industry and deter external firms from entering the industry. Merrill Lynch's cash management account is a classic example. By making major investments in information technology, they became the first securities brokers to offer a credit line, checking account (through BankOne), Visa credit card, and automatic investment in a money market fund, all in one account [26, 35]. Thus, large investments in computer-based information systems can make the stakes too high for some present or prospective players in an industry.

Building a Strategic IT Platform

Investing in information technology enables a firm to build a **strategic IT platform** that allows it to take advantage of strategic opportunities. In many cases, this results from a firm investing in advanced computer-based information systems to improve the efficiency of its own internal operations. Typically, this means acquiring hardware and software, developing telecommunications networks, hiring information system specialists, and training end users. Then, armed with this technology platform, the firm can **leverage investment in information technology** by developing new products and services. For example, the development by banks of remote banking services using automated teller machines was an extension of their expertise in teller terminal networks, which interconnect their branches.

Developing a Strategic Information Base

Information systems also allow a firm to **develop a strategic information base** that can provide information to support the firm's competitive strategies. Information in a firm's corporate databases has always been a valuable asset in promoting efficient operations and effective management of a firm. However, information about a firm's operations, customers, suppliers, and competitors, as well as other economic and demographic data, is now viewed as a strategic resource; that is, it is used to support strategic planning, marketing, and other strategic initiatives.

For example, many businesses are now using computer-based information about their customers to help design marketing campaigns to sell customers new products and services. This is especially true of firms that include several subsidiaries offering a variety of products and services. For example, once you become a customer of a subsidiary of Transamerica, you quickly become a target for marketing campaigns by their other subsidiaries, based on information provided by the Transamerica strategic information resource base. This is one way a firm can leverage its investment in transaction processing and customer accounting systems—by linking its databases to its strategic planning and marketing systems. This strategy helps a firm create better marketing campaigns for new products and services, build better barriers to entry for competitors, and find better ways to lock in customers and suppliers.

Information Systems and the Value Chain

Let's look at one final important concept that can help a manager identify opportunities for strategic information systems. The **value chain** concept was developed by Michael Porter [28] and is illustrated in Figure 9.6. It views a firm as a series, or chain, of basic activities that add value to its products and services and thus add a margin of value to the firm. In the value chain concept, some business activities are primary activities, others are support activities. This framework can highlight where competitive strategies can best be applied in a business. That is, managerial end users should try to develop a variety of strategic information systems for those basic activities that add the most value to a company's products or services, and thus to the overall business value of the firm. Figure 9.6 provides examples of how and where information systems technology can be applied to basic business activities using the value chain framework.

For example, Figure 9.6 shows that office automation systems can increase the productivity of office communications and support activities in management and administrative services. Employee skills database systems can help the human resource management function locate and assign employees to important positions and projects. Computer-aided design (CAD) systems can automate the design of products and processes as part of technology development. Finally, electronic data interchange (EDI) systems can help improve procurement of resources by providing online telecommunications links to a firm's suppliers.

FIGURE 9.6

The value chain of a firm. Note the examples of the variety of strategic information systems that can be applied to a firm's basic activities for competitive advantage.

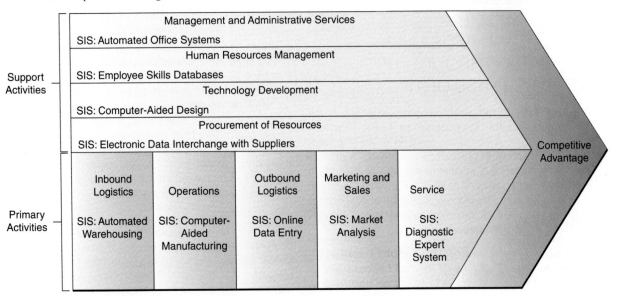

Other examples of strategic applications of information systems technology to primary business activities are identified in Figure 9.6. These include automated warehousing systems to support inbound logistic activities involving storage of inventory, computer-aided manufacturing (CAM) systems for manufacturing operations, and online order entry systems to improve *outbound logistics* activities that process customer orders. Information systems can also support marketing and sales activities by providing analyses of present and potential markets for goods and services, and can improve customer service by offering expert system diagnostic services to customers.

Thus, the value chain concept can help managers decide where and how to apply the strategic capabilities of information technology. It shows how various types of strategic information systems can be applied to the specific business activities that help a firm gain competitive advantages in the marketplace.

REAL WORLD CASE

ROYAL BANK, C.R. ENGLAND, AND USAA: THE BREAKTHROUGH STRATEGIC USE OF IT

William Davidson has spent six years studying some 70 businesses that have achieved major business breakthroughs—spectacular gains in growth, speed, service, efficiency, or product development. A professor of management at the University of Southern California and consultant at MESA Partners, Davidson is writing a book, *Breakthroughs of Champions,* that culls the lessons from their experiences. He spoke with *Fortune*'s Strat Sherman.

What do you mean you can have it all? Popular books like *The Discipline of Market Leaders* say that's nonsense—you have to focus on one kind of competence.

"Managers who accept such artificial restrictions are limiting their own potential. There is no inherent trade-off between, say, cost leadership and customer service. You can have simultaneous improvements in both—as well as in quality, cycle time, and precision, which is the tailoring of your products to individual customers. It's possible to do this and support business growth at the same time."

Royal Bank of Canada

"To see how precision works, look at Royal Bank of Canada. The essence of their breakthrough was creating a comprehensive customer database available online to all branches and offices. When a customer requests a loan, the bank can respond instantly now, but that's the least of it. The information in their database revealed enormous opportunities to serve their customers better. Their average customer—and they have 9 million—buys roughly three financial services from the Royal Bank and over 14 from other sources. Using this newfound customer knowledge, bank executives refocused their marketing efforts so completely on existing customers that they no longer have much interest in new ones. And the profitability of their existing relationships has soared."

C.R. England

"C.R. England, a private trucking company in Utah, is the best example I know of using technology to make information the main driver of business results. They measure everything from cargo temperature to the speed at which invoices are processed—and use the numbers to turbocharge results. Every worker has a customized set of performance measures, depending on what he or she does. All employees get a customized performance report each week, and the results show up vividly in their paychecks. This is perhaps the best-managed company we have encountered—managed within an inch of its life. And highly profitable: C.R. England has increased its truck fleet sevenfold in seven years, while revenues per truck are up by one-quarter."

USAA

"The insurer USAA is another example of a breakthrough company. A decade ago they set a goal of completing almost every customer transaction in the first conversation with the customer. An outrageous goal. They set up a new customer-service organization and gave all the service reps online access to an enterprisewide information infrastructure. They aligned everything in the organization to feed into that system. The program was a smashing success. Their overhead costs on some key policies are 75 percent below competitors', and their customer-service and satisfaction levels are the envy of the industry."

What are the key attributes of breakthrough companies?

"Aggressive use of advanced technology. An orientation to outrageous objectives rather than continuous improvement. Strong customer focus. Singleness of purpose. The discipline to do enterprisewide initiatives rather than local ones. And a mindset that recognizes unexpected new opportunities that appear along the way."

CASE STUDY QUESTIONS

1. Do you think the companies in this case are making breakthrough use of information technology? Why or why not?

2. What competitive IT strategies are being implemented by the companies in this case? Refer to Figure 9.5 to help you explain your choices.

3. How could Davidson's key attributes of breakthrough companies be used by other businesses? Give several examples.

Source: Adapted from Stratford Sherman, "You Can Have It All," *Fortune,* March 4, 1996, pp. 193–94. © 1996 Time Inc. All rights reserved.

Strategic Applications and Issues in Information Technology

Section II

How do most companies use information technology? Figure 9.7 illustrates various ways that organizations may view and use information technology. Companies may use information systems strategically, or may use them in defensive or controlled ways. For example, if a company emphasized strategic business uses of information technology, its management would view IT as a major competitive differentiator. It would then devote significant amounts of technology to support decision

Introduction

FIGURE 9.7

How a business may view and employ information technology.

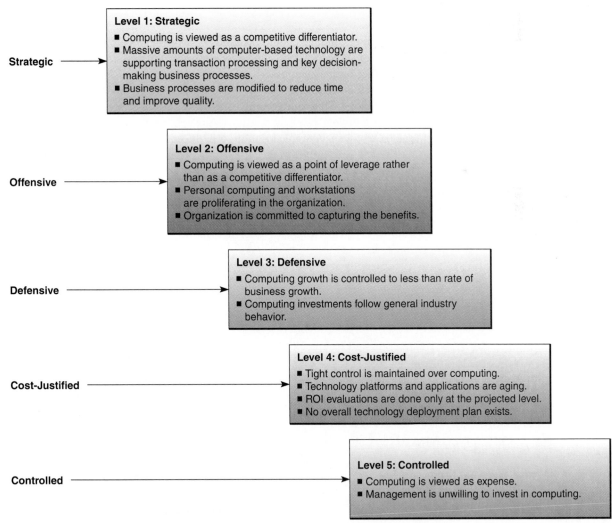

Strategic →
Level 1: Strategic
- Computing is viewed as a competitive differentiator.
- Massive amounts of computer-based technology are supporting transaction processing and key decision-making business processes.
- Business processes are modified to reduce time and improve quality.

Offensive →
Level 2: Offensive
- Computing is viewed as a point of leverage rather than as a competitive differentiator.
- Personal computing and workstations are proliferating in the organization.
- Organization is committed to capturing the benefits.

Defensive →
Level 3: Defensive
- Computing growth is controlled to less than rate of business growth.
- Computing investments follow general industry behavior.

Cost-Justified →
Level 4: Cost-Justified
- Tight control is maintained over computing.
- Technology platforms and applications are aging.
- ROI evaluations are done only at the projected level.
- No overall technology deployment plan exists.

Controlled →
Level 5: Controlled
- Computing is viewed as expense.
- Management is unwilling to invest in computing.

Source: Adapted from Richard Murray, "The Quest for World Class IT Capability," *Information Systems Management* (New York: Auerbach Publications), Summer 1991, p. 13. © 1991 Warren, Gorham & Lamont. Used with permission.

making, and to improve business processes. More and more businesses are beginning to use information systems strategically for competitive advantage. In this section, we will provide many examples of such strategic business applications of information technology.

Breaking Business Barriers

Figure 9.8 illustrates a useful framework for focusing on several vital capabilities of information technology that break traditional barriers to strategic business success. Two key capabilities of information technology seem obvious. First, computers and telecommunications networks break time barriers. Telecommunications is a lot faster than most other forms of communications. Second, computers and telecommunications break geographic barriers. Telecommunications networks enable you to communicate with people almost anywhere in the world as if you were there with them.

Two other business capabilities of information technology are not so obvious, or as easy to establish. First, information technology can break cost barriers. That is, computers and telecommunications networks can often significantly reduce the costs of business operations when compared with other means of information processing and communications. Second, telecommunications can break structural barriers. That is, computers and telecommunications networks can help a business develop strategic relationships by establishing new electronic linkages with customers, suppliers, and other business entities.

Figure 9.9 outlines examples of the four major strategic capabilities of information technology. This figure emphasizes how several strategic applications of information technology can help a firm capture and provide information quickly to end users at remote geographic locations at reduced costs, as well as supporting its strategic organizational objectives. For example, telecommunications links between the computers of traveling salespeople and those at regional sales offices can be used

FIGURE 9.8

Information technology can break time, geographic, cost, and structural barriers.

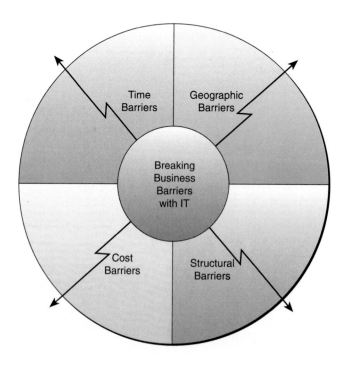

to transmit customer orders, thus breaking geographic barriers. Point-of-sale terminals and an online sales transaction processing network can break time barriers by supporting immediate credit authorization and sales processing. Teleconferencing can be used to cut costs by reducing the need for expensive business trips since it allows more people from remote locations to participate in meetings and collaborate on group projects. Finally, electronic data interchange systems are used by the business to establish strategic relationships with their customers and suppliers by making the exchange of electronic business documents fast, convenient, and tailored to the needs of the business partners involved. Let's now look at examples of such applications in more detail.

How can information technology shorten the intervals between the various critical steps in a business process? That's the focus of *interval reduction* and *just-in-time* operations. Their goal is to shorten the response time to customer demands and reduce inventory investment to a minimum, thus helping to make a company an *agile competitor*.

Breaking Time Barriers

- Producers who deliver their products and services in realtime relative to their competitors will have a strategic advantage. Operating in realtime means no *lag time* between identification and fulfillment of a need [11].
- Every major online use of IT in core operations moves firms toward just-in-time something—inventory, sales, distribution, publishing, scheduling, or reporting. Reducing time and inventory is one of the new business imperatives [20].

Toyota Motor Corp. is a classic example of the use of computers and telecommunications networks for interval reductions and just-in-time operations that resulted in a significant strategic advantage [11]. In the early 1980s, Toyota found to its dismay that while it took about 2 days to manufacture a car, it took about 25 to 30 days to process a customer's order for a car. From a total cost standpoint, Toyota then concluded that it was costing more to process the order on a car than to manufacture the car!

FIGURE 9.9

Examples of the strategic benefits of information technology.

Capabilities	Examples	Benefits
Break geographic barriers: Capture information about business transactions from remote locations	Transmission of customer orders from traveling salespeople to a corporate data center for order processing and inventory control	Provides better customer service by reducing delay in filling orders and improves cash flow by speeding up the billing of customers
Break time barriers: Provide information to remote locations immediately after it is requested	Credit authorization at the point of sale	Credit inquiries can be made and answered in seconds
Break cost barriers: Reduce the cost of more traditional means of communication	Video teleconferencing	Reduces expensive business trips; allows more people to participate in a meeting, thus improving the quality of decisions reached
Break structural barriers: Support linkages for competitive advantage	Electronic data interchange (EDI) of transaction data to and from suppliers and customers	Fast, convenient service locks in customers and suppliers

Toyota responded by developing a global telecommunications network that links the computers of its dealers and distribution centers to the computers at its headquarters in Toyota City, and the production and scheduling computers at its manufacturing centers. Its goal is to enable a customer in Japan to order a car that is not in inventory and have it delivered within 48 hours. As a result, Toyota gained a major competitive advantage measured by increases in customer satisfaction at the faster response times, and reductions in the costs involved in delivering a car from the factory to a customer.

Breaking Geographic Barriers

How can information technology break the geographic barriers that hinder the managerial control of operations, raise the cost of doing business, and limit the quality of services and the coverage of potential markets? Many businesses today operate from several locations and have customers or suppliers at distant locations. If a business is regional, national, or global in scope, then telecommunications networks become a vital component of its business operations. See Figure 9.10.

Telecommunications and computing technologies make it possible to distribute key business activities to where they are most needed, where they are best performed, or where they best support the competitive advantage of a business. Telecommunications networks link remote locations with company headquarters, other remote locations, and external entities such as suppliers, customers, and consultants. All of these entities can participate in business activities as if geographic barriers did not exist. Let's take a look at a few examples.

Citibank of New York moved its entire credit card operation to South Dakota during the 1980s because of high labor costs in New York City and restrictions by the State of New York on the interest rates it could charge for credit cards. Citibank uses leased satellite channels for data and voice communications, facsimile, and teleconferencing between its New York headquarters and its credit card operations center in South Dakota. Thus, Citibank's experience demonstrates that telecommunications networks enable a business to move part of its operations to distant locations with lower costs, a better workforce, or less restrictive government regulations [8].

FIGURE 9.10

Regional and global computing networks support distributed business operations.

John Feingersch/The Stock Market.

Mobil Oil Corporation is another example of how information technology can break geographic barriers. Mobil has a worldwide computing network for oil exploration consisting of several HP9000 minicomputers and over 1,000 personal computers and technical workstations. Mobil can pool the expertise of its scientists and engineers at 11 locations around the globe. For example, it may use E-mail and data communications to call on its engineers in Canada, Australia, Dallas, and Singapore to help analyze the feasibility of drilling for oil in sandstone off the coast of Nigeria. Or a Mobil scientist performing graphics-based analysis in Indonesia can send drawings in realtime to a colleague in Norway working a similar problem [15]. Thus, geographic barriers can effectively be ignored through the proper use of telecommunications for business operations.

How can information technology enable a business to gain strategic reductions in operating costs? Computers interconnected by telecommunications networks in key business areas can substantially reduce the costs of production, inventory, distribution, or communications for many business firms. Thus, information technology has helped companies cut labor costs, minimize inventory levels, reduce the number of distribution centers, and lower communications costs. Let's look at a specific example.

Breaking Cost Barriers

A few years ago, Hewlett-Packard Company (H-P) realized that it was spending $50 million to $100 million more each year than necessary on raw material purchases. That's because H-P is highly decentralized. H-P grants its operating divisions almost complete autonomy in purchasing and other operational decisions, "because they know their own needs best." However, because of this decentralization of purchasing, the company could not take advantage of high-volume discounts available from its suppliers.

Instead of centralizing purchasing, H-P used telecommunications networks to link the computers of divisional purchasing departments to a corporate procurement center's database. Each division at H-P still makes its own purchasing decisions. However, the corporate procurement office is able to integrate divisional purchasing information in the database to help it negotiate volume discounts for H-P's purchases, thus saving the company millions of dollars each year [20].

How can information technology enable a firm to break structural barriers that inhibit its operations or limit its drive for competitive advantage? Telecommunications networks can support innovations in the delivery of services, increase the scope and penetration of markets, and create strategic alliances with customers, suppliers, and even a firm's competitors. For example, automated teller machines shared by several banks and credit card companies placed in supermarkets and shopping malls break structural barriers between competing firms and expand the market for innovative financial services. Electronic data interchange (EDI) networks can create strategic links between a business and its customers and suppliers. They become "business partners," linked together by the convenience, efficiency, and the cost savings of their EDI network, and prospective customers for new types of services.

Breaking Structural Barriers

For example, Miller Brewing Company is a customer of Reynolds Metals Company and one of Reynolds's EDI business partners. Miller is helping Reynolds reduce the inventory of aluminum coils used at tin can manufacturing plants, and track the quality of aluminum that is received from Reynolds and other suppliers. Reynolds developed software that enables Miller to use its EDI network links to Reynolds to track in-transit inventories, as well as do materials forecasting and ordering and quality control monitoring. Thus, Reynolds's EDI network is helping it develop a new business alliance with one of its biggest customers [25].

Reengineering Business Processes

One of the most popular competitive strategies today is **business process reengineering** (BPR), most often simply called *reengineering.* In Chapter 1, we stressed that reengineering is more than automating business processes to make modest improvements in the efficiency of business operations. We defined reengineering as a fundamental rethinking and radical redesign of business processes to achieve dramatic improvements in cost, quality, speed, and service [17]. So BPR combines a strategy of promoting business innovation with a strategy of making major improvements to business operations so that a company can become a much stronger and more successful competitor in the marketplace. See Figure 9.11.

As Figure 9.11 points out, the potential payback of reengineering is high, but so is its level of risk and disruption to the organizational environment. Making radical changes to business processes to dramatically improve efficiency and effectiveness is not an easy task. While many companies have reported impressive gains, many others have failed to achieve the major improvements they sought through reengineering projects [20, 21]. That's why organizational redesign approaches are an important enabler of reengineering, along with the use of information technology. For example, one common approach is the use of self-directed teams, where managers become coaches and advisors to employees instead of supervisors. Another is the use of *case managers,* who handle almost all tasks in a business process, instead of splitting tasks among many different specialists [16, 17].

The Role of Information Technology

Of course, information technology plays a major role in reengineering business processes. The speed, information processing power, and ease-of-use of modern computer hardware, software, and networks can dramatically increase the efficiency of business processes, and communications and collaboration among the people responsible for their operation and management. For example, the order management process illustrated in Figure 9.12 is vital to the success of most companies. Many of them are reengineering this process with the help of the information technologies listed in Figure 9.13 [9].

FIGURE 9.11

How business process reengineering differs from business improvement.

	Spectrum of Reengineering	
	Business Improvement	**Business Reengineering**
Definition	Incrementally improving existing processes	Radically redesigning business systems
Target	Any process	Strategic business processes
Potential Payback	10%–50% improvements	10-fold improvements
Risk and Level of Disruption	Low	High
What Changes?	Same jobs, just more efficient	Big job cuts; new jobs; major job redesign
Primary Enablers	IT and work simplification	IT and organizational redesign

Source: Adapted from Colleen Frye, "Imaging Proves Catalyst for Reengineering," *Client/Server Computing,* November 1994, p. 54.

FIGURE 9.12

The order management process.

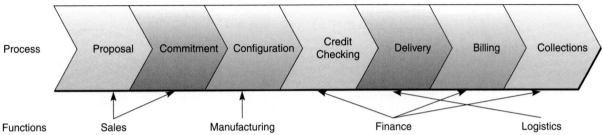

Source: Adapted and reprinted by permission of Harvard Business School Press from *Process Innovation: Reengineering Work through Information Technology* by Thomas H. Davenport (Boston: 1993), p. 248. Copyright © 1993 by Ernst & Young.

IBM Credit Corporation

The IBM Credit Corporation is one of the classic examples of how many companies are employing information technologies to reengineer business processes. IBM Credit reengineered a five-step credit application process that formerly took four specialists an average of more than seven days to complete. Now 55 percent of the credit requests are processed almost instantaneously by computers. The other 45 percent of credit applications are completely handled in one step and no more than four hours by case managers, called deal structurers, assisted by an easy-to-use computer-based credit processing system. In a few really tough cases, deal structurers consult and work as a team with a small group of credit experts. Now IBM Credit can process 100 times more credit requests than they formerly did with the same number of people [16, 17].

Ford Motor Company

Figure 9.14 shows how Ford Motor Company reengineered its procurement process. Procurement involves the purchasing, receiving, and accounts payable activities. Notice that the old process required the transmittal of five paper documents: (1) purchase order from purchasing to the vendor, (2) copy to accounts payable, (3) receiving document to accounts payable, (4) invoice from the vendor to accounts payable, and (5) check in payment from accounts payable to the vendor. More than 500 people in

FIGURE 9.13

Examples of information technologies that support reengineering the sales and order management processes.

- Prospect tracking and management systems.
- Portable sales force automation systems.
- Portable networking for field and customer site communications.
- Customer site workstations for order entry and status checking.
- Expert systems that match products and services to customer needs.
- Electronic data interchange and electronic funds transfer between firms.
- Expert systems for configuration, shipping, and pricing.
- Predictive modeling for continuous product replenishment.
- Composite systems that bring cross-functional information to employee workstations.
- Customer, product, and production databases.

Source: Adapted and reprinted by permission of Harvard Business School Press from *Process Innovation: Reengineering Work through Information Technology* by Thomas H. Davenport (Boston: 1993), p. 247. Copyright © 1993 by Ernst & Young.

FIGURE 9.14

How Ford reengineered its
procurement process.

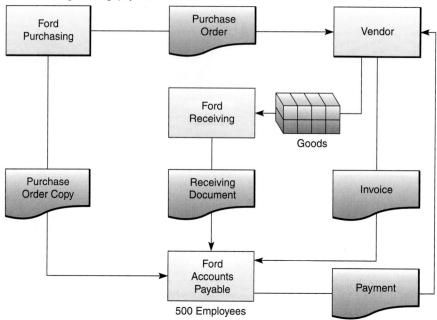

Before Reengineering: pay when invoice received.

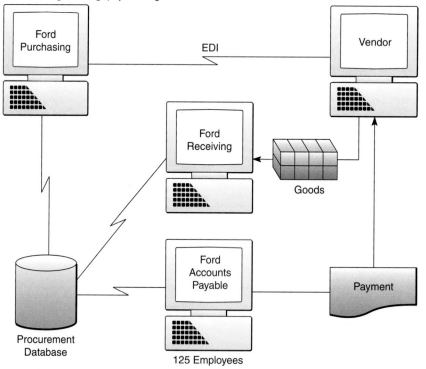

After Reengineering: pay when goods received.

accounts payable processed these documents. Much of this processing involved resolving discrepancies among the documents, especially when the items in the receiving document did not match the items in the purchase order or the vendor's invoice.

Ford reengineered this procurement process with the help of information technology. Instead of waiting to begin the payment process until a vendor sends an invoice, Ford's new system triggers payment when the goods are received. Notice that a check in payment is now the only paper document involved. Now, an electronic purchase order is transmitted by the purchasing department to the vendor using electronic data interchange (EDI). The purchasing department also enters the data into a procurement database. When goods from a vendor arrive at Ford, the receiving department uses their computers to see whether they match the purchase order information in the database. If they do, the database is updated to show that the goods have been accepted. Payment is then sent to the vendor by accounts payable, which now needs only 125 people for the procurement process [16, 17].

CIGNA Corporation, a leading worldwide insurance and financial services company, is our final reengineering example. CIGNA employs 50,000 people in almost 70 countries. Between 1989 and 1993, CIGNA completed more than 20 reengineering projects, saving over $100 million. At CIGNA,

CIGNA Corporation

> reengineering was refocused from excellence in operational business processes to enabling new business growth. Along the way, reengineering has begun to become part of the way that CIGNA employees and managers think. To CIGNA, business reengineering means "break-through innovation focused on customer needs." It is a vehicle to realign strategy, operations, and systems to deliver significantly increased financial results [6].

Thus, reengineering at CIGNA is a strategic business initiative. Figure 9.15 summarizes the objectives and accomplishments of reengineering programs of four major business areas at CIGNA. Major changes in business information systems and the use of information technology were involved in all of the projects. For example, CIGNA reengineered the corporate medical presale process by making major revisions to work activities and manual and computer-based procedures. The company reduced the time to deliver a quote to a customer for corporate medical insurance from 17 days to 3. Fourteen manual hand-offs of work from one person to another were reduced to three all-electronic transfers. See Figure 9.16.

Improving Business Quality

> No single approach to organizational change, including reengineering, is appropriate for all circumstances. Many companies have a portfolio of approaches to operational change including reengineering, continuous [quality] improvement, incremental approaches, and restructuring techniques. Some combine multiple approaches in one initiative—for example, using reengineering for a long-run solution and short-term process improvements in the current process to deliver quick benefit [10].

Thus, information technology can be used strategically to improve business performance in many ways other than in supporting reengineering initiatives. One important strategic thrust is continuous quality improvement, popularly called *total quality management* (TQM). Previous to TQM, quality was defined as meeting established standards or specifications for a product or service. *Statistical quality control* programs were used to measure and correct any deviations from standards [9].

FIGURE 9.15

Objectives and accomplishments of reengineering projects at CIGNA.

Project	Initial Objectives	Accomplishment
CIGNA Re	▪ To dramatically reduce cost and enhance technology infrastructure.	▪ Staff reduced by 50%. ▪ Operating expenses reduced by 42%. ▪ 1,200% transaction time improvement. ▪ Team-based organization. ▪ Systems reduced from 17 mainframe-based systems to five PC-based systems.
CIGNA International Life and Employee Benefits–UK	▪ 30% improvement in cost. ▪ 50% improvement in quality. ▪ 50% improvement in cycle time. ▪ 30% improvement in customer satisfaction. ▪ 14% growth in business.	▪ 30% improvement in cost. ▪ 75% improvement in quality. ▪ 100% improvement in cycle time. ▪ 50% improvement in customer satisfaction.
Global Risk Management	▪ More effective estimate on costs and better pricing of products sold to foreign subsidiaries of U.S. corporations. ▪ Leveraging information and expertise residing at CIGNA's foreign offices.	▪ New products offered to customers. ▪ 25% staff reduction. ▪ $25 million reduction in operating expenses. ▪ Client/server-based system that prices products considering local conditions and local losses.
Property and Casualty Claims Systems	▪ Improved working relationships between claims and systems, especially better communication. ▪ Faster response on systems changes. ▪ Better assessment of the business value of systems changes and new systems projects.	▪ Three organizational layers were flattened. ▪ Team-based organization. ▪ 32% reduction in systems staff. ▪ 63% reduction in reported systems problems. ▪ 100% accuracy on systems fixes. ▪ 43% reduction in systems requests.

Source: Adapted from J. Raymond Caron, Sirkka Jarvenpaa, and Donna Stoddard, "Business Reengineering at CIGNA Corporation: Experiences and Lessons from the First Five Years," *MIS Quarterly*, September 1994, p. 235. Reprinted with permission from the *MIS Quarterly*.

Total Quality Management

Total quality management is a much more strategic approach to business improvement. Quality is emphasized from the customer's viewpoint, rather than the producer's. Thus, quality is defined as meeting or exceeding the requirements and expectations of customers for a product or service. This may involve many features and attributes, such as performance, reliability, durability, responsiveness, aesthetics, and reputation, to name a few [27, 36].

FIGURE 9.16

The results of reengineering the process to deliver an insurance quote to a corporate customer at CIGNA International–United Kingdom.

Corporate Medical Presale Process	
Before Reengineering	**After Reengineering**
▪ Seventeen-day cycle time.	▪ Three-day cycle time.
▪ Fourteen hand-offs—manual	▪ Three hand-offs—all electronic.
▪ Seven authorization steps.	▪ Zero authorization steps.
▪ Six hours of total work.	▪ Three hours of total work.
▪ Four hours of value-added work.	▪ Three hours of value-added work.
▪ Two hours of rework.	▪ Zero hours of rework.

Source: Adapted from J. Raymond Caron, Sirkka Jarvenpaa, and Donna Stoddard, "Business Reengineering at CIGNA Corporation: Experiences and Lessons from the First Five Years," *MIS Quarterly*, September 1994, p. 240. Reprinted with permission from the *MIS Quarterly*.

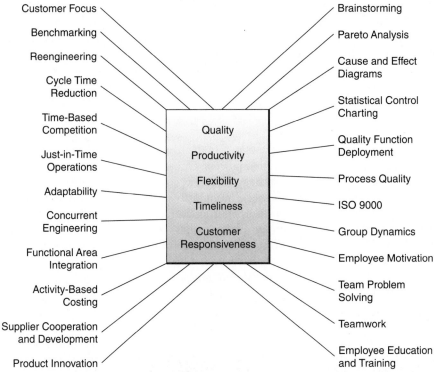

Customer Focus
Benchmarking
Reengineering
Cycle Time Reduction
Time-Based Competition
Just-in-Time Operations
Adaptability
Concurrent Engineering
Functional Area Integration
Activity-Based Costing
Supplier Cooperation and Development
Product Innovation

Quality
Productivity
Flexibility
Timeliness
Customer Responsiveness

Brainstorming
Pareto Analysis
Cause and Effect Diagrams
Statistical Control Charting
Quality Function Deployment
Process Quality
ISO 9000
Group Dynamics
Employee Motivation
Team Problem Solving
Teamwork
Employee Education and Training

FIGURE 9.17

The objectives and methodologies of total quality management.

Source: Adapted and reproduced from C. Carl Pegels, *Total Quality Management: A Survey of Its Important Aspects,* 1995, p. 6, with the permission of boyd & fraser publishing company. Copyright 1995 by boyd & fraser publishing company. All rights reserved.

Total quality management is also a much broader management approach than quality control. As Figure 9.17 illustrates, TQM may use a variety of tools and methods to seek continuous improvement of quality, productivity, flexibility, timeliness, and customer responsiveness. According to quality guru Richard Schonberger, companies that use TQM are committed to:

1. Even better, more appealing, less variable quality of the product or service.
2. Even quicker, less-variable response—from design and development through supplier and sales channels, offices, and plants all the way to the final user.
3. Even greater flexibility in adjusting to customers' shifting volume and mix requirement.
4. Even lower cost through quality improvement, rework reduction, and nonvalue-adding waste elimination [27].

Figure 9.18 summarizes examples of many improvements to business performance attributed by companies to their total quality management programs [27]. Information technology was significantly involved in most of these improvements, along with a variety of organizational, management, and work redesign initiatives. Let's look at a few examples involving information technology in more detail.

AMP Corporation is a leading manufacturer of electrical/electronic connectors and interconnection systems. It has 28,000 employees and operates 180 facilities in 36 countries, with sales approaching $4 billion in 1994. AMP promotes total quality

AMP Corporation

management in many ways, including several global online systems. One system, called Quality Scoreboard, enables over 2,500 managers at all levels to access key performance indicators for internal operations, customers, distributors, suppliers, and competitors. Managers can also view daily quality information about products manufactured or purchased by AMP. Quality Scoreboard can even initiate corrective action by managers. Another system, called Delivery Scoreboard, provides managers with daily shipping and scheduling performance results for the company [5].

Ford Motor Company

Ford is committed to designing quality into their cars, instead of relying on inspection during and after the production process. One key use of information technology that supports this quality strategy is an easy-to-use database of customer and quality information. The database is continuously updated with customer expectations and concerns, and lessons learned from customer feedback. This database is then accessed for information by quality professionals who are involved in the design and development, testing, and manufacturing-planning processes. Ford believes that the customer/quality database is a key element in increasing customer satisfaction. And that is important, since Ford estimates that each one-point gain in owner loyalty is worth $100 million in profit [5].

FIGURE 9.18

Examples of improvements gained through total quality management.

- **AMP.** On-time shipments improved from 65% to 95%, and AMP products have nationwide availability within three days or less on 50% of AMP sales.
- **Asea, Brown, Boveri.** Every improvement goal customers asked for—better delivery, quality responsiveness, and so on—was met.
- **Chrysler.** New vehicles are now being developed in 33 months versus as long as 60 months 10 years ago.
- **Eaton.** Increased sales per employee from $65,000 in 1983 to about $100,000 in 1992.
- **Fidelity.** Handles 200,000 information calls in four telephone centers; 1,200 representatives handle 75,000 calls, and the balance in automated.
- **Ford.** Use of 7.25 man-hours of labor per vehicle versus 15 man-hours in 1980; Ford Taurus bumper used 10 parts compared to 100 parts on similar GM cars.
- **General Motors.** New vehicles are now being developed in 34 months versus 48 months in the 1980s.
- **IBM Rochester.** Defect rates per million are 32 times lower than four years ago and on some products exceed six sigma (3.4 defects per million).
- **Pratt & Whitney.** Defect rate per million was cut in half; a tooling process was shortened from two months to two days; part lead times were reduced by 43%.
- **VF Corp.** Market response system enables 97% in-stock rate for retail stores compared to 70% industry average.
- **NCR.** Checkout terminal was designed in 22 months versus 44 months and contained 85% fewer parts than its predecessor.
- **AT&T.** Redesign of telephone switch computer completed in 18 months versus 36 months; manufacturing defects reduced by 87%.
- **Deere & Co.** Reduced cycle time of some of its products by 60%, saving 30% of usual development costs.

Source: Adapted and reproduced from C. Carl Pegels, *Total Quality Management: A Survey of Its Important Aspects,* 1995, p. 27, with the permission of boyd & fraser publishing company. Copyright 1995 by boyd & fraser publishing company. All rights reserved.

We are changing from a competitive environment in which mass-market products and services were standardized, long-lived, information-poor, and exchanged in one-time transactions, to an environment in which companies compete globally with niche market products and services that are individualized, short-lived, information-rich, and exchanged on an ongoing basis with customers [13].

Agility in competitive performance is the ability of a business to prosper in rapidly changing, continually fragmenting global markets for high-quality, high-performance, customer-configured products and services. An agile company can make a profit in markets with broad product ranges and short model lifetimes, can process orders in arbitrary lot sizes, and can offer individualized products while maintaining high volumes of production. Agile companies depend heavily on information technology to support and manage business processes, while providing the information processing capability to treat masses of customers as individuals [13].

Figure 9.19 illustrates that to be an agile competitor, a business must implement four basic strategies of agile competition. First, customers of an agile company feel enriched by products or services that they perceive as solutions to their individual problems. Thus, products can be priced based on their value as solutions, not on their cost to produce. Second, an agile company cooperates internally and with other companies, even competitors. This allows a business to bring products to market as rapidly and cost-effectively as possible, no matter where resources are located and who owns them. Third, an agile company organizes so that it thrives on change and uncertainty. It uses flexible, multiple organizational structures keyed to the requirements of different and constantly changing customer opportunities. Finally, an agile company leverages the impact of its people

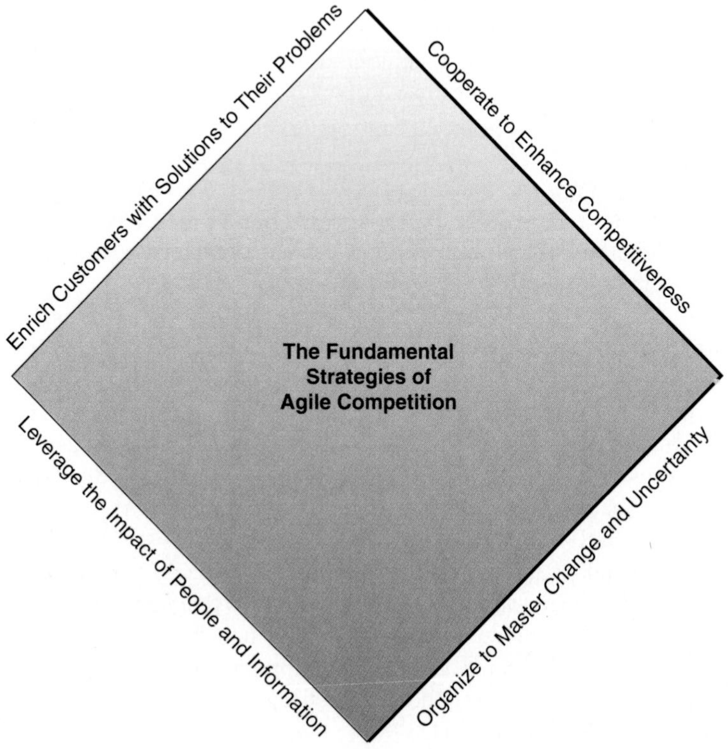

Becoming an Agile Competitor

FIGURE 9.19

The four fundamental strategies of agile competition.

The Fundamental Strategies of Agile Competition

Enrich Customers with Solutions to Their Problems

Cooperate to Enhance Competitiveness

Leverage the Impact of People and Information

Organize to Master Change and Uncertainty

and the information and knowledge that they possess. By nurturing an entrepreneurial spirit, an agile company provides powerful incentives for employee responsibility, adaptability, and innovation [13].

The Role of Information Technology

> The bottleneck to higher levels of performance in an agile company is not equipment but information flow, internally and among cooperating companies. Information is already an increasingly important and increasingly valuable component of consumer and commercial products. Packaging information, providing access to information, and information "tools"—for example, design software and database search software—will become increasingly valuable products in their own right, as well as increasingly valuable elements of hardware products, such as automobiles [13].

So information technology is a strategic requirement for agile product development and delivery. Information systems provide the information that people need to support agile operations, as well as the information built into products and services. Let's take a look at several examples.

Ross Operating Valves

Ross Operating Valves manufactures hydraulic valves in Madison Heights, Michigan; in Lavonia, Georgia; and in Frankfurt, Germany, and Tokyo, Japan. Ross uses a manufacturing system called Ross/Flex at the Lavonia plant. Ross/Flex consists of proprietary computer-aided design (CAD) software and a database of digitized valve designs. Ross/Flex enables valves to be custom-designed jointly by customers and by Ross "integrators"—engineers and skilled machinists. Designs are downloaded to computer-controlled machine tools. Prototypes are completed in one day at a typical cost of $3,000, one-tenth of the previous cost and time.

After the prototype is tested, customers can request changes to produce improved prototypes. When they are satisfied, customers can then approve production of the valves. Since introducing Ross/Flex in 1992 as a free service, business has increased dramatically and Ross has enjoyed extraordinary market success. In 1995, Ross began offering customers the option of remotely accessing its design software and database for a fee. Customers can then design their own valves and download them to Ross computer-controlled machinery for production [1, 13].

Ross/Flex demonstrates the strategic use of information technology to support agile competition. Ross (1) enriches customers with custom-designed solutions, (2) cooperates with them to enhance their own competitiveness, (3) organizes innovatively with teams of integrators who can easily handle changing customer needs, and (4) leverages their people and information resources to produce innovative and profitable business opportunities in a dynamic global market.

Motorola and Toshiba

Motorola manufactures customer-configured cellular pagers to order at its Boynton Beach, Florida, plant. Pagers are assembled, tested, packaged, and shipped using computer-controlled machinery, only hours after receiving the remotely entered customer orders. Motorola also has a built-to-order facility for two-way radios in Plantation, Florida. This plant produces 500 different models. The radios are made to individual customer order in two hours, compared to 10 days as recently as 1990 [13].

Toshiba manufactures more than 20 models of portable computers, each with many different customer-selected options. It assembles them on a single production line in batches of 20 per model, and can still make money on batches as small as 10 computers. At each work point on the production line, a notebook computer provides instructions for assembling the next model, the mix of options for each unit, and the number to be assembled [13].

Motorola and Toshiba both demonstrate the use of information technology to support agile competition. Many different models of products are quickly produced to order for their customers, using computer-controlled or computer-supported production lines. Thus, both companies are able to enrich their customers with products that they want, when they want them. And both are able to do so profitably even when producing small amounts of constantly changing made-to-order products.

Creating a Virtual Company

These days, thousands of companies, large and small, are setting up virtual corporations that enable executives, engineers, scientists, writers, researchers, and other professionals from around the world to collaborate on new products and services without ever meeting face to face. Once the exclusive domain of Fortune 500 companies with banks of powerful computers and dedicated wide area networks, remote networking is now available to any company with a phone, a fax, and E-mail access to the Internet or an online service [30].

In today's dynamic global business environment, forming a **virtual company** can be one of the most important strategic uses of information technology. A virtual company (also called a *virtual corporation* or *virtual organization*) is an organization that uses information technology to link people, assets, and ideas. Figure 9.20 outlines six basic characteristics of successful virtual companies. It emphasizes that to be successful, a virtual company must be an adaptable and opportunity-exploiting organization, providing world-class excellence in its competencies and technologies, which transparently create integrated customer solutions in business relationships based on mutual trust [13].

Figure 9.21 illustrates that a business that forms virtual companies typically uses an organizational structure called a **network structure.** Notice that this company (Firm A) has developed alliances with suppliers, customers, subcontractors, and competitors. Thus the network structure makes it easy to create flexible and adaptable virtual companies keyed to exploit fast-changing business opportunities [7].

Virtual Company Strategies

Why are people forming virtual companies? Several major reasons stand out and are summarized in Figure 9.22. People and corporations are forming virtual companies as the best way to implement key business strategies that promise to ensure success in today's turbulent business climate.

For example, in order to exploit a diverse and fast-changing market opportunity, a business may not have the time or resources to develop the manufacturing and distribution infrastructure, people competencies, and information technologies

- **Adaptability.** Able to adapt to a diverse, fast-changing business environment.
- **Opportunism.** Created, operated, and dissolved to exploit business opportunities when they appear.
- **Excellence.** Possess all-star, world-class excellence in the core competencies that are needed.
- **Technology.** Provide world-class information technology and other required technologies in all customer solutions.
- **Borderless.** Easily and transparently synthesize the competencies and resources of business partners into integrated customer solutions.
- **Trust-Based.** Members are trustworthy and display mutual trust in their business relationships.

FIGURE 9.20

Six basic characteristics of successful virtual companies.

FIGURE 9.21

A network structure facilitates the creation of virtual companies.

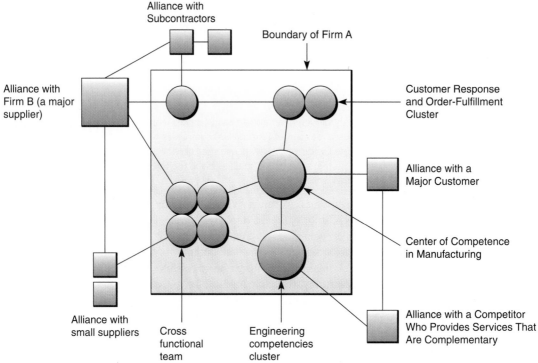

Source: Adapted from James I. Cash, Jr., Robert G. Eccles, Nitin Nohria, and Richard L. Nolan, *Building the Information-Age Organization: Structure, Control, and Information Technologies* (Burr Ridge, IL: Richard D. Irwin, 1994), p. 34.

needed. Only by quickly forming a virtual company of all-star partners can it assemble the components it needs to provide a world-class solution for customers and capture the market opportunity. Of course, computers, telecommunications networks, and other information technologies will be a vital component in creating a successful solution. Let's look at several examples.

Steelcase, Inc.

Steelcase, Inc., is a major U.S. maker of office furniture. It has formed a virtual company called Turnstone as a subsidiary. Turnstone sells office furniture and office products through catalogs designed and printed by a third-party company. Customers of Turnstone phone in credit card orders to a telemarketing company based in Denver, which transmits the order data to computers at warehouses operated by Excel Logistics, Inc., in Westerville, Ohio. From there the products are shipped to customers by Excel, or by another carrier it has hired as a subcontractor. Excel's computer systems handle all order processing, shipment tracking, and inventory control applications. So marketing and financial management and coordinating the virtual company's business partners are the only major functions left to Turnstone's managers [23].

IBM Ambra

IBM's Ambra is a classic example of a virtual company formed to take advantage of a limited market opportunity. Ambra was a virtual company subsidiary of the IBM Corporation, formed by IBM to produce and market a PC clone. Ambra's headquarters was in Raleigh, North Carolina. There 80 employees used global

- Share infrastructure and risk.
- Link complementary core competencies.
- Reduce concept-to-cash time through sharing.
- Increase facilities and market coverage.
- Gain access to new markets and share market or customer loyalty.
- Migrate from selling products to selling solutions.

FIGURE 9.22
Business strategies of virtual companies.

telecommunications networks to coordinate the activities of five companies that were the other business partners that made up the virtual company.

This included Wearnes Technology of Singapore, which did engineering design and subsystem development services, and manufactured or contracted for the Ambra PC components. SCI Systems manufactured the Ambra microcomputers in its assembly plants on a build-to-order basis from order data received by its computers from AI Incorporated. AI, a subsidiary of Insight Direct, a national telemarketing company based in Tempe, Arizona, received orders for Ambra computers from customers over its 800-number telephone lines. Merisel Enterprises provided the product and delivery database used by AI, and handled Ambra order fulfillment and customer delivery. Finally, another IBM subsidiary provided field service and customer support [13].

> Companies will continue to use the Internet as a marketing channel—a place to publish information about themselves and their products—as well as to communicate with customers and business partners. But the Internet is capable of far more. Viewing the 'net merely as a gigantic bulletin board or electronic-mail system badly misses the point. With its extraordinary scope and growth, this global network of networks' true future will be to support distributed applications across companies and geographic boundaries [3].

Connecting to the Internet is one of the fastest growing and most popular ways that companies are trying to create strategic business applications of information technology. Figure 9.23 illustrates some of the present and potential business uses of the Internet. Notice that customers, suppliers, business partners, as well as the company headquarters and remote employee sites can be interconnected by the Internet.

Many businesses, both large and small, are viewing the Internet as a way to create strategic collaboration, operations, marketing, and alliances. These major **strategic business uses of the Internet** are summarized in Figure 9.24. Companies are using the global E-mail, bulletin board, file transfer, and remote computing capabilities of the Internet to support concurrent realtime collaboration among employees and business partners. This enables strategic gains to be made in the efficiency of business processes for developing, producing, marketing, or maintaining products and services. These same capabilities are fostering the growth of strategic alliances, including virtual companies, among business partners.

Many companies are dedicating servers to handle the hypermedia databases and information products they are developing as home pages on the Internet's World Wide Web. This, typically, includes hyperlinked multimedia catalogs and promotional materials about a company's products and services that can be browsed using point-and-click browsing software like Mosaic or Netscape. Finally, some companies have begun to do online transaction processing on the Internet. This may involve electronic data interchange (EDI) between businesses and their

Using the Internet

Strategic Business Uses

FIGURE 9.23

Using the Internet for business.

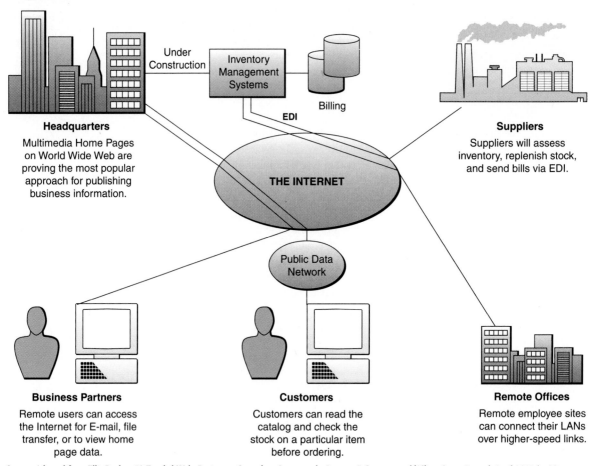

Source: Adapted from Ellis Booker, "A Tangled Web: Businesses Struggle to Leverage the Internet," *Computerworld/Client Server Journal,* April 1995, p. 19. Copyright 1995 by Computerworld, Inc., Framingham, MA 01701—Reprinted from *Computerworld.*

suppliers, or electronic funds transfer (EFT) between businesses and their customers. However, the Internet lacks sufficient security, such as widespread use of secure servers and browsers, standard authorization techniques, and encryption of all monetary transactions. Once security is assured, the use of the Internet for online transaction processing should grow dramatically [3, 34]. See Figure 9.25.

GE and Sun Microsystems

General Electric Co. has established home pages on the Internet for its GE Plastics and GE Capital Services subsidiaries. The GE Plastics home page contains more than 1,500 pages of data and photos, between 35 and 50 megabytes of data. One of the main benefits of GE's home pages is to reduce the need for customers to call the GE help desk's 800-number, which receives over 80,000 calls yearly. GE hopes its home pages will strengthen its relationships with customers, while significantly cutting its phone bills and help desk costs [3].

Sun Microsystems External Home Page is one of the most popular World Wide Web sites on the Internet. It has received over 50,000 accesses ("hits") from Internet users per month. Sun's External Home Page has 15 buttons hyperlinking customers,

- **Strategic Collaboration.** Realtime global communications and collaboration among employees and business partners to develop, produce, market, and maintain products and services.

- **Strategic Operations.** Global links to customers and suppliers using online ordering systems and electronic data interchange.

- **Strategic Marketing.** Promoting a company and its products and services by developing a variety of hyperlinked multimedia databases and information products for access by businesses and consumers.

- **Strategic Alliances.** Online global links to business partners. Electronic networking among the members of virtual companies.

FIGURE 9.24

Strategic business uses of the Internet.

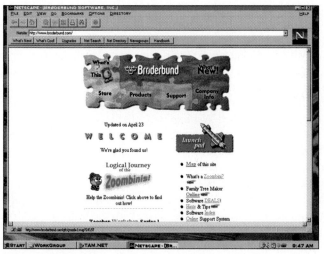

Courtesy of Brøderbund.

FIGURE 9.25

The Brøderbund and Sprint home pages on the Internet's World Wide Web.

Courtesy of Sprint.

employees, and other users to everything from organizational maps to daily electronic news feeds. Because the External Home Page was so popular with its own employees, Sun has developed a home page for internal use by its staff. Called Sun-Web, this intranet site is expected to improve communications and collaboration among Sun's employees worldwide [4].

Digital Equipment Corporation and IBM

Like other major corporations, Digital Equipment Corporation (DEC) and IBM, both leading computer manufacturers, make heavy use of the Internet. This includes sending and receiving thousands of E-mail messages daily, and providing standard and multimedia company or product information on servers. They also provide press releases, E-mail directories, and financial data. In addition, Digital has successfully used the remote computing capability of the Internet (Telenet) as a new way to market some of its computers. For example, Digital connected two models of its latest high-performance Alpha computers to the Internet. It then invited Internet users to "test drive" the systems remotely using their own software to operate the machines. Several thousand potential customers logged on to the machines in six months. This resulted in sales of Alpha computers worth over $5 million to customers who had tried them on the Internet [34].

IBM includes an Internet Access Kit with its OS/2 Warp operating system. It nurtures its relationship with OS/2 Warp users by providing easy access and 10 free hours on the IBM Global Network, also known as Advantis, and a World Wide Web point-and-click browser called WebExplorer. IBM has developed an extensive home page Web Site called the IBM Internet Connection. Employees of IBM exchange over 30,000 Internet E-mail messages a day with outsiders. IBM engineers also use the Internet to collaborate with other companies in joint product development. For example, software engineers in Hawthorne, New York, use the Internet to collaborate with developers at Bellcore in New Jersey. They use Telenet to work on high performance workstations at Bellcore that they share with the Bellcore researchers [24, 34].

The Challenges of Strategic IS

As we have seen in this chapter, the strategic use of information technology enables managers to look at information systems in a new light. No longer is the information systems function merely an operations necessity; that is, a set of technologies for processing business transactions, supporting business processes, and keeping the books of a firm. It is also more than a helpful supplier of information and tools for managerial decision making. Now the IS function can help managers develop competitive weapons that use information technology to implement a variety of competitive strategies to meet the challenges of the competitive forces that confront any organization. However, this is easier said than done.

> We have learned over the past decade that it is not *the technology* that creates a competitive edge, *but the management process that exploits technology;* that there are not instant solutions, only difficult, lengthy, expensive implementations that involve organizational, technical, and market-related risk; and that competitive advantage comes from doing something others cannot match. If technology magically created competitive advantage for everyone, then there would effectively be no competitive edge for anyone. If innovation were easy, everyone would be an innovator. It is not easy, as evidenced by the many barriers to transforming IT from a problem to an opportunity. Among these barriers are the troubled history of IT in large organizations, particularly the limitations of the business management process; the culture gap between business and IS people; the rapid pace of technological change; and the immense and persistent difficulties associated with trying to integrate the many incompatible components of IT into a corporate platform [20].

So successful strategic information systems are not easy to develop and implement, as Figure 9.26 illustrates. They may require major changes in the way a business operates, and in their relationships with customers, suppliers, competitors, and others. The competitive advantages that information technology produces can quickly fade away if competitors can easily duplicate them, and the failure of strategic systems can seriously damage a firm's performance. Many of the examples and cases in this chapter and text demonstrate the challenges and problems as well as the benefits of the strategic uses of information technology. Thus, the effective use of strategic information systems presents managers with a major managerial challenge.

Sustaining Strategic Success

Figure 9.27 illustrates some of the factors that contribute to the success and sustainability of strategic information systems. Sustained success in using information technology strategically seems to depend on three sets of factors [21, 22].

- **The Environment.** A major environmental factor is the structure of an industry. For example, is it *oligopolistic,* that is, a closed structure with a few major players; or is it a wide open and level competitive playing field? Competitive restrictions and unique situations are environmental factors

FIGURE 9.26

Examples of the success and failure of strategic information systems.

Initiative	Strategic Success: Automated Teller Machines	Strategic Failure: Home Banking
Stimulus	Cost structures of branches; pressure on margins	Successes of ATMs and corporate cash management systems; perceived large market of personal computer users
First Major Mover(s)	Citibank (1976)	Chemical Bank (Pronto system) (1980)
Customer Acceptance	Rapid and consistent; convenience the draw	Minimal; no player in United States or Europe ever established a critical mass of customers. Many entrants to the market dropped out, as did Chemical, in 1989.
Catch-up Moves	"Shared access" networks (Cirrus, Monec); bank-specific networks; regional bank joint ventures	Mainly small-scale pilots and market tests; 19 American banks entered and abandoned the market, 1984–1989
First-Mover Expansion	Expanded locations in New York and other states; kept other banks from adding their ATM cards to the Citibank electronic franchise	Pronto abandoned in 1989
Commoditization	Strategic necessity by 1982. Almost every bank in the United States began offering ATM services.	Already complete, even before the market is established. No unique delivery base. Fifteen banks in 1990 were offering services through the Prodigy personal computer-based system. Still no evidence of a real market.
Comments	Highlights dilemma of cooperate versus compete. Consumer pressures for shared access plus operating cost of own networks forced expensive retrofit of systems. Cooperation earlier would have been cheaper for many.	The classic instance of the unmet potential: no technology blockages, but no self-justifying benefits seen by target customers

Source: Adapted and reprinted by permission of Harvard Business School Press from *Shaping the Future: Business Design through Information Technology* by Peter G. W. Keen. Boston: 1993, p. 248. Copyright © 1993 by Peter G. W. Keen.

FIGURE 9.27

Key factors for sustaining strategic success in the use of information technology.

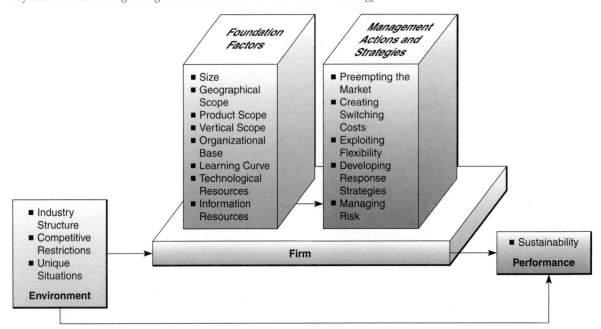

Source: Adapted from William Kettinger, Varun Grover, Subashish Guha, and Albert Segars, "Strategic Information Systems Revisited: A Study in Sustainability and Performance," *MIS Quarterly*, March 1994, p. 34. Reprinted with permission from the *MIS Quarterly*.

that involve political and regulatory restrictions to wide-open competition. For example, antitrust laws, patents, and government intervention can derail a company's plans for a preemptive business use of IT.

- **Foundation Factors.** Unique industry position, alliance, assets, technological resources, and expertise are foundation factors that can give a company a competitive edge in a market. If such a company develops a strategic business use of IT, they have a winning combination for strategic success.

- **Management Actions and Strategies.** None of the other factors mentioned will ensure success if a company's management does not develop and initiate successful actions and strategies that shape how information technology is actually applied in the marketplace. Examples include (1) preempting the market by being first and way ahead of competitors in a strategic business use of IT, (2) creating switching costs and barriers to entry, (3) developing strategies to respond to the catch-up moves of competitors, and (4) managing the business risks inherent in any strategic IT initiatives.

Figure 9.28 provides an overview of recent research findings on companies that are winners and losers in terms of their strategic use of information technology [21]. Sustained winners include Air Products and Chemicals, American Airlines, Bergen Brunswig, DEC, Toys 'Я' Us, and Federal Express. These companies' investment in a specific strategic use of information technology continued to improve both their profitability and market share from 5 to 10 years after launching their strategic information systems. Sustained losers like Chase Manhattan, Mellon Bank, and United Airlines continued to suffer losses in profitability and market share for 5 to 10 years

FIGURE 9.28

Winners and losers in sustaining strategic advantage with IT. Sustained winners increased profits and market share for at least 5 to 10 years by strategic uses of information technology.

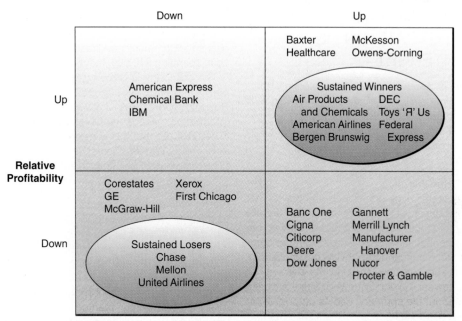

Source: Adapted from William Kettinger, Varun Grover, and Albert Segars, "Do Strategic Systems Really Pay Off? An Analysis of Classic Strategic IT Cases," *Information Systems Management* (New York: Auerbach Publications), Winter 1995, p. 39. © 1995 Warren, Gorham & Lamont. Used with permission.

after making specific attempts to use IT strategically. As you can see, other companies had mixed success since they could not sustain profitability and market share for up to five years after introducing their strategic information systems.

So the lesson is clear. Sustained success in the strategic use of information technology is not a sure thing. Success depends on many environmental and foundation factors, but also on the actions and strategies of a company's management team. As a future manager, developing strategic business uses of information technology may be one of your biggest managerial challenges.

COLUMBIA SPORTSWEAR, DEALERNET, AND ALASKA AIRLINES: STRATEGIC USE OF THE INTERNET

Free enterprise is discovering that for a relatively small investment of time and capital, global reach is now a computer and modem away. Forward-thinking companies are finding a new world of strategic potential and business opportunity via the Internet and the World Wide Web.

Columbia Sportswear

If Gert Boyle seems like one tough mother in her Columbia Sportswear advertisements, she's equally imposing in cyberspace. Her reading glasses low on her nose, Boyle flicks that same critical gaze from the computer screen at the command http://www.columbia.com. Click on Boyle and you pass through the gateway to Columbia Sportswear's World Wide Web site—a wealth of information about the company and its outdoor-wear products. Welcome to the Mothernet, the screen reads.

It's an image thing. Boyle's mug appears on many of the Web site's pages, reinforcing the Mother Knows Best marketing concept that Columbia has branded among the sports conscious. A series of mouse clicks might take you to Mom's Favorite of the Month, perhaps the Hoodoo Parka with technical descriptions of fabrics and construction methods. Type in your zip code and you get a list of dealers in your area that carry the Columbia line. You leave the Columbia Web site knowing everything you'd ever want to know about its products—and the feeling that maybe Boyle really does know best.

"The benefit for our company," say Columbia's Jon Alder, "is the ability to generate two-way communication with millions of our customers. I know that doesn't sound like much, but what could possibly be more important than providing a tool that allows us to communicate better? The cost has been quite low. Our intent is to take this slowly. From a business point of view our investment has been minimal."

DealerNet

Marty Rood, on the other hand, knows cars. Load up the DealerNet home page (http://www.dealernet.com) and you find a photo of a sedan speeding down a country highway. Click on the photo and you're taken to a colorful index with graphic links to resources that will help you choose a new car, locate a dealer, and even start down the road toward a purchase. Rood, a Seattle car dealer, gave up his profitable Lynnwood, Washington, Nissan-Volvo dealership to create the first Virtual Showroom on the Web, which now gives 320 dealers nationwide a chance to communicate directly with consumers interested in spending $10,000, maybe $50,000, on a new car.

The company is growing by about 30 auto dealers per month and was acquired last year by Reynolds + Reynolds Corp. (http://www.reyrey.com), a leader in information management systems for the auto industry. "They realized that this is where auto retailing is going," says Peter Wilson, DealerNet's operations manager. "They purchased us because we were the leader."

Alaska Airlines

Alaska Airlines recently became the nation's first carrier to offer its clients the opportunity to research, book, and pay for travel over the Internet.

The airline's new World Wide Web site (http://www.alaskaair.com) is "a truly unique vehicle for marketing and selling because it puts our product at the fingertips of customers—any time of the day or night," says Bill Ayer, vice president of marketing and planning. The system provides users side-by-side comparisons of all the flights of Alaska Airlines, and its sister carrier Horizon Air, as well as the times and lowest available fares in the markets they plan to fly, on the days they want to fly.

Customers may book flights, purchase tickets with a credit card, secure seat assignments, and be confirmed through the Web site with the airlines' ticketless Instant Travel option. Customers can also make a booking and hold it for 24 hours, and purchase the tickets later by phoning the airline or visiting a travel agent. Mileage Plan members use the system to redeem frequent flyer awards and check on their mileage accounts.

"We surveyed our frequent flyers and nearly half said they wanted the convenience of making travel plans on their home or office computers," Ayer says.

CASE STUDY QUESTIONS

1. Do you think the companies in this case are using the Internet strategically? Refer to Figure 9.24 to help you explain your answer.

2. What competitive IT strategies do you recognize being implemented by each of the companies in this case? Refer to Figure 9.5 to help you explain your choices.

3. How could other types of businesses use similar Internet strategies? Give several examples.

Source: Adapted from Don Campbell, "Working the Web," *Alaska Airlines Magazine,* March 1996, pp. 27–29.

Summary

- **The Role of Strategic Information Systems.** Information systems can play several strategic roles in businesses. They can help a business improve its operations, promote innovation, lock in customers and suppliers, create switching costs, raise barriers to entry, build a strategic IT platform, and develop a strategic information base. Thus, information technology can help a business gain a competitive advantage in its relationships with customers, suppliers, competitors, new entrants, and producers of substitute products. Refer to Figure 9.4 for a summary of the uses of information technology for strategic advantage.

- **Breaking Business Barriers.** Information technology can break traditional barriers to strategic business success. This includes time and geographic barriers broken by the speed and reach of global telecommunications networks. Information technology can also break cost barriers by significantly increasing the efficiency of business operations, and structural barriers by electronically linking a business to its customers, suppliers, and business partners.

- **Reengineering Business Processes.** Information technology is a key ingredient in reengineering business operations by enabling radical changes to business processes that dramatically improve their efficiency and effectiveness. IT can play a major role in supporting innovative changes in the design of work flows, job requirements, and organizational structures in a company.

- **Improving Business Quality.** Information technology can be used to strategically improve the quality of business performance. In a total quality management approach, IT can support programs of continual improvement in meeting or exceeding customer requirements and expectations in quality, services, cost, responsiveness, and other features that have a significant impact on a firm's competitive position.

- **Becoming an Agile Competitor.** A business can use information technology to help it become an agile company. Then it can prosper in rapidly changing markets with broad product ranges and short model lifetimes in which it must process orders in arbitrary lot sizes, and can offer individualized products while maintaining high volumes of production. An agile company depends heavily on IT to help it: (1) enrich its customers with customized solutions to their needs, (2) cooperate with other businesses to bring products to market as rapidly and cost-effectively as possible, (3) coordinate the flexible, multiple organizational structures it uses, and (4) leverage the competitive impact of its people and information resources.

- **Creating a Virtual Company.** Forming virtual companies has become an important competitive strategy in today's dynamic global markets. Information technology plays an important role in providing computing and telecommunications resources to support the communications, coordination, and information flows needed. Managers of a virtual company depend on IT to help them manage a network of people, knowledge, financial, and physical resources provided by many business partners to quickly take advantage of rapidly changing market opportunities.

- **Using the Internet.** Connecting to the Internet has become a key strategy for businesses seeking quick access to new markets. The Internet promises to be an attractive and cost-effective way for many companies to develop the strategic collaboration, operations, marketing, and alliances needed to solve and succeed in today's fast-changing global markets. Computing, telecommunications, and other information technologies are a necessary foundation for companies planning to implement such competitive strategies.

- **The Challenges of Strategic IS.** Successful strategic information systems are not easy to develop and implement. They may require major changes in how a business operates internally and with external stakeholders. Sustained success depends on many environmental and fundamental business factors, and especially on the actions and strategies of a company's management team. So developing strategic uses of information technology is a major managerial challenge.

Key Terms and Concepts

These are the key terms and concepts of this chapter. The page number of their first explanation is in parentheses.

1. Agile competitor (355)
2. Breaking business barriers (344)
   a. Cost barriers (347)
   b. Geographic barriers (346)
   c. Structural barriers (347)
   d. Time barriers (345)
3. Building a strategic IT platform (340)
4. Business process reengineering (348)
5. Competitive forces (335)
6. Competitive strategies (335)
7. Creating switching costs (339)
8. Developing a strategic information base (340)
9. Improving business operations (336)
10. Interorganizational information systems (339)
11. Leveraging investment in IT (340)
12. Locking in customers and suppliers (338)
13. Promoting business innovation (338)
14. Raising barriers to entry (339)

15. Strategic business use of the Internet (359)

16. Strategic information systems (334)

17. Strategic roles of information systems (336)

18. Total quality management (352)

19. Value chain (340)

20. Virtual company (357)

Review Quiz

Match one of the key terms and concepts listed above with one of the brief examples or definitions listed below. Try to find the best fit for answers that seem to fit more than one term or concept. Defend your choices.

_____ 1. A business must deal with customers, suppliers, competitors, new entrants, and substitutes.

_____ 2. Cost leadership, differentiation of products, and development of new products are examples.

_____ 3. Using investment in technology to keep firms out of an industry.

_____ 4. Making it unattractive for a firm's customers or suppliers to switch to its competitors.

_____ 5. Time, money, and effort needed for customers or suppliers to change to a firm's competitors.

_____ 6. Information systems that improve operational efficiency or promote business innovation are examples.

_____ 7. Information systems can help a business develop new products, services, and processes.

_____ 8. Information systems can help a business significantly reduce costs and improve productivity.

_____ 9. Information systems can help a business develop a strategic base of information.

_____ 10. A business can develop strategic capabilities in IT skills and resources.

_____ 11. Information systems can help a business develop electronic links to its customers and suppliers.

_____ 12. Highlights how strategic information systems can be applied to a firm's basic activities for competitive advantage.

_____ 13. A business can find strategic uses for the computing and telecommunications capabilities it has acquired to run its operations.

_____ 14. A business can use information systems to build barriers to entry, promote innovation, create switching costs, and so on.

_____ 15. A business can use information technology to develop low-cost ways to build close, convenient business relationships with global customers.

_____ 16. Information technology can help a business make radical improvements in business processes.

_____ 17. Programs of continual improvement in meeting or exceeding customer requirements or expectations.

_____ 18. A business can prosper in rapidly changing markets while offering its customers individualized solutions to their needs.

_____ 19. A network of business partners formed to take advantage of rapidly changing market opportunities.

_____ 20. Companies hope to use the Internet to gain a competitive advantage in their industry or in new markets.

Discussion Questions

1. Suppose you are a manager being pushed to use information technology to gain a competitive advantage in an important market for your company. What reservations might you have about doing so? Why?

2. How could a business use information technology to increase switching costs and lock in its customers and suppliers? Use business examples to support your answers.

3. How could a business leverage its investment in information technology to build a strategic IT platform that serves as a barrier to entry by new entrants into its markets?

4. Refer to the Real World Case on Royal Bank, C.R. England, and USAA in the chapter. How can aggressive use of information technology and setting outrageous objectives lead to breakthroughs in the strategic use of IT? Give several examples.

5. What strategic role can information technology play in business process reengineering and total quality management?

6. Will the rapid growth in business activity and business use of the Internet have a strategic impact on many companies? Explain.

7. How could a business use the Internet strategically? Be sure to include the concepts of breaking business barriers, forming a virtual company, and becoming an agile competitor in your answer.

8. Refer to the Real World Case on Columbia Sportswear, DealerNet, and Alaska Airlines in the chapter. Why could using the Internet to communicate better with customers be a strategic use of IT?

9. "Information Technology can't really give a company a strategic advantage, because most competitive advantages don't last more than a few years and soon become strategic necessities that just raise the stakes of the game." Discuss.

10. MIS author and consultant Peter Keen says: "We have learned over the past decade that it is not technology that creates a competitive edge, but the management process that exploits technology." What does he mean? Do you agree or disagree? Why?

Real World Problems

1. Aetna and Prudential: Competing with the Internet and Reengineering

"Don't think of us as some old, stodgy insurance company that's been around for over 150 years. We want to break that mold, cut loose, and have some fun." That statement, emblazoned on the home page of Aetna Life and Casualty's World Wide Web site, is the message nearly every insurance company is trying to convey these days. Actually, they don't have much choice. Mutual funds companies, banks, brokerages, and other competitors have been snatching insurers' customers for the better part of the past decade. That's why market leaders such as Aetna and The Prudential Insurance Company of America are leaning heavily on data warehousing, Internet services, business process reengineering, and other leading-edge information systems strategies to bring them closer to their customers.

More than 120 insurance companies worldwide have launched Web sites since 1994. The majority offer little more than advertising and marketing. To take a look at some of the more innovative sites, check out these Web addresses:

- http://www2.pcy.md.net/marketplace/aetna/
- http://www.spectra.net/mall/aig/
- http://www.itthartford.com
- http://www.prudential.com/
- http://www.massmutual.com/

Prudential is a good example of the business process reengineering taking place in the insurance industry. Prudential has instituted its Gibraltar project, an automated application process that focuses on the firm's midlevel insurance customers. Those clients, who fall into the $5,000 to $50,000 insurance policy range, represent 23 percent of the 500,000 policies Prudential wrote last year.

In the past, Prudential's 14,000 customer agents would spend up to an hour filling out a 10- to 12-page application on each prospect. The process was further hindered by Prudential's bureaucratic setup, in which customer applications were passed among a multitude of departments over a four- to six-week period before a policy was written, said Ernie Testa, vice president of underwriting at Prudential's South Plainfield, New Jersey, office.

Today, case managers gather all the customer information over the phone and enter it simultaneously into an event-driven, IBM OS/2 application. That frees up Prudential's agents to focus on selling products. The insurer can now generate an insurance policy—from start to finish—in about five days instead of several weeks, Testa said.

a. Why are insurance companies like Aetna using the Internet? Check out several Web sites as examples of what Aetna and others are doing.

b. Is Prudential's use of business process reengineering a strategic use of IT? Explain.

Source: Adapted from Thomas Hoffman, "Getting a Piece of the Web," *Computerworld*, March 4, 1996, pp. 1, 28. Copyright © 1996 by Computerworld, Inc., Framingham, MA 01701—Reprinted from *Computerworld*.

2. Ryder and Union Pacific: Using IT to Compete for Customers

Union Pacific Corp. employees have a Watchdog that tells them which train is carrying a customer's cargo. And at Ryder Systems, Inc., SAM's the "man" that helps district managers keep truck fleets in top profit-producing trim. After railroad deregulation in the mid-1980s, customer service and asset management shot to No. 1 on rail firms' priority lists. And truckers are similarly revamping procedures in the field and in the corporate office. The competitive pressures for both are high. Now more than ever, manufacturers and major grocery store chains are selecting providers that can meet tight, fast-changing schedules at the lowest cost.

Ryder

Ryder is a case in point. It has taken a decidedly strategic approach to managing its fleet of 200,000 vehicles used to deliver manufacturing products and consumer goods. The $5 billion company, famous for renting yellow moving vans to consumers, is primarily in the logistics business. No wonder, then, that asset management is considered a core competency. And no wonder SAM, which stands for simplified asset management, was the first client/server application to be rolled out over the Miami-based company's new $27 million frame-relay network.

The system, which was implemented late last year, is intended to help Ryder's 75 district managers get the most performance from each truck at the lowest cost and to manage the purchase, maintenance, fueling, and sale of vehicles that Ryder owns or leases to customers. By using their PCs or laptops to access a database on a local IBM RS/6000 or Novell NetWare server, managers can see the cost per mile to operate a particular truck or the total lifetime maintenance costs. Managers can compare truck performance within their fleet to determine best use—for lighter freight or shorter trips, for instance. If they need to get an enterprisewide comparison, they can access similar data from all 75 districts that are consolidated and stored on a DB2 database residing on an IBM 3090 mainframe.

Union Pacific

Union Pacific Corp. has centralized customer service. If a customer calls about shipment location, service representatives turn to Watchdog, an application using an Oracle relational database that contains customer records and the location of each train. Train locations are monitored using PC-like devices called automatic equipment identification readers that are mounted along the track, said Lynden Tennison, assistant vice president of information systems development.

The readers send out a radio signal that scans tags affixed to each car. This information is sent to a Tandem Computer processor via dial-up circuits. Using custom-built interfaces, the location of the train is routed back to the mainframe, which updates the Oracle database. When the shipments encounter delays, customers can be notified promptly to discuss alternatives that might mitigate the problem, Tennison said.

a. Is Ryder's asset management system a strategic use of IT? How about Union Pacific's customer service system? Explain your answers.
b. How could other types of businesses use similar strategies? Give several examples.

Source: Adapted from Candee Wilde, "Trains, Trucks, & Bucks," *Computerworld/Client Server Journal*, February 1996, pp. 38–40. Copyright © 1996 by Computerworld, Inc., Framingham, MA 01701—Reprinted from *Computerworld*.

3. Showtime and Sears: Reengineering Accounting and Finance

Reengineering has come to the accounting and finance functions and none too soon. Reengineering is affecting many areas of these functions. Accounts payable, accounts receivable, general ledger, and financial reporting are among the areas that may be targeted for reengineering. The desire to cut costs and save money aren't the only factors driving the trend. Globalization and the need for all parts of an organization to work together are bringing reengineering to some companies.

Showtime Networks., Inc., began reengineering its finance department three years ago. "There were such convoluted work flows and business processes, remnants of an age gone by, we decided it's time to really step back and rethink this," says Thomas Espeland, senior vice president of information services and technology at the New York–based cable TV programmer.

Sears, Roebuck and Co. in Hoffman Estates, Illinois, reengineered its budget-creation process. Managers of the financial department and other managers created budgeting standards for travel, supplies, and other expenses. The budgeting process, which used to take weeks, was cut to a few hours in many cases, says Steve Beitler, national manager for financial processes and systems at Sears.

Espeland says accounting and finance people are less forgiving of errors, such as those in software programming, than others because a company's books must be highly accurate. Beitler notes there are complications particular to accounting because it has "many more internal customers" than other functions in an organization. Changes in accounting systems ripple through the entire company. So both the risks and rewards in costs, quality, and efficiency in reengineering accounting and finance can have a strategic impact on a company.

a. Why are finance and accounting systems good candidates for business process reengineering?
b. What problems might arise in a BPR project in finance or accounting? How would you solve such problems?

Source: Adapted from Alan Horowitz, "Bean Zapping," *Computerworld*, April 22, 1996, p. 72. Copyright © 1996 by Computerworld, Inc., Framingham, MA 01701—Reprinted from *Computerworld*.

4. Banc One, Warner Bros., and United Video: Making Money on the Net

Having trouble cost-justifying an Internet-based electronic commerce project? Consider these signs of success.

- **Banc One Corp.** in Columbus, Ohio, invested several hundred thousand dollars last year to support an electronic data interchange-based service that corporate and academic libraries use to order publications (http://www.rowe.com). As the automated clearinghouse for the service, Banc One expects to bring in enough transaction revenue to break even this year and "make a few million dollars in the near future," said Steve Dieringer, group product manager of electronic services at the bank.

- **Warner Bros. Online,** which launched its World Wide Web site last fall (http://www.warnerbros.com), invested "tens of millions of dollars" for all the necessary hardware, software, and personnel to support Internet-based product sales from its Warner Bros. Studio Store, said James A. Banister, vice president of production and technology at the Burbank, California–based firm. Banister said he expects the venture to become profitable by year's end.

- **United Video Satellite Group,** which provides the Prevue channel on cable television, recently launched an Internet service that replaces fax-based communications with 3,000 cable network affiliates to post their pay-per-view events. It took United Video just one week to develop the system, said Brian Boyd, director of Internet services at the Tulsa, Oklahoma–based firm. Because the Internet infrastructure was already in place, company officials expect United Video to recoup its project investment through labor and other cost savings within 12 months.

Industry gurus back these claims. Gay Slesinger, an analyst at Giga Information Group, said Sun Microsystems had $12 million in product sales via the Internet last year and saved $1 million in customer support costs. Despite fears that Internet-based electronic commerce isn't secure, it is already a lucrative industry—and one that is expected to take off. The value of goods and services sold over the Internet last year was placed at $72 million, Slesinger said. The market could reach $200 billion by the year 2000 and $1 trillion by 2010, she added.

But even the early winners are complaining about ongoing technical challenges. Because busy signals are so common to end users attempting to access the Web, the Internet "won't be a good distribution network" for widespread sales of products and services until it achieves the same kind of reliability available with television programming, Banister said. Banister said he doesn't expect the Internet to reach that kind of reliability for another two to five years.

a. Why do you think the companies in this case have been successful in reaching profitability on the Internet?

b. What must occur before business profitability becomes commonplace on the Internet? Explain your answer.

Source: Adapted from Thomas Hoffman, "Net Worth," *Computerworld*, May 13, 1996, p. 69. Copyright © 1996 by Computerworld, Inc., Framingham, MA 01701—Reprinted from *Computerworld*.

Application Exercises

1. Strategic Marketing Information System for Action Products

Action Products is considering the development of a strategic marketing information system. The proposed system would use customer information gathered each time a sale is made to target mailings to those customers most likely to purchase particular product lines. The new system is expected to increase sales by improving market penetration. Because of the speculative nature of the system's benefits, only the first four years of operation are to be considered in evaluating its profitability.

The information systems department estimates that the system would cost $200,000 for initial development, to be completed in one year. Once the system becomes operational, its maintenance is expected to require $30,000 per year.

The best estimate of the impact of the system on sales is that it would increase sales from their current projected levels by 5 percent in the first year of operation and by 7.5 percent for the second, third, and fourth years of operation. The level of sales for products affected by this system is currently $18,500,000 and sales are expected to remain constant through the projection period unless the new system is developed. The marginal contribution of a dollar of sales to profits is 30 percent.

a. Based on these figures, construct a spreadsheet that displays all of the important elements of the costs and benefits of the proposed system. Your spreadsheet should include a row or column showing the net contribution of the system to Action Products' profits during the development year and each of the four years of operation.

b. Assume that Action Products requires a return on investment of at least 25 percent for this type of investment. Add a net present value calculation to your spreadsheet and determine whether this project would be justified.

c. If you have a spreadsheet with a goal-seeking function, find the level of initial development cost for the system that would produce a net present value of zero in question *b*, assuming that all other parameters remain unchanged.

d. Write a report summarizing your results and including a recommendation about the proposed system.

2. ABC Company Purchasing System

The information system that ABC Company uses for purchasing is substantially outdated. Inadequacies of the system require Purchasing Department employees to make numerous manual calculations and to call vendors to accommodate standard requests that could be generated automatically by a well-designed, modern, purchasing system. Three alternative solutions to this problem have been proposed: (1) Modification of the current system, (2) development of an entirely new system by ABC's IS department, and (3) purchase of a third-party purchasing software package and modification to meet ABC's needs. A spreadsheet will be used to estimate the costs and benefits of these alternatives over the next 10 years.

Modifying the existing system would be the least costly alternative; the modified system would cost $155,000 to develop and could be operational within a year.

Purchase of a third-party package would cost $225,000 plus an additional $125,000 to adapt it to meet ABC's needs. A purchased system could also be operational within a year.

Development of a new system by ABC's IS staff would take two years to complete and cost $475,000. The development cost would be spread evenly across the two years.

Benefits of the new system would come in the form of reduced time required by the purchasing staff to answer requests and process orders. These benefits have been measured in staff hours saved compared to the current system. The following table lists expected work hours per year saved (as compared to the current system) for each alternative. The amount of time saved is not identical since only an internally developed system can completely implement the desired improvements. The cost of an hour of work time by the average purchasing department employee is $17 including all fringe benefits. Assume that both the cost of a clerical hour and the number of hours saved will not change over the 10-year period.

System	Purchasing Department Hours Saved
Modification	3,500
Development	12,000
Purchase	7,000

a. Based on the preceding figures, develop a spreadsheet showing the costs and benefits of each alternative system over the next 10 years.

b. Modify your spreadsheet so that it includes calculations of the net present value of each investment assuming a required return on investment of 10 percent.

c. Describe which alternative you would choose and why you would choose it.

d. The time saved under each system was assumed to be constant over the entire period of operation. Do you think that this is a realistic assumption? If not, what pattern of savings would you expect for each alternative?

Review Quiz Answers

1.	5	6.	16	11.	10	16.	4
2.	6	7.	13	12.	19	17.	18
3.	14	8.	9	13.	11	18.	1
4.	12	9.	8	14.	17	19.	20
5.	7	10.	3	15.	2	20.	15

Selected References

1. Alter, Allan. "Jack Be Agile, Jack Be Quick." *Computerworld*, November 7, 1994.

2. Bakos, J. Yannis. "A Strategic Analysis of Electronic Marketplaces." *MIS Quarterly*, September 1991.

3. Booker, Ellis. "A Tangled Web: Businesses Struggle to Leverage the Internet." *Computerworld/Client Server Journal*, April 1995.

4. Booker, Ellis. "GE Places Services on the Internet." *Computerworld*, October 31, 1994.

5. Bowles, Jerry. "Quality 2000: The Next Decade of Progress." Special Advertising Supplement, *Fortune*, October 3, 1994.

6. Caron, J. Raymond; Sirkka Jarvenpaa; and Donna Stoddard. "Business Reengineering at CIGNA Corporation: Experiences and Lessons from the First Five Years." *MIS Quarterly*, September 1994.

7. Cash, James I., Jr.; Robert G. Eccles; Nitin Nohria; and Richard L. Nolan. *Building the Information-Age Organization: Structure, Control, and Information Technologies.* Burr Ridge, IL: Richard D. Irwin, 1994.

8. Clemons, Eric, and Michael Row. "Sustaining IT Advantage: The Role of Structural Differences." *MIS Quarterly*, September 1991.

9. Davenport, Thomas H. *Process Innovation: Reengineering Work through Information Technology.* Boston: Harvard Business School Press, 1993.

10. Davenport, Thomas H., and Donna Stoddard. "Reengineering: Business Change of Mythic Proportions." *MIS Quarterly*, June 1994.

11. Davis, Stanley. *Future Perfect.* Reading, MA: Addison-Wesley, 1989.

12. Frye, Colleen. "Imaging Proves Catalyst for Reengineering." *Client/Server Computing*, November 1994.

13. Goldman, Steven; Roger Nagel; and Kenneth Preis. *Agile Competitors and Virtual Organizations: Strategies for Enriching the Customer.* New York: Van Nostrand Reinhold, 1995.

14. Guha, Subashish; William Kettinger; and James Teng. "Business Process Reengineering: Building a Comprehensive Methodology." *Information Systems Management*, Summer 1993.

15. Halper, Mark. "Mobil Nets Unite Staff." *Computerworld*, January 11, 1993.

16. Hammer, Michael. "Reengineering Work: Don't Automate, Obliterate." *Harvard Business Review*, July–August 1990.

17. Hammer, Michael, and James Champy. *Reengineering the Corporation: A Manifesto for Business Revolution.* New York: HarperCollins, 1993.

18. Hopper, Max. "Rattling SABRE—New Ways to Compete in Information." *Harvard Business Review*, May–June 1990.

19. Jacobson, Ivar; Maria Ericsson; and Ageneta Jacobson. *The Object Advantage: Business Process Reengineering with Object Technology.* New York: ACM Press, 1995.

20. Keen, Peter G.W. *Shaping the Future: Business Design through Information Technology.* Boston, MA: Harvard Business School Press, 1991.

21. Kettinger, William; Varun Grover; Subashish Guha; and Albert Segars. "Strategic Information Systems Revisited: A Study in Sustainability and Performance." *MIS Quarterly*, March 1994.

22. Kettinger, William; Varun Grover; and Albert Segars. "Do Strategic Systems Really Pay Off? An Analysis of Classic Strategic IT Cases." *Information Systems Management*, Winter 1995.

23. King, Julia. "Logistics Providers Enable 'Virtual' Firms." *Computerworld,* July 18, 1994.

24. Lieberman, Philip. "A Guide to OS/2 Warp's Internet Access Kit." *Personal Systems,* March–April 1995.

25. Lindquist, Christopher. "Miller Finds Pardox Brew Tasty." *Computerworld,* February 8, 1993.

26. Neumann, Seev. *Strategic Information Systems: Competition through Information Technologies.* New York: Macmillan College Publishing Co., 1994.

27. Pegels, C. Carl. *Total Quality Management: A Survey of Its Important Aspects.* Danvers, MA: boyd & fraser publishing co., 1995.

28. Porter, Michael. *Competitive Advantage.* New York: Free Press, 1985.

29. Porter, Michael, and Victor Millar. "How Information Gives You Competitive Advantage." *Harvard Business Review,* July–August 1985.

30. Resnick, Rosalind. "The Virtual Corporation." *PC Today,* February 1995.

31. Roche, Edward M. *Telecommunications and Business Strategy.* Chicago: Dryden Press, 1991.

32. Schonberger, Richard. "Is Strategy Strategic? Impact of Total Quality Management on Strategy." *Academy of Management Executive,* August 1992.

33. Sprague, Ralph, Jr., and Barbara McNurlin. *Information Systems Management in Practice.* 3rd ed. Englewood Cliffs, NJ: Prentice Hall, 1993.

34. Tetzelli, Rick. "The Internet and Your Business." *Fortune,* March 7, 1994.

35. Wiseman, Charles. *Strategic Information Systems.* Burr Ridge, IL: Richard D. Irwin, 1988.

36. Zahedi, Fatemeh. *Quality Information Systems.* Danvers, MA: boyd & fraser publishing co., 1995.

Continuing Real World Case

Fast Freight, Inc.: Networking the Enterprise—Part III: Business Applications of IS

Business Benefits of Network Applications

Fast Freight's management and staff at all locations can utilize a variety of IS applications of the computer network to accomplish their assignments with speed and efficiency. When dispatchers need to know who is transporting a specific order, they can quickly check the card on the master board. When managers want to know how much freight has been handled through their depots over the past three months, they can call that up from the AS/400 through the PC workstations in their offices. When the executive vice president wants to know how much rail time delay has been incurred by the company's operations, he can get a report within an hour. And, when Fast Freight's major customer, Burlington Northern, needs tangible older documents to help settle a legal claim, they are electronically retrieved, reprinted, and faxed or sent by EDI to the proper office.

Clearly, Fast Freight's current three-tier, interconnected computer network contributes substantially to Fast Information Systems' mission of "efficient, on-time delivery with proper documentation" for its customers. The three-tier computer network developed by Fast Freight has provided a new level of efficiency for the corporation in both day-to-day operations and long-term customer service. By locating AS/400 computers in each strategic depot, Fast Freight has allowed end users at these facilities to quickly process and store data locally, make use of it when necessary, and exchange it quickly.

In fact, Fast Information Systems technicians are just finishing installing electronic data interchange (EDI) applications between the company and Burlington Northern. The EDI applications will eliminate mailing or faxing order documents between the railroad and Fast Freight as well as between Fast Freight's depots and the home office. This will improve efficiency and cut handling and paper costs as well as fax communication expenses. The EDI system will also increase efficiency of Fast Imaging's image processing services.

Because of Fast Freight's computer network, depot and repair facility managers can monitor day-to-day operations, coordinate service with other facilities, and access valuable decision-making information from headquarters. Conversely, administrators in Wenatchee can easily access data from any facility or office, helping them to monitor operations and troubleshoot problems throughout the company as well as having access to corporate data for major decision making and problem solving.

The use of the Novell image server eliminated countless hours of manual filing and retrieval of transportation documentation, not to mention storage space. As Jim Kellogg, Fast Freight's systems engineer stated, "We receive (via mail and fax) a semi-trailer load of documents every three months and it's growing." These truckloads of documentation have to be manually captured into the system. Soon the new EDI system will eliminate the bulk of that procedure. Still, Kellogg says the company needs 1 gigabyte of new storage each month to keep up with the demand and if more storage were available, they could do "five times the volume." To this end, Fast Imaging has installed optical disk equipment that will enable them to burn (make) their own CD–ROMs for document image storage. This will give them far greater storage capacity and increase their electronic document management business.

Case Study
Questions

1. What are the benefits of Fast Freight's IS applications to its business operations and management decision making?
2. Does Fast Freight use its information systems strategically for competitive advantage? Explain.
3. What future applications of information technology should be investigated by Jim Kellogg? How would they benefit Fast Freight's business operations, managerial decision making, or competitive advantage?

Development and Management

How can end users help develop information system solutions to solve business problems and pursue business opportunities? What managerial challenges do information systems pose for the end user managers of modern organizations? The three chapters of this module emphasize how managers and end users can develop and manage the use of information technology in a global information society.

Chapter 10, "Developing Business Solutions with Information Technology," introduces the traditional, prototyping, and end user approaches to the development of information systems, and discusses managerial issues in the implementation of information technology.

Chapter 11, "Enterprise and Global Management of Information Technology," emphasizes the impact of information technology on management and organizations, the importance of information resource management, and the managerial implications of global information technology.

Chapter 12, "Security and Ethical Challenges of Information Technology," discusses the controls needed for information system performance and security, as well as the ethical implications and societal impacts of information technology.

Developing Business Solutions with Information Technology

LEARNING OBJECTIVES

After reading and studying this chapter, you should be able to:

1. Describe and give examples to illustrate each of the steps of the information systems development cycle.

2. Explain how computer-aided systems engineering and prototyping have affected the process of systems development for end users and information systems specialists.

3. Identify the activities involved in the implementation process for organizational and technological change, and give examples of some of the major management techniques involved.

4. Discuss how end user resistance to changes in business processes or information technology can be minimized by end user involvement in systems development and implementation.

5. Describe several evaluation factors that should be considered in evaluating the acquisition of hardware, software, and IS services.

6. Identify the activities involved in the implementation of new information systems.

7. Use the systems development cycle and a model of information system components as problem-solving frameworks to help you propose information system solutions to simple business problems.

Section I   *Developing Information System Solutions*

Suppose the chief executive of a firm where you are the sales manager asks you to find a better way to get information to the salespeople in your company. How would you start? What would you do? Would you just plunge ahead and hope you could come up with a reasonable solution? How would you know whether your solution was a good one for your company? Do you think there might be a systematic way to help you develop a good solution to your chief executive's request? There is. It's a problem-solving process called the *systems approach*.

The Systems Approach

The **systems approach** to problem solving uses a systems orientation to define problems and opportunities and develop solutions. Studying a problem and formulating a solution involves the following interrelated activities:

1. Recognize and define a problem or opportunity in a systems context.
2. Develop and evaluate alternative system solutions.
3. Select the system solution that best meets your requirements.
4. Design the selected solution so that it meets your requirements.
5. Implement and evaluate the success of the designed system.

The Systems Development Cycle

The systems approach can be applied to the solution of many types of problems. However, when it is applied to the development of information system solutions to business problems, it is called **information systems development** or *application development*. Most computer-based information systems are conceived, designed, and implemented using some form of a systematic development process. In this process, end users and information specialists *design* information systems based on an *analysis* of the information requirements of an organization.

FIGURE 10.1

Developing information system solutions to business problems is typically a multi-step process or cycle.

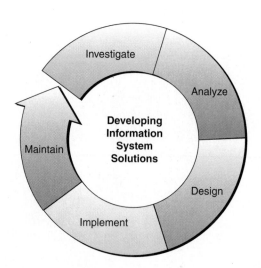

Thus, a major part of this process is known as *systems analysis and design.* However, as Figure 10.1 shows, several other major activities are involved in a complete development cycle.

When the systems approach is applied to the development of information system solutions, a multistep process or cycle emerges. This is frequently called the systems development cycle, or **systems development life cycle** (SDLC). Figure 10.2 summarizes what goes on in each stage of the traditional *information systems development cycle,* which includes the steps of (1) investigation, (2) analysis, (3) design, (4) implementation, and (5) maintenance.

You should realize, however, that all of the activities involved are highly related and interdependent. Therefore, in actual practice, several developmental activities can occur at the same time. So, different parts of a development project

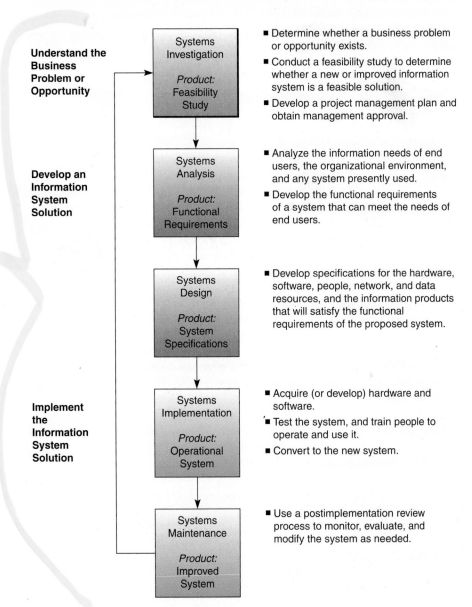

Understand the Business Problem or Opportunity

Systems Investigation

Product: Feasibility Study

- Determine whether a business problem or opportunity exists.
- Conduct a feasibility study to determine whether a new or improved information system is a feasible solution.
- Develop a project management plan and obtain management approval.

Develop an Information System Solution

Systems Analysis

Product: Functional Requirements

- Analyze the information needs of end users, the organizational environment, and any system presently used.
- Develop the functional requirements of a system that can meet the needs of end users.

Systems Design

Product: System Specifications

- Develop specifications for the hardware, software, people, network, and data resources, and the information products that will satisfy the functional requirements of the proposed system.

Implement the Information System Solution

Systems Implementation

Product: Operational System

- Acquire (or develop) hardware and software.
- Test the system, and train people to operate and use it.
- Convert to the new system.

Systems Maintenance

Product: Improved System

- Use a postimplementation review process to monitor, evaluate, and modify the system as needed.

FIGURE 10.2

The traditional information systems development cycle. Note how the five steps of the cycle are based on the stages of the systems approach. Also note the products that result from each step in the cycle.

can be at different stages of the development cycle. In addition, analysts may recycle back at any time to repeat previous activities in order to modify and improve a system they are developing.

Finally, you should realize that developments such as computer-aided systems engineering (CASE), prototyping, and end user development are automating and changing some of the activities of information systems development. These developments are improving the quality of systems development and making it easier for IS professionals, while enabling more end users to develop their own systems. We will discuss them shortly. Now, let's take a look at each step of this development process.

Systems Investigation

Do we have a business problem (or opportunity)? What is causing the problem? Would a new or improved information system help solve the problem? What would be a *feasible* information system solution to our problem? These are the questions that have to be answered in the **systems investigation** stage—the first step in the systems development process. This stage may involve consideration of proposals generated by an *information systems planning* process, which we will discuss in Chapter 11. The investigation stage includes the screening, selection, and preliminary study of proposed information system solutions to business problems such as those facing Auto Shack Stores as described in the case study example on page 383.

Feasibility Studies

Because the process of developing a major information system can be costly, the systems investigation stage frequently requires a preliminary study called a **feasibility study.** A feasibility study is a preliminary study to investigate the information needs of prospective users and determine the resource requirements, costs, benefits, and feasibility of a proposed project. You would use the methods of gathering information summarized in Figure 10.3 to collect data for a feasibility study. Then you might formalize the findings of this study in a written report that includes preliminary specifications and a developmental plan for the proposed system. If management approves the recommendations of the feasibility study, the **systems analysis** stage can begin.

The goal of feasibility studies is to evaluate alternative systems and to propose the most feasible and desirable systems for development. The feasibility of a proposed system can be evaluated in terms of four major categories, as illustrated in Figure 10.4.

The focus of **organizational feasibility** is on how well a proposed information system supports the objectives of the organization and its strategic plan for information systems. For example, projects that do not directly contribute to meeting an organization's strategic objectives are typically not funded. **Economic feasibility** is concerned with whether expected cost savings, increased revenue, increased profits, reductions in required investment, and other types of benefits will exceed the costs of developing and operating a proposed system. For example, if a project can't cover its

---

FIGURE 10.3

Ways to gather information for systems development.

- Interviews with employees, customers, and managers.
- Questionnaires to appropriate end users in the organization.
- Personal observation or involvement in business operations.

- Examination of documents, reports, procedures manuals, and other documentation.
- Development, manipulation, and observation of a model of the business operations.

CASE STUDY EXAMPLE

AUTO SHACK STORES: SOLVING A BUSINESS PROBLEM

Auto Shack Stores is a chain of auto parts stores in Arizona, with headquarters in Phoenix. The firm has grown to 14 stores in just 10 years, and it offers a wide variety of automotive parts and accessories. Sales and profits have increased each year, but the rate of sales growth has failed to meet forecasts in the last three years. Early results for 1996 indicate that the rate of sales growth is continuing to drop, even with the addition of two new stores in 1995. Adding the new stores was the solution decided on by corporate management last year to reverse the trend in sales performance.

In recent meetings of corporate and store managers, the issue of computer use has been raised. Auto Shack uses computers for various information processing jobs, such as sales transactions processing, analysis of sales performance, employee payroll processing, and accounting applications. However, sales transactions by customers are still written up by salespeople. Also, corporate and store managers depend on daily sales analysis reports that contain information that is always several days old.

Most store managers see the installation of a company-wide network of point-of-sale (POS) systems as a key to reversing Auto Shack's sales trends. They believe using networks of POS terminals in each store would drastically shorten the time needed by a salesperson to write up a sale. This would not only improve customer service, it would free salespeople to sell to more customers. The managers call these the *selling floor* benefits of POS systems.

Another major point raised is that POS systems would allow immediate capture and processing of sales transaction data. Up-to-date sales performance information could then be made available to managers at personal computer workstations connected into the company's telecommunications network. This would provide the capability for information on sales performance to be tailored to each manager's information needs. Currently, managers have to depend on daily sales analysis reports that use the same report format. Too much of a manager's time is being used to generate sales performance information not provided by the system. Managers complain they don't have enough time to plan and support sales efforts unless they make decisions without enough information.

The president of Auto Shack has resisted previous proposals to automate the selling process. He knows automation would involve a large initial investment and resistance to the technology by some salespeople and managers. He fears the loss of salesperson/customer interactions. He also fears that managers will become too dependent on computers if they have them in their offices. However, the continued disappointing sales performance has softened his position. Also, the president realizes that POS systems have become commonplace in all types of retail stores. Auto Shack's major competitors have installed such systems, and their growth continues to outpace his own firm's. The company is failing to achieve its goal of increasing its share of the automotive parts market.

The team of store managers and systems analysts from the information services department conducted a feasibility study of the POS options facing Auto Shack. The study team made personal observations of the sales processing system in action and interviewed managers, salespeople, and other employees. Based on a preliminary analysis of user requirements, the team proposed a new sales processing system. This new system features a telecommunications network of point-of-sale (POS) terminals and management workstations. After reviewing the feasibility study, the top management of Auto Shack gave the go-ahead for the development of the new POS system.

development costs, it won't be approved, unless mandated by government regulations or other considerations. **Technical feasibility** can be demonstrated if reliable hardware and software capable of meeting the needs of a proposed system can be acquired or developed by the business in the required time. Finally, **operational feasibility** is the willingness and ability of the management, employees, customers, suppliers, and others to operate, use, and support a proposed system. For example, if the software for a new system is too difficult to use, employees may make too many errors and avoid using it. Thus, it would fail to show operational feasibility. See Figure 10.5.

FIGURE 10.4

Organizational, economic, technical, and operational feasibility factors. Note that there is more to feasibility than cost savings or the availability of hardware and software.

Organizational Feasibility	Economic Feasibility
■ How well the proposed system supports the strategic objectives of the organization	■ Cost savings ■ Increased revenue ■ Decreased investment ■ Increased profits
Technical Feasibility	**Operational Feasibility**
■ Hardware and software capability, reliability, and availability	■ End user acceptance ■ Management support ■ Customer, supplier, and government requirements

Cost/Benefit Analysis

Feasibility studies typically involve **cost/benefit analysis**. If costs and benefits can be quantified, they are called tangible; if not, they are called intangible. Examples of **tangible costs** are the costs of hardware and software, employee salaries, and other quantifiable costs needed to develop and implement an IS solution. **Intangible costs** are difficult to quantify; they include the loss of customer goodwill or employee morale caused by errors and disruptions arising from the installation of a new system.

Tangible benefits are favorable results, such as the decrease in payroll costs caused by a reduction in personnel or a decrease in inventory carrying costs caused by a reduction in inventory. **Intangible benefits** are harder to estimate. Such benefits as better customer service or faster and more accurate information for management fall into this category. Figure 10.6 lists typical tangible and intangible benefits with examples. Possible tangible and intangible costs would be the opposite of each benefit shown.

Systems Analysis

What is **systems analysis**? Whether you want to develop a new application quickly or are involved in a long-term project, you will need to perform several basic activities of systems analysis. Many of these activities are an extension of those used in conducting a feasibility study. Some of the same information-gathering

FIGURE 10.5

Examples of how a feasibility study measured the feasibility of the POS system proposed for Auto Shack Stores.

Organizational Feasibility	Economic Feasibility
■ How well the proposed system fits the store's plans for integrating sales, marketing and financial systems	■ Savings in checkout costs ■ Increased sales revenue ■ Decreased investment in inventory ■ Increased profits
Technical Feasibility	**Operational Feasibility**
■ Capability, reliability, and availability of POS hardware and software	■ Acceptance of salespeople ■ Store management support ■ Customer acceptance

Tangible Benefits	Example
▪ Increase in sales or profits	▪ Development of computer-based products and services
▪ Decrease in information processing costs	▪ Elimination of unnecessary procedures and documents
▪ Decrease in operating costs	▪ Reduction in inventory carrying costs
▪ Decrease in required investment	▪ Decrease in inventory investment required
▪ Increased operational ability and efficiency	▪ Improvement in production ability and efficiency; for example, less spoilage, waste, and idle time

Intangible Benefits	Example
▪ New or improved information availability	▪ More timely and accurate information and new types of information
▪ Improved abilities in computation and analysis	▪ Analytical modeling
▪ Improved customer service	▪ More timely service response
▪ Improved employee morale	▪ Elimination of burdensome boring job tasks
▪ Improved management decision making	▪ Better information and decision analysis
▪ Improved competitive position	▪ Systems which lock in customers and suppliers
▪ Improved business and community image	▪ Progressive image as perceived by customers, suppliers, and investors

FIGURE 10.6

Possible benefits of computer-based information systems, with examples. Note that an opposite result for each of these benefits would be a cost or disadvantage of computer-based information systems.

methods are used, plus some new tools that we will discuss shortly. However, systems analysis is not a preliminary study. It is an in-depth study of end user information needs that produces *functional requirements* that are used as the basis for the design of a new information system. Systems analysis traditionally involves a detailed study of:

- The information needs of the organization and end users like yourself.
- The activities, resources, and products of any present information systems.
- The information system capabilities required to meet your information needs, and those of other end users.

An **organizational analysis** is an important first step in systems analysis. How can you improve an information system if you know very little about the organizational environment in which that system is located? You can't. That's why you have to know something about the organization, its management structure, its people, its business activities, the environmental systems it must deal with, and its current information systems. You must know this information in more detail for the specific end user departments that will be affected by the new or improved information system being proposed. For example, you cannot design a new inventory control system for a chain of department stores until you learn a lot about the company and the types of business activities that affect its inventory.

Organizational Analysis

FIGURE 10.7

An overview of the present sales processing system at Auto Shack Stores.

- When a customer wants to buy an auto part, a salesclerk writes up a sales order form. Recorded on this form are customer data, such as name, address, and account number, and product data, such as name, product number, and price. A copy of the sales order form is given to the customer as a receipt.

- Sales order forms are sent at the end of each day to the information services department. The next day they are entered into the computer system by data entry clerks using video terminals and stored on the mainframe computer's magnetic disk units.

- These daily sales transactions are used by a sales processing program to update a sales master file to reflect the sales of the day.

- Sales processing also involves the use of a sales analysis program to produce sales analysis reports that tell store managers the trends in sales for various types of auto parts.

Analysis of the Present System

Before you design a new system, it is important to study the system that will be improved or replaced (if there is one). You need to analyze how this system uses hardware, software, network, and people resources to convert data resources, such as transactions data, into information products, such as reports and displays. Then you should document how the information system activities of input, processing, output, storage, and control are accomplished. For example, you might note the format, timing, volume, and quality of input/output activities that provide *user interface* methods for interaction between end users and computers. Then, in the systems design stage, you can specify what the resources, products, and activities *should be* in the system you are designing. Figure 10.7 outlines the activities of the present sales processing system at Auto Shack Stores.

Functional Requirements Analysis

This step of systems analysis is one of the most difficult. You need to work with systems analysts and other end users to determine your specific information needs. For example, you need to determine what type of information you require; what its format, volume, and frequency should be; and what response times are necessary. Second, you must try to determine the information processing capabilities required for each system activity (input, processing, output, storage, control) to meet these information needs. Your main goal should be to identify what should be done, not how to do it. Finally, you should try to develop **functional requirements.** Functional requirements are end user information requirements that are not tied to the hardware, software, network, data, and people resources that end users presently use or might use in the new system. That is left to the design stage to determine. For example, Figure 10.8 outlines some of the key areas where functional requirements should be developed. Figure 10.9 shows examples of functional requirements for a sales transaction processing system at Auto Shack Stores.

FIGURE 10.8

Functional requirements specify information system capabilities required to meet the information needs of users.

- **User interface requirements.** The input/output needs of end users that must be supported by the information system, including sources, formats, content, volume, and frequency of each type of input and output.

- **Processing requirements.** Activities required to convert input into output. Includes calculations, decision rules, and other processing operations, and capacity, throughput, turnaround time, and response time needed for processing activities.

- **Storage requirements.** Organization, content, and size of databases, types and frequency of updating and inquiries, and the length and rationale for record retention.

- **Control requirements.** Accuracy, validity, safety, security, and adaptability requirements for system input, processing, output, and storage functions.

- **User Interface Requirements**
  Automatic entry of product data and easy-to-use data entry screens for salespeople.
- **Processing Requirements**
  Fast, automatic calculation of sales totals and sales taxes.
- **Storage Requirements**
  Fast retrieval and update of data from product, pricing, and customer databases.
- **Control Requirements**
  Signals for data entry errors and easy-to-read receipts for customers.

FIGURE 10.9

Examples of functional requirements for a sales transaction processing system at Auto Shack Stores.

Systems Design

Systems analysis describes *what* a system should do to meet the information needs of users. **Systems design** specifies *how* the system will accomplish this objective. Systems design consists of design activities that produce **system specifications** satisfying the functional requirements developed in the systems analysis stage. Figure 10.10 is a design overview of the new point-of-sale system proposed for Auto Shack Stores.

User Interface, Data, and Process Design

A useful way to look at systems design is illustrated in Figure 10.11. This concept focuses on three major products or *deliverables* that should result from the design stage. In this framework, systems design consists of three activities: **user interface, data, and process design.** This results in specifications for user interface methods and products, database structures, and processing and control procedures [1].

User Interface Design

The user interface design activity focuses on designing the interactions between end users and computer systems. Designers concentrate on input/output methods and the conversion of data and information between human-readable and machine-readable forms. As we will see shortly, user interface design is frequently a *prototyping* process, where working models or *prototypes* of user interface methods are designed and modified with feedback from end users. Thus, user interface design produces detailed specifications for information products such as display screens, interactive user/computer dialogues (including the sequence or flow of dialogue), audio responses, forms, documents, and reports.

- When a customer wishes to buy an auto part, the salesclerk enters customer and product data using an online POS terminal. The POS terminal has a keyboard for data entry and a video screen for display of input data, as well as data entry menus, prompts, and messages. POS terminals are connected in a telecommunications network to the store's mainframe computer, which uses a comprehensive sales transaction processing program.
- The POS terminal prints out a sales receipt for the customer that contains customer and product data and serves as a record of the transaction.
- The POS terminal transmits sales transaction data to the store's mainframe computer. This immediately updates the sales records in the company's database, which is stored on magnetic disk units.
- The computer performs sales analyses using the updated sales records in the company database. Afterward, sales performance information is available to corporate and store managers in a variety of report formats at their management workstations.

FIGURE 10.10

A design overview of the new point-of-sale system proposed for Auto Shack Stores.

FIGURE 10.11
Systems design can be viewed as the design of user interfaces, data, and processes.

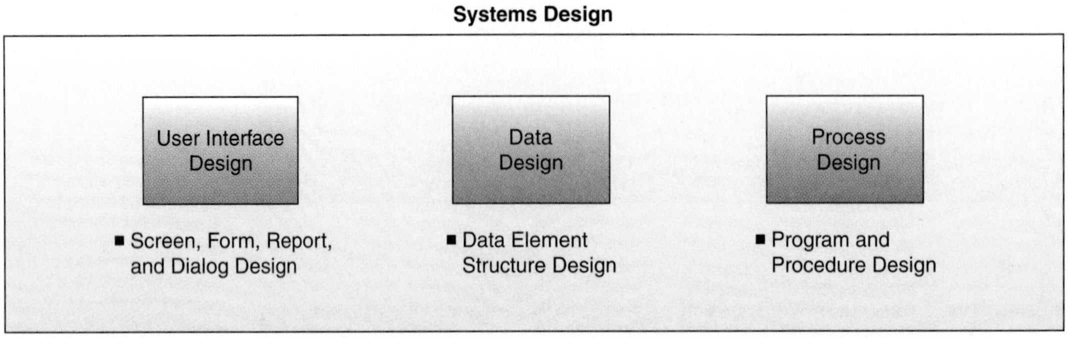

Systems Design

User Interface Design	Data Design	Process Design
▪ Screen, Form, Report, and Dialog Design	▪ Data Element Structure Design	▪ Program and Procedure Design

Data Design

The data design activity focuses on the design of the structure of databases and files to be used by a proposed information system. Data design frequently produces a *data dictionary,* which catalogs detailed descriptions of:

- The *attributes* or characteristics of the *entities* (objects, people, places, events) about which the proposed information system needs to maintain information.
- The relationships these entities have to each other.
- The specific data elements (databases, files, records, etc.) that need to be maintained for each entity tracked by the information system.
- The integrity rules that govern how each data element is specified and used in the information system.

Process Design

The process design activity focuses on the design of *software resources,* that is, the programs and procedures needed by the proposed information system. It concentrates on developing detailed specifications for the program modules that will have to be purchased as software packages or developed by custom programming. Thus, process design produces detailed program specifications and procedures needed to meet the user interface and data design specifications that are developed. Process design must also produce specifications that meet the functional control and performance requirements developed in the analysis stage.

System Specifications

The design of user interface methods and products, database structures, and processing and control procedures results in hardware, software, network, data, and personnel specifications for a proposed system. Systems analysts work with you so they can use your knowledge of your own work activities and their knowledge of computer-based systems to specify the design of a new or improved information system. The final design must specify what types of hardware resources (machines and media), software resources (programs and procedures), network resources (communications media and networks), and people resources (end users and information systems staff) will be needed. It must specify how such resources will convert data resources (stored in files and databases they design) into information products (displays, responses, reports, and documents). These specifications are the final product of the systems design stage, and are called the **system specifications.** Figure 10.12 outlines some of the key characteristics that should be included in system specifications. Figure 10.13 shows examples of system specifications that could be developed for a point-of-sale system at Auto Shack Stores.

- **User interface specifications:** The content, format, and sequence of user interface products and methods such as display screens, interactive dialogues, audio responses, forms, documents, and reports.

- **Database specifications:** Content, structure, distribution, and access, response, maintenance, and retention of databases.

- **Software specifications:** The required software package or programming specifications of the proposed system, including performance and control specifications.

- **Hardware and network specifications:** The physical and performance characteristics of the equipment and networks required by the proposed system.

- **Personnel specifications:** Job descriptions of persons who will operate the system.

FIGURE 10.12

System specifications specify the details of a proposed information system.

Computer-Aided Systems Engineering

Major changes are occurring in the traditional process of systems development that we described in this chapter. That's because the SDLC process has often been too inflexible, time-consuming, and expensive. In many cases, end user requirements are defined early in the process, and then end users are locked out until the system is implemented. Also, the backlog of unfilled user requests has grown to two to five years in many companies. Therefore, a **computer-aided systems engineering** (CASE) process has emerged due to the availability of a variety of software packages for systems and software development. CASE (which also stands for **computer-aided software engineering**) involves using software packages, called CASE tools, to perform many of the activities of the systems development life cycle. For example, software packages are available to help do business planning, project management, user interface design, database design, and software development. Thus, CASE tools make a computer-aided systems development process possible. See Figures 10.14 and 10.15.

Using CASE Tools

Figure 10.14 emphasizes that CASE packages provide many computer-based tools for both the *front end* of the systems development life cycle (planning, analysis, and design) and the back end of systems development (implementation and maintenance). Note that *server and workstation repositories* help integrate the use of tools at both ends of the development cycle. The *system repository* is a computerized

- **User Interface Specifications**
  Use handheld optical scanning wands to automatically capture product data on barcoded tags. Use data entry screens with key data highlighted for better readability.

- **Database Specifications**
  Develop databases that use a relational structure to organize access to all necessary customer and merchandise data.

- **Software Specifications**
  Develop or acquire a sales processing program that can accept entry of optically scanned bar codes, retrieve necessary product data, and compute sales amounts in less than 0.5 second. Acquire a relational database management package to manage stored databases.

- **Hardware and Network Specifications**
  Install POS terminals at each checkout station connected to a system of networked microcomputers in each store that are also connected to the corporate headquarters network.

- **Personnel Specifications**
  All hardware and software must be operable by regular store personnel. IS personnel should be available for hardware and software maintenance as needed.

FIGURE 10.13

Examples of system specifications for a new point-of-sale system at Auto Shack Stores.

FIGURE 10.14

The components of CASE. This is an example of the CASE software tools and repositories in an integrated CASE product.

CASE Software Tools

- The Planning Toolset begins the development process with information strategy planning from a high-level, business vantage point

- The Analysis Toolset focuses on correctly capturing detailed business requirements early in the development process

- The Design Toolset provides detailed specifications of the system solution

- The Information Integrator integrates system specifications, checks them for consistency and completeness, and records them in the repositories

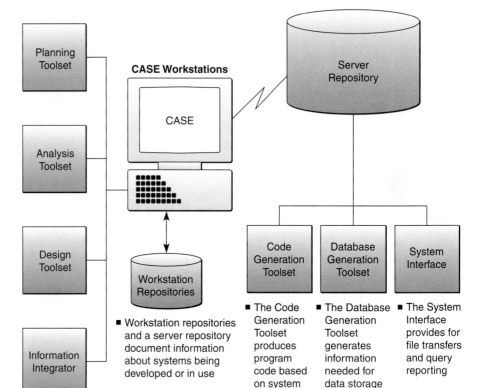

- Workstation repositories and a server repository document information about systems being developed or in use

- The Code Generation Toolset produces program code based on system specifications

- The Database Generation Toolset generates information needed for data storage and access

- The System Interface provides for file transfers and query reporting

FIGURE 10.15

Displays of a CASE software package. This package allows a systems analyst to interactively develop system specifications, use a variety of analysis and design tools, and design the format of screens and reports.

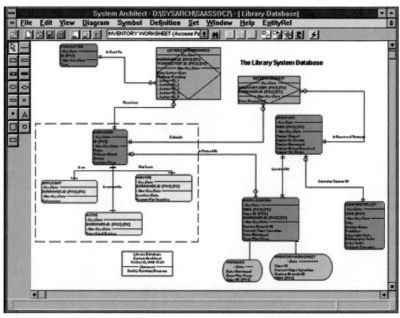

Courtesy of Popkin Software and Systems, Inc.

database for all of the details of a system generated with other systems development tools. The repository helps to ensure consistency and compatibility in the design of the data elements, processes, user interfaces, and other aspects of the system being developed.

Integrated CASE tools (called I-CASE) are now available that can assist all of the stages of systems development. Some of these CASE tools support *joint application design* (JAD), where a group of systems analysts, programmers, and end users can jointly and interactively design new applications. Finally, if the development of new systems can be called *forward engineering,* some CASE tools support *backward engineering.* That is, they allow systems analysts to inspect the logic of a program code for old applications, and convert it automatically into more efficient programs that significantly improve system effectiveness.

Prototyping

Microcomputer workstations and a variety of CASE and other software packages allow the rapid development and testing of working models, or **prototypes,** of new applications in an interactive, iterative process involving both systems analysts and end users. **Prototyping** not only makes the development process faster and easier for systems analysts, especially for projects where end user requirements are hard to define, but it has opened up the application development process to end users. These developments are changing the roles of end users and information systems specialists in systems development. See Figure 10.16.

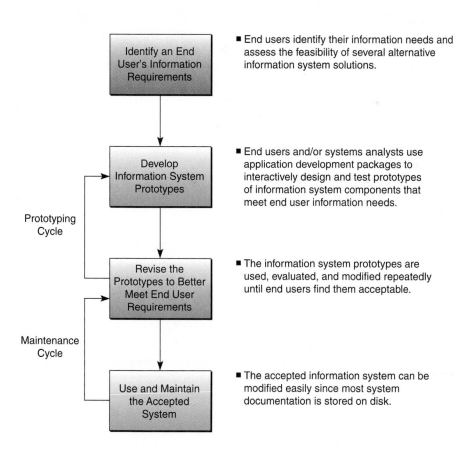

FIGURE 10.16

Application development using prototyping. Note how prototyping combines the steps of the traditional systems development cycle and changes the traditional roles of information systems specialists and end users.

FIGURE 10.17

Using an application development ment package to design a prototype employee personnel record screen.

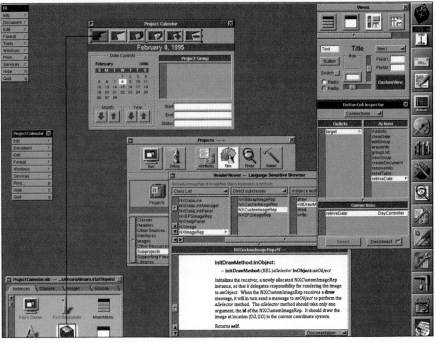

Courtesy of Quyen Systems, Inc.

The Prototyping Process

Prototyping can be used for both large and small applications. Typically, large systems still require using the traditional system development approach, but parts of such systems can frequently be prototyped. A prototype of an information system needed by an end user is developed quickly using a variety of application development packages. The prototype system is then repeatedly refined until it is acceptable to an end user.

As Figure 10.16 illustrates, prototyping is an iterative, interactive process that combines steps of the traditional systems development cycle. End users with sufficient experience with application development packages can do prototyping themselves. Alternatively, an end user can work with a systems analyst to develop a prototype system in a series of interactive sessions. For example, they could develop prototypes of management reports or data entry screens, such as the one illustrated in Figure 10.17.

The prototype is usually modified several times until the end user finds it acceptable. Any program modules not directly developed by the CASE software can then be coded by programmers using conventional programming languages. The final version of the application system is then turned over to the end user for operational use. Figure 10.18 outlines a typical prototyping-based systems development process.

End User Development

In a traditional systems development cycle, your role as a business end user is similar to that of a customer or a client. Typically, you will make a request for a new or improved system, answer questions about your specific information needs and information processing problems, and provide background information on your existing information systems. Systems analysts and other IS professionals work with you to

- A few end users and IS developers form a team to develop an application's specifications.
- Initial prototype schematic design developed.
- Schematic converted into simple point-and-click prototype using end user tools.
- A few screens and routine linkages are presented to users.
- After the team gets feedback from users, the prototype is reiterated.
- Further presentations and reiterations.
- Consultation with central IT developer/consultants to identify potential improvements and conformance to existing standards.
- Prototype converted to finished application.
- User review and sign-off.
- Application system loaded onto servers.

FIGURE 10.18

An example of a typical prototyping-based systems development process.

Source: Adapted from Larry Marion, "Application Development in the Decentralized Enterprise," Special Advertising Supplement, *Computerworld*, March 13, 1995, p. 12. Copyright © 1995 by Computerworld, Inc., Framingham, MA 01701—Reprinted from *Computerworld*.

analyze your problem and suggest alternative solutions. When you approve the best alternative, it is designed and implemented. Here again, you may be involved in a prototyping design process or be on an implementation team with IS specialists.

However, in **end user development,** IS professionals play a consulting role while you do your own application development. Sometimes a staff of user consultants may be available to help you and other end users with your application development efforts. For instance, a *user services* department or *information center* may provide assistance for both mainframe and microcomputer applications development. This may include training in the use of application packages; selection of hardware and software; assistance in gaining access to organization databases; and, of course, assistance in analysis, design, and implementing your application.

In end user development, you and other end users can develop new or improved ways to perform your jobs without the direct involvement of IS professionals. The application development capabilities built into a variety of end user software packages have made it easier for many users to develop their own computer-based solutions. For example, you can use an electronic spreadsheet package as a tool to develop a way to easily analyze weekly sales results for the sales managers in a company. Or you could use a database management package to design data-entry displays to help sales clerks enter sales data, or to develop monthly sales analysis reports needed by district sales managers. Figures 10.40 and 10.44 in the *Application Exercises* at the end of the chapter illustrate the basic activities of the spreadsheet and database application development process for end users.

End user development should focus on the fundamental activities of an information system: input, processing, output, storage, and control. Figure 10.19 illustrates these system components and the questions they address. In analyzing a potential application, you should focus first on the *output* to be produced by the application. What information is needed and in what form should it be presented? Next, look at the *input* data to be supplied to the application. What data are available? from what sources? and in what form? Then you should examine the *processing* requirement. What operations or transformation processes will be required to convert the available inputs into the desired output? Among software packages the developer is able to use, which package can best perform the operations required?

Doing End User Development

You may find that the desired output cannot be produced from the inputs that are available. If this is the case, you must either make adjustments to the output expected, or find additional sources of input data, including data stored in files and databases from external sources. The *storage component* will vary in importance in end user applications. For example, some applications require extensive use of stored data or the creation of data that must be stored for future use. These are better suited for database management development projects than for spreadsheet applications.

Necessary control measures for end user applications vary greatly depending upon the scope and duration of the application, the number and nature of the users of the application, and the nature of the data involved. For example, special procedures to restrict access to data are less needed if each application will be utilized either by only one individual serving as a developer/user or by a developer and a single additional user. Control measures are also needed to protect against accidental loss or damage to an end user file. The most basic protection against this type of loss is simply to make backup copies of application files on a frequent and systematic basis. Another example concerns spreadsheet applications that are used on a repeated basis or used by an individual other than its developer. Then it is a good idea to take advantage of the cell protection features of spreadsheet software to protect key cells from accidental erasure.

Checklist for End User Analysis and Design

Figure 10.20 outlines key questions you can use as a checklist to begin the process of analysis and design. Also included are answers that identify generic system components that are typically found in most computer-based information systems in business. Use this checklist as a tool to identify such components yourself in any information system you are studying. Then use it again as a source of design features you may want to suggest for a new or improved system.

FIGURE 10.19

End user development should focus on the basic information processing components of an information system.

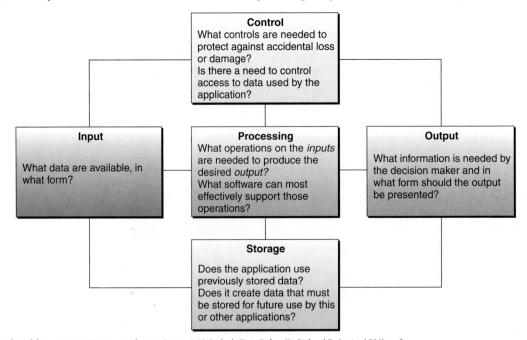

Source: Adapted from James N. Morgan, *Application Cases in MIS,* 2nd ed. (Burr Ridge, IL: Richard D. Irwin, 1996), p. 3.

An **IS component matrix** can be used to document the results of using the checklist for analysis and design [16]. As shown in Figure 10.21, an IS component matrix views an information system as a matrix of resources, products, and activities. It highlights how the activities of input, processing, output, storage, and control are accomplished, and how the use of people, hardware, network, and software resources supports the conversion of data resources into information products. An IS

The IS
Component Matrix

Input of Data Resources

Question: How are data captured and prepared for processing? How should they be? What data resources are or should be captured?

Answers: Input data are frequently collected from *source documents* (such as payroll time cards) and converted to machine-sensible data by a *keyboarding* data entry process. Other input may be captured directly by transaction terminals (such as point-of-sale terminals) using devices such as optical scanners. Input into the system typically consists of:

- **Transaction data.** *Example:* Data describing sales transactions are captured by a point-of-sale terminal.
- **Database adjustments.** *Example:* A change in a customer's credit limit, using an online terminal in the credit department or processing a "credit increase request form" mailed in by a customer.
- **Inquiries.** *Example:* What is the balance owed on a customer's account?
- **Output of other systems.** *Example:* The output of a sales transaction processing system includes data needed as input by an inventory control system to reflect transactions that change the amount of inventory on hand.

Processing of Data Resources

Question: How are data manipulated and transformed into information? How should they be? What processing alternatives should be considered?

Answers: Data resources are subjected to sorting, summarizing, calculating, and other manipulation activities. Processing alternatives include batch processing and realtime processing. *Examples*:

- Calculating employee payroll.
- Sorting employee record by employee number.
- Summarizing employee payroll costs.
- Realtime processing of sales data from point-of-sale terminals.
- Nightly batch processing of deposited checks by banks.

Output of Information Products

Question: How is information communicated to users? How should it be? What **information products** are and should be produced?

Answers: Output typically takes the form of the following information products:

- **Reports.** *Example:* A sales analysis report outlining the sales made during a period by sales territory, product, and salesperson.
- **Documents.** *Example:* A paycheck or sales receipt.
- **Displays or responses.** *Example:* A video terminal displays the balance owed on a customer's account. The same information can be transmitted to a telephone by a computer audio-response unit.
- **Control listings.** *Example:* Each time an employee paycheck is printed, a line on a listing known as a payroll register is also printed and recorded on magnetic tape. This helps provide an *audit trail* for control purposes.
- **Input to other systems.** *Example:* Part of the output of a payroll system serves as input to a labor-cost accounting system and the general ledger system of the firm.

FIGURE 10.20

A checklist for end user analysis and design.

FIGURE 10.20
Concluded

Storage of Data Resources

Question: How are **data resources** organized, stored, updated, and retrieved? How should they be?

Answers: Data resources are stored and organized into files and databases. This facilitates:

- Supplying data needed by the organization's information system applications. *Example:* The current credit balance of a customer is retrieved from a customer database by sales and accounting personnel.
- The updating of files and databases to reflect the occurrence of new business transactions. *Example:* A customer's credit balance is increased to reflect recent purchases on credit.

Control of System Performance

Question: How are input, processing, output, and storage activities monitored and controlled? How should they be? What control methods should be considered?

Answers: Input, processing, output, and storage activities must be controlled so that an information system produces proper information products and achieves its other objectives. Typical control methods include:

- **Input controls.** *Example:* Formatted data entry screens warn users if input data exceed specified parameters.
- **Processing controls.** Software may contain checkpoint routines that check the accuracy of intermediate results during processing.
- **Output controls.** *Example:* Computer users may check the accuracy of specified control totals in reports.
- **Storage controls.** *Example:* Databases may be protected by security programs that require proper identification and authorization codes by end users.

component matrix poses a fundamental question that should be answered by both end users and IS specialists: What resources are required to accomplish the activities that can produce the information products needed by end users?

Figure 10.22 illustrates the use of an IS component matrix to document the basic components of a sales processing system for a retail store. Note how it spotlights the activities needed, resources used, and products produced by this information system. Some cells are left blank because information for each cell may not be available or applicable. However, duplicate entries are also possible, because the same resources and products can be used to support several information system activities. Still, an IS component matrix serves its purpose by emphasizing the information system components used in a real world information system.

FIGURE 10.21

An IS component matrix highlights the resources needed to accomplish activities that produce information products needed by end users.

Information System Activities	Hardware and Network Resources		Software Resources		People Resources		Data Resources	Information Products
	Machines	Media	Programs	Procedures	Specialists	Users		
Input								
Processing								
Output								
Storage								
Control								

FIGURE 10.22

An example of an IS component matrix for a sales processing system at a chain of retail stores. Note how it emphasizes some of the basic activities needed, resources used, and products produced by this information system.

Information System Activities	Hardware and Network Resources		Software Resources		People Resources		Data Resources	Information Products
	Machines	Media	Programs	Procedures	Specialists	Users		
Input	POS terminals Management workstations	Bar tags Mag stripe Credit cards	Data entry program	Data entry procedures		Salesclerks Customers	Customer data Product data	Data entry displays
Processing	Mainframe computer Network servers Communications processors	Communications network media	Sales processing program Sales analysis program	Sales transaction procedures	Computer operators	Salesclerks Managers	Customer, inventory, and sales databases	Processing status displays
Output	POS terminals Management workstations	Paper reports and receipts	Report generator program Graphics programs	Output use and distribution procedures		Salesclerks Managers Customers		Sales analysis reports and displays Sales receipts
Storage	Magnetic disk drives	Magnetic disks	Database management program		Computer operators		Customer, inventory, and sales databases	
Control	Mainframe computer Network servers Communications processors POS terminals	Paper documents and control reports	Performance monitor program Security monitor program	Correction procedures	Computer operators Control clerks	Salesclerks Managers Customers	Customer, inventory, and sales databases	Data entry displays Sales receipts Error displays and signals

BOSTON BEER COMPANY: SPRINTING THROUGH SYSTEMS DEVELOPMENT

Scrap reengineering. Forget training. Sprint through systems development. And take no more than 24 hours to decide on a configuration. That's how $150 million Boston Beer Co. managed to implement a full suite of the notoriously complex SAP R/3 client/server software in just four months. R/3, by SAP America, is the leading client/server suite of accounting and finance software for midsize to large corporations.

Boston's total cost was less than $1 million—a minuscule and almost unheard-of amount—for software and new hardware at its Boston headquarters. "It's really not as difficult as it seems," said Timothy E. Ostrom, manager of the microbrewery's three-person IS department. "But I think a lot of executives make it sound that way because they want to be greeted as this great ball of fire for installing SAP," Ostrom said.

Maybe so, but Boston Beer took some very unconventional shortcuts to meet its self-imposed deadline. First, rather than assemble and train a big committee to hammer out how it should configure the software, the company turned the work over to three consultants from SAP.

"There's currently a shortage of SAP expertise. Big companies train their people then lose them," explained Martin Roper, the brewery's vice president of manufacturing and business development. "I'm not interested in training future SAP consultants. As a small company, I can't afford that," Roper said. This year, Boston Beer's total IS budget is approximately $1.3 million.

Boston Beer also couldn't afford any delays, so Roper streamlined configuration decisions, which other R/3 sites have been known to agonize over for weeks or months. When the SAP consultants asked for a configuration preference, Boston Beer made the decision in less than a day. SAP's R/3 has thousands of tables that must be configured, or customized, for the business.

The software suite runs a variety of applications, from order processing to accounting and production. It replaces several manual and mainframe systems to give the brewery a clearer picture of its beer inventory and profits.

Also unusual was the company's use of an earlier version of R/3 software instead of the current release. That was to minimize chances of any extra complications. Already, Boston Beer was adding two brewing locations and was in the throes of its initial public stock offering.

On the technology side, the company shifted its 200 employees off of dumb terminals and Macintoshes and onto networked PCs that run Windows 3.1. The R/3 software runs on a Hewlett-Packard UNIX machine with an Oracle database.

"With everything else going on, we were trying not to disrupt the existing business systems," Roper said. So Boston Beer decided to forgo the usual business process reengineering project. "The philosophy was to get up and running, then figure out how jobs would change," he said. "I think reengineering delays the process, and I'm real happy we didn't go that route."

Delaying reengineering "isn't a bad strategy," said Vinnie Mirchandani, an analyst at Gartner Group. "But Boston Beer may be very optimistic in thinking they'll go back and do it. Chances are they won't because after the euphoria of implementation dies down, the focus shifts to maintenance," he said.

CASE STUDY QUESTIONS

1. Why did Boston Beer sprint through systems development? Was it a good business decision? Explain.

2. What activities of the systems development and implementation process (see Figures 10.25 and 10.27) do you recognize in this case?

3. Do you agree with Boston Beer's decision to delay business process reengineering? Why or why not?

Source: Adapted from Julia King, "Boston Beer Brews Quick Hop to R/3," *Computerworld*, April 1, 1996, pp. 1, 121. Copyright © 1996 by Computerworld, Inc., Framingham, MA 01701—Reprinted from *Computerworld*.

Implementing Business Change with IT

Section II

Introduction

The implementation process is the next major stage that follows the investigation, analysis, and design stages of the systems development process introduced in Section I. Therefore, implementation is an important activity in the deployment of information technology to support the business changes planned by an organization and its end users.

Managing Organizational Change

IT increasingly changes jobs, skill needs, work, and relationships. Technical change has become synonymous with organizational change. Such change can be complex, painful, and disruptive. The people side of IT is often more difficult to anticipate and manage smoothly than is the technological side [9].

Typically, implementing changes in information technology is only part of a larger process of managing major changes in business processes, organizational structures, job assignments, and work relationships. Figure 10.23 illustrates some of the major managerial activities that organizations use to help manage business change. Notice that **change management** requires the involvement and commitment of top management and a formal process or organizational design. This supports changes in business and technology generated by the reengineering of business processes or other work redesign activities [20].

Human resource management is a major focus of other organizational change management activities shown in Figure 10.23. This includes activities such as developing innovative ways to measure, motivate, and reward performance. So is designing programs to recruit and train employees in the core competencies required in a changing workplace. Finally, change management involves analyzing and defining all changes facing the organization, and developing programs to reduce the risks and costs, and to maximize the benefits of change. For example, implementing a reengineered business process might involve developing a change *action plan,* assigning selected managers as *change sponsors,* developing employee *change teams,* and encouraging open communications and feedback about organizational changes. To summarize, change experts recommend:

- Involve as many people as possible in reengineering and other change programs.
- Make constant change part of the culture.
- Tell everyone as much as humanly possible about everything as often as possible, preferably in person.
- Make liberal use of financial incentives and recognition.
- Work within the company culture, not around it [14].

Implementing Information Technology

Any new way of doing things generates some resistance by the people affected. Thus, the reengineering of business processes, including the implementation of new computer-based work support technologies, can generate a significant amount of end user fear and reluctance to change. Figure 10.24 outlines many reasons for such **end user resistance,** some of which we explore in a discussion concerning societal

FIGURE 10.23

Some of the major activities involved in organizational change management.

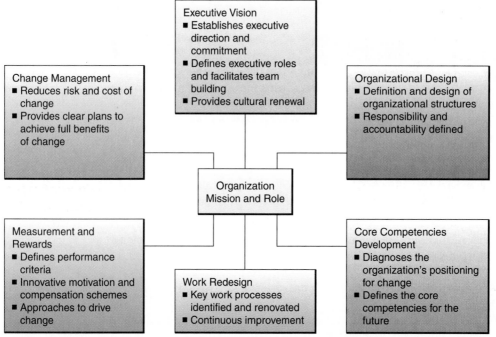

Source: Adapted and reprinted from Louis Fried and Richard Johnson, "Gaining the Technology Advantage: Planning for the Competitive Use of IT," *Information Systems Management* (New York: Auerbach Publications), Fall 1991. © 1991 Warren, Gorham & Lamont. Used with permission.

FIGURE 10.24

Reasons for user resistance to reengineering business processes.

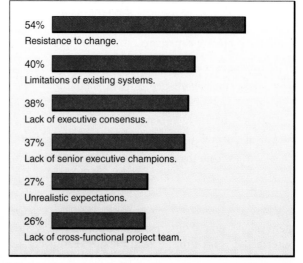

Toughest Tasks

- 54% Installing the information technology infrastructure.
- 53% Dealing with fear and anxiety throughout the organization.
- 46% Managing resistance by key managers.
- 42% Changing job functions, career paths, recruitment, or training.
- 42% Designing the new business process.
- 39% Having a clear vision of the new organization.

Major Obstacles

- 54% Resistance to change.
- 40% Limitations of existing systems.
- 38% Lack of executive consensus.
- 37% Lack of senior executive champions.
- 27% Unrealistic expectations.
- 26% Lack of cross-functional project team.

Source: Adapted from "Rocks in the Gears: Reengineering the Workplace," by Joseph Maglitta, *Computerworld*, October 3, 1994, p. 96. Copyright © 1994 by Computerworld, Inc., Framingham, MA 01701—Reprinted from *Computerworld*.

impacts of IT in Chapter 12. However, end user resistance can be minimized by formal **technology implementation** programs, which end user managers and IS consultants can develop to encourage user acceptance and productive use of reengineered business processes and new information technologies. So, one of the keys to solving problems of end user resistance is proper end user education and training, improved communications with IS professionals, and end user involvement in the development and implementation of new systems. See Figure 10.25.

Direct end user participation in systems development projects *before* a system is implemented is especially important in reducing the potential for end user resistance. This involvement helps ensure that end users assume ownership of a system, and that its design meets their needs. Systems that tend to inconvenience or frustrate users cannot be effective systems, no matter how technically elegant they are and how efficiently they process data. Let's look at two examples.

Federal Express emphasizes the change management value of on-the-job training. Fed Ex has installed more than 1,000 interactive video workstations for training of their couriers and customer service personnel. The workstations enable rapid learning of new products and services as they are rolled out. When Fed Ex, for example,

Federal Express Corporation

FIGURE 10.25

A technology implementation cycle. Technology implementation activities can minimize end user resistance to the changes brought on by new information technologies.

	Activity	Goal
1. **Preimplementation**	Gather data on workplace, personnel work, tasks, etc.	Determine planning alternatives, needed resources, and possible roadblocks
2. **Human design**	Study automated workplace and establish criteria for its human design	Eliminate deterrents and establish incentives for productivity, human physiology, and psychology
3. **Marketing**	Develop and implement a strategy for "selling" technical systems and the changes they cause	Introduce technology so that worker "buys" the system and "owns" the system
4. **Education**	Educate workers about the demands new technology will make on them and the benefits it will provide	Reduce worker stress concerning technology and increase confidence in the ability to use it productively
5. **Training**	Develop and implement a sequential, natural program of skill growth	Develop workers who are minimally computer competent and primed for additional computer skills evolution
6. **Documentation**	Compose and distribute documents that explain how the system works	Provide easy access to and effective assistance from reference materials so that workers can complete automated tasks
7. **Human communication**	Establish and maintain continuing means of communication with workers	Create opportunities for dialogue between workers and information technology, technicians, and management
8. **Postimplementation**	Compile evaluation of each phase into one document and review entire implementation process	Feed forward evaluation results to improve the next technology implementation

Source: Adapted from *Computerizing the Corporation: The Intimate Link Between People and Machines* by Vicki McConnell and Karl Koch (New York: Van Nostrand Reinhold, 1990), p. 100.

initiates international package delivery service to a new country, it uses the training systems to acquaint employees with customs requirements for the country. Fed Ex views the systems as a strategic advantage and has integrated them into many of its human resource policies. For example, under its policy of learning-based compensation, when a Federal Express employee completes a training module, the workstation automatically triggers an increase in the employee's compensation level in the payroll database [5].

TRW Information Services

TRW Information Services encourages employee "buy-in" for its reengineering projects by making reengineering efforts part of everyone's job. Over 200 employees are part of a reengineering team, which includes the executive vice president and general manager. Employee motivation is kept high through financial and travel bonuses. TRW publishes a special biweekly newsletter and provides a telephone hot-line to provide information on reengineering projects. These information sources help reduce anxiety by employees over rumors they might hear about possible job cuts [10].

Implementing Information Systems

The **implementation process** for newly designed information systems, involves a variety of acquisition, testing, documentation, installation, and conversion activities. It also involves the training of end users in the operation and use of the new information system. Thus, implementation is a vital step in ensuring the success of new systems. Even a well-designed system can fail if it is not properly implemented. See Figure 10.26. Figure 10.27 illustrates the major activities of the implementation process for new systems. In this section, we will concentrate on the acquisition and installation of IS resources and other managerial implementation issues. Figure 10.28 outlines examples of activities that Auto Shack Stores might use to implement new point-of-sale systems.

Acquiring Hardware, Software, and Services

Acquiring hardware, software, and external IS services is a major implementation activity. These resources can be acquired from many sources in the **computer industry**. For example, Figure 10.29 lists the top 10 mainframe, midrange, microcomputer, software, services, and data communications companies in 1996. Of course, there are many other firms in the computer industry that supply hardware, software, and services. For example, you can buy microcomputer hardware and software from mail-order firms like Dell and Gateway, or from retail chains like Computerland and MicroAge, while thousands of small consulting firms provide a broad range of IS services.

FIGURE 10.26

Why systems development projects succeed or fail.

Top five reasons for success:	Top five reasons for failure:
■ User involvement.	■ Lack of user input.
■ Executive management support.	■ Incomplete requirements and specifications.
■ Clear statement of requirements.	■ Changing requirements and specifications.
■ Proper planning.	■ Lack of executive support.
■ Realistic expectations.	■ Technological incompetence.

Source: Adapted from "Few IS Projects Come in on Time, on Budget," by Rosemary Cafasso, *Computerworld,* December 12, 1994, p. 20. Copyright © 1994 by Computerworld, Inc., Framingham, MA 01701—Reprinted from *Computerworld.*

FIGURE 10.27

An overview of the implementation process. Implementation activities are needed to transform a newly developed information system into an operational system for end users.

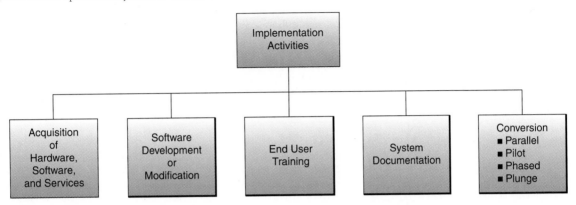

Hardware and Software Suppliers

Many larger business and professional organizations, educational institutions, and government agencies have employee purchase plans that let you buy computer hardware and software at substantial discounts. These *corporate buying* plans are arranged through negotiations with hardware manufacturers and software companies.

Original equipment manufacturers (OEMs) produce and sell computers by assembling components produced by other hardware suppliers. Plug-compatible manufacturers (PCMs) manufacture computer mainframes and peripheral devices that are specifically designed to be compatible (by just "plugging in") with the computers made by IBM, Digital Equipment Corporation, and others. Value-added resellers (VARs) specialize in providing industry-specific hardware and software from selected manufacturers.

Suppliers of IS Services

The major sources of **information systems services** are computer manufacturers, computer retailers, computer service centers, systems integrators, and independent consultants. These and other types of firms in the computer industry offer a variety of services.

- Evaluate and acquire new hardware and software. Hardware includes computer systems, POS terminals, and telecommunications processors and network facilities. Software includes network management programs and POS transaction processing packages.

- Develop computer programs or make any necessary modifications to software packages that are acquired.

- Prepare training materials and documentation on how to operate the new POS system for managers and salespeople.

- Educate and train managers, salespeople, and information systems personnel to operate the new system.

- Test the system and make corrections until it operates properly.

- Convert to the new system on a phased store-by-store basis to minimize disruption. Use the first store converted as a pilot installation to help with testing and training.

- Perform a postimplementation audit within 30 days of each store's conversion to determine if the new POS systems are achieving their expected advantages.

FIGURE 10.28

Examples of implementation activities for Auto Shack's new POS systems.

FIGURE 10.29

Major companies in the computer industry that provide mainframes, midrange computers, microcomputers, software, services, and data communications products. Note the position of IBM and international companies.

Microcomputer Systems			Servers and Midrange Systems			Mainframe Systems		
Rank	Company	Revenues ($ millions)	Rank	Company	Revenues ($ millions)	Rank	Company	Revenues ($ millions)
1	IBM	$12,949.2	1	IBM	$6,474.6	1	IBM	$6,474.6
2	Compaq Computer	9,176.0	2	Hewlett-Packard	3,650.2	2	Fujitsu	4,823.6
3	Apple Computer	8,533.5	3	AT&T	3,529.1	3	Hitachi	4,376.2
4	Fujitsu	6,431.5	4	Compaq Computer	3,256.0	4	NEC	3,870.0
5	Toshiba	5,690.1	5	NEC	2,515.5	5	Unisys	1,116.4
6	Hewlett-Packard	5,475.3	6	Tandem	1,846.2	6	Groupe Bull	795.0
7	NEC	5,224.5	7	Toshiba	1,820.8	7	Siemens Nixdorf	769.8
8	Dell Computer	4,558.0	8	Digital Equipment	1,689.4	8	Amdahl	758.0
9	Packard Bell	4,300.0	9	Fujitsu	1,607.9	9	Cray Research	412.4
10	Sun Microsystems	3,965.0	10	Siemens Nixdorf	1,226.3	10	Mitsubishi	290.2

Computer Software			IS Services			Data Communications		
Rank	Company	Revenues ($ millions)	Rank	Company	Revenues ($ millions)	Rank	Company	Revenues ($ millions)
1	IBM	$12,949.2	1	IBM	$20,143.2	1	AT&T	$3,244.5
2	Microsoft	7,418.0	2	EDS	12,422.1	2	NTT Data	3,172.0
3	Fujitsu	6,431.5	3	Digital Equipment	6,497.8	3	IBM	2,877.6
4	Computer Associates	2,460.9	4	Hewlett-Packard	6,257.5	4	Cisco Systems	2,667.8
5	NEC	2,322.0	5	CSC	3,895.0	5	3Com	1,962.8
6	Novell	1,897.2	6	Andersen Consulting	3,798.0	6	Matsushita	1,756.6
7	Oracle	1,526.9	7	Fujitsu	3,751.7	7	Bay Networks	1,700.0
8	SAP	1,349.2	8	Cap Gemini Sogeti	3,614.2	8	Motorola	1,457.3
9	Digital Equipment	1,299.6	9	Unisys	3,535.3	9	Hewlett-Packard	1,303.7
10	Hitachi	1,296.7	10	ADP	3,156.7	10	Alcatel	1,155.6

Source: Adapted and reprinted with permission of *Datamation* magazine from "The Datamation 100," *Datamation,* June 15, 1996, pp. 32–80. © 1996 by Cahners Publishing Company.

For example, *computer service centers* (or service bureaus) provide off-premises computer processing of customer jobs. *Systems integrators* take over complete responsibility for an organization's computer facilities when an organization outsources its computer operations. They may also assume responsibility for developing and implementing large systems development projects that involve many vendors and subcontractors. Many other services are available to end users, including computer rentals, systems design services, contract programming, consulting, education, and hardware maintenance.

Evaluating Hardware, Software, and Services

How do computer-using organizations evaluate and select hardware and software? Typically, they require suppliers to present bids and proposals based on system specifications developed during the design stage of systems development. Minimum acceptable physical and performance characteristics for all hardware and software requirements are established. Most large business firms and all government agencies formalize these requirements by listing them in a document called an RFP (request for proposal) or RFQ (request for quotation). Then they send the RFP or RFQ to appropriate vendors, who use it as the basis for preparing a proposed purchase agreement. See Figure 10.30.

ABC DEPARTMENT STORES INC.

PHONE (602)323-4557 BOX 5124 PHOENIX, ARIZONA 86581-0058

REQUEST FOR PROPOSAL

0001	1	1
REQUEST NO	PAGE	OF

1 ACME COMPUTER SUPPLY CO.
2704 E. MCDOWELL ROAD
PHOENIX, ARIZONA 85283

2

3

TERMS: (1) YOU ARE INVITED TO BID ON GOODS AND/OR SERVICES ITEMIZED BELOW.
(2) THIS REQUEST FOR PROPOSAL IS NOT INTENDED TO BE RESTRICTIVE. BRAND NAME OR MANUFACTURER'S NAME MAY BE USED FOR PURPOSE OF DESCRIPTION AND/OR TO ESTABLISH THE QUALITY DESIRED. BIDS ARE NOT RESTRICTED TO SUCH BRAND OR MANUFACTURER.
(3) THE ATTENTION OF THE BIDDER IS DIRECTED TO THE TERMS AND CONDITIONS ON THE REVERSE SIDE WHICH ARE INCORPORATED HEREIN.

WE RESERVE THE RIGHT TO REJECT ANY AND ALL BIDS.

RETURN THIS QUOTATION TO PURCHASING DEPT. AT ABOVE ADDRESS

DATE	BUYER	REQUISITION NO.	QUOTATION DUE DATE
6/24/9X	G. WILLIAMS	0001	7/24/9X

LINE	OBJECT CODE	QUANTITY	UNIT	PART NUMBER AND DESCRIPTION	UNIT PRICE	AMOUNT
1	08561	10	1	IMPACT DOT MATRIX PRINTER		
				MINIMUM SPECIFICATIONS:		
				FULLY COMPATIBLE WITH Microsoft Windows software		
				PRINTING SPEED: 200 CHARACTERS PER SECOND		
				PRINTING DIRECTION: BIDIRECTIONAL, LOGIC SEEKING		
				COLUMN WIDTH: 80 COLUMNS PICA		
				PAPER FEED: ADJUSTABLE SPROCKET FEED		
				PRINT HEAD: DISPOSABLE 24 PIN IMPACT DOT MATRIX		
				RIBBON TYPE: CARTRIDGE RIBBON		
				GRAPHICS CAPABILITY: HIGH-RESOLUTION GRAPHICS. SIX DENSITIES AND A GRAPHICS CHARACTER SET.		

IMPORTANT → SHOW ARIZONA AND LOCAL SALES TAX WHEN APPLICABLE. IF NOT SHOWN AS SEPARATE ITEM, IT WILL BE ASSUMED TO BE INCLUDED IN UNIT AND TOTAL PRICES.

SALES TAX

THIS IS NOT AN ORDER

TOTAL

SHIPMENT WILL BE MADE	TERMS	F.O.B. POINT
________ Days after Receipt of Order		ABC DEPARTMENT STORES PHOENIX, ARIZONA

We quote as shown, except as otherwise noted. The undersigned agrees that this proposal is a firm offer which shall be irrevocable and open for acceptance for ________ calendar days (60 calendar days unless otherwise specified) from the date set for submission of quotes.

SIGNATURE DATE

FIGURE 10.30

Example of a request for proposal (RFP). Note how it specifies the capabilities that must be met in the supplier's bid.

Computer users may use a scoring system of evaluation when there are several competing proposals for a hardware or software acquisition. They give each **evaluation factor** a certain number of maximum possible points. Then they assign each competing proposal points for each factor, depending on how well it meets the specifications of the computer user. Scoring each evaluation factor for several proposals helps organize and document the evaluation process. It also spotlights the strengths and weaknesses of each proposal. See Figure 10.31.

A formal evaluation process reduces the possibility of buying inadequate or unnecessary computer hardware or software. Badly organized computer operations, inadequate systems development, and poor purchasing practices may cause inadequate or unnecessary acquisitions. Therefore, it is necessary to use various methods of evaluation to measure key factors for computer hardware, software, and services. See Figures 10.32, 10.33, and 10.34.

Whatever the claims of hardware manufacturers and software suppliers, the performance of hardware and software must be demonstrated and evaluated. Independent hardware and software information services (such as the Datapro and Auerbach reporting services) should be used to gain detailed specification information and evaluations. Hardware and software should be demonstrated and evaluated. This can be done on the premises of the computer user or by visiting the operations of other computer users who have similar types of hardware or software. Other users are frequently the best source of information needed to evaluate the claims of manufacturers and suppliers. Vendors should be willing to provide the names of such users.

Large computer users frequently evaluate proposed hardware and software by requiring the processing of special benchmark test programs and test data. Users can then evaluate test results to determine which hardware device or software package displayed the best performance characteristics. Special software simulators may also be available that simulate the processing of typical jobs on several computers and evaluate their performances.

Hardware Evaluation Factors

When you evaluate computer hardware, you should investigate specific physical and performance characteristics for each hardware component to be acquired. This is true whether you are evaluating mainframes, microcomputers, or peripheral devices. Specific questions must be answered concerning many important factors. These **hardware evaluation factors** and questions are summarized in Figure 10.32.

Notice that there is much more to evaluating hardware than determining the fastest and cheapest computing device. For example, the question of possible obsolescence must be addressed by making a *technology* evaluation. The factor of ergonomics is also very important. Ergonomic factors ensure that computer hardware and software are user-friendly, that is, safe, comfortable, and easy-to-use. *Connectivity* is another important evaluation factor, since so many computer systems are now interconnected within wide area or local area telecommunications networks.

Software Evaluation Factors

You should evaluate software according to many factors that are similar to those used for hardware evaluation. Thus, the factors of performance, cost, reliability, availability, compatibility, modularity, technology, ergonomics, and support should be used to evaluate proposed software acquisitions. In addition, however, the **software evaluation factors** summarized in Figure 10.33 must also be considered. You should

---

FIGURE 10.31

Evaluating microcomputer operating systems. Note the use of a scoring system to evaluate operating systems based on eight key criteria.

	IBM OS/2 Warp	Microsoft Windows NT Workstation 3.5	Microsoft Windows 95 (Beta version)
Reliability	7.1	7.4	6.2
Recovery from failure	6.5	6.6	5.8
Multitasking	8.0	7.4	6.5
Speed	7.3	7.2	7.0
Technical support	7.0	6.2	5.8
Ease of use	7.7	7.0	7.3
Applications breadth	5.0	6.0	6.5
Memory management	7.4	6.8	6.6
Average rating	**7.0**	**6.8**	**6.5**

Source: Adapted from Michael Sullivan-Trainor, "IBM OS/2 Wins Tech Points," *Computerworld,* April 24, 1995, p. 118. Copyright © 1995 by Computerworld, Inc., Framingham, MA 01701—Reprinted from *Computerworld.*

answer the questions they generate in order to properly evaluate software purchases. For example, some software packages are notoriously slow, hard-to-use, or poorly documented. They are not a good choice, even if offered at attractive prices.

Most suppliers of hardware and software products and many other firms offer a variety of IS services to end users and organizations. Examples include assistance during installation or conversion of hardware and software, employee training, customer hot-lines, and hardware maintenance. Some of these services are provided without cost by hardware manufacturers and software suppliers. Other types of services can be contracted for at a negotiated price. Evaluation factors and questions for IS services are summarized in Figure 10.34.

Evaluating IS Services

Hardware Evaluation Factors	Rating
Performance What is its speed, capacity, and throughput?	
Cost What is its lease or purchase price? What will be its cost of operations and maintenance?	
Reliability What is the risk of malfunction and its maintenance requirements? What are its error control and diagnostic features?	
Availability When is the firm delivery date?	
Compatibility Is it compatible with existing hardware and software? Is it compatible with hardware and software provided by competing suppliers?	
Modularity Can it be expanded and upgraded by acquiring modular "add on" units?	
Technology In what year of its product life cycle is it? Does it use a new untested technology or does it run the risk of obsolescence?	
Ergonomics Has it been "human factors engineered" with the user in mind? Is it user-friendly, designed to be safe, comfortable, and easy to use?	
Connectivity Can it be easily connected to wide area and local area networks of different types of computers and peripherals?	
Environmental Requirements What are its electrical power, air-conditioning, and other environmental requirements?	
Software Is system and application software available that can best use this hardware?	
Support Are the services required to support and maintain it available?	
Overall Rating	

FIGURE 10.32

A summary of major hardware evaluation factors. Notice how you can use this to evaluate a computer system or a peripheral device.

FIGURE 10.33

A summary of selected software evaluation factors. Note that most of the hardware evaluation factors in Figure 10.32 can also be used to evaluate software packages.

Software Evaluation Factors	Rating
Efficiency Is the software a well-written system of computer instructions that does not use much memory capacity or CPU time?	
Flexibility Can it handle its processing assignments easily without major modification?	
Security Does it provide control procedures for errors, malfunctions, and improper use?	
Language Is it written in a programming language that is used by our computer programmers and users?	
Documentation Is the software well documented? Does it include helpful user instructions?	
Hardware Does existing hardware have the features required to best use this software?	
Other Factors What are its performance, cost reliability, availability, compatibility, modularity, technology, ergonomics, and support characteristics? (Use the hardware evaluation factor questions in Figure 10.32.)	
Overall Rating	

Other Implementation Activities

Testing

Testing, documentation, and training are keys to successful implementation of a new system. See Figure 10.35. The testing of a newly developed system is an important implementation activity. **System testing** involves testing hardware devices, testing and debugging computer programs, and testing information processing procedures. Programs are tested using test data that attempt to simulate all conditions that may arise during processing. In good programming practice (structured programming), programs are subdivided into levels of modules to assist their development, testing, and maintenance. Program testing usually proceeds from higher to lower levels of program modules until the entire program is tested as a unit. The program is then tested along with other related programs in a final systems *test*. If computer-aided software engineering (CASE) methodologies are used, such program testing is minimized because any automatically generated program code is more likely to be error-free.

An important part of testing is the production of tentative copies of displays, reports, and other output. These should be reviewed by end users of the proposed systems for possible errors. Of course, testing should not occur only during the system's implementation stage, but throughout the system's development process. For example, end users examine and critique input documents, screen displays, and processing procedures when a prototyping methodology is used during the systems design stage. Immediate end user testing is one of the benefits of a prototyping process.

Documentation

Developing good user **documentation** is an important part of the implementation process. Examples include manuals of operating procedures and sample data entry display screens, forms, and reports. During the implementation stage, system documentation manuals may be prepared to finalize the documentation of a large system.

Evaluation Factors for IS Services	Rating
Performance What has been their past performance in view of their past promises?	
Systems Development Are systems analysis and programming consultants available? What are their quality and cost?	
Maintenance Is equipment maintenance provided? What is its quality and cost?	
Conversion What systems development, programming, and hardware installation services will they provide during the conversion period?	
Training Is the necessary training of personnel provided? What is its quality and cost?	
Backup Are several similar computer facilities available for emergency backup purposes?	
Accessibility Does the vendor have a local or regional office that offers sales, systems development, and hardware maintenance services? Is a customer hot-line provided?	
Business Position Is the vendor financially strong, with good industry market prospects?	
Hardware Do they have a wide selection of compatible hardware devices and accessories?	
Software Do they offer a variety of useful system software and application packages?	
Overall Rating	

FIGURE 10.34

Evaluation factors for IS services. These factors focus on the quality of support services computer users may need.

When computer-aided systems engineering methods are used, documentation can be created and changed easily. Figure 10.36 illustrates the contents of system documentation stored in the repository of a CASE package.

Documentation serves as a method of communication among the people responsible for developing, implementing, and maintaining a computer-based system. Installing and operating a newly designed system or modifying an established application requires a detailed record of that system's design. Documentation is extremely important in diagnosing errors and making changes, especially if the end users or systems analysts who developed a system are no longer with the organization.

Training

Training is a vital implementation activity. IS personnel, such as user consultants, must be sure that end users are trained to operate a new system or its implementation will fail. Training may involve only activities like data entry, or it may also involve all aspects of the proper use of a new system. In addition, managers and end users must be educated in the fundamentals of information systems technology and its application to business operations and management. This basic knowledge should be supplemented by training programs for specific hardware devices, software packages, and end user applications. As we mentioned in Chapter 6, this educational role is a typical service of an organization's information center.

FIGURE 10.35
Testing, documentation, and training are keys to successful implementation.

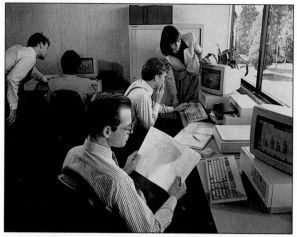

Howard Grey/Tony Stone Images.

Conversion Methods

The initial operation of a new computer-based system can be a difficult task. Such an operation is usually a **conversion** process in which the personnel, procedures, equipment, input/output media, and databases of an old information system must be converted to the requirements of a new system. Four major forms of system conversion are illustrated in Figure 10.37. They include:

- Parallel conversion.
- Phased conversion.
- Pilot conversion.
- Plunge or direct cutover.

Conversions can be done on a parallel basis, whereby both the old and the new system are operated until the project development team and end user management agree to switch completely over to the new system. It is during this time that

FIGURE 10.36

The contents of system documentation organized and stored using a CASE software package.

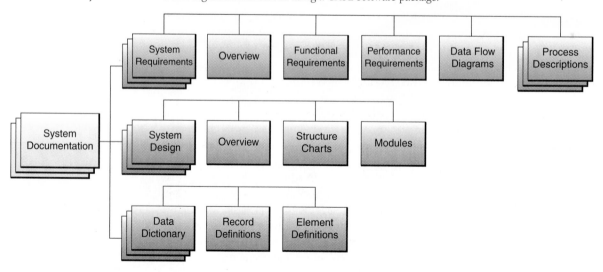

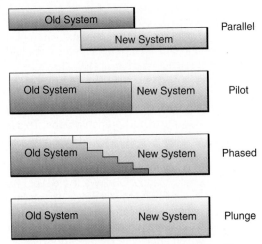

Parallel

Pilot

Phased

Plunge

Source: Adapted with the permission of Prentice Hall Inc., Upper Saddle River, NJ, from *Managing Information Technology: What Managers Need to Know* by E. Wainwright Martin, Daniel DeHayes, Jeffrey Hoffer, and William Perkins. © 1991, p. 299.

FIGURE 10.37

The four major forms of conversion to a new system.

the operations and results of both systems are compared and evaluated. Errors can be identified and corrected, and the operating problems can be solved before the old system is abandoned. Installation can also be accomplished by a direct cutover or *plunge* to the newly developed system. It can also be done on a phased basis, where only parts of a new application or only a few departments, branch offices, or plant locations at a time are converted. A phased conversion allows a gradual implementation process to take place within an organization. Similar benefits accrue from using a pilot conversion, where one department or other work site serves as a test site. A new system can be tried out at this site until developers feel it can be implemented throughout the organization.

Maintenance

Once a system is fully implemented and being operated by end users, the maintenance function begins. **Systems maintenance** is the monitoring, evaluating, and modifying of operational information systems to make desirable or necessary improvements. For example, the implementation of a new system usually results in the phenomenon known as the *learning curve*. Personnel who operate and use the system will make mistakes simply because they are not familiar with it. Though such errors usually diminish as experience is gained with a new system, they do point out areas where a system may be improved. Maintenance is also necessary for other failures and problems that arise during the operation of a system. End users and information systems personnel then perform a troubleshooting function to determine the causes of and solutions to such problems.

The maintenance activity includes a **postimplementation review** process to ensure that newly implemented systems meet the systems development objectives established for them. Errors in the development or use of a system must be corrected by the maintenance process. This includes a periodic review or audit of a system to ensure that it is operating properly and meeting its objectives. This audit is in addition to continually monitoring a new system for potential problems or necessary changes. Maintenance includes making modifications to a system due to changes in the business organization or the business environment. For example, new tax legislation, company reorganizations, and new business ventures usually require making a variety of changes to current business information systems.

MERRILL LYNCH AND COMERICA: EVALUATING WINDOWS NT VERSUS OS/2 WARP

Merrill Invests in NT

Merrill Lynch & Co. is bullish on Windows NT. The New York brokerage is rolling out Microsoft Corp.'s desktop and server operating system to 25,000 users as part of an $800 million plan to upgrade systems for its financial consultants.

"We looked at OS/2, which is a very good platform, but we felt NT is the future," said Ritch Gaiti, a first vice president and director of advanced office systems and technology at Merrill Lynch's Princeton, New Jersey, office. Gaiti said OS/2 lacks "longevity and acceptance," and UNIX "wasn't appropriate to support our branch-office environment."

These moves are an example of Wall Street's shift to Windows NT, according to Bob Rossettie, a financial services industry consultant at Ernst & Young in New York. Windows NT integrates more easily than UNIX or OS/2 with the Windows PCs that most financial services customers are using at home and at work. And most third-party banking and brokerage applications are being written for Windows NT, Rossettie said.

Comerica Banks on OS/2

Comerica, Inc, banks on IBM's OS/2 Warp to deliver scalability, multitasking, and high reliability to its tellers and customer service representatives at branches throughout Michigan. But Comerica's biggest payoff from its OS/2 Warp and Warp Server deployment has been extra time to devote to customers.

The overall reliability of OS/2 Warp Server and OS/2 Warp has allowed Comerica's network administrators to assume a proactive development stance rather than a reactive "fix-it" stance, according to Ken Milczynski, vice president and business area manager for Comerica's Branch Systems Development Technologies. "That gives

hours more time to spend with our end users and lets our end users spend more time with the bank's customers," Milczynski said.

Milczynski said the Detroit-based financial holding company opted to upgrade its older IBM OS/2 operating system to OS/2 Warp Server and OS/2 Warp in its corporate and branch offices. This is a trend mirrored by much of IBM's installed base—particularly in the financial and accounting industries.

A key reason for Comerica's satisfaction and increased deployment of OS/2 Warp and Warp Server is high reliability, according to Milczynski. Reliability—as in 100 percent uptime—is paramount to Comerica's 4,000 employees in its 280 branch offices and its 31 ComeriMart branches, which are located in grocery stores. For the ComeriMart sites, Comerica relies on OS/2 Warp server's Personally Safe and Sound, a backup and recovery service integrated into the core network operating system. This feature lets users dedicate one of the OS/2 Warp Servers as the backup server.

Another factor was that tests of OS/2 Warp found it uses "about 25 percent less memory than prior versions of OS/2, and it's well able to accommodate multitasking applications," Milczynski noted. The new integrated speech-enabled functions in the next version of OS/2 "may also be very appealing to our users in the future," he said.

IBM's technical support was also a key factor in Comerica's decision to upgrade to the OS/2 Warp server and operating system platforms. Milczynski said he and his fellow network administrators are able to directly call the OS/2 Warp engineers at IBM's laboratories in Boca Raton, Florida. "I'd say that's exactly the kind of return on investment we're looking for," Milczynski said.

CASE STUDY QUESTIONS

1. Do you agree with Merrill Lynch's decision to choose Windows NT over OS/2 and UNIX? Why or why not?

2. Do you agree with Comerica's decision to upgrade to OS/2 Warp? Why or why not?

3. What evaluation factors (see Figures 10.32, 10.33, and 10.34) were most important in these two decisions? Explain.

Source: Adapted from Thomas Hoffman, "Merrill Lynch Invests in NT," and Laura Didio, "Bank's Customer Service Boosted with OS/2 Warp," *Computerworld*, May 13, 1996, pp. 12, 72. Copyright © 1996 by Computerworld, Inc., Framingham, MA 01701—Reprinted from *Computerworld*.

Summary

- **The Systems Development Cycle.** End users and systems analysts should use a systems approach to help them develop information system solutions to business problems. This frequently involves an information systems development cycle where IS specialists and end users conceive, design, and implement computer-based information systems. The stages, activities, and products of the information systems development cycle are summarized in Figure 10.2.

- **CASE, Prototyping, and End User Development.** Major changes occurring in the traditional information systems development cycle include computer-aided systems engineering (CASE) software packages. These computerize and automate parts of the systems development process, and prototyping tools and methodologies, which promote an iterative, interactive process that develops prototypes of user interfaces and other information system components. Also, the application development capabilities built into end user software packages have made it easier for end users to develop their computer-based applications.

- **Implementing Business/IT Change.** Implementation activities include managing the introduction and implementation of changes in business processes, organizational structures, job assignments, and work relationships resulting from reengineering projects, strategic business alliances, and the introduction of new technologies. Companies use change management programs to reduce the risks and costs and maximize the benefits of such major changes in business and information technology.

- **Implementating IS.** The implementation process for information systems is summarized in Figure 10.38. Implementation involves acquisition, testing, documentation, training, installation, and conversion activities that transform a newly designed information system into an operational system for end users.

- **Evaluating Hardware, Software, and Services.** Business end users should know how to evaluate the acquisition of information system resources. Manufacturers and suppliers can be required to present bids and proposals based on system specifications developed during the design stage of systems development. A formal evaluation process reduces the possibility of incorrect or unnecessary purchases of computer hardware or software. Several major evaluation factors, summarized in Figures 10.32, 10.33, and 10.34, can be used to evaluate hardware, software, and IS services.

- **Acquisition**
  Evaluate and acquire necessary hardware and software resources and information system services. Screen vendor proposals.

- **Software Development**
  Develop any computer programs that will not be acquired externally as software packages. Make any necessary modifications to software packages that are acquired.

- **Training**
  Educate and train management, end users, and operating personnel. Use consultants or training programs to develop user competencies.

- **Testing**
  Test and make necessary corrections to the programs, procedures, and hardware used by a new system.

- **Documentation**
  Record and communicate detailed system specifications, including procedures for end users and IS personnel and examples of input/output displays and reports.

- **Conversion**
  Convert from the use of a present system to the operation of a new or improved system. This may involve operating both new and old systems in *parallel* for a trial period, operation of a *pilot* system on a trial basis at one location, *phasing* in the new system one location at a time, or an immediate *cutover* to the new system.

FIGURE 10.38

A summary of IS implementation activities.

Key Terms and Concepts

These are the key terms and concepts of this chapter. The page number of their first explanation is given in parentheses.

1. Change management (399)
2. Computer-aided systems engineering (389)
3. Computer industry (402)
4. Conversion methods (410)
5. Cost/benefit analysis (384)
6. Documentation (408)
7. Economic feasibility (382)
8. End user development (393)
9. End user resistance (399)
10. Evaluation factors (404)
    a. Hardware (406)
    b. Software (406)
    c. IS services (407)
11. External IS services (403)
12. Feasibility study (382)
13. Functional requirements (386)
14. Intangible
    a. Benefits (384)
    b. Costs (384)
15. IS component matrix (395)
16. IS implementation process (402)
17. Operational feasibility (383)
18. Organizational analysis (385)
19. Organizational feasibility (382)
20. Postimplementation review (411)
21. Prototype (391)
22. Prototyping (391)
23. Systems analysis (384)
24. Systems approach (380)
25. Systems design (387)
26. Systems development life cycle (381)
27. Systems investigation (382)
28. Systems maintenance (411)
29. System specifications (389)
30. System testing (408)
31. Tangible
    a. Benefits (384)
    b. Costs (384)
32. Technical feasibility (383)
33. Technology implementation (401)
34. User interface, data, and process design (387)

Review Quiz

Match one of the key terms and concepts listed above with one of the brief examples or definitions listed below. Try to find the best fit for answers that seem to fit more than one term or concept. Defend your choices.

_____ 1. Using an organized sequence of activities to study a problem or opportunity in a systems context.

_____ 2. Evaluating the success of a solution after it has been implemented.

_____ 3. Your evaluation shows that benefits outweigh costs for a proposed system.

_____ 4. The costs of acquiring computer hardware, software, and specialists.

_____ 5. Loss of customer goodwill caused by errors in a new system.

_____ 6. Increases in profits caused by a new system.

_____ 7. Improved employee morale caused by efficiency and effectiveness of a new system.

_____ 8. A multistep process to conceive, design, and implement an information system.

_____ 9. The first stage of the systems development cycle.

_____ 10. Determines the organizational, economic, technical, and operational feasibility of a proposed information system.

_____ 11. Cost savings and additional profits will exceed the investment required.

_____ 12. Reliable hardware and software are available to implement a proposed system.

_____ 13. Customers will not have trouble using a proposed system.

_____ 14. The proposed system supports the strategic plan of the business.

_____ 15. Studying in detail the information needs of users and any information systems presently used.

_____ 16. A detailed description of user information needs and the input, processing, output, storage, and control capabilities required to meet those needs.

_____ 17. The process that results in specifications for the hardware, software, people, network, and data resources and information products needed by a proposed system.

_____ 18. Systems design should focus on developing end user input/output methods, data structures, and programs and procedures.

_____ 19. A detailed description of the hardware, software, people, network, and data resources and information products required by a proposed system.

_____ 20. Acquiring hardware and software, testing and documenting a proposed system, and training people to use it.

_____ 21. Making improvements to an operational system.

_____ 22. Using software packages to computerize many of the activities in the systems development process.

_____ 23. A working model of an information system.

_____ 24. An interactive and iterative process of developing and refining information system prototypes.

_____ 25. Companies should try to minimize the risks and costs, and maximize the benefits of major changes in business and technology.

_____ 26. The source of hardware, software, and services for users.

_____ 27. Contracting with outside firms for computer processing, education, maintenance, and so on.

_____ 28. Performance, cost, reliability, technology, and ergonomics are examples.

_____ 29. Performance, cost, efficiency, language, and documentation are examples.

_____ 30. Maintenance, conversion, training, and business position are examples.

_____ 31. End users frequently resist the introduction of new technology.

_____ 32. User resistance to the introduction of IT can be overcome by their involvement and training.

_____ 33. Operate in parallel with the old system, use a test site, switch in stages, or cut over immediately to a new system.

_____ 34 Checking whether hardware and software work properly for end users.

_____ 35. A user manual communicates the design and operating procedures of a system.

_____ 36. New business ventures or legislation will probably require changes in some of our information systems.

_____ 37. Managers and business specialists can develop their own computer-based business applications.

Discussion Questions

1. Why have computer-aided systems development and prototyping methods become so popular? What are their limitations?

2. Refer to the Real World Case on Boston Beer Company in the chapter. What are the advantages and disadvantages of using consultants to do a company's systems development?

3. What applications software packages can be used by end users to help them do applications development? Give several examples.

4. Refer to the Real World Case on Merrill Lynch and Comerica. Does the overwhelming use of Windows operating systems make them the best choice for business PC users and network servers over OS/2 and UNIX? Explain your answer.

5. Pick a task you would like to computerize. How could you use the steps of the information systems development cycle as illustrated in Figure 10.2 to help you? Use examples to illustrate your answer.

6. How can a company use change management to minimize the risks and costs and maximize the benefits of changes in business and technology? Give several examples.

7. What are the three most important factors you would use in evaluating computer hardware? Computer software? Explain why.

8. Assume that in your first week on a new job you are asked to use a type of software package that you have never used before. What kind of user training should your company provide to you before you start?

9. Refer to the Real World Problem on WMX Technologies in the chapter. How can the systems development process be made more efficient and effective in developing and implementing new business/IT systems?

10. Assume a chain of retail stores is going to implement a new computer-based point-of-sale system. Should they use the parallel, plunge, phased, or pilot form of IS conversion? Which conversion strategy is best? Explain why.

Real World Problems

1. WMX Technologies: Workout in Systems Development

It often takes a year or more to design and deploy a new system. But what if you could encourage teamwork, make faster decisions and cut out wasteful processes along the way? WMX Technologies, Inc., an Oak Brook, Illinois–based environmental services firm, found that taking those steps helped it upgrade its billing system in just two months and save $11,000 on the project last year. The development team of end users and IS technicians was guided by a process-improved methodology called Workout, developed by Leap Technologies., Inc., in Chicago. It helps IS/business teams identify processes that need to be streamlined and then take action.

For WMX, the goal was to revamp an IBM mainframe-based billing system to track national accounts better and churn out customer invoices faster. WMX reengineered the system to enable about 20 end users in the billing department to download the mainframe data into PCs running Microsoft's Access database software.

Using Workout on that and several other projects yielded savings of $1.3 million last year. With more than 70 Workout teams in operation, WMX expects to save an additional $4.5 million this year, said John Biedry, WMX director of business. The methodology has other benefits for IS. "It's giving us a better understanding of the needs of our end users and their departments," said Patricia Anderson, manager of systems development at WMX.

In some ways, Workout is similar to total quality management (TQM), a philosophy of continuous process improvement. Like TQM, Workout emphasizes teamwork between departments—such as IS and accounting—to run through a list of deliverables, such as a decision about the appropriate graphical user interface for a system.

Unlike TQM, Workout is fast. Projects are done in six to eight weeks because ideas are acted on immediately. Without Workout, "It probably would have taken us a couple more months to get the new billing system in place," said Sharon Metz, supervisor of national accounts at WMX.

a. What business benefits did WMX derive from using Workout for business process reengineering?

b. How does Workout benefit the systems development process?

Source: Adapted from Thomas Hoffman, "Method to Upgrade Madness," *Computerworld,* April 1, 1996, p. 75. Copyright © 1996 by Computerworld, Inc., Framingham, MA 01701—Reprinted from *Computerworld.*

2. SAP America and Baxter Healthcare: Selecting Client/Server Software

When it comes to choosing client/server-based financial applications, the decision is frequently being made outside the information services department. "It seems that the CEO goes out to lunch with a SAP exec, has three martinis, and it's a done deal," says Jim Webber, head of Omicron, a consortium of East Coast–based information systems executives. "These decisions are being made at the top, without a lot of the disciplined cost/benefit analysis." Another analyst disagrees. "I think it's two martinis. But the SAP decision certainly seems to emanate from the top," says Barry Wilderman, vice president of application development strategies service at Meta Group, Inc.

IS managers and analysts alike agree that SAP America, Inc., has marketed its software to the executive suite so effectively that, quite often, neither IS nor managers of the lines of business are in on the decision. SAP's R/3, the leading enterprisewide financials package, is a "take-it-or-leave-it" purchase: You buy the whole suite of integrated applications—from general ledger to accounts payable—or none at all. Building on its integration strengths, SAP captured the imagination of senior management to the tune of $1.88 billion last year. Its closest competitor is Oracle Corp., with sales of $700 million. Yet, SAP is also winning over IS management. It has done so by fulfilling key functionality and technical requirements, such as the ability to handle high transaction volumes and do ad hoc reporting.

For example, Baxter Healthcare Corp. in Deerfield, Illinois, had a list of more than 500 requirements for its reengineering of mainframe financial systems to a client/server environment, says Steve Van Kuiken, director of new product development and SAP R/3 project director. His team screened some 50 packages. "SAP stood apart because of its breadth of functionality. Far and away, it met more of our requirements. It probably isn't as fully functional as our mainframe applications," he says, "but because of the integration, we'll have less reconciliation of the numbers, and we'll be able to close our books a lot faster."

a. Why did Baxter select SAP's R/3 software?

b. Do you think CEOs should decide to acquire software like SAP's R/3 without involving IS or business unit management? Explain.

Source: Adapted from Leslie Goff, "Doing the Power Lunch," *Computerworld,* March 25, 1996, p. 128. Copyright © 1996 by Computerworld, Inc., Framingham, MA 01701—Reprinted from *Computerworld.*

3. Northeast Utilities and Rochester Gas & Electric: Switching to Object-Based CASE Tools

How do you get from conventional systems development to object-oriented design? That's the problem facing an increasing number of corporate information systems shops as they begin serious client/server development. Large IS shops traditionally have used programming languages such as COBOL and PL/1, along with modeling techniques such as entity-relationship diagrams, for database design. But in the future, many developers say they will also need object-oriented capabilities to create complex, client/server applications.

"We realize objects can't do everything, but they're going to do an awful lot, eventually," said Douglas Stone, a computer scientist at Northeast Utilities, Inc., in Berlin, Connecticut. "We're looking for CASE tools that will bridge that gap."

The shift to an object-oriented approach for business development is long overdue, said David Sharon, president of CASE Associates, Inc. "It's natural evolution, but many IS professionals have been deeply rooted in their on-the-job experiences" with traditional development, he said. Indeed, many IS shops are concerned that their staffs won't be able to make the transition to object-oriented development and tools.

"People are telling us that 50 percent of the COBOL programmers in the world will not make the paradigm shift," said William Lamb, a senior analyst at Rochester Gas & Electric Co. in Rochester, New York. "That's not the tool I'm looking for if 50 percent of the programmers around here are going to be rendered useless."

That's why CASE tool sets that can help developers make the transition are crucial, Stone said. "We need something that will let us work up to that, so we can do entity-relationship diagrams in the right place and build object models in the right place. We have to move over in a coordinated fashion," he said.

a. Why is object-oriented design a problem for the IS departments of some companies?

b. How can CASE tools help solve this problem?

Source: Adapted from Frank Hays, "Tools Ease Migration to Object-Based Design," *Computerworld,* April 1, 1996, p. 52. Copyright © 1996 by Computerworld, Inc., Framingham, MA 01701—Reprinted from *Computerworld.*

4. U.S. Army National Guard and Army Reserve: Changing Technology and User Requirements

Sixty thousand diskless workstations, 10,000 UNIX servers, 2 million lines of Ada code, and multilevel security. It seemed like a good idea at the time. But that was then—1990—and this is $500 million later; and the $1.8 billion project to set up the world's largest client/server system for the U.S. Army National Guard and Army Reserve recently completed a major course correction.

The diskless X Window System terminals became full-fledged PCs, UNIX gave way to Microsoft Windows NT, custom Ada programs bowed to software packages, and the elaborate security was canceled due to lack of interest. The changes, plus earlier delays, pushed final implementation of the Reserve Component Automation System (RCAS) out to 2002, eight years later than planned. RCAS managers hope that cost savings from the restructured program will still allow the Army to complete the program within the original cost estimate.

The restructuring of RCAS is in part the result of rapid changes in technology that made 1990 assumptions increasingly obsolete as the huge project crept forward. Another issue was the apparent failure of program managers to get enough user input early on. RCAS is intended to support the day-to-day activities of 10,500 Guard and Reserve units at 4,000 sites in 11 functional areas such as logistics, finance, and training. It is also intended to enable the rapid mobilization of forces during wartime.

The custom programs written in the Ada programming language were needed to satisfy very complex multilevel security requirements. Databases were to have held a combination of unclassified, confidential, and secret data, with the operating system permitting access to just the data for which an individual user was cleared. But it turned out that little RCAS data are classified, so multilevel database security was scrapped in favor of point-to-point encryption.

Meanwhile, users already accustomed to Windows-based PCs said "no way" to the unfamiliar UNIX operating system and the limited diskless workstations. The revised system is "not some arcane system that is different from ones the soldier uses at work or at home," said Maj. Rusty Lingenfelter, director of information management at the Iowa Army National Guard in Johnston. "So they can come in on weekends and sit down to something that is familiar."

a. Is the failure of the original RCAS systems design due to developments in technology or lack of user involvement? Explain.

b. Could the major design and implementation problems of the RCAS project have been avoided? What should have been done differently?

Source: Adapted from Gary Anthes, "Army Changes Client/Server Attack," *Computerworld,* March 11, 1996, p. 73. Copyright © 1996 by Computerworld, Inc., Framingham, MA 01701—Reprinted from *Computerworld.*

Application Exercises

1. System Study Report

Study an information system described in a case study in this text or one used by an organization to which you have access. Write up the results in a **system study report.** Make a presentation to the class based on the results of your system study. Use the outline in Figure 10.39 as a table of contents for your report and the outline of your presentation. Use presentation software and/or overhead transparencies to display key points of your analysis.

2. ABC Company: End User Spreadsheet Development

Use an electronic spreadsheet and follow the basic activities of the end user spreadsheet application development process in Figure 10.40.

Create the ABC Company financial performance spreadsheet as shown in Figure 10.41, using the formulas shown in Figure 10.42. The basic parameters (control variables) in this spreadsheet are the amount of money initially invested, the ratio of expenses to revenue, the tax rate, and the rate of growth in revenue. These parameter values are placed in a control area at the top of the spreadsheet so they can be identified and changed easily to see their impact on the other calculations.

Other formulas simply reflect that profit is revenue minus expenses and after-tax profit is profit minus taxes. The sum and average functions complete the final two columns of the spreadsheet.

a. Enter $1,000 for 1996 sales, 60 percent for the ratio of expenses to revenue, 40 percent for the tax rate, and 10 percent for the rate of revenue growth. Notice how the spreadsheet as shown in Figure 10.41 is instantly generated and displayed. Store and print this spreadsheet.

b. Use the spreadsheet you created to perform what-if analysis. Change the 1996 revenue, the revenue growth rate, the expense ratio, or tax rate and observe the impact on profits. (For example, increase revenue for 1996 by $1,000, increase expenses to 65 percent of revenue, and decrease taxes to 25 percent of profit.) Print a copy of the spreadsheet with the results of these changes, then make at least one more set of changes to values of your own choosing and print a copy of those results as well.

c. Create graphics displays of parts of the spreadsheet you developed and get printouts of your graphs. Figure 10.43 shows examples of the kinds of graphs that might be generated. Make changes to your spreadsheet parameter values and note how the graph results change to reflect these changes.

d. Write a short explanation of what happened when you did a what-if analysis and its implications for a managerial end user.

FIGURE 10.39

Outline of a system study report.

- **Introduction to the organization and information system.** The name of the organization, what the organization does, and the type of information system studied.
- **Analysis of the current information system.** Identify the following system components in your report. Prepare an IS component matrix (see Figures 10.21 and 10.22 on pages 396 and 397) to summarize the components of your information system. Use the checklist in Figure 10.20 to help you identify the components that are or should be part of this information system.
  - Input, processing, output, storage, and control methods currently used.
  - Hardware, software, and people involved.
  - Data captured and information products produced.
  - Files and databases accessed and maintained.
- **Evaluation of the current information system.**
  - **Efficiency:** Does it do the job right? Is the information system well organized? Inexpensive? Fast? Does it require minimum resources? Process large volumes of data, produce many information products?
  - **Effectiveness:** Does it do the right job? The way the end users want it done? Give them the information they need, the way they want it? Does it support the objectives of the organization?
- **Design and implementation of an information system proposal.**
  - Do end users need a new system or just improvements? Why?
  - What exactly are you recommending they do?
  - Is it feasible? What are its benefits and costs?
  - What will it take to implement your recommendations?

FIGURE 10.40

The basic activities of the spreadsheet development process.

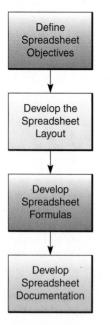

- What information and decision support should be provided by the spreadsheet?

- What should be the column and row headings of the spreadsheet? What other spreadsheet areas need to be specified?

- What mathematical relationships need to be expressed as formulas in the spreadsheet? What built-in spreadsheet functions can be used to perform spreadsheet calculations?

- What information about spreadsheet objectives, assumptions, values, and control measures needs to be documented?

FIGURE 10.41

An example of a simple financial spreadsheet for the ABC Company.

ABC Company: Financial Performance					
	1996	1997	1998	Total	Average
Revenue	$1,000.00	$1,100.00	$1,210.00	$3,310.00	$1,103.33
Expenses	600.00	660.00	726.00	1,986.00	662.00
Profit	400.00	440.00	484.00	1,324.00	441.33
Taxes	160.00	176.00	193.60	529.60	176.53
Profit after taxes	$ 240.00	$ 264.00	$ 290.40	$ 794.40	$ 264.80

FIGURE 10.42

These formulas and functions are the spreadsheet business model for the financial spreadsheet in Figure 10.41.

	A	B	C	D	E	F
1			ABC Company: Financial Performance			
2						
3	Performance parameters					
4	1996 Revenue	1000				
5	Annual revenue growth	0.1				
6	Ratio expenses to revenue	0.6				
7	Tax rate	0.4				
8						
9						
10		1996	1997	1998	Total	Average
11	Revenue	=B4	=B11*(1+$B5)	=C11*(1+$B5)	=SUM(B11:D11)	=AVERAGE(B11:D11)
12	Expenses	=B11*$B6	=C11*$B6	=D11*$B6	=SUM(B12:D12)	=AVERAGE(B12:D12)
13	Profit	=B11−B12	=C11−C12	=D11−D12	=SUM(B13:D13)	=AVERAGE(B13:D13)
14	Taxes	=B13*$B7	=C13*$B7	=D13*$B7	=SUM(B14:D14)	=AVERAGE(B14:D14)
15	Profit after taxes	=B13−B14	=C13−C14	=D13−D14	=SUM(B15:D15)	=AVERAGE(B15:D15)

3. Student Scores: End User Database Development

Use a database management software package and follow the basic activities of the end user database development process in Figure 10.44. Create a Student Exam Scores database table to store the sample data in Figure 10.45. Each student record includes the student's name, Social Security number, gender, and grades for three exams.

a. Create the Student Exam Scores table, enter the data records for the seven students shown below, and get a printed listing of the Student Exam Scores table.

b. Edit the Student Exam Scores file by changing at least two exam scores and add at least one new student record. Choose any values you want for these changes and additions. When you have completed these changes, get another printed listing of the Student Exam Scores table.

c. Use a database query to retrieve a printed listing of all students whose score on the first exam was 85 or higher, similar to Figure 10.46.

d. Create and print a report showing the exam scores and total points earned by students sorted in ascending order by total points, similar to Figure 10.47.

FIGURE 10.43

Examples of a bar graph and pie chart of the data in the spreadsheet shown in Figure 10.41.

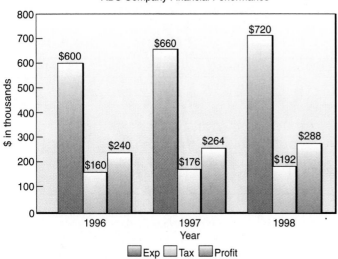

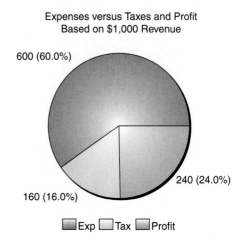

FIGURE 10.44

The basic activities of the end user database development process.

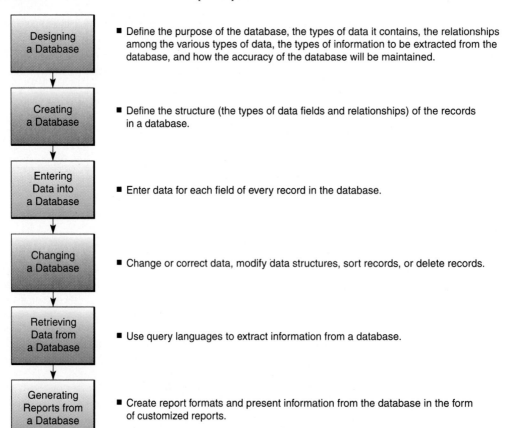

- Designing a Database
  - ■ Define the purpose of the database, the types of data it contains, the relationships among the various types of data, the types of information to be extracted from the database, and how the accuracy of the database will be maintained.

- Creating a Database
  - ■ Define the structure (the types of data fields and relationships) of the records in a database.

- Entering Data into a Database
  - ■ Enter data for each field of every record in the database.

- Changing a Database
  - ■ Change or correct data, modify data structures, sort records, or delete records.

- Retrieving Data from a Database
  - ■ Use query languages to extract information from a database.

- Generating Reports from a Database
  - ■ Create report formats and present information from the database in the form of customized reports.

Sample Student Exam Scores

Name	Soc. Sec. #	Gender	Exam 1	Exam 2	Exam 3
Bevins, M.	386-27-1894	Female	88	84	91
Davidson, P.	684-76-9013	Male	72	79	74
Gorton, A.	713-23-9870	Male	93	90	94
Jones, J.	593-94-7826	Female	57	63	61
Miller, G.	774-92-6927	Female	96	94	98
Perkins, P.	657-83-6204	Male	53	59	64
Shaw, J.	546-68-0632	Female	76	74	79

FIGURE 10.45
Sample student exam scores.

Name	Social Security Number	Gender	Exam 1
Bevins, M.	386-27-1894	Female	88
Gorton, A.	713-23-9870	Male	93
Miller, G.	774-92-6927	Female	96

FIGURE 10.46
The results of a database query for all students whose score on the first exam exceeded 85 percent.

FIGURE 10.47
A Student Exam Scores report.

Summary of Student Performance

Name	Social Security Number	Gender	Exam 1	Exam 2	Exam 3	Total
Perkins, P.	657-83-6204	Male	53	59	64	176
Jones, J.	593-94-7826	Female	57	63	61	181
Davidson, P.	684-76-9013	Male	72	79	74	225
Shaw, J.	546-68-0632	Female	76	74	79	229
Bevins, M.	386-27-1894	Female	88	84	91	263
Gorton, A.	713-23-9870	Male	93	90	94	277
Miller, G.	774-92-6927	Female	96	94	98	288
Average			76.428571	77.571429	80.142857	234.14286

Review Quiz Answers

1. 24
2. 20
3. 5
4. 31b
5. 14b
6. 31a
7. 14a
8. 26
9. 27
10. 12
11. 7
12. 32
13. 17
14. 19
15. 23
16. 13
17. 25
18. 34
19. 29
20. 16
21. 28
22. 2
23. 21
24. 22
25. 1
26. 3
27. 11
28. 10a
29. 10b
30. 10c
31. 9
32. 33
33. 4
34. 30
35. 6
36. 28
37. 8

Selected References

1. Allen, Brandt, and Andrew Boynton. "Information Architecture —In Search of Efficient Flexibility," *MIS Quarterly,* December 1991.

2. Belmonte, Richard, and Richard Murray. "Getting Ready for Strategic Change." *Information Systems Management,* Summer 1993.

3. Cafasso, Rosemary. "Few IS Projects Come in on Time, on Budget." *Computerworld,* December 12, 1994.

4. Cooprider, Jay, and John Henderson. "Technology-Process Fit: Perspectives on Achieving Prototyping Effectiveness." *Journal of Management Information Systems,* Winter 1990–91.

5. Davenport, Thomas H. *Process Innovation: Reengineering Work through Information Technology.* Boston: Harvard Business School Press, 1993.

6. Forte, Gene, and Ronald Norman. "CASE: A Self-Assessment by the Software Engineering Community." *Communications of the ACM,* April 1992.

7. Guha, Subashish; William Kettinger; and James Teng. "Business Process Reengineering: Building a Comprehensive Methodology." *Information Systems Management,* Summer 1993.

8. Hershey, Gerald, and Donna Kizzier. *Planning and Implementing End User Information Systems.* Dallas: South Western Publishing, 1992.

9. Keen, Peter G. W. *Shaping the Future: Business Design through Information Technology.* Boston: Harvard Business School, 1991.

10. Maglitta, Joseph. "Rocks in the Gears: Reengineering the Workplace." *Computerworld,* October 3, 1994.

11. McConnell, Vicki, and Karl Koch. *Computerizing the Corporation: The Intimate Link between People and Machines.* New York: Van Nostrand Reinhold, 1990.

12. Mische, Michael. "Transnational Architecture: A Reengineering Approach." *Information Systems Management,* Winter 1995.

13. Morgan, James N. *Application Cases in MIS.* 2nd ed. Burr Ridge, IL: Richard D. Irwin, 1996.

14. Murray, Richard, and Richard Hardin. "The IT Organization of the Future." *Information Systems Management,* Fall 1991.

15. Murray, Richard, and Dorothy Trefts. "Building the Business of the Future: The IT Imperative." *Information Systems Management,* Fall 1992.

16. O'Brien, James A., and Craig A. VanLengen. "Evaluating Information Systems Documentation Techniques." *Journal of Information Systems Education,* Fall 1992.

17. Orlikowsky, Wanda. "CASE Tools as Organizational Change: Investigating Incremental and Radical Changes in Systems Development." *MIS Quarterly,* September 1993.

18. Pei, Daniel, and Carmine Cutone. "Object-Oriented Analysis and Design." *Information Systems Management,* Winter 1995.

19. Sprague, Ralph, and Barbara McNurlin. *Information Systems Management in Practice.* 3rd ed. Englewood Cliffs, NJ: Prentice Hall, 1993.

20. Vessey, Iris, and Robert Glass. "Applications-Based Methodologies: Development by Application Domain." *Information Systems Management,* Fall 1994.

21. Watson, Hugh, and Mark Frolick. "Determining Information Requirements for an EIS." *MIS Quarterly,* September 1993.

22. Whitten, Jeffrey; Lonnie Bentley; and Vic Barlow. *Systems Analysis and Design Methods.* 3rd ed. Burr Ridge, IL: Richard D. Irwin, 1994.

Enterprise and Global Management of Information Technology

LEARNING OBJECTIVES

After reading and studying this chapter, you should be able to:

1. Identify the major ways information technology has affected managers.
2. Explain how problems of information system performance can be solved by management involvement in IS planning and control.
3. Identify how information technology is affecting the structure and activities of organizations.
4. Identify the five major dimensions of the information resource management concept and explain how they affect the management of the information systems function.
5. Identify several cultural, political, and geoeconomic challenges that confront managers in the management of global information technology.
6. Explain the effect on global IT strategy of the trend toward a transnational business strategy by international business organizations.
7. Identify several considerations that affect the choice of IT applications, IT platforms, data definitions, and systems development methods made by a global business.

Section I

Managing Information Resources and Technologies

Introduction

The strategic and operational importance of information technology in business is no longer questioned.

> What is less clear is how business executives can ensure that their firms benefit from new opportunities afforded by IT and avoid its well-known, oft-repeated pitfalls: botched development projects; escalating costs with no apparent economic benefit; organizational disruption; and technical glitches. Competence and confidence in handling IT will clearly be key to effective management in the coming decade. Senior executives can no longer delegate IT policy and strategic decision making to technical professionals [16].

Thus, there is a real need for business end users to understand how to manage this vital organizational function. In this section, we will explore how IT has affected managers and organizations, and stress the concept of *information resource management* as a key framework for managing information technology by both end user managers and IS managers. So whether you plan to be an entrepreneur and run your own business, a manager in a corporation, or a managerial-level professional, managing information system resources and technologies will be one of your major responsibilities. See Figure 11.1.

Managers and Information Technology

When computers were first introduced into business, predictions were made that there would be significant changes in management and organizations. The information processing power and programmed decision-making capability of computer-based information systems were supposedly going to cause drastic reductions in employees, including middle management and supervisory personnel. Centralized computer systems would process all of the data for an organization, control all of its operations, and make most of its decisions [19].

FIGURE 11.1

Information technology is having a major impact on the management, structure, and work activities of organizations.

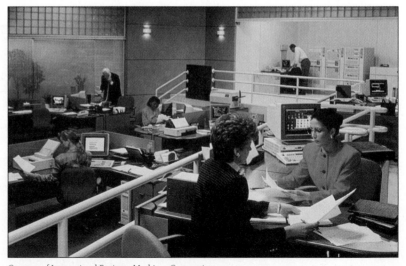

Courtesy of International Business Machines Corporation.

This did not prove to be the case. Changes in organizational structure and types of personnel did occur, but they were not as dramatic as predicted. Naturally, highly automated systems do not require as many people as manual methods. Therefore, there have been significant reductions in the number of people required to perform manual tasks in many organizations. For example, computerized accounting systems have drastically reduced the need for clerical accounting personnel, and factory automation has greatly reduced the demand for many types of factory workers. However, these reductions were countered by dramatic increases in sales and service personnel, knowledge workers, and managers as businesses increased the depth and scope of their operations. It was also countered to some extent by the need for more technicians and professionals to develop and run the computer-based information systems of organizations [23].

Now, however, a variety of forces seem to be causing a significant change in the structure and distribution of managers in organizations in which information technology plays a major role. For example, Peter Drucker, the visionary management scholar and author, predicts that by the end of the 1990s, the typical large business will have fewer than half the levels of management and no more than one-third of the managers it had in the 1980s. He also predicts that information technology will allow the structure of information-based organizations to be more like those of hospitals, universities, and symphony orchestras. They will be *knowledge-based*, "composed largely of specialists who direct and discipline their own performance through organized feedback from colleagues, customers, and headquarters" [13].

As Figure 11.2 illustrates, the competitive pressures of the business and technology environment of the 1990s are forcing major firms to rethink their use and management of information technology. Many business executives now see information technology as an *enabling technology* for managing the *cooperative advantage* that business units must have to successfully confront the competitive measures they face. For example, telecommunications networks and more cost-effective hardware

---

FIGURE 11.2

Information technology must be managed to meet the challenges of the business and technology environment of the 1990s.

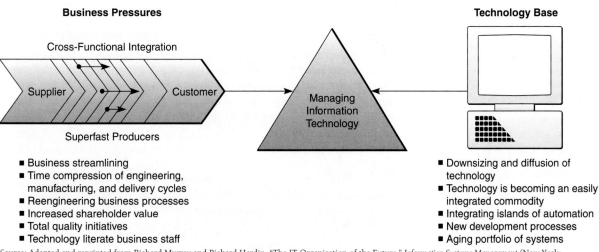

Source: Adapted and reprinted from Richard Murray and Richard Hardin, "The IT Organization of the Future," *Information Systems Management* (New York: Auerbach Publications), Fall 1991, p. 69. ©1991 Warren, Gorham & Lamont. Used with permission.

FIGURE 11.3

Information technologies are
enablers of innovation in
managerial processes.

- Executive information systems that provide realtime information.
- Electronic linkages to external partners in strategic processes.
- Computer-based simulations that support learning-oriented planning.
- Electronic conferencing and group decision support systems.
- Expert systems for planning and capital allocation.
- Information technology infrastructure for communications and group work.

Source: Adapted and reprinted by permission of Harvard Business School Press from *Process Innovation: Reengineering Work through Information Technology* by Thomas H. Davenport. Boston: 1993, p. 286. Copyright © 1993 by Ernst & Young.

and software are enabling individuals, business units, and organizations to be "wired together" in close business relationships that can provide the communication and coordination needed in today's competitive global marketplace [25].

Thus, **information technology**, that is, the technologies of modern computer-based information systems, is once again being portrayed as a major force for organizational and managerial change. Thanks to telecommunications networks and personal computers, computing power and information resources are now more readily available to more managers than ever before. In fact, these and other information technologies are already promoting innovative changes in managerial decision making, organizational structures, and managerial work activities in companies around the world [12]. See Figure 11.3.

For example, the decision support capability provided by information systems technology is changing the focus of managerial decision making. Managers freed from number crunching chores must now face tougher strategic policy questions in order to develop realistic alternatives for today's dynamic competitive environment. The use of telecommunications networks, electronic mail, and electronic meeting systems to coordinate work activity is another example of the impact of information technology on management. Middle managers no longer need to serve as conduits for the transmission of operations feedback or control directives between operational managers and top management. Thus, forecasters see drastic reductions in the layers and numbers of middle management, and the dramatic growth of work groups consisting of task-focused teams of specialists [13, 23].

Finally, information technology presents managers with a major managerial challenge. Managing the information system resources of a business is no longer the sole province of information systems specialists. Instead, **information resource management** (IRM) has become a major responsibility of all managers. That is, data and information, computer hardware and software, telecommunications networks, and IS personnel should be viewed as valuable resources that must be managed by all levels of management to ensure the effective use of information technology for the operational and strategic benefit of a business.

Information Systems Performance

As Figure 11.4 illustrates, the information systems function has performance problems in many organizations. The promised benefits of information technology have not occurred in many documented cases. Studies by management consulting firms, computer user groups, and university researchers have shown that many businesses have not been successful in managing their computer resources and information services departments. Figure 11.4 dramatizes the results of research on the types of problems that arise when new information technologies, especially client/server networks,

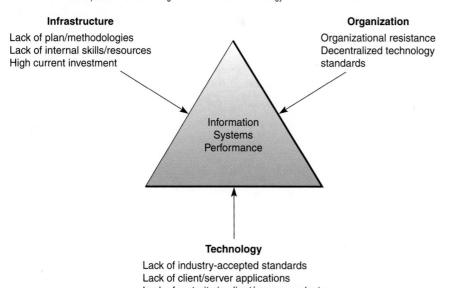

Infrastructure
Lack of plan/methodologies
Lack of internal skills/resources
High current investment

Organization
Organizational resistance
Decentralized technology standards

Information Systems Performance

Technology
Lack of industry-accepted standards
Lack of client/server applications
Lack of maturity in client/server products

FIGURE 11.4

Performance problems in information systems. New information technologies can cause infrastructure, organization, and technology problems in an organization.

Source: Adapted and reprinted from John Levis and Peter Von Schilling, "Lessons from Three Implementations: Knocking Down Barriers to Client/Server," *Information Systems Management* (New York: Auerbach Publications), Summer 1994, p. 21. © 1994 Warren, Gorham & Lamont. Used with permission.

are implemented in many businesses [20]. Thus, it is evident that in many organizations information technology is not being used effectively, efficiently, or economically [12, 23]. For example:

- Information technology is not being used *effectively* by companies that use IT primarily to computerize traditional business processes instead of using it for decision support and innovative processes and products to gain competitive advantages.

- Information technology is not being used *efficiently* by information services groups that provide poor response times, frequent downtimes, incompatible systems, unintegrated data, and applications development backlogs.

- Information technology is not being used *economically* in many cases. Information technology costs have risen faster than other costs in many businesses, even though the cost of processing each unit of data is decreasing due to dramatic price reductions and improvements in hardware and software technology.

What is the solution to problems of poor performance in the information systems function? There are no quick and easy answers. However, the experiences of successful organizations reveal that the basic ingredient of high-quality information systems performance is extensive and meaningful *involvement* of managers and end users in the *governance* of the IS function [4, 25]. This should be the key ingredient in shaping the response of management to the challenge of improving the business value of information technology.

Proper involvement of managers in the management of IT requires the development of governance structures that encourage the active participation of managerial end users in planning and controlling the business uses of IT. Thus, many organizations have developed policies and procedures that require managers to be involved in IT

Management Involvement and Governance

decisions that affect their business units. This helps managers avoid IS performance problems in their business units in the key areas outlined in Figure 11.4. Without this high degree of involvement, managers cannot hope to improve the strategic business value of information technology. Figure 11.5 illustrates several major levels of **management involvement** and governance of information technology.

- Many organizations use an *executive information technology committee* of top management to do strategic information system planning and to coordinate the development of major information systems projects. This committee includes senior management of the major divisions of the firm, as well as the **chief information officer** (CIO) of the organization, who is the senior executive responsible for governance of the IS function.

- A *steering committee* of business unit managers, operating managers, and management personnel from the information services department may be created to oversee the progress of critical systems development projects. The committee meets on a regular basis to review progress made, to settle disputes, and to change priorities, if necessary.

- Development of decision support and work group systems requires managerial involvement in the prototyping process for such projects. End user managers must also accept their responsibility for managing the resources and quality of information services provided to their business units and work groups.

Let's now look at two actual examples of management involvement and governance of information technology in business [2].

Hughes Space and Communications Co.

Hughes has established rules, institutions, and a process to manage information, according to CIO Gary R. Osborn. To manage a specific item of information, the business unit divides responsibility between "process owners," such as a manufacturing vice president, and the IS department. Process owners are the sources of data who

FIGURE 11.5

Levels of management involvement in IS governance. Successful information systems performance requires the involvement of managers in IS governance.

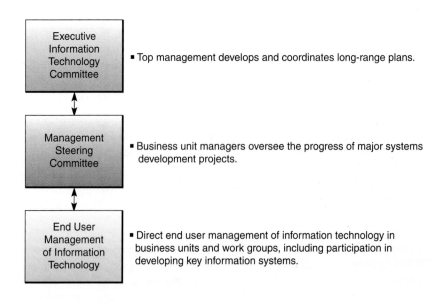

define their quality, accuracy, and accessibility. IS sets rules distinguishing different kinds of data and dictating how data are formatted on the system. A policy board meets every two to four weeks to decide changes in information policy. Broader information issues are discussed, along with corporate issues, in a quarterly meeting of senior Hughes executives. Osborn sits on both boards.

Chemical Banking Corporation

After Chemical Bank and Manufacturers Hanover Trust Co. merged, a business technology management council was established to set technology direction for the combined companies. The council is chaired by Denis J. O'Leary, Chemical's executive vice president and CIO. It includes the top IS executives from both central IS and Chemical's business units, senior non-IS executives from Chemical business units, and the controller's office. The council sets policies, standards, and guidelines that direct technology policies for both line managers and IS managers. The council has spun off subcommittees such as the two-year-old information management committee. The committee is cochaired by O'Leary, the CFO, and the head of credit policy. It establishes rules and principles for managing information across the company.

Organizations and Information Technology

One way to understand the organizational impact of information technology is to view an **organization as a sociotechnical system.** In this context, people, tasks, technology, culture, and structure are the basic components of an organization. Figure 11.6 illustrates this conceptual framework, which was first developed by Harold Leavitt [18]. This concept emphasizes that to improve an organization's performance, managers must (1) change one or more of these components and (2) take into account the relationships among these interdependent components. This is especially important for the proper use of information technology. In the past, firms have used information systems technology to automate organizational tasks without giving sufficient consideration to its strategic impact on the organization. Thus, a major managerial challenge of information technology is to develop information systems that promote strategic improvements in how an organization supports its people, tasks, technology, culture, and structure.

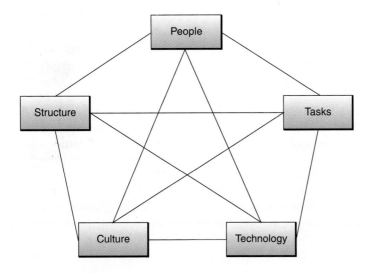

FIGURE 11.6

Organizations as sociotechnical systems. Information systems must accommodate the people, tasks, technology, culture, and structure components and relationships of an organization.

People

Managers are individuals with a variety of preferences for information and diverse capabilities for effectively using information provided to them. As we pointed out in Chapter 8, information systems must produce information products tailored to meet managers' individual needs, as management information, decision support, and executive information systems can do.

Tasks

The tasks of many organizations have become quite complex and inefficient over time. In many cases, information technology has been used to do the same old thing, only faster. However, as we discussed in Chapter 9, IT can play a major role in fighting organizational complexity by supporting the **reengineering of business processes.** For example, IT developments such as electronic data interchange dramatically reduce the need for several departments to be involved in preparing, authorizing, checking, and sending paper business documents. This can eliminate many manual tasks and required procedures, and significantly improve communication and strategic cooperation between organizations.

Technology

The technology of computer-based information systems continues to grow more sophisticated and complex. However, this technology should not dictate the information needs of end users in the performance of their organizational tasks. It should accommodate the management culture and structure of each organization. For example, executive information systems have shown they can overcome many of the objections of top executives to the lack of individual and task flexibility of previous types of management information systems.

Culture

Organizations and their subunits have a culture that is shared by managers and other employees. That is, they have a unique set of organizational values and styles. For example, managers at some organizations share an informal, collegial, entrepreneurial spirit that stresses initiative, collaboration, and risk taking. Managers at other organizations may stress a more formal "do it by the book," "go through the chain of command," or "don't risk the stockholders' money" approach. Naturally, the designs of information systems and information products must accommodate such differences. For example, managers in a corporate culture that encourages entrepreneurial risk taking and collaboration will probably favor executive information systems that give them quick access to forecasts about competitors and customers, and E-mail and groupware systems that make it easy to communicate with colleagues anywhere.

Structure

Organizations structure their management, employees, and job tasks into a variety of organizational subunits. However, we have just mentioned how Drucker and others are emphasizing that information technology must support a process of *organizational redesign.* So the IS function must no longer assume a hierarchical, centralized, organizational structure that it supports by centralizing processing power, databases, and systems development at the corporate headquarters level. This type of structure emphasizes gathering data into centralized databases and producing reports to meet the information needs of functional executives.

Instead, IT must be able to support a more decentralized, collaborative type of organizational structure, which needs more interconnected client/server networks, distributed databases, downsized computers, and systems development resources distributed to business unit and work group levels. Thus, information technology must emphasize quick and easy communication and collaboration among individuals, business units, and other organization work groups, using electronics instead of paper. For example, information technologies such as E-mail, groupware, and desktop videoconferencing enable the development of interorganizational information systems and network organizational structures that are vital to the formation of the virtual companies discussed in Chapter 9.

Information resource management (IRM) has become a popular way to emphasize a major change in the management and mission of the information systems function in many organizations. IRM can be viewed as having five major dimensions. Figure 11.7 illustrates this conceptual framework [27].

Information Resource Management

- **Strategic Management.** Information technology must be managed to contribute to a firm's strategic objectives and competitive advantages, not just for operational efficiency or decision support.
- **Functional Management.** Information technology and information systems can be managed by functional organizational structures and managerial techniques commonly used throughout other business units.
- **Resource Management.** Data and information, hardware and software, telecommunications networks, and IS personnel are vital organizational resources that must be managed like other business assets.
- **Technology Management.** All technologies that process, store, and communicate data and information throughout the enterprise should be managed as integrated systems of organizational resources.
- **Distributed Management.** Managing the use of information technology and information system resources in business units or work groups is a key responsibility of their managers, no matter what their function or level in the organization.

Strategic Management

The IRM concept emphasizes a strategic management view that we emphasized in Chapter 9 and have stressed throughout this text. That is, the IS function must manage information technology so that it makes major contributions to the profitability and strategic objectives of the firm. Thus, the information systems' function must change from an *information services utility* focused only on serving a firm's transaction processing or decision support needs. Instead, it must become a producer or packager of information products or an *enabler* of organizational structures and business

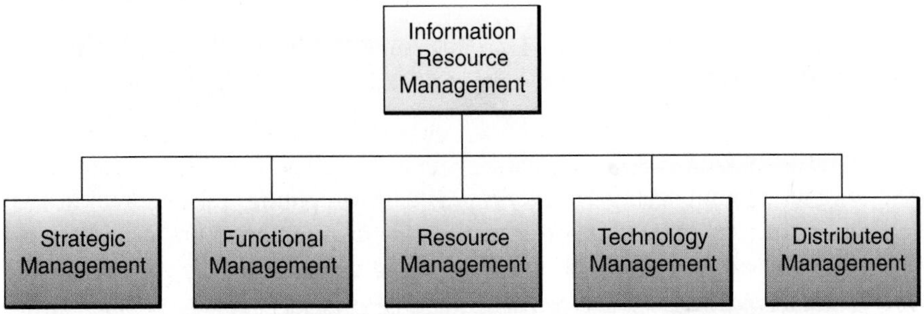

FIGURE 11.7

The information resource management (IRM) concept. Note that there are five major dimensions to the job of managing information systems resources.

Information Resource Management

Strategic Management | Functional Management | Resource Management | Technology Management | Distributed Management

Source: Adapted from James A. O'Brien and James N. Morgan, "A Multidimensional Model of Information Resource Management," *Information Resources Management Journal,* Spring 1991, p. 4. Copyright © 1991, *Information Resources Management Journal,* Idea Group Publishing, Harrisburg, PA. Reprint by permission.

processes that can give a firm a comparative advantage over its competitors. As we saw in Chapter 9, companies can develop strategic information systems to gain a competitive edge. Thus, information resource management focuses on developing and managing information systems that significantly improve operational efficiency, promote innovative products and services, and build strategic business alliances and information resources that can enhance the competitiveness of an organization.

The Chief Information Officer

Many companies have created a senior management position, the **chief information officer** (CIO), to oversee all use of information technology in their organizations. Thus, all traditional computer services, telecommunications services, office automation systems, and other IS technology support services are the responsibility of this executive. Also, the CIO does not direct day-to-day information service activities. Instead, CIOs concentrate on long-term planning and strategy. They also work with other top executives to develop strategic information systems that help make the firm more competitive in the marketplace. Several firms have filled the CIO position with executives from outside the IS field to emphasize the strategic business role of information technology. Figure 11.8 illustrates how new CIOs (most of whom had previous management experience outside of the IS function) spend their time [3].

Strategic Information Systems Planning

Strategic IS management requires strategic IS planning. See Figure 11.9. Companies do strategic information systems planning with four main objectives in mind.

- **Business Alignment.** Aligning investment in information technology with a company's business vision and strategic business goals.
- **Competitive Advantage.** Exploiting information technology to create innovative and strategic business information systems for competitive advantage.
- **Resource Management.** Developing plans for the efficient and effective management of a company's information system resources, including IS personnel, hardware, software, data, and network resources.
- **Technology Architecture.** Developing technology policies and designing an information technology architecture that integrates the internetworked computer systems, databases, and applications of the organization [7].

The strategic IS planning process illustrated in Figure 11.10 is *business driven*, not *technology driven*. Notice that a business vision and business drivers, such as business process reengineering to achieve the best industry practices and the needs of customers and business partners, are what drive the planning process. Companies can develop business/IT strategies based on the strategic opportunities that are revealed. Only then can the IT architecture for the company be designed.

The Information Technology Architecture

Figure 11.10 also shows that the **IT architecture** that is created by the strategic-planning process is a conceptual design, or *blueprint*, that includes the following major components:

- **Technology Platform.** Computer systems, system and application software, and telecommunications networks provide a computing and communications infrastructure, or *platform*, that supports the use of information technology in the business.
- **Data Resources.** Many types of operational specialized databases, including data warehouses, analytical databases, and external data banks (as discussed in Chapter 5), store and provide data and information for business processes and managerial decision support.

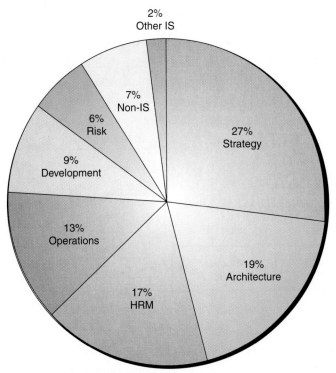

FIGURE 11.8
How CIOs spend their time.

Source: Adapted from Lynda Applegate and Joyce Elam, "New Information Systems Leaders: A Changing Role in a Changing World," *MIS Quarterly*, December 1992, p. 481. Reprinted with permission from the *MIS Quarterly*.

- **Applications Portfolio.** Business applications of information technology are designed as a diversified *portfolio* of information systems that support key business functions as well as crossfunctional business processes. In addition, an applications portfolio should include support for interorganizational

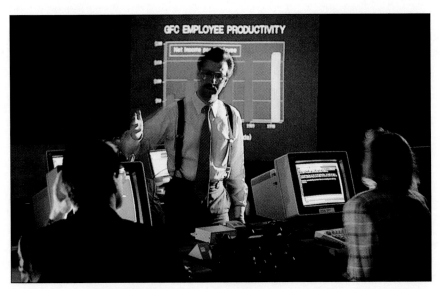

Seth Resnick/Liaison International.

FIGURE 11.9
Strategic business planning is a vital ingredient for the successful use of information technology.

FIGURE 11.10

Strategic planning uses a business vision and business drivers to create an IT architecture and tactical IS plans for the business use of information technology.

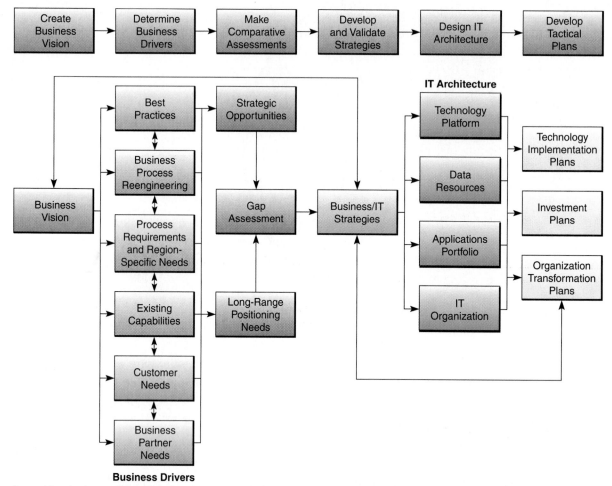

Source: Adapted and reprinted from Michael Mische, "Transnational Architecture: A Reengineering Approach," *Information Systems Management* (New York: Auerbach Publications), Winter 1995, p. 21. © 1995 Warren, Gorham & Lamont. Used with permission.

business linkages, managerial decision making, end user computing and collaboration, and strategic initiatives for competitive advantage.

- **IT Organization.** The organizational structure of the IS function within a company, and the distribution of IS specialists among corporate headquarters and business units can be designed or redesigned to meet the changing strategies of a business. The form of the IT organization depends on the managerial philosophy, business vision, and business/IT strategies formulated during the strategic planning process.

Tactical IS planning is the last stage of the planning process shown in Figure 11.10. Tactical IS planning produces project proposals for the development of new or improved information systems that implement the IT architecture created during strategic IS planning. These projects are then evaluated, ranked, and fitted into a multiyear development plan. Finally, a resource allocation plan is developed to specify the IS resources, financial commitments, and organizational changes needed to implement the strategic IT development plan of the company.

Operational information systems planning involves detailed planning for the accomplishment of new systems development projects, including the preparation of operating budgets and the development of plans, procedures, and schedules for each project. Such planning is an important part of a *project management* effort that plans and controls the implementation of systems development projects. This is necessary if a project is to be completed on time and within its proposed budget and if it is to meet its design objectives. Now, let's take a look at one company's planning process.

S.C. Johnson & Son, more commonly known as Johnson Wax, emphasizes a *portfolio management* approach in its use of IS planning [15]. Johnson divides all IT applications into six portfolios according to the business function they support. These include sales, marketing, distribution, finance, manufacturing, and logistics. Each portfolio consists of a mix of computer-based applications that keep a particular business function operating successfully. An IS specialist serves as the manager of each application portfolio. Johnson's annual goals for the portfolio usually require portfolio managers to lower the portfolio's fixed costs and come up with innovative IT solutions.

The general managers of each Johnson business unit meet regularly with the IS staff to define major goals for improvements in business processes in their units. For example, they might want a 15 percent reduction in the cost of closing a sale, or a 5 percent reduction in inventory levels. Then an information technology team headed by a portfolio manager develops an IT strategy to meet these business goals. Finally, the IT team proposes system development projects to create new systems or enhance present systems to the general managers to meet their business units' goals.

S.C. Johnson & Son, Inc.

Functional Management

The IRM concept stresses that managerial functions and techniques common to most businesses and organizational structures must be used to manage information technology. IS managers must use managerial techniques (such as planning models, financial budgets, project management, and functional organization) just as they do with other major resources and activities of the business.

In many large organizations, the information systems function is organized into a departmental or divisional unit. We will use the name *information services department* for this group, though such names as information systems, computer services, data processing, EDP, MIS, and IRM department are also used. Information services departments perform several basic functions and activities. These can be grouped into three basic **IS functions**: (1) systems development, (2) operations, and (3) technical services. Figure 11.11 illustrates this grouping of information services functions and activities in a functional IS organizational structure.

Centralization versus Decentralization

Experience has shown that modern computer-based information systems can support either the **centralization or decentralization** of information systems, operations, and decision making within computer-using organizations. For example, centralized computer facilities connected to all parts of an organization by telecommunications networks allow top management to centralize decision making formerly done by lower levels of management. It can also promote centralization of operations, which reduces the number of branch offices, manufacturing plants, warehouses, and other work sites needed by the firm.

On the other hand, there is an increasing trend toward downsized and distributed networks (of microcomputers and server computers at multiple work sites) that allow top management to delegate more decision making to middle managers. Management can also decentralize operations by increasing the number of branch offices (or other company units) while still having access to the information and communications capabilities they need to control the overall direction of the organization.

Computer-based information systems can encourage either the centralization or decentralization of information systems, business operations, and management. The philosophy of top management, the culture of the organization, the need to reengineer its operations, and its use of aggressive or conservative competitive strategies all play major roles with information technology in shaping the firm's organizational structure and information systems architecture [24, 3].

Changing Trends

Companies continue to use a variety of organizational arrangements for the delivery of information services. In the early years of computing, when computers could barely handle a single department's workload, decentralization was the only option. Subsequently, the development of large mainframe computers and telecommunications networks and terminals caused a centralization of computer hardware and software, databases, and information specialists at the corporate level of organizations. Next, the development of minicomputers and microcomputers accelerated a **downsizing** trend, which prompted a move back toward decentralization by many business firms. Distributed processing networks of micro- and minicomputers at the corporate, department, work group, and end user levels came into being. This promoted a shift of databases and information specialists to some departments, and the creation of information centers to support end user computing.

FIGURE 11.11

A functional organizational structure for an information services department. Note the activities that take place under each of the major functions of information services.

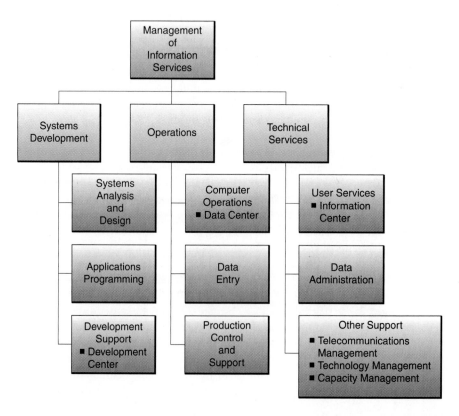

Lately, the trend has been to establish tighter control over the information resources of an organization, while still serving the strategic needs of its business units. This has resulted in a centralizing trend at some organizations and the development of hybrid structures with both centralized and decentralized components at others. Some companies have even spun off their information systems function into IS *subsidiaries* that offer information processing services to external organizations as well as to their parent company.

Other corporations have **outsourced**, that is, turned over all or part of their information systems operation to outside contractors known as *systems integrators* or facilities management companies. Such changes in the organizational alignment of the information systems function are expected to continue into the future. Organizations will continue to experiment with ways to both control and encourage the use of information system resources to promote end user productivity and the achievement of their strategic objectives. Figure 11.12 is a *business-focused* organizational structure for an IS department. Figure 11.13 illustrates how IS personnel can be organized into *delivery teams* and assigned to business units [31].

FIGURE 11.12

A business-focused organizational structure assigns delivery teams of IS specialists to business units and functions.

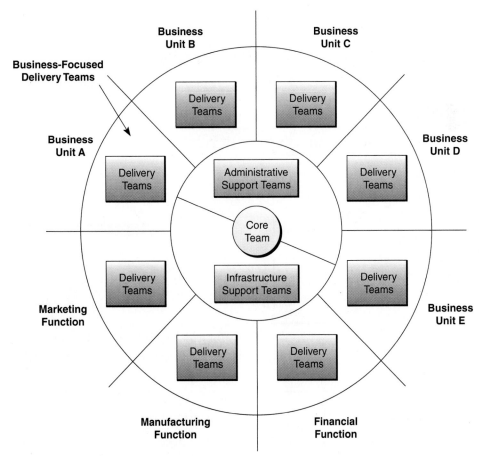

Source: Adapted and reprinted from Robert Sloan and Hal Green, "Manufacturing Decision Support Architecture," *Information Systems Management* (New York: Auerbach Publications), Winter 1995, p. 15. © 1995 Warren, Gorham & Lamont. Used with permission.

Let's take a quick look at the recent experiences of two major corporations to dramatize how radically businesses are restructuring their IS functions.

DuPont Corporation

DuPont slashed annual spending on its total IS function from $1.2 billion in 1989 to $770 million in 1994, a 40 percent cut. DuPont, which generated $38 billion in sales in fiscal 1994, also cut the number of people working in IS services by over 30 percent in the same period, from 7,000 to 4,800 employees. Nearly 200 data centers (computer centers) spread throughout the global company were merged into 40, according to Cinda Hallman, vice president of IS at DuPont. She says that IS can now move away from cost cutting and work on integrating their customers and suppliers [21].

Del Monte Foods

Del Monte outsourced all of its data centers to Electronic Data Systems Corporation several years ago, so it no longer runs its own IS computer operations. Del Monte has been aggressively implementing a Top 20 plan to develop strategic applications of information technology for its top 20 customers and suppliers. Del Monte is also

FIGURE 11.13

How an IS delivery team could be organized.

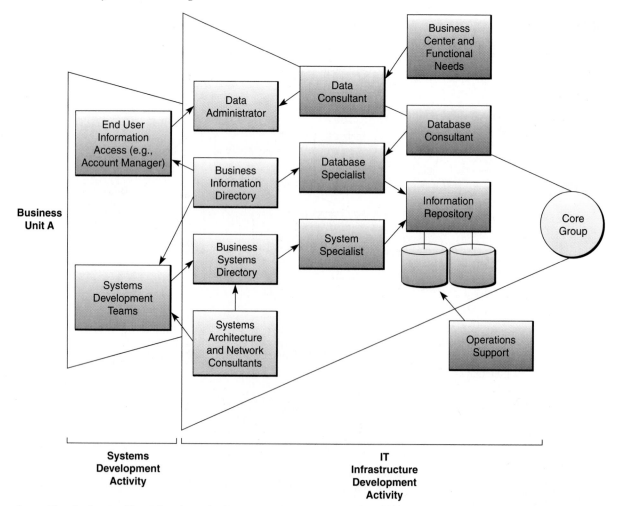

Source: Adapted and reprinted from Robert Sloan and Hal Green, "Manufacturing Decision Support Architecture," *Information Systems Management* (New York: Auerbach Publications), Winter 1995, p. 14. © 1995 Warren, Gorham & Lamont. Used with permission.

pursuing strategic alliances outside of its company walls, says David A. McPherson, CIO and vice president. He says that the cost savings from business reengineering projects at Del Monte are used to finance such new IS programs [21].

Managing Systems Development

Systems development management means managing activities such as systems analysis and design, prototyping, applications programming, project management, quality assurance, and system maintenance for all major systems development projects. Planning, organizing, and controlling the systems development function of an information services department is a major managerial responsibility. It requires managing the activities of systems analysts, programmers, and end users working on a variety of information systems development projects. In addition, many systems development groups have established **development centers**, staffed with consultants to the professional programmers and systems analysts in their organizations. Their role is to evaluate new applications development tools and help information systems specialists use them to improve their application development efforts.

Managing IS Operations

IS operations management is concerned with the use of hardware, software, network, and personnel resources in the corporate or business unit **data centers** (computer centers) of an organization. Operational activities that must be managed include data entry, equipment operations, production control, and production support.

Most operations management activities are being automated by the use of software packages for computer system performance management. These **system performance monitors** monitor the processing of computer jobs, help develop a planned schedule of computer operations that can optimize computer system performance, and produce detailed statistics that are invaluable for effective planning and control of computing capacity. Such information evaluates computer system utilization, costs, and performance. This evaluation provides information for capacity planning, production planning and control, and hardware/software acquisition planning. It is also used in quality assurance programs, which stress quality control of services to end users. See Figure 11.14.

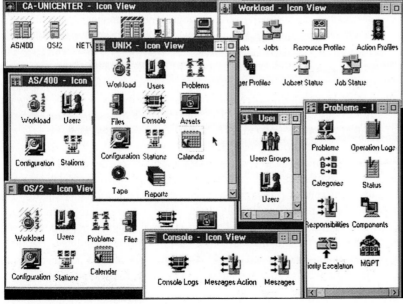

FIGURE 11.14

A computer system performance monitor in action. The CA-UNICENTER package can monitor and manage a variety of computer systems and operating systems.

Courtesy of Computer Associates, Inc.

System performance monitors also supply information needed by **chargeback systems** that allocate costs to users based on the information services rendered. All costs incurred are recorded, reported, allocated, and charged back to specific end user departments, depending on their use of system resources. Under this arrangement, the information services department becomes a service center whose costs are charged directly to computer users, rather than being lumped with other administrative service costs and treated as an overhead cost.

Many performance monitors also feature *process control* capabilities. Such packages not only monitor but automatically control computer operations at large data centers. Some use built-in expert system modules based on knowledge gleaned from experts in the operations of specific computer systems and operating systems. These performance monitors provide more efficient computer operations than human-operated systems. They also are leading toward the goal of "lights out" data centers, where computer systems can be operated unattended, especially after normal business hours.

Resource Management

From an information resource management point of view, data and information, hardware and software, telecommunications networks, and IS personnel are valuable resources that should be managed for the benefit of the entire organization. If plant and equipment, money, and people are considered vital organizational resources, so should its data, information, and other information system resources. This is especially true if the organization is committed to building a strategic information resource base to be used for strategic IT applications, and if it wants to develop innovative products and services that incorporate information systems technology. We discussed managing data as an organizationwide resource through programs of data administration and data resource management in Chapter 5. In this chapter, let's now look at several human resource management issues.

Human Resource Management of IT

The success or failure of an information services organization rests primarily on the quality of its people. Many computer-using firms consider recruiting, training, and retaining qualified IS personnel as one of their greatest challenges. Managing information services functions involves the management of managerial, technical, and clerical personnel. One of the most important jobs of information services managers is to recruit qualified personnel and to develop, organize, and direct the capabilities of existing personnel. Employees must be continually trained to keep up with the latest developments in a fast-moving and highly technical field. Employee job performance must be continually evaluated and outstanding performances rewarded with salary increases or promotions. Salary and wage levels must be set, and career paths must be designed so individuals can move to new jobs through promotion and transfer as they gain in seniority and expertise.

For example, many firms provide information services personnel with individual career paths, opportunities for merit salary increases, project leadership opportunities, and attendance at professional meetings and educational seminars. These opportunities help provide the flexible job environment needed to retain competent personnel. Challenging technological and intellectual assignments and a congenial atmosphere of fellow professionals are other major factors frequently cited in helping to retain information services personnel [1]. Figures 1.4 and 1.5 in Chapter 1 illustrated some of the job categories, salaries, and career paths available to information systems professionals.

An information resource management philosophy emphasizes that all technologies that process, store, and deliver data and information must be managed as integrated systems of organizational resources. Such technologies include telecommunications and office automation systems, as well as traditional computer-based information processing. These "islands of technology" are bridged by IRM and become a primary responsibility of the CIO, since he is in charge of all information technology services. Thus, the information systems function can become "a business within a business," whose chief executive is charged with strategic planning, research and development, and coordination of all information technologies for the strategic benefit of the organization [8, 9].

Technology Management

The rapid growth of telecommunications networks in computer-using firms has made **telecommunications management** a major technology management function. This function manages the wide area networks for applications such as online transaction processing, electronic data interchange, and electronic mail, and the local area networks for work group and end user computing. These networks require a major commitment of hardware and software resources, as outlined in Chapter 4. They also require the creation of managerial and staff positions to manage their use. Thus, telecommunications management is responsible for overseeing all telecommunications services provided to end users and the information services function.

Telecommunications Management

Telecommunications managers are usually responsible for evaluating and recommending the acquisition of communications media, communications carriers, and communications hardware and software for end user, departmental, and corporate telecommunications networks. They work with end user managers to improve the design, operational quality, and security of an organization's telecommunications networks and services. Network managers typically manage the operation of specific wide area and local area telecommunications networks. They monitor and evaluate telecommunications processors (such as network and file servers), network control software (such as network operating systems), and other common network hardware and software resources to ensure a proper level of service to the users of a network.

Telecommunications networks need a lot of managing to operate efficiently and effectively. That's why the quality of an organization's telecommunications managers and staff is a vital concern. Acquiring, training, and retaining good *network managers* or *administrators* should be a top priority. For example, even a small LAN needs a network manager who is responsible for its management and maintenance. New workstations and software must be installed, data and program files must be maintained, operations problems must be diagnosed and solved, and network security must be maintained. So manageability is a key managerial concern in any decision involving an organization's telecommunications activities.

The management of rapidly changing technology is important to any organization. Changes in information technology have come swiftly and dramatically and are expected to continue into the future. Developments in information systems technology have had, and will continue to have, a major impact on the operations, costs, management work environment, and competitive position of many organizations. Therefore, many firms have established separate groups to identify, introduce, and monitor the assimilation of new information systems technologies into their organizations, especially those with a high payoff potential [8]. These organizational units are called *technology management, emerging technologies*, or *advanced technology* groups.

Advanced Technology Management

Such advanced technology groups (ATGs) typically report to the chief information officer and are staffed with former senior systems analysts and other specialists in information systems technology. Their job is to monitor emerging technological developments and identify innovative developments that have high potential payoffs to the firm. Then they work with end user managers and information services management to introduce new technologies into the firm. They also audit a firm's current applications of technology so they can recommend improvements.

Distributed Management

Responsibility for managing information technology is increasingly being distributed to the managers of an organization at all levels and in all functions. Information resource management is not just the responsibility of an organization's chief information officer. If you're a manager, IRM is one of your responsibilities, whether you are a manager of a company, a department, a work group, or a functional area. This is especially true as telecommunications networks and developments such as cooperative processing, end user computing, work group computing, and interorganizational information systems drive the responsibility for managing information systems out to all of an organization's functional and work group managers [24, 25].

Managing End User Computing

As we saw in Chapter 6, the number of people in organizations who use or want to use computers to help them do their jobs has outstripped the capacity of many information services departments. As a result, a revolutionary change to end user computing has developed. End users now use personal computer workstations, software packages, and local area networks to develop and apply computer-based information systems to their own business activities. Organizations have responded by creating an **end user services,** or *client services*, function to support and manage this explosion in end user computing.

End user computing provides both opportunities and problems for end user management. Establishing an **information center** in an organization or end user department is one solution. However, other organizations have dismantled their

---

FIGURE 11.15

Three strategies for managing end user computing.

User Autonomy
Equipment (primarily microcomputers) is purchased without corporate standards. End users are fully responsible for design and support of systems. End users totally control the budget.

User Partnership
Equipment and software are purchased by end users using a corporate standard. Applications are developed by end users. Systems training and support are given by the IS function. Budget responsibility is shared.

Central Control
Equipment and software are purchased by the IS function. Applications are developed by both end users and IS staff. The IS staff provides support and training. The budget is controlled by the IS function.

Source: Adapted from Thomas Clark, "Corporate Systems Management: An Overview and Research Perspective," *Communications of the ACM,* February 1992, p. 65. Copyright © 1992, Association for Computing Machinery, Inc. By permission.

information centers and distributed end user support specialists to departments and other work groups. For example, some firms create user liaison positions, or "help desks," with end user "hot-lines." IS specialists with titles such as *user consultant, account executive*, or *business analyst* may be assigned to end user work groups. These specialists perform a vital role by troubleshooting problems, gathering and communicating information, coordinating educational efforts, and helping end users with application development. Their activities improve communication and coordination between end user work groups and the corporate information services department and avoid the runaround that can frustrate end users.

In addition to these measures, most organizations must still establish and enforce policies concerning the acquisition of hardware and software by end users. This ensures their compatibility with existing hardware and software systems. Even more important is the development of applications with proper controls to promote correct performance and safeguard the integrity of corporate and departmental databases. We will discuss such IS controls in Chapter 12. Figure 11.15 summarizes three basic strategies organizations use to manage end user computing [9].

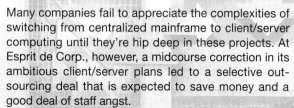

REAL WORLD CASE

ESPRIT DE CORP.: OUTSOURCING IS DEVELOPMENT AND OPERATIONS

Many companies fail to appreciate the complexities of switching from centralized mainframe to client/server computing until they're hip deep in these projects. At Esprit de Corp., however, a midcourse correction in its ambitious client/server plans led to a selective outsourcing deal that is expected to save money and a good deal of staff angst.

"Esprit is not a technology-driven company, and I was not able to afford an MIS staff with significant depth at different skill sets," said Peter Hanelt, chief operating officer at the $300 million apparel maker. The missing skill sets included distributed database management and UNIX expertise. So Esprit decided last month to expand its outsourcing arrangement with Software Maintenance Specialists (SMS) in Santa Ana, California. With the estimated $15 million, five-year extension, the SMS contract now includes installation of client/server hardware and software, network management, and application development.

SMS will now support a select group of Esprit's information systems operations in several client/server initiatives over the next few years. That support includes the rollout of an electronic data interchange order fulfillment system with retailers and an IBM RS/6000 server–based retail management system.

The San Francisco–based women's and children's clothing wholesaler began working with SMS in October 1994 to outsource its mainframe processing.

By expanding the outsourcing deal, Esprit expects to reduce its client/server initiation costs by several hundred thousand dollars over the next five years.

"The outsourcing arrangement gives us the ability to ramp up and ramp down on personal resources when needed," explained Chuck Bell, director of systems applications at Esprit. The move also should enable Esprit to meet its original four-year development plan that the company wasn't meeting on its own. In addition, the outsourcing relationship should enable Esprit to tackle its client/server projects faster than if it hired outside contractors to handle each independent phase, Hanelt said. Esprit's 25 IS staffers were picked up by SMS to support the selective outsourcing functions. Hanelt declined to discuss how much the client/server project cost.

The deal makes sense for Esprit because it allows the company to retain strategic control over its client/server migration while enabling it to off-load nonessential activities such as equipment installation to SMS. Esprit's approach also maps with industry trends. "It's a great strategy. User companies can shorten their time of implementation and get accountability from these vendors," said Allie Young, a senior analyst at Dataquest Worldwide Services. Efficiency is particularly important for Esprit and other players in the women's apparel industry, where profit margins continue to get squeezed.

CASE STUDY QUESTIONS

1. Do you think Esprit's outsourcing of IS development and operations is a good business decision? Why or why not?

2. When should a company consider outsourcing an IS function? Its entire IS operation?

3. What are the benefits of not outsourcing a company's IS management, development, or operations?

Source: Adapted from Thomas Hoffman, "Esprit Alters the Fit of Its Outsourcing," *Computerworld*, January 22, 1996, p. 62. Copyright © 1996 by Computerworld, Inc., Framingham, MA 01701—Reprinted from *Computerworld*.

Global Information Technology Management

It's no secret that international dimensions are becoming more and more important in managing a business in the global economies and markets of the 1990s. Whether you become a manager in a large corporation or the owner of a small business, you will be affected by international business developments, and deal in some way with people, products, or services whose origin is not from your home country. For example:

> The global corporation may have a product that was designed in a European country, with components manufactured in Taiwan and Korea. It may be assembled in Canada and sold as a standard model in Brazil, and in the United States as a model fully loaded with options. Transfer pricing of the components and assembled product may be determined with an eye to minimizing tax liability. Freight and insurance may be contracted for relet through a Swiss subsidiary, which earns a profit subject only to cantonal taxes. The principal financing may be provided from the Eurodollar market based in London. Add the complexities of having the transactions in different countries, with foreign exchange hedge contract gains and losses that sometimes offset trading losses and gains, and one has a marvelously complex management control problem [17].

So international issues in business management are vitally important today. This means that international issues in accounting, marketing, finance, production/operations, human resource management, and, of course, information systems and information technology are also very important to business success. Properly designed and managed information systems using appropriate information technologies are a key ingredient in international business. They provide vital information resources needed to support business activity in global markets. See Figure 11.16.

Figure 11.17 illustrates the major dimensions of the job of managing **global information technology** that we will cover in this section. Notice that all global IT activities must be adjusted to take into account the cultural, political, and geoeconomic challenges that exist in the international business community. Developing appropriate

The International Dimension

Global IT Management

Jon Feingersh/The Stock Market.

FIGURE 11.16

Business managers must now deal with international and global issues.

FIGURE 11.17

The major dimensions of
global IT management.

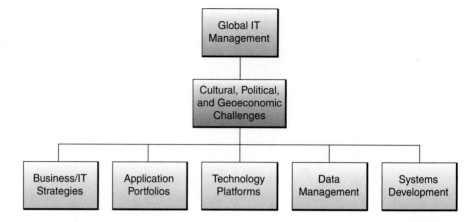

FIGURE 11.17

The major dimensions of
global IT management.

business and IT strategies for the global marketplace should be the first step in **global
IT management.** Once that is done, end user and IS managers can move on to developing the *portfolio of applications* needed to support *business/IT strategies*; the hardware,
software, and telecommunications technology *platforms* to support those applications;
the *data management* methods to provide necessary databases; and finally the *systems
development* projects that will produce the global information systems required.

Cultural, Political, and Geoeconomic Challenges

"Business as usual" is not good enough in global business operations. The same
holds true for global IT management. There are too many cultural, political, and
geoeconomic (geographic and economic) realities that must be confronted in order
for a business to succeed in global markets. As we have just said, global IT management must focus on developing global business IT strategies and managing global
application portfolios, technologies, platforms, databases, and systems development
projects. But managers must also accomplish that from a perspective and through
methods that take into account the cultural, political, and geographic differences that
exist when doing business internationally.

For example, a major *political challenge* is that many countries have rules regulating or prohibiting transfer of data across their national boundaries (*transborder
data flows*), especially personal information such as personnel records. Others severely restrict, tax, or prohibit imports of hardware and software. Still others have *local
content* laws that specify the portion of the value of a product that must be added in
that country if it is to be sold there. Other countries have *reciprocal trade agreements*
that require a business to spend part of the revenue they earn in a country in that
nation's economy [28].

Geoeconomic challenges in global business and IT refer to the effects of geography
on the economic realities of international business activities. The sheer physical distances
involved are still a major problem, even in this day of electronic telecommunications and
jet travel. For example, it may still take too long to fly in specialists when IT problems
occur in a remote site. It is still difficult to communicate conveniently across the world's
24 time zones. It is still difficult to get good-quality telephone and telecommunications
service in many countries. There are still problems finding the job skills required in some
countries, or enticing specialists from other countries to live and work there. Finally,
there are still problems (and opportunities) in the great differences in the cost of living
and labor costs in various countries [23]. All of these geoeconomic challenges must be
addressed when developing a company's global business and IT strategies.

Cultural challenges facing global business and IT managers include differences in languages, cultural interests, religions, customs, social attitudes, and political philosophies. Obviously, global IT managers must be trained and sensitized to such cultural differences before they are sent abroad or brought into a corporation's home country. Other cultural challenges include differences in work styles and business relationships. For example, should one take one's time to avoid mistakes, or hurry to get something done early? Should one go it alone or work cooperatively? Should the most experienced person lead, or should leadership be shared? The answers to such questions depend on the culture you are in and highlight the cultural differences that might exist in the global workplace. Let's take a look at a recent example.

The Republic of Singapore

Located on the tip of the Malaysian peninsula, the city-state nation of Singapore is one of the economic powerhouses of Asia. Singapore is also a preeminent user of information technology for strategic advantage in business and government. A recent study demonstrated the role of cultural differences between the United States and Singapore in the use of electronic meeting systems as group support systems (GSS) [32]. For example:

1. Singaporean groups had higher premeeting consensus than U.S. groups.
2. All groups in both cultures had the same level of postmeeting consensus.
3. Change in consensus was greater in United States groups than in Singaporean groups.
4. After controlling for premeeting consensus, influence among participants was more equal in Singaporean groups than in U.S. groups.
5. In Singaporean groups, a GSS led to unequal influence among participants in groups with a high level of agreement before their meeting.

Thus, the use of group support systems is a good example of how culture can affect the impact of information technology. Singaporean culture places a high priority on group harmony and the maintenance of social structure. When there is a high premeeting agreement within a group, cultural pressure promotes an acquiescence of group members' opinions to that of a dominant member of the group. Therefore, group members are sufficiently satisfied with a group solution to suppress their personal opinions in favor of supporting cultural norms. Thus, GSS voting tools enable a team with an initially high level of consensus to discover rapidly their accord and quickly reach agreement on an issue [32].

The Global Company

What does it mean to be a **global company**? How does one know if a business is truly a global company? Here's one definition:

> A global company is a business that is driven by a global strategy, which enables it to plan and treat all of its activities in the context of a whole-world system, and therefore serve its local and global customers with excellence [6].

Figure 11.18 illustrates this view of a global company. It emphasizes that a global company balances its strategies and activities to ensure serving customers in each locality with sensitivity and excellence, while still implementing a whole-world strategy that serves its global customers with excellence. Becoming a global company is a major undertaking, a process requiring fundamental business transformation. According to MIS professor and international consultant Richard Nolan, becoming a global company is a multiyear process, driven by the vision of achieving a fundamentally different state

FIGURE 11.18

What it means to be a global company.

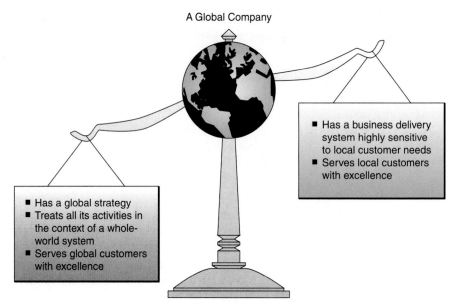

A Global Company

- Has a business delivery system highly sensitive to local customer needs
- Serves local customers with excellence

- Has a global strategy
- Treats all its activities in the context of a whole-world system
- Serves global customers with excellence

Source: Adapted and reprinted by permission of Harvard Business School Press from *Globalization, Technology, and Competition: The Fusion of Computers and Telecommunications in the 1990s* by Stephen P. Bradley, Jerry A. Hausman, and Richard L. Nolan. Boston: 1993, p. 245. Copyright © 1993 by the President and Fellows of Harvard College.

than the current one, and involving simultaneous changes in just about every aspect of the business [6]. Figure 11.19 emphasizes the scope of the changes required to become a global company.

IBM Corporation

IBM is a global company, deriving more than 60 percent of its revenue from outside the United States. IBM continues to study how to improve its structure, operations, and management, in response to the challenges of being global. IBM's 500 largest international customers represent more than 20 percent of the company's revenue, more than $13 billion; this customer base is growing approximately twice as fast as IBM's domestic base. The demands of these international customers are a powerful business incentive. Also, IBM's strategy is to cooperate with its thousands of business partners around the world. Working with its global business partners, many of which are intent on making use of IBM's international dimensions, has raised new and difficult issues for IBM management. However, IBM believes the business opportunity inherent in being global opens the field for new applications and services that the company is eager to exploit [6].

Rosenbluth Travel

Rosenbluth Travel is one of the five largest firms in the travel industry in the United States, with annual sales over $1.3 billion. Its success is characterized by:

- Rapid and creative innovation driven by closeness to its market and a clear vision of its corporate customers' changing needs.
- Aggressive use of information technology (IT) to build infrastructure for the delivery of services and to form a platform for continued innovation [6].

Rosenbluth offers global travel services in an effort to keep pace with customers that have globalized their operations in response to market pressure, competitor actions, and changing supplier relations. Rosenbluth chose a unique

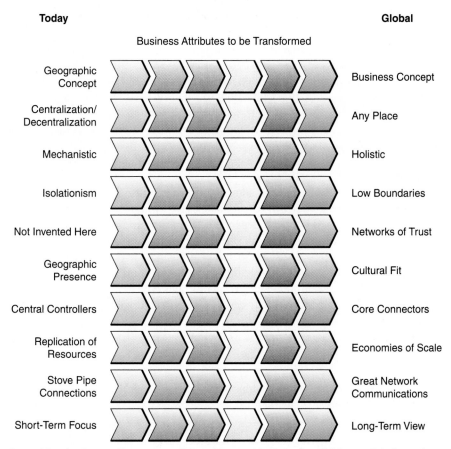

FIGURE 11.19

What it takes to become a global company.

Today   **Global**

Business Attributes to be Transformed

Geographic Concept	→	Business Concept
Centralization/ Decentralization	→	Any Place
Mechanistic	→	Holistic
Isolationism	→	Low Boundaries
Not Invented Here	→	Networks of Trust
Geographic Presence	→	Cultural Fit
Central Controllers	→	Core Connectors
Replication of Resources	→	Economies of Scale
Stove Pipe Connections	→	Great Network Communications
Short-Term Focus	→	Long-Term View

Source: Adapted and reprinted by permission of Harvard Business School Press from *Globalization, Technology, and Competition: The Fusion of Computers and Telecommunications in the 1990s* by Stephen P. Bradley, Jerry A. Hausman, and Richard L. Nolan. Boston: 1993, p. 58. Copyright © 1993 by the President and Fellows of Harvard College.

structure for globalization, the Rosenbluth International Alliance (RIA). Rather than relying on expansion through development of its own offices abroad and attempting to develop local travel management expertise and to capture the necessary shares of foreign markets, the company chose to work with the best foreign partners it could find. RIA, a cooperative alliance of independent agencies, comprises 32 partners spanning 37 countries. The benefits of this approach are as follows:

- Even for multinational corporate clients, the bulk of travel is regional or local, requiring local expertise. RIA's structure reflects this.
- When necessary, local markets can be linked. Providing service for traveling executives and resolving unanticipated problems require more than presence; they require local expertise coupled with global access to information. RIA's structure reflects this as well.
- The need for global coordination is expected to increase as clients demand consolidated reporting of travel patterns and global travel management services. RIA's structure, being flexible, can evolve as global travel support needs change [6].

Global Business and IT Strategies

How much of a business need is there for **global information technology**? That is, do we need to use IT to support our company's international business operations? Figure 11.20 helps answer these questions by showing that many firms are moving toward **transnational strategies** in which they integrate their global business activities through close cooperation and interdependence among their international subsidiaries and their corporate headquarters. Businesses are moving away from (1) *multinational* strategies where foreign subsidiaries operate autonomously; (2) *international* strategies in which foreign subsidiaries are autonomous but are dependent on headquarters for new processes, products, and ideas; or (3) *global* strategies, where a company's worldwide operations are closely managed by corporate headquarters [17, 24].

In the transnational approach, a business depends heavily on its information systems and appropriate information technologies to help it integrate its global business activities. Instead of having independent IS units at its subsidiaries, or even a centralized IS operation directed from its headquarters, a transnational firm moves to integrate its IS operations. Thus, a transnational business tries to develop an integrated and cooperative worldwide hardware, software, and telecommunications architecture for its IT *platform*. Figure 11.21 illustrates how a transnational business and IT strategy for a global company can be implemented with an integrated network organizational structure [6].

FIGURE 11.20

Companies operating internationally are moving toward a transnational business strategy. Note some of the chief differences between international, global, and transnational business and IT strategies.

International	Global	Transnational
■ Autonomous operations.	■ Global sourcing.	■ Virtual operations.
■ Region specific.	■ Multiregional.	■ World markets.
■ Vertical integration.	■ Horizontal integration.	■ Transparent order fulfillment and customers.
■ Specific customers.	■ Some transparency of customers and production.	■ Transparent manufacturing.
■ Captive manufacturing.	■ Some cross regionalization.	■ Global sourcing.
■ Customer segmentation and dedication by region and plant.		■ Dynamic resource management.

	Information Technology Characteristics	
■ Standalone systems.	■ Regional decentralization.	■ Logically consolidated, physically distributed.
■ Decentralized/no standards.	■ Interface dependent.	■ Common data.
■ Heavy reliance on interfaces.	■ Some consolidation of applications and use of common systems.	■ Integrated systems.
■ Multiple systems, high redundancy and duplication of services and operations.	■ Reduced duplication of operations.	■ Specialized workstation-based applications.
■ Lack of common systems and data.	■ Some worldwide IT standards.	■ Transnational IT policies and standards.

Source: Adapted and reprinted from Michael Mische, "Transnational Architecture: A Reengineering Approach," *Information Systems Management* (New York: Auerbach Publications), Winter 1995, p. 18. © 1995 Warren, Gorham & Lamont. Used with permission.

The applications of information technology developed by global companies depend on their business and IT strategies and their expertise and experience in IT. However, their IT applications also depend on a variety of **global business drivers,** that is, business requirements caused by the nature of the industry and its competitive or environmental forces. One example would be companies like airlines or hotel chains that have *global customers,* that is, customers who travel widely or have global operations. Such companies will need global IT capabilities for online transaction processing so they can provide fast, convenient customer service to their customers or face losing them to their competitors. The economies of scale provided by global business operations are another business driver that requires the support of global IT applications [15].

Companies whose products are available worldwide would be another example of how business needs can shape global IT. For example, Coca-Cola or Pepsi might use teleconferencing to make worldwide product announcements, and use computer-based marketing systems to coordinate global marketing campaigns. Other companies with global operations have used IT to move parts of their operations to lower-cost sites. For example, Citibank moved its credit card processing operations to Sioux Falls, South Dakota; American Airlines moved much of its data entry work to Barbados; and other firms have looked to Ireland and India as sources of low-cost software development [15, 21]. Figure 11.22 summarizes some of the business requirements that make global IT a competitive necessity.

Of course, many global IT applications, particularly finance, accounting, and office applications, have been in operation for many years. For example, most multinational companies had global financial budgeting and cash management systems, and more recently office automation applications such as fax and E-mail systems. However, as global operations expand and global competition heats up, there is increasing pressure for companies to install global transaction processing applications for their customers and suppliers. Examples include global point-of-sale (POS) and customer service systems for customers and global electronic data interchange (EDI)

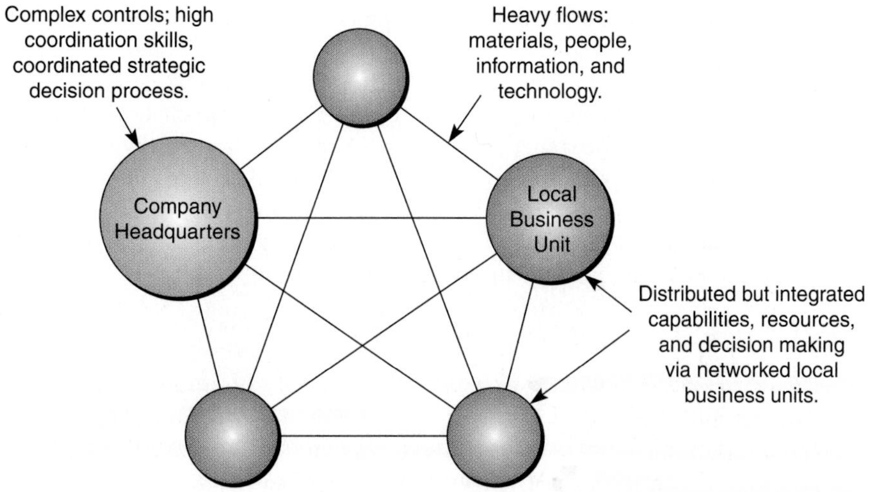

Global Business and IT Applications

Complex controls; high coordination skills, coordinated strategic decision process.

Heavy flows: materials, people, information, and technology.

Company Headquarters

Local Business Unit

Distributed but integrated capabilities, resources, and decision making via networked local business units.

FIGURE 11.21

An example of how a transnational business and IT strategy can be implemented with an integrated network organizational structure.

Source: Adapted and reprinted by permission of Harvard Business School Press from *Globalization, Technology, and Competition: The Fusion of Computers and Telecommunications in the 1990s* by Stephen P. Bradley, Jerry A. Hausman, and Richard L. Nolan. Boston: 1993, p. 86. Copyright © 1993 by the President and Fellows of Harvard College.

FIGURE 11.22

Business drivers for global IT. These are some of the business reasons behind global IT applications.

Global customers. Customers are people who may travel anywhere or companies with global operations. Global IT can help provide fast, convenient service.

Global products. Products are the same throughout the world or are assembled by subsidiaries throughout the world. Global IT can help manage worldwide marketing and quality control.

Global operations. Parts of a production or assembly process are assigned to subsidiaries based on changing economic or other conditions. Only global IT can support such geographic flexibility.

Global resources. The use and cost of common equipment, facilities, and people are shared by subsidiaries of a global company. Global IT can keep track of such shared resources.

Global collaboration. The knowledge and expertise of colleagues in a global company can be quickly accessed, shared, and organized to support individual or group efforts. Only global IT can support such electronic collaboration.

Source: Adapted from Blake Ives and Sirkka Jarvenpaa, "Applications of Global Information Technology: Key Issues for Management," *MIS Quarterly*, Volume 15, Number 1, March 1991, p. 40. Reprinted with permission from the *MIS Quarterly*.

systems for suppliers. Figure 11.23 illustrates the distribution of global IT applications based on whether they are single-purpose or collaborative systems owned by a single global company, or a cooperative venture involving several companies [29].

Chase Manhattan Bank

Chase Manhattan Bank is an example of a global company with global information systems for customer service. At Chase's Global Securities Services (GSS), more than 200 managers around the world use the Account Service Planning and Analysis (ASPA) system. ASPA, along with two related systems, helps GSS develop service and production plans, as well as monitor success against these plans according to customer service expectations and revenue targets. By quickly analyzing specific customer service data by various dimensions, Chase is able to identify key service problems in its global transaction processing systems and drill down through countries and customer accounts anywhere in the world, zero in on the problem, and take corrective action to prevent recurrence.

A customer service manager in any of Chase's service centers around the world can check for problems in performance with a few mouse clicks on her PC. A typical problem could be something like dividend or settlement payments taking longer than normal. Once a service problem is identified, the GSS customer service manager can use the system to analyze the situation and, working with the customer—who may be unaware of the problem—put together a program that will correct the problem within a specific time limit [4].

Global IT Platforms

The choice of *technology platforms* (also called the *technology infrastructure*) is another major dimension of global IT management. That is, what hardware, software, telecommunications networks, and computing facilities will be needed to support our global business operations? Answering this question is a major challenge of global IT management. The choice of a global IT platform is not only technically complex but also has major political and cultural implications.

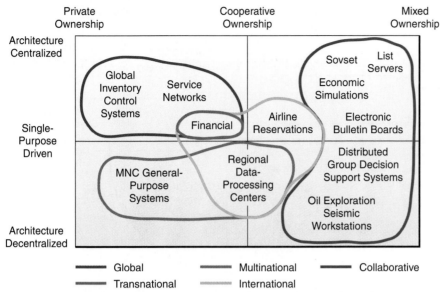

FIGURE 11.23

Families of global IT applications and information systems.

Source: Adapted with permission of Prentice Hall Inc., Upper Saddle River, NJ, from Edward M. Roche, *Managing Information Technology in Multinational Corporations.* © 1992, p. 50.

For example, hardware choices are difficult in some countries because of high prices, high tariffs, import restrictions, long lead times for government approvals, lack of local service or spare parts, and lack of documentation tailored to local conditions. Software choices can also present unique problems. Software packages developed in Europe may be incompatible with American or Asian versions, even when purchased from the same hardware vendor. Well-known U.S. software packages may be unavailable because there is no local distributor, or because the software publisher refuses to supply markets that disregard software licensing and copyright agreements [14].

Telecommunications network and computing facilities decisions also present major challenges in global IT management. In Chapter 4, we discussed some of the managerial challenges posed by telecommunications network technologies. Obviously, global telecommunications networks that cross many international boundaries make such issues even more complex.

Figure 11.24 shows that companies with global business operations usually establish or contract with systems integrators for additional data centers in their subsidiaries in other countries. These data centers meet local and regional computing needs, and even help balance global computing workloads through communications satellite links. However, offshore data centers can pose major problems in headquarter's support, hardware and software acquisition, maintenance, and security.

> Establishing locations for international data centers presents several challenges: overlapping working hours; local computing and labor regulations; potential theft; sabotage and terrorism; unreliable power sources; availability of completely redundant network backup capability; and the like [15].

That's why many global companies turn to systems integrators like EDS or IBM to manage their overseas operations. See Figure 11.25.

Business Structure   **IT Structure**

FIGURE 11.24
Global business and technology structures. Note how a global IT structure reflects a company's global business structures.

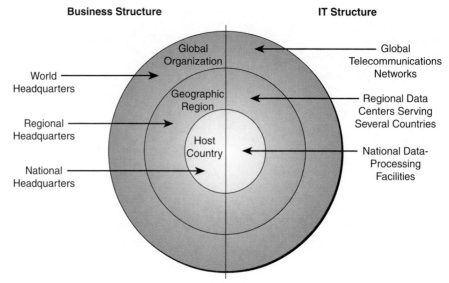

Source: Adapted with permission of Prentice Hall Inc., Upper Saddle River, NJ, from Edward M. Roche, *Managing Information Technology in Multinational Corporations.* © 1992, p. 34.

Global Data Issues

Global data issues have been a subject of political controversy and technology barriers in global business operations for many years. A major example is the issue of **transborder data flows** (TDF), in which business data flow across international borders over the telecommunications networks of global information systems. Many countries view transborder data flows as violating their national sovereignty because TDF avoid customs duties and regulations for the import or export of goods and services. Other countries may view TDF as a violation of their privacy legislation since, in many cases, data about individuals are being moved out of the country without

FIGURE 11.25

The global telecommunications command center of Electronic Data Systems.

Bill Gallery/Stock Boston.

stringent privacy safeguards. Still others view transborder data flows as violating their laws to protect the local IT industry from competition, or their labor regulations for protecting local jobs [7].

Figure 11.26 outlines some of the fears and responses of several countries to global data issues. Notice that this includes not only transborder data flows but also regulation of files and databases stored in a host country. Recent research seems to indicate that data issues have not been as much of a problem for global business as had been feared. This is due primarily to difficulties in enforcing such laws, and to efforts by host countries to encourage foreign investment. However, the data issues that still seem politically sensitive are those that affect the movement of personal data in payroll and personnel applications [7, 15].

Other important global data issues are concerned with global data management and standardization of data. Common data definitions are necessary for sharing data among the parts of an international business. Differences in language, culture, and technology platforms can make global data standardization quite difficult. For example, a sale may be called "an 'order booked' in the United Kingdom, an 'order scheduled' in Germany, and an 'order produced' in France" [29]. However, businesses are moving ahead to standardize data definitions and structures. By involving their subsidiaries in data modeling and database design, they hope to develop a global data architecture that supports their global business objectives [14].

Country	Presumed Fear	Actual Response
Brazil	Information colonialism and a lack of development of a domestic information industry.	All companies must maintain copies of all databases physically within the country; offshore processing is prohibited.
Canada	Exportation of corporate information to headquarters in other countries (especially the United States). Abuses of the personal privacy of its citizens. Loss of cultural and national sovereignty.	1980 Banking Act prohibits processing data transactions outside of the country unless approved by the government. Limitations on the number of direct access links for international data transmission and limitations on satellite usage.
France	Basically the same as Canada.	Imposition of taxes on and duties on information and information transfers. Requires every database maintained in France to be registered with the government.
Germany	A lack of development of a domestic information industry. Abuses of personal privacy.	Regulations that favor the domestic information industry and control of private leased telecommunications lines that connect to public communications networks. Data records on German nationals must be kept in Germany.
Sweden	Abuses of privacy. Domestic economic data may not be accessible if stored abroad.	Has a data protection law and a commission to license and approve all data systems. Prohibits offshore processing and storage of data.
Taiwan	National and economic security.	Government monitoring of data transmissions.

FIGURE 11.26

Global data issues. Note the fears and responses by some countries to the issues of transborder data flows and control of global databases.

Source: Adapted from William Carper, "Societal Impacts and Consequences of Transborder Data Flows," in Shailendra Palvia et al., *The Global Issues of Information Technology Management*, p. 443. Copyright © 1992, Idea Group Publishing, Harrisburg, PA. Reprinted by permission.

Global Systems Development

Just imagine the challenges of developing efficient, effective, and responsive applications for business end users domestically. Then multiply that by the number of countries and cultures that may use a global IT system. That's the challenge of managing global systems development. Naturally, there are conflicts over local versus global system requirements, and difficulties in agreeing on common system features such as multilingual user interfaces and flexible design standards. And all of this effort must take place in an environment that promotes involvement and "ownership" of a system by local end users. Thus, one IT manager estimates that

> it takes 5 to 10 times more time to reach an understanding and agreement on system requirements and deliverables when the users and developers are in different countries. This is partially explained by travel requirements and language and cultural differences, but technical limitations also contribute to the problem [15].

Other systems development issues arise from disturbances caused by systems implementation and maintenance activities. For example: "An interruption during a third shift in New York City will present midday service interruptions in Tokyo." Another major development issue relates to the trade-offs between developing one system that can run on multiple computer and operating system platforms, or letting each local site customize the software for its own platform [15]. See Figure 11.27.

Several strategies can be used to solve some of the systems development problems that arise in global IT [15, 29]. First is transforming an application used by the home office into a global application. However, often the system used by a subsidiary that has the best version of an application will be chosen for global use. Another approach is setting up a *multinational development team* with key people from several subsidiaries to ensure that the system design meets the needs of local sites as well as corporate headquarters.

A third approach is called *parallel development*. That's because parts of the system are assigned to different subsidiaries and the home office to develop at the same time, based on the expertise and experience at each site. Another approach is the concept of *centers of excellence*. In this approach, an entire system may be assigned for development to a particular subsidiary based on their expertise in the business or technical dimensions needed for successful development. Obviously, all of these approaches require managerial oversight and coordination to meet the global needs of a business.

FIGURE 11.27

The global use of information technology depends on international systems development efforts.

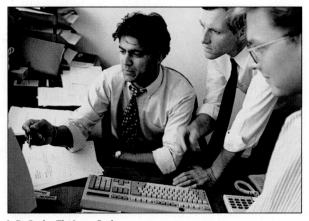

L. D. Gordon/The Image Bank.

Most companies fail to have in place a coherent information *technology* strategy. Their IT infrastructure does not match or facilitate their emerging global *business* strategy. Few multinationals have discovered the potential of computer and communications technology to transform their operations on a global basis. A company may have a single product sold globally, but no globally rationalized product database. It may be fighting a battle for centralized control when the business strategy needs to be different for each national market. It most likely has many different national data centers when it could better serve strategy with regionalized data processing of selected applications and resources [29].

Now that we have covered the basic dimensions of global IT management, it is time to acknowledge that much work remains to be done to implement global IT strategies. As a future managerial end user or IS manager, the global business success of the company you work for will be in your hands. But now at least you know the dimensions of the problems and opportunities that arise from the use of information technology to support global business operations.

First, you must discover if your company has a global business strategy and a strategy for how information technology can support global business operations. If not, you can begin to play a role, however small, in developing such strategies. Then you must discover or help develop the IT applications to support your global business activities. This includes providing your ideas for the hardware, software, and telecommunications platform and databases you need to do business globally. This process can be a gradual one. For example, as a managerial end user, you can follow the lead of a global corporation that laid out the five basic actions it had to accomplish to become a truly successful global company, as shown in Figure 11.28.

As a managerial end user, global IT management will be one of your many managerial responsibilities. Like other areas of global business management, it requires an added dimension of sensitivity to the cultural, political, and geoeconomic realities of doing business with people in other countries. But it also offers an exciting challenge of competing successfully in a dynamic global arena to bring your products or services to customers throughout the world.

You and Global IT Management

FIGURE 11.28

Basic steps toward becoming a global company.

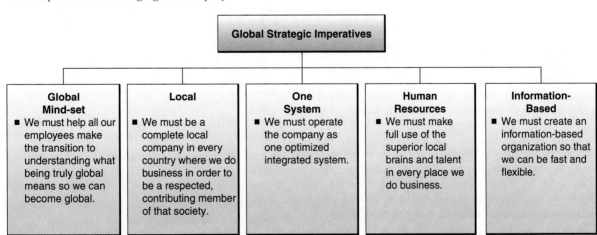

Source: Adapted and reprinted by permission of Harvard Business School Press from *Globalization, Technology, and Competition: The Future of Computers and Telecommunications in the 1990s* by Stephen P. Bradley, Jerry A. Hausman, and Richard L. Nolan. Boston: 1993, p. 248. Copyright © 1993 by the President and Fellows of Harvard College.

REAL WORLD CASE

EASTMAN KODAK AND OTHERS: GOING GLOBAL IN IT MANAGEMENT

Vaughn Hovey knows what's involved in a global integration project. A few years ago, the manager of IT supplier and alliance management at Eastman Kodak Co. was involved in a project to consolidate 17 data centers in the United States, Canada, Germany, France, Japan, England, Brazil, and Mexico down to 7.

Kodak chose IBM for the three-year job in 1990 because of its global reach. IBM's Integrated Systems Solution Corp. (ISSC) coordinated its work with IBM units in Europe and Japan. "We were looking for one global supplier who could be flexible in working relationships and provide common processes around change and problem management," Hovey says.

"The data center operations included multiprotocol network connections; a Pan-Asian, Pan-European network; and physical backbone management," says Gordon Myers, ISSC's general manager of consulting services and managed operations. "In addition," he notes, "we did network management in Europe, RS/6000 server implementations in Latin America, and LAN-based electronic-mail management in North America." "Migration went virtually without a hitch," Hovey recalls. The cost? Upwards of "hundreds of millions," Myers says. "Kodak was the first large company to engage in a contract of this type."

With Latin America in the throes of massive privatization, China building a new IT infrastructure, and American and European companies scrambling to gain better control of worldwide subsidiaries, the push for global integration is proceeding rapidly toward a tighter, if not more recentralized, vision of IS.

"There is a difference between true multinational companies and global companies," observes Frank Callan, a vice president of global business development with Electronic Data Systems based in Plano, Texas. "Typically, global companies' reporting lines are different; their products drive their individual geographies. By contrast, multinationals have geographies that are more autonomous and choose which products move into various markets.

"As multinationals struggle to move toward the global mind-set, local geographies feel left out of the mainstream," Callan observes. "System developers can get caught up in political battles, and you start to see a pushback—a reluctance of the local geographies to adopt what headquarters has dictated."

Respecting global business differences is trickier than it may seem. Countries such as Japan don't accept imported business practices. "The way you do invoicing and handle the tax system is unique in Japan," says George Kadifa, group vice president for manufacturing practices, Oracle Services. The dilemma is "how to ensure that you design business processes that are global in nature, but still take care of local requirements, such as different geographic requirements," he says.

"There is the major issue of international coordination," Kadifa says. "You've got to avoid duplication and inefficiencies. But how do you ensure that local requirements are met while you're not creating an independent solution as you go? It requires complex methodology and structure to manage global rollouts," Kadifa says. The methodology involves the integration of implementation plans at the systems and technical level, the network architecture level, the data repository level, and finally at the people level of operations and training.

Cap Gemini Sogeti, a French company with operating units in the United States and Europe, has a global idea. "Our approach in staffing an international job is to have our local operating units form a global team," says Mike Meyer, executive vice president of Cap Gemini America, Inc. "About three years ago, we made a $40 million investment to become more transnational, to adopt a common language, English, for all our documentation and business correspondence, and to adopt common service offerings no matter which country we go into," Meyer says.

Large companies want global staffing muscle and centralized control, he argues. "It makes us more sensitive to the marketplace. More and more companies are putting one global project manager in charge; they want to work with a global firm on a worldwide basis—what's implied by that is the strong desire to look and feel and act as one company." Gemini accomplishes this by using a common methodology and quality management system across all its operating units around the world.

CASE STUDY QUESTIONS

1. Why do you think Kodak decided to consolidate its global data centers and chose ISSC to do the job?

2. How would you solve the business/IT challenges identified by Frank Callan of EDS and George Kadifa of Oracle Services?

3. Do you agree with Cap Gemini's move to become a transnational company? Why or why not?

Source: Adapted from Arielle Emmett, "Going Global," *Computerworld*, February 26, 1996, pp. SI/15–16. Copyright © 1996 by Computerworld, Inc., Framingham, MA 01701—Reprinted from *Computerworld*.

Summary

- **Managers and IT.** Information technology is changing the distribution, relationships, resources, and responsibilities of managers. That is, IT is eliminating layers of management, enabling more collaborative forms of management, providing managers with significant information and computing resources, and confronting managers with a major information resource management challenge.

- **IS Performance.** Information systems are not being used effectively, efficiently, or economically by many organizations. The experiences of successful organizations reveal that the basic ingredient of high-quality information system performance is extensive and meaningful management and user involvement in the governance of information technology. Thus, managers may serve on executive steering committees and create an IS management function within their business units.

- **Organizations and IT.** The people, tasks, technology, culture, and structure of an organization affect how it will organize and use information technology. Thus, many variations exist, which reflect the attempts of organizations to tailor their organizational structures and applications to their particular business activities and management philosophy, as well as to the capabilities of centralized or distributed information systems. Lately, the trend has been to a combination of centralized and distributed arrangements for the management of information technology.

- **Information Resource Management.** Managing the use of information technology in an organization has become a major managerial responsibility. End user managers should use an information resource management approach to manage the data and information, hardware and software, telecommunications networks, and people resources of their business units and work groups for the overall benefit of their organizations. The information systems function in an organization may be headed by a chief information officer who oversees the organization's strategic use of information technology (strategic management). IRM also involves managing data and IS personnel (resource management), telecommunications and advances in information technologies (technology management), and end user computing (distributed management). The activities of information services can be grouped into basic functional categories such as systems development, operations, and technical services (functional management).

- **Managing Global IT.** The international dimensions of managing global information technology include dealing with cultural, political, and geoeconomic challenges posed by various countries, developing appropriate business and IT strategies for the global marketplace, and developing a portfolio of global IT applications and a technology platform to support them. In addition, database management methods have to be developed and systems development projects managed to produce the global information systems that are required to compete successfully in the global marketplace.

- **Global Business and IT Strategies and Issues.** Many businesses are becoming global companies and moving toward transnational business strategies in which they integrate the global business activities of their subsidiaries and headquarters. This requires that they develop a global IT platform, that is, an integrated worldwide hardware, software, and telecommunications architecture. Global companies use this IT platform to develop and deliver global IT applications that meet their unique global business requirements. Global IT and end user managers must deal with restrictions on the availability of hardware and software, restrictions on transborder data flows and movement of personal data, and difficulties with developing common data definitions and system requirements.

Key Terms and Concepts

These are the key terms and concepts of this chapter. The page number of their first explanation is in parentheses.

1. Centralization or decentralization (437)
   a. Information systems
   b. Operations and management
2. Chargeback systems (442)
3. Chief information officer (434)
4. Cultural, political, and geoeconomic challenges (448)
5. Data center (441)

6. Development center (441)
7. Downsizing (438)
8. End user services (444)
9. Global business drivers (453)
10. Global company (449)
11. Global information technology (447)
12. Global IT management (447)
    a. Applications (453)
    b. Business/IT strategies (452)

   c. Data issues (456)
   d. IT platforms (454)
   e. Systems development (458)
13. Human resource management of IT (442)
14. Impact of information technology
    a. On management (426)
    b. On organizations (431)
15. Information center (444)

16. Information resource management (433)

    a. Five dimensions of IRM (433)

17. Information services functions (437)

18. Information systems performance (428)

19. Management involvement (429)

20. Operations management (441)

21. Organizations as sociotechnical systems (431)

22. Outsourcing IS Operations (439)

23. Strategic IS planning (434)

24. System performance monitor (441)

25. Systems development management (441)

26. Technology management (443)

27. Telecommunications management (443)

28. Transborder data flows (456)

29. Transnational strategy (452)

Review Quiz

Match one of the key terms and concepts listed above with one of the brief examples or definitions listed below. Try to find the best fit for answers that seem to fit more than one term or concept. Defend your choices.

_____ 1. Managers now have a lot of information, information processing power, and responsibility for information systems.

_____ 2. Information technology affects the people, tasks, technology, culture, and structure of organizations.

_____ 3. Information system resources can be distributed throughout an organization or consolidated in corporate data centers.

_____ 4. Information systems can help management increase the number of regional and branch offices or consolidate operations.

_____ 5. The management of data, information, hardware, software, and IS personnel as organizational resources.

_____ 6. Managing information technology is a distributed, functional responsibility focusing on the strategic management of IS resources and technologies.

_____ 7. Computers have not been used efficiently, effectively, and economically.

_____ 8. A management steering committee is an example.

_____ 9. End users need information centers or other forms of liaison, consulting, and training support.

_____ 10. Includes the basic functions of systems development, operations, and technical services.

_____ 11. An executive that oversees all information systems technology for an organization.

_____ 12. Managing systems analysis and design, computer programming, and systems maintenance activities.

_____ 13. Planning and controlling data center operations.

_____ 14. Corporate locations for computer system operations.

_____ 15. A support group for an organization's professional programmers and systems analysts.

_____ 16. A support group for an organization's end users.

_____ 17. Rapidly changing technological developments must be anticipated, identified, and implemented.

_____ 18. Using outside contractors to provide and manage IS operations.

_____ 19. Telecommunications networks and their hardware and software must be developed, administered, and maintained.

_____ 20. Software that helps monitor and control computer systems in a data center.

_____ 21. The cost of IS services may be allocated back to end users.

_____ 22. Recruiting and developing information services employees.

_____ 23. Develops a business vision, business/IT strategies, and an IT architecture for the IS function.

_____ 24. Many business firms are replacing their mainframe systems with networked microcomputers.

_____ 25. A business that is driven by a global strategy.

_____ 26. Using IT to support a company's international business operations.

_____ 27. Integrating global business activities through cooperation among international subsidiaries and corporate headquarters.

_____ 28. Differences in customs, governmental regulations, and the cost of living are examples.

_____ 29. Global customers, products, operations, resources, and collaboration.

_____ 30. Applying IT to global transaction processing systems is an example.

_____ 31. The goal of some organizations is to develop an integrated worldwide hardware, software, and telecommunications platform.

_____ 32. Transborder data flows and security of personnel databases are top concerns.

_____ 33. Standardizing computer systems, software packages, telecommunications networks, and computing facilities.

_____ 34. Agreement is needed on common user interfaces and other design features in global IT.

_____ 35. Global telecommunications networks move data across national boundaries.

Discussion Questions

1. What has been the impact of information technology on the work relationships, activities, and resources of managers?

2. What can end user managers do about performance problems in the use of information technology and the development and operation of information systems in a business?

3. Refer to the Real World Case on Esprit de Corp. in the chapter. Outsourcing an IS function is a make-or-buy decision. What are several major factors that must be considered by a business making an outsourcing decision? Explain.

4. How is information technology affecting the structure and work roles of modern organizations? For example, will middle management wither away? Will companies consist primarily of self-directed project teams of knowledge workers? Explain your answer.

5. Should the IS function in a business be centralized or decentralized? What recent developments support your answer?

6. Refer to the Real World Case on Eastman Kodak and Others in the chapter. Do you agree that "respecting global business differences is trickier than it may seem"? Explain your answer.

7. What do you think are the most important cultural, political, or geoeconomic challenges facing managers of global companies? Why?

8. What are several major dimensions of global IT management? How would cultural, political, or geoeconomic challenges affect each of them?

9. Why do you think firms with global business operations are moving away from multinational, global, and international strategies toward a transnational business strategy? How does this affect global IT management?

10. What important business drivers or requirements do you think are most responsible for a company's use of global IT? Give several examples to illustrate your answer.

Real World Problems

1. AmeriData Technologies and National Bank of Maryland: Outsourcing IS Services Management

To say AmeriData is growing is like saying the Internet has generated a *little* interest lately. From 1992 revenues of just over $64 million, the company topped $1 billion in 1994—that's a 300 percent growth rate a year. Revenue projections for 1995 hover around $1.5 billion. Those are some of the stats for AmeriData, the top-ranked systems integrator in terms of customer satisfaction in a *Computerworld* survey of the largest 25 companies that developed and managed IS services for other corporations.

Much of that growth is due to the company absorbing some 30 independent companies, including consultants, value-added resellers, and distributors. Founded in 1968, the company has offices in 130 cities around the world. In the United States, 70 offices house AmeriData's six distribution centers, 600 salespeople, and a total of 2,300 employees, including almost 1,000 consultants, engineers, and technicians. Last year, the company acquired part of Control Data Systems' international business for $34 million, opening new integration opportunities overseas.

"The company is built on a regional business model," says Lee Stagni, AmeriData's vice president of marketing. "Within the regions, we offer configuration integration for our customers as well as higher level consulting—both are driven from the field." AmeriData's business model has a decidedly protective bent. While most organizations welcome the flexibility and freedom made possible by the PC, they also pine for the old days when a single big vendor—

IBM, for example—handled all the details, says CEO James K. McLeary. "It's that seamless experience that we are trying to bring back for our customers," he says, "while also giving them the freedom of an à la carte menu."

AmeriData's philosophy and capabilities made a convert of Deborah Hirsch, staff assistant for technology at First National Bank of Maryland in Baltimore. "They have become our vendor of choice for all hardware procurement," she says. "They also provided an integration process for our servers and workstations across 180 locations." Hirsch uses words like *flexible, thorough,* and *sensitive* to describe AmeriData's performance. "I don't have to give them detailed instructions, because they know what we will want when we decide to upgrade a site." When AmeriData did First National Bank's file-server rollout, for example, "it was accomplished without any First National people and they achieved a 96 percent accuracy rate."

a. Why do companies hire systems integrators like AmeriData?

b. Why do you think AmeriData has been so successful as a systems integrator?

Source: Adapted from Alan Earls, "Who to Choose?" *Computerworld,* February 26, 1996, p. SI/4. Copyright © 1996 by Computerworld, Inc., Framingham, MA 01701—Reprinted from *Computerworld.*

2. Duke Power Co. and Oracle Corporation: Failure in Managing Systems Development

Duke Power Co. pulled the plug on a $23 million object-based customer information system after Oracle Corp. failed to deliver it within a promised two-year window. Duke executives declined to disclose how much money the company lost through its abandoned Project Sea Green effort. Oracle was supposed to deliver the object-based customer system in one "big bang" by the end of last year, Duke officials said. But the utility balked when Oracle asked for yet another two years to complete it. A former Duke systems analyst said "zero percent" of the object investment is recoverable. The Charlotte, North Carolina–based utility is consequently being forced to take a $12 million charge against its fiscal 1995 revenue, said the systems analyst, who asked to remain anonymous.

Even the Oracle executive who led the Duke project acknowledged its shortcomings. "The object-oriented methods and tools proved not to be scalable to a problem of this size and complexity," said Steve Perkins, a vice president at Oracle Consulting who oversaw the CIS project. The main difficulty, he said, was developing object-oriented computer-aided software engineering tools that could handle the data models that Oracle consultants developed during their two years on the Duke job.

But the CIS project isn't completely undone. Duke is applying the business rules and data models that Oracle created to replace a 22-year-old IBM mainframe-based CIS with a client/server IBM DB2 architecture. The resuscitated project is aptly named Phoenix "for the mythical bird that rises from the ashes," said Hugh McCutcheon, the new project manager. Unlike the Oracle project, Phoenix will be delivered in seven phases through March 2000, and user acceptance will be closely tracked during that time. That tracking "gives the business users a chance to see the system as it's being rolled out and suggest changes where they're needed," McCutcheon explained. "Contrast that to having someone develop what is your company's most important system over a two-year period, installing it over a weekend, and not knowing what you're getting."

Even though Phoenix is a "less ambitious" effort than the object-based scheme, McCutcheon noted that it has many of the same goals. Those include electronic bill payments via electronic data interchange (EDI) and the Internet. All utilities are under immense time pressure to create modernized CISs because deregulation will soon allow now-captive customers to choose their energy supplier.

a. Why did Project Sea Green fail at Duke Power?
b. Do you think Project Phoenix is more likely to succeed? Why or why not?

Source: Adapted from Thomas Hoffman and Julia King, "Utility Unplugs Object Project," *Computerworld,* February 26, 1996, pp. 1, 125. Copyright © 1996 by Computerworld, Inc., Framingham, MA 01701—Reprinted from *Computerworld.*

3. Nestlé and R.R. Donnelley: Proactive Global Technology Management

When he joined Nestlé, S.A., five years ago as senior vice president of information technology and logistics, Jean Claude Dispaux created a team of eight senior information technology managers who are his eyes and ears around the world. It is Dispaux's way of maintaining "dotted-line" control of the global IS and logistics infrastructure in a decentralized federated organization. It is also Dispaux's way of gathering data on technology trends from the field, which helps him plan for the skills that Nestlé's IS department will need in the future.

Known as the Coordination Group, Nestlé's IS SWAT team works with operating units around the world. Its head, Oliver Gouin, reports directly to Dispaux at company headquarters in Vevey, Switzerland. Every member of the Coordination Group has worked for many years at Nestlé, and Dispaux tries to limit tenure on the team to no more than three years. The group is international in composition. Currently, there is one Frenchman, a Spaniard, a Canadian, an American, an Italian, and three Swiss—one French-speaking and two German-speaking.

Alan Guibord, vice president of information technology at R.R. Donnelley & Sons Co., takes a similar approach. He has created a research and development group that studies a range of computing and communications developments and recommends implementation. The group also serves as a window for identifying skills Guibord will need to develop in his IS department.

Guibord's group at Donnelley consists of 18 people. Currently, it is studying the Internet's advanced messaging, remote computing, and high-bandwidth communications, such as asynchronous transfer mode. Every quarter the group assembles a handful of vendors to address trends and discuss Donnelley's specific technology needs. For example, at a recent meeting, Donnelley hosted eight telecommunications vendors who made presentations on approaches to Donnelley's networking needs.

a. Why do companies need to do technology management?
b. Do you prefer Nestlé's or Donnelley's approach to technology management? Explain.

Source: Adapted from Bruce Rayne, "Staffing for the Future," *Computerworld Leadership Series,* April 15, 1996, p. 6. Copyright © 1996 by Computerworld, Inc., Framingham, MA 01701—Reprinted from *Computerworld.*

4. Cisco Systems and KPMG Peat Marwick: Global IS Development and Implementation

Some companies, such as Cisco Systems, Inc., already have worldwide private or value-added networks in place but require major upgrades to new databases and functional business applications, especially in client/server systems. Cisco Systems' eight-month worldwide rollout of Oracle databases and applications—a complete revamp of its business computing—cost $10 million and involved more than 1,200 users, 10 primary sites in the United States, Canada, and Japan, and more than 100 corporate sales offices, says Peter Solvik, chief information officer for the $3 billion internetworking company headquartered in San Jose, California.

The company chose KPMG Peat Marwick as the primary systems integrator for the project. Oracle Services was selected as a technical subcontractor to provide performance tuning and development standards. The project involved installing and customizing all the Oracle applications— from order entry to manufacturing to financials, about 14 modules in all—and making them accessible from Cisco's San Jose computing facility to global users across the company's worldwide private network. A team of 100 professionals from KPMG, Oracle Services, Cisco, and outside consulting firms coordinated the project, handling project management, applications development, business function analysis, and technical support. For both Canada and Japan, the design work was done in San Jose.

A project such as this requires more than a passing interest from the top. "Cisco's senior management backed the project with dollars and freed up senior people in the organization to make it happen," says Mark Lee, KPMG's senior manager of strategic services consulting. "They had

a sense of urgency," Lee says. "It's my impression that when clients don't have a sense of urgency, and they don't have enough full-time people on the integration job, projects tend to fail." "To my knowledge there's never been a core system mainframe replacement done for an entire corporation in eight months," says Cisco's Solvik. "It's very successful; we're on time, within budget, and meeting the core objectives."

a. Why did Cisco succeed in its global systems development and implementation project?

b. What can other companies do to manage systems development projects more effectively based on Cisco's experience?

Source: Adapted from Arielle Emmett, "Going Global," *Computerworld*, February 26, 1996, pp. SI/15–16. Copyright © 1996 by Computerworld, Inc., Framingham, MA 01701—Reprinted from *Computerworld*.

Application Exercises

1. ABC Company Global Internet Site Management

ABC Company operates a large and expanding number of sales offices throughout the globe. Increasingly, communications among employees at these diverse locations are handled through the Internet. In addition, many customers and vendors worldwide use the Internet to communicate with ABC's employees. You have been asked to maintain a file to track the available Internet facilities at all of ABC's offices and to record Internet address information on each site. An employee is to be assigned responsibility for managing Internet and World Wide Web activities at each site; however, this assignment has

not been made at all sites at this time. Some sites have a Web page in place while others do not. Your file is to track this set of information. A sample of relevant data follows.

a. Create a database table to store the preceding information and the sample data.

b. Print a report showing the Internet manager and the World Wide Web address for all sites having a World Wide Web page.

c. Run and print a query listing all information available about sites with an Internet manager but without a World Wide Web page.

Site	Country	Internet/WWW Manager	Web Page Completed	Internet Address
Atlanta	United States	Jones, P.	Yes	abcatl.com
Brussels	Belgium	Landis, J.	No	abcbru.com
Cairo	Egypt	Powers, G.	Yes	abccai.com
Dallas	United States		No	abcdal.com
Frankfurt	Germany	Alters, A.	No	abcfra.com
Honolulu	United States	Tower, V.	Yes	abchon.com
Los Angeles	United States		No	abclax.com
Mexico City	Mexico	Ruiz, R.	No	abcmex.com
Osaka	Japan	Chang, A.	Yes	abcosk.com
São Paulo	Brazil	Morris, M.	Yes	abcspo.com
Toronto	Canada	Walls, W.	No	abctor.com

2. Managing Systems Maintenance at Action Products

Modifying systems in response to user requests is a major aspect of systems maintenance for the information systems department at Action Products Company. Users can request changes to information systems by filling out a change request form and sending it to the group charged with maintenance responsibilities for the affected system.

Users have often complained of long response times to their change requests and lack of follow-up to ensure that the changes made solve the problem reported. To expedite the processing of change requests, Action Products has assigned you the authority and responsibility for coordinating change requests.

You have decided to maintain a database file providing summary information about each change request. You will record the requesting user's name, the date the request was made, and the name of the information system to be modified. You will then make an assignment of the new request to an appropriate maintenance team and record that information as well.

Once a request has been added to your database file, its progress toward completion will be recorded under the Completion status variable. A request will be listed as IP (for in-process) as soon as you assign it to a maintenance team. Once the changes have been completed, you are to be notified by the maintenance team. At that point, you will change the status to PA (for pending approval). You then will notify the user who submitted the request to evaluate the changes and inform you that the changes are either accepted (status AC) or rejected (status RE). A user who rejects the changes must submit a new change request form to describe any further modifications required. A set of sample data follows.

a. Create a database table to store this information and enter the sample data shown.
b. Create and print a report categorized by maintenance team numbers that summarizes the status of all change requests.
c. Perform and get printed listings of the following queries:
1. Retrieve all available data on request whose status is IP sorted in order from oldest to most recent.
2. Retrieve the request number data and status of all requests assigned to team PO3.
3. Retrieve a count of the number of change requests in each completion status.

Requesting User	Request ID No.	Request Date	System Affected	Maint. Team Assigned	Completion Status
Davis, L.	7843	04/07/96	Payroll	PO3	AC
Evans, G.	7844	04/09/96	Acct. Rec.	PO2	RE
Morris, M.	7845	04/09/96	Inventory	PO1	PA
Allen, J.	7846	04/12/96	Payroll	PO3	IP
Jones, P.	7857	04/28/96	Order Proc.	PO2	AC
Lewis, R.	7872	05/07/96	Inventory	PO1	AC
Evans, G.	7879	05/18/96	Acct. Rec.	PO2	IP
Norton, M.	7886	05/22/96	Inventory	PO1	IP
Powers, R.	7889	05/24/96	Payroll	PO3	IP

Review Quiz Answers

1. *14a*
2. *14b*
3. *1a*
4. *1b*
5. *16*
6. *16a*
7. *18*
8. *19*
9. *8*
10. *17*
11. *3*
12. *25*
13. *20*
14. *5*
15. *6*
16. *15*
17. *26*
18. *22*
19. *27*
20. *24*
21. *2*
22. *13*
23. *23*
24. *7*
25. *10*
26. *11*
27. *29*
28. *4*
29. *9*
30. *12a*
31. *12b*
32. *12c*
33. *12d*
34. *12e*
35. *28*

Selected References

1. Alavi, Maryam, and Gregory Young. "Information Technology in an International Enterprise: An Organizing Framework." In *The Global Issues of Information Technology Management*, ed. Shailendra Palvia et al. Harrisburg, PA: Idea Group Publishing, 1992.
2. Alter, Allan. "Profiles in Governance." In "A More Perfect Union," *Computerworld*, November 28, 1994.
3. Applegate, Lynda, and Joyce Elam. "New Information Systems Leaders: A Changing Role in a Changing World." *MIS Quarterly*, December 1992.
4. Bowles, Jerry. "Quality 2000: The Next Decade of Progress," *Fortune*, Special Advertising Supplement, October 3, 1994.

5. Boynton, Andrew; Robert Zmud; and Gerry Jacobs. "The Influence of IT Management Practice on IT Use in Large Organizations." *MIS Quarterly,* September 1994.

6. Bradley, Stephen P.; Jerry A. Hausman; and Richard L. Nolan. *Globalization, Technology, and Competition: The Fusion of Computers and Telecommunications in the 1900s.* Boston: Harvard Business School Press, 1993.

7. Carper, William. "Societal Impacts and Consequences of Transborder Data Flows." In *The Global Issues of Information Technology Management,* ed. Shailendra Palvia et al. Harrisburg, PA: Idea Group Publishing, 1992.

8. Cash, James I., Jr.; Robert G. Eccles; Nitin Nohria; and Richard L. Nolan. *Building the Information-Age Organization.* Burr Ridge, IL: Richard D. Irwin, 1994.

9. Clark, Thomas. "Corporate Systems Management: An Overview and Research Perspective." *Communications of the ACM,* February 1992.

10. Corett, Michael. "Outsourcing and the New IT Executive." *Information Systems Management,* Fall 1994.

11. Couger, J. Daniel. "New Challenges in Motivating MIS Personnel." *Handbook of IS Management.* 3rd ed. Boston: Auerbach, 1991.

12. Davenport, Thomas H. *Process Innovation: Reengineering Work through Information Technology.* Boston: Harvard Business School Press, 1993.

13. Drucker, Peter. "The Coming of the New Organization." *Harvard Business Review,* January–February 1988.

14. Frenzel, Carroll. *Management of Information Technology.* Boston: boyd & fraser, 1992.

15. Ives, Blake, and Sirkka Jarvenpaa. "Applications of Global Information Technology: Key Issues for Management." *MIS Quarterly,* March 1991.

16. Keen, Peter G. W. *Shaping the Future: Business Design through Information Technology.* Boston: Harvard Business School, 1991.

17. King, William, and Vikram Sethi. "A Framework for Transnational Systems." In *The Global Issues of Information Technology Management,* ed. Shailendra Palvia et al. Harrisburg, PA: Idea Group Publishing, 1992.

18. King, William, and Vikram Sethi. "An Analysis of International Information Regimes." *International Information Systems,* January 1992.

19. Leavitt, H. J., and T. L. Whisler. "Management in the 1980s." *Harvard Business Review,* November–December 1985.

20. Levis, John, and Peter Von Schilling. "Lessons from Three Implementations: Knocking Down Barriers to Client/Server." *Information Systems Management,* Summer 1994.

21. Maglitta, Joseph. "CIOs Warned to Get Their Shops in Shape." *Computerworld,* November 7, 1994.

22. Manheim, Marvin. "Global Information Technology: Issues and Strategic Opportunities." *International Information Systems,* January 1992.

23. McFarlan, F. Warren. "The Expert's Opinion." *Information Resources Management Journal,* Fall 1991.

24. Mische, Michael. "Transnational Architecture: A Reengineering Approach." *Information Systems Management,* Winter 1995.

25. Murray, Richard, and Richard Hardin, "The IT Organization of the Future." *Information Systems Management,* Fall 1991.

26. Niederman, Fred; James Brancheau; and James Wetherbe. "Information Systems Management Issues for the 1990s." *MIS Quarterly,* December 1991.

27. O'Brien, James A., and James N. Morgan. "A Multidimensional Model of Information Resource Management." *Information Resources Management Journal,* Spring 1991.

28. Palvia, Shailendra; Prashant Palvia; and Ronald Zigli, eds. *The Global Issues of Information Technology Management.* Harrisburg, PA: Idea Group Publishing, 1992.

29. Roche, Edward M. *Managing Information Technology in Multinational Corporations.* New York: Macmillan, 1992.

30. Rochester, Jack, and David Douglass. "Building a Global IT Infrastructure." *I/S Analyzer,* June 1991.

31. Sloan, Robert, and Hal Green. "Manufacturing Decision Support Architecture." *Information Systems Management,* Winter 1995.

32. Watson, Richard; Teck Hua Ho; and K. S. Raman. "Culture: A Fourth Dimension of Group Support Systems." *Communications of the ACM,* October 1994.

Security and Ethical Challenges of Information Technology

CHAPTER OUTLINE

LEARNING OBJECTIVES

After reading and studying this chapter, you should be able to:

1. Outline several types of information system controls, procedural controls, and facility controls that can be used to ensure the quality and security of information systems.

2. Discuss ways to control the performance and security of end user computing systems.

3. Identify several ethical principles that affect the use and management of information technology.

4. Identify several ethical issues in how information technology affects employment, individuality, working conditions, privacy, crime, health, and solutions to societal problems.

5. Identify what end users and IS managers can do to lessen the harmful effects and increase the beneficial effects of information technology.

Section I

Security and Control Issues in Information Systems

Why Controls Are Needed

As a manager, you will be responsible for the control of the quality and performance of information systems in your business unit. See Figure 12.1. Like any other vital business asset, the resources of information systems hardware, software, networks, and data need to be protected by built-in controls to ensure their quality and security. That's why controls are needed. Computers have proven that they can process huge volumes of data and perform complex calculations more accurately than manual or mechanical information systems. However, we know that (1) errors do occur in computer-based systems, (2) computers have been used for fraudulent purposes, and (3) computer systems and their software and data resources have been accidentally or maliciously destroyed.

There is no question that computers have had some detrimental effects on the detection of errors and fraud. Manual and mechanical information processing systems use paper documents and other media that can be visually checked by information processing personnel. Several persons are usually involved in such systems and, therefore, cross-checking procedures are easily performed. These characteristics of manual and mechanical information processing systems facilitate the detection of errors and fraud.

Computer-based information systems, on the other hand, use machine-sensible media such as magnetic disks and tape. They accomplish processing manipulations within the electronic circuitry of a computer system. The ability to check visually the progress of information processing activities and the contents of databases is significantly reduced. In addition, a relatively small number of personnel may effectively control processing activities that are critical to the survival of the organization. Therefore, the ability to detect errors and fraud can be reduced by computerization. This makes the development of various control methods a vital consideration in the design of new or improved information systems.

Effective controls are needed to ensure **information system security,** that is, the accuracy, integrity, and safety of information system activities and resources. Controls can minimize errors, fraud, and destruction in an information services organization. Effective controls provide **quality assurance** for information systems. That is, they can make a computer-based information system more free of errors and fraud and able to provide information products of higher quality than manual types of

FIGURE 12.1

Managers are responsible for the control of the quality and performance of information systems in their business units.

Bob Krist/Tony Stone Images.

information processing. This can help reduce the potential negative impact (and increase the positive impact) that information technology can have on business survival and success and the quality of life in society.

What Controls Are Needed

Three major types of controls must be developed to ensure the quality and security of information systems. These control categories, illustrated in Figure 12.2, are:

- Information system controls.
- Procedural controls.
- Facility controls.

Information System Controls

Information system controls are methods and devices that attempt to ensure the accuracy, validity, and propriety of information system activities. Controls must be developed to ensure proper data entry, processing techniques, storage methods, and information output. Thus, information system controls are designed to monitor and maintain the quality and security of the input, processing, output, and storage activities of any information system. See Figure 12.3.

Input Controls

Have you heard the phrase *garbage in, garbage out* (GIGO)? Figure 12.4 shows why controls are needed for the proper entry of data into an information system. Examples include passwords and other security codes, formatted data entry screens, audible error signals, templates over the keys of key-driven input devices, and prerecorded and prenumbered forms. Input of source documents can also be controlled by registering them in a logbook when they are received by data entry personnel. Realtime systems that use direct access files frequently record all entries into the system on magnetic tape control logs that preserve evidence of all system inputs. Computer software can include instructions to identify incorrect, invalid, or improper input data as it enters the computer system. For example, a data entry program

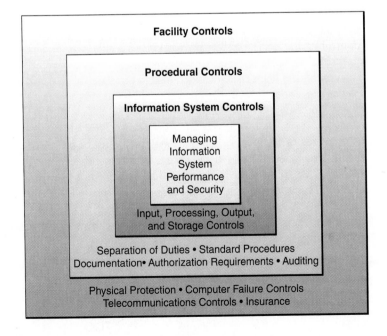

FIGURE 12.2

The controls needed for information system security. Specific types of controls can be grouped into three major categories: information system, procedural, and facility controls.

FIGURE 12.3

Example of information system controls. Note that they are designed to monitor and maintain the quality and security of the input, processing, output, and storage activities of an information system.

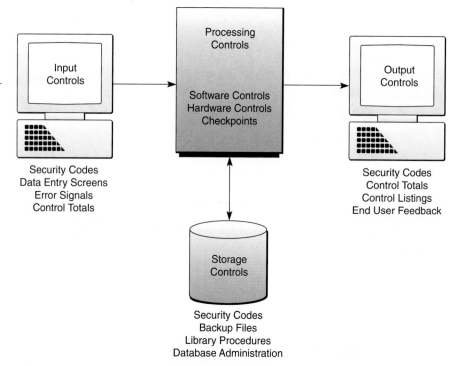

Input Controls

Security Codes
Data Entry Screens
Error Signals
Control Totals

Processing Controls

Software Controls
Hardware Controls
Checkpoints

Output Controls

Security Codes
Control Totals
Control Listings
End User Feedback

Storage Controls

Security Codes
Backup Files
Library Procedures
Database Administration

can check for invalid codes, data fields, and transactions. Also, the computer can be programmed to conduct "reasonableness checks" to determine if input data exceed certain specified limits or are out of sequence. This includes the calculation and monitoring of selected **control totals.**

Data entry and other systems activities are frequently monitored by the use of control totals. For example, a record count is a control total that consists of counting the total number of source documents or other input records and comparing this total to the number of records counted at other stages of input preparation. If the totals do not match, a mistake has been made. Batch totals and hash totals are other forms of control totals. A *batch total* is the sum of a specific item of data within a batch of transactions, such as the sales amounts in a batch of sales transactions. *Hash totals* are the sum of data fields that are added together for control comparisons only. For example, employee Social Security numbers could be added to produce a control total in the input preparation of payroll documents.

Processing Controls

Once data are entered correctly into a computer system, it must be processed properly. Processing controls are developed to identify errors in arithmetic calculations and logical operations. They are also used to ensure that data are not lost or do not go unprocessed. Processing controls can include hardware controls and software controls.

Hardware Controls

Hardware controls are special checks built into the hardware to verify the accuracy of computer processing. Examples of hardware checks include:

- **Malfunction detection circuitry** within a computer or telecommunications processor that can monitor their operations. For example, parity checks are made to check for the loss of the correct number of bits in every byte of data processed or transmitted on a network. Another example is *echo checks* that

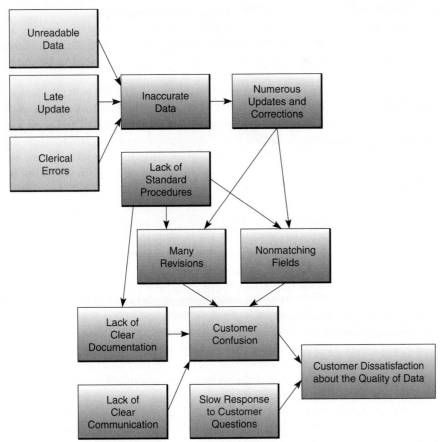

FIGURE 12.4

Garbage in, garbage out. Input controls are needed for the proper entry of data into a computer system.

Source: Adapted and reproduced from *Quality Information Systems* by Fatemeh Zahedi, p. 397, with permission of boyd & fraser publishing company. Copyright 1995 by boyd & fraser publishing company. All rights reserved.

require a device or circuit to return a signal to verify that it was properly activated. Other examples are redundant circuitry checks, arithmetic sign checks, and CPU timing and voltage checks.

- **Redundant components.** For example, multiple read-write heads on magnetic tape and disk devices check and promote the accuracy of reading and recording activities.
- **Special-purpose microprocessors and associated circuitry** that may be used to support *remote diagnostics* and maintenance. These allow off-site technicians to diagnose and correct some problems via a telecommunications link to the computer.

Software Controls

Some software controls ensure that the right data are being processed. For example, the operating system or other software checks the internal file labels at the beginning and end of magnetic tape and disk files. These labels contain information identifying the file as well as provide control totals for the data in the file. These internal file labels allow the computer to ensure that the proper storage file is being used and that the proper data in the file have been processed.

Another major software control is the establishment of checkpoints during the processing of a program. *Checkpoints* are intermediate points within a program being processed where intermediate totals, listings, or "dumps" of data are written on magnetic tape or disk or listed on a printer. Checkpoints minimize the effect of processing errors or failures, since processing can be restarted from the last checkpoint (called a *rollback*), rather than from the beginning of the program. They also help build an **audit trail**, that allows transactions being processed to be traced through all of the steps of their processing.

Many input, processing, output, and storage controls may be provided by specialized system software packages known as **system security monitors.** System security monitors are programs that monitor the use of a computer system and protect its resources from unauthorized use, fraud, and destruction. Such programs provide the computer security needed to allow only authorized users to access the system. For example, identification codes and passwords are frequently used for this purpose. Security monitors also control the use of the hardware, software, and data resources of a computer system. For example, even authorized users may be restricted to the use of certain devices, programs, and data files. Finally, such programs monitor the use of the computer and collect statistics on any attempts at improper use. They produce reports to assist in maintaining the security of the system. See Figure 12.5.

Output Controls

How can we control the quality of the information products produced by an information system? Output controls are developed to ensure that information products are correct and complete and are transmitted to authorized users in a timely manner. Several types of output controls are similar to input control methods. For example, output documents and reports are frequently logged, identified with route slips, and visually verified by input/output control personnel. Control totals on output are usually compared with control totals generated during the input and processing stages. Control listings can be produced that provide hard copy evidence of all output produced.

Prenumbered output forms can be used to control the loss of important output documents such as stock certificates or payroll check forms. Distribution lists help input-output control personnel ensure that only authorized users receive output.

FIGURE 12.5

Using CA-UnicenterStar, the security monitor module of the CA-UNICENTER performance monitor system.

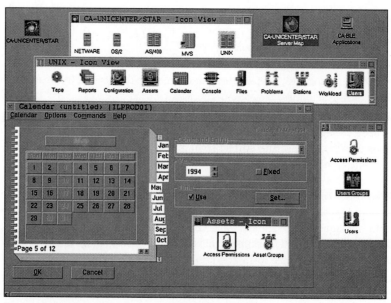

Courtesy of Computer Associates, Inc.

Access to the output of realtime processing systems is controlled typically by security codes that identify which users can receive output and the type of output they are authorized to receive. Finally, end users who receive output should be contacted for feedback on the quality of the output. This is an important function of systems maintenance and quality assurance activities.

How can we protect our data resources? First, control responsibilities for files of computer programs and organizational databases may be assigned to a librarian or database administrator. These employees are responsible for maintaining and controlling access to the libraries and databases of the organization. Second, many databases and files are protected from unauthorized or accidental use by security programs that require proper identification before they can be used. Typically, the operating system or security monitor protects the databases of realtime processing systems from unauthorized use or processing accidents. Account codes, passwords, and other **security codes** are frequently used to allow access to authorized users only. A catalog of authorized users enables the computer system to identify eligible users and determine which types of information they are authorized to receive.

Typically, a three-level password system is used. First, an end user logs on to the computer system by entering his or her unique identification code or user ID. The end user is then asked to enter a *password* in order to gain access into the system. Finally, to access an individual file, a unique file name must be entered. In some systems, the password to read the contents of a file is different from that required to write to a file (change its contents). This feature adds another level of protection to stored data resources. However, for even stricter security, passwords can be scrambled, or *encrypted*, to avoid their theft or improper use.

Many firms also use *backup files* that are duplicate files of data or programs. Such files may be stored off-premises; that is, in a location away from the computer center, sometimes in special storage vaults in remote locations. Many realtime processing systems use duplicate files that are updated by telecommunication links. Files are also protected by *file retention* measures that involve storing copies of master files and transaction files from previous periods. If current files are destroyed, the files from previous periods are used to reconstruct new current files. Usually, several generations of files are kept for control purposes. Thus, master files from several recent periods of processing (known as *child, parent, grandparent* files, etc.) may be kept for backup purposes.

Storage Controls

Facility controls are methods that protect physical facilities and their contents from loss or destruction. Computer centers are subject to such hazards as accidents, natural disasters, sabotage, vandalism, unauthorized use, industrial espionage, destruction, and theft of resources. Therefore, physical safeguards and various control procedures are necessary to protect the hardware, software, network, and vital data resources of computer-using organizations.

Facility Controls

Encryption of data and the use of fire wall computers have become important ways to protect computer network resources. Passwords, messages, files, and other data can be transmitted in scrambled form and unscrambled by computer systems for authorized users only. This process is called **encryption.** Typically, it involves using a special mathematical algorithm, or key, to transform digital data into a scrambled code before they are transmitted, and to decode the data when they are received. Special

Encryption and Fire Walls

FIGURE 12.6

The encryption process of the controversial Clipper chip proposed by the U.S. government. The Clipper microprocessor would allow law enforcement surveillance of encrypted data transmissions and files.

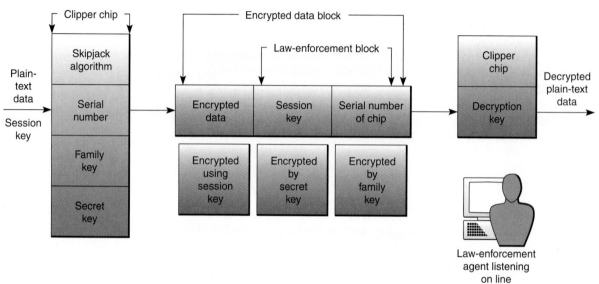

Source: Adapted and reprinted from "Crypto Policy and Business Privacy," by Winn Schwartau, *PC Week,* June 28, 1993, p. 207. Copyright © 1993, Ziff-Davis Publishing Company.

microprocessors and software packages can be used for the encryption process. There are several competing encryption standards, including DES (Data Encryption Standard), RSA (by RSA Data Security); PGP (pretty good privacy), a popular encryption program available on the Internet; and the Skipjack algorithm of the U.S. government's proposed Clipper encryption microprocessor chip. See Figure 12.6.

Another important method for control and security of telecommunications networks is the use of **fire wall** computers. A network fire wall is a computer system that protects computer networks from intrusion by serving as a filter and safe transfer point for access to and from other networks. It screens all network traffic, and only allows authorized transmissions in and out of the network. Fire walls have become an essential component of organizations connecting to the Internet, because of its vulnerability and lack of security. Figure 12.7 illustrates the Internet fire wall system of AT&T [35].

Fire walls can deter, but not completely prevent, unauthorized access (hacking) into computer networks. In some cases, a fire wall may allow access only from trusted locations on the Internet to particular computers inside the fire wall. Or it may allow only "safe" information to pass. For example, a fire wall may permit users to read E-mail from remote locations but not to run certain programs. In other cases, it is impossible to distinguish safe use of a particular network service from unsafe use and so all requests must be blocked. The fire wall may then provide substitutes for some network services (such as E-mail or file transfer) that perform most of the same functions but are not as vulnerable to penetration [35].

Physical Protection Controls

Providing maximum security and disaster protection for a computer installation requires many types of controls. Only authorized personnel are allowed access to the computer center through such techniques as identification badges for information services personnel, electronic door locks, burglar alarms, security police, closed-circuit

FIGURE 12.7

AT&T's Internet fire wall system.

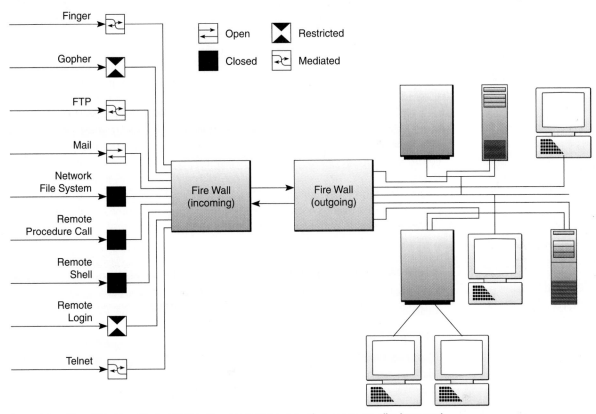

Source: Adapted from "Wire Pirates" by Paul Wallich. Copyright © 1994 by Scientific American, Inc. All rights reserved.

TV, and other detection systems. The computer center should be protected from disaster by such safeguards as fire detection and extinguishing systems; fireproof storage vaults for the protection of files; emergency power systems; electromagnetic shielding; and temperature, humidity, and dust control.

Biometric controls are a fast-growing area of computer security. These are security measures provided by computer devices that measure physical traits that make each individual unique. This includes voice verification, fingerprints, hand geometry, signature dynamics, keystroke analysis, retina scanning, face recognition, and genetic pattern analysis. Biometric control devices use special-purpose sensors to measure and digitize a *biometric profile* of an individual's fingerprints, voice, or other physical trait. The digitized signal is processed and compared to a previously processed profile of the individual stored on magnetic disk. If the profiles match, the individual is allowed entry into a computer facility or given access to information system resources.

Biometric Controls

Sorry, the computer is down is a well-known phrase to many end users. A variety of controls can prevent such computer failure or minimize its effects. Computers fail for several reasons—power failure, electronic circuitry malfunctions, mechanical malfunctions of peripheral equipment, hidden programming errors, and computer

Computer Failure Controls

operator errors. The information services department typically takes steps to prevent equipment failure and to minimize its detrimental effects. For example, computers with automatic and remote maintenance capabilities may be acquired. A program of preventive maintenance of hardware may be established. Adequate electrical supply, air conditioning, humidity control, and fire prevention standards must also be set. A backup computer system capability may be arranged with other computer-using organizations. Major hardware or software changes should be carefully scheduled and implemented to avoid problems. Finally, computer operators should have adequate training and supervision.

Many firms also use **fault tolerant** computer systems to ensure against computer failure. These systems have multiple central processors, peripherals, and system software. This may provide a *fail-safe* capability where the computer system continues to operate at the same level even if there is a major hardware or software failure. However, many fault tolerant computer systems offer a *fail-soft* capability where the computer system can continue to operate at a reduced but acceptable level in the event of a major system failure. Figure 12.8 outlines some of the fault tolerant capabilities used in many computer systems and networks.

Procedural Controls

Procedural controls are methods that specify how the information services organization should be operated for maximum security. They facilitate the accuracy and integrity of computer operations and systems development activities.

Separation of Duties

Separation of duties is a basic principle of procedural control. It requires that the duties of systems development, computer operations, and control of data and program files be assigned to separate groups. For example, systems analysts and computer programmers may not be allowed to operate corporate mainframes or make changes to data or programs being processed. In addition, a librarian or database

FIGURE 12.8

Methods of fault tolerance in computer-based information systems.

Layer	Threats	Fault Tolerant Methods
Applications	Environment, hardware and software faults	Application-specific redundancy and rollback to previous checkpoint
Systems	Outages	System isolation, data security, system integrity
Databases	Data errors	Separation of transactions and safe updates, complete transaction histories, backup files
Networks	Transmission errors	Reliable controllers; safe asynchrony and handshaking; alternative routing; error-detecting and error-correcting codes
Processes	Hardware and software faults	Alternative computations, rollback to checkpoints
Files	Media errors	Replication of critical data on different media and sites; archiving, backup, retrieval
Processors	Hardware faults	Instruction retry; error-correcting codes in memory and processing; replication; multiple processors and memories

Source: Adapted from Peter Neumann, *Computer-Related Risks* (New York: ACM Press), p. 231. Copyright © 1995, Association for Computing Machinery, Inc. By permission.

administrator has the responsibility for maintaining a library of data files and program files. Finally, a production control section may monitor the progress of information processing jobs, data entry activities, and the quality of input/output data. This is an important *quality assurance* function.

Typically, an IS organization develops and maintains manuals of standard procedures for the operation of information systems. Following standard procedures promotes uniformity and minimizes the chances of errors and fraud. It helps employees know what is expected of them in operating procedures and output quality. It is important that procedures be developed for both normal and unusual operating conditions. For example, procedures should tell employees what to do differently when their computers are not working. Finally, system, program, and operations documentation must be developed and kept up-to-date to ensure the correct processing of each application. Documentation is also invaluable in the maintenance of a system as needed improvements are made.

Standard Procedures and Documentation

Requests for systems development, program changes, or computer processing are frequently subjected to a formal review before authorization is given. For example, program changes generated by maintenance programmers should be approved by the manager of programming after consultation with the manager of computer operations and the manager of the affected end user department. Conversion to new hardware and software, installation of newly developed information systems, and changes to existing programs should be subjected to a formal notification and scheduling procedure. This minimizes their detrimental effects on the accuracy and integrity of ongoing computer operations.

Authorization Requirements

Natural and man-made disasters do happen. Hurricanes, earthquakes, fires, floods, criminal and terrorist acts, and human error can all severely damage an organization's computing resources, and thus the health of the organization itself. Many organizations, like airlines and banks, for example, are crippled by losing even a few hours of computing power. Many firms could survive only a few days without computing facilities. That's why organizations develop **disaster recovery** procedures and formalize them in a *disaster recovery plan*. It specifies which employees will participate in disaster recovery and what their duties will be; what hardware, software, and facilities will be used; and the priority of applications that will be processed. Arrangements with other companies for use of alternative facilities as a disaster recovery site and offsite storage of an organization's databases are also part of an effective disaster recovery effort.

Disaster Recovery

In Chapter 6, we outlined some of the risks of end user application development. We also discussed measures companies are taking to ensure the quality and security of end user applications. However, what many firms are beginning to realize is that, in many cases, end user–developed applications are performing extremely important business functions. Instead of merely being systems for personal productivity or decision support, these applications are supporting the accomplishment of important business activities that are critical to the success and survival of the firm. Thus, they can be called *company-critical* end user applications.

Figure 12.9 outlines controls that can be observed or built in to all *company-critical end user applications*. Many companies are insisting on such end user controls to protect themselves from the havoc that errors, fraud, destruction, and other hazards could

Controls for End User Computing

FIGURE 12.9
Criteria and controls for
company-critical end user
applications.

- Methods for testing user-developed systems for compliance with company policies and work procedures.
- Methods for notifying other users when changes in mission-critical user-developed systems are planned.
- Thorough documentation of user-developed systems.
- Training several people in the operation and maintenance of a system.
- A formal process for evaluating and acquiring new hardware and software.
- Formal backup and recovery procedures for all user systems.
- Security controls for access to user and company computer systems, networks, and databases.

cause to these critical applications and thus to the company itself. The controls involved are those that are standard practice in applications developed by professional IS departments. However, such controls were ignored in the rush to end user computing.

Figure 12.9 emphasizes a major point for managerial end users. Who is ultimately responsible for ensuring that proper controls are built into company-critical applications? End user managers are! This emphasizes once again that all managers must accept the responsibility for managing the information system resources of their work groups, departments, and other business units.

Auditing Information Systems

An information services department should be periodically examined, or *audited*, by internal auditing personnel from the business firm. In addition, periodic audits by external auditors from professional accounting firms are a good business practice. Such audits should review and evaluate whether proper and adequate information system controls, procedural controls, facility controls, and other managerial controls have been developed and implemented. There are two basic approaches for **auditing information systems**—that is, auditing the information processing activities of computer-based information systems. They are known as (1) auditing around the computer and (2) auditing through the computer.

Auditing around the computer involves verifying the accuracy and propriety of computer input and output without evaluating the computer programs used to process the data. This is a simpler and easier method that does not require auditors with programming experience. However, this auditing method does not trace a transaction through all of its stages of processing and does not test the accuracy and integrity of computer programs. Therefore, it is recommended only as a supplement to other auditing methods.

Auditing through the computer involves verifying the accuracy and integrity of the computer programs that process the data, as well as the input and output of the computer system. Auditing through the computer requires a knowledge of computer operations and programming. Some firms employ special EDP auditors for this assignment. They may use special test data to test processing accuracy and the control procedures built into the computer program. The auditors may develop special test programs or use audit software packages. See Figure 12.10.

EDP auditors use such programs to process their test data. Then they compare the results produced by their audit programs with the results generated by the computer user's own programs. One of the objectives of such testing is to detect the presence of unauthorized changes or patches to computer programs. Unauthorized program patches may be the cause of unexplainable errors or may be used for fraudulent purposes.

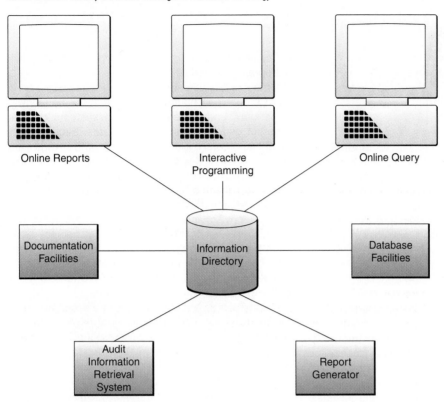

FIGURE 12.10

An example of the capabilities of an audit software package.

Auditing through the computer may be too costly for some computer applications. Therefore, a combination of both auditing approaches is usually employed. However, both auditing approaches must effectively contend with the changes caused by computer-based information systems to the *audit trail*.

An **audit trail** can be defined as the presence of documentation that allows a transaction to be traced through all stages of its information processing. This journey begins with a transaction's appearance on a source document and ends with its transformation into information on a final output document. The audit trail of manual information systems was quite visible and easy to trace. However, computer-based information systems have changed the form of the audit trail. Information formerly available to the auditor in the form of visual records is no longer available or is recorded on media that can be interpreted only by machines. For example, realtime transaction processing systems have increased the invisibility of the traditional audit trail. Paper documents and historical files are frequently eliminated when remote terminals and direct access files are used.

Such developments make the auditing of such systems a complex but vital assignment. Therefore, auditing personnel should be included on the project team of all major systems development projects and consulted before smaller critical systems projects are implemented. In addition, auditing personnel should be notified of changes to major computer programs caused by program maintenance activities. Such procedures give the auditor the opportunity to suggest methods of preserving the audit trail. The auditor can also ensure that adequate controls are designed into systems being developed or modified.

UNION PACIFIC RAILROAD: CONFRONTING THE MILLENNIUM BUG

It sounds like the plot of the next James Bond thriller: defective computer chips and software time bombs hiding since the 1950s detonate at exactly 12:01 A.M., January 1, 2000. Computers worldwide are tricked into interpreting the new millennium, A.D. 2000, as the year 1900. The current date format fails, and the world is catapulted into unpredictable high-tech chaos.

Unfortunately, this scenario is no Hollywood movie. The countdown is real and will affect corporations large and small. In fact, the year 2000 problem—also called the millennium bug—may be the single, most dangerous conundrum ever to threaten the world's computer infrastructure. If ignored, it has the potential to adversely affect every computer with a date chip and knock out common software applications such as spreadsheets, accounting packages, PIMs, and E-mail systems as well as mass hardware/software systems such as city traffic signals, global ATM machines, and telecommunications networks.

"Forty years ago, nobody expected program code would be around at the turn of the century," admits Dick Kearny, the partner in charge of Global Year 2000 at KPMG Peat Marwick. "Programmers in the '60s, '70s, and '80s were just trying to conserve what was then precious computer storage space," explains Kearny. "Instead of registering the century and year using four digits, they just put in the year to represent the century using only the last two digits so 86 automatically means 1986; but unfortunately, 00 translates to 1900, not the year 2000." The problem is, there's no quick fix for many older systems. According to Kearny, thousands of computers are running mountains of fragile code that's responsible for handling millions of critical business applications, which are not equipped for year 2000 dates. The fear is that these applications have existed for so long and have been altered and revised in so many undocumented ways that no one knows how to untangle them.

Union Pacific Railroad

The Union Pacific Railroad is facing the issue head-on. Jim Fox is director of information systems at Union Pacific. Jim's job centers around bringing the railroad into the next century—a problem no one at Union Pacific even considered until last year when the company discovered its computers weren't capable of making a stop after December 31, 1999.

Omaha, Nebraska–based Union Pacific—one of the most modern and largest railroads in the country—is dependent upon three mainframe systems cobbled together over the past 20 to 25 years. Each environment has several million lines of code with several thousand programs. Unfortunately, 83 percent of these programs use some type of date logic, explains Fox, and all are affected by the year 2000 date change.

The first sign of date derailment appeared when the Information Services group ran into problems with applications that handled five-year car scheduling, budgeting, and forecasting. Contracts with vendors and suppliers were affected, as were all normal financial reporting and human resources applications for computing wages, benefits, and retirement.

Union Pacific's first step was hiring Viasoft Inc., one of the many year 2000 consultant groups. With Viasoft, Union Pacific did a complete assessment of its mainframe computers and developed a plan of action. Viasoft's Impact 2000 revealed the size of the problem, the time involved to fix it, the resources required, and the cost.

"Based on Viasoft's findings, we grouped our applications into three categories," says Fox. "Our highest priority was those applications that we were not going to replace but that were already experiencing some year 2000 limitations. Those had to be converted immediately. The second group was systems that we were not going to replace and were not experiencing any year 2000 problems. And our lowest priority was systems we expected to replace instead of converting."

The company's goal is to be completely year 2000 ready by December 31, 1998, in order to have "one full year to make sure everything works," says Fox. The company expects to spend millions of dollars before the project is complete. Fox admits that one of the hardest parts of the process is "knowing you're going to spend all that money and not get any real return on your investment—except, of course, company survival."

CASE STUDY QUESTIONS

1. Is the millennium bug a major business problem? Why or why not?

2. Why didn't businesses move earlier to solve this problem? What can they do now?

3. Do you think that Union Pacific is moving effectively to solve their year 2000 problems? Explain.

Source: Adapted from Michael Cahlin, "The Millennium Bug," *PC Today*, June 1996, pp. 88–89. *PC Today*, 125 W. Harvest Drive, Lincoln, NE 68501.

Ethical and Societal Challenges of Information Technology

Section II

The Ethical Dimension

Ethical questions are involved in many strategic decisions, such as investment in human resources, modernization, product development and service, marketing, environmental decisions, and executive salaries. Often strategic issues are threats or opportunities that may significantly affect the firm's performance and are characterized by their novelty, complexity, and speed. Obviously, such threats or opportunities may involve a large ethical component. For example, Johnson & Johnson had to remove Tylenol from store shelves, and Manville Corporation quickly decided how to preserve the company's assets while meeting its obligations to victims during asbestos liability suits [17].

Whether we are in an ethical crisis or not is a subject of debate. But what is not debatable is that we are in the midst of an **information revolution,** in which information technology has dramatically magnified our ability to acquire, manipulate, store, and communicate information. Thanks to information technology, we have electronic tools that let us retrieve and communicate information in seconds to practically any person, in any place, at any time of the day. Thanks to IT, we can now communicate easily, work cooperatively, share resources, and make decisions, all electronically. But also thanks to information technology, it has now become possible to engage in ethical or unethical business practices electronically anywhere in the world.

That's why it is important for you to understand the ethical dimensions of working in business and using information technology. As a future managerial end user, it will be your responsibility to make decisions about business activities and the use of IT, which will always have an ethical dimension that must be considered. See Figure 12.11.

For example, should you electronically monitor your employees' work activities and electronic mail? Should you let employees use their work computers for private business or take home copies of software for their personal use? Should you electronically access your employees' personnel records or workstation files? Should

Tom Carroll/Phototake.

FIGURE 12.11

Managers must consider the ethical dimension of the business use of IT. Computer networks managed from this control room are designed to control refinery processes, ensure worker safety, and protect environmental quality.

you sell customer information extracted from transaction processing systems to other companies? These are a few examples of the types of decisions you will have to make that have a controversial ethical dimension. So let's take a closer look at ethical considerations in business and information technology.

Ethical Foundations

There are several **ethical philosophies** that you can use to help guide you in ethical decision making. Four basic ethical philosophies are: egoism, natural law, utilitarianism, and respect for persons [10]. Briefly, these alternative ethical philosophies are:

Egoism. What is best for a given individual is right.

Natural law. Humans should promote their own health and life, propagate, pursue knowledge of the world and God, pursue close relationships with other people, and submit to legitimate authority.

Utilitarianism. Those actions are right that produce the greatest good for the greatest number of people.

Respect for persons. People should be treated as an end and not as a means to an end; and actions are right if everyone adopts the moral rule presupposed by the action.

There are many **ethical models** of how humans apply their chosen ethical philosophies to the decisions and choices they have to make daily in work and other areas of their lives. For example, one theory focuses on people's decision-making processes, and stresses how various factors of our perceptions of them affect our ethical decision-making process. Figure 12.12 illustrates this model. Notice how individual attributes; personal, professional, and work environments; and government/legal and social environments may affect our decision processes and lead to ethical or unethical behavior.

Another example is a *behavioral stage* theory, which says that people go through several stages of *moral evolution* before they settle on one level of ethical reasoning. Figure 12.13 illustrates the stages in this model of ethical behavior. In this model, if you reach the final stage of moral evolution, your actions are guided by self-chosen ethical principles, not by fear, guilt, social pressure, and so on.

Business Ethics

Business ethics can be subdivided into two separate areas [18]. The first concerns the illegal, unethical, or questionable practices of managers or organizations, their causes, and their possible remedies. The second is concerned with the numerous ethical questions that managers must confront as part of their daily business decision making. For example, Figure 12.14 outlines some of the basic categories of ethical issues and specific business practices that have serious ethical consequences. Notice that the issues of employee privacy, security of company records, and workplace safety are highlighted because they have been major areas of ethical controversy in information technology.

How can managers make ethical decisions when confronted with business issues such as those listed in Figure 12.14? Several important alternatives based on theories of *corporate social responsibility* can be used [29,30].

- **The stockholder theory** holds that managers are agents of the stockholders, and their only ethical responsibility is to increase the profits of the business without violating the law or engaging in fraudulent practices.

- **The social contract theory** states that companies have ethical responsibilities to all members of society, which allow corporations to exist based on a social contract. The first condition of the contract requires companies to enhance

FIGURE 12.12

A model of ethical decision making. Note the factors that may affect our ethical decision-making process.

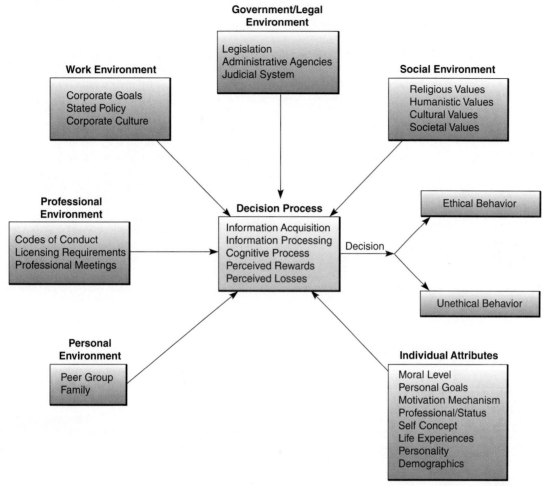

Source: Adapted from "A Behavioral Model of Ethical and Unethical Decision Making" by Michael Bonner, Clarence Gratto, Jerry Gravander, and Mark Tuttle, *Journal of Business Ethics,* June 1987, pp. 265–280. Copyright © 1987. Reprinted by permission of Kluwer Academic Publishers.

the economic satisfaction of consumers and employees. They must do that without polluting the environment or depleting natural resources, misusing political power, or subjecting their employees to dehumanizing working conditions. The second condition requires companies to avoid fraudulent practices, show respect for their employees as human beings, and avoid practices that systematically worsen the position of any group in society.

- **The stakeholder theory** maintains that managers have an ethical responsibility to manage a firm for the benefit of all of its *stakeholders*, which are all individuals and groups that have a stake in or claim on a company. This usually includes the corporation's stockholders, employees, customers, suppliers, and the local community. Sometimes the term is broadened to include all groups who can affect or be affected by the corporation, such as competitors, government agencies, special interest groups, and the media. Balancing the claims of conflicting stakeholders is obviously not an easy task for managers.

FIGURE 12.13
Stages of moral evolution. Note how people may evolve in their moral orientation through several levels of ethical reasoning.

Stages of Morality		Illustrative Behavior
Level 1: Preconventional morality		
Stage 1	Punishment orientation	Obeys rules to avoid punishment
Stage 2	Reward orientation	Conforms to obtain rewards or to have favors returned
Level II: Conventional morality		
Stage 3	Good-boy/good-girl orientation	Conforms to avoid disapproval of others
Stage 4	Authority orientation	Upholds laws and social rules to avoid censure of authorities and guilt about not "doing one's duty"
Level III: Postconventional morality		
Stage 5	Social-contact orientation	Actions guided by principles commonly agreed on as essential to the public welfare—upheld to retain respect of peers and self-respect
Stage 6	Ethical principle orientation	Actions guided by self-chosen ethical principles (that usually value justice, dignity, and equality)—upheld to avoid self-condemnation

Source: Adapted from "Education for the Moral Development of Managers: Kohlberg's Stages of Moral Development and Integrative Education" by Gerald D. Baxter and Charles A. Rarick, *Journal of Business Ethics,* June 1987, pp. 243–248. Copyright © 1987. Reprinted by permission of Kluwer Academic Publishers.

Ethical and Societal Dimensions of IT

Figure 12.15 illustrates several important aspects of the ethical and societal dimensions of information technology. It emphasizes that the use of information technology in business has major impacts on society, and thus raises serious ethical considerations in areas such as privacy, crime, health, working conditions, individuality, employment, and the search for societal solutions through IT. However, you should realize that information technology can have a beneficial effect as well as a negative effect in each of these areas. For example, computerizing a production process may

FIGURE 12.14
Basic categories of ethical business issues. Information technology has caused ethical controversy in the areas of employee privacy, security of company records, and workplace safety.

Equity	Rights	Honesty	Exercise of Corporate Power
Executive Salaries	Corporate Due Process	Employee Conflicts of Interest	Political Action Committees
Comparable Worth	Employee Health Screening	*Security of Company Records*	*Workplace Safety*
Product Pricing	*Employee Privacy*	Inappropriate Gifts	Product Safety
	Sexual Harassment	Advertising Content	Environmental Issues
	Affirmative Action	Government Contract Issues	Disinvestment
	Equal Employment Opportunity	Financial and Cash Management Procedures	Corporate Contributions
	Shareholder Interests	Questionable Business Practices in Foreign Countries	Social Issues Raised by Religious Organizations
	Employment at Will		Plant/Facility Closures and Downsizing
	Whistle-blowing		

Source: Adapted from The Conference Board, "Defending Corporate Ethics," in Peter Madsen and Jay Shafritz, *Essentials of Business Ethics* (New York: Meridian, 1990), p. 18.

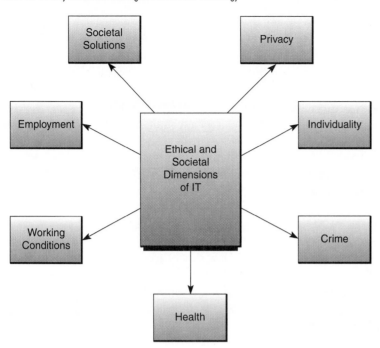

FIGURE 12.15

Major aspects of the ethical and societal dimensions of information technology. Remember that IT can have both a positive and a negative effect on society in each of the areas shown.

have the adverse effect of eliminating jobs, and the beneficial effect of improving the working conditions and job satisfaction of employees that remain, while producing products of higher quality at less cost. So your job as a managerial end user should involve managing your work activities and those of others to try to minimize the negative effects of IT and maximize its beneficial effects. That would represent an ethically responsible use of information technology.

Ethics and Information Technology

To help you in making such ethical choices, it might be helpful to keep in mind four **ethical principles** that can serve as guidelines in the implementation of any form of technology [22]. Figure 12.16 illustrates some of the ethical risks that may arise in the use of IT.

- **Proportionality.** The good achieved by the technology must outweigh the harm or risk. Moreover, there must be no alternative that achieves the same or comparable benefits with less harm or risk.
- **Informed Consent.** Those affected by the technology should understand and accept the risks.
- **Justice.** The benefits and burdens of the technology should be distributed fairly. Those who benefit should bear their fair share of the risks, and those who do not benefit should not suffer a significant increase in risk.
- **Minimized Risk.** Even if judged acceptable by the other three guidelines, the technology must be implemented so as to avoid all unnecessary risk.

Information Ethics

Another way to understand the ethical dimensions of IT is to consider the basic ethical issues that arise from its use to gather, process, store, and distribute information. Richard Mason [10] has posed four basic ethical issues that deal with the vulnerability of people to this aspect of information technology. It is based on the concept that information forms the intellectual capital of individual human beings. However, information systems can rob people of their intellectual capital. For example, people can lose information without compensation and without their permission. People can also be denied access to information or be exposed to erroneous information. Mason summarizes these four ethical issues with the acronym PAPA—privacy, accuracy, property, and accessibility.

- **Privacy.** What information about one's self or one's associations must a person reveal to others, under what conditions, and with what safeguards? What things can people keep to themselves and not be forced to reveal to others?
- **Accuracy.** Who is responsible for the authenticity, fidelity, and accuracy of information? Similarly, who is to be held accountable for errors in information and how is the injured party to be made whole?
- **Property.** Who owns information? What are the just and fair prices for its exchange? Who owns the channels, especially the airways, through which information is transmitted? How should access to this scarce resource be allocated?
- **Accessibility.** What information does a person or an organization have a right or a privilege to obtain, under what conditions, and with what safeguards?

FIGURE 12.16

Ethical considerations of the potential harms or risks of the business use of IT.

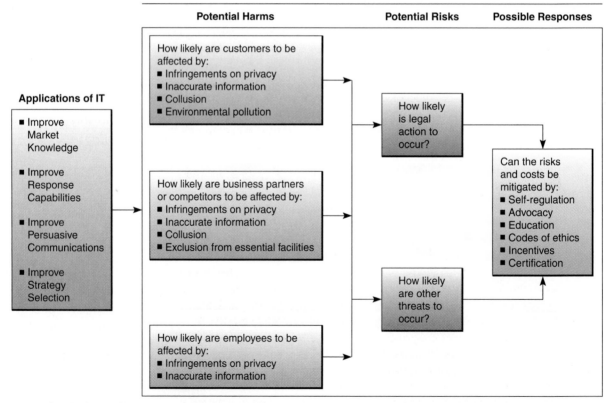

Source: Adapted and reprinted by permission of Harvard Business School Press from Robert C. Blattberg, Rashi Glazer, and John D. C. Little, *The Marketing Information Revolution.* Boston: 1994, p. 291. Copyright © 1994 by the President and Fellows of Harvard College.

In answering these questions, Mason proposes the development of a new social contract, where information technology will help ensure everyone's right to fulfill his or her human potential. In this new social contract, information systems should be designed to ensure accuracy and not invade a person's privacy. Channels of information should be protected and information made accessible to avoid information illiteracy or deprivation. Finally, information systems should be designed to protect an individual's intellectual capital from unauthorized exposure, loss, or damage. Developing, protecting, and enforcing this social contract then becomes the responsibility of end users, managers, and IS professionals.

The impact of information technology on **employment** is a major ethical concern and is directly related to the use of computers to achieve automation. There can be no doubt that the use of information technology has created new jobs and increased productivity, while also causing a significant reduction in some types of job opportunities. Computers used for office information processing or for the numerical control of machine tools are accomplishing tasks formerly performed by many clerks and machinists. Also, jobs created by information technology within a computer-using organization require different types of skills and education than do the jobs eliminated by computers. Therefore, individuals may become unemployed unless they can be retrained for new positions or new responsibilities.

IT and Employment

However, there can be no doubt that information technology has created a host of new job opportunities for the manufacture, sale, and maintenance of computer hardware and software, and for other information system services. Many new jobs, such as systems analysts, computer programmers, and computer operators, have been created in computer-using organizations. New jobs have also been created in service industries that provide services to the computer industry and to computer-using firms. Additional jobs have been created because information technology makes possible the production of complex industrial and technical goods and services that would otherwise be impossible to produce. Thus, jobs have been created by activities that are heavily dependent on information technology, in such areas as space exploration, microelectronic technology, and scientific research.

A frequent criticism of information technology concerns its negative effect on the **individuality** of people. Computer-based systems are criticized as impersonal systems that dehumanize and depersonalize activities that have been computerized, since they eliminate the human relationships present in noncomputer systems. Although it is more efficient for an information system to deal with an individual as a number than as a name, many people feel a loss of identity when they seem to be "just another number."

IT and Individuality

Another aspect of the loss of individuality is the regimentation of the individual that seems to be required by some computer-based systems. These systems do not seem to possess any flexibility. They demand strict adherence to detailed procedures if the system is to work. The negative impact of IT on individuality is reinforced by horror stories that describe how inflexible and uncaring computer-based systems are when it comes to rectifying their own mistakes. Many of us are familiar with stories of how computerized customer billing and accounting systems continued to demand payment and send warning notices to a customer whose account has already been paid, despite repeated attempts by the customer to have the error corrected.

However, computer-based systems can be ergonomically engineered to accommodate **human factors** that minimize depersonalization and regimentation. People-oriented and user-friendly information systems can thus be developed. The computer hardware, software, graphical user interface, and other IT capabilities that make such systems possible are increasing rather than decreasing. For example, use of microcomputers has dramatically improved the development of people-oriented end user and work group information systems. Even everyday products and services have been improved through microprocessor-powered "smart" products.

IT and Working Conditions

Information technology has eliminated monotonous or obnoxious tasks in the office and the factory that formerly had to be performed by people. For example, word processing and desktop publishing make producing office documents a lot easier to do, while robots have taken over repetitive welding and spray painting jobs in the automotive industry. In many instances, this allows people to concentrate on more challenging and interesting assignments, upgrades the skill level of the work to be performed, and creates challenging jobs requiring highly developed skills in the computer industry and within computer-using organizations. Thus, information technology can be said to upgrade the *quality of work* because it can upgrade the quality of working conditions and the content of work activities.

Of course, it must be remembered that some jobs created by information technology—data entry, for example—are quite repetitive and routine. Also, to the extent that computers are utilized in some types of automation, IT must take some responsibility for the criticism of assembly-line operations that require the continual repetition of elementary tasks, thus forcing a worker to work like a machine instead of like a skilled craftsperson. Many automated operations are also criticized for relegating people to a "do-nothing" standby role, where workers spend most of their time waiting for infrequent opportunities to push some buttons. Such effects do have a detrimental effect on the quality of work, but they must be compared to the less-burdensome and more creative jobs created by information technology.

Computer Monitoring

One of the most explosive ethical issues concerning the quality of work is **computer monitoring**. That is, computers are being used to monitor the productivity and behavior of millions of employees while they work. Supposedly, computer monitoring is done so employers can collect productivity data about their employees to increase the efficiency and quality of service. However, computer monitoring has been criticized as unethical because it monitors individuals, not just work, and is done continually, thus violating workers' privacy and personal freedom. For example, when you call to make a reservation, an airline reservation agent may be timed on the exact seconds he or she took per caller, the time between calls, and the number and length of breaks taken. In addition, your conversation may also be monitored [9, 11]. See Figure 12.17.

Computer monitoring has been criticized as an invasion of the privacy of employees because, in many cases, they do not know that they are being monitored or don't know how the information is being used. Critics also say that an employee's right of due process may be harmed by the improper use of collected data to make personnel decisions. Since computer monitoring increases the stress on employees who must work under constant electronic surveillance, it has also been blamed for causing health problems among monitored workers. Finally, computer monitoring has been blamed for robbing workers of the dignity of their work. In effect, computer monitoring creates an "electronic sweatshop," where workers are forced to work at a hectic pace under poor working conditions.

Political pressure is building to outlaw or regulate computer monitoring in the workplace. For example, a Privacy for Consumers and Workers Act has been introduced in both houses of the U.S. Congress. This proposed law would regulate

Jon Feingersh/Uniphoto Picture Agency.

FIGURE 12.17
Computer monitoring can be used to record the productivity and behavior of people while they work.

computer monitoring, and protect the worker's right to know and right to privacy. Public advocacy groups, labor unions, and many legislators are pushing for action. In the meantime, lawsuits by monitored workers against employers are increasing rapidly. Jury awards to workers have been in the hundreds of thousands of dollars [10]. So computer monitoring of workers is one ethical issue that won't go away.

Privacy Issues

Information technology makes it technically and economically feasible to collect, store, integrate, interchange, and retrieve data and information quickly and easily. This characteristic has an important beneficial effect on the efficiency and effectiveness of computer-based information systems. However, the power of information technology to store and retrieve information can have a negative effect on the **right to privacy** of every individual. For example, confidential E-mail messages by employees are monitored by many companies. Confidential information on individuals contained in centralized computer databases by credit bureaus, government agencies, and private business firms has been stolen or misused, resulting in the invasion of privacy, fraud, and other injustices. The unauthorized use of such information has seriously damaged the privacy of individuals. Errors in such databases could seriously hurt the credit standing or reputation of an individual. See Figure 12.18.

Some of the important privacy issues being debated in business and government include the following [30]:

- Accessing individuals' private E-mail conversations and computer records (*violation of privacy*).
- Always knowing where a person is, especially as mobile and paging services become more closely associated with people rather than places (*computer monitoring*).
- Using customer information to market additional business services (*computer matching*).
- Collecting telephone numbers and other personal information to build individual customer profiles (*unauthorized personal files*).
- Using automated equipment either to originate calls or to collect caller information (*caller identification*).

E-Mail Privacy

Companies differ on their privacy policies, especially as they apply to electronic mail. For example, First Bancorporation of Ohio vows that it will never monitor the E-mail system used by its more than 1,000 employees. It views E-mail correspondence as private. However, Eastman Kodak's policy states that it retains the right to monitor employee E-mail. But the company says that it will exercise that right only if there is reason to suspect that an employee is involved in illegal or unauthorized activity. The Bank of Boston, on the other hand, has a written policy banning all use of computers for personal business, and warns employees that it will actively monitor E-mail to enforce that policy. To underscore its reasons, the bank revealed that it had discovered an employee running a gambling operation and handicapping dog races over its E-mail system [25, 31].

Computer Matching

Unauthorized use or mistakes in the **computer matching** of personal data are another controversial threat to privacy. Individuals have been mistakenly arrested and jailed, and people have been denied credit because their physical profiles or Social Security numbers have been used to match them incorrectly or improperly with the wrong individuals. A newer threat is the unauthorized matching of computerized information about you extracted from the databases of sales transaction processing systems, and sold to *information brokers* or other companies. You are then subjected to a barrage of unsolicited promotional material and sales contacts [11]. See Figure 12.19.

Such developments were possible before the advent of computers. However, the speed and power of large computer systems networked to direct access databases and remote terminals greatly increases the potential for such injustices. The trend toward nationwide telecommunications networks with integrated databases by business firms and government agencies substantially increases the potential for the misuse of computer-stored information.

Privacy Laws

In the United States, the Federal Privacy Act strictly regulates the collection and use of personal data by governmental agencies (except for law enforcement investigative files, classified files, and civil service files). The law specifies that individuals have the right to inspect their personal records, make copies, and correct or remove erroneous

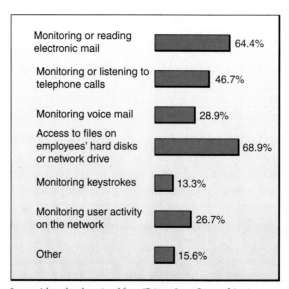

FIGURE 12.18

Areas covered by a privacy policy in a survey of companies.

Source: Adapted and reprinted from "Privacy Issue Comes of Age in a Networked World" by Laura Smith, *PC Weekly*, June 28, 1993, p. 202. Copyright © 1993, Ziff-Davis Publishing Company.

or misleading information. It also specifies that federal agencies (1) must annually disclose the types of personal data files they maintain, (2) cannot disclose personal information on an individual to any other individual or agency except under certain strict conditions, (3) must inform individuals of the reasons for requesting personal information from them, (4) must retain personal data records only if it is "relevant and necessary to accomplish" an agency's legal purpose, and (5) must "establish appropriate administrative, technical, and physical safeguards to ensure the security and confidentiality of records" [10, 11, 34].

The U.S. Congress enacted the Electronic Communications Privacy Act and the Computer Fraud and Abuse Act in 1986. These federal **privacy laws** are a major attempt to enforce the privacy of computer-based files and communications. These laws prohibit intercepting data communications messages, stealing or destroying data, or trespassing in federal-related computer systems. In 1988 the Computer Matching and Privacy Act became law in the United States. It regulates the matching of data held in federal agency files to verify eligibility for federal programs. Such legislation should emphasize and accelerate the efforts of systems designers to use hardware, software, and procedural controls to maintain the accuracy and confidentiality of computerized databases.

Computer Libel and Censorship

The opposite side of the privacy debate is the right of people to know about matters others may want to keep private (freedom of information), the right of people to express their opinions about such matters (freedom of speech), and the right of people to publish those opinions (freedom of the press). One of the biggest battlegrounds in the debate are the bulletin boards, E-mail boxes, and online files of the Internet and public information networks such as Prodigy, CompuServe, and America Online. The weapons being used in this battle include *flame mail*, libel laws, and censorship.

Flaming is the practice of sending extremely critical, derogatory, and often vulgar E-mail messages (*flame mail*), or electronic bulletin board postings to other users on the Internet or online services. Flaming is especially prevalent on some of the bulletin

FIGURE 12.19

Why companies do computer matching.

	Customer (Internal Information)	Customer (External Information)	Prospect
Acquire	1. Profile own customers based on existing transaction data.	2. Acquire new information about existing customers from a third party.	3. Acquire information about prospective customers from a third party.
Use	4. Target own customer for new or repeat business.	5. Market-research or cross-market own customers for new business.	6. Target prospective customers for new business.
Transfer	7. Transfer information about own customers within organization.	8. Transfer information about customers to a third party.	9. Transfer information about prospects to other third parties.

Source: Adapted from "How Did They Get My Name? An Exploratory Investigation of Consumer Attitudes toward Secondary Information Use" by Mary Culnane, *MIS Quarterly*, September 1993, p. 347. Reprinted with permission of the *MIS Quarterly*.

FIGURE 12.20

Examples from the
computer libel and censorship debate, and software
piracy controversy.

Flaming liability
Online service provider Prodigy Services Co. is under legal siege for defamatory remarks
posted against a business.
  Long Island–based securities firm Stratton Oakmont, Inc., filed a $200 million libel
suit against the user who posted the defamatory comments and against Prodigy for
failing to remove the offending message. Prodigy already screens E-mail for obscenities
or racist comments; the flame in question accused Stratton Oakmont of fraudulent
securities offerings.

Cyberspace censorship?
Against the objections of civil liberties activists, Pittsburgh-based Carnegie Mellon University
has decided to cut sexually oriented newsgroups from its Internet servers because some of
these online discussion forums are dedicated to posting explicit digitized photographs.
Pennsylvania obscenity laws prohibit distribution of such images. These images have been
downloaded or viewed more than 6 million times at the school, according to a study by one
Carnegie Mellon research associate.

Copycat
David LaMacchia, a 20-year-old student at MIT, is in court for using the school's Internet
servers to distribute copyrighted software.
  LaMacchia faces charges of conspiracy to commit wire fraud. A conviction could bring
him as many as five years in federal prison, plus fines well beyond the scope of ordinary
school loans.
  The twist for the defense is that LaMacchia collected no money for his efforts and
neither uploaded nor downloaded any of the copyrighted programs. He only operated
a bulletin board that made such activities possible.

Source: Adapted from "Cyberspace and the Law," by Derek Slater, *Computerworld,* December 5, 1994, p. 115.
Copyright © 1994 by Computerworld, Inc., Framingham, MA 01701—Reprinted from *Computerworld.*

board systems of special interest discussion groups such as the Internet's Usenet. There
have been several incidents of racist or defamatory messages that have led to calls for
censorship and lawsuits for libel. In addition, the presence of sexually explicit photographs and text at Internet locations has triggered lawsuits and censorship actions by
the institutions involved [28]. Most recently, the Communications Decency Act of the
U.S. Telecommunications Deregulation and Reform Bill of 1996 bans the sending of
"indecent" material over the Internet and online services without ensuring that children
won't have access to it [38]. See Figure 12.20 and Application Exercise 2.

Computer Crime

Computer crime is a growing threat caused by the criminal or irresponsible actions
of a small minority of computer professionals and end users who are taking advantage of the widespread use of computers and information technology in our society.
It thus presents a major challenge to the ethical use of IT. Computer crime also poses
serious threats to the security of computer-based information systems and makes the
development of effective control methods a top priority. See Figure 12.21.

Computer Crime Laws

One way to understand computer crime is to see how current **laws** define it. A
good example of this is the U.S. Computer Fraud and Abuse Act of 1986. In a nut-
shell, this law says that computer crime involves access of "federal interest" computers (used by the federal government), or operating in interstate or foreign
commerce (1) with intent to defraud, (2) resulting in more than a $1,000 loss, or
(3) to gain access to certain medical computer systems. Trafficking in computer
access passwords is also prohibited. Penalties for violations of this law are severe.

Mode	Misuse Type
External	
1. Visual spying	Observing of keystrokes or screens
2. Misrepresentation	Deceiving operators and users
3: Physical scavenging	Dumpster-diving for printout
Hardware misuse	
4. Logical scavenging	Examining discarded/stolen media
5. Eavesdropping	Intercepting electronic or other data
6. Interference	Jamming, electronic or otherwise
7. Physical attack	Damaging or modifying equipment, power
8. Physical removal	Removing equipment and storage media
Masquerading	
9. Impersonation	Using false identities external to computer systems
10. Piggybacking attacks	Usurping communications lines, workstations
11. Spoofing attacks	Using playback, creating bogus nodes and systems
12. Network weaving	Masking physical whereabouts or routing
Pest programs	Setting up opportunities for further misuse
13. Trojan horse attacks	Implanting malicious code, sending letter bombs
14. Logic bombs	Setting time or event bombs (a form of Trojan horse)
15. Malevolent worms	Acquiring distributed resources
16. Virus attacks	Attaching to programs and replicating
Bypasses	Avoiding authentication and authority
17. Trapdoor attacks	Utilizing existing flaws
18. Authorization attacks	Password cracking, hacking tokens
Active misuse	Writing, using, with apparent authorization
19. Basic active misuse	Creating, modifying, using, denying service, entering false or misleading data
20. Incremental attacks	Using salami attacks
21. Denials of service	Perpetrating saturation attacks
Passive misuse	Reading, with apparent authorization
22. Browsing	Making random or selective searches
23. Inference, aggregation	Exploiting database inferences and traffic analysis
24. Covert channels	Exploiting covert channels or other data leakage
Inactive misuse	Willfully failing to perform expected duties, or committing errors of omission
Indirect misuse	Preparing for subsequent misuses, as in offline preencryptive matching, factoring large numbers to obtain private keys, autodialer scanning

FIGURE 12.21

Types of computer crime. Note the many ways that computer systems and networks have been misused for criminal purposes.

Source: Adapted from *Computer-Related Risks* by Peter Neumann (New York: ACM Press), p. 102. Copyright © 1995, Association for Computing Machinery, Inc. By permission.

They include 1 to 5 years in prison for a first offense, 10 years for a second offense, and 20 years for three or more offenses. Fines could range up to $250,000 or twice the value of the stolen data [9, 11].

The Data Processing Management Association (DPMA) defines computer crime more specifically. In its Model Computer Crime Act, the DPMA defines computer crime as including (1) the unauthorized use, access, modification, and destruction of hardware, software, data, or network resources; (2) the unauthorized release of information; (3) the unauthorized copying of software; (4) denying an end user access to his or her own hardware, software, data, or network resources; and (5) using or conspiring to use computer resources to illegally obtain information or tangible property.

Examples of Computer Crime

Another way to understand computer crime is to examine examples of major types of criminal activity involving computers. Typically, this involves the theft of money, services, software, and data; destruction of data and software, especially by *computer viruses*; and malicious access, or *hacking* of computer networks, and violations of privacy.

Money Theft

Many computer crimes involve the theft of money. They frequently involve fraudulent alteration of computer files to cover the tracks of the thieves, or to swindle money from others based on falsified records. For example, in the famous Volkswagen AG case of 1987, a group of company executives altered computerized foreign exchange accounting files to hide their theft of almost $253 million. In the most famous computer swindle, The Equity Funding Case of 1977, a group of con artists used a large insurance company's computers to generate thousands of falsified insurance policies with a face value of over $2 billion. The policies were then used as collateral to swindle investors out of more than $600 million for worthless stock in a fictitious company.

We do not know the extent of other major computer frauds, though losses from automated teller machines (ATMs) are smaller, but numerous. Financial institutions do not usually report them, because they fear a loss of consumer confidence and increases in insurance premiums. A lot of unsuccessful frauds have been reported, but many have been foiled more by accident than by vigilance. For example, in 1988, the Union Bank of Switzerland was automatically processing a money transfer of $54.1 million, when a computer failure caused a manual check of the transaction that revealed it was fraudulent [23].

Service Theft

The unauthorized use of a computer system is called service theft. A common example is unauthorized use of company-owned microcomputers by employees. This may range from doing private consulting or personal finances to playing video games. So, if it's unauthorized use of someone else's computer, it's service theft. More serious cases are also more blatant. In one example, the manager of a New York state university computer center and his assistant secretly used the school's computer to provide a variety of commercial computing services to their business clients.

Software Theft

Computer programs are valuable property and thus are the subject of theft from computer systems. However, unauthorized copying of software, or **software piracy**, is also a major form of software theft. Several major cases involving the unauthorized copying of software have been widely reported. These include lawsuits by the Software Publishers Association, an industry association of software developers, against major corporations that allowed unauthorized copying of their programs. Lotus Development Corporation and other software companies have also won lawsuits against competitors who marketed copies or clones that had the look and feel of their popular software packages.

Unauthorized copying is illegal because software is intellectual property that is protected by copyright law and user licensing agreements. For example, in the United States, commercial software packages are protected by the Computer Software Piracy and Counterfeiting Amendment to the Federal Copyright Act. In most cases, the purchase of a commercial software package is really a payment to license its fair use by an individual end user. Therefore, many companies sign *site licenses* that allow them to legally make a certain number of copies for use by their employees at a particular location. Other alternatives are *shareware*, which allows you to make copies of software for others, and *public domain software*, which is not copyrighted.

Making illegal changes to data is another form of computer crime. For example, an employee of the University of Southern California was convicted of taking payments from students and changing their grades in return. Other reported schemes involved changes in credit information, and changes in Department of Motor Vehicles' records that facilitated the theft of the cars to which the records referred. More recently, employees of the U.S. Social Security Administration were indicted for selling confidential personal information to *information brokers*. Also indicted were Virginia state police and other officers who sold criminal histories from the National Crime Information Center databases [4].

Data Alteration or Theft

One of the most destructive examples of computer crime involves the creation of **computer viruses** or *worms*. Virus is the more popular term but, technically, a virus is a program code that cannot work without being inserted into another program. A worm is a distinct program that can run unaided. In either case, these programs copy annoying or destructive routines into the networked computer systems of anyone who accesses computers infected with the virus or who uses copies of magnetic disks taken from infected computers. Thus, a computer virus or worm can spread destruction among many users. Though they sometimes display only humorous messages, they more often destroy the contents of memory, hard disks, and other storage devices. Copy routines in the virus or worm spread the virus and destroy the data and software of many computer users.

Computer Viruses: Destruction of Data and Software

Computer viruses enter a computer system typically through illegal or borrowed copies of software, or through network links to other computer systems. Copies of software downloaded from electronic bulletin boards can be another source of viruses. A virus usually copies itself into the files of a computer's operating system. Then the virus spreads to main memory and copies itself onto the computer's hard disk and any inserted floppy disks. The virus spreads to other computers through telecommunications links or floppy disks from infected computers. Thus, as a good end user computing practice, you should avoid using software from questionable sources without checking for viruses. You should also regularly use vaccine programs that can help diagnose and remove computer viruses from infected files on your hard disk or in a network. See Figure 12.22.

Hacking, in computerese, is the obsessive use of computers, or the unauthorized access and use of networked computer systems. Illegal hackers (also called *crackers*) may steal or damage data and programs. One of the issues in hacking is what to do about a hacker who commits only electronic breaking and entering; that is, gets access to a computer system, reads some files, but neither steals nor damages anything. This situation is common in computer crime cases that are prosecuted. In California, a court found that the typical computer crime statute language prohibiting malicious access to a computer system did apply to any users gaining unauthorized access to others' computer systems [10].

Malicious Access

Widely publicized attacks by hackers on the Internet have splashed the open electronic playground with a dose of cold reality and sent newcomers scrambling to beef up network security plans. In recent years, as the Internet has changed from the casual chat line of the academic and research communities to the playground of the computationally hip, attacks have increased. The influx has created a new breed of intruder who uses sophisticated software programs designed to automatically probe the Internet looking for system weaknesses [2].

Crime on the Internet

Someone breaks into computer systems at Rice University and steals files of thousands of passwords, changes passwords, and destroys several files. Someone takes over a student's account on a computer at Northern Arizona University and

FIGURE 12.22

An example of the display of a computer vaccine program to eliminate computer viruses.

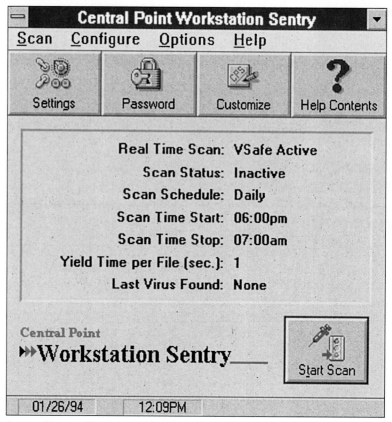

Courtesy of Symantec Corporation.

sends a racist E-mail message to over 15,000 Internet users worldwide. Someone breaks into computers at IBM, Sprint, and an Internet service provider and sends an *electronic mail bomb* of thousands of angry E-mail messages to *Wired* magazine and a pair of *Newsday* reporters, jamming their Internet mailbox and knocking them off the Net. Someone breaks into the heavily protected computer networks of General Electric, causing them to disconnect from the Internet for three days. The Computer Emergency Response Team (CERT) of Carnegie Mellon University notices that someone is using network monitoring software (*sniffers*) to capture passwords over 110 times in 10 months on the Internet [1, 12].

These are just some of the computer crimes that hackers commit on the Internet each day, according to CERT. Figure 12.23 shows that computers connected to the Internet are vulnerable to hacking in many different ways. Services such as Gopher, FTP (file transfer protocol), electronic mail, or a network file system may be used to extract passwords or other vital files or to plant data that will cause a system to welcome intruders. A cracker may also use services that allow one computer on a network to execute programs on another computer—including remote procedure call (rpc), remote shell (rshell), and remote login (rlogin). This allows the intruder to gain *privileged access* directly. Telnet, a tool for interactive communication with remote computers, or Finger, a service that provides data about users, can help a cracker discover information to plan other attacks. A hacker may telnet to a computer's E-mail port, for example, to find out whether a particularly vulnerable mail program is running or to determine whether certain privileged user accounts may be easily accessible.

FIGURE 12.23

Hackers can break into the Internet by using the vulnerability of its services to break into files, steal passwords, and take over an Internet server.

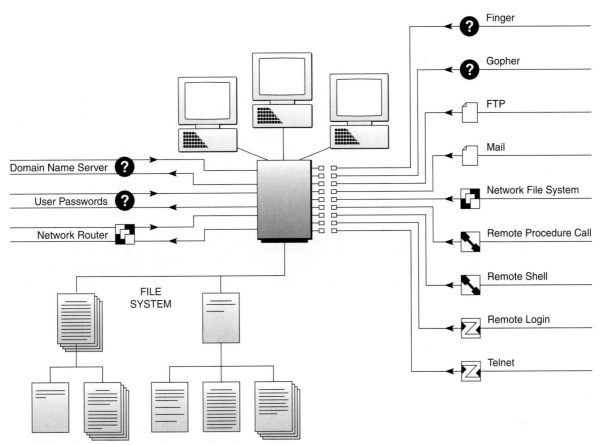

Source: Adapted from "Wire Pirates" by Paul Wallich. Copyright © 1994 by Scientific American, Inc. All rights reserved.

How can companies and end users protect themselves from such intruders? Password encryption and fire wall computers are tops on the list, followed by tight security management of a company's networks and encryption of sensitive files and databases. Frequent changing of user passwords helps, but a list of one-time passwords (only used once) carried by an end user is a lot better. In *challenge-response* password encryption systems, users carry a special calculator that encrypts a number provided by the system that they can use as a password into the system. Encryption of private E-mail messages and other data by popular E-mail and groupware packages is another good security measure for the Internet [35].

The use of information technology in the workplace raises a variety of **health issues**. Heavy use of computers is reportedly causing health problems like job stress, damaged arm and neck muscles, eye strain, radiation exposure, and even death by computer-caused accidents. For example, *computer monitoring* is blamed as a major cause of computer-related job stress. Workers, unions, and government officials criticize computer monitoring as putting so much stress on employees that it leads to health problems [10, 11].

Health Issues

People who sit at PC workstations or visual display terminals (VDTs) in fast-paced, repetitive keystroke jobs can suffer a variety of health problems known collectively as *cumulative trauma disorders* (CTDs). Their fingers, wrists, arms, necks, and backs may become so weak and painful that they cannot work. Many times strained muscles, back pain, and nerve damage may result. In particular, some computer workers may suffer from *carpal tunnel syndrome*, a painful, crippling ailment of the hand and wrist that typically requires surgery to cure [19].

Prolonged viewing of video displays causes eyestrain and other health problems in employees who must do this all day. Radiation caused by the *cathode ray tubes* (CRTs) that produce most video displays is another health concern. CRTs produce an electromagnetic field that may cause harmful radiation of employees who work too close for too long in front of video monitors. Some pregnant workers have reported miscarriages and fetal deformities due to prolonged exposure to CRTs at work. However, several studies have failed to find conclusive evidence concerning this problem. Still, several organizations recommend that female workers minimize their use of CRTs during pregnancy [10, 11].

Ergonomics

Solutions to some of these health problems are based on the science of **ergonomics**, sometimes called *human factors engineering*. The goal of ergonomics is to design healthy work environments that are safe, comfortable, and pleasant for people to work in, thus increasing employee morale and productivity. Ergonomics stresses the healthy design of the workplace, workstations, computers and other machines, and even software packages. Other health issues may require ergonomic solutions emphasizing *job design*, rather than workplace design. For example, this may require policies providing for work breaks from heavy VDT use every few hours, while limiting the CRT exposure of pregnant workers. Ergonomic job design can also provide more variety in job tasks for those workers who spend most of their workday at computer workstations. See Figure 12.24.

FIGURE 12.24

Ergonomic factors in the workplace. Note that good ergonomic design considers tools, tasks, the workstation, and environment.

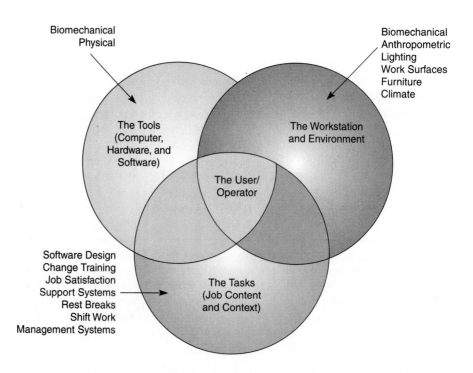

Societal Solutions

Before we conclude this section, it would be good to emphasize that information technology can have many beneficial effects on society. We can use information technology to solve human and social problems through **societal solutions** such as medical diagnosis, computer-assisted instruction, governmental program planning, environmental quality control, and law enforcement. For example, computers can help diagnose an illness, prescribe necessary treatment, and monitor the progress of hospital patients. Computer-assisted instruction (CAI) allows a computer to serve as tutor, since it uses conversational computing to tailor instruction to the needs of a particular student. This is a tremendous benefit to students, especially those with learning disabilities.

Information technology can be used for crime control through various law enforcement applications. For example, computerized alarm systems allow police to identify and respond quickly to evidences of criminal activity. Computers have been used to monitor the level of pollution in the air and in bodies of water, to detect the sources of pollution, and to issue early warnings when dangerous levels are reached. Computers are also used for the program planning of many government agencies in such areas as urban planning, population density and land use studies, highway planning, and urban transit studies. Computers are being used in job placement systems to help match unemployed persons with available jobs. These and other applications illustrate that information technology can be used to help solve the problems of society.

You and Ethical Responsibility

As a managerial end user, you have a responsibility to do something about some of the abuses of information technology in the workplace. Whether you are a manager, end user, or IS professional, you should accept the ethical responsibilities that come with your work activities. That includes properly performing your role as a vital human resource in the computer-based information systems you help develop and use in your organization. In this section, we have outlined several ethical principles that can serve as the basis for ethical conduct by managers, end users, and IS professionals. But what more specific guidelines might help your ethical use of information technology?

One way to answer this question is to examine statements of responsibilities contained in codes of professional conduct for IS professionals. A good example is the code of professional conduct of the Data Processing Management Association (DPMA), an organization of professionals in the computing field. Its code of conduct outlines the ethical considerations inherent in the major responsibilities of an IS professional. Figure 12.25 is a portion of the DPMA code of conduct.

The DPMA code provides guidelines for ethical conduct in the development and use of information technology. End users and IS professionals would live up to their ethical responsibilities by voluntarily following such guidelines. For example, you can be a **responsible end user** by (1) acting with integrity, (2) increasing your professional competence, (3) setting high standards of personal performance, (4) accepting responsibility for your work, and (5) advancing the health, privacy, and general welfare of the public. Then you would be demonstrating ethical conduct, avoiding computer crime, and increasing the security of any information system you develop or use.

As a managerial end user, you should insist that the ethical and societal dimensions of information technology be considered when computer-based information systems are being developed and used. For example, a major design objective should be to develop systems that can be easily and effectively used by people.

FIGURE 12.25

Part of the DPMA standards of professional conduct. This code can serve as a model for ethical conduct by end users as well as IS professionals.

DPMA Standards of Professional Conduct

In recognition of my obligation to my employer I shall:

- Make every effort to ensure that I have the most current knowledge and that the proper expertise is available when needed.
- Avoid conflicts of interest and ensure that my employer is aware of any potential conflicts.
- Protect the privacy and confidentiality of all information entrusted to me.
- Not misrepresent or withhold information that is germane to the situation.
- Not attempt to use the resources of my employer for personal gain or for any purpose without proper approval.
- Not exploit the weakness of a computer system for personal gain or personal satisfaction.

In recognition of my obligation to society I shall:

- Use my skill and knowledge to inform the public in all areas of my expertise.
- To the best of my ability, ensure that the products of my work are used in a socially responsible way.
- Support, respect, and abide by the appropriate local, state, provincial, and Federal laws.
- Never misrepresent or withhold information that is germane to a problem or a situation of public concern, nor will I allow any such known information to remain unchallenged.
- Not use knowledge of a confidential or personal nature in any unauthorized manner to achieve personal gain.

Source: Adapted from Bruce E. Spiro, "Ethics in the Information Age," *Information Executive,* Fall 1989, p. 40.

The objectives of the system must also include protection of the privacy of the individuals and the defense of the system against computer crime. Control hardware, software, and procedures must be included in the systems design. The potential for misuse and malfunction of a proposed system must be analyzed and controlled with respect to all of an organization's present and potential stakeholders, individuals, and society as a whole.

It should be obvious to you that many of the detrimental effects of information technology are caused by individuals or organizations that are not accepting the ethical responsibility for their actions. Like other powerful technologies, information technology possesses the potential for great harm or great good for all humankind. If managers, end users, and IS professionals accept their ethical responsibilities, then information technology can help make this world a better place for all of us.

PACIFIC NORTHWEST NATIONAL LABORATORY AND OTHERS: ABUSING INTERNET ACCESS IN THE WORKPLACE

Employers who give Internet access to their staffs are sending out a message: Look at porn, lose a paycheck.

Faced with international controversies over pornography and hate speech on the Internet, employers are setting policies to limit Internet usage to business purposes. They also are penalizing employees who send out abusive electronic mail, "flame" people on Usenet, or visit inappropriate sites on the World Wide Web. And they are cautioning employees to remember that out on the 'net, they represent their companies, not just themselves.

"Employees are under the misapprehension that the First Amendment applies in the workplace—it doesn't," said Neal J. Friedman, a Washington attorney who specializes in online law. "Employees need to know they have no right of privacy and no right of free speech using company resources."

Employers are hitting the hardest when sex and pornography are involved. Consider these recent examples: Some 98 employees at Pacific Northwest National Laboratory in Richland, Washington, were disciplined last month when audits of system usage revealed that they used lab computers on their own time to access pornographic sites on the Web. Pacific Northwest National Laboratory became suspicious that employees were abusing the Internet when the staff set up sniffers to measure 'net traffic and found lots of hits going out to *Playboy* and *Penthouse* sites.

- Kmart Corp. in Troy, Michigan, fired web-master Rod Fournier in November when he created a hot link from a single period at the end of a sentence on the Kmart home page to his personal home page. That page, in turn, contained a link to a site that spoofed the controversy over Internet pornography.

- At Sandia National Labs in Albuquerque, New Mexico, 64 employees, contractors, and college interns were disciplined in August and September for reading pornography on company time and their own time.

The heaviest offenders were suspended without pay for up to a month, while others received shorter unpaid suspensions and letters of reprimand.

For most companies, an Internet usage policy is straightforward. It generally informs employees that their Internet access is a company resource that should be used only for their jobs.

"3M's policy is simply put: that the Web must be used for business purposes. If people get on and abuse it, then you've got a problem with that individual and need to handle it," said Luke Crofoot, a marketing services supervisor at 3M in St. Paul, Minnesota. Crofoot said he opposes draconian measures to control Internet use. "What really gets under my skin is the people who want to censor the world and place on me the burden of creating the infrastructure of what should and should not be censored," he said. Trying to control employee use of the Internet is nonproductive, he added. It is better to educate people about how to use the Internet and accept that at first they will spend a lot of time online looking up nonbusiness-related content, Crofoot said.

That approach may work for companies that give employees a lot of independence, said Barry Weiss, a partner at Gordon & Glickson, a Chicago law firm that specializes in information technology legal issues. But for firms that want more control over their employees, the best solution is to develop detailed Internet usage policies, he added. Companies that have detailed Internet usage policies in place or are developing them include The Chase Manhattan Bank NA; Johnson Controls, Inc.; Pioneer Hi-Bred International Inc.; and Monsanto Co.

"The Internet is essentially a communications tool," Weiss said. "It's important that companies think about the different ways that information will be communicated. They want to define policies and procedures to avoid risk so that this new technology will be used in an effective way."

CASE STUDY QUESTIONS

1. How are some employees abusing the online access provided by their companies?

2. What should companies do to curb such abuses of their computing resources?

3. Do you agree with Neal Friedman that "employees . . . have no right of privacy and no right of free speech using company resources"? Why or why not?

Source: Adapted from Mitch Wagner, "Firms Spell Out Appropriate Use of Internet for Employees," *Computerworld*, February 5, 1996, pp. 56–58. Copyright © 1996 by Computerworld, Inc., Framingham, MA 01701—Reprinted from *Computerworld*.

Summary

- **IS Security and Control.** One of the most important responsibilities of the management of computer-using business firms is to assure the security and quality of its information services activities. Controls are needed that ensure the accuracy, integrity, and safety of the information system activities and resources of the organization and its end users. Such controls attempt to minimize errors, fraud, and destruction, and can be grouped into three major categories: (1) information system controls, (2) procedural controls, and (3) facility controls, as summarized in Figures 12.2 and 12.3.

- **The Ethical Foundations of IT.** Business and IT activities involve many ethical considerations. Various ethical philosophies and models of ethical behavior may be used by people

in forming ethical judgments. These serve as a foundation for ethical principles and codes that can serve as guidelines for dealing with ethical business issues that may arise in the use of information technology.

- **Ethical and Societal Dimensions of IT.** Information technology raises serious ethical and societal issues in terms of the impact of IT on employment, individuality, working conditions, computer monitoring, privacy, computer matching, health, and computer crime. Managerial end users and IS professionals can help solve the problems of improper use of IT by assuming their ethical responsibilities for the ergonomic design, beneficial use, and enlightened management of information technology in our society.

Key Terms and Concepts

These are the key terms and concepts of this chapter. The page number of their first explanation is in parentheses.

1. Auditing information systems (480)
2. Audit trail (481)
3. Biometric controls (477)
4. Business ethics (484)
5. Computer crime (494)
   a. Examples (496)
   b. Laws (494)
6. Computer matching (492)
7. Computer monitoring (490)
8. Computer virus (497)
9. Control for end user computing (479)
10. Control totals (472)
11. Disaster recovery (479)

12. Encryption (475)
13. Ergonomics (500)
14. Ethical and societal dimensions of IT (486)
    a. Employment (489)
    b. Individuality (489)
    c. Health (499)
    d. Privacy (491)
    e. Societal solutions (501)
    f. Working conditions (490)
15. Ethical models (484)
16. Ethical philosophies (484)
17. Ethical principles (487)

18. Facility controls (475)
19. Fault tolerant (478)
20. Fire wall (476)
21. Hacking (497)
22. Human factors (489)
23. Information system controls (471)
24. Information system security (470)
25. Privacy laws (493)
26. Procedural controls (478)
27. Responsible end user (501)
28. Security codes (475)
29. Software piracy (496)
30. System security monitor (474)

Review Quiz

Match one of the key terms and concepts listed above with one of the brief examples or definitions listed below. Try to find the best fit for answers that seem to fit more than one term or concept. Defend your choices.

_____ 1. Ensuring the accuracy, integrity, and safety of information system activities and resources.

_____ 2. A computer system that acts as a safe transfer point for access to and from other networks by a company's networked computers.

_____ 3. Control totals, error signals, and security codes are examples.

_____ 4. The separation of the duties of computer programmers and computer operators is an example.

_____ 5. Fire and access detection systems are examples.

_____ 6. Software that can control access and use of a computer system.

_____ 7. A computer system can continue to operate even after a major system failure if it has this capability.

_____ 8. Periodically examine the accuracy and integrity of computer processing.

_____ 9. The presence of documentation that allows a transaction to be traced through all stages of information processing.

_____ 10. Managerial end users are responsible for information system controls in their business units.

_____ 11. Using your voice or fingerprints to identify you electronically.

_____ 12. A plan to continue IS operations during an emergency.

_____ 13. The sum of subtotals must equal a grand total.

_____ 14. Scrambling data during its transmission.

_____ 15. Passwords, user IDs, and account codes are examples.

_____ 16. Examples are egoism, natural law, utilitarianism, and respect for persons.

_____ 17. Ethical choices may result from decision-making processes or behavioral stages.

_____ 18. Managers must confront numerous ethical questions in their businesses.

_____ 19. Ethical guidelines in the use of information and information technology.

_____ 20. Employees may have to retrain or transfer.

_____ 21. Computer-based systems may depersonalize human activities.

_____ 22. Constant long-term use of computers at work may cause health problems.

_____ 23. Personal information is in computer-accessible files.

_____ 24. Computer-based monitoring of environmental quality is an example.

_____ 25. Tedious jobs are decreased and jobs are made more challenging.

_____ 26. Using computers to identify individuals that fit a certain profile.

_____ 27. Regulate the collection, access, and use of personal data.

_____ 28. Using computers to monitor the activities of workers.

_____ 29. People have a variety of needs when operating computers.

_____ 30. Using computers to steal money, services, software, or data.

_____ 31. It is illegal to access a computer with intent to defraud.

_____ 32. Unauthorized copying of software.

_____ 33. Electronic breaking and entering into a computer system.

_____ 34. A program makes copies of itself and destroys data and programs.

_____ 35. Designing computer hardware, software, and workstations that are safe, comfortable, and easy to use.

_____ 36. End users should act with integrity and competence in their use of information technology.

Discussion Questions

1. What can be done to improve security on the Internet? Give several examples of controls and other security measures.

2. How do IS controls, procedural controls, and facility controls improve IS performance and security? Give several examples to illustrate your answer.

3. What artificial intelligence techniques can a business use to improve computer security and fight computer crime?

4. What controls are needed for end user computing? Give an example of three controls that could be used at your school or work.

5. What is disaster recovery? How could it be implemented at your school or work?

6. Refer to the Real World Case on the Union Pacific Railroad in the chapter. What should PC end users do about the millennium bug? Explain your answer.

7. Is there an ethical crisis in business today? What role does information technology play in unethical business practices?

8. What business decisions will you have to make as a manager that have both an ethical and IT dimension? Give several examples to illustrate your answer.

9. Refer to the Real World Case on Pacific Northwest National Laboratory and Others in the chapter. Is abuse of online access a problem at your university or place of work? Why or why not?

10. What would be examples of one positive and one negative effect for each of the ethical and societal dimensions of IT illustrated in Figure 12.15? Give it a try.

Real World Problems

1. Charles Schwab & Co. and Lombard Institutional Brokerage: Using Encryption and Fire Walls on the Net

Online trading has been a lucrative venture for the few start-up brokerages that have leaped into the fray in the past few months. But security concerns and slow response times on the Internet have kept more established investment bankers from plunging into cybertrading.

Charles Schwab & Co. started an Internet-based trading site with a few hundred customers across the United States. Schwab expects to extend these services for general availability in a few weeks, said Gideon Sasson, senior vice president of electronic brokerage technology at the San Francisco–based brokerage. Schwab is using Secure Socket Layer (SSL) and RSA encryption technologies with Netscape Communications Commerce Server software to protect its IBM RS/6000 Web server, Sasson said. He declined to name the fire wall technologies that Schwab is using.

Information systems managers at online brokerages such as Lombard Institutional Brokerage (http://www.lombard.com) dismiss the security scare, claiming the encryption capabilities in Netscape's Secure Commerce Server software and other fire wall protection are up to the task. Lombard uses two Livingston Enterprises FireWall IRX routers that have built-in filtering logic with the ability to act as a fire wall and a router at the same time, said John MacIlwaine, director of information technology at Lombard, which gets 15 percent of its trading revenue from its cyberservice. Lombard uses hardware logic at the network level to prevent unauthorized access into its Sun Microsystems SPARC1000 Web servers, MacIlwaine said. Netscape's Commerce Server with standard SSL protection is used to encrypt transactions over the 'net.

a. What concerns have kept most securities brokers from trading on the Internet?

b. Why do Schwab and Lombard believe they have solved such problems?

Source: Adapted from Thomas Hoffman, "Bull or Bear?" *Computerworld,* April 22, 1996, pp. 57, 59. Copyright © 1996 by Computerworld, Inc., Framingham, MA 01701—Reprinted from *Computerworld.*

2. Database America and Yahoo, Inc.: Privacy on the Internet

Information systems managers who build business sites on the Internet are beginning to trip privacy alarms, and it's forcing them to start thinking about ethical issues that, until now, they've been able to blissfully ignore. Yahoo, Inc., and Database America Cos. triggered just such an alert over a new service that lists the names, addresses, and telephone numbers of 90 million people nationwide.

The problem? The database, Yahoo People Search at http://www.yahoo.com/search/people, included unlisted phone numbers and addresses for people such as police

officers, judges, and prosecutors who feared their lives would be in danger if malefactors found out where they lived. The resulting hue and cry forced Database America, which owns the list, to delete information about people whose phone numbers are unlisted in phone company white pages. The move was spurred by complaints from worried law enforcement officials.

Privacy issues will be heightened further when Netscape Communications Corp. includes a button linking to white page services in the next version of its Navigator browser, due out soon. At issue are privacy concerns raised by the Internet, where information that has always been publicly available but difficult to find is now shipped into people's living rooms on their PCs.

"Online, there's a heightened concern about privacy. The public has taken the opinion that online usage should be kept confidential," said Paul Sagan, editor and president of new media at Time, Inc., which runs the Pathfinder site on the World Wide Web (http://pathfinder.com) for parent company Time Warner, Inc. "There's a concern about Big Brother—that there's so much information flowing online and aggregated about you, that a person can find out a lot about you with very little effort."

Name and address directories such as Database America's are culled from phone books, marketing lists, and public records such as driver's license and voter registration lists. Until recently, these were expensive collections, often available only to savvy marketers and investigators who knew where to find them. Now, the same information is available for less than $100 on CD-ROM or free on the Internet.

Robert Hoffer is general manager and vice president of new media at Database America. The company provides its database of 90 million names to several Web sites, including Yahoo. Database America also sells the database to CD-ROM publishers. Reacting to privacy concerns, the company removed unlisted phone numbers from the database. "We think the white pages are a good place to make a stand with the privacy issue," he said. "If you have opted to be listed, you've opted to make that information public. And if you've opted to be unlisted, you've opted for privacy."

a. Should unlisted phone numbers and addresses be available as an Internet service? Why or why not?

b. Do you agree with Robert Hoffer that if you have asked to be listed in a telephone directory's white pages, your telephone number and address can be made available to anyone as an Internet service?

Source: Adapted from Mitch Wagner, "Web on Privacy Alert," *Computerworld,* April 29, 1996, pp. 1, 16. Copyright © 1996 by Computerworld, Inc., Framingham, MA 01701—Reprinted from *Computerworld.*

3. Soren Ragsdale and Jeff Slaton: Spamming and Flaming on the Internet

While Soren Ragsdale was away from his PC—at a 7-Eleven, in fact, buying a Big Gulp—the electronic thunderbolt struck. Someone, and Ragsdale has his ideas about who, had forged an electronic-mail message in his name. The crass note promoted a bogus business that Ragsdale supposedly was starting. Then came the spam: The ne'er-do-well sent the E-mail to hundreds of Internet Usenet groups and thousands of users worldwide.

Thus began the torrent, says Ragsdale, a student at Arizona State University in Tempe. Within hours, more than 40,000 angry responses spammed into his Internet account at school. Ragsdale suspects the message that lit this flaming wildfire was forged by Jeff "Spam King" Slaton, with whom Ragsdale has waged a lengthy flame war. Jeff Slaton has made a career of spamming the Usenet for start-up companies that want to advertise on the Internet. Ragsdale hates Slaton and his spam and has created a Web site to let the world know it.

Ragsdale and Slaton are poster children for the all out war approach on the Internet. Slaton, for example, has talked about suing the Internet service provider that hosts Ragsdale's anti-spam and anti-Slaton opinions, Ragsdale says. The Spam King couldn't be reached for comment. He regularly changes his E-mail address and telephone number to stay ahead of a rabid pack of Slaton-haters.

Most 'netters don't expect the trouble to die down. For example, Charles Hymes, a doctoral candidate in human/computer interaction at the University of Michigan, says: "The reason Jeff Slaton isn't going away is the same reason you don't have slimy lawyers going away: There will always be people with no morals who think they can make money."

a. How does the Ragsdale/Slaton incident demonstrate spamming and flaming?

b. Are spamming and flaming ethical practices? What can be done to curb such activities?

Source: Adapted from Kim Nash, "The Enforcers," *Computerworld*, April 15, 1996, pp. 103–104. Copyright © 1996 by Computerworld, Inc., Framingham, MA 01701—Reprinted from *Computerworld*.

4. National Computer Security Association: Combatting Computer Viruses

If you have 1,000 PCs in your organization, you can expect to get hit by a computer virus about 120 times this year. So says the National Computer Security Association (NCSA). According to the poll of 300 midsize and large companies

and government agencies, the chances of encountering a virus today is about one in 100 PCs per month, about five to 10 times higher than early last year.

Occurrences of older viruses such as Form and Stealth have increased, but the most dramatic rise is for the Word concept virus, a so-called macro virus that was unknown just a year ago. It infected 36 percent of the sites surveyed and was responsible for half of all virus encounters. Word concept rides in documents created by Microsoft Word. Unlike other viruses that typically load when a user boots from an infected floppy diskette, Word concept macro code can travel as electronic mail. It can infect a PC when the document is opened. "There is no question the No. 1 virus threat today is from macro viruses," said a security manager at a Fortune 100 manufacturer. He said his company, which he asked not be named, had set up a very strong, centralized computer incident response office where users can go for help. That's lacking at many companies, he said.

The companies surveyed said three-quarters of viruses came from diskettes, and 15 percent came from unknown sources. Nine percent of the viruses came from E-mail attachments, which weren't a virus source before the creation of the Word concept virus last year. "Electronic mail and viruses weren't even an issue a year ago," said Peter Tippett, president of the NCSA. NCSA estimated total losses in North America due to computer viruses last year at $1 billion. They will amount to $2 billion to $3 billion this year, according to the NCSA. See Figure 12.26.

In the survey, 97 percent of companies polled said they use antivirus software. "Most companies say they own antivirus software for most of their machines," Tippett said. "But what this boils down to is, people aren't using it." Another problem, Tippett said, is that often a PC is scanned for viruses only when it is booted, which allows it to become infected and pass along a virus to other machines between scans. He said users should employ continuously running antivirus software, particularly to catch the new macro viruses.

a. How do the newest computer viruses infect and harm PC users?

b. What should you do to protect yourself from computer viruses?

Source: Adapted from Gary Anthes, "Old, New Viruses Swarm PC Users," *Computerworld*, May 6, 1996, p. 55. Copyright © 1996 by Computerworld, Inc., Framingham, MA 01701—Reprinted from *Computerworld*.

Application Exercises

1. Computer Ethics: The Clipper Chip Controversy

In April 1993, the Clinton administration proposed a new standard for encryption technology, developed with the

National Security Agency. The new standard is a plan called the Escrowed Encryption Standard. Under the standard, computer chips would use a secret algorithm called Skipjack to encrypt information.

FIGURE 12.26

Facts about computer viruses.

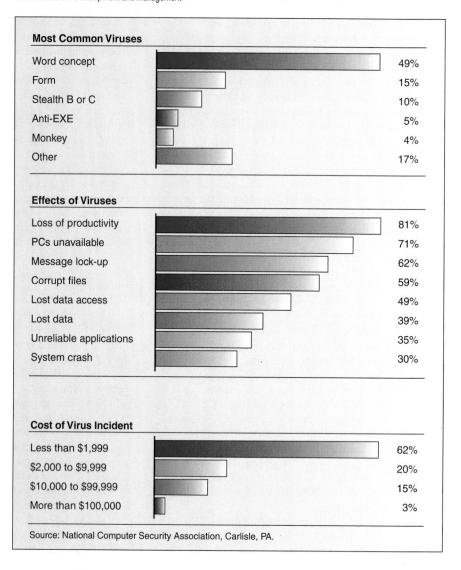

The Clipper Chip

The Clipper Chip is a semiconductor device designed to be installed on all telephones, computer modems, and fax machines to encrypt voice communications. The Clipper Chip contains a powerful algorithm that uses an 80-bit encryption scheme that is considered impossible to crack with today's computers within a normal lifetime. Clipper uses a long key, which could have as many as 1,024 values. The only way to break Clipper's code would be to try every possible combination of key values. A single supercomputer would take a billion years to run through all of Clipper's possible keys.

The chip also has secret government master keys built in that would be available only to government agencies. Proper authorization, in the form of a court order, would be necessary to intercept communications.

The difference between conventional data encryption chips and the Clipper Chip is that the Clipper contains a law enforcement access field (LEAF). The LEAF is transmitted along with the user's data and contains the identity of the user's individual chip and the user's key—encrypted under the government's master key. This would stop eavesdroppers from breaking the code by finding out the user's key. Once an empowered agency knew the identity of the individual chip, it could retrieve the correct master key, use that to decode the user's key, and so decode the original scrambled information. (Refer back to Figure 12.6 for an illustration of the Clipper Chip.)

The Government's Case

The Clinton administration's proposed new standards for encryption technology—the Clipper Chip—was supposed to be the answer to the individual's concern for data security and the government's concern for law enforcement. Law-abiding citizens would have access to the encryption they need and the criminal element would be unable to use encryption to hide their illicit activity.

Despite opposition from the computer industry and civil libertarians, government agencies are phasing in the Clipper technology for unclassified communications. Commercial use of Clipper is still entirely voluntary, and there is no guarantee it will be adopted by any organizations other than government ones. Yet several thousand Clipper-equipped telephones are currently on order for government use.

The Justice Department is evaluating proposals that would prevent the police and FBI from listening in on conversations without a warrant. A possible solution to the concerns about privacy invasion would be to split the decryption key into two or more parts and give single parts to trustees for separate government agencies. In theory, this would require the cooperation of several individuals and agencies before a message could be intercepted. This solution could compromise the secrecy needed to conduct a clandestine criminal investigation, but the Justice Department is investigating its feasibility.

The Opponents' Case

Computer industry and civil libertarian opponents of the plan have criticized its implementation on several counts:

- Terrorists and drug dealers would circumvent telephones if the telephones had the Clipper Chip. Furthermore, they might use their own chip.
- Foreign customers would not buy equipment from American manufacturers if they knew that their communications could be intercepted by United States government agents.
- The integrity of the "back door" system could be compromised by unscrupulous federal employees, thus violating the privacy of citizens.
- The remote possibility exists that an expert cryptologist could somehow break the code and sell the information to privacy violators.

The Ethical Dilemma

No method of data encryption will always protect individual privacy and society's desire to stop criminal activities. Electronic funds transfer systems and the information superhighway have made the need for private communications more important than ever before. Society's problems with drugs and terrorism complicate the issues, highlighting the sensitive balance among the individual's right to privacy, society's need to protect itself, and everyone's fear of Big Brother government tools.

a. Briefly summarize the ethical case for the Clipper Chip.

b. Briefly summarize the ethical case against the Clipper Chip.

c. What is your position? Explain your ethical reasoning, identifying any ethical principles you are using to support your position on this controversy.

Source: Adapted from Edward H. Freeman, "When Technology and Privacy Collide," *Information Systems Management,* Spring 1995, pp. 43–46 (New York: Auerbach Publications). Copyright © 1995 Warren, Gorham & Lamont. Used with permission.

2. The Communications Decency Act: An Ethical Debate

The Telecommunications Deregulation and Reform Bill, enacted into law by the U.S. Congress in February 1996, contains the Communications Decency Act, co-sponsored by Senator Jim Exon, Democrat from Nebraska, and Senator Dan Coats, Republican from Indiana. The Act has raised an ethical controversy and is not being enforced while it is challenged in the courts as unconstitutional.

In June of 1996, a U.S. federal court panel of three judges ruled that the Act was an unconstitutional violation of free speech. In their decision, the judges said:

- "As the most participatory form of mass speech yet developed, the Internet deserves the highest protection from government intrusion."
- "Any content-based regulation of the Internet, no matter how benign the purpose, could burn the global village to roast the pig."
- "Just as the strength of the Internet is chaos, so the strength of our liberty depends upon the chaos and cacophony of the unfettered speech the First Amendment protects."

Senator Exon and Marc Rotenberg, director of the Electronic Privacy Information Center (EPIC), a public interest research center in Washington, D.C., debated some of the provisions and ethical and societal implications of the legislation in the pages of *Computerworld.*

Senator Jim Exon: For the Act

Our law will shield children from pornography that is only a few clicks away on their computers and will make it illegal to engage children in sexual conversations online. It will impose penalties on people who transmit pornographic material via computer networks that are accessible to children. The maximum penalty for such an offense would be up to two years in jail and a fine of up to $250,000.

Don't let opponents of the legislation fool you: Nothing in it applies to constitutionally protected speech between consenting adults. It simply says a person can't use a computer to transmit or display indecent material in a way that is openly accessible to a person under 18 years of age.

This law will be enforced the same way as our existing pornography laws: If someone files a complaint, law enforcement will investigate. Federal privacy laws haven't been repealed. Cybercops won't surf the 'net to look for violators. Indecent communications simply must be conducted in a place that is out of reach for children.

Access for children can be restricted in several ways, including requiring use of a verified credit card, debit account, adult access code, or adult personal identification number.

The Supreme Court already has approved such means for limiting child access to telephone dial-a-porn services.

Parents, schools, and a responsible industry still must be involved in the effort to make the Internet safer. But does anyone really think that parents can monitor all of their children's waking hours? We need the added deterrent of law so that those who would pervert the network will think twice.

Opponents forsake reason when they say they want to protect children from indecency, seduction, and harassment but maintain that the overriding issue is freedom of access to anything by anybody. Tell that to a parent who has had a child lured away by a deviant on a computer network. Hardly a day goes by without another story about the mix of depravity and children on the 'net. How many more are never reported?

There is too much of the self-serving philosophy of the hands-off elite. They seem to rationalize that the framers of the Constitution plotted to make certain that the profiteering pornographer, the pervert, and the pedophile be free to practice their pursuits in the presence of children on a taxpayer-created and subsidized computer network. That is nonsense.

Marc Rotenberg: Against the Act

Regulating the Internet isn't like regulating radio or television. No World Wide Web site operator is licensed. No scarce spectrum is used. Regulating speech on the Internet is like telling bookstore owners, newsstand operators, and librarians which books to stock and which magazines to sell. It's like the government telling people who use the telephone which words they can use.

Supporters of the legislation say it will protect children from the evils of dirty pictures. That's crazy, too. Young kids aren't interested in dirty pictures. Like all campaigners against sexuality, all the publicity-seeking moralists have accomplished is to splash the stuff they most fear across the front pages of the nation's newspapers. They might as well put a blinking arrow on top of the *Playboy* home page and say, "Don't look here!"

Of course, parents should be free to select materials that are appropriate for their children, and Internet users should be able to reject material that is objectionable. If you really don't like an online service's policy or content, cancel your membership.

But be careful when people tell you which words you can speak and which books you can read. Once they start drawing lines, they rarely stop. Parody, criticism, satire, adult conversation, literature, and art all would become suspect.

The legislation gives federal investigators the right to comb through Web sites, newsgroup posts, and even private electronic mail to find evidence of indecent speech. Use a word that someone doesn't like, and you could get thrown in jail. The bill even threatens the right to use privacy technologies, such as encryption, because the government now will have the right to open private E-mail if it suspects the message contains offensive language. Flaming becomes a criminal offense.

The supporters of government censorship will say they don't intend to eliminate the acceptable stuff, just the bad stuff. And that's exactly the problem the First Amendment was designed to avoid. It gives us the right and the responsibility to decide for ourselves what is objectionable and what isn't. It forces us to make choices when we are confronted with controversial ideas and new viewpoints. We don't need the First Amendment to protect greeting card prose. We need it to protect the openness and diversity of a free society.

The Ethical Question

Can society's right to protect children from online pornography and pedophiles coexist with the individual's right to freedom of expression on the Internet?

a. Briefly summarize the ethical case for the Communications Decency Act.

b. Briefly summarize the ethical case against the Communications Decency Act.

c. What is your position? Explain your ethical reasoning, identifying any ethical principles you are using to support your position on this controversy.

Source: Adapted from Senator Jim Exon and Marc Rotenberg, "Internet Privacy: How Far Should Federal Regulation Go?" *Computerworld*, February 19, 1996, pp. 74–76, and Gary Anthes, "Net Forces Laud Rulings," *Computerworld*, June 17, 1996, p. 4. Copyright © 1996 by Computerworld, Inc., Framingham, MA 01701—Reprinted from *Computerworld*.

Review Quiz Answers

1. 24	10. 9	19. 17	28. 7
2. 20	11. 3	20. 14a	29. 22
3. 23	12. 11	21. 14b	30. 5a
4. 26	13. 10	22. 14c	31. 5b
5. 18	14. 12	23. 14d	32. 29
6. 30	15. 28	24. 14e	33. 21
7. 19	16. 16	25. 14f	34. 8
8. 1	17. 15	26. 6	35. 13
9. 2	18. 4	27. 25	36. 27

Selected References

1. Anthes, Gary. "Internet Hackers Hit GE, Others." *Computerworld,* December 5, 1994.

2. Anthes, Gary, and James Daly. "Internet Users Batten Down Hatches." *Computerworld,* February 7, 1994.

3. Austin, Nancy. "Personal versus Professional Ethics: Handling the Job/Ethics Clash." *Working Women,* September 1992.

4. Betts, Mitch. "Personal Data More Public than You Think." *Computerworld,* March 9, 1992.

5. Bloom, Paul; Robert Adler; and George Milne. "Identifying the Legal and Ethical Risks and Costs of Using New Information Technologies to Support Marketing Programs." In *The Marketing Information Revolution,* ed. Robert C. Blattberg, Rashi Glazer, and John D. C. Little. Boston: Harvard Business School Press, 1994.

6. Carey, Jane, ed. *Human Factors in Information Systems: An Organizational Perspective.* Norwood, NJ: Ablex, 1991.

7. Cash, James I., Jr.; Robert G. Eccles; Nitin Nohria; and Richard L. Nolan. *Building the Information-Age Organization: Structure, Control, and Information Technologies.* Burr Ridge, IL: Richard D. Irwin, 1994.

8. Cheswick, William, and Steven Bellovin. "In Depth: Repelling the Wily Hacker." *Computerworld,* May 16, 1994.

9. Culnane, Mary. "How Did They Get My Name?: An Exploratory Investigation of Consumer Attitudes toward Secondary Information Use." *MIS Quarterly,* September 1993.

10. Dejoie, Roy; George Fowler; and David Paradice, eds. *Ethical Issues in Information Systems.* Boston: boyd & fraser, 1991.

11. Dunlop, Charles, and Rob Kling, eds. *Computerization and Controversy: Value Conflicts and Social Choices.* San Diego: Academic Press, 1991.

12. Elmer-DeWitt, Phillip. "Terror on the Internet." *Time,* December 12, 1994.

13. Freeman, Edward, ed. *Business Ethics: The State of the Art.* New York: Oxford University Press, 1991.

14. Freeman, Edward. "When Technology and Privacy Collide: Encoded Encryption and the Clipper Chip." *Information Systems Management,* Spring 1995.

15. Fried, Louis. "Information Security and New Technology." *Information Systems Management,* Summer 1994.

16. Ganesan, Ravi, and Ravi Sandhu, guest editors. "Security in Cyberspace." Special Section, *Communications of the ACM,* November 1994.

17. Harrington, Susan. "What Corporate America Is Teaching about Ethics." *Academy of Management Executive* 5, no. 1 (1991).

18. Kallman, Earnest, and John Grillo. *Ethical Decision Making and Information Technology: An Introduction with Cases.* New York: Mitchel McGraw-Hill, 1993.

19. Keppler, Kay. "A New Kind of Cutting Edge." *AI Expert,* February 1995.

20. Knouse, Stephen, and Robert Giacalone. "Ethical Decision Making in Business." *Journal of Business Ethics,* May 1992.

21. Madsen, Peter, and Jay Shafritz, eds. *Essentials of Business Ethics.* New York: Meridian, 1990.

22. McFarland, Michael. "Ethics and the Safety of Computer Systems." *Computer,* February 1991.

23. Neumann, Peter. *Computer-Related Risks.* New York: ACM Press, 1995.

24. Ranier, Rex, Jr.; Charles Snyder; and Houston Carr. "Risk Analysis for Information Technology." *Journal of Management Information Systems,* Summer 1991.

25. Rothfeder, Jeffrey. "Computers May Be Personal, but Are They Private?" *Beyond Computing,* January–February 1994.

26. Schuler, Doug, guest editor. "Social Computing." Special Section, *Communications of the ACM,* January 1994.

27. Schwartau, Winn. "Crypto Policy and Business Privacy." *PC Week,* June 28, 1993.

28. Slater, Derek. "Cyberspace and the Law." *Computerworld,* December 5, 1994.

29. Smith, H. Jefferson, and John Hasnas. "Debating the Stakeholder Theory." *Beyond Computing,* March–April 1994.

30. Smith, H. Jefferson, and John Hasnas. "Establishing an Ethical Framework." *Beyond Computing,* January–February 1994.

31. Smith, Laura. "Privacy Issue Comes of Age in a Networked World." *PC Week,* June 28, 1993.

32. Solomon, Robert. *Ethics and Excellence: Cooperation and Integrity in Business.* New York: Oxford University Press, 1992.

33. Stark, Andrew. "What's the Matter with Business Ethics?" *Harvard Business Review,* May–June 1993.

34. Straub, Detmar, and Rosann Collins. "Key Information Liability Issues Facing Managers: Software Piracy, Proprietary Databases, and Individual Rights to Privacy." *MIS Quarterly,* June 1990.

35. Wallich, Paul. "Wire Pirates." *Scientific American,* March 1994.

36. Wolinsky, Carol, and James Sylvester. "From Washington: Privacy in the Telecom Age." *Communications of the ACM,* February 1992.

37. Zahedi, Fatemeh. *Quality of Information Systems.* Danvers, MA: boyd & fraser, 1995.

38. Zoglin, Richard. "We're All Connected." *Time,* February 12, 1996.

Continuing Real World Case

Fast Freight, Inc.: Networking the Enterprise — Part IV: Issues in IT Management

Telecommunications Issues

As efficient as Fast Freight's system seems, a problem area is telecommunications. According to Jim Kellogg, senior systems engineer, Fast Freight spends between $12,000 and $15,000 a month on telephone line charges, and "the quality of service is not that great" in the Wenatchee Valley. Still, for Fast Freight, those expenses are less than the cost of leased lines to connect their facilities in a private wide area network. However, MCI Communications recently completed installation of a fiber optic network into the valley. This development could lead to Fast Freight's establishment of their own wide area networks in the Pacific Northwest and the rest of the country. Building such networks would enhance the efficiency of their EDI and electronic data management applications.

Jim Kellogg also stressed that Fast Freight's IS staff chose a token ring local area network over Ethernet because of quality, not speed. They preferred the token ring network's "one item at a time around the ring" operating principle rather than the "data collision" concept of a faster Ethernet network. The complexity of their three-tier network drove the decision, as well as the different applications that would be running simultaneously at any given time. As Jim Kellogg pointed out, "We'd rather give up some speed than chance losing a system."

The Client/Server Debate

Changing computer network hardware and software is a perennial topic at Fast Freight. Typically, debates rage around several key issues. One concerns substituting PCs for the video terminals connected to the AS/400 midrange systems at the freight depots. Most of the IS staff and most managers believe that using PCs as terminals is unnecessary and will cause increased training costs and security problems. However, the new operating manager of Fast Administrative, the subsidiary for administrative and accounting services for Fast Freight, thinks otherwise.

Karen Hilstead is a CPA who holds an MBA from a nearby state university. Her argument is that PCs will increase the productivity and skill level of employees. But even more important, she believes PCs will prepare them for the new generation of client/server business application software that is being installed in many companies. Hilstead is a leading proponent of a move toward client/server computing, starting first with the accounting and administrative applications at Fast Freight, and then moving into freight operations and other areas. Hilstead argues that new client/server applications will give the company more flexibility and agility in meeting the operational and strategic challenges of its fast-paced, fast-changing business environment.

Hilstead does have a few allies in corporate management and on the IS staff. They agree with her that the client/server model for business computing would be better for the company's future than the current midrange computer/video terminal network installed at Fast Freight. Even Jim Kellogg has warmed up to client/server since IBM began touting the AS/400 as a family of servers that could be used in client/server applications.

The Master Schedule Board

Fast Freight's IS staff has been designing and developing their multilevel network system for several years and has constantly sought to improve it. However, Jim Kellogg admitted that they had not yet found a high-tech alternative to the master schedule board on which information cards on shipments in process are visually monitored by dispatchers. When Kellogg was asked if the dispatchers could use their terminal displays to track the trucks, freight, or schedules of a given order, he replied that "the dispatchers do it more quickly manually than on a computer keyboard." He insisted that dispatchers have found it quicker to utilize this master information board they have developed rather than call shipment scheduling information up on their terminal screens. Kellogg indicated that they have tried several approaches to this matter and "what works now has proven to be the best."

Kellogg did admit that the scheduling software does not provide shipment information quick enough through a manual keyboard inquiry. He also admitted that Fast Freight's dispatchers are not as well trained as they should be in using the shipment scheduling and tracking software. Kellogg indicated that the IS staff was working on several alternatives, such as the use of a quicker macro inquiry command, or the use of a voice-activated device for dispatchers. In any event, Kellogg insisted that Fast Freight's multilevel computer network has been well thought out, developed, and integrated into the operations and administrative environment of the company.

Security Measures

Since it is so vital to the business operations of the company, the security of Fast Freight's computer network is a top concern. All company data and image databases are backed up daily by tape backup systems. Through a control system of passwords and multilevel codes, only authorized personnel (dispatchers, operators, managers) can access Fast Freight's systems. Only managers can access certain parts of the main system in the home office. In fact, managers and administrators have a system of their own at the company headquarters in Wenatchee.

In addition, Fast Freight has developed a disaster recovery plan that designates its freight depot in South Seattle as a "hot site." That is, the depot will be used as an alternative corporate computing site in case of a major computer failure at the Wenatchee headquarters. Thus, South Seattle features a large AS/400 model similar to that at Wenatchee, as well as increased telecommunications lines, a network server, and more PCs than at other depots. So Jim Kellogg and the IS staff think that Fast Freight has established a secure computing environment for its networked computing systems.

Case Study Questions

1. What should Fast Freight do to solve the problems it is having in telecommunications?
2. Should Fast Freight move from video terminals to PCs? To client/server systems and applications? Explain.
3. Should Fast Freight replace its master schedule board with a high-tech alternative? What would you recommend?
4. Are Fast Freight's security measures adequate for its business? Explain. What other security measures would you recommend?
5. Do you have any other suggestions for improvements in IS management or the use of IT that you would recommend to the management of Fast Freight? Explain the reasons for your suggestions.

Glossary for Managerial End Users

Accounting Information Systems
Information systems that record and report business transactions, the flow of funds through an organization, and produce financial statements. This provides information for the planning and control of business operations, as well as for legal and historical record-keeping.

Active Data Dictionary
A data dictionary that automatically enforces standard data element definitions whenever end users and application programs use a DBMS to access an organization's databases.

Ada
A programming language named after Augusta Ada Byron, considered the world's first computer programmer. Developed for the U.S. Department of Defense as a standard high-order language.

Ad Hoc Inquiries
Unique, unscheduled, situation-specific information requests.

Agile Competition
The ability of a company to profitably operate in a competitive environment of continual and unpredictable changes in customer preferences, market conditions, and business opportunities.

Algorithm
A set of well-defined rules or processes for the solution of a problem in a finite number of steps.

Analog Computer
A computer that operates on data by measuring changes in continuous physical variables such as voltage, resistance, and rotation. Contrast with Digital Computer.

Analytical Database
A database of data extracted from operational and external databases to provide data tailored to online analytical processing, decision support, and executive information systems.

Analytical Modeling
Interactive use of computer-based mathematical models to explore decision alternatives using what-if analysis, sensitivity analysis, goal-seeking analysis, and optimization analysis.

Applet
A small limited-purpose application program, or small independent module of a larger application program.

Application Development
See Systems Development.

Application Generator
A software package that supports the development of an application through an interactive terminal dialogue, where the programmer/analyst defines screens, reports, computations, and data structures.

Application Portfolio
A planning tool used to evaluate present and proposed information systems applications in terms of the amount of revenue or assets invested in information systems that support major business functions.

Application Software
Programs that specify the information processing activities required for the completion of specific tasks of computer users. Examples are electronic spreadsheet and word processing programs or inventory or payroll programs.

Application-Specific Programs
Application software packages that support specific applications of end users in business, science and engineering, and other areas.

Arithmetic-Logic Unit (ALU)
The unit of a computing system containing the circuits that perform arithmetic and logical operations.

Artificial Intelligence (AI)
A science and technology whose goal is to develop computers that can think, as well as see, hear, walk, talk, and feel. A major thrust is the development of computer functions normally associated with human intelligence, for example, reasoning, inference, learning, and problem solving.

ASCII: American Standard Code for Information Interchange
A standard code used for information interchange among data processing systems, communication systems, and associated equipment.

Assembler
A computer program that translates an assembler language into machine language.

Assembler Language
A programming language that utilizes symbols to represent operation codes and storage locations.

Asynchronous
Involving a sequence of operations without a regular or predictable time relationship. Thus operations do not happen at regular timed intervals, but an operation will begin only after a previous operation is completed. In data transmission, involves the use of start and stop bits with each character to indicate the beginning and end of the character being transmitted. Contrast with Synchronous.

Audio-Response Unit
An output device of a computer system whose output consists of the spoken word. Also called a voice synthesizer.

Audit Trail
The presence of media and procedures that allow a transaction to be traced through all stages of information processing, beginning with its appearance on a source document and ending with its transformation into information on a final output document.

Automated Teller Machine (ATM)
A special-purpose transaction terminal used to provide remote banking services.

Automation
The automatic transfer and positioning of work by machines or the automatic operation and control of a work process by machines, that is, without significant human intervention or operation.

Auxiliary Storage
Storage that supplements the primary storage of the computer. Same as Secondary Storage.

Back-End Processor
Typically, a smaller general-purpose computer that is dedicated to database processing using a database management system (DBMS). Also called a database machine.

Background Processing
The automatic execution of lower-priority computer programs when higher-priority programs are not using the resources of the computer system. Contrast with Foreground Processing.

Backward-Chaining
An inference process that justifies a proposed conclusion by determining if it will result when rules are applied to the facts in a given situation.

Bar Codes
Vertical marks or bars placed on merchandise tags or packaging that can be sensed and read by optical character-reading devices. The width and combination of vertical lines are used to represent data.

Barriers to Entry
Technological, financial, or legal requirements that deter firms from entering an industry.

BASIC: Beginner's All-Purpose Symbolic Instruction Code
A programming language developed at Dartmouth College that is popular for microcomputer and time-sharing systems.

Batch Processing
A category of data processing in which data are accumulated into batches and processed periodically. Contrast with Realtime Processing.

Baud
A unit of measurement used to specify data transmission speeds. It is a unit of signaling speed equal to the number of discrete conditions or signal events per second. In many data communications applications it represents one bit per second.

Binary
Pertaining to a characteristic or property involving a selection, choice, or condition in which there are two possibilities, or pertaining to the number system that utilizes a base of 2.

Biometric Controls
Computer-based security methods that measure physical traits and characteristics such as fingerprints, voice prints, retina scans, and so on.

Bit
A contraction of "binary digit." It can have the value of either 0 or 1.

Block
A grouping of contiguous data records or other data elements that are handled as a unit.

Bootstrap
A technique in which the first few instructions of a program are sufficient to bring the rest of itself into the computer from an input device.

Branch
A transfer of control from one instruction to another in a computer program that is not part of the normal sequential execution of the instructions of the program.

Buffer
Temporary storage used to compensate for a difference in rate of flow of data, or time of occurrence of events, when transmitting data from one device to another.

Bug
A mistake or malfunction.

Bulletin Board System (BBS)
A service of personal computer networks in which electronic messages, data files, or programs can be stored for other subscribers to read or copy.

Bundling
The inclusion of software, maintenance, training, and other products or services in the price of a computer system.

Bus
A set of conducting paths for movement of data and instructions that interconnects the various components of the CPU.

Business Ethics
An area of philosophy concerned with developing ethical principles and promoting ethical behavior and practices in the accomplishment of business tasks and decision making.

Business Information System
Information systems within a business organization that support one of the traditional functions of business such as marketing, finance, or production. Business information systems can be either operations or management information systems.

Business Process Reengineering (BPR)
Restructuring and transforming a business process by a fundamental rethinking and redesign to achieve dramatic improvements in cost, quality, speed, and so on.

Byte
A sequence of adjacent binary digits operated on as a unit and usually shorter than a computer word. In many computer systems, a byte is a grouping of eight bits that can represent one alphabetic or special character or can be packed with two decimal digits.

C
A low-level structured programming language developed by AT&T–Bell Laboratories. It resembles a machine-independent assembler language and is popular for software package development.

Cache Memory
A high-speed temporary storage area in the CPU for storing parts of a program or data during processing.

Capacity Management
The use of planning and control methods to forecast and control information processing job loads, hardware and software usage, and other computer system resource requirements.

Case-Based Reasoning
Representing knowledge in an expert system's knowledge base in the form of cases, that is, examples of past performance, occurrences, and experiences.

Cathode Ray Tube (CRT)
An electronic vacuum tube (television picture tube) that displays the output of a computer system.

CD–ROM
An optical disk technology for microcomputers featuring compact disks with a storage capacity of over 500 megabytes.

Cellular Radio
A radio communications technology that divides a metropolitan area into a honeycomb of cells to greatly increase the number of frequencies and thus the users that can take advantage of mobile phone service.

Central Processing Unit (CPU)
The unit of a computer system that includes the circuits that control the interpretation and execution of instructions. In many computer systems, the

CPU includes the arithmetic-logic unit, the control unit, and primary storage unit.

Change Management
Managing the process of implementing major changes in information technology, business processes, organizational structures, and job assignments to reduce the risks and costs of change, and optimize its benefits.

Channel
A path along which signals can be sent. More specifically, a small special-purpose processor that controls the movement of data between the CPU and input/output devices.

Chargeback Systems
Methods of allocating costs to end user departments based on the information services rendered and information system resources utilized.

Check Bit
A binary check digit; for example, a parity bit.

Check Digit
A digit in a data field that is utilized to check for errors or loss of characters in the data field as a result of data transfer operations.

Checkpoint
A place in a program where a check or a recording of data for restart purposes is performed.

Chief Information Officer
A senior management position that oversees all information technology for a firm concentrating on long-range information system planning and strategy.

Client/Server Network
A computing environment where end user workstations (clients) are connected to micro or mini LAN servers and possibly to mainframe superservers.

Clock
A device that generates periodic signals utilized to control the timing of a computer. Also, a register whose contents change at regular intervals in such a way as to measure time.

Coaxial Cable
A sturdy copper or aluminum wire wrapped with spacers to insulate and protect it. Groups of coaxial cables may also be bundled together in a bigger cable for ease of installation.

COBOL: COmmon Business Oriented Language
A widely used business data processing programming language.

Code
Computer instructions.

Cognitive Science
An area of artificial intelligence that focuses on researching how the human brain works and how humans think and learn, in order to apply such findings to the design of computer-based systems.

Cognitive Styles
Basic patterns in how people handle information and confront problems.

Cognitive Theory
Theories about how the human brain works and how humans think and learn.

Common Carrier
An organization that supplies communications services to other organizations and to the public as authorized by government agencies.

Communications Satellite
Earth satellites placed in stationary orbits above the equator that serve as relay stations for communications signals transmitted from earth stations.

Competitive Advantage
Developing products, services, processes, or capabilities that give a company a superior business position relative to its competitors and other competitive forces.

Competitive Forces
A firm must confront (1) rivalry of competitors within its industry, (2) threats of new entrants, (3) threats of substitutes, (4) the bargaining power of customers, and (5) the bargaining power of suppliers.

Competitive Strategies
A firm can develop cost leadership, product differentiation, and business innovation strategies to confront its competitive forces.

Compiler
A program that translates a high-level programming language into a machine-language program.

Computer
A device that has the ability to accept data; internally store and execute a program of instructions; perform mathematical, logical, and manipulative operations on data; and report the results.

Computer-Aided Design (CAD)
The use of computers and advanced graphics hardware and software to provide interactive design assistance for engineering and architectural design.

Computer-Aided Engineering
The use of computers to simulate, analyze, and evaluate models of product designs and production processes developed using computer-aided design methods.

Computer-Aided Manufacturing (CAM)
The use of computers to automate the production process and operations of a manufacturing plant. Also called factory automation.

Computer-Aided Planning (CAP)
The use of software packages as tools to support the planning process.

Computer-Aided Software Engineering (CASE)
Same as Computer-Aided Systems Engineering, but emphasizing the importance of software development.

Computer-Aided Systems Engineering (CASE)
Using software packages to accomplish and automate many of the activities of information systems development, including software development or programming.

Computer Application
The use of a computer to solve a specific problem or to accomplish a particular job for an end user. For example, common business computer applications include sales order processing, inventory control, and payroll.

Computer-Assisted Instruction (CAI)
The use of computers to provide drills, practice exercises, and tutorial sequences to students.

Computer-Based Information System
An information system that uses computer hardware and software to perform its information processing activities.

Computer Crime
Criminal actions accomplished through the use of computer systems, especially with intent to defraud, destroy, or make unauthorized use of computer system resources.

Computer Ethics
A system of principles governing the legal, professional, social, and moral responsibilities of computer specialists and end users.

Computer Generations
Major stages in the historical development of computing.

Computer Graphics
Using computer-generated images to analyze and interpret data, present information, and do computer-aided design and art.

Computer Industry
The industry composed of firms that supply computer hardware, software, and services.

Computer-Integrated Manufacturing (CIM)
An overall concept that stresses that the goals of computer use in factory automation should be to simplify, automate, and integrate production processes and other aspects of manufacturing.

Computer Matching
Using computers to screen and match data about individual characteristics provided by a variety of computer-based information systems and databases in order to identify individuals for business, government, or other purposes.

Computer Monitoring
Using computers to monitor the behavior and productivity of workers on the job and in the workplace.

Computer Program
A series of instructions or statements, in a form acceptable to a computer, prepared in order to achieve a certain result.

Computer System
Computer hardware as a system of input, processing, output, storage, and control components. Thus a computer system consists of input and output devices, primary and secondary storage devices, the central processing unit, the control unit within the CPU, and other peripheral devices.

Computer Terminal
Any input/output device connected by telecommunications links to a computer.

Computer Virus or Worm
Program code that copies its destructive program routines into the computer systems of anyone who accesses computer systems that have used the program, or anyone who uses copies of data or programs taken from such computers. This spreads the destruction of data and programs among many computer users. Technically, a virus will not run unaided, but must be inserted into another program, while a worm is a distinct program that can run unaided.

Concentrator
A special-purpose computer that accepts information from many terminals using slow-speed lines and transmits data to a main computer system over a high-speed line.

Concurrent Processing
The generic term for the capability of computers to work on several tasks at the same time, that is, concurrently. This may involve specific capabilities such as overlapped processing, multiprocessing, multiprogramming, multitasking, parallel processing, and so on.

Connectivity
The degree to which hardware, software, and databases can be easily linked together in a telecommunications network.

Context Diagram
The highest level data flow diagram. It defines the boundaries of a system by showing a single major process and the data inputs and outputs and external entities involved.

Control
(1) The systems component that evaluates feedback to determine whether the system is moving toward the achievement of its goal and then makes any necessary adjustments to the input and processing components of the system to ensure that proper output is produced. (2) A management function that involves observing and measuring organizational performance and environmental activities and modifying the plans and activities of the organization when necessary.

Control Listing
A detailed report that describes each transaction occurring during a period.

Control Totals
Accumulating totals of data at multiple points in an information system to ensure correct information processing.

Control Unit
A subunit of the central processing unit that controls and directs the operations of the computer system. The control unit retrieves computer instructions in proper sequence, interprets each instruction, and then directs the other parts of the computer system in their implementation.

Conversion
The process in which the hardware, software, people, network, and data resources of an old information system must be converted to the requirements of a new information system. This usually involves a parallel, phased, pilot, or plunge conversion process from the old to the new system.

Cooperative Processing
Information processing that allows the computers in a distributed processing network to share the processing of parts of an end user's application.

Cost/Benefit Analysis
Identifying the advantages or benefits and the disadvantages or costs of a proposed solution.

Critical Success Factors
A small number of key factors that executives consider critical to the success of the enterprise. These are key areas where successful performance will assure the success of the organization and attainment of its goals.

Cross-Functional Information Systems
Information systems that are integrated combinations of business information systems, thus sharing information resources across the functional units of an organization.

Cursor
A movable point of light displayed on most video display screens to assist the user in the input of data.

Cybernetic System
A system that uses feedback and control components to achieve a self-monitoring and self-regulating capability.

Cylinder
An imaginary vertical cylinder consisting of the vertical alignment of data tracks on each surface of magnetic disks that are accessed simultaneously by the read/write heads of a disk device.

Data
Facts or observations about physical phenomena or business transactions. More specifically, data are objective measurements of the attributes (characteristics) of entities such as people, places, things, and events.

Data Administration
A data resource management function that involves the establishment and enforcement of policies and procedures for managing data as a strategic corporate resource.

Data Bank
A comprehensive collection of libraries of data.

Database
A collection of logically related records or files. A database consolidates many records previously stored in separate files so that a common pool of data records serves many applications.

Database Administration
A data resource management function that includes responsibility for developing and maintaining the organization's data dictionary, designing and monitoring the performance of databases, and enforcing standards for database use and security.

Database Administrator
A specialist responsible for maintaining standards for the development, maintenance, and security of an organization's databases.

Database Management Approach
An approach to the storage and processing of data in which independent files are consolidated into a common pool, or database, of records available to different application programs and end users for processing and data retrieval.

Database Management System (DBMS)
A set of computer programs that controls the creation, maintenance, and utilization of the databases of an organization.

Data Center
An organizational unit that uses centralized computing resources to perform information processing activities for an organization. Also known as a computer center.

Data Communications
See Telecommunications.

Data Design
The design of the logical structure of databases and files to be used by a proposed information system. This produces detailed descriptions of the entities, relationships, data elements, and integrity rules for system files and databases.

Data Dictionary
A software module and database containing descriptions and definitions concerning the structure, data elements, interrelationships, and other characteristics of an organization's databases.

Data Entry
The process of converting data into a form suitable for entry into a computer system. Also called data capture or input preparation.

Data Flow Diagram
A graphic diagramming tool that uses a few simple symbols to illustrate the flow of data among external entities, processing activities, and data storage elements.

Data Management
Control program functions that provide access to data sets, enforce data storage conventions, and regulate the use of input/output devices.

Data Model
A conceptual framework that defines the logical relationships among the data elements needed to support a basic business or other process.

Data Modeling
A process where the relationships between data elements are identified and defined to develop data models.

Data Planning
A corporate planning and analysis function that focuses on data resource management. It includes the responsibility for developing an overall information policy and data architecture for the firm's data resources.

Data Processing
The execution of a systematic sequence of operations performed upon data to transform it into information.

Data Resource Management
A managerial activity that applies information systems technology and management tools to the task of managing an organization's data resources. Its three major components are database administration, data administration, and data planning.

Data Warehouse
A central source of data that has been extracted from various organizational databases and standardized and integrated for use throughout an organization.

Debug
To detect, locate, and remove errors from a program or malfunctions from a computer.

Decision-Making Process
A process of intelligence, design, and choice activities that result in the selection of a particular course of action.

Decision Support System (DSS)
An information system that utilizes decision models, a database, and a decision maker's own insights in an ad hoc, interactive analytical modeling process to reach a specific decision by a specific decision maker.

Demand Reports and Responses
Information provided whenever a manager or end user demands it.

Desktop Accessory Package
A software package that provides features such as a calculator, note page, alarm clock, phone directory, and appointment book that is available as a pop-up window on a computer display screen at the touch of a key.

Desktop Publishing
The use of microcomputers, laser printers, and page-makeup software to produce a variety of printed materials, formerly done only by professional printers.

Desktop Videoconferencing
The use of end user computer workstations to conduct two-way interactive video conferences.

Development Centers
Systems development consultant groups formed to serve as consultants to the professional programmers and systems analysts of an organization to improve their application development efforts.

Digital Computer
A computer that operates on digital data by performing arithmetic and logical operations on the data. Contrast with Analog Computer.

Digitizer
A device that is used to convert drawings and other graphic images on paper or other materials into digital data that are entered into a computer system.

Direct Access
A method of storage where each storage position has a unique address and can be individually accessed in approximately the same period of time without having to search through other storage positions. Same as Random Access. Contrast with Sequential Access.

Direct Access Storage Device (DASD)
A storage device that can directly access data to be stored or retrieved, for example, a magnetic disk unit.

Direct Data Organization
A method of data organization in which logical data elements are distributed randomly on or within the physical data medium. For example, logical data records distributed randomly on the surfaces of a magnetic disk file. Also called direct organization.

Direct Input/Output
Devices such as terminals that allow data to be input into a computer system or output from the computer system without the use of machine-readable media.

Disaster Recovery
Methods for ensuring that an organization recovers from natural and human-caused disasters that affect its computer-based operations.

Disk Pack
A removable unit containing several magnetic disks that can be mounted on a magnetic disk storage unit.

Distributed Databases
The concept of distributing databases or portions of a database at remote sites where the data are most frequently referenced. Sharing of data is made possible through a network that interconnects the distributed databases.

Distributed Processing
A form of decentralization of information processing made possible by a network of computers dispersed throughout an organization. Processing of user applications is accomplished by several computers interconnected by a telecommunications network, rather than relying on one large centralized computer facility or on the decentralized operation of several independent computers.

Document
(1) A medium on which data have been recorded for human use, such as a report or invoice. (2) In word processing, a generic term for text material such as letters, memos, reports, and so on.

Documentation
A collection of documents or information that describes a computer program, information system, or required data processing operations.

Downsizing
Moving to smaller computing platforms, such as from mainframe systems to networks of personal computers and servers.

Downtime
The time interval during which a device is malfunctioning or inoperative.

Generator
A software package for a decision support system that contains modules for database, model, and dialogue management.

Duplex
In communications, pertaining to a simultaneous two-way independent transmission in both directions.

EBCDIC: Extended Binary Coded Decimal Interchange Code
An eight-bit code that is widely used by mainframe computers.

Echo Check
A method of checking the accuracy of transmission of data in which the received data are returned to the sending device for comparison with the original data.

Economic Feasibility
Whether expected cost savings, increased revenue, increased profits, and reductions in required investment exceed the costs of developing and operating a proposed system.

EDI: Electronic Data Interchange
The electronic transmission of source documents between the computers of different organizations.

Edit
To modify the form or format of data. For example: to insert or delete characters such as page numbers or decimal points.

Edit Report
A report that describes errors detected during processing.

EFT: Electronic Funds Transfer
The development of banking and payment systems that transfer funds electronically instead of using cash or paper documents such as checks.

Electronic Data Processing (EDP)
The use of electronic computers to process data automatically.

Electronic Document Management
An image processing technology in which an electronic document may consist of digitized voice notes and electronic graphics images, as well as digitized images of traditional documents.

Electronic Mail
The transmission, storage, and distribution of text material in electronic form over communications networks.

Electronic Meeting Systems (EMS)
The use of video and audio communications to allow conferences and meetings to be held with participants who may be geographically dispersed or may be present in the same room. This may take the form of group decision support systems, teleconferencing, or other methods.

Electronic Spreadsheet Package
An application program used as a computerized tool for analysis, planning, and modeling that allows users to enter and manipulate data into an electronic worksheet of rows and columns.

Emulation
To imitate one system with another so that the imitating system accepts the same data, executes the same programs, and achieves the same results as the imitated system.

Encryption
To scramble data or convert it, prior to transmission, to a secret code that masks the meaning of the data to unauthorized recipients. Similar to enciphering.

End User
Anyone who uses an information system or the information it produces.

End User Collaboration
Using networked computers to share resources, communicate ideas, and coordinate work efforts among end user work groups.

End User Computing Systems
Computer-based information systems that directly support both the operational and managerial applications of end users. Also, the direct, hands-on use of computers by end users.

Enterprise Analysis
A planning process that emphasizes how computer-based information systems will improve the performance and competitive position of a business enterprise. This includes planning how information systems can support the basic business processes, functions, and organizational units of an organization.

Enterprise Model
A conceptual framework that defines the structures and relationships of business processes and data elements, as well as other planning structures, such as critical success factors, and organizational units.

Entity Relationship Diagram (ERD)
A data planning and systems development diagramming tool that models the relationships among the entities in a business process.

Entropy
The tendency of a system to lose a relatively stable state of equilibrium.

Ergonomics
The science and technology emphasizing the safety, comfort, and ease of use of human-operated machines such as computers. The goal of ergonomics is to produce systems that are user-friendly: safe, comfortable, and easy to use. Ergonomics is also called human factors engineering.

Evaluation Criteria
Key areas in which a proposed solution will be evaluated.

Exception Reports
Reports produced only when exceptional conditions occur, or reports produced periodically that contain information only about exceptional conditions.

Executive Information Systems (EIS)
An information system that provides strategic information tailored to the needs of top management.

Executive Support System (ESS)
An executive information system with additional capabilities, including data analysis, decision support, electronic mail, and personal productivity tools.

Expert System (ES)
A computer-based information system that uses its knowledge about a specific complex application area to act as an expert consultant to users. The system consists of a knowledge base and software modules that perform inferences on the knowledge and communicate answers to a user's questions.

Facilities Management
The use of an external service organization to operate and manage the information processing facilities of an organization.

Facsimile
The transmission of images and their reconstruction and duplication on some form of paper at a receiving station.

Fault Tolerant Systems
Computers that have multiple central processors, peripherals, and system software and that are able to continue operations even if there is a major hardware or software failure.

Feasibility Study
A preliminary study that investigates the information needs of end users and the objectives, constraints, basic resource requirements, cost/benefits, and feasibility of proposed projects.

Feedback
(1) Data or information concerning the components and operations of a system. (2) The use of part of the output of a system as input to the system.

Fiber Optics
The technology that uses cables consisting of very thin filaments of glass fibers that can conduct the light generated by lasers at frequencies that approach the speed of light.

Field
A data element that consists of a grouping of characters that describe a particular attribute of an entity. For example: the name field or salary field of an employee.

Fifth Generation
The next generation of computing, which will provide computers that will be able to see, hear, talk, and think. This would depend on major advances in parallel processing, user input/output methods, and artificial intelligence.

File
A collection of related data records treated as a unit. Sometimes called a data set.

File Maintenance
The activity of keeping a file up-to-date by adding, changing, or deleting data.

File Management
Controlling the creation, deletion, access, and use of files of data and programs.

File Processing
Utilizing a file for data processing activities such as file maintenance, information retrieval, or report generation.

Financial Information Systems
Information systems that support financial managers in the financing of a business and the allocation and control of financial resources. Include cash and securities management, capital budgeting, financial forecasting, and financial planning.

Fire Wall Computer
A computer that protects computer networks from intrusion by screening all network traffic and serving as a safe transfer point for access to and from other networks.

Firmware
The use of microprogrammed read only memory circuits in place of hardwired logic circuitry. See also Microprogramming.

Floating Point
Pertaining to a number representation system in which each number is represented by two sets of digits. One set represents the significant digits or fixed-point "base" of the number, while the other set of digits represents the "exponent," which indicates the precision of the number.

Floppy Disk
A small plastic disk coated with iron oxide that resembles a small phonograph record enclosed in a protective envelope. It is a widely used form of magnetic disk media that provides a direct access storage capability for microcomputer systems.

Flowchart
A graphical representation in which symbols are used to represent operations, data, flow, logic, equipment, and so on. A program flowchart illustrates the structure and sequence of operations of a program, while a system flowchart illustrates the components and flows of information systems.

Foreground Processing
The automatic execution of the computer programs that have been designed to preempt the use of computing facilities. Contrast with Background Processing.

Format
The arrangement of data on a medium.

FORTRAN: FORmula TRANslation
A high-level programming language widely utilized to develop computer programs that perform mathematical computations for scientific, engineering, and selected business applications.

Forward Chaining
An inference strategy that reaches a conclusion by applying rules to facts to determine if any facts satisfy a rule's conditions in a particular situation.

Fourth-Generation Languages (4GL)
Programming languages that are easier to use than high-level languages like BASIC, COBOL, or FORTRAN. They are also known as nonprocedural, natural, or very-high-level languages.

Frame
A collection of knowledge about an entity or other concept consisting of a complex package of slots, that is, data values describing the characteristics or attributes of an entity.

Frame-Based Knowledge
Knowledge represented in the form of a hierarchy or network of frames.

Front-End Processor
Typically a smaller, general-purpose computer that is dedicated to handling data communications control functions in a communications network, thus relieving the host computer of these functions.

Functional Requirements
The information system capabilities required to meet the information needs of end users. Also called system requirements.

Fuzzy Logic Systems
Computer-based systems that can process data that are incomplete or only partially correct, that is, fuzzy data. Such systems can solve unstructured problems with incomplete knowledge, as humans do.

General-Purpose Application Programs
Programs that can perform information processing jobs for users from all application areas. For example, word processing programs, electronic spreadsheet programs, and graphics programs can be used by individuals for home, education, business, scientific, and many other purposes.

General-Purpose Computer
A computer that is designed to handle a wide variety of problems. Contrast with Special-Purpose Computer.

Generate
To produce a machine-language program for performing a specific data processing task based on parameters supplied by a programmer or user.

Generator
A computer program that performs a generating function.

Gigabyte
One billion bytes. More accurately, 2 to the 30th power, or 1,073,741,824 in decimal notation.

GIGO
A contraction of "Garbage In, Garbage Out," which emphasizes that information systems will produce erroneous and invalid output when provided with erroneous and invalid input data or instructions.

Global Company
A business that is driven by a global strategy so that all of its activities are planned and implemented in the context of a whole-world system.

Global Information Technology
The use of computer-based information systems and telecommunications networks using a variety of information technologies to support global business operations and management.

Globalization
Becoming a global enterprise by expanding into global markets, using global production facilities, forming alliances with global partners, and so on.

Goal-Seeking Analysis
Making repeated changes to selected variables until a chosen variable reaches a target value.

Graphical User Interface
A software interface that relies on icons, bars, buttons, boxes, and other images to initiate computer-based tasks for users.

Graphics
Pertaining to symbolic input or output from a computer system, such as lines, curves, and geometric shapes, using video display units or graphics plotters and printers.

Graphics Pen and Tablet
A device that allows an end user to draw or write on a pressure sensitive tablet and have the handwriting or graphics digitized by the computer and accepted as input.

Graphics Software
A program that helps users generate graphics displays.

Group Decision Making
Decisions made by groups of people coming to an agreement on a particular issue.

Group Decision Support System (GDSS)
A decision support system that provides support for decision making by groups of people.

Groupware
Software packages that support work activities by members of a work group whose workstations are interconnected by a local area network.

Hacking
(1) Obsessive use of a computer. (2) The unauthorized access and use of computer systems.

Handshaking
Exchange of predetermined signals when a connection is established between two communications terminals.

Hard Copy
A data medium or data record that has a degree of permanence and that can be read by people or machines.

Hardware
(1) Machines and media. (2) Physical equipment, as opposed to computer programs or methods of use. (3) Mechanical, magnetic, electrical, electronic, or optical devices. Contrast with Software.

Hash Total
The sum of numbers in a data field that are not normally added, such as account numbers or other identification numbers. It is utilized as a control total, especially during input/output operations of batch processing systems.

Header Label
A machine-readable record at the beginning of a file containing data for file identification and control.

Heuristic
Pertaining to exploratory methods of problem solving in which solutions are discovered by evaluation of the progress made toward the final result. It is an exploratory trial-and-error approach guided by rules of thumb. Opposite of algorithmic.

Hierarchical Data Structure
A logical data structure in which the relationships between records form a hierarchy or tree structure. The relationships among records are one to many, since each data element is related only to one element above it.

High-Level Language
A programming language that utilizes macro instructions and statements that closely resemble human language or mathematical notation to describe the problem to be solved or the procedure to be used. Also called a compiler language.

Homeostasis
A relatively stable state of equilibrium of a system.

Host Computer
Typically a larger central computer that performs the major data processing tasks in a computer network.

Human Factors
Hardware and software capabilities that can affect the comfort, safety, ease of use, and user customization of computer-based information systems.

Human Information Processing
A conceptual framework about the human cognitive process that uses an information processing context to explain how humans capture, process, and use information.

Human Resource Information Systems (HRIS)
Information systems that support human resource management activities such as recruitment, selection and hiring, job placement and performance appraisals, and training and development.

Hybrid AI Systems
Systems that integrate several AI technologies, such as expert systems and neural networks.

Hypermedia
Documents containing multiple forms of media, including text, graphics, video, and sound, that can be interactively searched, like Hypertext.

Hypertext
A methodology for the construction and interactive use of text material, in which a body of text in electronic form is indexed in a variety of ways so it can be quickly searched by a reader.

Icon
A small figure on a video display that looks like a familiar office or other device such as a file folder (for storing a file), a wastebasket (for deleting a file), or a calculator (for switching to a calculator mode).

Image Processing
A computer-based technology that allows end users to electronically capture, store, process, and retrieve images that may include numeric data, text, handwriting, graphics, documents, and photographs. Image processing makes heavy use of optical scanning and optical disk technologies.

Impact Printers
Printers that form images on paper through the pressing of a printing element and an inked ribbon or roller against the face of a sheet of paper.

Index
An ordered reference list of the contents of a file or document together with keys or reference notations for identification or location of those contents.

Index Sequential
A method of data organization in which records are organized in sequential order and also referenced by an index. When utilized with direct access file devices, it is known as index sequential access method, or ISAM.

Inference Engine
The software component of an expert system, which processes the rules and facts related to a specific problem and makes associations and inferences resulting in recommended courses of action.

Information
Information is data placed in a meaningful and useful context for an end user.

Information Architecture
A conceptual framework that defines the basic structure, content, and relationships of the organizational databases that provide the data needed to support the basic business processes of an organization.

Information Center
A support facility for the end users of an organization. It allows users to learn to develop their own application programs and to accomplish their own information processing tasks. End users are provided with hardware support, software support, and people support (trained user consultants).

Information Float
The time when a document is in transit between the sender and receiver, and thus unavailable for any action or response.

Information Processing
A concept that covers both the traditional concept of processing numeric and alphabetic data, and the processing of text, images, and voices. It emphasizes that the production of information products for users should be the focus of processing activities.

Information Quality
The degree to which information has content, form, and time characteristics that give it value to specific end users.

Information Resource Management (IRM)
A management concept that views data, information, and computer resources (computer hardware, software, networks, and personnel) as valuable organizational resources that should be efficiently, economically, and effectively managed for the benefit of the entire organization.

Information Retrieval
The methods and procedures for recovering specific information from stored data.

Information Superhighway
An advanced high-speed network that would connect individuals, households, businesses, government agencies, libraries, schools, universities, and other institutions with interactive voice, video, data, and multimedia communications.

Information System
A set of people, procedures, and resources that collects, transforms, and disseminates information in an organization. Or a system that accepts data resources as input and processes them into information products as output. Also, a system that uses the resources of hardware (machines and media), software (programs and procedures), people (users and specialists), and networks (communications media and network support) to perform input, processing, output, storage, and control activities that transform data resources into information products.

Information System Resources
People, hardware, software, data, and networks are the resources of an information system.

Information Systems Development
See Systems Development.

Information System Specialist
A person whose occupation is related to the providing of information system services. For example: a systems analyst, programmer, or computer operator.

Information Systems Planning
A formal planning process that develops plans for developing and managing information systems that will support the goals of the organization. This includes strategic, tactical, and operational planning activities.

Information Technology (IT)
Hardware, software, telecommunications, database management, and other information processing technologies used in computer-based information systems.

Information Theory
The branch of learning concerned with the likelihood of accurate transmission or communication of messages subject to transmission failure, distortion, and noise.

Input
Pertaining to a device, process, or channel involved in the insertion of data into a data processing system. Opposite of Output.

Input/Output (I/O)
Pertaining to either input or output, or both.

Input/Output Interface Hardware
Devices such as I/O ports, I/O busses, buffers, channels, and input/output control units, which assist the CPU in its input/output assignments. These devices make it possible for modern computer systems to perform input, output, and processing functions simultaneously.

Inquiry Processing
Computer processing that supports the realtime interrogation of online files and databases by end users.

Instruction
A grouping of characters that specifies the computer operation to be performed.

Intangible Benefits and Costs
The nonquantifiable benefits and costs of a proposed solution or system.

Integrated Circuit
A complex microelectronic circuit consisting of interconnected circuit elements that cannot be disassembled because they are placed on or within a "continuous substrate" such as a silicon chip.

Integrated Packages
Software that combines the ability to do several general-purpose applications (such as word processing, electronic spreadsheet, and graphics) into one program.

Integrative Information Systems
Information systems that combine the capabilities of several types of information systems.

Intelligent Agent
A special-purpose knowledge-based system that serves as a software surrogate to accomplish specific tasks for users.

Intelligent Terminal
A terminal with the capabilities of a microcomputer that can thus perform many processing and other

functions without accessing a larger computer.

Interactive Processing
A type of realtime processing in which users can interact with a computer on a realtime basis.

Interactive Video
Computer-based systems that integrate image processing with text, audio, and video processing technologies, which makes interactive multimedia presentations possible.

Interface
A shared boundary, such as the boundary between two systems. For example, the boundary between a computer and its peripheral devices.

Internet
The Internet is a rapidly growing network of thousands of business, educational, and research networks connecting millions of computers and their users in over 100 countries.

Internetwork Processor
Communications processors used by local area networks to interconnect them with other local area and wide area networks. Examples include bridges, routers, hubs, and gateways.

Internetworks
Interconnected local area and wide area networks.

Interoperability
Being able to accomplish end user applications using different types of computer systems, operating systems, and application software, interconnected by different types of local and wide area networks.

Interorganizational Information Systems
Information systems that interconnect an organization with other organizations, such as a business and its customers and suppliers.

Interpreter
A computer program that translates and executes each source language statement before translating and executing the next one.

Interrupt
A condition that causes an interruption in a processing operation during which another task is performed. At the conclusion of this new assignment, control may be transferred back to the point where the original processing operation was interrupted or to other tasks with a higher priority.

Intranet
An Internet-like network of interconnected networks within an organization, whose Web-like browsing software provides easy access to network resources, the Internet, and other networks.

Inverted File
A file that references entities by their attributes.

IS Component Matrix
A matrix that documents how hardware, software, people, network, and data resources support an information system's input, processing, output, storage, and control activities to produce information products for end users.

IT Architecture
A conceptual design for the implementation of information technology in an organization, including its hardware, software, and network technology platforms, data resources, application portfolio, and IS organization.

Iterative
Pertaining to the repeated execution of a series of steps.

Job
A specified group of tasks prescribed as a unit of work for a computer.

Job Control Language (JCL)
A language for communicating with the operating system of a computer to identify a job and describe its requirements.

Joystick
A small lever set in a box used to move the cursor on the computer's display screen.

K
An abbreviation for the prefix kilo-, which is 1,000 in decimal notation. When referring to storage capacity it is equivalent to 2 to the 10th power, or 1,024 in decimal notation.

Key
One or more fields within a data record that are used to identify it or control its use.

Keyboarding
Using the keyboard of a microcomputer or computer terminal.

Knowledge Base
A computer-accessible collection of knowledge about a subject in a variety of forms, such as facts and rules of inference, frames, and objects.

Knowledge-Based Information System

An information system that adds a knowledge base to the database and other components found in other types of computer-based information systems.

Knowledge Engineer

A specialist who works with experts to capture the knowledge they possess in order to develop a knowledge base for expert systems and other knowledge-based systems.

Knowledge Workers

People whose primary work activities include creating, using, and distributing information.

Language Translator Program

A program that converts the programming language instructions in a computer program into machine language code. Major types include assemblers, compilers, and interpreters.

Large-Scale Integration (LSI)

A method of constructing electronic circuits in which thousands of circuits can be placed on a single semiconductor chip.

Layout Forms and Screens

Tools used to construct the formats and generic content of input/output media and methods for the user interface, such as display screens and reports.

Light Pen

A photoelectronic device that allows data to be entered or altered on the face of a video display terminal.

Line Printer

A device that prints all characters of a line as a unit.

Liquid Crystal Displays (LCDs)

Electronic visual displays that form characters by applying an electrical charge to selected silicon crystals.

List Organization

A method of data organization that uses indexes and pointers to allow for non-sequential retrieval.

List Processing

A method of processing data in the form of lists.

Local Area Network (LAN)

A communications network that typically connects computers, terminals, and other computerized devices within a limited physical area such as an office, building, manufacturing plant, or other worksite.

Locking in Customers and Suppliers

Building valuable relationships with customers and suppliers that deter them from abandoning a firm for its competitors or intimidating it into accepting less-profitable relationships.

Logical Data Elements

Data elements that are independent of the physical data media on which they are recorded.

Logical System Design

Developing general specifications for how basic information systems activities can meet end user requirements.

Loop

A sequence of instructions in a computer program that is executed repeatedly until a terminal condition prevails.

Machine Cycle

The timing of a basic CPU operation as determined by a fixed number of electrical pulses emitted by the CPU's timing circuitry or internal clock.

Machine Language

A programming language where instructions are expressed in the binary code of the computer.

Macro Instruction

An instruction in a source language that is equivalent to a specified sequence of machine instructions.

Magnetic Disk

A flat circular plate with a magnetic surface on which data can be stored by selective magnetization of portions of the curved surface.

Magnetic Drum

A circular cylinder with a magnetic surface on which data can be stored by selective magnetization of portions of the curved surface.

Magnetic Ink

An ink that contains particles of iron oxide that can be magnetized and detected by magnetic sensors.

Magnetic Ink Character Recognition (MICR)

The machine recognition of characters printed with magnetic ink. Primarily used for check processing by the banking industry.

Magnetic Tape

A plastic tape with a magnetic surface on which data can be stored by selective magnetization of portions of the surface.

Mag Stripe Card

A plastic wallet-size card with a strip of magnetic tape on on surface; widely used for credit/debit cards.

Mainframe

A larger-size computer system, typically with a separate central processing unit, as distinguished from microcomputer and minicomputer systems.

Management Functions

Management as a process of planning, organizing, staffing, directing, and controlling activities.

Management Information System (MIS)

A management support system that produces prespecified reports, displays, and responses on a periodic, exception, or demand basis.

Management Levels

Management as the performance of planning and control activities at the strategic, tactical, operational levels of an organization.

Management Support System (MSS)

An information system that provides information to support managerial decision making. More specifically, an information-reporting system, executive information system, or decision support system.

Managerial End User

A manager, entrepreneur, or managerial-level professional who personally uses information systems. Also, the manager of a department or other organizational unit that relies on information systems.

Managerial Roles

Management as the performance of a variety of interpersonal, information, and decisional roles.

Manual Processing

(1) Data processing that requires continual human manipulation and intervention and uses simple data processing tools such as paper forms, pencils, and filing cabinets. (2) All data processing that is not automatic, even if it utilizes machines such as typewriters and calculators.

Manufacturing Information Systems

Information systems that support the planning, control, and accomplishment of manufacturing processes. This includes concepts such as computer-integrated manufacturing (CIM) and technologies such as computer-aided manufacturing (CAM) or computer-aided design (CAD).

Marketing Information Systems
Information systems that support the planning, control, and transaction processing required for the accomplishment of marketing activities, such as sales management, advertising, and promotion.

Mass Storage
Secondary storage devices with extra-large storage capacities such as magnetic or optical disks.

Master File
A data file containing relatively permanent information that is utilized as an authoritative reference and is usually updated periodically. Contrast with Transaction File.

Mathematical Model
A mathematical representation of a process, device, or concept.

Media
All tangible objects on which data are recorded.

Megabyte
One million bytes. More accurately, 2 to the 20th power, or 1,048,576 in decimal notation.

Memory
Same as Storage.

Menu
A displayed list of items (usually the names of alternative applications, files, or activities) from which an end user makes a selection.

Menu Driven
A characteristic of interactive computing systems that provides menu displays and operator prompting to assist an end user in performing a particular job.

Meta Data
Data about data; data describing the structure, data elements, interrelationships, and other characteristics of a database.

Microcomputer
A very small computer, ranging in size from a "computer on a chip" to a small typewriter-size unit.

Micrographics
The use of microfilm, microfiche, and other microform to store data in greatly reduced form.

Microprocessor
A microcomputer central processing unit (CPU) on a chip without input/output or storage capabilities in most cases.

Microprogram
A small set of elementary control instructions called microinstructions or microcode.

Microprogramming
The use of special software (microprograms) to perform the functions of special hardware (electronic control circuitry). Microprograms stored in a read-only storage module of the control unit interpret the machine language instructions of a computer program and decode them into elementary microinstructions, which are then executed.

Microsecond
A millionth of a second.

Middleware
Software that helps diverse networked computer systems work together, thus promoting their interoperability.

Midrange Computer
A computer category between microcomputers and mainframes. Examples include minicomputers, network servers, and technical workstations.

Millisecond
A thousandth of a second.

Minicomputer
A small (e.g., the size of a desk) electronic, digital, stored-program, general-purpose computer.

Model Base
An organized collection of conceptual, mathematical, and logical models that express business relationships, computational routines, or analytical techniques. Such models are stored in the form of programs and program subroutines, command files, and spreadsheets.

Modem
(MOdulator-DEModulator) A device that converts the digital signals from input/output devices into appropriate frequencies at a transmission terminal and converts them back into digital signals at a receiving terminal.

Monitor
Software or hardware that observes, supervises, controls, or verifies the operations of a system.

Mouse
A small device that is electronically connected to a computer and is moved by hand on a flat surface in order to move the cursor on a video screen in the same direction. Buttons on the mouse allow users to issue commands and make responses or selections.

Multidimensional Structure
A database model that uses multidimensional structures (such as cubes or cubes within cubes) to store data and relationships between data.

Multimedia Presentations
Providing information using a variety of media, including text and graphics displays, voice and other audio, photographs, and video segments.

Multiplex
To interleave or simultaneously transmit two or more messages on a single channel.

Multiplexer
An electronic device that allows a single communications channel to carry simultaneous data transmission from many terminals.

Multiprocessing
Pertaining to the simultaneous execution of two or more instructions by a computer or computer network.

Multiprocessor Computer Systems
Computer systems that use a multiprocessor architecture in the design of their central processing units. This includes the use of support microprocessors and multiple instruction processors, including parallel processor designs.

Multiprogramming
Pertaining to the concurrent execution of two or more programs by a computer by interleaving their execution.

Multitasking
The concurrent use of the same computer to accomplish several different information processing tasks. Each task may require the use of a different program, or the concurrent use of the same copy of a program by several users.

Nanosecond
One billionth of a second.

Natural Language
A programming language that is very close to human language. Also called very-high-level language.

Network
An interconnected system of computers, terminals, and communications channels and devices.

Network Architecture
A master plan designed to promote an open, simple, flexible, and efficient telecommunications environment through the use of standard protocols, standard communications hardware and software interfaces, and the design

of a standard multilevel telecommunications interface between end users and computer systems.

Network Data Structure
A logical data structure that allows many-to-many relationships among data records. It allows entry into a database at multiple points, because any data element or record can be related to many other data elements.

Neural Networks
Computer processors or software whose architecture is based on the human brain's meshlike neuron structure. Neural networks can process many pieces of information simultaneously and can learn to recognize patterns and programs themselves to solve related problems on their own.

Node
A terminal point in a communications network.

Nonimpact Printers
Printers that use specially treated paper and that form characters by laser, thermal (heat), electrostatic, or electrochemical processes.

Nonprocedural Languages
Programming languages that allow users and professional programmers to specify the results they want without specifying how to solve the problem.

Numerical Control
Automatic control of a machine process by a computer that makes use of numerical data, generally introduced as the operation is in process. Also called machine control.

Object
A data element that includes both data and the methods or processes that act on that data.

Object-Based Knowledge
Knowledge represented as a network of objects.

Object-Oriented Language
An object-oriented programming (OOP) language used to develop programs that create and use objects to perform information processing tasks.

Object Program
A compiled or assembled program composed of executable machine instructions. Contrast with Source Program.

OEM: Original Equipment Manufacturer
A firm that manufactures and sells computers by assembling components

produced by other hardware manufacturers.

Office Automation (OA)
The use of computer-based information systems that collect, process, store, and transmit electronic messages, documents, and other forms of office communications among individuals, work groups, and organizations.

Office Management Systems
Office automation systems that integrate a variety of computer-based support services, including desktop accessories, electronic mail, and electronic task management.

Offline
Pertaining to equipment or devices not under control of the central processing unit.

Online
Pertaining to equipment or devices under control of the central processing unit.

Online Analytical Processing (OLAP)
A capability of some management, decision support, and executive information systems that supports interactive examination and manipulation of large amounts of data from many perspectives.

Online Transaction Processing (OLTP)
A realtime transaction processing system.

Open Systems
Information systems that use common standards for hardware, software, applications, and networking to create a computing environment that allows easy access by end users and their networked computer systems.

Operand
That which is operated upon. That part of a computer instruction that is identified by the address part of the instruction.

Operating Environment Package
Software packages or modules that add a graphics-based interface between end users, the operating system, and their application programs, and that may also provide a multitasking capability.

Operating System
The main control program of a computer system. It is a system of programs that controls the execution of computer programs and may provide scheduling, debugging, input/output control, system accounting, compilation, storage assignment, data management, and related services.

Operational Feasibility
The willingness and ability of management, employees, customers, and sup-

pliers to operate, use, and support a proposed system.

Operation Code
A code that represents specific operations to be performed upon the operands in a computer instruction.

Operations System
A basic subsystem of the business firm that constitutes its input, processing, and output components. Also called a physical system.

Operation Support System (OSS)
An information system that collects, processes, and stores data generated by the operations systems of an organization and produces data and information for input into a management information system or for the control of an operations system.

Opportunity
A basic condition that presents the potential for desirable results in an organization or other system.

Optical Character Recognition (OCR)
The machine identification of printed characters through the use of light-sensitive devices.

Optical Disks
A secondary storage medium using laser technology to read tiny spots on a plastic disk. The disks are currently capable of storing billions of characters of information.

Optical Scanner
A device that optically scans characters or images and generates their digital representations.

Optimization Analysis
Finding an optimum value for selected variables in a mathematical model, given certain constraints.

Organizational Feasibility
How well a proposed information system supports the objectives of an organization's strategic plan for information systems.

Output
Pertaining to a device, process, or channel involved with the transfer of data or information out of an information processing system. Opposite of Input.

Outsourcing
Turning over all or part of an organization's information systems operation to outside contractors, known as systems integrators or facilities management companies.

Packet
A group of data and control information in a specified format that is transmitted as an entity.

Packet Switching
A data transmission process that transmits addressed packets such that a channel is occupied only for the duration of transmission of the packet.

Page
A segment of a program or data, usually of fixed length.

Paging
A process that automatically and continually transfers pages of programs and data between primary storage and direct access storage devices. It provides computers with multiprogramming and virtual memory capabilities.

Parallel Processing
Executing many instructions at the same time, that is, in parallel. Performed by advanced computers using many instruction processors organized in clusters or networks.

Parity Bit
A check bit appended to an array of binary digits to make the sum of all the binary digits, including the check bit, always odd or always even.

Pascal
A high-level, general-purpose, structured programming language named after Blaise Pascal. It was developed by Niklaus Wirth of Zurich in 1968.

Pattern Recognition
The identification of shapes, forms, or configurations by automatic means.

PCM: Plug Compatible Manufacturer
A firm that manufactures computer equipment that can be plugged into existing computer systems without requiring additional hardware or software interfaces.

Pen-Based Computers
Tablet-style microcomputers that recognize handwriting and hand drawing done by a pen-shaped device on their pressure-sensitive display screens.

Performance Monitor
software package that monitors the essing of computer system jobs, develop a planned schedule of r operations that can optimize system performance, and tailed statistics that are uter system capacity ntrol.

Periodic Reports
Providing information to managers using a prespecified format designed to provide information on a regularly scheduled basis.

Peripheral Devices
In a computer system, any unit of equipment, distinct from the central processing unit, that provides the system with input, output, or storage capabilities.

Personal Information Manager (PIM)
A software package that helps end users store, organize, and retrieve text and numerical data in the form of notes, lists, memos, and a variety of other forms.

Physical System Design
Design of the user interface methods and products, database structures, and processing and control procedures for a proposed information system, including hardware, software, and personnel specifications.

Picosecond
One trillionth of a second.

Plasma Display
Output devices that generate a visual display with electrically charged particles of gas trapped between glass plates.

Plotter
A hard-copy output device that produces drawings and graphical displays on paper or other materials.

Pointer
A data element associated with an index, a record, or other set of data that contains the address of a related record.

Pointing Devices
Devices that allow end users to issue commands or make choices by moving a cursor on the display screen.

Pointing Stick
A small buttonlike device on a keyboard that moves the cursor on the screen in the direction of the pressure placed upon it.

Point-of-Sale (POS) Terminal
A computer terminal used in retail stores that serves the function of a cash register as well as collecting sales data and performing other data processing functions.

Port
(1) Electronic circuitry that provides a connection point between the CPU and input/output devices. (2) A connection point for a communications line on a CPU or other front-end device.

Postimplementation Review
Monitoring and evaluating the results of an implemented solution or system.

Presentation Graphics
Using computer-generated graphics to enhance the information presented in reports and other types of presentations.

Prespecified Reports
Reports whose format is specified in advance to provide managers with information periodically, on an exception basis, or on demand.

Private Branch Exchange (PBX)
A switching device that serves as an interface between the many telephone lines within a work area and the local telephone company's main telephone lines or trunks. Computerized PBXs can handle the switching of both voice and data in the local area networks that are needed in such locations.

Problem
A basic condition that is causing undesirable results in an organization or other system.

Procedure-Oriented Language
A programming language designed for the convenient expression of procedures used in the solution of a wide class of problems.

Procedures
Sets of instructions used by people to complete a task.

Process Control
The use of a computer to control an ongoing physical process, such as petrochemical production.

Process Design
The design of the programs and procedures needed by a proposed information system, including detailed program specifications and procedures.

Processor
A hardware device or software system capable of performing operations upon data.

Program
A set of instructions that cause a computer to perform a particular task.

Programmed Decision
A decision that can be automated by basing it on a decision rule that outlines the steps to take when confronted with the need for a specific decision.

Programmer
A person mainly involved in designing, writing, and testing computer programs.

Programming
The design, writing, and testing of a program.

Programming Language
A language used to develop the instructions in computer programs.

Programming Tools
Software packages or modules that provide editing and diagnostic capabilities and other support facilities to assist the programming process.

Project Management
Managing the accomplishment of an information system development project according to a specific project plan, in order that a project is completed on time, within its budget, and meets its design objectives.

Prompt
Messages that assist a user in performing a particular job. This would include error messages, correction suggestions, questions, and other messages that guide an end user.

Protocol
A set of rules and procedures for the control of communications in a communications network.

Prototype
A working model. In particular, a working model of an information system that includes tentative versions of user input and output, databases and files, control methods, and processing routines.

Prototyping
The rapid development and testing of working models, or prototypes, of new information system applications in an interactive, iterative process involving both systems analysts and end users.

Pseudocode
An informal design language of structured programming that expresses the processing logic of a program module in ordinary human language phrases.

Public Information Networks
Networks provided by various organizations and companies to personal computer users that offer a variety of computing and other information services.

Quality Assurance
Methods for ensuring that information systems are free from errors and fraud

and provide information products of high quality.

Query Language
A high-level, humanlike language provided by a database management system that enables users to easily extract data and information from a database.

Queue
(1) A waiting line formed by items in a system waiting for service. (2) To arrange in or form a queue.

RAID
Redundant arrays of independent disks. Magnetic disk units that house many interconnected microcomputer hard disk drives, thus providing large, fault tolerant storage capacities.

Random Access
Same as Direct Access. Contrast with Sequential Access.

Random Access Memory (RAM)
One of the basic types of semiconductor memory used for temporary storage of data or programs during processing. Each memory position can be directly sensed (read) or changed (write) in the same length of time, irrespective of its location on the storage medium.

Reach and Range Analysis
A planning framework that contrasts a firm's ability to use its IT platform to reach its stakeholders, with the range of information products and services that can be provided or shared through IT.

Read Only Memory (ROM)
A basic type of semiconductor memory used for permanent storage. Can only be read, not "written," that is, changed. Variations are Programmable Read Only Memory (PROM) and Erasable Programmable Read Only Memory (EPROM).

Realtime
Pertaining to the performance of data processing during the actual time a business or physical process transpires, in order that results of the data processing can be used to support the completion of the process.

Realtime Processing
Data processing in which data are processed immediately rather than periodically. Also called online processing. Contrast with Batch Processing.

Record
A collection of related data fields treated as a unit.

Reduced Instruction Set Computer (RISC)
A CPU architecture that optimizes processing speed by the use of a smaller number of basic machine instructions than traditional CPU designs.

Redundancy
In information processing, the repetition of part or all of a message to increase the chance that the correct information will be understood by the recipient.

Register
A device capable of storing a specified amount of data such as one word.

Relational Data Structure
A logical data structure in which all data elements within the database are viewed as being stored in the form of simple tables. DBMS packages based on the relational model can link data elements from various tables as long as the tables share common data elements.

Remote Access
Pertaining to communication with the data processing facility by one or more stations that are distant from that facility.

Remote Job Entry (RJE)
Entering jobs into a batch processing system from a remote facility.

Report Generator
A feature of database management system packages that allows an end user to quickly specify a report format for the display of information retrieved from a database.

Reprographics
Copying and duplicating technology and methods.

Resource Management
An operating system function that controls the use of computer system resources such as primary storage, secondary storage, CPU processing time, and input/output devices by other system software and application software packages.

Robotics
The technology of building machines (robots) with computer intelligence and humanlike physical capabilities.

Routine
An ordered set of instructions that may have some general or frequent use.

RPG: Report Program Generator
A problem-oriented language that utilizes a generator to construct programs that produce reports and perform other data processing tasks.

Rule
Statements that typically take the form of a premise and a conclusion such as If-Then rules: If (condition), Then (conclusion).

Rule-Based Knowledge
Knowledge represented in the form of rules and statements of fact.

Scenario Approach
A planning approach where managers, employees, and planners create scenarios of what an organization will be like three to five years or more into the future, and identify the role IT can play in those scenarios.

Schema
An overall conceptual or logical view of the relationships between the data in a database.

Scientific Method
An analytical methodology that involves (1) recognizing phenomena, (2) formulating a hypothesis about the causes or effects of the phenomena, (3) testing the hypothesis through experimentation, (4) evaluating the results of such experiments, and (5) drawing conclusions about the hypothesis.

Secondary Storage
Storage that supplements the primary storage of a computer. Synonymous with Auxiliary Storage.

Sector
A subdivision of a track on a magnetic disk surface.

Security Codes
Passwords, identification codes, account codes, and other codes that limit the access and use of computer-based system resources to authorized users.

Security Monitor
A software package that monitors the use of a computer system and protects its resources from unauthorized use, fraud, and vandalism.

Semiconductor Memory
Microelectronic storage circuitry etched on tiny chips of silicon or other semiconducting material. The primary storage of most modern computers consists of microelectronic semiconductor storage chips for random access memory and read only memory (ROM).

Structured Decisions
involving procedures that can specified, but not

enough to lead to a definite recommended decision.

Sensitivity Analysis
Observing how repeated changes to a single variable affect other variables in a mathematical model.

Sequential Access
A sequential method of storing and retrieving data from a file. Contrast with Random Access and Direct Access.

Sequential Data Organization
Organizing logical data elements according to a prescribed sequence.

Serial
Pertaining to the sequential or consecutive occurrence of two or more related activities in a single device or channel.

Server
A computer that supports telecommunications in a local area network, as well as the sharing of peripheral devices, software, and databases among the workstations in the network.

Service Bureau
A firm offering computer and data processing services. Also called a computer service center.

Smart Products
Industrial and consumer products, with "intelligence" provided by built-in microcomputers or microprocessors that significantly improve the performance and capabilities of such products.

Software
Computer programs and procedures concerned with the operation of an information system. Contrast with Hardware.

Software Package
A computer program supplied by computer manufacturers, independent software companies, or other computer users. Also known as canned programs, proprietary software, or packaged programs.

Software Piracy
Unauthorized copying of software.

Software Suites
A combination of individual software packages that share a common graphical user interface and are designed for easy transfer of data between applications.

Solid State
Pertaining to devices such as transistors and diodes whose operation depends on the control of electric or magnetic phenomena in solid materials.

Source Data Automation
The use of automated methods of data entry that attempt to reduce or eliminate many of the activities, people, and data media required by traditional data entry methods.

Source Document
A document that is the original formal record of a transaction, such as a purchase order or sales invoice.

Source Program
A computer program written in a language that is subject to a translation process. Contrast with Object Program.

Special-Purpose Computer
A computer designed to handle a restricted class of problems. Contrast with General-Purpose Computer.

Spooling
Simultaneous peripheral operation online. Storing input data from low-speed devices temporarily on high-speed secondary storage units, which can be quickly accessed by the CPU. Also, writing output data at high speeds onto magnetic tape or disk units from which it can be transferred to slow-speed devices such as a printer.

Stage Analysis
A planning process in which the information system needs of an organization are based on an analysis of its current stage in the growth cycle of the organization and its use of information systems technology.

Standards
Measures of performance developed to evaluate the progress of a system toward its objectives.

Storage
Pertaining to a device into which data can be entered, in which they can be held, and from which they can be retrieved at a later time. Same as Memory.

Strategic Information Systems
Information systems that provide a firm with competitive products and services that give it a strategic advantage over its competitors in the marketplace. Also, information systems that promote business innovation, improve operational efficiency, and build strategic information resources for a firm.

Strategic Opportunities Matrix
A planning framework that uses a matrix to help identify opportunities with strategic business potential, as

well as a firm's ability to exploit such opportunities with IT.

Structure Chart
A design and documentation technique to show the purpose and relationships of the various modules in a program.

Structured Decisions
Decisions that are structured by the decision procedures or decision rules developed for them. They involve situations where the procedures to follow when a decision is needed can be specified in advance.

Structured Programming
A programming methodology that uses a top-down program design and a limited number of control structures in a program to create highly structured modules of program code.

Structured Query Language (SQL)
A query language that is becoming a standard for advanced database management system packages. A query's basic form is SELECT . . . FROM . . . WHERE.

Subroutine
A routine that can be part of another program routine.

Subschema
A subset or transformation of the logical view of the database schema that is required by a particular user application program.

Subsystem
A system that is a component of a larger system.

Supercomputer
A special category of large computer systems that are the most powerful available. They are designed to solve massive computational problems.

Superconductor
Materials that can conduct electricity with almost no resistance. This allows the development of extremely fast and small electronic circuits. Formerly only possible at super cold temperatures near absolute zero. Recent developments promise superconducting materials near room temperature.

Switch
(1) A device or programming technique for making a selection. (2) A computer that controls message switching among the computers and terminals in a telecommunications network.

Switching Costs
The costs in time, money, effort, and inconvenience that it would take a cus-tomer or supplier to switch its business to a firm's competitors.

Synchronous
A characteristic in which each event, or the performance of any basic operation, is constrained to start on, and usually to keep in step with, signals from a timing clock. Contrast with Asynchronous.

System
(1) A group of interrelated or interacting elements forming a unified whole. (2) A group of interrelated components working together toward a common goal by accepting inputs and producing outputs in an organized transformation process. (3) An assembly of methods, procedures, or techniques unified by regulated interaction to form an organized whole. (4) An organized collection of people, machines, and methods required to accomplish a set of specific functions.

System Flowchart
A graphic diagramming tool used to show the flow of information processing activities as data are processed by people and devices.

Systems Analysis
(1) Analyzing in detail the components and requirements of a system. (2) Analyzing in detail the information needs of an organization, the characteristics and components of presently utilized information systems, and the functional requirements of proposed information systems.

Systems Approach
A systematic process of problem solving that defines problems and opportunities in a systems context. Data are gathered describing the problem or opportunity, and alternative solutions are identified and evaluated. Then the best solution is selected and implemented, and its success evaluated.

Systems Context
Recognizing systems, subsystems, and components of systems in a situation. Also called a systemic view.

Systems Design
Deciding how a proposed information system will meet the information needs of end users. Includes logical and physical design activities, and user interface, data, and process design activities that produce system specifications that satisfy the system requirements developed in the systems analysis stage.

Systems Development
(1) Conceiving, designing, and implementing a system. (2) Developing information systems by a process of investigation, analysis, design, implementation, and maintenance. Also called the systems development life cycle (SDLC), information systems development, or application development.

Systems Development Tools
Graphical, textual, and computer-aided tools and techniques used to help analyze, design, and document the development of an information system. Typically used to represent (1) the components and flows of a system, (2) the user interface, (3) data attributes and relationships, and (4) detailed system processes.

Systems Implementation
The stage of systems development in which hardware and software are acquired, developed, and installed, the system is tested and documented, people are trained to operate and use the system, and an organization converts to the use of a newly developed system.

Systems Investigation
The screening, selection, and preliminary study of a proposed information system solution to a business problem.

Systems Maintenance
The monitoring, evaluating, and modifying of a system to make desirable or necessary improvements.

System Software
Programs that control and support operations of a computer system. System software includes a variety of programs, such as operating systems, database management systems, communications control programs, service and utility programs, and programming language translators.

System Specifications
The product of the systems design stage. It consists of specifications for the hardware, software, facilities, personnel, databases, and the user interface of a proposed information system.

System Support Programs
Programs that support the operations, management, and users of a computer system by providing a variety of support services. Examples are system utilities and performance monitors.

Tangible Benefits and Costs
The quantifiable benefits and costs of a proposed solution or system.

Task Management
A basic operating system function that manages the accomplishment of the computing tasks of users by a computer system.

Technical Feasibility
Whether reliable hardware and software capable of meeting the needs of a proposed system can be acquired or developed by an organization in the required time.

Technological Implementation
Formal programs of implementation-support activities to encourage user acceptance and productive use of reengineered business processes and new information technologies.

Technology Implementation
Methods for ensuring end user acceptance and productive use of newly installed information system technologies.

Technology Management
The establishment of organizational groups to identify, introduce, and monitor the assimilation of new information system technologies into organizations.

Telecommunications
Pertaining to the transmission of signals over long distances, including not only data communications but also the transmission of images and voices using radio, television, and other communications technologies.

Telecommunications Channel
The part of a telecommunications network that connects the message source with the message receiver. It includes the physical equipment used to connect one location to another for the purpose of transmitting and receiving information.

Telecommunications Controller
A data communications interface device (frequently a special-purpose mini- or microcomputer) that can control a telecommunications network containing many terminals.

Telecommunications Control Program
A computer program that controls and supports the communications between computers and terminals in a telecommunications network.

Telecommunications Monitors
Programs that control and support communications between the computers and terminals in a telecommunications network.

Telecommunications Processors
Multiplexers, concentrators, communications controllers, and cluster controllers that allow a communications channel to carry simultaneous data transmissions from many terminals. They may also perform error monitoring, diagnostics and correction, modulation-demodulation, data compression, data coding and decoding, message switching, port contention, and buffer storage, and serve as an interface to satellite and other communications networks.

Telecommuting
The use of telecommunications to replace commuting to work from one's home.

Teleconferencing
The use of video communications to allow business conferences to be held with participants who are scattered across a country, continent, or the world.

Telephone Tag
The process that occurs when two people who wish to contact each other by telephone repeatedly miss each other's phone calls.

Teleprocessing
Using telecommunications for computer-based information processing.

Terabyte
One trillion bytes. More accurately, 2 to the 40th power, or 1,009,511,627,776 in decimal notation.

Text Data
Words, phrases, sentences, and paragraphs used in documents and other forms of communication.

Throughput
The total amount of useful work performed by a data processing system during a given period of time.

Time Sharing
Providing computer services to many users simultaneously while providing rapid responses to each.

Total Quality Management
Planning and implementing programs of continuous quality improvement, where quality is defined as meeting or exceeding the requirements and expectations of customers for a product or service.

Touch-Sensitive Screen
An input device that accepts data input by the placement of a finger on or close to the CRT screen.

Track
The portion of a moving storage medium, such as a drum, tape, or disk, that is accessible to a given reading head position.

Trackball
A rollerball device set in a case used to move the cursor on a computer's display screen.

Transaction
An event that occurs as part of doing business, such as a sale, purchase, deposit, withdrawal, refund, transfer, payment, and so on.

Transaction Document
A document produced as part of a business transaction. For instance: a purchase order, paycheck, sales receipt, or customer invoice.

Transaction File
A data file containing relatively transient data to be processed in combination with a master file. Contrast with Master File.

Transaction Processing Cycle
A cycle of basic transaction processing activities including data entry, transaction processing, database maintenance, document and report generation, and inquiry processing.

Transaction Processing System (TPS)
An information system that processes data arising from the occurrence of business transactions.

Transaction Terminals
Terminals used in banks, retail stores, factories, and other work sites that are used to capture transaction data at their point of origin. Examples are point-of-sale (POS) terminals and automated teller machines (ATMs).

Transborder Data Flows (TDF)
The flow of business data over telecommunications networks across international borders.

Transform Algorithm
Performing an arithmetic computation on a record key and using the result of the calculation as an address for that record. Also known as key transformation or hashing.

Transnational Strategy
A management approach in which an organization integrates its global business activities through close cooperation and interdependence among its headquarters, operations, and international subsidiaries, and its use of appropriate global information technologies.

Turnaround Document
Output of a computer system (such as customer invoices and statements) that is designed to be returned to the organization as machine-readable input.

Turnaround Time
The elapsed time between submission of a job to a computing center and the return of the results.

Turnkey Systems
Computer systems where all of the hardware, software, and systems development needed by a user are provided.

Unbundling
The separate pricing of hardware, software, and other related services.

Universal Product Code (UPC)
A standard identification code using bar coding, printed on products that can be read by the optical supermarket scanners of the grocery industry.

Unstructured Decisions
Decisions that must be made in situations where it is not possible to specify in advance most of the decision procedures to follow.

User-Friendly
A characteristic of human-operated equipment and systems that makes them safe, comfortable, and easy to use.

User Interface
That part of an operating system or other program that allows users to communicate with it to load programs, access files, and accomplish other computing tasks.

User Interface Design
Designing the interactions between end users and computer systems, including input/output methods and the conversion of data between human-readable and machine-readable forms.

Utility Program
A standard set of routines that assists in the operation of a computer system by performing some frequently required process such as copying, sorting, or merging.

Value-Added Carriers
Third-party vendors who lease telecommunications lines from common carriers and offer a variety of telecommunications services to customers.

Value-Added Resellers (VARs)
Companies that provide industry-specific software for use with the computer systems of selected manufacturers.

Value Chain
Viewing a firm as a series or chain of basic activities that add value to its products and services and thus add a margin of value to the firm.

Videotex
An interactive information service provided over phone lines or cable TV channels.

Virtual Company
A form of organization that uses information technology to link the people, assets, and ideas of a variety of business partners, no matter where they may be located, in order to exploit a business opportunity.

Virtual Machine
Pertaining to the simulation of one type of computer system by another computer system.

Virtual Memory
The use of secondary storage devices as an extension of the primary storage of the computer, thus giving the appearance of a larger main memory than actually exists.

Virtual Reality
The use of multisensory human/computer interfaces that enable human users to experience computer-simulated objects, entities, spaces, and "worlds" as if they actually existed.

VLSI: Very-Large-Scale Integration
Semiconductor chips containing hundreds of thousands of circuits.

Voice Mail
A variation of electronic mail where digitized voice messages rather than electronic text are accepted, stored, and transmitted.

Voice Recognition
Direct conversion of spoken data into electronic form suitable for entry into a computer system. Also called voice data entry.

Volatile Memory
Memory (such as electronic semiconductor memory) that loses its contents when electrical power is interrupted.

Wand
A handheld optical character recognition device used for data entry by many transaction terminals.

What-If Analysis
Observing how changes to selected variables affect other variables in a mathematical model.

Wide Area Network (WAN)
A data communications network covering a large geographic area.

Window
One section of a computer's multiple-section display screen, each of which can have a different display.

Wireless LANs
Using radio or infrared transmissions to link devices in a local area network.

Word
(1) A string of characters considered as a unit. (2) An ordered set of bits (usually larger than a byte) handled as a unit by the central processing unit.

Word Processing
The automation of the transformation of ideas and information into a readable form of communication. It involves the use of computers to manipulate text data in order to produce office communications in the form of documents.

Work Group Computing
End user computing in a work group environment in which members of a work group may use a local area network to share hardware, software, and databases to accomplish group assignments.

Workstation
A computer terminal or micro- or minicomputer system designed to support the work of one person. Also, a high-powered computer to support the work of professionals in engineering, science, and other areas that require extensive computing power and graphics capabilities.

World Wide Web (WWW)
A network of multimedia Internet information sources.

Name Index

Organization Index

Subject Index

Storage (continued)
  capacities of computers, 60–61
  CD–R disks, 76
  CD–ROM disks, 76–77, 225–233
  controls, 475
  direct and sequential access, 72–73, 185–186
  erasable optical disks, 76–77
  magnetic disk storage, 74–75
  magnetic tape storage, 75–76
  optical disk storage, 76–77
  secondary storage devices, 60
  storage capacity elements, 61
  storage trends and trade-offs, 71–72
  WORM disks, 76–77
Story board, 227
STRATEGEM (software), 293
Strategic advantage, fundamentals of, 334–342; see also other Strategic entries
  agile competitor, becoming an, 355–357
  challenges of strategic IS, 362–363
    success/failure examples, 363
  competitive strategy concepts, 334–342
  Internet
    strategic uses, 359–362
    strategic uses, examples, 360–362
  strategic IS, 14, 32
  strategic roles of IS, 336–340
    building strategic IT platform, 340
    creating switching costs, 339
    developing information base, 340
    improving operations, 336–337
    locking in customers and suppliers, 338–339
    promoting innovation, 338
    raising barriers to entry, 339
  value chain and IS, 340–341
  virtual company, 357–359
Strategic applications and issues, 343–365
  breaking business barriers with IT, 344–347
    cost barriers, 347
    geographic barriers, 346–347
    structural barriers, 347
    time barriers, 345–346
  business process reengineering (BPR), 348–351
  levels of IT use, 343
  overview, 343–344
  total quality management (TQM), 351–354
Strategic information systems, 14, 32
Strategic IS planning, objectives of, 434
  business alignment, 434
  competitive advantage, 434
  resource management, 434
  technology architecture, 434
Strategic management, 433–436
  chief information officer (CIO), 434
  IT architecture, 434–437
  strategic IS planning, 434

Strategic transaction processing systems, 260
Structural barriers, 347
Structured (programmable) decisions, 282
Structured query language; see SQL
Style sheets, 221
Subject area databases (SADB), 171
Subschemas, 184
Subscribers, 143
Supercomputer, 48
  systems, 53
Supermicros, 51
Superminis, 51
Superservers, 130
Support processor, 57–58
Switching costs, 339
Switching on networks, 148
  alternatives, 151–152
Symbolic languages, 104–105
Synchronous transmission, 151
System concepts; see also other System(s) entries
  adaptive system, 21
  basic components/functions, 18
  control, 19–20
  feedback, 19–20
  input, 18
  interface, 20
  open system, 20
  output, 18
  processing, 18
  system, defined, 18
System development
  management, 441
  programs defined/described, 98
System for Individual Marketing and Review (SIMR), 316
System management programs, defined/described, 98
System Network Architecture (SNA), 149
System resources, 22–25
  data resources, 23–25
  hardware resources, 22–23
  network resources, 25
  people resources, 22
  software resources, 23
Systems analysis, 382, 384–387
  functional requirements analysis, 386–387
  organizational analysis, 385–386
  present-system analysis, 386
Systems design, 387–389
  data design, 388
  process design, 388
  system specifications, 388–389
  user interface design, 387
Systems development
  cycle, 380–382
  global, 458
Systems investigation, 382–384

Systems investigation (continued)
  cost/benefit analysis, 384
  feasibility studies, 382, 384
System software; see also Operating systems (software) and Programming languages
  database management systems, 103
  defined, 88
  major functional categories, defined/described, 98
    system development programs, 98
    system management programs, 98
    system support programs, 98
  overview, 98
  programming packages, 108–109
  sort programs, 103
  as systems resources, 23
  system support monitors, 103
  system support programs, 103
  telecommunications monitors, 103
  utility programs, 103
System specifications, 388–389
System support (software) programs, 103
  defined/described, 98
System testing, 408
System W (software), 293

Tactical IS planning, 436
Tangible benefits, 384, 385
Tangible costs, 384
Task management software, 100–101
  multiprogramming, 100
  multitasking, 100
  time-sharing, 100
  virtual machines, 101
Technical feasibility, 382
Technological dimension of IS, 4
Technology implementation cycle, 401
Technology management, 443–444
  advanced technology management, 443–444
  telecommunications management, 443
Technology platform, 434
Telecommunications
  carriers, 120, 141–142
  channels (lines; links), 125, 138
  defined, 54, 120–121
  management, 443
  monitors (software), 103, 126
  software packages, 145
  telecommunication monitors, 103
Telecommunications Deregulation and Reform Bill (1996), 122, 156, 494, 509
Telecommunications network model, components of, 125–126
  channels and media, 125
  computers, 126
  control software, 126